CONRAD WEISER

THE INDIAN COUNTRY

Based on a map of the British and French settlements of North America (London, 1755), showing the "Bounds of the SIX NATIONS"

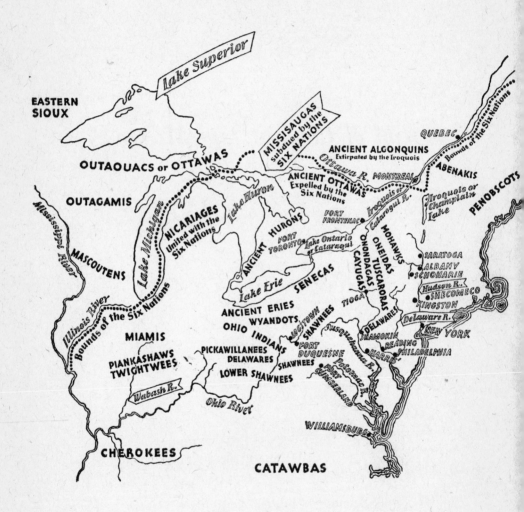

CONRAD WEISER

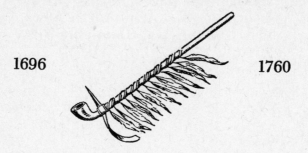

1696   1760

Friend of Colonist and Mohawk

By

PAUL A. W. WALLACE

Philadelphia

UNIVERSITY OF PENNSYLVANIA PRESS

London: Humphrey Milford

Oxford University Press

1 9 4 5

Copyright 1945

PAUL A. W. WALLACE

Manufactured in the United States of America

To

CHARLES BERWIND MONTGOMERY

whom I met on the road to Weiser's

FOREWORD

CONRAD WEISER, Pennsylvania's Indian ambassador, was one of the world's great originals, a hot-headed, true-hearted, whimsical Jack-of-all-trades; a farmer and the owner of a tannery, one of the founders of Reading, Pennsylvania, a colonel on active service during the French and Indian War, the first President Judge of Berks County, a faithful husband and the father of fourteen children, a monk at Ephrata, a pillar of the Lutheran Church, a promoter of Moravian missions, a rebel in New York and a prisoner in an Albany jail, a hymn-writer, traveler, statesman, linguist, diplomat, and woodsman. That is Conrad Weiser in a nutshell.

His career introduces us to the whole colonial scene from New York to the Carolinas, taking in the seacoast towns, the frontier settlements, the forests of the Alleghenies, and the long houses and cabins of the Indians on the Hudson, Mohawk, Delaware, Susquehanna, and Ohio Rivers. He bought books from Benjamin Franklin and taught Poor Richard what he knew about the Six Nations Indians. He corresponded with Thomas Lee, the "President of Virginia." He quarreled with Governor Denny of Pennsylvania. In the conduct of Indian affairs, he was the rival of George Washington and of Sir William Johnson. He introduced Count Zinzendorf to the Shawnees and saved his life in the Wyoming Valley. He traveled through the woods with Peter Boehler, whom good Methodists remember as the man who caused John Wesley's second conversion. He was the adviser of Thomas Penn, Proprietor of Pennsylvania, and the adviser of General Forbes who captured Fort Duquesne. He was at home on Society Hill in Philadelphia as well as at John Harris' Ferry on the fringe of civilization. He gave his daughter in marriage to Henry Melchior Muhlenberg, the "Patriarch of the Lutheran Church in America." His first grandchild grew up to become the famous General John Peter Gabriel Muhlenberg of Washington's staff in the Revolutionary War.

In his day, everybody knew him. Governors, churchmen, and Indian chiefs relied on his advice and took him as much for granted as they took the sun in heaven. The Iroquois named him Tarachiawagon, He Who Holds the Heavens. During the French and Indian War, settlers beyond the Blue Mountains called him "Father" and appealed to him for protection. His home was the battalion headquarters for the Delaware-Susquehanna line. He organized the intelligence service. During the black fall of 1755, he was for a time Pennsylvania's main defense, receiving a blanket commission from the Governor to do whatever was necessary for the safety of the province. With a volunteer army he plugged the gap in the Blue Mountains and broke the force of the Indian attack.

He went everywhere, saw everyone, did everything. Yet through all the excitements of his public life he liked best to be at home with his *Frau liebste*, his *Kinder*, and his *Kieh*.

There was never any man like him, and never will be. He reminds us of nobody and of everybody. He was as vital and various as the life of nature changing through the seasons: mystic and matter-of-fact; an honest monk and a passionate husband; a religious enthusiast, antisectarian, yet the chief lay worker of his time for the Lutheran Church in America; a hymn-writer in German, and in English the author of some excellent journals of adventure in the woods; a military strategist; a student of the law; a lover of books; a traveler through the wilds who knew the Shamokin Trail like a village street, and visited the distant towns of Oswego, Onondaga, and Logstown; above all a lover of the little Tulpehocken home to which he came back finally to die.

To avoid the confusion to which the modern reader is liable by reason of the double sets of dates found in early records, all events before 1752 (when the modern calendar was officially adopted in Great Britain and her colonies) have in this book been dated in conformity with modern usage to the extent that the calendar year is assumed to have begun on January 1, not March 25 as formerly. Thus an event dated February 16, 1738 (Old Style), or 1738/9 in Weiser's journals, is here dated February 16, 1739.

On the other hand, monthly reckonings prior to September 1752 follow the Julian calendar, which Weiser used, rather than the Gregorian calendar, which the Moravians used—to the considerable confusion of anyone following Weiser's 1745 itinerary to Onondaga through the pages of the Bethlehem Diary, since the Moravians were eleven days ahead in their reckoning.

In 1752, by dropping eleven days from the month of September, the colonies adopted the Gregorian calendar and got rid of the confusion.

I have met with so much kindness in the course of this study that any adequate acknowledgment would require a supplementary volume.

The briefest list of those to whom I am chiefly indebted must include the names of three State Archivists of Pennsylvania: Dr. H. H. Shenk, Professor of History at Lebanon Valley College, who first drew my attention to Conrad Weiser as a subject for biography; Dr. Curtis W. Garrison; and Dr. Henry W. Shoemaker. It must include also the members of the staff of the Department of Archives, Harrisburg, Pa.

I wish to make special acknowledgment to Dr. Julian P. Boyd, formerly Librarian of the Historical Society of Pennsylvania and now Librarian at Princeton University; to many members of the staff at the H.S.P., especially to Miss Townsend, Miss Miller, Miss Bond, and Mr. Givens; to Dr. G. W. Clemens, Curator of the Historical Society of Berks County; to Miss Lillian D. Harbaugh of the Juniata College Library; to Miss Winifred V. Eisenberg of the Krauth Memorial Library, Lutheran Theological Seminary, Mt. Airy, Pa.; to Dr. W. N. Schwarze, former President of Moravian College, and Professor Kenneth G. Hamilton, Moravian Archives, Bethlehem, Pa.; to Dr. St. George L. Sioussat, Chief of the Division of Manuscripts, Library of Congress; to Mr. Arthur Stevenson, Schoharie County Historian, and Mr. Myron Vroman, Curator of the Old Stone Fort Museum, Schoharie, N.Y.; to the late Mr. Donald MacPherson, Historian of Delaware County, N.Y., and his son, Mr. Malcolm MacPherson; to Mrs. Howell Souder, who permitted me to make a transcript of Conrad Weiser's "Diary"; to Mrs. K. T. Anderson of Augustana College, who let me examine Conrad Weiser's Account Book; to Mr. Guy S. Klett of Philadelphia; to Mr. C. W. Unger of Pottsville, Pa.; to Dr. Cornelius Weygandt and Dr. F. G. Speck of the University of Pennsylvania; to Miss Helen Ethel Myers, Librarian, Lebanon Valley College; to Mr. J. Bennett Nolan of Reading; to the late Dr. John Baer Stoudt and his son, Dr. John Joseph Stoudt, of Allentown; to Mrs. C. M. Steinmetz of Reading; to Dr. William J. Hinke, Auburn, N.Y.; to Mr. Francis-J. Audet, Ottawa, Ont.; to Mr. John M. Okie, Lansdowne, Pa.; to Dr. P. B. Gibble, Palmyra, Pa.; to Dr. Hubertis Cummings, Harrisburg; to Dr. W. N. Fenton, Smithsonian Institution, Washington, D. C.

I can never forget the hospitality I have received from the Indians whose ancestors shared Conrad Weiser with the English. Their thoughtful courtesy has been unfailing whenever I have gone to them for help, whether at Onondaga, N.Y., or on the Six Nations Reserve near Brantford, Ont. In particular I am indebted to Sharenkhowane (Chief William D. Loft), one of the last duly appointed *royaners* of the Mohawks, Six Nations Reserve, Ont., and his daughter, Dawendine (Mrs. Arthur Winslow); to the late Chief Joseph Montour, whom I visited on the Delaware Line, Six Nations Reserve, and who there taught me that the Delawares are still a people; to the late Chief Jacob Hess, "pagan preacher" of the Cayugas, Ohsweken, Ont.; to Mr. Williams of the Tuscaroras, at Little Buffalo (near the village of "69 Corners"), Six Nations Reserve; to Major E. P. Randle, Superintendent of the Six Nations, Brantford; and to "Chief" Emerson Metoxen of the Oneidas, now living at Wayne, Pa., who traveled the Shamokin Trail with me and explored Weiser's route to Onondaga, where he introduced me to the present head chief of the Six Nations in the United States.

I owe much to the late Dr. George Wheeler of Germantown, who generously shared with me his books and magazines, as well as his own intimate knowledge of the Pine Grove region and the lower end of the Shamokin Trail.

Above all, I am indebted to the late Charles Berwind Montgomery, who helped me with books, maps, transcripts, and clues to historical riddles all along the way, and who generously shared with me his vast knowledge of Pennsylvania colonial manuscripts and his profound understanding of the people and causes figuring in them.

Annville, Pennsylvania   P. A. W. W.
December 1944

CONTENTS

PART I: DISTANT FIELDS

PART II: THE CHAIN OF FRIENDSHIP

xi

PART III: WEAK LINKS

PART IV: BLACK WAMPUM

CONTENTS

PART V: THE CHAIN HOLDS

MAPS

xiv

Part I

DISTANT FIELDS

CONRAD WEISER'S FAMILY

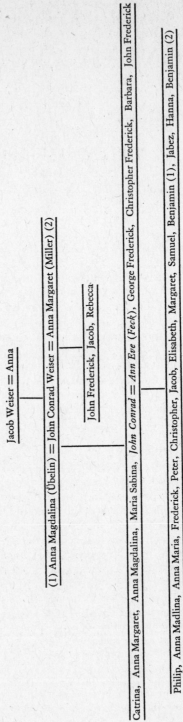

Jacob Weiser = Anna

(1) Anna Magdalina (Übelin) = John Conrad Weiser = Anna Margaret (Miller) (2)

John Frederick, Jacob, Rebecca

Catrina, Anna Margaret, Anna Magdalina, Maria Sabina, John Conrad = Ann Eve (Feck), George Frederick, Christopher Frederick, Barbara, John Frederick

Philip, Anna Madlina, Anna Maria, Frederick, Peter, Christopher, Jacob, Elisabeth, Margaret, Samuel, Benjamin (1), Jabez, Hanna, Benjamin (2)

CHAPTER I

CONRAD WEISER

. . . Receives the Queen's Bounty

I

EARLY in the morning of June 13, 1710, the ship *Lyon* (of Leith, Captain Stevens commander) [1] drew into New York harbor with an escort, H.M.S. *Feversham*.[2] On board the Lyon were 402 "poor Palatines," among them thirteen-year-old Conrad Weiser (whom Count Zinzendorf in good time was to style the Emperor of the Iroquois) with his father and seven brothers and sisters.

It was good to see land: the sands, the Fort, the Battery outside its walls, the neat rows of houses, with rock, mountain, and forest in the background. It was better yet to feel solid ground underfoot when they disembarked at Nutten Island, now called Governor's Island. Conrad had been on board since Christmas: some five months in English waters, where the *Lyon* and nine other ships of the convoy had puttered about between London and Plymouth awaiting final orders; and seven or eight weeks on the ocean, where Conrad lay sick and bewildered in the midst of tossing death. The passengers were packed tightly below decks, amid smells, darkness, and vermin, with a subsistence allowance of sixpence a day per head.[3] Poor food and bad water prepared the way for typhus, the "Palatine fever." The little children died, almost all of them, and a great number of their elders. Some two hundred souls were lost, a third of the passenger list. The ship's doctor, Thomas Benson, tells us that he "administered aid and Medicines, to above 330 p'sons which have all been sick at One time in the said passage, and none but himselfe to assist them; during all the said time . . ."[4]

Years later, after Conrad had become famous throughout the colonies, he wrote down for his children what he knew about his own early life. It was little enough. The uprooting had been complete, and the voyage from Plymouth to New York had interposed a dark barrier to recollection. His real life began on that Tuesday morning in mid-June of 1710.

This is what he had to tell of his origin:

Anno 1696 the 2 November I Conrad Weiser was born in Europe in the land of Würtenberg in the county of Herrenberg the place is called Astät and baptized at Kupingen nearby as my father has told me

I say I was born the 2 November 1696

My Father was named Joh: Conrad Weiser My Mother Anna Magdalina *gebohren* Übelin My grand Father Jacob Weiser My greatgrand Father also Jacob Weiser. chief magistrates [*schultheissen*] in the town of gross astach in the county of Backnang likewise in the land of Würtenberg in the said place

3

my Ancestors from of Old have been born and there lie buried both on my Father's and on my Mother's side.[5]

It was a well-established little feudal world that Conrad had entered. The Weisers were a good burgher family, probably of peasant extraction but by 1696 well entrenched socially in their corner of Württemberg, being connected by marriage with the best families in the neighborhood. Conrad's uncle, John Michael Weiser, was at that time *Schultheiss* or mayor of Gross Aspach, as Conrad's grandfather (and his great-grandfather, too, if we may accept the statement of the Autobiography unsupported by any evidence in the town records) had been before him. A great-uncle, John Conrad Weiser, was town clerk in Backnang, the county seat.[6] This uncle cut something of a dash, flourishing a coat of arms which he had acquired in 1691: a shield emblazoned with a swan and three red roses.[7] He was apparently the "rich uncle" of the family, and it is not improbable that our two John Conrads, father and son, were named after him.[8]

Conrad was a son of the regiment, and so it came about that he entered the world, not at the family seat of Gross Aspach, but at the tiny village of Affstät, some twenty miles southeast of Stuttgart, where his father, a corporal in the Württemberg Blue Dragoons, was then stationed.[9] But Conrad was to remember nothing in later years of these army beginnings. His father soon got his discharge from the Blue Dragoons and settled down to work as a baker in Gross Aspach, where by 1700 we find him one of six representatives of the Bakers' Guild, which had a membership of four hundred.[10]

Gross Aspach was not much bigger than Affstät, but it had a better tone. Whereas Affstät did not even have a church (Conrad had to be carried to the village of Kuppingen for baptism), Gross Aspach had both a church and a school. The parson, Master Erhard Hägelin, was somewhat preoccupied at the time, finding it necessary to supplement his clerical income by engaging in a wine business on the side.[11] Johannes Blumhard,[12] the schoolmaster, on the other hand, was a man of both piety and learning. Conrad never forgot the passages of scripture Master Johannes made him learn by heart.[13]

Gross Aspach was a farming community, lying about thirty miles northeast of Stuttgart in a shallow valley drained by the Klöpferbach. This little stream is a tributary of the Murr, the waters of which in turn flow into the Neckar and so find their way to the Rhine. The Klöpferbach cuts the town in two, separating what was in Conrad's day the baronial part belonging to Baron von Sturmfeder from the ducal part belonging to the Duke of Württemberg. Church, parsonage, and tithe-barn lay in the baronial section, but the ducal section contained the townhall. Since Conrad's relatives were ducal magistrates, we may suppose that Conrad himself was brought up on the ducal side of the brook.[14]

The town lies nested between the escarpments of the Backnang Basin, at the center of a colorful pattern of farms, vineyards, orchards, and woodlands. It is so snug a place that it may seem difficult to understand how any man as well established there as John Conrad Weiser was in 1709 should leave its shelter and take his family on a dangerous voyage to an uncertain destination on the other side of the world. But John Conrad knew very well what he was doing.

In those days Württemberg was none too friendly to her people. While men starved, Duke Eberhard Ludwig played with his mistress, Christiana Wilhelmina von Grävenitz—an expensive lady who wanted her Stuttgart to be like Versailles and used the dukedom's revenues to that end. The Duke denied her nothing, from palaces to midsummer snow. When she wanted to go sleighing in summer, the Duke had the streets covered with salt for her. "I am the Pope in my country," said Eberhard Ludwig.[15]

By 1709, the valley in which Gross Aspach lay seemed about to revert to the wolves as it had done in the Thirty Years' War when, human society having crumbled, wild creatures came out of the Black Forest and down off the Löwenstein Mountains to possess it. John Conrad saw what his grandfather had seen before him: war and pestilence sweeping the country, with taxes following like looters at their heels. In 1707 a French army under Marshall Villars had marched plundering through the town.[16] Marauding military mobs terrorized the neighboring hamlets. Disease followed the troops, the hideous "Hot Fever," which struck people in the prime of life and killed them in two days. As if war and pestilence were not enough, the elements took a hand and in 1708–9 plagued the country with the coldest winter known in a hundred years. The frost came in October and stayed till April.[17] Orchards and vineyards were ruined, among them the vineyards of John Conrad Weiser.

When the cold left, the fever returned. It struck at the Weisers. In the Gross Aspach register of deaths for 1709 is this entry:

"May 1. was buried here: Anna Magdalena, Wife of John Conrad Weiser Burgher and Baker, who died very suddenly of the fever in the 43rd Year of her Life, while she was pregnant with her 15th child." [18]

She was "Buried beside Her Ancestors," wrote Conrad for his children; "she was a god-fearing woman and much loved by Her neighbors.

"Her motto was Jesus I live for thee, I die for thee, thine am I in life and death." [19]

II

With the death of Anna Magdalina, the family broke up. John Conrad Weiser set off for England and America, taking most of his children with him.

His decision to leave must have been made suddenly. No doubt, of course, he had seen the "Golden Book" [20] (with Queen Anne's picture in it) advertising the delights of America, and had heard of Kocherthal's party of Germans who had gone to New York in 1708.[21] Certainly he had heard the stirrings of the migratory movement which, by the spring of 1709, was pouring people by the thousands out of the Palatinate and Württemberg into the Rhine voyage bound for England. But it is hardly likely that he had planned to embark on any such adventure while Anna Magdalina was expecting another child. It is more probable that the shock of her death made him jump impulsively, as he was to continue to do at every crisis that subsequently confronted him in America, at something new, some plan to wrench from circumstances by main strength the satisfactions that life seemed bent on denying him. The hasty way in which he wound up his affairs at Gross Aspach lends color to this suggestion.

In the same year namely 1709 [wrote Conrad in the Autobiography] my Father moved away from gross astach, the 24 June, he took eight children with him, my eldest sister Catrina remained there with Her husband Conrad Boss, by whom she had already had two children. my Father left them his house fields and meadows, vineyard and gardens, they could pay him no more than 75 guilders, the rest amounting to 600 guilders my Father was to get later, but he never did. and it has now been made a present to Them.

In about two months we reached london in England along with several thousand germans whom queen Anne of most glorious memory had taken under her care, and was Furnishing with Food.[22]

Conrad tells us no more about the journey to London than is found in that brief passage from the Autobiography. We wish he had told us more. We should like to know whether the Weisers left home on one of the high, two-wheeled, covered carts containing food, clothes, and bedding, which so many other emigrants from Württemberg used at that time. If so, did they pull the cart by hand, as was the custom, or did John Conrad spend some of his guilders on a horse? If they followed the common track, they went down the Neckar Valley to the Rhine and there took a boat for Rotterdam.[23]

The Rhine journey was a long one, broken by stops at more than thirty customs stations on the way.[24] The Weisers made good time, but even so they spent nearly a month on this part of their travels alone. To so wide-awake a man as John Conrad, the delays must have been trying, in view of the uncertainties ahead. No one knew how long England would continue to welcome the folk who had been pouring down the Rhine since early spring. At first all had seemed well. Queen Anne, whose late husband the Prince of Denmark was of German stock and a Lutheran, had felt warmly disposed toward the distressed Protestants of Germany, and Parliament was with her. England regarded herself as the champion of the Protestant cause in Europe. Besides, England could use these sturdy people to protect her American frontier. A naturalization act was passed in March to encourage the newcomers.[25] The Duke of Marlborough interested himself personally in their welfare.[26] Transport ships were provided, with the approval of the Queen, to bring the Palatines (such they were all called, from whatever region they came) over to England, there to await the disposition of the government.

In April, May, and June they came by thousands. On June 14, James Dayrolle, British Resident at the Hague, wrote to London that

. . . upon the continuation of H. M. Bounty or any other encouragement, you may have half Germany if you please, for they are all flying away not only from the Palatinate, but from all other countrys in the neighborhood of the Rhine. . . . The expenses may be great but are necessary, if you are in want of these people for the plantations, as my Lord Townshend seems to be of opinion you are, otherwise they must perish where they come to lye at Briel.[27]

The stream flowed on till, by July, it had become a flood that alarmed London. Accommodations could not be provided fast enough. Disease threatened. The labor market was glutted. The government took fright. On July 23 Secretary Boyle instructed Lord Townshend "to request the Dutch to prevent any further embarkation." [28]

Fortunately for the Weisers there was no cable then, and a letter from London to Rotterdam took the better part of a week. So that we find in the record of embarkations at Rotterdam that the Dutch agents van Toren and van Gent embarked a party of Palatines, July 27, on a vessel that sailed for London the next day. In the list of this last official embarkation, we find this entry:

Weiser, Johan Koenrat & vrouw & 8 ch.[29]

"John Conrad Weiser and eight children"—so much we might have expected. But what about the *wife?* Perhaps it was a clerk's error. What clerk would enter a crowd of young children on such a journey without presupposing a mother to look after them? Or perhaps—what's in a name? John Conrad made Anna Margaret Miller his wife a few months later in New York. Was she already a privileged member of the party when they embarked at Rotterdam? And was this anticipation of the marital state a cause of the hatred which all the children showed for their stepmother afterward?

The appearance of John Conrad's name on the official embarkation list shows that the Weisers were not among those who paid their own way across to London, and that they were not among those who had their transportation paid for them by private charity. John Conrad Weiser and his family had accepted the Queen's Bounty.

III

Once arrived in London the Weisers with the rest of the Palatines were caught up in the political currents of Queen Anne's England, where Whig and Tory battled for place and perquisite.

During this time the boy Conrad kept his eyes and his ears open. He may not have seen the sights and met the people for which Queen Anne's London has since become famous. He could not read what Dick Steele and Jonathan Swift wrote about the Palatines in the *Tatler*. But he heard the common talk of his compatriots in the tent colony on Blackheath, and all the bustle and controversy that surrounded his father wherever he went.

The Palatines in London created a commotion from the start, and soon became a political storm center. It is not difficult to understand how this should be so if we look at the situation for a moment from the Englishman's point of view. When from ten to thirty thousand foreigners (the estimates vary and it does not concern us to settle the figures here) descended on London babbling a strange tongue like a flock of migratory blackbirds, they not only provided talk for the coffee houses, gossip for the *Tatler*,[30] and a sight for the populace, but they also provided a nice problem for the politicians. It was not simply a matter of finding them immediate shelter and subsistence. Sixteen hundred tents from the ordnance stores [31] went far to take care of the one, while an allowance of something under a shilling a day per person, with permission to beg on the streets, provided for the other.[32] The real problem for the politicians was how to dispose of these dark-skinned, stocky, round-headed men of Alpine race (progenitors of the modern "Pennsylvania Dutch") in such a way as to serve the fortunes of the Whig party.

The plan that appealed most to the politicians was one that touched a note of patriotic pride. It was pushed by Joseph Addison's friend, Col. Robert Hunter. For the upkeep of her navy, England was dependent on the purchase of tar and pitch from the Scandinavian countries. Why not employ the Palatines to extract these necessaries from the pine forests of her own colonies in North America? It was decided to ship between three and four thousand willing Palatines to the New World for this purpose, and Col. Hunter, recently appointed Governor of New York, was put in charge of the experiment.

The Board of Trade knew that the Palatines, being "very necessitous," would have to be subsisted at the Queen's expense for at least a year, that is, "till they can reap the fruit of their labour." [33] But the Board indulged in a little pipe-dreaming to assure themselves that the Queen would receive a good return on her investment. The Palatines, said their Lordships,

. . . will be a good barrier between Her Majesty's Subjects and the French & their Indians in those parts, and in process of time by intermarrying with the neighbouring Indians (as the French do) they may be capable of rendring great Service to Her Majesty's Subjects there; and not only very much promote the Fur Trade, but likewise the increase of Naval Stores, which may be produced in great plenty . . .[34]

"In process of time"—there was the rub. In the end great benefits might ensue, but meanwhile who was to foot the bill? The same taxpayer, undoubtedly, who had already complained of the cost of maintaining the tent colony on Blackheath. The Whigs were frightened. What would the taxpayer (politicians' incubus) say to the cost of a long ocean voyage followed by a year's subsistence for these colonists in the New World?

Governor Hunter advanced a solution. Let the Palatines pay for themselves. Let the sums expended for their maintenance be regarded as a debt for them to work off, like redemptioners. Instead of giving them land in outright grant, as originally proposed, there should be "reservations." He asked the Board of Trade, December 1, to consider "whether it be not advisable that they be servants to the Crown for a certain Term, or at least 'till they have repaid the Expences the Crown is at in setting them to work, and subsisting them whilst they can not subsist themselves . . ."[35]

This reservation was accepted by the Board of Trade, which, on December 5, recommended that each family among them be given a grant of forty acres of land "after they shall have repaid by the produce of their labour the charges the publick shall be at in settling and subsisting them there . . ." [36]

A covenant, embodying these reservations, was drawn up and presented to the Palatines for their signature. It was therein stipulated that the Palatines should stay wherever the governor put them until their debt was discharged, and that they should not leave the province without his express permission.[37]

If we are astonished that so independent a man as John Conrad Weiser should have put his signature to a document that bound him for an indefinite time to the land like a serf, we should remember that he was keen enough to sense the veering winds of English politics and wise enough to wish to put the Atlantic Ocean as quickly as possible between himself and a falling government. It was plain that the Whigs were on their way out, and as plain that no help could be looked for from the Tories when they came in. Among these latter there was even talk of sending the Palatines back to Germany. It was better for John Conrad to sign anything that would get him to America, where he might hope to straighten things out somehow in the free air of the New World.

CHAPTER 2

... *Gathers Pine Knots in Livingston's Bush*

I

June 13 1710 [writes Weiser] we came to Anchor at new-york in north America, and in the same Autumn were settled at lewenstein's Manor at the Queen's expence.

Here in levingston or as the High Germans say lewenstein's manor we were to burn tar and cultivate hemp For the Queen in payment for our transportation, From holland to England and from England to New-York . . . but it did not work out . . .

THE adventures of the Palatines during their two years at Livingston Manor provided a drama in which young Conrad Weiser watched his father play the leading rôle. It was the beginning for the boy of a hard training in the school of disillusionment and resistance that stiffened his back for the man's work that lay ahead of him in Pennsylvania.

The Palatines in their covenant with the government in England had agreed to settle "in such place or places as shall be allotted to us in the Province of New York." [1] Governor Hunter planted them in tents near the Hudson River, about a hundred miles above New York, in the vicinity of a great pine forest that was expected, in the Governor's words "to serve all Europe with Tarr." [2]

The settlers were divided into five, and later seven, squads or villages over each of which a headman presided, John Conrad Weiser being one. Commissions were issued to certain men as justices of the peace "to hear small causes" among their people. The chief of these was John Conrad Weiser.

Ground was cleared and log huts were erected. In the East Camp, where the Weisers lived, each family was assigned a lot forty feet wide and fifty feet deep. Stones were gathered and outdoor "bake-ovens" were built, so many for each community. House furniture, tables and chairs, was carved out of the forest.

But this was not the friendly wilderness the Palatines had dreamed of in London. It was late fall when they first broke sod, and the winter set in cold. They were poorly clothed and insufficiently fed, through fault of the agents entrusted with their supply. Instead of dealing with friendly Indians as they had expected, they had to do with commissioners who treated them like serfs. The bits of land assigned to them seemed an insult to men who had been among the best farmers in Europe.

As the story is usually told, Governor Hunter is made to be the villain of the piece. But Hunter deserves more sympathy than blame. He sank his fortune and wrecked his career in the Palatine affair. Before his unlucky dealings with these people, and particularly before his contention with the Weisers, he had had an honorable and successful career. Though a poor man's son born into an aristocratic age, he had turned his good friends, good looks, and good luck in a profitable marriage to the best advantage until in 1709 (through the influence, it is said, of his friend Joseph Addison, one of the under-secretaries of state) he was appointed to succeed Lovelace as Governor of New York and to handle the Palatine experiment.

Hunter was a man of warm, enthusiastic temperament, and, when he sailed from London with his ten shiploads of Palatines and eight thousand pounds of Whig money to finance the colony, his head was full of projects that grew like mushrooms in the fertile soil of inexperience. In advocating the tar experiment he had assured their Lordships of the Board of Trade that in a year the colonists would be able to support themselves, and soon after would repay, in goods produced, the cost of transporting and providing for them. One good workman, it was calculated, could produce six tons of tar in a year. Six hundred men, by the economies of mass production, could make seven thousand tons. The figures were almost too good: England could not use such quantities of tar. But what England did not use, Spain and Portugal could; and thus the Palatines would have introduced England to a new and profitable source of foreign trade.

Founded on such fantasies, the Livingston Manor project was bound to crash. But Hunter was one of the last to read the signs. When the Palatines reached their quarters in the fall, it seems only then to have occurred to him that the newcomers would need support not for one year only but for two or more. The first year was already lost, and the second could not see enough land cleared for their subsistence. Other difficulties appeared when Hunter came to know something about the process of tar manufacture. The trees had to be prepared for two years by cutting and barking to concentrate the sap before they could be felled and the burning for resin extraction begun.

The worst of the Governor's misfortunes came from the other side of the ocean. The Whigs had fallen out of office and the Tories had tumbled in before he and his contingent landed at New York. Henceforth the Palatines, as far as help from the government in England was concerned, might have been wrecked on an atoll in the Pacific. The Treasury never spent another penny in their support, and Governor Hunter, like the man of honor he was, had to support them with his own purse and credit. Hoping ultimately to be repaid by the government for the fortune he was losing, he plunged ever deeper into debt to keep the Palatines at work, and continued to write encouraging letters to London. "I have now prepared neare 100,000 trees," said he, "and in ye fall sett them to work about ye second preparation. . . . That no hands may be idle we employed the boys and girls in gathering knotts whilst their fathers were barking, out of which hee [Sackett] has made about threescore barrells of good tarr, and hath kills ready to sett on fire for about as much more soe soone as he getts casks ready to receive it." [3]

Sackett was a local farmer who had persuaded the Governor (who understood nothing about the tar business) that he (Sackett) understood everything; and who, having been put in charge of production, had proceeded with great energy and confidence to have his hundred thousand trees barked in the wrong way. In the end some two hundred barrels of tar (made out of knots gathered by the children) was all that this gigantic experiment yielded—not enough to pay for the special rum ration issued to keep unwilling Palatines at work.

Both the politicians and the colonists were bound to be disappointed. The scheme embodied in the covenant was born of the wedlock of two contradictory purposes: to provide good farms for the Palatines and at the same time tar for the navy. It would have taken more than a government edict to bring the pitch pine and good farm land together. The pitch pine loves sand and gravel, a rocky, sterile soil. Governor Hunter's agents had examined the valley of Schoharie Creek, which flows out of the Catskill Mountains to join the Mohawk River, but had found the land here unsuitably good. "These lands however," wrote the Governor to the Lords of Trade, July 24, 1710, "I believe will be no ways fitt for the design in hands, being very good lands which here bears no pines . . ." [4] There was no such obstacle to settlement at Livingston Manor, where a soil was found sufficiently lean to offer nature's stepchild, the *pinus rigida*, a congenial home. Whether even here the pitch pine grew in sufficient abundance to give the experiment prospect of success is a matter of technical dispute that we may leave to the botanic historians for settlement.

If the Palatines had known then that their labors at tar making could never, in New York, pay their debt and set them free, they could hardly have been more bitter against the government than their other grievances had made them. They did not forget that most of their young children had died at sea. Since landing, their families had been further reduced by the binding out, at the Governor's instance, of such children as were capable of service in order to lessen the cost of providing for the colony. But for the present their principal grievance lay in the person of their "Patrone," Robert Livingston.

This ingenious scoundrel had a strangle-hold on the Governor and the Palatines both. He had become Hunter's political ally. He sold him land for the colony, and soon was appointed Inspector of Palatines and President of the Palatine Court (which had authority to inflict corporal punishment short of mutilation and death). He lent money to the Palatines and to their overseers. Most important of all, he had the contract for supplying them with food. They were to receive daily the equivalent of a four pence halfpenny loaf and a quart of ship's beer. Three days a week they were to have meat; on other days, fish, cheese, peas, or butter as a substitute. The salted meat (delivered by weight) turned out to be one-eighth salt and almost uneatable.[5] The bread allowance was kept short weight by the trick of failing to register properly the weight of the barrels in which the flour was delivered.[6] The Palatines soon learned that no good was to be expected from the tight-lipped, eel-nosed rascal who had been set over them. A few years before this, Robert Livingston had been under suspicion of involvement, financially, with Captain Kidd, the privateer, who is still remembered in Madagascar as no angel. Captain Kidd was hanged in 1701, but Robert Livingston, exonerated by the court, lived cannily on to show the world how a prudent man may share Captain Kidd's brand of social solicitude and still keep a moist skin above his neck. Robert Livingston was the only creature who got any good out of the Palatine tar experiment.

Another grievance developed when the Palatines discovered the full import of the covenant they had signed at Plymouth. They had agreed to stay "in such place or places as shall be allotted to us." When men began to leave the Manor, under pressure of distress if not of actual starvation, it was ordered that such persons must obtain a ticket of leave for some specified place, and that if they abandoned that place they were to be brought back and punished. If any person left the Manor without a ticket, a hue and cry was to be started after him, and on apprehension he was to be thrown into the common gaol.

The whole Livingston Manor episode was a whirligig of suspicion and disaster. Livingston cheated the Palatines; for this they blamed Governor Hunter; Hunter, ruined by supporting them out of his own pocket, hated them for their ingratitude; the ministry failed to support him because, in part at least, of his connection with Robert Livingston. "I think it unhappy," wrote Lord Clarendon to Lord Dartmouth, March 8, 1711, "that Colº Hunter at his first arrival in his Government fell into so ill hands, for this Levingston has been known many years in that Province for a very ill man . . . guilty of most notorious frauds . . . My Lord, upon the whole matter I am of opinion that if the Subsistence proposed is allowed, the consequence will be that Levingston and some others will get Estates, the Palatines will not be the richer." [7]

By the time Hunter himself had learned that, as he put it, Livingston was "the most selfish man alive," [8] it was too late; the harm had been done. The government in England, the Palatines in New York, were determined to dabble no more in pitch.

In addition to all their genuine grievances, the Palatines, through the growth of a curious legend, had mistakenly come to believe themselves entitled to another. They had been defrauded, they persuaded themselves, of lands actually set aside for them by the Queen in the beautiful Schoharie Valley. "For the Indian deputies," writes Conrad in his Autobiography, "who were in England at the time the german People were lying in tents on Blackheath had made a present to Queen Anna of this schochary that she might settle these People upon it."

Conrad is wrong in his chronology. The Palatines had left their tents and entered their ships three months before Hendrick and the three other "Indian Kings" reached England. Be that as it may, Hendrick did offer these lands to Governor Hunter on his return to New York,[9] and the Palatines had at one time been encouraged to believe that they would be settled on them. When conditions grew insufferable at Livingston Manor, they set themselves with biblical fervor on possessing this land of Canaan

—"the promised land of Scorie" as they called it. And John Conrad Weiser was destined to be their Moses.

II

Bad food and poor clothing made the first fall, winter, and spring at Livingston Manor hard enough for fourteen-year-old Conrad Weiser to bear, but the changes that came in the family circle were still harder. During these months he lost all his brothers and gained a harsh stepmother.

I have already said that my Father was a Widower when he left germany [he writes], and landed with eight children in New-york 1710. there both my brothers George fridrick and Gristoph fridrick were bound out By the Governor to long Island with my then sick Father's consent the following winter that is to say in december my youngest brother Joh: friderich died in about the sixth year of his age and was buried in Livingston's Bush . . .[10]

Some time in the spring of 1711, probably early in April to judge from the Subsistence Accounts, John Conrad Weiser married Margretha Müller. "It was an unfortunate marriage," writes Conrad, "and the cause of the family's all becoming scattered. At last I was the only one left with my Father. except for the three Children he had by my stepmother, viz., Johann friderich & Jacob Weiser and Rebecca everything went crab-fashion, and one misfortune after another befell our family, in which I was always involved I often did not know where to turn and learned to pray to God, and the bible became to me a very helpful book" [11]

The spring of 1711 found the Palatines in general dangerously unsettled. One of the commissioners wrote to the Governor about threatening talk he had heard from five men seated about a fire.

One said, "We came to America to establish our families—to secure lands for our children, on which they will be able to support themselves after we die; and that we cannot do here."

"What is to be done in that case but to have patience?" replied another.

"Patience and Hope," retorted the first, "make fools of those who fill their bellies with them." [12]

For a time the impatient ones had their way, and the Palatines went on strike; but Robert Livingston was in a position to show them that patience and hope, with meat three times a week, were better subsistence than no meat at all. On May 26 he wrote a letter to the Provincial Secretary at New York telling of "ye finall Submission of all the . . . Tounes on our Side & ye 2 Tounes on ye oyr Side . . . we sent ye Palatines to work on Munday & I hope they are now Convinced of their Error." [13]

It is not difficult to imagine by what means the man who had once been Captain Kidd's patron, and was now President of the Palatine Court and purveyor of Palatine rations, persuaded those dependent on him of their error.

The military campaign of 1711, for which a large number of the Palatines volunteered, demonstrated the loyalty of these people to their new fatherland, but at the same time it provided them with a fresh grievance. The forty men in Captain John Conrad Weiser's company from Queensbury went with the rest of the Palatine contingent, consisting of some three hundred men, to Albany to join other forces from New York, New Jersey, and Connecticut (of Pennsylvania's quota, not a man turned up).[14] Governor Hunter, on March 29, left them "upon their march beyond Albany towards the lakes," with a large body of Indians of the Five Nations to follow, intending to coöperate with the English fleet in the reduction of Canada. Meanwhile Admiral Walker, of drawing-room fame, pirouetted on and off the rocks in the Gulf of St. Lawrence (during the course of which adventures the *Feversham*, which had escorted the *Lyon* to New York the year before, was wrecked[15]), and sailed for home after accomplishing nothing more to his credit than getting a rôle for himself in the French Canadian legend of *L'Amiral Fantôme*. The Palatines marched home again and were discharged without pay.

The return of some three hundred armed and angry men ("they found their Families almost starv'd, no provision having been given them during their absence"[16]) brought the unsettlement at Livingston Manor to a head. The Palatines, led by John Conrad Weiser,[17] informed the Governor that their present lands were worthless, and that they were resolved to have "the lands given them by the Queen." Repeated conferences with the Governor, who had the covenant read aloud to them in German, failed to disturb their determination to have the lands at "Scorie." The terms of the contract were clear enough, obliging them to remain where the Governor put them till they had paid off their debt to the Queen; but they declared they would rather lose their lives than stay where they were.

At last the Governor (as the Palatines complained later through their representative, John Conrad Weiser, in London) "in a passion stamp'd on the Ground & said here is your Land (meaning the almost Barren Rocks) where you must live & dye."[18] Seeing a body of armed insurgents at hand, he deployed his own troops and gave orders to fire if the Palatines did not submit to being disarmed.

The climax came in the fall of 1712. The Governor, moved by the collapse of his fortune under the drain of supporting the colony without help from the Treasury, informed the Palatines that from now on they would have to support themselves. This they could do, he said, either from the produce of the lands on which they were now settled, or by hiring themselves out to the people of the province—remembering always that they were still bound by the covenant and under obligation to return to the manufacture of tar whenever the Governor called them.

"Then the People Scattered over the whole province of new-york," wrote Weiser for his children. "Many remained where they were   about 150 families determined to remove to schocharih (a place about 40 English Miles to the West of Albany). They therefore sent deputies to the land of the Maquas to consult with the Indians about it who allowed them to occupy schochary . . . my Father was the First of the german deputies"[19]

A few families, impatient for their "promised land," cut a fifteen-mile passage through the worst part of the forest and hurried into the valley. Their sufferings during the winter and spring were intense. The rest of the Palatines, even those whose hearts were set on the Schoharie, were too prudent to throw themselves into the wilderness unprepared.

In November 1713 [actually 1712: Conrad is frequently wrong about these early dates] when the above-mentioned deputies had returned from the Maqua country to lewenstein Manor the people moved the same Autumn to Albany and Shonechtady so as to be able to move in the spring to schochary bread was excessively dear. the people worked hard For Their daily bread and the Inhabitants were very kind and did Much good to the german newcomers, though for that matter there were some ill-disposed persons too, my Father reached Shenechady the same fall where he remained with his family over winter with a man named Johannes Meyndert.[20]

CHAPTER 3

. . . *Lives Among the Mohawks*

FROM Schenectady in 1712 Conrad Weiser set out on his first adventure among the Indians. A number of Mohawks, including Hendrick, Terachjoris, and three other sachems, had come down from their castles by way of Schenectady to Albany in order to meet Mr. Andrews, the new missionary sent out at their request by the Society for the Propagation of the Gospel.[1] A heavy snowfall held up travel on the trails for some time after the welcoming ceremonies had been completed on November 15, but by the twentieth the Indians were on their way back to their castles.[2]

"A chief Of the Maqua [Mohawk] Nation Named Qua y nant," writes Conrad, "visited my Father   they agreed that I should go with quaynant to his country to learn the Maqua language   I went with Him and reached the Maqua country towards the end of November. . . ."[3]

Old John Conrad had now one less mouth to feed. All the boys had in one way or another been provided for. That eased the immediate problem of subsistence. Looking into the future, he no doubt saw the advantage to be gained for his people in their Schoharie venture by training up for them an interpreter independent of the Governor's interest. His son Conrad, just turned sixteen, was young enough to master the Mohawk tongue, which Mr. Andrews speaks of as so "Extream hard to be learnt" that it is "almost impossible for any to learn it perfectly except they begin wth it when Children."[4]

It was Conrad's first long absence from the family circle, and he was half-terrified among the strangers with whom he took up his lodging: black-haired, brown-skinned people who wore mantles of blanket cloth or bearskin, who greased their bodies with clarified bear's fat, and who called themselves the Ho-dé-no-sau-nee or People of the Long House, the doors of which were kept by the Mohawk nation on the east and the Seneca nation on the west. Mr. Andrews, who was also spending his first winter among them, found them astonishing to look at. They "cut their hair off from one side of their heads," he wrote, "and some of that on the other they tie up in Knots upon the Crown with ffeathers, Tufts of ffur upon their Ears and some of them wear a Bead fastened to their Noses with a Thread hanging down to their Lips, Bead and Wampum about their Hocks and wrists."[5]

Mr. Andrews does not tell us that different nations of Indians had different modes of hair-dress and body decoration, and that it was only the warriors who went in for shaved heads: it was a sign of their profession. Visiting French Mohawk warriors (the Caughnawagas or Praying Indians settled near Montreal) were almost bald, having had the hairs of the head pulled out except for a tuft on the crown. Visiting Senecas from their home region about Niagara fluttered the hearts of Mohawk girls with their nose beads. But the tribal meaning of such ornaments would at first be lost on a boy like Conrad, whose excitement would spring from the very strangeness of the costumes and colors and smells and sounds that mingled all about him.

The Mohawks lived in towns. Dyiondarogon, the so-called Lower Castle, which consisted "of 40 or 50 Wigwams or houses, pallizadoed Round," [6] and contained about 460 men, women, and children, stood near the mouth of Schoharie Creek beside the new English fort where Mr. Andrews held services in the Queen's Chapel. The Upper Castle, Canajoharie, was a town of twenty or thirty houses [7] where "King" Hendrick lived and his brothers Abraham and Nicholas. Besides these two main towns there were other smaller villages (with "7 or 8 houses in a Town" [8]) along the Mohawk Valley and its tributaries.

Twenty-four miles south of Dyiondarogon was a small castle called "Eskaharie," where some forty Mohawks lived; [9] and about eight miles to the south of it, at a bend in Schoharie Creek under the nose of Onistagrawa or Corn Mountain, where the cultivation of maize is said to have been brought to a state of perfection, was a still smaller village under the head-ship of Karighondonte. Some evidence points to this village, situated on a broad flat valley enfolded by a spur of the Catskill Mountains, within a mile or two of the present town of Middleburgh, N.Y., as the scene of Conrad's first residence among the Mohawks.[10]

Conrad spent a winter that lasted four or five snow-bound months in a Mohawk long house "made of Mats & bark of Trees together with poles about 3 or 4 yards high"; [11] and, although each of the several compartments in the house had its separate fire, he suffered much from the cold.

Like most young people in contact with strangers, Conrad took the virtues of his hosts for granted and marked only their vices. He was hungry and blamed them for improvidence. Their violence when in drink so frightened him that he often ran away to hide in fear of his life. Yet despite this he felt a strong pull on his affections, which was to last during life, made by Chief Quaynant and his family circle. Among those of Conrad's generation (I speak thus broadly since in counting relationship among the Mohawks those whom we call cousins ranked in certain cases as brothers and sisters) were Jonathan Cayenquiloquoa and his brother Moses, the Song [12]—good warriors both in their time, and friends to the English colonies. There was also a girl who, some forty years later, was to be the foster mother of Conrad's son Sammy when he in his turn was training to be an interpreter.

II

Who were the Ho-dé-no-sau-nee, these People of the Long House who repelled and at the same time attracted Conrad, and, by laying hold on his love and his fear, seized his attention and engaged his sympathies so deeply that he came in time to have a more thorough understanding of their mind and way of life than any other white man of his day?

The Mohawks, keepers of the eastern door, were a part of the Five Nations Confederacy (the Iroquois) whose chief towns and council fires dotted the forest along the Ambassadors' Road between the Hudson River and Niagara. From east to west there were, first, the Mohawks (more properly the *Caniengas*, the People of the Flint—Mohawk being a name given them in derision by their enemies the Delawares), whose nation, having originated the League, was known as the Eldest Brother; then the Oneidas, or People of the Standing Stone; the Onondagas, or People of the Mountain; the Cayugas, the Great-Pipe People; [13] and the Senecas, or People of the Great Hill.[14]

They were divided into two groups, the Elder Nations and the Younger Nations; the Mohawks, Onondagas, and Senecas comprising the first group, and the Oneidas and Cayugas (and later the Tuscaroras) the second. The Senecas and Mohawks, as befitted their position as guardians of the two doors of the Long House, had the greatest name in war, though there were famous warriors also among the other nations. The Onondagas, as befitted the central position which they held in the League—in more than the geographical sense—were known as the most philosophical and the most sage in council. They preserved the finest traditions of the Iroquois peoples and were, at the time at which we first meet them, the least injured of all the Five Nations by the corrosive acid of the white man's culture.

The Council of the Confederacy met at the chief village of the Onondagas, and sachems of this tribe were custodians of the Council Brand— the Fire that Never Dies—as well as of the wampum belts on which the records of the Confederacy were preserved. Today an Indian village named Onondaga, on the outskirts of Syracuse, still stands as a monument to the ancient confederacy whose impress was felt a thousand miles through the woods, and whose orders went unchallenged from Lake Ontario to Chesapeake Bay and from the Delaware River to beyond the Ohio.

"The 5 Indian Nations," reported Governor Dongan of New York in 1687, "are the most warlike people in America & are a bulwark between us & the French & all other Indians. *They goe as far as the South Sea, the North West passage & Florida to warr.*" [15]

"The most warlike people in America." We have known it from childhood: war whoops, scalps, dripping tomahawks and all; naked bodies gliding through the woods on noiseless moccasins; not a twig snaps and only the melancholy call of the loon breaks the unearthly stillness.

Forget the melodrama. The Iroquois were human, man for man neither more brave nor more cunning, and indeed no more cruel, than their white brothers. They had much the same aptitudes, the same fears, the same hopes, even some of the same vices. But there was a difference that made it difficult for people of European stock, especially in the early eighteenth century, to understand them. Their *mores* were those of a transitional culture between a savage and a civilized state. The Five Nations were just emerging from a Dark Age of warfare and wandering, and beginning to enjoy the fruits of a great experiment in social and political organization associated with the names of Deganaweda and Hiawatha.

Hiawatha, an Onondaga Indian with a poet's vision of a warless world and an orator's skill in moving people, after having been driven out of his own nation by the snake-haired dictator Atotarho, made himself a canoe and paddled down the Mohawk River to one of the Mohawk castles, where he found refuge. The Mohawks adopted him and put themselves behind his proposal for a league of Iroquois nations—a league that was intended to be strong enough and broad enough to embrace ultimately all of human kind.

That is the legend as given by Horatio Hale in *The Iroquois Book of Rites* (Philadelphia, 1883). The official version of the Iroquois, however, gives to Deganaweda the honor of having originated the League, as we read in Duncan Campbell Scott's "Traditional History of the Confederacy of the Six Nations" (*Transactions of the Royal Society of Canada*, 1911) and in Arthur C. Parker's *The Constitution of the Five Nations* (Albany, 1916). The fact seems to be that Deganaweda with his bundle of sticks, each of which was weak but which together were unbreakable, provided the symbol of union; and, with his extraordinary mind for organization, Deganaweda (assisted by Hiawatha) worked out the details of a plan by which the nations might be interlocked in the meshes of a firm but flexible net of family union. So it was that, some time before the white men appeared, five independent peoples of Iroquois stock organized a league of nations, sometimes called Kayanerenh-kowa, the Great Peace, with an ingenious system of clans that bound the different peoples comprising it with the closest family ties, and so by one step gained peace among themselves and security from their enemies.

They were now ready to advance the next step and build what we call a civilization for themselves. Their genius seemed to promise it—if the white man with his mastery of machines did not crush them before they were well started.

They had a deep sense of human brotherhood, the Ho-dé-no-sau-nee, fostered by a religion of love. They believed in a great spirit, Tarachia-wagon, the Holder of the Heavens, who cared for his people and desired them to care for one another. They told their children how he had appointed to each of the Five Nations its own place to dwell in, and how he had taught them the use of corn and other fruits of the earth. They approached him, this Father of the Peoples, not by way of church and altar, bell, book, and candle, but through nature, finding as Wordsworth did that "there is a spirit in the woods." The precepts of the Great Spirit they obeyed with a fidelity that put most Christians to shame.

The teachings of Christ and his apostles [writes Weiser] [16] are more congenial to them than to [many so-called Christians]: for when it is said Owe no man anything save to love one another Rom 13:8 Be not anxious for the morrow Matth 6:34 He that is greatest among you shall be your servant Matth 23:11 . . . That is what they actually practice without calling themselves Christian, while many who bear the name never give such things a thought.

. . . If the word religion means a formal belief in certain written Articles of Faith, such as, prayer, singing, churchgoing, baptism, the Lord's Supper, or other well-known Christian ordinances, or even heathen worship, then we can truly say: the Indians, or so-called Iroquois, and their neighbors have no religion, for of such a one we see and hear nothing among them. But if by the word religion we understand the knitting of the soul to God, and the intimate relation to, and hunger after the highest Being arising therefrom, then we must certainly allow this apparently barbarous people a religion, for we find traces among them that they have a united trust in God, and some-time (although quite seldom) united appeals to Him.

Whatever the story books may tell us to the contrary, the Five Nations were not at heart a bloodthirsty and cruel people. Conrad found them gentle—as long as the rum trader was absent. "One can be among them for thirty years and more," he wrote, "and never once see two sober Indians fight or quarrel." Mr. Andrews at the Lower Castle, writing in 1712/3, found them (except when in liquor "a civil peaceable quiet people . . . Extream kind to each other . . ." [17]

Horatio Hale, in *The Iroquois Book of Rites*, confirms Weiser's estimate of them:

Instead of a race of rude and ferocious warriors, we find . . . a kindly and affectionate people, full of sympathy for their friends in distress, considerate to their women, tender to their children, anxious for peace, and imbued with a profound reverence for their constitution and its authors. We become conscious of the fact that the aspect in which these Indians have presented themselves to the outside world has been in a large measure deceptive and factitious. The ferocity, craft and cruelty, which have been deemed their leading traits, have been merely the natural accompaniments of wars of self-preservation, and no more indicated their genuine character than the war-paint, plume and tomahawk of the warrior displayed the customary guise in which he appeared among his own people. The cruelties of war, when war is a struggle for national existence, are common to all races. The persistent desire for peace, pursued for centuries in federal unions, and in alliances and treaties with other nations, has been manifested by few as steadily as by the countrymen of Hiawatha. The sentiment of universal brotherhood which directed their polity has never been so fully developed in any branch of the Aryan race, unless it may be found incorporated in the religious quietism of Buddha and his followers.[18]

The people of this "Confederate Republic," as Lewis Evans calls them in his map of 1749, were democrats on the Anglo-Saxon model: a liberty-loving people, who harnessed their freedom with tradition and ceremony to keep it under control. Impatient of restraint yet masters of themselves, they could endure any hardship except slavery. In captivity they died. They held to a system of hereditary chiefs or *royaners* (the Delawares called such council chiefs "sachems," and this word is the one commonly used in contemporary records), yet they exercised the right of deposing any chief, as Hendrick was deposed in the winter of 1712–13, and of choosing other leaders at any time to guide them in council or in war. Joseph Brant was not a *royaner*, yet he led them in the hegira to Canada. There were forty-nine of these hereditary chieftainships, each perpetuating the name of one of the founders of the League, as Atotarho, Hiawatha, etc. Descent was, from our point of view, in a zigzag line, commonly through a sister of the last incumbent, for theirs was a matriarchal system, and relationship was traced through the female line. On the death of a *royaner*, the head woman of the family in which his chieftainship ran chose a successor and proposed his name to the council. Her recommendation was seldom rejected.

The Ho-dé-no-sau-nee respected their chiefs, but there was no snobbery. Their great men were as poor as the poorest, for *noblesse oblige*, and they shared whatever they possessed. Shickellamy, the great pro-consul at Shamokin, died in rags. Their language took no cognizance of social grades. In conversation there was no *Sie* and *du* to juggle with, Conrad Weiser noticed, according as the social status of one's interlocutor was above or below one's own. There were no words for "Your Majesty," "Your Highness," or "Your Excellency." They called the English governor "Brother."

Their justice was simple but sufficient. They had no police and they needed none. Their code of honor was seldom broken. They recognized two crimes: theft and murder. Sex crimes were unknown among them. They administered one punishment: death. But it was seldom needed. Fear of public disapproval was usually sufficient to keep the slate clean. In one particular only did their justice conspicuously fail. Violence committed by a man in liquor was overlooked, for rum was acknowledged to be a power above the human will, and their sense of social obligation had not yet had time to build a code, such as that which guarded sex, to fend off this newly imported evil.

III

The strength of the Ho-dé-no-sau-nee is not to be explained by the number of their fighting men, which was small, but by that of their allies, which was enormous. If the prestige of the League had depended on the two or three thousand men they were able to put into the field, even though these were the best fighting men in the woods, they could never have held their empire together. They owed their power chiefly to the wise statesmanship by which they made it profitable to most of the Indian nations in their world to respect the Great Peace and accept its protection. "No people," wrote James Logan to John Penn, "have a truer Notion of Justice than they, nor more strictly insist on it . . ." [19]

Though the nations comprising the Confederacy had a language of their own, each speaking a dialect of the common tongue, they were not very different in blood from the Algonquin peoples surrounding them. The custom of adopting prisoners of war, and so assimilating conquered peoples, made any sharp racial distinction impossible. But the ethos of the Five

Nations was their own. Their strong but loose-bound union (like that of the modern British Commonwealth), symbolized in the Fire that Never Dies at Onondaga; the bold and significant Iroquoian myths with which they fed the minds of their children; the body of historical tradition which they preserved by means of wampum belts and ceremonial chants; the sense of international responsibility felt by members of a league that sought to preserve peace along with justice among all peoples as far as their wampum belts could reach—all these together gave the man of the Five Nations a distinctive character. He was the *civis romanus* of the woods.

If we stop to cast up the accomplishments of this people, whose total number—men, women, and children—was probably never in excess of fifteen or twenty thousand; and if we remember that from their towns in what is now the State of New York they conquered their enemies in an ever-widening circle that overlapped the present boundaries of New England, Pennsylvania, the Virginias, North Carolina, Kentucky, Ohio, Indiana, Illinois, Michigan, and Ontario; that they made alliances beyond that circle, established protectorates, offered asylum to harried peoples who turned to them from all sides of their empire for help, and by these means maintained order for generations over a territory almost equal in size to western Europe—we may begin to see that the story of the Five Nations is one of the great stories of mankind.

Even now, after they have been broken up and dispersed over a number of reservations in the United States and Canada, the Five Nations (now Six) are still a people. If they are no longer a powerful one, we in our time of prosperity have no cause to look on them with condescension. In the infant days of the English colonies in America, we were dependent on them for our preservation. A little more than two hundred years ago, some of their chiefs spoke these words, as told by Conrad Weiser in one of his first recorded translations, to the Governor of New France who was preparing to make war against the English:

Corlaer [the Province of New York in the person of its governor] is our Brother. He came to us when he was but very little, and a Child, we suckled him at our Breasts; we have nursed him & taken Care of him till he is grown up to be a Man; he is our Brother & of the same Blood. He and We have but one Ear to hear with, One Eye to see with and one Mouth to speak with. We will not forsake him, nor see any Man make War with him without assisting.[20]

In 1755, when our population was eighty times that of the Six Nations, we still sought, and received, their protection; and Conrad Weiser is chiefly remembered for having given us the determining advantage of their assistance in the French and Indian War. Today no honor is too high for this marvelous people to whom we owe in large measure our national existence.

CHAPTER 4

. . . Finds Himself in a Dungeon

I

CONRAD WEISER, during the winter of 1712–13, was in no mood to see the virtues of the Ho-dé-no-sau-nee nor indeed to say a good word about anything. He was preoccupied with his own troubles. Not only did he suffer much from the excessive cold, being "but badly clothed," as he tells us, but "towards spring also from hunger, for the Indians had almost nothing to eat. A bushel of Indian corn was worth five to six shillings." [1]

His fear of drunken Indians had grounds enough. At the best of times the effect of liquor on the Indians was not to make Pickwicks of them, comfortably maudlin and amusing, but to turn them into "mad distracted Creatures," as Mr. Andrews wrote that same winter from what he saw of them at the Lower Mohawk Castle, and to set them "doing any mischiefe; some are for burning their houses others for killing their wives and Children." [2]

In 1713 they had special reason to turn their rage against the whites. A rumor spread along the Mohawk Valley that the English were resolved "to kill and destroy all who had Black Pates," [3] in other words, all Indians. During the summer a belt of wampum two hands broad came up from Conestoga in Pennsylvania with word that the governor intended to cut off the Five Nations in revenge for their support of the Tuscaroras in the war the latter were waging against North Carolina.

The rumor was unfounded, but it was one that easily gained credence in the uncertain state of Indian relations. The Five Nations some time before this, on receiving an appeal for help from the Tuscaroras, who were of Iroquoian stock and were hard beset when their ancient enemies the Catawbas received the backing of the Carolina whites, had offered them sanctuary on their lands in Pennsylvania and New York, and even proposed to take them into the League "on the cradle-board," that is, to give them a voice at the Great Council without allotting them permanent seats or royanerships, so that Deganaweda's roster of chiefs should remain undisturbed. With the inclusion of the Tuscaroras, which took place some time about 1710, [4] though their migration to the north by way of the Tuscarora Path or Path Valley took the better part of a hundred years to complete, the Five Nations became Six and were thenceforth so called. At the same time the Six Nations, now at war with North Carolina, wondered how they stood with the people of New York who owed allegiance to Carolina's "female king." The woods were tingling with apprehension. In Fort Hunter, where a small English garrison at the mouth of the Schoharie overlooked the stockaded "ferst castel" [5] of the Mohawks, fears were entertained of an Indian rising that, despite the presence of the new missionary, might destroy the fort and everybody in it.

Toward the end of July, soon after the Six Nations had received the warning belt from Conestoga, Conrad Weiser left the *Wilder Hook* (as the Dutch named the bend in Schoharie Creek where Karighondonte had his town), and returned to his own people. His father was now settled only a mile or two away, on the other side of the creek. He had moved into the valley in March with a party of 150 families, using "sledges thro' the snow which then Cover'd the ground about 3 foot deep." [6] The village where he had settled, which bore his name, Weisersdorf, had some forty log houses,[7] set along a street later known as the Clauver Wye, which may still be seen in the town of Middleburgh, rambling in a westerly direction over the flats toward the mouth of the Little Schoharie.

The neighborhood was full of sweet clover and Indians—Mohicans (there was a village of them across the creek from the *Wilder Hook* and the mountain to the south was called the *Moheganter*), Mohawks, Tuscaroras, Oneidas, Delawares. This was border country, exposed to the French. One of Governor Hunter's reported reasons for declining to settle the Palatines here in the first place was the difficulty of defending it. Karighondonte, it is to be remembered, was himself a French Indian. Some of his "nation," as the three hundred Indians who had gathered under his leadership were sometimes called, being suspicious of the newcomers and insulting, the Palatines "were obliged," as John Conrad put it, "to keep fair with the Friendly Indians amongst Whom they dwelt, which was the only way to be protected & live in Peace." [8] The young interpreter was soon called on to show his skill. He writes:

I had made a good beginning, that is to say I had learned the greater part Of the Mohawk language, An English mile From my Father's house there lived several Mohawk families with the mohawks always around going out Hunting and coming back difficulties often cropped up, so that I had Much interpreting to do but without pay   there was No one else to be found among our people who understood the Language, so that I became Completely master of the Language. so Far as my Years and other circumstances permitted.[9]

In the main, circumstances were favorable. The geographical situation was the best possible for such training, for, while the Schoharie was then beyond the bounds of white civilization, the fact that the three chief rivers of the Atlantic seaboard (the Hudson, Delaware, and Susquehanna) headed in the mountains of the Mohawk country made it one of the cosmopolitan centers of Indian life. The Palatine settlement itself was at the hub of important Indian trails: to the Mohawk River at the Lower and again at the Upper Mohawk Castle; to the Hudson at Albany and again at Catskill; to the headwaters of the Delaware, some twenty miles away, at Lake Utsayantha; to Lake Otsego (where Fenimore Cooper was to have his home), and what was later known as Cherry Valley; to the Adaquighung or Charlotte Branch of the Susquehanna; and, *via* Cookose on the Mohawk Branch of the Delaware, directly to the Susquehanna itself at the important Indian settlement of Oquage. The Susquehanna valley gave all the Six Nations their best highway, whether by water or by trail, to Pennsylvania and the southern colonies. The Schoharie was, in consequence, a much-traveled valley, and contained within its boundaries fragments of many Indian nations. Karighondonte's village contained both Mohawks and Delawares, the latter a people who were held in subjection by the Six Nations and denominated "women," but who were winning a curious revenge by making their nickname Mohaw-wuk or Mohawk, which means "man-eater" or "louse," stick to their chief enemies, the Caniengas.[10] No place in America could have been better suited for Conrad's introduction to the currents of Indian politics, customs, and prejudices, in preparation for his later career as an Indian ambassador.

But Conrad's eyes were not set on distant horizons. "About this time," he writes, "I became ill and thought I would die and would have been glad to die, my stepmother was a stepmother indeed, through her influence I was harshly treated by my Father, I had no other friend to turn to and had to endure hunger and cold, I often made up my mind to Run away, but the Sickness mentioned put a bridle and bit in my mouth I was bound as if with rope to give obedience and stay with my Father" [11]

No doubt it was of this same period, when, surrounded by embittered people intent on their grievances, he developed a hearty grievance of his own, that he wrote in his Onondaga Journal of 1737: "I had, at a previous period of my life, wished that I had never heard of a God, either from my parents or other people, for the idea I had of him led me away from him. I thought the Atheists more happy than those who cared much about God." [12]

It was out of this "great anguish," as he calls it, that Conrad found his religion. The very violence of his distress and the loneliness of his situation caused him to look inward and to discover resources within himself. He had embarked thus early on a search for spiritual reality that was to lead him through many strange adventures in the ensuing years. He was by nature richly endowed with spiritual faculty, but he lacked the help of any ordered teaching to guide his thought. Perhaps it was as well. At least it assured him a more intimate contact with the unseen world than if he had approached it through conventional intermediaries. He learned little from tradition but much from experience. If he had relied on the teaching of the schools, he might have become only another of the violent sectarians who disturbed the church fellowship of the time. As it was he grew up into the wise tolerance of one who could define religion as "an attraction of the soul to God"; [13] and who, worshipping earnestly with the Lutherans, the Reformed, the Moravians, the Seventh Day German Baptists, and the People of the Long House, found his God among them all.

II

At Weisersdorf Conrad found everyone in extremest poverty. Only the kindness of the Indians, who showed them where to find food in the woods, and the charity of Albany and Schenectady people, who lent them equipment, kept the colony going. "one borrowed a horse here another maybe a cow there and plow harness," wrote Conrad. "they banded together and broke so Much sod as to have almost enough corn to Eat Next year. but this year we suffered great hunger, and people made many a meal of the wild *patatas* and Ground Beans which grew in great Plenty the *patates* were called *ochnanada* By the Indians and the Ground Beans *otachragara* when we wanted Flour we had to go some 35 or 40 Miles For it and then beg it on credit, one got a bushel of wheat here another a bushel or two there and we were often 3 or 4 days Away from home before we got back to our folks who were waiting in pain and tears for bread." [14]

Conrad was not romancing when he wrote thus of his hardships. The Rev. John F. Haeger, describing the misery of the "poor Palatines" in a letter of July 6, 1713, says that "they boil grass and ye children eat the leaves of the trees. . . . I have seen old men and women crie that it should have almost moved a stone." [15]

"the people had settled in villages," continues Conrad, "of which there were seven . . . named . . . after the deputies who had been sent from Lewensteins Manor to the Mohawk country.[16] . . . Here then the People lived for some years without preachers and without magistrats Fairly peaceably each man did what seemed right to him" [17]

Once established, there were no better settlers in America than these Schoharie Palatines. They resembled the New England Puritans in that they had the fear of the Lord in their hearts; but they did not have the Puritan conviction of sin. They enjoyed life frankly and were tolerant of their neighbors. They loved heartily, ate freely, and believed in witches, though they did not hang them. They were not given to mortifying the flesh. *Nach 'm Essen, en ka Dabak; un' DAS schteht in d'r Bibel* [18]—so runs the saying among their descendants in Pennsylvania today: "After food, a chew of tobacco; and THAT is in the Bible."

Above all, they liked to be their own masters and to work their own land. Here on the Schoharie the land was theirs by right of various purchases they had made from Karighondonte and others: one such purchase being made with three hundred pieces of eight. In all they had a ten-mile tract running down the valley from a burned oak stump marked by the Indians with a turtle and a snake.[19] This marker was near the mouth of the Little Schoharie, not far above the present town of Middleburgh.

As soon as they had arrived, they had set to work cutting down trees and putting up shelters—which they needed at once, for within a week of their coming four babies were born. "From logs they cut blocks," wrote the chronicler Simms in 1845, "which answered the purposes of chairs and tables." [20] Bedsteads, he tells us, they dispensed with for the time. Men lie soft on ground that is their own. Outdoor "bake-ovens" were built and shared by neighboring families. Hartmansdorf, one of the larger villages, is said to have had seven. Judge Brown, the first historian of the Schoharie (he was born in 1745 of Palatine parents and was brought up on

the Schoharie) tells us that "the new inhabitants soon began to think themselves well off. By their industry, and great fertility of the soil, they soon
got plenty to eat—wore more moggisins—buckskin breeches and jackets
of leather, which they plentifully obtained of the Indians." [21] "They Had
a Horse": [22] a gray bought by nine persons at Weisersdorf. John Conrad
Weiser undoubtedly had a share in it.

But meanwhile a cloud had drifted over the colony. Orders had come
from the Governor "not to goe upon the land," as they themselves afterwards expressed it, "& he who did so should be declar'd a Rebell." [23] In
their relations with Governor Hunter the Palatines believed themselves to
be reënacting the story of Pharaoh and the Israelites. It is to be feared that
these "laborious and honest but . . . headstrong ignorant people," [24] as
Governor Burnet afterwards described them, were too intent on their
grievances to do justice to Governor Hunter. The latter, according to
Judge Brown, sent an agent, Bayard, into the Schoharie Valley to give a
deed to "every householder who would make known to him the boundaries
of the land he had taken." [25] But the Palatines were beyond reason, a
prey to what Judge Brown calls "black ignorance." Suspecting a plot to
deprive them of their new lands, they besieged the agent in the house of
Hans Jerry Schmidt of Schmidtsdorf, firing some sixty shots into the
house through the straw roof. Mr. Bayard, who had pistols, shot back, kept
the crowd off during the day, and escaped under cover of night to Schenectady. Governor Hunter, it is said, gave the Palatines still another chance
to get deeds for their lands, this time on payment of "one ern of corn," [26]
but no one appeared to take the offer. The Governor in the end granted
away the Schoharie lands to certain "Gentlemen of Albany," among whom
were Rip van Dam and Robert Livingston, the latter a son of the one-
time "Patrone" of the Palatines. It now became the care of these "Gentlemen of Albany" to make the Palatines choose between paying for the
land on which they were settled or leaving it.

When the elderly Adam Vroman, a Dutchman from Albany, arrived
in 1715 and took up lands across the creek from Weisersdorf, John Conrad
eyed him as an intruder and set out to get rid of him. Certainly Vroman
had some right to his land, for he had bought it of the Indians; but certainly
also the Weisers and their Indian friends had some cause for complaint,
since between 1711 and 1714 Vroman's Indian deed for 260 acres had
grown into a government patent for over a thousand. [27]

When Vroman first came, the Palatines warned him to keep off. When
he disregarded the warning, ploughed his acres under Corn Mountain,
and sowed grain, the Palatines drove their horses over his new-sown fields
at night. To disturb his slumbers, they led horses with bells about their
necks up and down past the Indian house where he lodged. They waited
till his new stone house was getting well up, and then one night they came
and tore it down. But Vroman won out in the end. He persisted, raised
his crops, built his house, and when he died left Onistagrawa behind
him as a monument to his stubbornness; for the beaky little eminence

that overlooks the site of Weisersdorf, the Wilder Hook, and all the arena
of these early quarrels, goes now by the name of Vroman's Nose.

On July 9, 1715, Vroman wrote a letter to Governor Hunter, laying
all his troubles at the door of the Weisers, father and son:

John Conradus Wiser has been the Ring Leader among the Indians and now
he is turn'd their Interpreter so that this Wiser and his Son talk with the
Indians very often and have made treates for them and have been busy to buy
Land at many places which is Contrary to your Excellencys Proclamation,
and has made the Indians drunk to that degree to go and mark of Land with
them: and I am no wayes secure of my Life their for after I came away they
went and pulld my son off of the waggon and beat him and said they would
kill him or his father or any body Else that came their so that my son was
forced to come away: Likewise they say they care for nobody   John Conradus Wiser & 2 or 3 more has made their Escape by way of Boston and have
said they will go for England but has left his son which is their Interpreter to
the Indians and every day tells the Indians many Lyes, whereby much mis-
cheife may Ensue more than we now think off . . .[28]

It is not surprising that a few days later Governor Hunter should have
issued instructions to all justices of the peace in the counties of Albany
and Duchess to arrest on sight "one John Conrade Wiser a Covenanted
Servant of his Majesty, who has been Guilty of Several Mutinous Riotous
and other disobedient & illegal practices is now skulking in your County
to avoid punishment . . . and to cause him to be sent down in safe Custody
to the City of New York That he may be proceeded against as the Nature
of his Crimes shall require." [29] The Governor even thought proper to
warn the Lords of Trade in London about this "Jean Conrad Weizer,"
leader of seditions and creator of confusion among the Five Nations, who,
says his Excellency, has fled to Boston and "gives out that he is bound
for England instructed by the Indians." [30]

According to Simms, a tradition has been handed down in the Vroman
family that that same autumn, after Adam Vroman and his son had left
the Wilder Hook and gone to Schenectady for the winter, a man named
Moore from Weisersdorf murdered the agent, Truax, whom Vroman
had left behind. Moore escaped, says the legend, and went to Pennsylvania,
where he later confessed.[31] There was, in fact, a Johannes Mohr living
in Weisersdorf about that time (see the Simmendinger list [32]), and we do
find the name of Hans Moore in the Tulpehocken tax list for 1725,[33] but
the confession is not among our documents.

Sheriff Adams came one day to Weisersdorf with a special warrant to
take John Conrad Weiser "dead or a life," [34] as John Conrad reported
the incident afterwards in London. The sheriff was no more welcome
than Vroman had been, but this time (Weiser meanwhile having had
warning and made his escape) the women took charge of the entertainment. They were led by Magdalena Zeh, who perhaps thought of herself
as another Barbara Walch, the heroine of Shorndorf, Württemberg, who
had once marched a body of women to the town hall with brooms and

mops and shown the town council its duty.[35] Magdalena and her gossips knocked the sheriff down, beat him, dragged him through barnyard puddles, rode him on a rail seven miles through the settlements, broke two of his ribs, and destroyed the sight of one eye.[36] In such manner, observed John Conrad, was Sheriff Adams "prevented." [37] Governor Hunter said "he would hang John Conrad Weiser." [38]

"After this circumstance," writes Judge Brown, to whom we turn for conclusion of the episode, "the Schoharie people got very shy to go to Albany—made the practice to send their wives for salt, or not to enter Albany but on Sundays, and then out again." Nothing happening for a long time, however, the Weisersdorfers grew so "tame" that one day a good number of their menfolk ventured to enter the town, where-upon the sheriff and a posse sallied out and "took every one of them and clapped them to jail. The most notorious were put in the dungeon, among whom was young Conrad Wiser." [39]

The prisoners were not to be released until they had signed papers recognizing the title of the "Gentlemen of Albany" to the Schoharie lands. "Young Conradt Wiser soon got tired of his dungeon, resolved to agree to take a lease and pay rent; so did all the rest that were in jail." [40]

The Palatine trust in Albany chivalry was due for a shock. Even one of their women (was it Magdalena Zeh?) was arrested. Her retention in prison was one item in the catalogue of complaints that John Conrad Weiser afterwards tried to lay before the Throne.

The spirit of the colony was all but broken, but the Palatines made one last move. They despatched three deputies, John Conrad Weiser, William Scheff, and John Walrath, to London to lay their grievances before the sovereign.[41] Queen Anne "of most glorious memory" was no more, but it was hoped her successor, George I, who spoke German, would be as generous as she had been to her wards.

The journey was disastrous from beginning to end, a trail of false hopes and broken lives. A flaming sword seemed to turn every way to keep this people out of their Eden. To begin with, the delegates were captured by pirates and stripped of everything. John Conrad Weiser was three times tied up and flogged. Reaching England at last in poverty, the deputies contracted debts and were thrown into prison, where Walrath died. When at last, after a weary while, fresh funds reached them from New York and they managed to get their petition at last before the authorities, Colonel Hunter, who had returned to England, appeared against them and ruined their case. Scheff and Weiser quarreled ("they both had hard heads," observed the younger Conrad [42]). Scheff returned alone to New York, where he died a few weeks after his arrival. John Conrad stayed on in England, interviewing the Penns and others, but nothing came of it. When at last he returned to America he had little more positive to show for his five years' labors in the Circumlocution Offices of Georgian England than a personal letter of recommendation from John Carteret, Secretary of State in Walpole's cabinet and one of the few Englishmen of the time who could speak German.

Lord Carteret to the Governor of New York [43]
Whitehall April 30th 1723

Gov[r] of New York
Sir

M[r] John Conrad Weiser who acts as Deputy on behalf of the Palatines at New York, being upon his return thither, I give him this Letter to recommend him to you desiring that you will give him all due encouragemen[t] & Protection. I am &ca

CARTERET

But the Palatines were to have the last word in the quarrel with Governor Hunter after all. Remembering their short flour rations and bad salt pork at Livingston Manor, they refused to sign a certificate to the effect that the Governor "had subsisted them pursuant to y[e] Queens orders"; and so Robert Hunter, now relieved of his governor's commission, failed to receive reimbursement from the government for his personal outlay on the Palatines' behalf.[44]

When John Conrad returned to New York, he found his Schoharie colony broken up. Some of the people, it is true, had humbled themselves and purchased title to the land from the Gentlemen of Albany. Others had accepted free government land farther north, at Stone Arabia. Still others turned their eyes to the south, having heard of rich lands in Pennsylvania, to which, indeed, Governor Keith of that province had invited them. John Conrad while in England had petitioned the Lords of Trade to let his people settle in the "Schettery" (Swatara) region of Pennsylvania.[45] But he returned from overseas too late to join the party of Palatines who, as his son tells us,

. . . united and cut a Way from schochary to the SusqueHana River brought Their goods over and made Canoes and descended the stream to the Mouth of Suartaro Creek and drove Their Cattle overland that was in the spring of the Year 1723. From there they came to tulpehockin and this is the beginning of the tulpehockin Settlements . . . others followed . . . took lands without permission of the authorities . . . and against the will of the Indians for the land had not yet been bought from Them, there was no one among the People to control them, everyone did as he liked and Their strong Self-will has stood in their way to this hour.[46]

John Conrad did not follow them for twenty-three years. He had other schemes in his head and private battles to fight: first on the Delaware River, where his unauthorized purchase of Minisink lands from the Indians brought him into conflict with the Proprietors of Pennsylvania and forced him to make another retreat; afterwards on the borders of New England, where his son visited him near Shecomeco. It was not until he reached the ripe age of eighty-six that the old "Rebell" came down to the Tulpehocken and there rounded out his career by dying under his son Conrad's roof.

Before we leave the story of Conrad's unhappy adolescence, we must take notice of an unpleasant story that tradition has connected with his name: the story of a foot race he won from an Indian rival by knocking him down.

"In the summer of 1713 or '14," writes Simms, "a *stump* was given by the Indians to their German neighbors at Weiser's dorf, to run a foot race, offering to stake on the issue, a lot of dressed deer-skins against some article the Germans possessed; possibly, their old mare. The challenge was accepted, and a son of Conrad Weiser was selected, to run against a little dark Indian, called the most agile on foot of all the tribe." [47]

The course was at Weisersdorf, starting half a mile above the village, and ending just beyond the first house in the town.

They had to run very close to the house, and Weiser, being on the outside as they approached it side by side, sprang with all his might against his competitor. The sudden impetus forced the Indian against the building, and he rebounded and fell half dead upon the ground. Weiser then easily won the race . . .[48]

That the story does Conrad no credit is, of course, no reason for disputing its authenticity. It may not square with what we know of Conrad's subsequent dealings with the Indians, which were honorable; but it squares very well with the unsociable temper he exhibited in his 'teens. The legend has no better authority than the garrulous Simms, who recorded it, without citing his own source, in two different versions published in 1845 and 1882. But there has recently come to my attention a curious bit of substantiating evidence. The story of the foot race gives a possible solution of the riddle of Conrad's Indian name of *Siguras* (or *Zihguras* as Conrad first spells it in 1736, *Segoruras* as it is spelled in Richard Peters' diary in 1758 [49]).

No such word as Siguras is now known among the Mohawks. But Chief William Loft (a *royaner* whose title, *Sharenkhowane*, comes second after that of Hiawatha in the Roll of the Chiefs) suggested to me at Ohsweken, Ontario, in 1937 that the old word may be the equivalent of the modern *sa-gor-yos*, meaning *the killer*.

"The name *Sagoryos*," explained Chief Loft, "would be applied to a warrior. Or it might be given in fun to someone who had knocked another down."

Conrad, the Killer. No wonder the chiefs changed Conrad's name when they came to know him better.

CHAPTER 5

. . . Brings His Ann Eve to Pennsylvania

ONCE his father was out of the way, Conrad Weiser settled down. "In 1720," he writes, "while my father was in England I took my Ann Eva to wife and was married by the rev. Johan friderich Heger reformed preacher the 22 november. in My Father's house at schochary" [1]

Ann Éve (as her father spells the name in his will [2]) was born in 1700. She was not, as some of her descendants would like to believe, an Indian. Henry Muhlenberg, her son-in-law, speaks of her as "a German Christian person of evangelical parentage." [3] She was the daughter of John Peter Feck (or Feg) and Anna Maria his wife, who had come out with the Palatines to New York in 1710. The Weisers and the Fecks there saw much of each other. "Johannis Feeg" is listed as one of the volunteers under Captain John Conrad Weiser for the Canada expedition of 1711.[4] Afterwards John Peter brought his family to the Schoharie and lived at Weisersdorf,[5] where his daughter Ann Eve no doubt marveled at the young interpreter's exploits, as she was to do more than half a century later at those of her grandson, General John Peter Muhlenberg, whose successes under Washington she lived to see.

A great number of Conrad Weiser's letters have been preserved. That there are no love letters among them is no reflection either on Conrad's heart or on his Ann Eve's. He had no reason to write to her since she had never learned to read. But she must have been lovable. Conrad's phrase, "my Ann Eve," suggests affection, as does also the birth of their fourteen children—several of them while Conrad was trying to live the life of a monk. If Ann Eve was like her daughter, Anna Maria, then Henry Muhlenberg's description of his young bride as "pure in heart, pious, unpretentious, meek, and active," [6] explains not only Conrad's life-long attachment to his home, but also the ever-widening circle of friends who found it a haven. Before Reading or Lebanon in Pennsylvania were heard of, the "Weisers" had a place on the map.

From the day of his marriage, Conrad's family takes first place in the Autobiography. He has little to say thereafter about himself and nothing at all about his grievances. He records the births, baptisms, and deaths of his children; and, with the arrival of his last child, Benjamin, in 1744, the Autobiography stops suddenly without so much as a hint of the public honors Conrad's adventures in the Indian world had brought him in that same year.

1722 the 7th September my Son philip was born and baptized by Joh. Bernhard von dühren luth. preacher his sponsors were philip braun and his wife the 13 January 1725 my daughter Anna Madlina was born, she was baptized by Joh. Jacob oehl refor. preacher Her sponsors were Christian Bauch Junior and my sister BarBara

1727 my daughter Maria was born the 24 June and baptized by Willm Christoph Birckenmeyer luth. Preacher Her sponsors nicklas feg & his wife

1728 the 24 december my Son friderich was born he was baptized by Joh. Bernhard von dühren luth. preacher his sponsors were nicklas feg and his wife

these four were born to me at schochary

then in the Year 1729 I went to pensilvania and settled at tulpehockin where the following children were born to me . . .[7]

We need not spur after him in this patriarchal gallop; but, leaving the rest of the children to make their appearance in due course, we turn back for a last view of the Weisers at Schoharie.

Ann Eve was pretty well tied to the house by the four children who came in the six years between 1722 and 1728, but Conrad was much on the trail. Early in 1721 he was sent to New York with a petition to the new governor, William Burnet, whom he found friendly but firm. In 1726 we find Conrad traveling as far into the wilderness as Otseninky (now Binghamton, N.Y.) on the Susquehanna.[8] We do not know whether he went there on foot by the trail that ran southwest from Weisersdorf past Mount Utsayantha, down the Mohawk Branch of the Delaware to Cookose, and thence over one range of hills to Oquage and over a second range to Otseninky; or whether he took the short and well-worn trail which the Palatines had used in 1723, over to the Adaquighung or Charlotte Branch of the Susquehanna and so down by canoe. We do know that eleven years later he was back in Otseninky as Pennsylvania's ambassador to the Six Nations, and was glad to have a bite of bread here (it was a time of famine) with one of his old Indian acquaintances.

He was restless at Weisersdorf and wanted to get away. It was no place to bring up a large family; there was not enough land available. On May 10, 1723, he with Johannes Lawyer, Jr., and Peter Wagoner, gave Caquayodighe and some other Indians the value of fifteen pounds in Indian goods in exchange for a large tract of land on Otsquage Creek not far from the Upper Mohawk Castle.[9] On the twentieth of June the three partners petitioned the government to recognize the grant.[10] But by the time the patent was forthcoming, which was not until July 8, 1725, Conrad's interest seems to have evaporated, for he did not enter into possession.

His heart was no longer in New York. Perhaps the sympathy his later career was to evince for the dispossessed Indians was an outgrowth of his own experience in that province. He had watched men like Adam Vroman and Rip van Dam squeeze their way into the Schoharie Valley as they and their like were squeezing a way, with the connivance of the law, into all the lands held by the Mohawks. Vroman by now was entrenched securely, owning the best pasture lands in the neighborhood of Weisersdorf. Conrad wanted to own a farm somewhere where there was room for expansion.

For a time he watched his father negotiating with the Delaware Indians for a purchase of their Minisink lands. By 1726 old John Conrad had actually bought one tract on the Delaware River, and was proposing to buy others, somewhere east of the present town of Stroudsburg, on which to settle the New York Palatines.[11] But the scheme collapsed when James Logan, the Provincial Secretary of Pennsylvania, wrote a threatening letter on August 1, 1727, warning John Conrad in the name of "common sense, & honesty," not to trespass on the Penns' domain.[12]

Then young Conrad turned his eyes to the region where his father-in-law, John Peter Feck, was already established.

". . . in the Year 1729 I went to pensilvania and settled at tulpehockin." [13]

We wish he had told us more about that journey. A removal in those days from the Catskills to the South Mountains, with a wife and four children, one of them in arms, was an adventure worth recording.

Tradition (which has been too active with Conrad Weiser's career for a biographer's peace of mind) is insistent that Conrad came by the Susquehanna route, as the fifteen families had done in 1723. It is perilous to battle with tradition when there is no documentary evidence to support a contrary opinion, but at the same time it is cowardly to leave the field uncontested. Here are some suggestions.

Between Vroman's Nose and Eagle Peak, where Weiser finally settled, there were shorter routes than the four-hundred-mile journey by way of the Susquehanna River and Swatara Creek. Conrad could have saved nearly a hundred miles, and for half the journey might have had the help of a wagon, if he had gone to Albany, down the Hudson to Esopus (Kingston), and thence by way of the old Dutch mining road (the Rondout-Neversink Road, named after rivers that it crossed) to the Minisink region where his father had recently made friends with the Indians. From the Minisinks there was an Indian trail over the mountains and across the Schuylkill River to the Fecks at Tulpehocken.

Or, again, he could have saved a hundred miles if he had come all the way by the Delaware trail, following a path that led up the Schoharie, across to Lake Utsayantha, down the banks of the Delaware past Cookose and Lackawaxen to the Minisinks, and so on as before.[14] Can we picture the Weisers, with Frederick only a few months old, picking their way on horseback over windfalls and through streams, Ann Eve perhaps carrying the baby strapped to an Indian cradle-board on her back? Or shall we, for the sake of the baby, suppose that the family came by boat from Albany, via the Hudson and the sea to New York and Philadelphia, and thence by road as Conrad's father was to come in 1746?

On behalf of the Susquehanna route it must be admitted that in 1729 that river was already familiar to him as far at least as Otseninky, and certainly the Susquehanna Valley was then the most commonly used route of Indian travel between the Mohawk country and Pennsylvania. Along its course, at least as far as Shamokin (our Sunbury), Conrad would have found Indians who understood the Mohawk tongue; and, paddling up the Swatara and (probably) the Quittapahilla to the site of the present city of Lebanon, he would have found only a light land passage intervening between the place where he had to leave his canoe and the end of his journey.

> *O false and treacherous Probability*
> *Enemy of truth, and friend to wickedness . . .*

It is well to get back to certainties. One thing we know: by whatever route he came, Conrad never left the mountains for long. The thick ribs of the Alleghenies (the Endless Mountains, as the Six Nations called them) interposed barrier after barrier to the traveler, who had either to climb them or circumvent them by the winding river courses.

The last range of these mountains, called the Kittatinny or Blue Mountains, overlooks, between the Gaps of the Susquehanna and Schuylkill Rivers, what is now known as Lebanon Valley; and it was here that the Weisers at length came to ground. Today the cities of Reading and Harrisburg stand at the gateways, east and west, of Lebanon Valley; but, when Conrad first came, the Indians still owned the valley; and from crest to crest of the Blue and South Mountains that flanked it the forest stretched unbroken except where some Delawares or Shawnees had made clearings for their corn, or where the Palatines were setting up their homesteads and extending their plantations.

Conrad chose his first acres with an eye to his children's children. The soil was rich and his neighbors were industrious; the community was bound to prosper. An Indian purchase was in the air, and title could soon be made secure. The plot he selected was on a new patch of road soon to be connected with others leading to Philadelphia; and behind, to the south, was vacant land offering any amount of room for expansion.

A temporary log house sheltered the family while he and his neighbors put up a permanent one. There was a spring close by, in a comfortable hollow at the foot of what came to be known as Weiser's Mountain or Eagle Peak, a friendly, shaggy little outpost of the Lehigh or South Mountains which he, his boys, and friends who stayed the night, used to climb. Eagles nested on its crest, 1,100 feet above the sea. The boys watched them circling in the sky.

He built his house of stone: square, solid, simple in plan. There was one main room, kitchen, dining-room, and sitting-room combined, at one end of which was a great fireplace with a bake-oven built into the wall behind. Here was baking enough and to spare for the company of travelers—soldiers, missionaries, Indian chiefs, governors, surveyors, botanists, etc.—who soon learned to make Weiser's a stopping place. Below was a cool cellar, and above were raftered sleeping quarters under the eaves.

Beside the house was a knoll (soon to serve for a burial plot) from which, when the trees were cut down, Conrad could look north through a gap in the hills to the sea-blue line of the Kittatinny Mountain, a stiff line broken only by the notch at *Rund Kop* or Round Head where the Shamokin Trail came over and where, thirty-seven years later, he was to build Fort Henry as the pivot of provincial defense in the French and Indian War.

Part II

THE CHAIN OF FRIENDSHIP

CHAPTER 6

. . . *Helps to Shape a New Indian Policy*

I

THERE is little record of Conrad Weiser's activities during his first two years in Pennsylvania; but we know that he was busy enough, building, ploughing, sowing, reaping, and entering eagerly into community affairs. He joined the little Lutheran congregation at Rieth's Church, became an elder, and even conducted service at times in the absence of a regular pastor. He impressed himself so well upon township and county that in February 1732 he was appointed with four other substantial citizens "to View and lay out" a road "from Simon Pickles plantation to Sculkill," [1] and next year signed a petition to have this continued to meet "ye Road that goeth from Oley to Philad^a." [2] In 1733 he was appointed Overseer of the Poor for Tulpehocken Township.[3]

Ann Eve was busy, too. There were four additions to the family in less than three years.

1730 the 27 february my Son Peter was born and 1731 the 15 february two Sons were born to me they were named Christoph and Jacob the First lived fifteen weeks, the other thirteen weeks when they were released from the evil of this life and passed into a Blessed Eternity 1732 the 19 June my daughter Elisabeth was born [4]

It was not only house, township, and county that engaged Conrad's attention. Before the end of 1731 he had entered the provincial service, and by 1732 was an important figure in it. This came about through his friendship with two remarkable men: James Logan, the Provincial Secretary at Philadelphia, and Shickellamy, the Six Nations' proconsul at Shamokin.

Shickellamy (as his Oneida name, *Swatane*, meaning "Our Enlightener," was rendered in the Delaware tongue) had been sent by the Onondaga Council to keep an eye on Pennsylvania's Indians in the Six Nations' interest.[5] Since he first appeared on the provincial scene at about the time of the Shawnee troubles of 1728 (when old Chief Kakowatchiky, after a mix-up in which shots were exchanged by a band of his warriors with some white people, sent a letter to the governor demanding the return of the gun one of his men had lost on the battlefield [6]), official Pennsylvania liked to think that Shickellamy had come specifically to keep the Shawnees in line. And for this they were thankful, since they did not know how to do it for themselves. Later, when the Governor and his council had come to know the Six Nations better, they learned that Shickellamy had been entrusted with the care of all the Indians on Pennsylvania's border, Delawares, Shawnees, Nanticokes (or Conoys), Conestogas, etc., and that it would be as well if the province handled Indian affairs through him.

For such a position no man could have been better suited. He had the tact that was needed in handling a subject and sensitive people like the Delawares, who, having been reduced to the status of "women" (i.e., denied the right to participate in war), suffered from a sense of thwarted pride. He had also the firmness that was needed in dealing with the white men, whose pride knew no bridle at all. Shickellamy was simple in his manner and quiet of speech (he was not one of the Indian orators produced in such abundance by the Six Nations), but a just, generous, far-sighted statesman and gentleman, carrying on the best traditions of Hiawatha and Deganaweda, whose Great Peace it was his function to uphold. He could neither read nor write, but his word was law in all the hinterland of Pennsylvania, and "Shickellamy his Mark" (a turtle, sign of his clan) was the strongest bond procurable in these woods.

James Logan, an Irish-born, English-educated Quaker of Scotch descent, had been brought to the province by William Penn in 1699, and left there to look after the Penn family interests. He was a better man for that purpose than William Penn himself, being, though a Quaker, not "a strict professor." Like other Friends of those days, he believed it better to outmaneuver an opponent than to meet him in battle; but, unlike them, he believed that all government rests ultimately on force. With France claiming all the continent except a fringe on the Atlantic coast (and casting jealous eyes on that, too) James Logan advocated military preparedness.

Benjamin Franklin tells a story—apocryphal it may be, but still bearing the stamp of Logan's character—that on his voyage to America with William Penn, when their ship the *Canterbury* was chased by an armed vessel which appeared to be a pirate, William Penn with most of the Quakers retired below while James Logan remained on deck and was quartered to a gun. When the danger was over, William Penn rebuked his secretary for resorting to arms. Logan replied, "I being thy servant, why did thee not order me to come down, but thee was willing enough that I should stay and help fight the ship when thee thought there was danger." [7]

Logan, whom Count Zinzendorf called a Quaker prince, was a man of many interests and a scholarly, scientific bent of mind. Besides collecting books (the Library Company of Philadelphia was founded by Benjamin Franklin on the famous Loganian Library) and publishing translations of Cato and Cicero, he contributed a number of papers to the Royal Society in London on botany, astronomy, electricity, etc. His scientific papers were ingenious. He loved to experiment, to follow a clue, to approach truth by the method of triangulation. The same methods he applied to the study of Indian affairs, gathering through a long life (he lived till 1752) an enormous knowledge of the Indians, and, at the same time, in turning his knowledge into diplomatic channels, evincing some fondness for Polonius' maxim, "By indirections find directions out." He was a born chess player.

There is a tradition that Conrad Weiser first met Shickellamy in the hunting woods of New York, where the latter was pleased to find a white man who could speak his language (the Oneida being closest to the Mohawk of all the Six Nations tongues), and pleased also to find himself talking with a man who understood Indian statecraft, for Weiser's early apprenticeship had taught him something about the League, its traditions, imperial problems, and council ceremonial. The two became fast friends.

Weiser's first recorded meeting with James Logan was on December 10, 1731, when Weiser appeared before the Governor and Council at Philadelphia as interpreter for Shickellamy. Shickellamy had brought an answer from the Six Nations to an invitation sent them by Brother Onas (i.e., the Governor of Pennsylvania, *Onas* being an Indian word meaning *feather, quill, or pen*—punning on the name of the Proprietor), to visit the council fire at Philadelphia. The invitation had been sent because it was believed that a close alliance with the Six Nations was essential to the province's security. Indian affairs were getting out of hand, and Brother Onas needed to lean on the arm of Hiawatha.

The immediate dangers threatening Indian relations in Pennsylvania had grown out of the white man's appropriation of Indian lands. There were four main trouble centers. The first was on the Susquehanna. The lands draining into this river south of the Blue Mountains had been bought by William Penn in 1786 of Governor Dongan of New York. The sale, however, was not recognized by the Six Nations who had formerly owned these lands and who, they said, had deeded them to New York only *in trust*. New York had no right to sell, they contended, without their consent, and that had never been given. Undoubtedly one of Pennsylvania's motives in seeking an alliance with the Six Nations was to get that consent. We shall see in a later chapter how this was done.

The second place of danger was on the Delaware. The west bank of that river north of Philadelphia as far as the present town of Matamoras was spotted with points of friction. The *Lenni Lenapi* (or Delaware Indians as they were now more commonly called), unlike their "Uncles" the Six Nations, did not sell land as a nation, and their deeds were not ratified by a common council. Local chiefs, men often of uncertain authority and undefined jurisdiction, sold land every now and again from motives of friendship or thirst, not infrequently even over the heads of the Indian residents.

"The Delaware Indians Some time agoe," complained the Shawnees, who were technically guests of the Delawares, "bid us Departt for they was Dry and wanted to Drink yᵉ land away whereupn wee told them Since Some of you are Gone to ohioh wee will go there also   wee hope you will nott Drink thatt away too" [8]

To such deeds, it might be, the signatures of one or two neighboring chiefs were appended, or perhaps the signatures of the Indians actually living on the land at the time. After such a document had been signed and payment made, it might happen that other chiefs of the neighborhood, or Indians from another district who had moved in (there was frequent immigration from the Jerseys) declined to recognize the sale, and proceeded to bother the white settlers, levying blackmail to wet their whistles. This danger was gravest at the Forks of the Delaware (the site of today's Easton and Bethlehem), where Delaware and Shawnee communities were found side by side with the white men.

A third center of danger lay in what is now called Lebanon Valley, whose fertile limestone soil had recently drawn to itself hundreds of Palatine farmers. The dispute here was much simpler than in the other two regions. The whites were unquestionably in the wrong. The valley was inhabited by Delawares and Shawnees. They had not sold it, yet they were being "egregiously abused" [9] by the newcomers, who were clearing the land for crops and raising cattle. What complicated the problem for the provincial government was that, to turn the settlers off now, would have been to do them as great an injustice as they were doing to the Indians, since they had entered the valley in good faith on Governor Keith's invitation. The only thing to do, as it appeared to the authorities, was to make honest men of the Palatines by purchasing the valley for them as soon as possible from the Indians.

There was need of haste. Some of the Shawnees and Delawares had already left the valley and gone off in a temper to the Ohio which had thus become the fourth, and, indeed, the most serious trouble center of them all.

On the Ohio they had come under the influence of the French. William Penn in his day had had little difficulty in keeping friends with the Shawnees and Delawares. Alone, they were not difficult to handle. But now that the French were come into the picture everything was changed. By 1731 it was reported that the French had swung the Shawnees on the Ohio into their orbit, and it was feared they might soon swing the Delawares as well. Once the French had seduced even a distant part of the Pennsylvania Indians, it was feared sedition might spread and infect those nearer home. But how could the Ohio danger be averted? An army? Not yet. France and England were technically at peace, and, besides, the Quaker Assembly in Philadelphia would not stand for fighting. Traders? Pennsylvania's traders were already swarming out there, but they were dangerous allies. They made Pennsylvania as many enemies as friends in the woods. John Sergeant in 1741 found that the Shawnees had a prejudice against Christians, at least Protestants, "derived it seems from the French, and confirmed by their own observation of the behaviour of that vile Sort of men, the Traders, that go among them; for they said (which I believe is an unhappy and reproachful truth) that they would lie, cheat, and debauch their women, and even their wives, if their husband were not at home." [10]

In 1731 the Indian colony on the Ohio was already recognized by astute observers like James Logan as the "little cloud no bigger than a man's hand." By 1755 it was big enough to swallow Braddock's army.

William Penn's Indian policy, which was to deal in a friendly way with local chiefs and not to lift one's eyes too anxiously to the horizon, had broken down. To the west, the French were known to be busy and hostile; it was feared that the Six Nations to the north were inclined to be the same. It was rumored that these latter were egging on a western nation to attack Pennsylvania because of her abuse of their tributaries within her borders. A restless white population was getting out of hand, killing Indians and thus playing into the hands of their enemies. Old Chief Sassoonan at Shamokin might talk much in his cups about the chain of friendship between his people and Brother Onas remaining bright as long as the sun, moon, and stars should endure; but the bibulous oratory of an aging chief could not forever restrain his young people, who did not forget how four white men in 1728 had, without provocation, attacked an old Indian with his women folk: how they had shot the old man in the breast with a gun charged with a bullet and ten swan shot, beaten out the brains of two Indian women with guns and axes, and set upon two Indian girls who ran away. One of these last they shot at with bow and arrow but, missing, pursued her and brought her back. The other they knocked down with a gun "and left her there." [11] Finding her unexpectedly alive the next day, though "much hurt about the head and face," they ordered her into the house of one of the murderers. ". . . most Certainly," wrote Samuel Nutt at the time, "such actions will Create the greatest antipathy betwixt the several nations of Indians & the Christians." [12]

"Christians." No wonder Kakowatchiky, the Shawnee chief, told Count Zinzendorf that the religion of the white man was not in his heart but in his mouth; and no wonder George Boone (uncle of the famous Daniel), under whose roof the Indian girls "(one of which is Crippled)" [13] just mentioned succeeded in finding refuge, wrote to Governor Gordon two days after the murders to say that the white inhabitants of the neighborhood had fled expecting an Indian uprising, and expressing his own fear that unless the government sent arms and ammunition the province would be "laid desolate and destroyed." [14]

For the time being, however, the Indians controlled themselves and the danger appeared to pass; but James Logan knew that the constant pressure of white settlers advancing into Indian lands, unauthorized and officially discouraged (except on the Maryland border where settlement was encouraged as a means of keeping Lord Baltimore's province in its place), made conflict almost inevitable—unless he could find some alchemic formula capable of turning Penn's Sylvania into the Forest of Arden. Meanwhile, in the absence of such a formula, he permitted himself to hope that the policy of William Penn—the tactful pressure of brotherly love—might somehow lead the Indians to embrace the white man's ways and submit gracefully to national extinction.

To this end Logan cultivated the friendship of certain young men of Sassoonan's connection, especially Opekasset and Shackatawlin, who were considered the most likely to succeed him. How successful he was may be seen from his letter to John Penn of August 2, 1731:

. . . we kept the old King with his next heirs, and some others of their People, not only near us, but closely in our Interest. . . . But now it has most unhappily so faln out, that Opekasset the eldest and next heir died last Spring of the Small pox, and Shachatawlin the truest, honestest young fellow I ever knew amongst the Indians, and whom I had brought to love my family as his nearest Relations, was lately kill'd by a sudden Stab from the old King Sassoonan's own hand in his liquor, So that none of that family but the unhappy old man who sorrows almost to death for the Accident, is now left for us to treat with, except such as we doubt are disaffected.[15]

The situation was grave, if not desperate. With hot-headed Scotch-Irish settlers on the border spilling Indian blood, French agents fretting up the Indians to avenge themselves, and a Quaker Assembly determined to block any military measures taken even for defense, James Logan was hard put to it to find a solution.

He wrote confidentially to his brother: "I am not at all satisfy'd that these parts will long be held by Brit." [16]

Of course there was the old stand-by: the Six Nations—"our only Security agst the ffrench in case of a Rupture," as Logan said in the letter to John Penn.[17] The Six Nations' war hatchet had long been regarded by the English colonies as a universal cure-all, more particularly as a silver bullet to be used against the French bogey. But the present emergency was beyond such a remedy. The Six Nations could hardly be expected to use the war hatchet against their own tributaries.

Then light came to James Logan. He had found his formula.

Not the war hatchet but the wampum belt of the Six Nations was the *unum necessarium*, the one thing needful. Their councils, their prestige, their restraining authority might be used to keep Pennsylvania's Indians (all tributary to the Six Nations) in line. The only difficulty was to get the Six Nations to use their power on Pennsylvania's behalf. It was at this point that Conrad Weiser (if we may suppose, as I think we should, an earlier acquaintance with Logan than the meeting on December 10) made his contribution. He knew as well as Shickellamy, and could explain without the embarrassment of confiding such intimate matters to an interpreter, how proud the Six Nations were, how jealous they were of their "nephews" the Delawares, and how anxious they were to maintain the prestige of the Onondaga Council, without which their empire would dissolve. It was reasonable to suppose that, if Pennsylvania publicly recognized the Six Nations' sovereignty over all Indians living in the territories granted to William Penn by King Charles, the Six Nations would in return exercise that sovereignty with an eye to His Majesty's interest. In a word, they would police Pennsylvania's woods in return for Pennsylvania's recognition of their sole right to do so.

II

This, then, was the new Indian policy: "to strengthen the hands of the Six Nations, and enable them to be the better answerable for their Tributaries." [18]

Chief credit for the formulation of the policy must go to James Logan. He had long recognized the importance of a well-implemented Six Nations alliance, and had been fumbling about for a means of getting it. But he did not take his final step without assistance. Both Shickellamy and Conrad

Weiser were in a position to show him how the trick could be turned and how best to use the alliance once he had got it. It is an odd coincidence, if it is nothing more, that Logan came to this knowledge so shortly after these two men had entered the province. It is useless, however, to try to apportion the honors. It is better to say simply that Pennsylvania's new Indian policy was the joint product of three men: Logan, Weiser, Shickellamy. Certainly Logan and Weiser were, when the records first show them together, already deep in each other's confidence; and certainly, also, they were both deep in Shickellamy's.

Two days after writing to John Penn, Logan proposed to the Council in Philadelphia that the French attempt to win over the Shawnee *émigrés* on the Ohio should be countered by a treaty with the Six Nations, "who have an absolute Authority as well over the Shawanese as all our Indians," [19] the object of the treaty being to persuade the Confederacy to bring the refractory Indians back across the Alleghenies and out of the French sphere of influence. The Council approved. Pennsylvania was to be put under the Six Nations' wing—if the Six Nations would have her.

Logan was much excited about the new policy, as he had reason to be, for it was his most noteworthy contribution to Indian affairs; but, being a Scot as well as a Quaker, he was cautious about advertising it. There were difficulties in the way. The Penns might not like it because of the expense it would entail. A treaty of alliance with the Six Nations involved the giving of presents, not once but time and time again, like the virtual tribute the Province of New York was paying yearly to the Confederacy. He tried to prepare John Penn. "There is an absolute necessity," he warned him, "(if this Country is to be preserv'd to the English Interest) of falling on further and not inexpensive measures." [20] He knew also that the Quakers might not like it because it meant supporting the imperial pretensions of the Iroquois—and the Quakers, through the Assembly, controlled Pennsylvania's purse strings. Therefore he was guarded about committing himself, even to the Penns, too explicitly on paper. He knew the Latin maxim, *Verba volunt, scripta manent,* and he hoped to see one of the Penns shortly in the province where he could talk it all over safely in private.

Writing, August 26, 1731, to inform John, Thomas, and Richard Penn (the three Proprietors) of the projected treaty, which he called an affair "of vast importance," he explained that "The intended Subject of the Treaty is to putt them [the Six Nations] if possible on measures to Strengthen both themselves and us. I must not be more particular here. If we can Succeed it may prove of Advantage to others of these Colonies." [21]

So it came about that, to launch the new Indian policy, Governor Gordon of Pennsylvania gave Shickellamy a message for the Six Nations, inviting them to send "some of their old wise men of Authority" to talk over with Brother Onas "some affairs concerning their own security and the peace of these countries." [22]

On his return from the Six Nations country a few months later, Shickellamy stopped at Tulpehocken and asked Conrad Weiser to come with him to the city as his interpreter. This Conrad agreed to do, and, mounting his horse, he joined the Cayuga Sehackqui and the Indian woman who were already members of Shickellamy's entourage, and proceeded with them to Philadelphia. The "poor Palatine," who had been an outlaw in New York and had seen the inside of an Albany dungeon, made a triumphal entry on this his first recorded visit to the capital of Pennsylvania. He was not on foot, alone, with a bun under each arm and one in his mouth, as Benjamin Franklin had been on his arrival in Philadelphia a few years before, but riding on horseback, in state, under the aegis of the vice-regent or "half-king" of the Six Nations Confederacy.

If Weiser had been reading Titan Leed's *Pennsylvania Almanack* of the preceding year, 1730, he knew what to expect to see when he turned off the Germantown road on to Second Street and entered the metropolis: "Tall Wessels" riding at anchor, "well built streets," and "the distant prospect clear" (whatever it was, for the author gave no detail). Did he know also, from reading the *Almanack,* that the littlenesses of human nature were not to be found in this favored community in which Apollo had erected his throne, that

Here solid Sense does every bosom warm
Here noise and nonsense have forgot to charm;

did he know, in a word, that, as Thomas Webb warbled (a versifier thought to be from Weiser's own neighborhood),[23] Philadelphia "(if the wishing muse inspir'd does Sing)" was to become "the Athens of mankind"?

To the Governor and Council Shickellamy reported, through Conrad Weiser and John Scull, interpreters, that the Six Nations thanked the Governor "very kindly" for his invitation, but said that, "the Winter now coming on," they must defer their visit till the spring. He added, as recorded in the Minutes of Council, December 10, 1731, that the chiefs of these nations were now grown very old and unfit to bear the fatigue of a long journey, but that they would certainly visit their brethren when the days grew longer and the sun gave more heat; in confirmation whereof they sent a small bundle of "Indian drest Deer Skins." [24]

It is to be noticed that Conrad Weiser had entered Pennsylvania's Indian affairs in the service of the Six Nations. He was a Mohawk by adoption, a friend of some of their chiefs, and he had lived for sixteen years in the fatherland of the Confederacy. From this time on, though he received compensation from the Province and came to be officially styled "Province Interpreter," the Six Nations regarded him as their man. "When we adopted him," said Canasatego in 1742, "we divided him into two equal Parts, one we kept for ourselves and one we left for You."

After spending four days in town, Conrad and his company set off for home. They had not gone far when James Logan, seized with one of those after-thoughts which, it must be suspected, were a part of his diplomatic technique, wrote Weiser a letter that discloses an astonishing trust, from one of his suspicious nature, unless we may suppose an earlier acquaintance than the official records show.

James Logan to Conrad Weiser [25]
Stenton 15th of Dec[br] 1731 aftern.

ffr[d] Conradt Wiser

As we talk'd not of Shekallemy's going up again to the 5 Nations, till just as they were upon going away, It came not into my mind to mention what I have Since thought of, which is, that, About ten dayes agoe some of our Traders coming home from Ohio, have told us, that after the Shawanese who went to Canada this last Summer with some french men came back to their town on Ohio, they put up a french flag or Colours in their town, as if they would Say, they are in league with the french and all one as french men. We were troubled to hear this, for the Shawanah Indians have been in league with our Government above thirty years and the Land on Ohio belongs to the 5 Nations. We heard this very lately & long since Shekallemy first went up, and we are willing our brethren of the five Nations Should know this, that they may think of it, and when their Chiefs came down to us, we may discourse of it together. We have Sent to the Shawanese to come back and live with us as our friends, for so we desire. Tell this to Shekallemy and Se-hachquè that they may mention it after they have delivered their first message, but not as a part of their message, or as if they were sent back about it, but only occasionally as a piece of News. We wish the Shawanese would be good and honest and joyn with the 5 Nations. Pray deliver this in the best manner thou canst to these 2 Indians, & make them fully understand the meaning of this Letter in every part. I wish you well on your Journey and am

Thy Loving friend
J. Logan

PS

I desire Shekallemy & Sehachquey may not mention a syllable of this to any of the Shawanese or to any other but the Chiefs of the 5 Nations after they have delv[d] the rest of their Message and desire them to be sure to Say that the reason of Shekallemy's coming back again was a mistake in the Interpretation

J. L.

III

The visit of the Six Nations chiefs was delayed, but at last on the 18th of August, 1732, Conrad Weiser arrived in town with a large delegation headed by Tyoninhogarao or "Open Door," who was a Seneca of the wolf clan and a *royaner*, forty-ninth and last in Deganaweda's Roll of the Chiefs. With him were his speaker, Hetaquantagechty, also a Seneca chief; several other chiefs of the Seneca, Cayuga, and Oneida nations; and a number of less distinguished Indian followers. Though there were delegates from only three of the United Nations, these were empowered to do business in the name of the whole Confederacy.

The "treaty," as such conferences were called, proceeded in the leisurely fashion prescribed by Indian etiquette, and lasted well over two weeks. Out of it all there came no treaty at all in the modern sense. No axis was formed. There were no protocols, no signatures, no secret clauses. But it was a great success. Confidence was established between the two parties, the Chain of Friendship was cleared of rust, and the road cleared for important negotiations later.

On August 23, Thomas Penn, who had arrived in America within the week, opened the conference formally (Conrad Weiser interpreting) with a characteristic burst of rhetoric and self-praise. He put everything in superlatives, especially the Penn family's benevolence. Thomas knew how to trade on his father's reputation. Hetaquantagechty replied for the Six Nations, matching Thomas Penn's Rotary Club manner

> *With more hauteur, as might an old Castilian*
> *Poor noble meet a mushroom rich civilian.*

Throughout the proceedings the Indians showed themselves superior to their hosts at the council table. There was less bark and more bite in what they had to say. They turned a neat compliment to Thomas Penn, the Proprietor, in whose coming at so opportune a time they professed to see the hand of the Ruler of Heaven and Earth. There was a glint of humor when they reported the reply they had made recently to the French governor, whom they called Onontio, when he proposed that they "sitt still and look on" while he made war on the English: "Onontejo," they had said, ". . . you are not wise to make War with Corlaer . . . we shall joyn him, and if we fight with you, we may have our Father Onontejo to bury in the Ground . . . be wise & live in Peace." [26]

Their courtesy was perfect. They yielded the initiative to the English, who had called the conference, allowing themselves to be questioned about their relations with the French and advised in the matter of their alliances. They betrayed no open resentment at the paternal tone Thomas Penn adopted toward them. When they spoke, though they used the quaint metaphors good form demanded of them in formal address, they not only achieved an admirable explicitness of statement but also managed to convey delicate overtones of meaning that are not wholly lost in Weiser's translation.

It is perhaps too much to read a tacit rebuke of Thomas Penn's condescension into Hetaquantagechty's speech when he told how the Six Nations had nursed and protected their brother, the province of New York, "till he is grown up to be a Man." [27] But certainly this and other of their speeches served notice on the Proprietor that filial piety was not what he and his province might expect from the Six Nations.

Logan was no doubt satisfied with the outcome. While the proposal on which the English had particularly set their hearts (that the Six Nations should exercise their authority to recall the Shawnees from the Ohio) was deftly parried by Hetaquantagechty's suggestion that the readiest way to bring the Shawnees back would be to recall the English traders who were out on the Ohio with them—nevertheless the chiefs showed that they were not unsympathetic to English fears in the matter. They informed the Governor's Council that on their way to town "They saw Cocowatchy . . . gave him a pipe of peace wth a bag of Tob: telling him he must not follow the rest of his people to Ohio but turn his back on it & his face this way of w[ch] he was glad." [28] The tone of the Philadelphia proceedings had been cordial, and the Indians seemed pleased not only with the present of flints, shirts, kettles, knives, tobacco tongs, combs, vermilion, etc., but more especially with Brother Onas' offer to keep a Fire burning in Philadelphia for them "to sitt down by & take Council together." This, coupled with Thomas Penn's advice to them to strengthen themselves by extending their alliances, they took "as a Sure Token of Brotherly Love towards them." [29]

It was not, in years to come, solely the logic of power politics that held the Six Nations and Pennsylvania together. As important as the new Indian policy itself was the personality of the two men who administered it, Conrad Weiser and Shickellamy. That the chiefs in Philadelphia understood this, we know from their request made on this occasion that future conferences should be "managed by the means of Shekallamy and Conrad Weyser, the Interpreter"; [30] and that the Governor and Council understood it, we know from the Council Minutes of August 30, 1732:

It was then considered, what might be proper to be given Shekallamy for his Trouble in the two Journeys he had performed at the Desire of this Government with Messages to the Six Nations, And likewise the Reward to Conrad Weyser, who had accompanied the Indians hither from Tulpahockin, had been very carefull of them, and was extremely Serviceable on this present Treaty; And it being observed, that these Men were not only very acceptable to the Indians, as appeared by their late Recommendation of them, but likewise seemed to be Persons of Truth & Honesty, on which Account it would be necessary to give them all due Encouragement; It is resolved that the Sum of Eight pounds be paid to Shekallamy, & Twelve pounds to Conrad Weyser, together with the Charges he may have necessarily expended for the Indians in their Journey hither." [31]

Thus the year 1732 had seen the beginning of Pennsylvania's planned attempt to clean up the four main trouble centers in Indian relations: the lower Susquehanna, the Forks of the Delaware, the Ohio, and Lebanon Valley. The last of these was disposed of in the same year. On September 7, Sassoonan, Pesquetamen [Pisquetomen], Lapahpaton [Lapachpiton], and others, signed a release of the lands "lying between those Hills called Lechaig Hills & those called Keckachtanemin Hills . . . and between the Branches of Delaware River on the Eastern Side of the said Land and the Branches or Streams running into the River Sasquehannah on the Western Side of the said Land" [32]—a transaction by which the better part of Lebanon Valley and a good deal more to the east of it passed into the Proprietors' hands.

The four trouble centers had been reduced to three. But the Susquehanna, Forks of the Delaware, and Ohio problems still remained, and were not so easily to be settled. We shall see in good time what "toil, blood, tears, and sweat" it took to dispose of them.

CHAPTER 7

. . . *Escapes the Tulpehocken Confusion*

I

AFTER the Indian purchase of 1732, Conrad set about getting title to his land. In June 1733, while down in Philadelphia interpreting again for Shickellamy, he got the Surveyor General to write a letter on his behalf to John Taylor, a surveyor in Lancaster County, and delivered it himself. "The Prop^r," it ran, "is desireous that Conradt Wiser Shall be Accommodated in the best manner the place where he is Settled will afford, and therefore would have thee Survey it Accordingly, and if he thinks fit to take another parcell where Vacant, it may also be Survey'd" [1]

A formal warrant followed in 1734 and another in 1735, each for one hundred acres. In May 1736, the whole two-hundred-acre tract, lying on the new road (now part of Pennsylvania Route 422, the Benjamin Franklin Highway from Philadelphia) extending south to "a Barren Mountain," and enclosing not only the site of the present Weiser Park but also a good portion of what is now the town of Womelsdorf, was surveyed for him by Franklin's friend and Junto partner, William Parsons.[2] The patent was signed in Philadelphia, October 6, 1736.[3]

Everything Weiser touched at this time seemed to prosper. His farm was a success. His plantation spread and climbed until it reached the summit of Eagle Peak and embraced over eight hundred acres. He owned horses and cattle. He became County Ranger. He invested widely in real estate, established a tannery,[4] lent money and collected when necessary through the courts. Soon he had become the acknowledged business leader in his community and was a model of steady industry and common sense.

But it was otherwise with his religious life. There the rebel in him still found play, and this, uniting with a natural strain of mysticism which the times encouraged, led him into the strangest interlude in his career: six years spent in an effort to shake off the world and follow the monkish pattern of the Ephrata Solitary.

The sight of Conrad Weiser among the doves and lilies, of a hard-fisted pioneer farmer and woodsman wooing the Virgin Sophia in company with Seventh Day German Baptists of Rosicrucian tendencies, gowned, sandaled, and cowled, gives a jolt to the imagination. We naturally ask the question that old Menno Light of the haunted mill house on the Quittapahilla at Annville (the property was once Conrad Weiser's) propounded one night to the headless ghost that stood before him: *Kan das sei?*—"Can this be?"

It not only could be but it had to be. Granted Conrad's emotional temperament (controlled most of the time but never tamed); granted the passionate desire for peace which his early uprooting and unhappy boyhood in New York had planted deep in his heart; and granted also the violent storms that wrecked the church life of his little Tulpehocken community—it is evident that Conrad's escape to the shelter of Ephrata was a thing not to be avoided when Conrad Beissel, the hermit evangelist of the Cocalico, called him to come.

Conrad Beissel was a product of one of those "awakenings" that for a hundred years past had been sending waves of religious exiles across the Atlantic. These devout people, whether English Puritans and Quakers or German Baptists and Moravians, were all moved by much the same spirit. They hoped to find rest from this world, and in the peace of primitive places the conditions requisite for the absorption of man's soul in God's.

Beissel, a baker of Eberbach, had been driven out of Germany and had come to Pennsylvania "to spend his life in solitude with God." [5] That he was sincere in his religion is, I think, not to be disputed; but whether in his Cocalico retirement he became absorbed in God or in himself is a question for the psychologists rather than the theologians to determine. Point by point, there is not much to attract one to Beissel. He was a vain, undersized, garrulous man, unreasonable, jealous, and at times vindictive. But he had the power of a cultist in a time of confusion. He was dreadfully in earnest. He promised absorption in the Eternal, and broke up families to accomplish it. He was feared, hated, and ridiculed; but he was also worshipped. As he went about the country, he collected disciples as a night-flare collects fish. Women forsook their husbands to come to him. Scandals sprang up with every step he took; but still men and women with the purest intent left all and followed him. When he walked in the street, female devotees came after him singing hymns. They followed him through all weathers. When exhausted, they were carried after him, still singing, "so that the people ran to the street to behold the wonder." [6]

Men made over their property to him and asked for no accounting. Following his example, men (and women, too) in the Conestoga region became hermits; and when the spirit moved him to renounce the hermit life and organize a monastic community on the banks of the Cocalico, they followed him hypnotically to Ephrata. His word to them was both the law and the prophets. If what he said seemed a little incoherent, it was the more evident that he spoke not from man but from God, whose thought (so they argued) cannot be bound by the fetters of human reason. When he gave orders and then contradicted them, he was the more reverenced: he had unveiled the secrets of the Ineffable. He pronounced marriage to be "the penitentiary of carnal man," [7] and exposed himself mercilessly to the temptations of the flesh. He preached temperance and was frequently drunk. "Truly," said his biographer in the *Chronicon Ephratense*, "God used him to manifest forth the wonders of eternity."

His brain was fertile as a ripe cheese. He believed that the elimination of human waste was not a necessary function of the body.[8] He avoided pork as unclean, and proscribed also geese, since these contributed their feathers to man's luxurious indulgence. When he preached, he closed his eyes, and on opening them not infrequently found most of his hearers gone, they "not being able to endure the Spirit's keenness." [9] He spoke rapidly, without reflection, even without a text, "so that the testimony in its delivery might not be weakened by written knowledge. . . . In his delivery, however, he was too fast, because he had to hurry after the Spirit"; and he "often concerned himself but little about the rules of language." [10]

This latter circumstance did not deter him from writing and publishing. He once composed a hymn of forty-three stanzas. He was the author of *Ninety Nine Mystical Sayings*. When asked by a scholar who traveled far to meet him why there were not a round hundred, he replied that "as the number 99 was reached he was stopped in the spirit." [11] There could be no reply to such a man. When rationalistic persons were by, such, that is, as "sought to catch and confine his discourse in the meshes of reason," he would be moved to contradict himself so as to throw his hearers into "a holy confusion." [12]

He kept his house open day and night. "Whoever was tempted, fled to him as to a city of refuge; and as soon as his threshold was reached, the blood avenger had to abandon him." [13] Wives fled to him from their husbands. The husbands beat him up now and again, but it was never proved against him that he indulged in other sweets than those of temptation.

The legends that spring up as soon as a famous man is gone are like a death mask: they show the impress that he has left on the minds of his fellows, and often are a better indication of the quality of his life than a catalogue of facts. The legend of Beissel's ghost, pursuing delinquent Dunkers from beyond the grave, gives a measure of the awe he inspired while alive.

After his death it seems that Christiania Luther and her husband Christian, abstaining from the love feasts of the Ephrata settlement, incurred Father Beissel's ghostly displeasure and learned that his was an ill spook to cross.

Christiania being in her own room by her Self [we read in a contemporary manuscript] was Visited . . . by the Deceased Conrad Pysall and he in a very angry and voilent rage fell upon her. taking her by the throat. So y^t She was allmost Strangled by [him] but in her Angush Calling Lord Jesus help me the S^d spirit departed . . . the same night about 12 clock. something Came to the same Christiania door. She hearing ye Door open & shut was much Surprised & applyd her Self immediately in prayer to our blessed Lord, her husband was then at rest in a little rome Just by & they were both awake, but She heard a voice which Said the Father is Coming. but by reason of her fervent prayers he had not the power to enter, but said Audibly I will goe and fetch Spirits Enough to help me to enter. hereupon the Spirit departed hastily and went out. but soon returned again, with a great Number with him So many as if the rome to her apprehension was quite full of them, the mean time her husband was still lying upon his bed in fervent Exercise & meditation; but the Exercise of the woman being through Christs assistance too powerfull for all the Spirits. they then left her and fell upon the husband, Catcht him by the throat as if it intended to Strangle him   Under this great Struggle & Voilent Exercise which lasted for Some time he Cryed out O Lord Jesus protect me. upon which the Spirit Departed . . .[14]

II

It is clear that a man of Weiser's vigor and good sense would not in normal times have bowed himself before such a moon-calf deity; but in 1735 times were not normal. In order to understand the forces at work in Tulpehocken which, by that year, had attained sufficient power to drive Conrad into Beissel's net, it is necessary to look back over the years during which they were shaping and taking direction.

When Weiser came to Pennsylvania, he was resolved to live down the turbulence of his early years: no longer to be the wanderer and outlaw, hating God, hating the government, hating his relatives and neighbors and himself. He intended to fit in, to work for church and state, raise a good family, and hoe his own garden. He was happy to make himself useful to the government in Philadelphia, which was the easier to do since the authorities there were eager for his services, they having found honest interpreters difficult to come by and understanding ones almost impossible. At the same time he entered whole-heartedly into the religious life of his local community, and attached himself at once to Rieth's Church.

At the outset, Rieth's was a union congregation, composed of adherents of the Lutheran and Reformed Churches. Leonhart Rieth gave a plot of land, Christopher Lechner gave his services as master builder or chief carpenter, and a log meetinghouse was erected in 1727 by the Tulpehocken Creek, east of the present town of Stouchburg. For furniture, there was a pulpit; a walnut table four feet in length, oval shaped, with carved legs, which served as altar; and seats made of hewn logs.[15] There was no pastor; but missionary preachers visited the spot occasionally, such as John Philip Böhm for the Reformed and John Bernard von Dühren of Schoharie for the Lutherans, who baptized, married, held holy communion, and thus kept alive respect for the church ordinances.

Conrad was not oppressed by the religious seclusion of a frontier community. He had resources within himself, and his reading encouraged independent living and thinking. He was not only a great Bible reader, but also a student of the works of Dr. Spener, the founder of pietism, of August Herman Francke, who had made the University of Halle a center of pietism, and of Johann Arndt, mystical author of the *Wahres Christentum* and the *Paradies Gärtlein*, to whom the Pietists looked back with reverence. From these authors, who sought to counteract the controversial side of the Reformation by insisting less on the Christ who died *for* us and more on the Christ who lives *in* us, Weiser derived sound nourishment for his mind.

He soon became a leader in his church, and, as elder, assembling the congregation on Sundays and other holy days, read them a good sermon and catechized their children.[16] Under Weiser's influence, Rieth's Church was a citadel of pietism in the wilderness: ". . . they sang, prayed, exhorted, admonished, and searched their own souls and one another's," [17] wrote Muhlenberg of this idyllic community in its days of grace. All went well, he tells us, as long as the spirit of unity and humility prevailed among them and they followed the clear word of God with vigilance, not turning their eyes outward to the fashions of the world's churches.

The coming of the Reverend John Peter Miller strengthened for a time the pietistic influence in the community, and gave Conrad Weiser a warm friend. Peter Miller was a young man of twenty when he came out from the Palatinate in 1730. He got himself ordained by the Presbyterians in Philadelphia and at once went out to the frontier to which he had felt a call, serving the Reformed congregations at Tulpehocken, Cocalico, and Conestoga. He was a cultured, scholarly, friendly man, devout and thoughtful; a pietist, but reasonable and not subject to emotional spasms. The stages on his religious journey are found plotted along an unswerving course, for his mind was trained to follow principles, and the chief of these he had mastered in youth.

Before he came to America he had become a mystic, a follower of Jacob Böhme (or Behmen), the cobbler of Görlitz, who expounded the mysteries of Enoch (who walked with God) and of the Virgin Sophia, spouse of the soul. To Peter Miller's way of thinking, the goal of life was absorption in the eternal, in God's infinite mind. As time went on and the pressure of daily life, with its increasing tempo of controversy at Tulpehocken, threatened to destroy the contemplative calm he sought, he came to feel that his goal could be achieved only by withdrawal from the world. In this opinion he was encouraged by the wave of revivalism then sweeping the province.

As was to be expected in a time of religious enthusiasm, and especially among newcomers to America where loneliness and awe of the surrounding forest put strange pressure on the imagination, fantasy was altogether too common a bedfellow with mysticism. New sects were born, and old sects divided to follow will-o'-the-wisps of the spirit. Among the many strange cults in Pennsylvania at this time were the Newborn, who believed themselves to be in the same state as Adam before the fall—sinless; and the New Mooners, who thought prayers were more effective during the early phases of the moon. Kelpius on the Wissahickon had gathered about him a group who came to be known as the Society of the Woman in the Wilderness. Conrad Biessel set up as a hermit and leader of hermits on the Conestoga and afterwards on the Cocalico, wooing the Virgin Sophia and keeping Saturday holy.

The German Baptists or "Dunkers," who were leaders in the "great awakening," were as a whole among the most sober and collected of these "dreaming saints" or enthusiasts. Their religion was simple. They did justly, loved mercy, walked humbly before their God. Their plainness of manner and dress, their attempts to revive the customs of the early Christians (such as feet-washing, love-feasts, immersion) appealed to what was strongest in Peter Miller. He visited them, allowed them to call him Brother and to wash his feet.[18] How much better, it seemed to him, was this brotherly simplicity than the denominational controversies that were already creeping into Rieth's Church—and for which Peter Miller himself was (though innocently) partly the cause.

For it seemed that, now that the Reformed at Rieth's had a special pastor for their thirty-odd families, the Lutherans, who numbered more than forty families, were under the necessity of getting one, too. They turned to Caspar Leutbecker for help. Leutbecker was a free-lance preacher of Moravian connections. He was a gentle soul, well meaning though not wholly unregardful of self, who found the bluster employed by some of his fellow pastors not only unchristian but also ineffective, meekness providing a better channel for the attainment of one's ends. His enemies called it guile.

When the Lutherans approached him, Leutbecker, who claimed to have been ordained by the late Court Pastor Böhm in London, said he knew just the man they wanted, and would, if they wished, send for him through the present Court Pastor Ziegenhagen. The Lutherans accordingly wrote a formal call, promising the invited pastor thirty pounds a year in addition to perquisites, and Conrad Weiser put the letter into Leutbecker's hand.[19] It would be well, suggested Leutbecker, if the congregation meanwhile built a parsonage in anticipation of the new pastor's arrival. This they did in the space of six weeks. During the building of the parsonage, Leutbecker preached regularly at Rieth's Church, and so won the hearts of the congregation that, when they received news (from Leutbecker) that Ziegenhagen's man had died at sea, the Lutherans invited Leutbecker himself to be their permanent pastor.

Weiser protested because, as he tells us, he had begun to doubt whether Leutbecker had really sent the letter entrusted to him.[20] It was suspected by some that Leutbecker had never intended otherwise than to occupy the new parsonage himself. Such doubts, however, were slow to mature in the presence of the gentle Moravian, whose sermons were pleasing and whose ministry was assiduous. He instructed "not only the parents of such children as were brought to be baptized"—so runs the report of the elders, endorsed some years later by Justice Conrad Weiser, "but also the sponsors, with regard to the importance of the Sacrament of baptism, and also indicated to us who was qualified and unqualified for the Lord's Supper, which fidelity the dear God blessed to so very many dear hearts that all the congregation rejoiced thereat." [21]

But not for long. Doubts of Leutbecker's ingenuousness grew. There came a cleavage in the congregation. Some few remained with Leutbecker. The greater number attached themselves to Caspar Stoever. Weiser withdrew altogether, for he found himself between the devil and the deep sea. He suspected Leutbecker, but Stoever he hated.

Caspar Stoever was the *enfant terrible* of the early Lutheran Church in Pennsylvania. He was a born trouble maker, enormously active and brutally orthodox. From his home in New Holland he preached and pounded his way over a large section of the province, establishing new churches and disrupting as many as he founded. Everywhere he left confusion in his wake. He never stayed long in a pastorate, perhaps because his followers (some of whom found gunpowder more congenial arguments in religious controversy than texts of scripture) soon turned any neighborhood to which he came into a bear garden. He was a good starter but not a good organizer. He could teach men to fight, but not to live together. He won supporters but not friends. All the early accounts we have of his work, and they are many, were written by his enemies. He was the only Lutheran leader of that time in Pennsylvania not in sympathy with the Halle pietists.

Whether chief blame for the Tulpehocken Confusion, as this renowned church *melée* came to be called, should be laid at the door of Leutbecker or Stoever, we cannot say with any greater certainty than Weiser did. In 1742 he attested that it had grown out of Pastor Stoever's interference with Leutbecker's ministry, Stoever having taken advantage of a reprimand Leutbecker gave a drunken church member who brought his child for baptism and who was twice sent away with instructions to come back sober.[22] In 1747, however, Weiser said that the attestation had been got from him by a trick of the Moravian party and published without his consent.[23] Be that as it may, one thing is clear: Weiser's plain disgust with the whole church quarrel, the precise causes of which he probably no more understood than do the church historians of today who still delight to find—though not to make—a confusion.

Leutbecker was a pacifist who believed in appeasement; Stoever was a fighter who took all he could get. Leutbecker and his party agreed to let the Stoeverites have the use of Rieth's Church one Sunday in each month. Stoever and his party meant to get it wholly into their possession, Sundays and week days included. When the Moravian party "put a lock on the gate in front of the church to keep the cattle from entering the graveyard," Stoever's people broke the lock. "And when we put another in place," continues the report of the Moravians (first endorsed, and then disavowed, by Conrad Weiser), "they got another entrance, which is still to be seen, just as if we wished to keep them out of the grave yard."

On the contrary! Feeling now ran so high that the Moravians would gladly have seen the Stoeverites in the graveyard for good and all. It was actually rumored (and believed in some Lutheran circles) that the Moravians prayed their enemies to death. When Conrad Weiser fell sick— we shall finish this story in good time.

The report goes on:

Meantime our pastor [Leutbecker] continued to preach sometimes in the church, when we were without a tumult; but sometimes he had to vacate in order to prevent a tumult, till at last by unheard of abuses and scurrility Stiever so urged on his people that we were quite put out of the church, and had to have our services in the minister's house.

In the end, the Stoeverites drove Leutbecker not only out of his church but out of the parsonage as well, throwing stones through his windows, putting gunpowder in his firewood (to explode in his stove),[24] and finally worrying him to his death at George Lescher's house in 1738.

Weiser did not wait for this finale before making up his mind about the church.

"I stayed home," he said.[25]

Pastor Miller, disappointed at seeing his sheep turning into goats before his eyes, resigned his charge.

The idyl of Rieth's Church was ended.

It was unfortunate that Weiser's first venture in church leadership should have ended so disastrously. His untrained mind could not operate easily outside the range of his own immediate experience, and that experience had now made it certain that he should never thereafter be entirely at home among what the world calls "church people."

He returned, after some years of religious wanderings, to the Lutherans, and before he died was the most prominent of their laymen in America; but it was long before he would take communion with them, and his son-in-law, Muhlenberg, found him "not churchly enough" for edification— a man of good foundations, as the Patriarch described him, but with a denominational superstructure of straw.

III

Meanwhile Conrad Beissel from his hermitage on the Cocalico (the Den of Serpents [26] had not yet changed its Indian name to the Biblical Ephrata) watched the Tulpehocken Confusion with satisfaction. The field was being made ready for the harvest. He desired to gather in Peter Miller, and to that end he "bowed his knee before God." [27] The Solitary needed a good preacher, someone of culture and standing, a young man who might in time grow into leadership in the new monastic community that was already taking shape in Beissel's mind, especially someone beyond the reach of scandal, for it was rumored abroad on the one hand that the Cocalico hermits (male and female) were no better than they should be, and on the other hand that they were agents of the Pope sent up from Mexico with gold to buy converts to Catholicism.[28]

When Beissel came reconnoitering to the Tulpehocken, he was received, as the Ephrata *Chronicon* tells us, by "the teacher" (Peter Miller) and the elders (chief among whom was Conrad Weiser) "with the consideration due to him as an ambassador of God."

Sober he seemed and very sagely sad.

Weiser and Miller found him ready to listen to their griefs. They discussed the problem of salvation with him, and confessed their disillusionment with the churchly way of life. They knew he must understand, for in No. 35 of his *Mystical Sayings* [29] (which book Peter Miller subsequently translated into English) he had written: "The Fruit of the Wise is Peace and Concord: but Folly is found there, where Men hate Peace."

Folly they had found in abundance at Rieth's Church, but where was peace to be had?

Watchman, tell us of the night,
What its signs of promise are.

Beissel was ready with an answer. If they wished to enter into God's peace, they must pass through the Red Sea of baptism,[30] oppose the world in everything,[31] and woo the Virgin Sophia.

It is unnecessary, and perhaps impossible, to define Sophia closely. She was something to be apprehended rather than comprehended: "Wisdom and Spirit of the universe," the divine female principle, the mirror of God and messenger of God, the Holy Ghost—Böhme's followers disputed much over the meaning of the term. What matter? The Virgin Sophia could be felt, as God's wings are felt, and her fruits were in experience. The wooing of her was the sublimation of all earthly instinct, a being caught up into the soul of God.

Weiser and Miller were dazzled by the bearded hermit, whose face shone with an inner light and who seemed to walk in an aura of God's peace. He once won a bride from her bridegroom at the marriage service.[32] Small wonder that he caught up these men bewildered by the Tulpehocken Confusion.

When Beissel returned to Ephrata, Conrad Weiser and Peter Miller accompanied him over the mountain some six miles on his way. They were to go with him all the way a little later.

The winning of Peter Miller was a great thing, and the Solitary rejoiced at it, but within reason, for it was not unexpected: Beissel had been on his knees about it for some time. But the catching of Conrad Weiser in the same net was a triumph without prevision and beyond parallel. The *Chronicon Ephratense* glows with satisfaction over it for many pages.

Since we do not have Weiser's own account of his conversion, we must rely for our information on the *Chronicon;* and this we may safely do since the author was Peter Miller, who, though writing after Weiser's death, had been in 1735 Weiser's most intimate friend.[33]

Among the seceders from the Tulpehocken church, says the *Chronicon,*

. . . was C. W., an elder of the Lutheran faith, a man who had received from God remarkable natural gifts and sound judgment, and therefore carried great weight with him into whatever sphere he might turn, whether that of nature or of the church. . . .

C. W. visited the Superintendent [Beissel] in his solitude in the Settlement. During this visit he was so enmeshed by the Philadelphian "little strength" [34] that Wisdom finally drew him into her net. Among other things the Superintendent asked him, what the young preachers were doing; and when he heard that B. R. had taken a wife, he sighed deeply and said, "Good God! they are spoiling in one's very hands." . . . On retiring, the Superintendent promised him a visit, which also followed soon after, though then taking in only his house and the teacher. Not long afterwards, however, he made another extended visit thither, on which the spirit of revival spread itself over that entire region . . . But, good God! a great hill had yet to be surmounted ere that disgrace was overcome which distinguished God's people from the children of this world. And this rested so heavily upon the Settlement at that time that superhuman power was needed to break through it.

In this whole matter, however, God made use of the faithfulness of the aforementioned C. W. For through his prudence it was that a great visitation, in which the heads of the revival were engaged, came to the Settlement. Now it was that the Superintendent had the wished-for opportunity to spread his net and catch men for the virgin Sophia . . .[35]

After much debate "concerning the counsels of God towards fallen man," Peter Miller decided to let himself be baptized, and Conrad Weiser with several others followed his decision. "Accordingly," continues the *Chronicon*, "they were baptized together under the water, after the teaching of Christ; which was done on a Sabbath in May of the year 1735." [36]

The water was that of the Millbach (Mill Creek), a small tributary of the Tulpehocken. The place is now marked by a shrine erected on the grounds of the Millbach House near Nemanstown, Pa.

"Thus," concludes the *Chronicon* of this episode, "the teacher, schoolmaster, three elders, besides various other households, went over from the Protestants to this new awakening; while for some time after the door was kept open for the Babylonian refugees." [37]

Ann Eve must be listed for the time among the Babylonians. She was nursing Sammy, who was born April 23, 1735, and caring for Margaret, who was born January 28, 1734. While, after attending to these two, she bustled about the bake-oven preparing food for the rest of her eight children and listening at the same time to Beissel's rapt conversation with her husband at the other end of the room, she may have turned over in her mind the very thought that John Donne had put into a couplet more than a hundred years before:

> *From thinking us all soul, neglecting thus*
> *Our mutual duties, Lord deliver us.*

CHAPTER 8

... *Lives in Two Worlds*

I

AFTER baptism, Conrad Weiser found himself on the horns of a dilemma. As a follower of Beissel and Jacob Böhme, he tried to live in the realm of the spirit, and to this end grew a long beard and fasted the flesh off his bones until his friends hardly recognized him. But as a husband, father, and Indian interpreter he had duties of a worldly nature that he could not ignore. The name given him when, a little later, he entered the Zionitic Brotherhood, was Enoch, no doubt in recognition of his dilemma. Enoch, according to Jacob Böhme, lived in two worlds: his soul dwelt in Paradise, his body in the flesh. Conrad Weiser as Brother Enoch was confronted with a problem more difficult than that with which Hamlet had confounded himself: he had to be and not to be at the same time.

In the shock of his "awakening," Conrad acted with the same whole-hearted abandon that had inspired him when he tore down Vroman's house at the Wilder Hook. His overcharged feelings had to explode. Something uncompromising had to be done, like destroying one's bridges behind one or perishing at the stake. The Burning of the Books served the purpose.

A day or two after the baptism, Conrad Weiser, Peter Miller, and others of the new "water saints" who had "dived for salvation" in the Millbach, collected all the devotional books of the old faith they could lay their hands on, both Lutheran and Reformed, stripping the learned Peter Miller's library for their purpose, and solemnly burned them at Gottfried Miller's house [1] on the north bank of the Tulpehocken (east of the present Rehrersburg Road). Into the fire went the Heidelberg Catechism, Luther's Catechism, the Psalter, the *Exercise of Godliness*—in all thirty-six books. Conrad Weiser is said to have been "the chief familiar," directing the play of torch and pitchfork by which these emblems of fallen priestcraft were consumed.

There is a tradition that even Arndt's *Paradies Gärtlein* (*Garden of Paradise*) was thrown on to the pyre with the rest of the priestly vanities —though, indeed, with hesitation. Certain of the torch-bearers thought this was going too far. The *Paradies Gärtlein* was popularly believed (like *The Long Lost Friend* in some parts of the "Dutch Country" today) to be divinely protected from fire and flood. To have it in one's possession was to ensure one's life against both; to attempt to destroy it by either was to go against Providence. But into the fire it went, presumably because the pastor, elder, and schoolmaster who were present were too much emancipated to heed the warnings of folklore—in which they erred. Folklore was to have the last word. Tradition has it that next morning the *Paradies Gärtlein* was found unburned, its edges crisped but the printed pages intact. The miracle was noised about the countryside, so increasing the book's fame as a charm that Christopher Saur of Germantown printed an American edition.

II

It is not easy to live on two planes. Conrad Weiser found renunciation of the world simple enough in the excitement of baptisms and burnings, but more difficult in the common run of life at home. For Peter Miller, of course, there was no such problem. He was a bachelor. All he had to do was to get the brethren to build him a hermitage at the foot of Weiser's Mountain, which they did; and there he lived by himself, putting on godliness as he took off flesh, until in November he moved to Ephrata, where Kedar, the first of the Kloster buildings, had just been erected, and entered Beissel's monastery.

Weiser did not become a hermit. For reason: he had Ann Eve, Philip, Madlina, Maria, Frederick, Peter, Elisabeth, Margaret, and little Sammy to look after. Neither did he go at once with Peter Miller into the monastery. There were two classes of membership in the Ephrata community: the Solitary and the Households. The Solitary subjected themselves to the utmost rigors of the monastic life. They lived in cells, fasted, had but little sleep—and that only on narrow boards with blocks of wood for pillows. "I know men here," wrote Weiser a little later, "who more than once have fasted for seven days and nights and from one year's end to another have not had one full meal, have allowed themselves only 3 or 4 hours sleep at the most in the 24 . . ." [2] Those of the Households, on the other hand, lived a more normal life. It was necessary that they should do so, since the Solitary depended on them for support. But while the Householders had one foot in the world, they had the other in the Kloster. They were united with their stricter brethren in submission to Beissel, the "Superintendent." They joined as much as possible in the community services. When they heard the Ephrata bell ring, those of them who were within earshot (i.e., within a radius of four miles) assembled their families for services like those held in the Kloster. Like the celibates, they wooed the Virgin Sophia by the mortification of the flesh, and husbands abjured intercourse with their wives.

After his conversion, Weiser continued for some years to live on the plantation. He had, of course, relinquished his position as elder in the Lutheran congregation; but he was now ready to accept guardianship of the Sabbatarian flock. He became their "teacher"—with such curious consequences to himself that it is necessary to give this episode its full setting.

The Tulpehocken community was both a triumph and a tribulation to Conrad Beissel. The capture of Conrad Weiser and Peter Miller was the greatest single victory he was to win over the powers and principalities of this world. But the victory was too overwhelming to be satisfactory. Weiser and Miller drew with them under the waters of the Millbach numbers of good Tulpehocken householders who could not be accommodated at Ephrata and were difficult to minister to from a distance. Ephrata was over the mountain, twelve miles due south of Weiser's plantation. In seeking to provide a "teacher" for the new community, Beissel met with repeated disappointment. Peter Miller having declined to serve, Michael Welfare (*Wohlfart*) entered upon the office. But the violence of his preaching was an offense to a congregation already rendered touchy by five years of the Confusion, and he "had to retire in shame and disgrace," [3] as the pious *Chronicon Ephratense* records. After him came one of the Solitary, Brother Elimelech (known to the world as Emanuel Eckerling) —"a born priest," as the *Chronicon* observes scornfully, "who possessed all the endowments for spiritual perversion. But as these people were too good for perversion"—and as, besides, he preached inordinately long sermons—"he fared even worse than the former." [4]

The stage was now set for Brother Weiser, whose overthrow the *Chronicon* proceeds to record with sad and sly complacency. The story that emerges from the allegorical, ambiguous style of that extraordinary book, in which reason is discredited as worldly and unreason held up as divine, but in which nevertheless a healthy humor is found perpetually wrestling with mysticism on the mat, is somewhat in the vein of *The Pilgrim's Progress*. At least it is the story of the conflict between Christian (Conrad Weiser) and Apollyon (woman). And the woman is his wife.

Unhappily for the welfare of Weiser's soul, his teaching like his charity began at home. If we are asked

> *Whether the devil tempted her*
> *By a High Dutch interpreter,*

we might reply by reminding the reader of what happened to Adam when Eve polished the apple. In the act of persuading Ann Eve that the separation of husband and wife was the way to salvation, Conrad was overtaken by the very temptations he was seeking to avoid. The peril of these "spiritual courtings," as the *Chronicon* calls them, reached a crisis some time in October. The *Chronicon* gives no dates, but we observe that Benjamin was born July 18, 1736.

We must let the *Chronicon* tell the story.

After the priestly chair was now empty again among the awakened, C. W. incautiously seated himself in it, and thereby opened the door for the tempter to try him. For while according to the manner of those times matrimonial bonds were considerably weakened through baptism, there were spiritual courtings through which the void in his side might easily have been filled again; although the temptation thereto lay only in the conditions, while the will for it was not there. The Superintendent once washed his feet, and as he noticed from the feeling of the feet to what temptations he was most exposed, he said to him: "The Brother must take heed against the female sex." Nevertheless the blood-avenger meanwhile got him into his power and tried to destroy him. [Mark, dear reader, this account agrees with that of Zipporah; [5] for she did not belong to Moses' people, wherefore also Moses sent her home again. That she saved her son from the destroying angel through the blood of the covenant, showed great wisdom in her.] He hurriedly notified the Super-intendent and sought his aid, who paid him a visit, when they opened their hearts to each other in private; whereupon the Superintendent took his burden upon himself, so that the good Brother was freed from all temptation. . . .

In this severe trial this Brother (C. W.) in his God-enamored condition found himself, and because he did not take sufficient heed to himself the tempter assailed him anew, and would probably have overcome him, had not God put it into the heart of the Sister to seek out the covenant and have her-self rebaptized by the Superintendent. Then the cords of the tempter were torn, and they again became as strangers to each other.[6]

In other words, Ann Eve herself joined the community, accepting (in principle) the spiritual doctrine of twin beds. But, as the *Chronicon* in-sinuates in the parable of Zipporah, Ann Eve fell away again and returned to her baking.

We can imagine Ann Eve, who from all accounts was not much of a Böhmist, to have been a trifle impatient with the Virgin Sophia. A woman with eight children on her hands and more to come, must have found herself plentifully occupied with things on this side of eternity. If she contemplated the Virgin Sophia, I dare say there was green in her eye. She had been a good wife to Conrad, had borne him ten children, had traveled with him through the wilderness from the Catskills to the South Mountains, and had now made herself the respected mistress of a stone house facing the Philadelphia Road. She was not going to be put away. In subsequent years, after the monastery on Zion had been erected and good Brother Enoch, entering it, had come to make Ephrata the center of his life, the Indians and the crops nevertheless still took him frequently over the mountain to the house where Ann Eve presided, and where the stork continued to put in an honest appearance.

Surely it is the strangest version on record of the eternal triangle: Ann Eve, Conrad, and the Virgin Sophia. Ann Eve won out, for she had the truth on her side: "It is not good for man to live alone." *Un' das Schteht in der Bibel.*

Two of Weiser's children entered the Kloster: his eldest son, Philip, for a time (veiled reference is made to his mother's sacrifice of him in the story of Zipporah) and little Madlina to stay. Philip's career as a celibate lasted no longer than his father's; Anna Madlina died during her novitiate.

Conrad Weiser contributed to Ephrata money, time, and his name. His mere presence in the community gave it standing. But Conrad was more than a mere figurehead. He threw himself furiously into the activities of the Brethren: praying, fasting, preaching, singing, and going on pilgrimages. He was one of the band who undertook a missionary journey in the summer of 1736.[7] With a staff in his hand and sandals on his feet, wearing a long robe girt about the waist with a rope, he took his place among the twelve gaunt brethren who proceeded in single file from village to village preach-ing (among other things) the gospel of marital separation to heads of families in Pennsylvania and New Jersey. It is as well that he left his own children behind him on this expedition.

There is no dodging the paradox. The whole Ephrata episode in Conrad's life seems fantastic and unreal. No amount of explanation can make it otherwise. Granted his excitability, his past uneasy life, his consequent desire to shake off the world; granted the pietistic spirit of the time, the personal influence of Peter Miller, and the spell of Beissel's mystical moonshine—granted all that, for the father of eight, nine, ten, eleven children (they kept coming) to continue honestly attempting the celibate life and the wooing of the Virgin Sophia seems quite outside the bounds of human credibility. Peter Miller we can understand, for he was by nature a recluse. Conrad Beissel we can understand, for he had a cast in his eye. But for Conrad Weiser, an honest, practical-minded farmer, woodsman, interpreter, Indian ambassador, plantation owner, happily married, a faithful husband, and the father of what came in time to be fourteen children: for him to play monk and dabble in Böhmist theosophy—truly, as the *Chronicon* said slyly of another, "God made use of him to manifest forth the wonders of eternity."

CHAPTER 9

... *Entertains the Onondaga Council*

I

AFTER 1732 the new Indian policy seemed to have bogged down. The Shawnees had not been brought back from the Ohio, the Delawares were increasingly obstreperous at the Forks, and the Six Nations had not given Brother Onas a release for the Susquehanna lands. In some respects the situation had even grown worse. It was feared in Pennsylvania that Maryland was trying to steal a march on her sister province and was negotiating with the Six Nations to get these same Susquehanna lands for herself.

That is why Weiser, when he learned from messengers sent by Heta-quantagechty that some fifteen chiefs of the Onondaga Council had set out from their country for Philadelphia intending "to Settle their affairs with their brethren there," [1] was so much concerned that he not only sent a letter on September 1, 1736,[2] to notify James Logan, but followed it up with another next day [3] in fear lest the first might have miscarried. Logan, who, as President of the Council, had been the acting governor since the death of Patrick Gordon, was as much excited in his Quaker way as Weiser, and wrote him several letters urging him to leave his farm even though this was sowing time (" 'tis hoped thou may hire a man that may be trusted to do this for thee in thy Stead" [4]), hurry north to meet the chiefs at the Indian town of Shamokin, show them every courtesy while "insinuating" himself into their councils (this was a Logan touch), and escort them to Philadelphia with as much decency as was compatible with frugality—which last was a proper Penn touch, "Saint" Thomas being still in the province and actually at Logan's elbow when he wrote.[5]

Accordingly, on Sunday, September 12, we find Conrad Weiser at Shamokin, watching the East Branch of the Susquehanna River for sight of the three or four expected canoes bearing the chiefs. Conrad was not entirely at ease. This was by far the most important assignment he had yet received from the government, and he was not quite sure how to go about it. Great issues were involved, as Logan had reminded him, with respect both to Indian and intercolonial relations. But it was not this that worried Conrad (he was never a man to balk at responsibility) so much as the mere prospect of meeting the Great Council, chiefs of the Fire That Never Dies. In the back of his mind was an awe of these men. It is true he had plenty of independence and self-confidence, but he was at the same time a hero worshipper and strongly influenced by that subtle atmosphere surrounding persons of position and character. These men whom he was about to welcome at Shamokin were the "very chiefs" of the Six Nations, *royaners;* and they comprised so considerable a portion of Deganaweda's roster that they came with the powers of the Onondaga Council itself.

Among them were two of the "vere greatest mans" [6] (as he explained excitedly to Logan) of the Oneida nation, which had special jurisdiction over the lands in dispute; and other chiefs of continental fame, such as Tocanuntie, the "Black Prince," whose name ranked so high in the lists of battle and of council that the French at this time would conduct no treaty with the Six Nations which he did not attend.

When at last the canoes came into view on the broad river that flows here between forested mountains, Weiser was astonished to see a flotilla, "about 18 Canoes full and a white flagg." [7] For a moment (I think for the last moment in his whole career as an ambassador) his nerve faltered. "I was troublet in my mind," he wrote to President Logan, "dit not know what to say or what to doe . . ." But his instinct did not fail him. As the chiefs came to shore, surrounded by swarms of men, women, and children, in blanket cloth mantles and buckskins, some feathered and painted, Conrad shook hands with them. It was exactly the right thing to do, and they responded warmly. There was Tocanuntie, Hanickhungo, Tahashwangarorus, Saguchsanyunt, Sawuntga, and a host of others: Onondagas, Senecas, Oneidas, Cayugas, and Tuscaroras. There were no Mohawks among them, the Mohawks having no manner of claim to these lands on the lower Susquehanna.

During the next few hours Conrad learned much, as the letter he dashed off for James Logan's benefit discloses, of the procedure of the Onondaga Council, and what means the chiefs used to keep their councils close. There was no question of "insinuating" himself into their minds. The chiefs were old stagers at the game of diplomacy, and knew how to keep their councils out of the reach of strangers.

Conrad Weiser to James Logan [8]

TulpehoKin Sept[r] the 16[d]
1736

Sir

. . . after the[y] landit and had taken up quarters Some in Houses and Some out dors they Inquired whoe the white man was that shook hand with them on the watter side   they was told that it was the five nations Interpreter. They Called a Counsel that Evening in olumapies [i.e., Sassoonan's] House and Send for me   Imediatly I went there and was orderet to seet down betwix two of the oldest man in the Company. they ask mey whether I was Zihguras   I told them ies,   they semd to be mighty glad   they ask me whether I had any thing to say   they was now purpos gathered to have a little Convers or discours with me. I told th. I had—and begun soon after   Brethren I am very glad to see you   I am send up to this place by your Brother pen. he heard of your Coming down but did not well know whether it was true or not therfore he send me to meet you to let you know his hearty desire in seeing you in philadelfia and so have all the rest of the Chief man in that town a hearty desire to see you. therfore Brethren let me desire you to loose no time in your way till you get ther.

they received it very kindly and after I Sat about an our. I took my leave the desired me not to goe Sleep before the Counsel brok up. I and Hatquantagechte and Shykelemo went a way to gether. I ask Hatqua[te] why he did not stay there   he told me he was not iet alowet to do so till the Chiefs send for him. about two ours after they send for Hotqua^te and Shyk⁰ about an Hour after they Came bak and told me that ther would be a Counsel in the Moring, to give me answer upon what was said. with some other directions. next morning before Sun ris they Send for me again   when they war all Meet after I Sad down among them, their speaker begun. Brother we ar very glad to see you here. it has ben a very good thought of our brother Pen to Send you to meet us. We give him many thanks for his so doing and now we will dispatch you to him with this letter (Showing this inClosed streng of wampon to me) We let our Brother pen and the Chief men of philadelfia our brethren Know that we the chief of the five nations (of ten towns) (110 in Company) ar Come to Shomokin and desyn to Set out next day after to morrow at longst if not to morrow for philadelfia over Tulpehokin we desire our brother pen that he May Send a Cupple of his waggons to Carry our Buntels and unable people to travle to philadelphia. ther is Such a great number of us we leave it intirely to him whether he can find houss-room for us in that town   we ar willing to be out dors as we are used to doe. we desire also of him to send to the Canastoge Indians and to the Caniaios that one or two of the Chiefs of both sort may Come and meet us in philadilfy and tell them that we send far them. those that have ben in philadelfy tells us your goods lye allone if was upon the street about the shops where the Shop Kepers Sells, we desire that it may be Kept in house while we are there   it may be Seen for all when the shop is open we will be very carefull hoping the same of you—

I left them the 13^d in the afternoon   ther is 110 of them as said before with womens and children betwixt 40 or 50 man most of them people of authority and the very Chiefs. *I could not perseive the last syne of their Knowing anything from Maryland therefor I thought not feet to mention any thing.* Especially as the Concludit to follow me next day. ther is but two among them I Remember I have seen befor   all the rest ar Strangers to me, and my person unknown to them besides 3 or 4

they keep their buisnes Intirely Close from Hotquantagechte and ShyKelmo and from Some of their very Company. I have no particular frind among them as iet   they sem to be of a very frindly disposition Especially the oonontagers of whom I took particular notice. ther is about 7 or 8 Elderly man of them. Hotquanta^te tells me they ar the wisest of their nation and the only chiefs. there is not one of the Canienkos   they promised to overtak them Some where but is not Come iet. if they dont Come I think it more good than harm. I Expect them all at my house against the 18^d or 19^d how I shall doe with this great number of Indians I desir your order for at present and nothing Els   my Credit is good Every where. Shykelimo thinks and Hotqu^te that they must have the victuals raw and let their wimans Boil it and so much as you think feet and not as they can eat or wast—

I hope none of the delawars will Come   olumpies is Sick Bisquit, also   the rest is abroad but they want one Chief man of Every Nation of Indians about that River for what End is not to be Known for Certain iet. I think it is for Sak of the land which they Intend to tread for with our proprietor as I am told in private by a Indian of their Companie acquainted with me. but he Stopt Imediatly telling me   you will hear in philadelfia. I have no More at present   I remain

Sir   yours to Serve
Conrad Weiser

I had not time to writ this over again I hope you will mak the best of it and Excuse me I had not time Enouf to goe down meself hired this young man to Carry this and Stay for yours pray let him be dispatched so soon as posible

it would have ben very well taken of them if I had brought a streng of wampon to acquaint them with the news of our Governors deat. and another Streng to tell them no to be disCuragd etc. Each about 1½ foot long all which may be don. at your house befor the get to place where they be quartered

it is my opinion that our proprietor will want Bilts of wampon and the Government also if they Could be had in time it would dispatch buisness.

II

It took more than tact, it took statesmanship, to get so large a company safely and happily down through the settlements to the outskirts of Philadelphia; but, with the expenditure of fifteen pounds for such things as fresh beef, an occasional dram, and wagons to help those who were lame, Weiser accomplished it.[9] On September 25 he wrote to Logan from Perkiomen ("Beriomen"), where the company halted a day "because for the rain," to say that he could perceive in his charges "nothing but good disposition," and that they would reach Stenton (the President's suburban home) on the 27th.[10]

At this time there was an election on in the city, and it was thought advisable to delay their entry until the stream of political argument had been turned off at the spigot. They were therefore entertained three days and nights at Stenton, where they were received by James Logan with as much cordiality as his failing health would permit, and where they were also welcomed by Thomas Penn and members of the Provincial Council who rode out specially to meet them. At this meeting, wampum was exchanged and all things were done gravely and in a manner befitting the dignity of the Onondaga Council. When Thomas Penn (through Conrad Weiser) delivered the chiefs three strings of wampum, the first to brighten their eyes and put away all grief, the second to desire them to open their hearts and speak with frankness, and the third to welcome them and promise them shelter—they responded with that strange, deep, musical call of approval, "Jo-ha," which never failed to impress those who heard it: a call that ran solemnly round the assembly, the representatives of each nation separately taking it up in turn. "Yoh-ha-hau (Jo-hah)," as an observer described it a few years later at Lancaster, "denotes Approbation, being a loud Shout or Cry consisting of a few notes, pronounced by all the Indians in a very musical Manner in the Nature of our Huzzas." [11]

We shall meet the "Jo-ha" so frequently in the treaties that it will be well here to give the full description of its music and significance that Conrad Weiser prepared for the *American Magazine* of December 1744:

When any Proposals are made by them in their Treaties with the white People, or by the white People to them, they make the Io-hau, or Shout of Approbation, which is performed thus: The Speaker after a Pause, in a slow

Tone pronounces the U. . . . huy; all the other Sachems in perfect silence: so soon as he stops, they all with one voice, in exact Time, begin one general Ió, raising & falling their Voices as the Arch of a Circle, & then raise it as high as at first, & stop at the Height at once, in exact time, & if it is of great Consequence, the Speaker gives the U. . . . huy thrice, & they make the Shout as often. It is usual, when the white People speak to them, and they give a Belt or String of Wampum, for the Interpreter to begin the U. . . . huy, & the Indians make the Shout [12]

Weiser brought his charges into town on the last day of September, and on October 2 a public conference was held in the Great Meeting House. The whole town was there: the Proprietor, the President, the Council, the Mayor, and the Recorder, "with divers Gentlemen, and a very large Audience that filled the House and its Galleries." [13] When the Indians came in, treading noiselessly on sepacs or moccasins, and took their seats, their brown faces, some painted with streaks of cinnabar or vermilion, and the red and blue blankets which they wore thrown loosely over the shoulder and kept to the body with the left hand, [14] threw a splash of rich color against the thinner, sharper tints of city faces and city costumes.

President Logan explained the occasion to the general audience. These chiefs, he said, "of whom there never at any time before had been so great a Number met in this Province," [15] had come with an answer to proposals made by this government four years ago. Then he turned the conference over to the Indians, since they had called it, and thereafter the public followed its proceedings through the medium of Conrad Weiser, Interpreter.

Hanickhungo, the Speaker, rose and, addressing Brother Onas, the President, and the gentlemen of the Council, touched on three points, each of which he fortified with a belt of wampum or some suitable present. Presenting a belt of white wampum eleven rows wide and decorated with four black St. George's crosses, he thanked his brethren for the council fire kindled in their city at which the chiefs were now come to warm themselves. Presenting a bundle of skins in the hair, he cleared the road between Philadelphia and the Six Nations country of any trees that might have fallen since the last meeting in 1732. With a large beaver coat he brightened the chain of friendship between the English and the Six Nations with all their dependents and allies, cleaned it of rust and spots, and proclaimed the desire of his people that it should "endure until this Earth passeth away & is no more seen."

This business of the Fire, Road, and Chain (symbols of international amity) was the rhetorical high-water mark of the treaty. It was conventional but very far from meaningless. It was like the ratifying of a treaty of alliance between modern states. That it should have been undertaken by the Onondaga Council was of vast significance, not only to Pennsylvania, but to the English colonies as a whole.

But the Six Nations, though they had a taste for poetry in their councils, were a practical people. They knew that "fair words butter no parsnips," and that lasting friendship is based on common interest. This foundation they proceeded to lay by clearing up the dispute about the Susquehanna lands. The week of October 3 was devoted to this matter.

The Onondaga Council had not come down to haggle. They had come to have their moral right to the lands admitted, and then to settle on almost any terms that were agreeable to Brother Onas. It was to be a contract between gentleman. In private conferences at the house of Thomas Penn the arguments on both sides were gone into thoroughly and in the end a satisfactory compromise was reached. To call it a sale would be to misread the Indian mind. Rather let us say that, in return for Penn's recognition of their ownership of the lands, the Six Nations surrendered them gladly.

On Monday, October 11, Conrad Weiser signed as witness to a deed by which the Six Nations released to Brother Onas

. . . all the said River Susquehannah, with the Lands lying on both sides thereof, to Extend Eastward as far as the heads of the Branches or Springs which run into the said Susquehannah, And all the lands lying on the West side of the said River to the setting of the Sun, and to extend from the mouth of the said River Northward, up the same to the Hills or mountains called in the language of the said Nations, the Tyannuntasacta, or Endless hills, and by the Delaware Indians, the Kekkachtanin Hills . . .[16]

For this huge tract, the province gave a few guns, blankets, hats, garters, tobacco pipes, looking glasses, pots of vermilion, etc. It was not very generous, especially since, in consideration of this payment, the Provincial Council cut to one-third the value of the courtesy present it had previously decided to give its guests. But the Six Nations were satisfied. The payment of any price at all was a recognition of the justice of their position, and was therefore of the highest value to them both because it raised their prestige among surrounding Indian nations and also because it provided a precedent for the similar claims they were on the point of pressing against Maryland and Virginia.

The Onondaga Council was pleased with Conrad Weiser. He had served them well as an interpreter. They knew from unhappy experience that all their skill in debate was lost when the interpreter who conveyed their thoughts was incompetent or partial. The chiefs informed James Logan, as the latter reported to the Council afterwards, "that they had found Conrad faithfull & honest, that he is a true good Man, & had spoke their Words & our Words and not his own . . ." They presented him "with a drest Skin to make him Shoes & two deer Skins to keep him warm. . . ."

The Council responded by giving Shickellamy a gift of six pounds' worth of any goods he liked. It was fitting to do this since, by the treaty of 1732, he and Weiser had been appointed together "as fitt & proper Persons to goe between the six Nations & this Government, & to be employed in all Transactions with one another, whose Bodies the Indians said were to be equally divided between them & us, we to have one half & they the other. . . ."[17]

Conrad and Shickellamy made a good team. Weiser had no trouble with the many Indian deputations he escorted through the province as long as

Shickellamy was alive. And Weiser never forgot that his body was divided, as the chiefs had said. He felt himself bound by a double loyalty: to the Six Nations and to Pennsylvania. It is the measure of his success as an ambassador that, by holding to a course within the bounds of the common interests of the two peoples, he kept the respect of both parties to the end. After his death, Seneca George spoke of him as "a great Man, and one-half a Seven Nation Indian [the League was expanding], & one-half an Englishman."

Before leaving the city, the Indians had their amusement. They went about to see the sights. Conrad conducted a party to the waterside and took them, at a cost of two pounds, aboard one of the ships in harbor.[18] This was of special interest to them. But it was not the masts and yards, the capstan and cable, and all the evidences of the white man's ingenuity and power that interested them. The Indians had little curiosity about mechanical inventions. The sailing ship had other significance for them. They saw in it a symbol of the white man's coming to their world, and a reminder of the welcome they had given him. The allegory of the ship first tied to the bushes, then to a tree, and at last to a rock was to become a council-fire classic. In time to come Conrad Weiser was to hear it many times—at Onondaga and out on the Ohio—spoken in reproach when the Indian found himself crowded by his own guest off the land.

III

On their way out of town, the Indians stopped at Stenton, but their call was cut short by a sudden illness of the President. They went on under Weiser's escort to Tulpehocken.

It was a sad homecoming for Conrad. He found several of the children ill, little Benjamin (three months old) dead.[19] But there was little time for private grief. The Indians stayed about the plantation for ten days, and there was important business to attend to. Indeed, if we consider the mis-understandings to which it gave rise in later years, the business done on Weiser's plantation may be considered the climax of the treaty, for it was here that the chiefs signed a release of any rights they might have had to lands south of the Blue Mountains as far east as the Delaware River.[20]

Twenty years later the Quakers and others of the anti-proprietary party smelled brimstone in the transaction. The Proprietors, they said, had tricked the Six Nations into assuming title to lands that rightfully belonged to the Delawares; and by thus bringing Delaware lands under the Six Nations auction block they caused an Indian war and drenched the province in blood.

". . . fourteen Days after the Deed of 1736 was granted," wrotes Charles Thomson in *An Enquiry into the Causes of the Alienation of the Delawares and Shawanese Indians* (Philadelphia, 1759),

a few of the *Indians* who remained in Town were drawn in to sign a Writing, declaring that they meant to extend the Grant to *Delaware*; but this was not an Act of the whole, nor was any Consideration paid, and every Circumstance considered, or only this one, *viz.* how *Indians* commonly debauch themselves with Liquor, after they think publick Business is over, it may be said this was done in a Manner not the farthest removed from all Suspicion of Chicanery.[21]

"This charge is false," said Conrad flatly when he read the lines. "The whole Page is nothing but Falsehood." [22]

Thomson's printed libel has been enshrined by later writers as if it were the Apostle's Great Toe. Conrad Weiser's written "Observations" on it have been ignored. But a reading of the original documents (many of which were not seen by Charles Thomson) shows conclusively that Weiser was right. Here are the facts.

While the Six Nations chiefs were in Philadelphia, James Logan and Thomas Penn told them of the difficulties they were having with the Indians at the Forks. Certain Delawares were asking pay for lands that had long since been bought and paid for. There were no formal demands from tribal councils, but individual Indians bothered settlers with demands for "compensation." It was blackmail on a large scale, and was becoming dangerous. It was not enough to buy these Indians off: they took the money and came back for more. Before 1755 some districts, notably the Moravian settlements around Bethlehem and Nazareth, had been paid for a number of times. The Proprietors were in an ugly dilemma. To pay brought no final settlement of the demands, yet not to pay might bring bloodshed.

When the chiefs left Philadelphia and called at Stenton on their way home, it had been the President's intention, as we learn from him, to ask their assistance in handling this problem.[23] It was reasonable to do so. The Forks Indians were subject to their Uncles, the Six Nations; and it was as much the responsibility of the Six Nations to prevent Delaware trespass upon Brother Onas' land as it was the responsibility of Brother Onas to prevent white settlers from trespassing on Indian lands.

Nootamis, a Jersey Delaware, was the Indian who was causing the President chief concern at the moment. It was feared that he was "Endeavouring to raise war between y[e] Indians and English." Logan and the chiefs had discussed him at some length in Philadelphia.

This man [wrote Logan to Weiser October 18] while he lived in Jersey pretended that a relation of his on this Side of Delaware left him his lands by will and Accordingly he came over and Claimed a great Quantity of Land to which the other had no right and made himself very troublesome, hereupon the Proprietors John & Thomas with divers other and me amongst the Rest in May 1735 met them at Pennsbury and there produced a Deed with witnesses yet living who had been present at & Signed the treaty proving the Indians who had been y[e] rightfull owners of that Land had long before sold it to our Proprietors. Nootamis and his Associates being thus baffled and greatly disappointed have resolved as I am very lately told to apply to these Chiefs of the 5 Nations on their Return and Endeavour to procure from them some Colour of a Grant by which they may Still Claim.[24]

While the chiefs of the Six Nations were at Stenton on their way home in October 1736, Logan was taken ill ("I just died away for a minute and exceedingly frighted my wife who was with me" [25]), and the Indians left before any means had been concerted of forestalling Nootamis' fraud. On recovering, Logan wrote to Weiser, entrusting to him the handling of this business. The chiefs were to be asked to sign a large document containing two engagements: first, a release of any right they might conceivably have had to lands on the Delaware in Pennsylvania (this to forestall Nootamis); and second, a promise never to sell lands lying within the bounds of the Province to any other than Brother Onas.

As for the first point, "These Nations," wrote Logan, "have in reality no manner of Pretence to any Land on ye waters of Delaware . . . They do not grant us any Land on Delaware therefore observe to them that this is not at all intended by it but they only release and quit all their claims there and as they make none it is in reality nothing & yet may prevent disputes hereafter. . . ." [26]

The President did not intend, and Weiser did not understand, that the chiefs were to sign a document transferring title (as has since been charged) from the Delawares to themselves. By this release the Six Nations were merely to put their seal to certain sales the Delawares had already made, and to serve notice on Nootamis that there could be no hope of drumming up a new Six Nations deed to supersede an old Delaware one. Neither in 1736 nor at any other time during Weiser's career (except for an outburst of rhetoric by Canasatego in 1742—an outburst that unfortunately has been quoted as though this rum-guzzling windjammer were the Iroquois Blackstone) did the Six Nations deny the right in principle of the Delawares to own land. What they did deny was the right of the Delawares to retain perpetual title to lands they had already sold.

"I desired to put this much down in writing," said Weiser in a letter to Count Zinzendorf in 1742, "that the five nations have not sold the land in question [i.e., at the Forks of the Delaware] to the proprietor but only validated the sale that the Delaware Indians made . . ." [27]

The Six Nations explained to Conrad Weiser at Easton in 1758 that by the 1736 release of lands on the Delaware they intended nothing other "than an acknowledgment that they were convinced we had fairly bought them of the Indians"; [28] and Conrad Weiser at the same Easton treaty told the Governor and Council that he joined in opinion with the Indians, "& always conceiv'd the matter in the same Light." [29]

On October 25, at Conrad Weiser's house in Tulpehocken, the Indians signed the release:

We the Chiefs of the Six Nations of Indians . . . who have lately at Philadelphia . . . released . . . All our Right . . . to all the Lands on both sides the River Sasquehannah from the Mouth thereof as far Northward . . . as that Ridge of Hills called the Tyoninhasachta or endless Mountains, Westward to the setting of the Sun and Eastward to the farthest springs of the Waters running into the said River, Do hereby further declare, That our true intent and Meaning by the said Writing was and is to release, And we do hereby more expressly release to the said Proprietors their Heirs and Successors forever All our Right, Claim and Pretensions whatsoever to all and every the Lands lying Within the Bounds and Limits of the Government of Pennsylvania, Beginning Eastward on the River Delaware as far Northward as the said Ridge or Chain of endless Mountains as they cross the Country of Pennsilvania from the Eastward to the West—And further as we have made the firmest League of friendship with our brethren of Pennsylvania and are become as one People with them—We do hereby promise and engage for ourselves and our Children and their Children, That neither We nor they nor any in Authority in our Nations will at any time bargain sell grant or by any means make over to any person or persons whatsoever whether White Men or Indians other than to the said Proprietors the Children of William Penn or to persons by them authorized and appointed to agree for and receive the same, any lands within the limits of the Government of Pennsilvania as 'tis bounded Northward with the Government of New York and Albany—But when we are willing to dispose of any further rights to Land within the said limits of Pensilvania. We will dispose of them to the said William Penn's Children and to no other persons whatsoever. In Witness whereof we have in behalf of all our Nations signed this further Writing being distinctly read and interpreted to us by our Friend Conrad Wyser the twenty fifth day of October 1736.[30]

Tocanuntie, Hanickhungo, Tahashwangarorus [Shickellamy], Saguchsanyunt, Sawuntga, Coxhayion, etc., put their marks to the document, and presented a belt of wampum by way of confirmation. Conrad Weiser, his father-in-law John Peter Feck, and his brother-in-law Leonard Feck, signed as witnesses.[31]

Conrad Weiser to James Logan [32]

Sir

this is to let you know that the Greatest part of the Indian is gone from here yesterday the Sinickers ar here still because of their being drunk they have Syned the larger deed after had it in Consideration from Morning till night 15 of the Chiefs have Synd and four of their youger people have syned for Wittnes and two of my Neighbors besides me. it went very hart about Syning over their right upon delaware because the sayd they had nothing to doe there about the land, they war afaired they Shoud doe anything a mis to their gosens the delawars.

I must be Short desyn to See you after I Come from Mahonyay to where I must goe to Carry up Some of their goods with about 10 Horses there is no help for it they ar disabled to Carry for Sicknes and Strong liquors Sak. they Charges will be some what larger then you Mobt Expect I must finish because for the bearers Sak   I remain   Sir   Yours

CONRAD WEISER

octbr the 27
  1736

PS I found one of my Children burryied after I Came whom and Some Sick.

A day or two after signing the release, some of the chiefs "in a very earnest manner" desired Conrad to write a letter for them to the Proprietor and the President, introducing their request, in Logan's vein, "as a Matter which they had forgot to mention at the Treaty at Philadelphia." They dictated it to him "Paragraph by Paragraph," [33] and Conrad presented it to Thomas Penn a few days later in Philadelphia.

We the Chiefs of the Six Nations, [ran the letter] . . . desire . . . of our Brethren Onas and James Logan never to buy any Land of our Cousins the Delawares, and Others whom we treat as Cousins; they are people of no Virtue, and have no where a Fire burning and deal very often unjust with our Friends and Brethren the English.

Let it be manifest to all People, that if so be the Delawares our Cousins and Other whom we treat as Cousins, offering to sell any Land to the Europeans, that no Body may buy it of them, for they have no Land remaining to them; and if they offer to sell they have no good design.[34]

Four chiefs set their mark to this: Tocanuntie, Hanickhungo, Saguchsanyunt, and Saristaquo.

This letter, like the second release, has been much misunderstood. The Six Nations were not here attempting to deprive the Delawares of title to land. They were merely saying in their way what James Logan had asked them to say in his: that the Delawares had no lands left to sell—or, as Canasatego less elegantly put it a few years later, that their lands had all gone through their guts. This was the interpretation put upon it by John Penn in England when he wrote to thank James Logan for his assistance to his brother at the treaty. "what gives me a Particular pleasure," he said, "is, the message they send back with relation to the Indians about the Forks that they had no Land to sell which agrees with our thoughts at Pennsbury, when Wee believed them to be Jersey Indians who came over the River after the Sale made to my Father . . ."[35]

With the purchase of the Susquehanna lands the three chief trouble centers had been reduced to two; and one of these, the Forks of the Delaware, was in process of liquidation.

CHAPTER 10

. . . Crosses the Endless Mountains

ON December 20, 1736, President Logan received a letter from Governor Gooch of Virginia expressing his desire to negotiate a peace between the Six Nations and the Southern Indians (the Cherokees and Catawbas), and proposing that Pennsylvania should send a messenger to invite the Six Nations to a conference for that purpose at Williamsburg in the spring.[1] Weiser was consulted. He saw at once how important Virginia's proposal was. Ever since his first winter among the Mohawks, he had known that the war between the Six Nations and the Southern Indians was a threat to the English colonies. Virginia and the Carolinas, which were allied with the Catawbas, might at any moment drag down Pennsylvania's alliance with the Six Nations into the muck of an Indian war. It seemed to the Indians that Pennsylvania and Virginia, being under the same king, should be one people, and it was difficult to understand why they should speak with two mouths. Already the steps taken by Virginia to keep Six Nations war parties out of the province had put great strain on Iroquois patience and laid all English-speaking white men under suspicion.

Weiser offered to go himself with the message to Onondaga.[2] For the moment Ephrata was forgotten in the glow of a great public cause. It might have been sufficient to send Shickellamy, but Weiser's going would be a compliment to the Confederacy that might help to smooth away the obstacles that were plainly visible on the path to peace. The Six Nations, however willing they might be in principle to end the war that was draining away their best manhood, distrusted the Catawbas and had little enough reason to like Virginia. More than a diplomatic despatch was needed to overcome their suspicion of peace proposals coming from such a source. If the message was to be effective, it must be backed by the presence of someone close to the heart of Brother Onas and someone in whom they themselves had confidence.

Weiser received his formal instructions from the President's hand on January 22, and with it a belt of wampum to confirm his embassy. In his instructions he was given considerable latitude. "If they hesitate about the Place or time of meeting," wrote Logan, "which last, 'tis doubted, may prove too Early for them, Settle both in the best manner in thy power . . . but let Dispatch be pressed and used in the whole. And whatever is agreed to, be Sure if possible to fix this point as Præliminary, that from the time of this Proposal, none of their young men or Warriours as they Call them shall in any manner attack or goe near those Southern Indians . . ."[3]

Conrad left Philadelphia the following day. Some preparations had to be made at Tulpehocken, but he hoped to set out again in a few days and to reach Onondaga "in 25 Days at farthest from this time," as Logan wrote to Gooch on January 22.[4]

If Conrad expected to be in Onondaga by February 16, he misread the signs. Bad weather kept him at Tulpehocken for four weeks, and it would have been better for him if he had kept off the trail for another six weeks longer. "This has been recon'd the hardest Winter Known here this thirty Years," wrote Margaret Freame to her brother John Penn, March 2.[5] Frost and thaw, snow, ice, rain, and floods, made travel through the woods all but impossible. The ice-break on the Schuylkill at Philadelphia scattered twelve-foot cakes of ice, "Like Vast Numbers of tomb Stones tumble'd and Chursh'd together," [6] over fences and about the fields and orchards. Under such conditions one can imagine what the trails were like, and especially the fords.

By the end of February, however, the winter seemed to Conrad to be about over. Finding "the Ground dry and the Rivalets shallow," [7] Weiser set out, hiring "Stoffel" Stump to accompany him. An Onondaga Indian, Owisgera by name, who had been taken ill at the treaty in the Fall and had remained at Weiser's over the winter, seemed now strong enough to accompany them.

Before they reached the mountains, the weather broke again, and winter set in once more, severe as ever. The story of the "misrys and Famine" [8] encountered on this, the most adventurous of all Weiser's journeys through the woods, has been told by Conrad himself in two excellent journals, one in English intended for the Council at Philadelphia, and the other in German for his family and friends. Both possess a tang of the forest that any rewriting would lose. The story must be told in Conrad's words.

We shall follow chiefly the German version, as translated by his great-grandson, Hiester H. Muhlenberg, permitting ourselves the use of occasional interpolations from the other journal, which gives a better account of the diplomatic proceedings.[9]

On the 27th of February, I left home for Onontago, which is the place where the allied Six Nations hold their council. It is situated in the center of these nations, on a river which enters into the great lake Onontario, from which the great St. Lawrence flows. I took with me as travelling companions, Stoffel Stump, a white man, and an Onontager Indian, who had been lying sick here since last summer, but had now recovered. His name was Owis-gera.

The 28th, we remained at Tolheo, on account of the bad weather, and to procure some necessaries for our journey.

The 1st of March we started from Tolheo, which is the last place in the inhabited part of Pennsylvania, and the same day we reached the top of Kiditanny mountain. The snow was about a foot deep.

The 2d and 3d, we found nothing but ice under the new fallen snow on the north side of the mountain, which caused dangerous falls to ourselves and our horses.

The 4th we reached Schomocken, but did not find a living soul at home who could assist us in crossing the Susquehannah River.

The 5th we lay still; we had now made about eighty miles.

The 6th we observed smoke on the other side of the river, about a mile

THE ONONDAGA TRAIL

Based on Claude J. Southier's Map of New York Province, 1776, with detail from Lewis Evans' Map of 1749, etc.

- ▬▬▬ ONONDAGA TRAIL
- ▪▪▪ OTHER TRAILS AND ROADS
- ⊞ ✕ TOWNS AND SETTLEMENTS
- ▲ ⚑ INDIAN VILLAGES
- ～～ RIVERS   ⌃⌃ MOUNTAINS

Lake Ontario

⊞ OSWEGO

Oneida Lake

▲ ONEIDA

Mohawk River

SARATOGA ⊞

FORT JOHNSON

▲ CANASORAGY

Salt Pits

▲ ONONDAGA where the General Council of the Confederate Republic of the Six Nations meets

CANAJOHARIE (Upper Mohawk Castle)
Otsego Lake

▲ FT. HUNTER

Lower Mohawk Castle

Schoharie Cr.

⊞ SCHOHARIE   ⊞ ALBANY

⊞ WEISERSDORF

ONAGARECHNY MT.
Where Indian Corn, Tobacco, Squash and Pompions were first found by the natives.

Canoes may come from this Lake with a Fresh to Pens[a]

Charlotte R.

Catskill Cr.

Mohegander

1743 & 1745 →   ← 1737
Gooseberry Mountain

Mohawk Branch of Delaware

CATSKILL ⊞

Livingston Manor

⚑ OQUAGA
OTSENINGO

Susquehanna River

▲ COOKOSE

Popoxtunk Branch of Delaware

Neversink R.

KINGSTON (Esopus) ⊞   ⊞ RHINE-BECK

✕ OWEGO

Cayuga Branch Chemung River

✕ TIOGA

Delaware River

Rondout R.

Hudson River

Susquehanna River

Oscalui (Sugar Cr.)

Towanda Cr.

Lackawaxen Creek

Diadactom Lycoming Cr.

✕ OSTUAGA (MONTOURSVILLE)
Muncy Cr. (Canaserago)

▲ WYOMING

DUPUY'S
BROADHEAD'S ⊞

NEW YORK ⊞

Path to Wyoming

▲ NESCOPEC

Lehigh R.

NAZARETH ⊞
EASTON ⊞   ⊞ PHILIPPSBURG

BETHLEHEM ⊞

AMBOY ⊞

BRUNSWICK ⊞

▲ SHAMOKIN

A path to Shamokin scarce passible for 3 steep Mountains

Delaware River

⊞ KINGSTON

Juniata R.

⊞ TOLHEO

Lehigh Hills

Oley Hills

Tohicon Cr.
Neshaming Cr.

⊞ READING   GERMANTOWN

WEISER'S ⊞
Eagle Peak

⊞ EPHRATA

Schuylkill River

⊞ BORDENTOWN

HARRIS' Susquehanna River

⊞ LANCASTER

⊞ PHILADELPHIA

⊞ NEWCASTLE

Atlantic Ocean

above our camp. We went up opposite the place, and saw a small hut. An Indian trader was induced, by the repeated firing of our pieces, to come over, who took us across safely in two trips, but not without great danger, on account of the smallness of the canoe, and the river being full of floating ice. We were obliged to leave our horses behind, as it was impossible to get them across. We again lay still to-day.

The 7th we started from here along one branch of the river. The main stream comes from the north-east; we went to the north-west. We found that we had commenced our journey at the wrong time; all the streams were filled with water and swollen, particularly those we had to cross. An old Shawano, by name Jenoniowana, took us across the creek at Zilly Squachne. I presented him with some needles and a pair of shoe-strings; he was very thankful, and behaved as if he thought he had received a great present.

On the 8th we reached the village where Shikilimo lives, who was appointed by the President to be my companion and guide on the journey. He was, however, far from home, on a hunt. The weather became bad and we laid by . . .

We turn now for a moment to the English journal.

I advised with Hetoquantagechty a chief Man of the Senakas about the affair I was sent for. He told me that I must provide more wampum to Confirm every Article in my Instruction and that it was very necessary to get Shykelimy to go along He being a Man whom the Six Nations count a wise Man and give Credit to what he advises. accordingly I sent for him. He was gone to Pexton . . . in the mean time I met some Warriors that were sent to tell those Indians thereabout to make ready, that about forty Men were to be at Shomockin next Day to go to War against the Cataquees I showd to these Indians the Belt of Wampum and told them what I had in Charge from the Government of Pennsylvania and told them further that I was assured the Six Nations would accept of the message and therefore (Says I) I lay a stop to your Journey. they went back and carried all the rest back to Scahandowany the place where they Live and where I found them comeing down they being Shawanees and Mohawks—

We return to the German journal.

. . . the waters rose still higher, and no Indian could be induced to seek Schikelimo until the 12th, when two young Indians agreed to go out in search of him.

On the 16th they returned with word that Shikelimer would return by the next day, which so happened. The waters had again risen, by reason of the warm wind and rain, which melted the snow in the forests. Several Indians arrived by water from the Six Nations, who reported that the snow was still waist-deep in the forests, and that it was not possible to proceed without snow-shoes.

The Indians at this place were out of provisions; our little stock was soon exhausted, as there was a numerous family in the house where we lodged. We had expected, on leaving home, to supply ourselves with provisions at this place, in which we were entirely disappointed. I saw a new blanket given for about one-third of a bushel of Indian-corn. Here we already began to suffer the pangs of hunger, and other troubles forced themselves on us. It was with great difficulty that I procured a small quantity of corn-meal and a few beans for the journey.

The 21st we ventured to proceed on our journey to Onontago. There were now five of us, as Shikelimo accompanied me, and we were joined by a warrior who had been on a war expedition to Virginia, and was going home in the same direction as we were traveling. In the forenoon we reached the large creek Kanasoragu. It was very high; and we were taken over in a canoe, not without great danger. The next day two English traders attempted to cross, but their canoe was overturned by the force of the current; one of them was drowned and the other only escaped by swimming.

To-day we passed a place where the Indians, in former times, had a strong fortification on a height. It was surrounded by a deep ditch; the earth was thrown up in the shape of a wall, about nine or ten feet, and as many broad. But it is now in decay, as from appearance it had been deserted beyond the memory of man.

The 22d we came to a village called Ostuaga, from a high rock which lies opposite. However, before we came in sight of the village, we reached a large creek, which looked more dreadful than the one of yesterday. After repeated firing of our guns, two young Indians came from the village to see what was to be done. They brought, at our request, a canoe from the village, and took us across. We quartered ourselves with Madam Montour, a French woman by birth, of a good family, but now in mode of life a complete Indian. She treated us very well according to her means, but had very little to spare this time, or, perhaps, dared not let it be seen, on account of so many hungry Indians about. She several times in secret gave me and Stoffel as much as we could eat, which had not happened to us before for ten days; she showed great compassion for us, saying that none of the Indians where we were going had anything to eat, except the Onontagers, which my Indian fellow-travellers refused to believe, until we found it true by experience.

The 23d we lay still on account of rainy weather. Two Indians arrived by water in a canoe made of elk-skins, who said that in the wilderness the snow was still knee-deep. I received from Madam Montour some provisions for the journey. We have now advanced one hundred and thirty miles.

The 24th we proceeded on our journey from here, and in the forenoon found the snow two feet deep; but as it had been very cold during the night, it was frozen so hard that we could walk over the surface without breaking often through the crust. In the afternoon we came to a thick forest, where the snow was three feet deep, but not frozen so hard, which made our journey fatiguing. We were between two high and steep mountains; a small creek flowing through the valley in an opposite direction to our course. The valley was not broader than the bed of the stream, and on both sides were frightfully high mountains and rocks, overgrown with carell or palmwood. The passage through here seemed to me altogether impossible, and I at once advised to turn back.[10] The Indians, however, encouraged me to persevere, stating that in a little distance the mountains were farther apart, and that we could easily proceed. I agreed at last to go on: the Indians took the lead, and clambered with hands and feet along the side of the mountain; we followed after. I had a small hatchet in my hand, with which I broke the ice to give us a foothold. There was considerable danger of freezing our feet, as we were often obliged to cross the stream, and had no space to keep our feet warm by exercise. After climbing in this way, we reached a point where the valley began to widen and become more spacious. We made a fire, and waited for our Onontager Indian, who was far behind; he being still weak from the illness he had undergone. In these three hours we had not advanced over one mile. The wood was altogether of the kind called by the English, spruce, so thick that we could not, generally, see the sun shine. After we had warmed ourselves and taken some food, we proceeded onward, and in the evening made our camp under the spruce trees. We broke branches to cover the snow where we lay down, and this constituted our beds. We made a large fire on the top of the snow, which was three feet deep. In the morning the fire had burned down to the ground, and was as if in a deep hole. We slept soundly after our hard day's journey, but were all stiff in the morning from the cold, which, during the night, had been excessive. We prepared breakfast, which consisted of a little Indian corn and beans, boiled in water.

The 25th, after breakfast, we proceeded on our journey. The snow was no deeper, and before noon we reached a stream which is a branch of the Otzuachtan river, which we had left yesterday. The stream we are now on the Indians call Dia-daclitu, (die berirte, the lost or bewildered) which in fact deserves such a name. We proceeded along this stream between two terrible mountains; the valley being, however, now about a half mile in width, and the stream flowed now against this, and then against the other mountain, among the rocks. Here we held a long council as to the best mode of procedure; whether to remain in the valley, and consequently be obliged to cross the stream repeatedly, or to endeavor to proceed along the sides of the mountains, as we had done yesterday. As it was very cold to wade the creek often, we determined to try the mountain's side. As we were clambering along the mountains, before we had proceeded a quarter of a mile, Shikelimo had an unlucky fall which nearly cost him his life. He had caught hold of a flat stone, sticking in the root of a fallen tree, which came loose, and his feet slipping from under him, he fell at a place which was steeper than the roof of a house. He could not catch hold of anything, but continued slipping on the snow and ice for about three rods, when his pack, which he carried in Indian fashion, with a strap round his breast, passed on one side of a sapling and he on the other, so that he remained hanging by the strap until we could give him assistance. If he had slipped half a rod further he would have fallen over a precipice about one hundred feet high, upon the other craggy [spitzige] rocks. I was two steps from him when he fell. We were all filled with terror, but were obliged to proceed until we reached a place where we could descend into the valley, which did not take place for a quarter of an hour. When we reached the valley Shikelimo looked around at the height of the steep precipice on which he had fallen. We looked at him: he stood still in astonishment, and said: "I thank the great Lord and Creator of the world, that he had mercy on me, and wished me to continue to live longer."

We soon came to the before-mentioned water, which had a strong current; we therefore cut a pole twelve or fifteen feet long, of which we all took hold, and so waded together, in case that if any one should lose his footing, he could hold on to the pole. The water reached to the waist, but we crossed safely. We had to suffer from excessive cold, because the hard frozen snow was still eighteen inches deep in the valley, and prevented us from walking rapidly; neither could we warm ourselves by walking, because we had to cross the stream six or seven times. The wood was so thick, that for a mile at a time we could not find a place of the size of a hand, where the sunshine could penetrate, even in the clearest day. This night we prepared a place to sleep in the same manner as last night.

During the night it began to storm, and the wind blew terribly, which seemed to me strange. The Indians say that in this whole valley, which is about sixty miles long, it storms in this manner, or snows, every night. It is such a desolate region that I often thought I must [die of oppression; I called it the Dismal Wilderness—*die Grausame wüste*].

The 26th, we passed the whole day in travelling along the stream; the mountains continued high, and we were obliged to wade over the creek many times, but it began to diminish in size, so that we could cross it several times on fallen timber. To-day, Tawagarat fell with such violence from one log on another, that he fainted and lay in that state for considerable time. We became very much fatigued today, from so often wading the creek in such cold weather; we also became very hungry; the provision was poor, and little of that. This night we built a hut of branches, because it again became cloudy; it stormed again terribly, and snowed at times as if it wished to bury us, but it never lasted long, and in the morning there was little snow on the ground.

The Indians believe that an Otkan (an evil spirit) has power in this valley, that some of them could call him by name, and brought him sacrifices by which he could be appeased. I asked if any of our party could do this, or knew his name. They answered no, that but few could do this, and they were magicians.

The 27th we followed up the valley and creek; the hills became lower as we continued to ascend, because we had been following up this water from the time we left Madam Montour's. At noon we reached the summit of the mountain. Before we had quite reached the summit, we saw two skulls fixed on poles, the heads of men who had been killed there a long time before, by their prisoners, who had been taken in South Carolina. The prisoners, who were two resolute men, had found themselves at night untied, which, without doubt, had been done by the Okton, and having killed their captors and taken possession of their arms, had returned home.

One of the wonders of nature is to be seen here. The creek already mentioned, is flowing as if on a summit or height of land; runs with a rapid current towards or against a linden tree, where it divides into two streams; the one stream becomes the water up which we have been travelling for three days, and flowing to the south, empties not far from the Indian village of Astuage, into the Quinaston river. The other stream flows to the north, and empties into the Susquehannah river, two hundred miles above Schomoken. Both streams finally again unite their waters at Schomoken, where the Otquinachson river empties into the Susquehannah. The stream flowing to the north is called the Dawantaa (the fretful or tedious).[11]

We travelled down this stream, and towards evening reached a place where the snow had entirely disappeared, in a grove of white oak trees. The south wind blew very warm, and the weather was pleasant; it seemed as if we had escaped from hell; we lay on the dry ground. I cooked for supper as much as I thought would give us plenty to eat, as we hoped soon to reach the Susquehannah river, where our Onontager had persuaded us that we would find provisions in plenty.

The 28th we eat our last meal for breakfast, as we believed that by evening at farthest, we would reach the river, and started immediately after. The warm south wind was still blowing, and the sun shining. We left the Dawantaa to the right hand, and about ten o'clock reached a water called Oscalui (the fierce) [*grausam*]. This is a rapid, impetuous stream, because it flows among the mountains, and because the wind has melted the snow in the high forests. We first cut down a long pine tree, but it did not reach the other shore, and was carried away by the current. The Indians advised that we should wade through, holding to a long pole; but I would not agree to that, because the water was too deep. We knew not what to do—while we were cutting down the tree, the water had risen a foot. As we could not agree on what was to be done, and were irritable from hunger, the Indians began to abuse Stoffel, who, they said, was to blame that I had not followed their advice. When I took his part, they treated me the same way—called me a coward who loved his life, but must die of hunger on this spot. I said, it is true we Europeans love our lives, but also those of our fellow-creatures; the Indians, on the contrary, loved their lives also, but often murdered one another, which the Europeans did not do, and therefore the Indians were cruel creatures, whose advice could not be followed in circumstances like the present. They then wished to make a raft, and thus cross to the other side, which it was impossible to do at this place, on account of the rapidity of the current, and the rocks in the bed of the stream. I said to them, that I had so far followed their advice, but I now required them to follow mine, and to follow the stream downwards until we reached a quiet place, even if we had to go to the Susquehannah river, because on level land the water was not so rapid as among the hills and mountains. Shikelimo answered, that I did not know how far it was to the Susquehannah river; they knew it better than I did; it was an impossibility. This he said to frighten me, but I knew it could not be more than a short day's journey, by following the course we were traveling, because I examined the compass several times every day; I could also tell it by the mountains on the right hand side of the stream, as we descended, which appeared to become lost; whereas, up the stream they appeared much higher, from which a sound judgment would infer, that a man had not far to go to find the current lessen or cease. Shikelimo retorted, that he was the guide, as being a person who had traveled the route often, while I had never done so; he would cross there; if I refused, I must bear the blame if I lost my life by hunger or any other accident. He would also complain to the Governor, Thomas Penn, and James Logan, of my folly, and excuse himself. The others spoke much to the same purpose, particularly Tawagarat, who was returning from the wars, who said openly, that he was too proud to obey an European. I answered them all, and in particular Shikelimo—it is true, he was appointed by the Governor to be my guide, but not my commander, and since he would not guide me on the path I wished to go, namely, down the creek, and wished to be my master, I set him free from his duty—he might go where he pleased. I intended to be my own guide, and positively to take my own course, with my fellow-traveller Stoffel, but I would still advise him to obey me this time, which I did as a friendly request at parting. I then took my pack and moved off, the Onontager followed me immediately—Shikelimo did not hesitate long, after he saw that I was in earnest, and soon followed. Tawagarat remained behind, because, as he said, he was too proud and obstinate to follow me. We had not gone more than a mile down stream, when I observed that nature had provided every- thing necessary for a safe crossing; the current had ceased entirely, and there was much dry pine timber, which is the lightest wood that can be found for such purposes. Here I threw down my pack, and ordered my companions to do the same. On their inquiring the reason, I said we would cross here. Shikelimo observed the fine opportunity, he was glad, fired off his gun, and shouted to make our companion who remained behind hear. We went to work, and in an hour and a half we had a raft of the dry pine timber mentioned, ready, and passed over safely. Stoffel and the Onontager crossed again, to fetch two hatchets which we had forgotten, and all was done without any danger. We turned again upstream, until we struck our path. My Indian companions thanked me for my good counsel, and for resisting their wishes so boldly. We traveled rapidly, for the purpose of reaching the Susquehannah river this evening, where some Indians resided, and when we came in sight of it, we sat down to rest; yet we were in trouble for our obstinate Tawagarat, who had remained behind. After we had been sitting there for half an hour, we heard a shout, and soon appeared Tawagarat at full speed, but very wet. On his questioning us as to how we had crossed, the Onontager related the mode, at which he was surprised, and stated that he had tied several pieces of wood together, and pushed off into the water, but was so hurried away by the current (in spite of his efforts with a pole), that he reached a small island which was just above the place we crossed at, where the raft separated, and he was obliged to wade the remaining distance, with the water up to his arm-pits. I reproved him for his pride and obstinacy; he acknowledged that he had acted foolishly, that he had heard our firing, but was already engaged in making his raft.

We proceeded on our journey, well pleased that we were all together again, and the same evening reached some Indians living on the Susquehannah river, where we, however, found nothing but hungry people, who sustained life with the juice of the sugar-trees. We, however, procured a little weak soup, made of corn meal. I had a quantity of Indian trinkets with me, but could procure no meal. My only comfort this evening was, that whoever labors or is tired will find sleep sweet.

The 29th we proceeded on our journey at an early hour, but without breakfast; reached a dangerous place where the path on the bottom-land was overflowed by the river, which was not very high, and we had to cross a very high mountain, which was not much better than the one where Shikelimo had met with his fall. We passed safely, and towards evening we were also safely ferried, in a canoe, over the great branch of the Susquehannah river. All the streams are very high, for the [snows] had been uncommonly deep this winter. This water is called Dia-ogon, and comes from the region of the Sinicker and Gaiuckers. There are many Indians living here, partly Gaiuckers, partly Mahikanders. We went into several huts to get meat, but they had nothing, they said, for themselves. The men were mostly absent, hunting; some of the old mothers asked us for bread. We returned to our quarters with a Mahikander, who directed his old grey-headed mother to cook a soup of Indian-corn. She hung a large kettle of it over the fire, and also a smaller one with potash, and made them both boil briskly. What she was to do with the potash was a mystery to me, for I soon saw that it was not for the purpose of washing, as some of the Indians are in the practice of doing, by making a lye, and washing their foul and dirty clothes. For the skin of her body was not unlike the bark of a tree, from the dirt, which had not been washed off for a long time, and was quite dried in and cracked; and her finger-nails were like eagles' claws. She finally took the ash kettle off the fire, and put it aside until it had settled, and left a clear liquor on top, which she carefully poured into the kettle of corn. I inquired of my companions why this was done; and they told me it was the practice of these and the Shawanos, when they had neither meat nor grease, to mix their food with lye prepared in this manner, which made it slippery, and pleasant to eat. When the soup was thus prepared, the larger portion was given to us, and out of hunger I quietly eat a portion, which was not of a bad taste. The dirty cook, and the unclean vessel, were more repulsive. After I had eaten a little, and quieted the worst cravings of hunger, I took some of my goods, and quietly left the hut, without being noticed by my companions, and went into another hut, gave the old grey-headed mother twenty-four needles and six shoe-strings, and begged her to give me some bread made of Indian-corn, if it were only as much as I could eat at one meal. She immediately gave me five small loaves of about a pound weight, of which I and Stoffel eat two the same evening. The Indians eat so much of the soup that they became sick. We had intended to take a day of rest here, if we could have procured meat, but had to be content to proceed on our journey.

The 30th we proceeded on our journey without anything to eat except the remaining [3] loaves, which were divided among us five. We passed a dangerous creek by wading in the shallow water, and passing the stream on a half fallen tree, which hung across the water. The current was frightful. An Indian from the last village, who was to help us over the water, and show us the path, fell into the water so that we saw neither hide nor hair; but soon rose, and saved himself by swimming to the opposite shore to the one we were trying to reach. Towards evening we arrived at the branch Owego; the Indian village was on the other side of the river, about a mile off. All the bottom land between us and the village was under water, and the current was rapid. We fired our guns three times, but no one would hear or show himself. If we had not seen the smoke of the huts, we would have thought the village was deserted. We began to prepare a fire and wood for a camp; and having made a long day's journey with hungry stomachs, were about to retire to sleep in that condition, and had already laid down, when a great storm came up from the west, with thunder and lightening, and such a violent rain, that it was almost incredible. We could not find a place to lie down, but stood the whole night around the fire. Towards morning it became very cold, and ice formed in every direction; the day before having been very warm, and succeeded by the thunder-storm, of which it was the cause. At dawn we again commenced firing our pieces, on which a canoe with some women at last came from the village, to take us across the river, as we supposed. But they only came over the bottom land to the edge of the river, where they called to us that there were no men in the village, and the women could not venture to cross the raging flood; which was of so unusual a height that the bottom land was flooded, which had not been the case for many years, and in particular as their canoe was so small. Tawagarat, whose home was there, called to them to venture. When they heard that it was Tawagarat, they came across in safety, and stepped on shore; one of them spoke not a word, but wrapped her face in her blanket. The others gave the canoe to the Indians to ferry us across, and afterwards to bring the women. All which was done in three times crossing backwards and forwards, but not without great and imminent danger. One party landed here, the other there, in dry places; but still had to pass sundry hollows and ditches, in water up to the breast, for the land is very uneven. I went first in the canoe; four of us, of whom two were Indians, went back with the canoe. I had new reasons to praise the protection of God, who had rescued us from such imminent peril; the water flew between the trees like arrows from a bow, where if we had struck one, of which there were so many, we must have perished. The Indians gladly received us into their huts, and showed us their compassion. Some of them were old acquaintances of mine from Schochry [Schohary]; they gave us food repeatedly, but each time only a little, so as not to injure our health. They were Caiuckers. All the men were absent hunting, except a couple of old grey-headed men, who had lodged at my home in Schochary some fifteen or sixteen years ago, and had shown me many favors according to their ability. Tawagarat remained here, and lodged in the hut of his mother-in-law; the woman who had hidden her face was his wife, and did so from modesty. Such is the custom among the virtuous women of the Indian tribes. We remained here to-day to recruit ourselves a little, and also to procure provisions for the further progress of our journey.

April the 1st, we still remained here; by my reckoning we are now two hundred and eighty miles from home.

April the 2d, we started about noon on our journey and reached the water called Ononto, and were immediately taken across in a canoe. Several families of Onontagers live here, with one of whom, an old acquaintance, we took up our lodgings, and were well treated.

The 3d, we reached the village Otsen-inky, inhabited by Onontagers and Shawanos. I was at this place in 1726, but find my old acquaintances of that period partly absent, partly dead. We still had five days journey, according to the report of these Indians, from here to Onontago, the object of our tiresome journey, as we could not take the nearest route by reason of the numerous creeks, and must keep upon the hills. The family with whom we lodged had not a mouthful to eat. The larger part of this village had been living for more than a month on the juice of the sugar-tree, which is as common here as hickory in Pennsylvania. We shared our small stock of provisions with sundry sick and children, who stood before us in tears while we were eating. From the time we left Madam Montour's, I generally gave to each one of us his daily portion;   if I gave of my own portion a part to these poor creatures, I met with no sour looks, but if I took from the capital stock to give to them, my companions showed great dissatisfaction. But this did not hinder a thief from stealing, while we were asleep, the remainder of our stock of bread, which was but small. This was the first misfortune that happened to us; the second was, that we heard the snow was still knee deep in the direction we were to travel, and that it was impossible to proceed;   the third was, that the rainy weather in which we had arrived was turned to snow, of which eighteen inches fell in one night;   the worst was, that we had nothing to eat, and our bodily strength began to fail from many trials both of hunger and cold. Here we were obliged to remain and pass the time in distress. I could, to be sure, purchase with needles and shoe strings, sugar made from the juice of the tree already mentioned, on which we sustained life, but it did not agree with us;   we became quite ill with much drinking to quench the thirst caused by the sweetness of the sugar. My companion Stoffel became impatient and out of spirits, and wished himself dead. He desired me to procure a canoe in which to float down the streams until we reached Pennsylvania, which might have been done in six or eight days, but not without provisions, and not without considerable danger, as the Susquehannah was very high and rapid, and we did not know the channel in such a swollen state of water.

But I was now determined on no account to return home without accomplishing the object of my mission, in particular as I knew the danger of the river. Two weeks before, I would gladly have turned back, as I foresaw all the difficulties we must undergo and conquer, but no one then would turn back or see the difficulties I feared. Stoffel wished he had followed my advice at that time. I was now, however, so resigned to misery, that I could have submitted to the greatest bodily hardships without resistance, since I had been relieved from the tortures of the mind by the wonderful hand of God.

I had, at a previous period of my life, wished that I had never heard of a God, either from my parents or other people, for the idea I had of him led me away from him. I thought the Atheists more happy than those who cared much about God. Oh, how far man is removed from God, yes, inexpressibly far, although God is near, and cannot impart the least thing to corrupt man until he has given himself up without conditions, and in such a manner as cannot be explained or described, but may be experienced in great anguish of body and mind. How great is the mercy of the Lord and how frequent; his power, his goodness, and his truth are everywhere evident. In short, our God created the heavens; the gods of the heathen are idols.

But to return to our affairs. I called the Indians together, represented to them the importance of my errand, stated what I was commanded to do by both the governments of Virginia and Pennsylvania, and required of them, as faithful allies of the English, and particular friends of the government of Pennsylvania, to furnish me with provisions for my party so that I could reach Onontago, the end of my journey. Because the business related especially to the allied 6 Nations, for whose sake, their brother, Thomas Penn, had taken such an interest in the affair, and had sent me such a journey at an inclement time of year, for the purpose of preventing further bloodshed unnecessarily and out of mere revenge, and that they might possess their lands and raise their provisions in peace. In the next place I required them to send out two messengers on snow-shoes as soon as possible, in advance, who should make known my approach, so that the councilmen of all the Six Nations could be called together, which would require three weeks. There was an old war-chief from Onontago present, by whose interference both points were agreed to, only no one knew where to procure provisions for us, or for the two Indian messengers. By general consent, a hut was broken into, whose occupants were far absent on a hunt, and so much corn was taken as was judged sufficient to enable us to reach Onontago. The two runners received a share, and the balance about one-third of a bushel, was given to us, which we thankfully received. I had it pounded at the house we occupied, which was done without loss. Hunger is a great tyrant, he does not spare the best of friends, much less strangers. Kaloping, a Frenchman, who had been taken captive when a boy, but now an Indian in appearance, if not worse, together with another young Indian, were sent off to notify my arrival to the council at Onontago. The last fall of snow was rapidly disappearing, as the weather had again become warm.

The 6th of April the runners started. In the meanwhile, an Indian had the kindness to invite me privately to supper. I took Stoffel with me; he gave us to eat by night on two occasions. A third time, another old acquaintance presented me with four small loaves one evening, which I immediately divided among my companions, and the surrounding hungry children.

These Indians often came to my lodgings, or invited me to their huts, for the purpose of talking (they are very inquisitive), and thus we passed the hungry hours away, in relating old or new events or traditions, and smoking tobacco, which they have in plenty. Among other things, I asked them how it happened that they were so short of provisions now, while twelve years ago they had a greater supply than all the other Indians; and now their children looked like dead persons, and suffered much from hunger. They answered, that now game was scarce, and that hunting had strangely failed since last winter; some of them had procured nothing at all;—that the Lord and Creator of the world was resolved to destroy the Indians. One of their seers, whom they named, had seen a vision of God, who had said to him the following words:—You inquire after the cause why game has become scarce. I will tell you. You kill it for the sake of the skins, which you give for strong liquors, and drown your senses, and kill one another, and carry on a dreadful debauchery. Therefore have I driven the wild animals out of the country, for they are mine. If you will do good, and cease from your sins, I will bring them back; if not, I will destroy you from off the earth.

I inquired if they believed what the seer had seen and heard? They answered, yes, some believed it would happen so; others also believed it, but gave themselves no concern about it. Time will show, said they, what is to happen to us; rum will kill us, and leave the land clear for the Europeans, without strife or purchase.

The Indians living here are on an arm of the Susquehannah, which comes out of high mountains, and is a rapid stream. I saw the children here walking up and down the banks of the stream, along the low land, where the high water had washed the wild potatoes, or ground acorns, out of the ground. These grow here on a long stem or root, about the size of a thick straw, and there are frequently from five to ten hanging to such a root, which is often more than six feet long. The richer the soil, the longer they grow, and the greater the quantity in the ground. The largest are of the size of a pigeon's egg, or larger, and look much in size and shape like black acorns. I thought of the words of Job, Chapter 30, 3–8, while these barbarians were satisfying their hunger with these roots, and rejoicing greatly when they found them in large numbers, and dug them up.

On the 7th we agreed to leave this place at once, and again to pass through a great wilderness, to reach the end of our journey. We started at eight o'clock in the morning from this miserable place, where more murders occur than in any other nation. It is called by the Indians, in particular, a den of murderers, where every year so many are swallowed up. About noon we met our messengers returning, who said it was impossible to proceed, on account of the deep snow in the mountains, which was more than knee-deep. We debated long, and it was decided, by a majority of voices, to postpone the journey until better weather and roads. The before-mentioned old war-chief had accompanied us, because he was a leading man in the war-council at Onontago, and wished to accompany me, for the purpose of advancing my business to a favorable termination. He was a grey-headed man of seventy years, as he showed by circumstantial proofs. He advised me, confidently, to proceed on the journey, and promised to guide us by such a route, that if we used our best efforts, we would, by tomorrow evening, reach a country where the snow had disappeared, by reason of the open forests. After two days of fatigue and trouble, said he, you will be better off than by turning back, with your business undone, after having already undergone so many hardships from cold, snow, high water, and hunger. I was pleased with his well-meant advice (for he often called me his son and child), and bade him lead on; for he was much interested in the object of my mission. We proceeded on our journey; rainy weather set in, and before night we were in snow up to the knees. We made a hut this evening, of the bark of the linden-trees, which we peeled off. It rained the whole night, with a warm south wind, which converted the snow into slush.

The 8th we traveled from early in the morning until evening, with great rapidity, in constant rain, through a dreadful thick wilderness, such as I had never seen. We frequently fell into holes and ditches, where we required the assistance of the others to extricate ourselves. We all lost courage. This was the hardest and most fatiguing day's journey I had ever made; my bodily strength was so exhausted that I trembled and shook so much all over, I thought I must fall from weariness, and perish. I stepped aside, and sat down under a tree to die, which I hoped would be hastened by the cold approaching night. When my companions remarked my absence, they waited for me some time, then returned to seek me, and found me sitting under a tree. But I would not be persuaded to proceed, for I thought it beyond my power. The entreaties of the old chief, and the sensible reasoning of Shikelimo (who said that evil days were better for us than good, for the first often warned us against sins, and washed them out, while the latter often enticed us to sin), caused me to alter my resolution, and I arose. But I could not keep up with the old man, who was the leader, and a good walker. He often waited for the whole party. We slept on the snow again that night; it rained the whole night, but not violently.

The 9th we prepared breakfast before day, and set out early in cloudy weather. Before noon we got out of the thick forests into scattered groves, where the snow had disappeared, as the old man had assured us. We seemed to have escaped out of all our troubles in this delightful region, especially as the sun broke through the clouds, and cheered us with his warm rays. If the snow and the forests had remained the same as yesterday, we must all have perished before reaching Onontaga. But hunger was still pinching us; to eat a little corn-meal soup was of no benefit, for it was only meal and water; the wheat bread and good meal had not only left the stomach, but the limbs also. We were now on high mountains, and to-day we passed the first waters flowing into the great Lake Onontario, or the St. Lawrence, out of which the famous river St. Lawrence flows, which passes through New France, or Canada. From all appearances, this is the most elevated region in North America; we passed several small runs on the left hand, which join the last just mentioned. To the right were others, which joined the Susquehannah; a day's journey from here, there are waters emptying into the Hudson to the east, and to the west, at some distance, are the waters joining the Meshasippia. We reached several small lakes and ponds, at one of which the Indians said an evil spirit, in the shape of a great snake, resided, who was frequently visible. The Indians refused to drink here.

The 10th we left our camp quite early, as we hoped to reach the end of our journey this day. About noon we passed the hill on which, by Indian tradition, corn, pumpkins, and tobacco first grew, and were discovered by an extraordinary vision. As we felt sure of reaching Onontago, we cooked the balance of our meal in a great hurry, and hastened onward. It began to rain hard. To-day we made forty miles, the timber was principally sugar-trees. This evening, we reached the first village of Onontago, to our great delight. Not a soul remained in the houses, all came running out to see us; they had been made acquainted with our coming by the old chief, a quarter of an hour previously, who had preceded us for that purpose. They came in crowds to the house we occupied. I found here several acquaintances, but they were surprised at my miserable aspect; one said it is he; another said no, it is another person altogether. It is not the custom among these people, for a stranger who has come from a distance to speak until he is questioned, which is never done until he has had food set before him, and his clothes dried, in which things they did not allow us to want.

Honor and praise, glory and power, be given to the Almighty God who rescued us from so many and various evils and dangers, and saved us from death and destruction, from doubt and despair, and other hazards.

For description of the diplomatic proceedings, we turn again to the English journal.

. . . the Chiefs of this Town came to our Lodging immediately to enquire what our design was to come such a great way at such a Season of the Year. I told them that I was sent by the Governm^t of Pennsylvania with a message of Moment and desired them to send immediately to the Chief Town which was about five Miles off to desire the Chiefs of the Onondaga Town to kindle their ffire with all Speed   I sent a string of Wampum to Signify the Earnestness of the Message—

On the 11th the Messengers came back early in the Morning with the Answer that their fire was kindled and a burning (that is) that some of the Chiefs of every of the Six Nations was there and that I should be welcome to deliver to them what I had from their Brethren of Philadelphia. we set out directly. when we got to the Town they brought Us to the House of Annuwarrogoe which was one of the best Houses in Town after we had Eat some Victuals some of the Chiefs came in to Us received Us to their ffire with a string of Wampum and told me that they would be ready to hear me speak when I pleased at such time or Day I should appoint but being say they you have Suffered so much for want of Victuals in comeing such a great way through Snow and Waters we would have you to rest your Self first and recover your Spirits again for you look like Dead Men. after having considered a little with Shykelimy I returned them thanks for their readiness and told them that my Instruction binds me to all reasonable Dispatch and that I was resolved to speak to them to Morrow and that Howbeit I was somewhat Poor of Body nevertheless I was Capable enough to Execute my Charge to which they all made a Sign at once to Signifye their being very much pleased. they appointed the House where I Lodged for Council next Morning and so Departed. Next Day in the Morning they met and the Speaker Takanunty signified to me that they were ready to hear me   I divided the whole Instruction into two Head Articles—

The first the desire of the Governor of Virginia to call or invite them to Williamsburg to a Treaty of Peace with the Southern Indians the Cherikees and Cataquees. To signifye the strong and earnest request of the said Governor I laid down a large string of wampum (520) to Confirm the truth thereof. Secondly the desire and request of the Province of Pennsylv^a Viz^t that their ffriends and Brethren had sent me up to take hold of their Brethren the Six Nations Hatchet 'till the Six Nations had held a Treaty of Peace with their Enemies the Southern Indians the Cherikees and Cataquees who now Cry for

Peace as also the good advice as becomes Brethren word for word as is mentioned in my Instruction to Signifye the great desire of their Brethren the Chief Persons of Philadelphia I laid down or delivered to them the Belt of Wampum I received from the Presid^t after all was delivered to them I told them I had at present no more to say and that I now leave it to them when they would give me their answer—

After the whole Assembly had Eat together they went to Council in another House. before night they sent to me to let me know that they were ready to give me their answer that Evening. accordingly they assembled at my Lodging and the Wampum I had deliver'd to them was tied to a stick and hung up in the middle of the House for every Body to see. and the whole that I had said to them was repeated by their Speaker and then He came to the answer. He spoke as a Man of great Authority and Prudence loud & Slow and great Silence and order was kept during the whole. their answer was as follows.—

Brethren we let you know that we have considered all that was said to us in the Morning in behalf of our Brother Asaryquoh (so they call the Governors of Virginia) and in behalf of our Brethren Onas James Logan and all the Chief Men or Council of Philadelphia *whom we Love dearly finding them always with an upright Heart* We must let you know that we cannot come to Williamsburg to a Treaty of Peace there is no Road to that place, we never travel through Bushes to Treatys of Peace it is too dangerous and we have no ffire at Williamsburg and if we shoud take a Stump of ffire to go there we cannot get there without running the Risque of our Lives for our Brother Asaryquoh has made a ffence or Wall about his Country and told us not to go over it he would hang us. and that ffence or Wall stands to this Day. and our Brother Asaryquoh's People are very Cross every where in his Country. We therefore give our Brother Asaryquoh an Invitation or a call to come to Albany together with the Chiefs of the Southern Indians the Cherikees and Cataquees his Friends, where we have a fire Burning under the Shadow of some Green Bushes, and we will treat with him and the Southern Indians in the presence of our Brethren the Governor of New York and the Commissioners of Indian Officers in Albany upon reasonable Terms, Such a thing cant be done in a corner it must be done by Publick ffire. We cannot appoint the time when he will or shall come He has Ships and Sloops enough we desire him to make what hast he. can and send word to Us when he is yet afar of. we will take all our Old Chief Men to Albany to the Treaty of Peace. and if our Brother Onas would be pleased to come to the Treaty we would be very glad, then our old People would see and know him (In Confirmation of what He said they handed a string of Wampum to me, and that string of Wampum I gave them was taken off from the Stick and put by—

As for the desire of our Brethren of Philadelphia to take hold of our Hatchet We Grant it. and it shall be put up for one Day and one Night (that is one Summer and one Winter) now Ensuing however some of our Warriours are abroad yet to the South as soon as they come home it shall be taken from them also and put up for the said time. In Confirmation of what we said to perform the Cessation. We give to our Brethren of Philadelphia this Belt of Wampum and we are very much pleased with their puting their hand to this Work we return them our thanks. then the Belt of Wampum I gave them was taken off from the Stick and put by and the Speaker begun again—

Brethren Asaryquoh Onas and James Logan we must now let you know that we have great Reason to doubt the truth of the matter that they Cataquees are Inclined to a Peace much less cry out for Peace, they are a very Proud People their Heart is not upright but Deceitfull we believe that they have cheated our Brother Asaryquoh in telling our Brother that they want to make Peace or have a design to Cheat Us. for if their Heart was upright they would have come long ago to our ffire in Onandago they know and all Nations of Indians know that we always treat Messengers or Peace makers kindly in the hottest of the War and send them away in Peace or after having due Proof of their upright Heart or good design granted their request we are a People that is given to War but we go to War when we want to be revenged we never hurted Messengers that came to us on Business we treat them with the best that we have and let them go in Peace and give them Safeguards if required. As for the Cherikees we cant tell much of them we never heard what Language they use we believe they are a more reasonable People they have been upon the way to come to us. but the Cataquees sent them back calling them fools told them that they would never make Peace with the Six Nations a handfull of People 'till all their Bones were scattered upon the Earth they said further we are a double Men are not afraid of any Body upon the Earth. however you shall and will find that we are a People that will Act upright and Prudent and will come to Peace if they give due Proof of having a good design and upright heart—

Next day Messengers went to the Nations with all Speed as to the Oneidoes Tuscarorys Mohawks and to the Cajoogoes and Tsanontowano or Seneckers to carry the News and Proclaim the Cessation of Arms.

We pick up the German journal again.

. . . After all was over, a feast was prepared. The food was brought in by other chiefs, and set down in the middle of the house in a variety of vessels. Each one brought his own dish and spoon, and helped himself to as much as he chose. After the feast was over, the discourse turned on the events of our journey. At a signal from the Speaker they all went away, to allow us to retire to rest. I received in the evening already an intimation of the answer, which was full and satisfactory.

The 13th, Shikelimo was very sick, and also Stoffel, which was probably caused by imprudence in eating; but in two days they were again well.

The 14th, the Council again assembled, together with all the males who were at home, and the whole of my message was repeated by the Speaker, and I was asked if it was correctly stated in all points. On my answering yes, the Speaker proceeded, and their answer was given at large, with the remark that I should comprehend it fully, so as to be enabled to report it correctly to the Governor of Virginia and Onas. They agreed to the truce, but decided against Williamsburg, and chose Albany as the place of the congress, all which can be seen in my English Journal more at large, with all the speeches and incidents.

These Indians wished me to remain with them a month, until my strength should be restored; they showed every possible kindness to me, and we had no scarcity of food.

I became very sick, so that I expected to die; for half an hour I could neither hear nor see. My host gave me medicine after I had recovered my senses, and could tell him to what cause I attributed this sudden attack; the medicine made a strong impression on my stomach and bowels, succeeded by a violent vomiting. After taking the medicine, I was ordered to walk briskly until it operated, which took place in about half a mile from the village, where I lay until I became insensible. Towards evening I was found by several Indians, who led me home, where a bed had been provided. At midnight I was well; other medicine was then given to me, and in the morning I arose perfectly restored, except that I felt weak.

I went with my host and another old friend to see a salt spring, of which there are great numbers, so that a person cannot drink of every stream, on account of the salt water. The Indians boil handsome salt for use. These Indians, who are otherwise called Onon-tagers (people of the hills), are the handsomest, wisest, and bravest of the Six Nations. They live in huts made of bark, which are very convenient; some of them are 50, 60, to 100 feet long, generally about 12 or 13 feet wide. In this length there are generally four to five fires, and as many families, who are looked upon as one. The country is hilly, but there is a small valley which is very fertile, and yields almost incredible crops of corn, which is plentiful about here. The Europeans from Oswego, as well as Niagara, often come here for corn.

These Indians did all in their power to detain me longer, but I could not be content. I was tired of the Indian country and affairs. At my request, they procured provisions for my return journey, and also a man to carry them and my pack.

On the 17th [says the English journal at this point] they met again in Council and told me that they now desired of their Brother Onas to come to the Treaty of Peace and be present as their particular ffriend for (Say they) the Governor of Virginia is a particular ffriend of the Southern Indians and we must needs have one of our particular ffriends on our Side we assure him that we always take his good advice very kindly—

We resume the German journal.

On the 18th we took leave (together with Stoffel and Shikelimo), for the purpose of returning home, if it should please the Supreme Being. The gods of the heathen are idols; the God of Israel created the heavens: he has a strong arm, but is patient, merciful, of great kindness, and is found by those who seek him. He is God.

This evening we reached the place where Indians make bark canoes, on a creek passing by the village of Otsen-inky, of which we have already spoken. We peeled a chestnut tree, and made a canoe. Caxhayen, who accompanied us, understood this work completely. The weather set in bad, so that we had to lie by under a bark shelter. Snow fell a foot deep.

On the 22d we embarked in our newly-made bark canoe, and pushed off. Caxhayen returned home. The first day we met many obstacles from fallen timber. This creek is about the size of the Tulpenhacken. We had to unload the canoe several times to mend it. We crossed several lakes, and before night reached a more rapid stream which flowed among the hills with such rapidity as can hardly be described. We shot several ducks, which are very plenty, and missed a deer and a bear.

On the 23d we reached deeper water, a river which comes from Oneido, joining it at this point. The water was very high and rapid. Saristaqua of Otsen-inky, who was hunting, fired his gun on seeing us, and called to us. We turned to shore, which we reached in a few minutes, but had been carried down a mile since he had fired. He joined us, and I related what had taken place in Onontago, at which he was pleased. We left him, entered our canoe again, and at night reached Otsen-inky. Fired at a bear and missed.

The 24th we pushed off early, and in half an hour reached the Susquehannah river. Passed, today, Onoto and Owego, down to the Dia-gon. We found that at the last village we had forgotten our Onontago salt.

The 25th we embarked early. Got a companion, a relative of Shikelimo, but who was of little use, except to help us eat. We passed the spot which we first reached after leaving the desolate wilderness, the mouth of Oshcalui and Dawantaa. Shot several ducks and a turkey. Passed several fine bodies of land, partly levelled, partly timbered.

The 26th we reached Scahanto-wano, where a number of Indians live, Shawanos and Mahikanders. Found there two traders from New York, and three men from the Maqui country, who were hunting land; their names were Ludwig Rasselman, Martin Dillenbach and Pit de Niger. Here there is a large body of land, the like of which is not to be found on the river.

A significant item in the English journal belongs to this part of the journey.

. . . we met several of the Shawanees and Delaware Indians who had fled from Pexton and Canaclackqueeny for the Cataquees had killed or carried away some Prisoners a few Days ago   Shykelimy told me that it appears now as the Council had told Us in Onandago about the Cataquees and he desired me to let the President of Philadelphia know it that he may write to the Governor of Virginia to prevent such doings. I met a Shawanee Indian in his flight who told me that his Son a Boy of about ten or twelve Years old was carried away by the Cataquees a few Days ago.

We bring the narrative to a close with the German journal.

On the 27th we embarked. About noon we met some Pennsylvania traders, who gave us some run.

On the 28th we reached Shomoken: here Shikelimo took leave of us and went home. Stoffel accompanied him, to bring the things we had left in his care, as saddles and bridles, and returned this evening on horseback. In the meanwhile, I had paddled down the river, on this side, to inquire after my horse of the Indians, who were now encamped here. When I went on shore and looked into the forest, the first object I saw was my horse, about twenty rods off, and, in fact, not far from the spot where I had left him when going up. Stoffel's horse could not be found at this time.

The 29th we set off over the country, on the 30th we reached Talheo, and, on the 1st day of May reached home in safety. Honour and praise, power and glory be given to Almighty God forever and ever.

CHAPTER II

... *Cleans up After the Walking Purchase*

I

WEISER'S journey to Onondaga in 1737 pointed the way to a united Indian policy. Virginia and Pennsylvania congratulated themselves on the success of their collaboration. It was a great thing to have brought the Six Nations to an armistice with the Catawbas, with whom they had been at war these many years.

Logan sent Weiser's journal to Governor Gooch, and the latter, "highly pleased," despatched a messenger at once to the Cherokees and Catawbas, informing them of the truce and the treaty. He planned, on receiving their answer, to send it to Onondaga by Conrad Weiser again.[1]

But Governor Gooch's chickens were not to be hatched. The Catawbas sent his messenger back to him again with a flat "No." It had happened that, at the very time the messenger was among them announcing peace, a Six Nations war party that had left the north before Weiser reached Onondaga and that consequently knew nothing of the truce, killed four or five Catawbas in their own country. The Catawbas were bent upon revenge.[2]

This put Pennsylvania in a difficulty. If, after the Six Nations had buried the hatchet, they should themselves "feel the Edge of that of others whom they Engaged not to annoy," [3] Brother Onas might be suspected of bad faith. With all speed the Six Nations must be warned. A message was prepared and given to Weiser to forward in haste to Onondaga.[4]

So Weiser set out again with Christopher Stump, this time to let the Onondaga Council know that the Catawbas would not hear of peace until they were revenged, and to warn the Six Nations to be on their guard. It was an unpleasant embassy, and Weiser's record, if he kept one, has not been preserved. All that we know of the journey is found in two small items. The first is in the Minutes of Council for September 27, 1737, in which it is stated that the new message to the Six Nations, drawn up by President Logan, "was by him laid before the Board and being read & approved, is Ordered to be forwarded by Conrad Weiser, now in town." [5] The second is in the Penns'

Account of Indian Expences [6]

1737. Sep. 28 [To Cash] p^d C Weiser for a Message to ye 5 Nations £ 20 " "
     d^o p^d C. Stump going wth C. Weiser to d^o   £ 10 " " [7]

When, early next spring, Logan learned that the Catawbas were in a better frame of mind, preparations were pushed again for the meeting at

Albany. But again there came a sudden turn for the worse. The Catawbas murdered certain emissaries of the Six Nations. That was the end of the peace conference, as James Logan very well knew. He wrote finis to the affair in a letter of September 24, 1738, to Governor Gooch, in which he said, "I am truly Sorry that all that passed in those late transactions between us about your Southern Indians Should by the Villany of Some of them, in committing those Barbarous Murthers on your ffrontiers at length terminate in nothing." [8]

"We are ingaged in a Warr with the Catawbas," said the Six Nations, "which will last to the End of the World." [9]

II

Sometime during the summer of 1738 Weiser made a mysterious journey with his good friend William Parsons to Wyoming. Reference to this journey is so conspicuously excluded from the official records that we are led to think James Logan was engaged in something on behalf of the Proprietors that he did not wish the general citizenry (including his critics in the Assembly) to know about.

To explain this, it is necessary to look back upon the notorious Walking Purchase. Weiser was not directly concerned in that transaction itself, but since he was to be deeply concerned in some of its consequences, it is well to have a clear sight of it before we go on with the main story of Weiser's life.

In 1734 Thomas Penn produced a copy of an old deed (the original having, it seems, been lost) by which some Delaware chiefs had conveyed to William Penn a tract of land near the Delaware River, the bounds of which extended from a certain point "back into the woods, as far as a man can go in a day and a half," and thence to the river again. Such terms of measurement were common enough in the days of Indian occupation, when men shared land as they shared the winds of heaven. The phrasing did not encourage precise measurement (it was not intended to), but the meaning was clear. Penn was to be allowed the use of a strip of land some thirty miles long and a few miles deep. The Delawares had no expectation that the line would ever be paced off. When, however, they found that the white men insisted on taking the Walk literally, they said that an ordinary walk was intended, with time out for meals and no puffing or straining.

The men who signed the deed were easy-going gentlemen of the woods who wanted to do a good turn for a friend, and took no thought for the morrow. The men who, fifty years later, had the line run out, were gentlemen of a different breed. They wore wigs, read Latin, and despised

> . . . the poor Indian whose untutored mind
> Sees God in stones and hears him in the wind.

Besides, they were in the provincial service, and it was their business to take close thought for the morrow and the next day. They set out to make an innocent phrase cover all the lands still claimed by the Delawares in Pennsylvania, and so to settle their most vexing Indian problem.

It was a nasty business, but it was not as wicked as the political enemies of the Proprietors made it out to be. Thomas Penn, James Logan, and James Steel (the Receiver General), who were in charge, did not create the problem which the Walk was intended to solve. Much of the land involved had been fairly bought and paid for. But the Delawares were a scattered people who kept no Fire burning (i.e., had no common council with authority over their people), and the more shiftless among them, as already noticed, took advantage of that fact. They sold land and, when settlers moved in, denied the sale and demanded compensation. A land racket of dangerous proportions had grown up. The Proprietors were resolved to stop all that. So far so good. It was necessary for the orderly development of the province. The regret is that the method they used was simply that of outsmarting the worst sort of Indian at his own game, and by this means they gave the Delawares a legitimate grievance in place of a pretended one.

The less savory elements of the Walking Purchase were kept out of the official records, but enough has leaked out to enable us to see that every step was well calculated in advance, and that the affair moved with precision from the first traveling of the line in 1735 to the expulsion of the Delawares in 1742.

In the spring of 1735, the Proprietors engaged Timothy Smith and John Chapman to clear a way for the Walk.[10] Three persons "who can travel well" were employed to see "how far that day & half Travelling will reach up the Country."[11] This was only a preliminary step, but all pains were taken to stretch the elastic terms of the deed to cover the utmost extent of territory. Horses and riders were hired to carry provisions for the walkers. "Rum Sugar & Lime Juce"[12] were sent to Timothy Smith to help the walkers get well beyond the West Branch (or Lehigh River) so as to bring the lands now occupied by the important cities of Bethlehem and Easton into the purchase. There was some delay, which put the proprietorial government into a considerable sweat, as the letters of James Steel disclose; but before the summer was over the walk had been accomplished, and the information gained by it was turned over to surveyors and draughtsmen who showed Thomas Penn and James Logan how, by the use of a little plane geometry, a walk of a day and a half could be made to take in a stretch of some 150 miles of the best land along the river—indeed, all the lands still claimed by the Delawares in the province.

Before the final Walk was made, there were other preliminaries of a political nature to be attended to. It was evident enough that the Delawares would protest. It was feared that they might appeal to their Uncles, the Six Nations (as Nootamis threatened to do in 1736). First, then, the Six Nations must be prepared. We have already seen how James Logan availed himself of his illness to have the Six Nations, out of the public eye, surrender by the "after-thought" deed of October 25, 1736, any rights they might have had to the Delaware lands. Their authority should never be used to protect their Nephews against the Proprietors. Logan's plan worked even better than he had hoped. The Six Nations chiefs, having no doubt been informed in Philadelphia of the vast territory supposed to be embraced by the terms of the old deed, wrote the letter already quoted requesting the Proprietors not to buy any more land of the Delawares since they had already sold all they had ever possessed.

The next step was to get the Delawares to confirm the earlier deed. This had been attempted in 1734 and again in 1735, without success. The Delawares had hedged. But in August 1737 it was finally accomplished. Thomas Penn, through the interpreter Barefoot Brunston, reminded the Delawares "as well of the Justice of William Penn as of his great Love for all the Indians." [13] Chief Manawkyhickon agreed that Thomas Penn's father was "a good Man," and expressed his own desire to "continue the same Love and Friendship that had subsisted between Wm Penn and all the Indians"; but he said he hesitated about signing a confirmation of the deed, since the Proprietor knew "how the Lines mentioned in the deed . . . are to run" while the Indians did not. [14]

When a very innocent-looking (and it is to be feared misleading) draught was made by old Mr. Andrew Hamilton and shown to the Indians, their doubts were resolved. [15] Manawkyhickon, Lappawinzoe, Nootamis, and Tisheekunk put their marks to the confirmation. That was on August 25, 1737. [16]

Preliminaries thus disposed of, the Proprietors moved fast. On August 27 instructions were issued for the final Walk. James Steel wrote to "Friend Solomon Jennings" [17] (described by the same Quaker correspondent three years before as "a Person of ill fame") to undertake this service with such assistants as should be provided for him. On the same day Steel wrote to Timothy Smith, Sheriff of Bucks, to engage the walker who had "held out the best" when the line was walked before: "and be Shoor," wrote Steel, "to chose the best Ground and Shortest way that can be found." [18] In the end, three men were selected: Solomon Jennings, James Yates, and Edward Marshall. Surveyors were instructed to lay out, from the information obtained in the preliminary scamper of 1735, the best and shortest route to the desired end. Trees were felled and a path cleared.

Young Joseph Knowles (nephew of the sheriff) has left a good account of what happened on the final day and a half:

I Joseph Knowles living with Timothy Smith . . . Do say that I went some time before, to Carry the Chean & help to clear a Road. (as directed by my Uncle Timothy Smith) When the Walk was performed, I was then present, & Carryed Provisions liquors, & Beding. About Sun riseing, we set out from John Chapmans Corner, at Wrightstown & Travelled untill we came to the forks of Delaware (as near as I can remember) was about One of the Clock the same day. The Indians then began to look Sullen & Murmured that the men walked so fast, and Severall times that Afternoon, Called out, and Say'd to them you Run, thats not fair, you was to Walk, The men appointed to Walk, paid no regard to the Indians, But was urged by Timothy Smith & the rest of the Proprietors party to proceed untill the sun was down, we was near the Indian town in the forks. The Indians denyed us going to the Town, on Excuse of a Canteco, We lodged in the Woods that night. Next morning being dull rayny weather, we sett out by the Watches, & Two of the three Indians, that walked the day before, came and Travelled with us about, Two or three Miles, & then left us, being Verry much Dissatisfied, & we proceeded by the Watches untill Noon [19]

Friend Solomon Jennings (who loved his bottle) gave up the first day and Yates the second, but Marshall kept on. When he threw himself down on the ground at noon, he had reached a spur of the Broad Mountain near Mauch Chunk. Sixty-four English miles had grown out of thirty.

And that was not all. By the terms of the old deed, a line was to be run from the point where the Walk ended back to the Delaware River. It might have been expected to take the shortest way, as indeed it would have done if this had been the Forest of Arden. But this was the Forest of Penn and Ink. The line was squared off at a right angle from the Walk and run parallel to the Delaware, which here makes a great bend, following a course that took four days to walk before the river was reached again at the mouth of Lackawaxen Creek. A set-square had completed what Marshall had begun, and finished off one of the greatest land frauds in our history.

James Hughes of Bedminster, who attended the surveyors in running the line to the North Branch of the Delaware, informed John Watson that "as he & the Survey[rs] Returned from runing the Line they called a[t] Tattamins who informed 'em that the Indians since the Walk had poisoned to Death One Lappakoo, An Indian who Against the Minds of the Indians in general, had consented to the Walk; and now see it so unreasonably performed were so incensed against him as to put him to Death." [20]

Edward Marshall lived to an unhappy old age. In 1769 he complained to Richard Smith, who visited him on his island in the Delaware, that the Proprietors had not rewarded him for his services.[21] Be that as it may, the Indians did not neglect him. They killed his wife and his son and wounded his daughter. He himself escaped.

Thomas Penn, on the other hand, was very well pleased with himself. He wrote complacently to inform his brother John in London about the Walk, "which," he said "takes in as much Ground as any Person here ever expected." [22]

"Am pleased," replied John, "you have got the Confirmation of the Delaware Indian's at an Easy rate." [23]

The rate seemed less easy after Braddock's defeat.

III

We can now understand why Weiser and Parsons made the trip to Wyoming, and why Parsons was given money "to purchase sundrys for y[e] Indians." [24] Kakowatchiky, the Shawnee chief, was living in the Wyoming Valley. Some of his people lived at the Forks and on the Minisink lands within the bounds of the Walking Purchase. It was a matter of urgency to Brother Onas, since the French were flirting with the Shawnees, that these restless and tameless Indians should feel no resentment against the province. About the time the confirmation deed was received from the Delawares, James Logan had evinced an interest in the Shawnees, not on the Ohio as heretofore but in the eastern part of the province, and had written to Conrad Weiser about them. "I believe the Proprietor would be pleased," said he, August 6, 1737, "to see thee in town, as soon as it can suit thy conveniency but first endeavour to learn what number of Shawanese there are above, on or near Sasquehannah what towns of them and who are their Chiefs, yet we would not have thee travel for it. Perhaps Allumapis who as Pesqueetamen Sayes is now at Tulpyhockin can inform thee." [25]

Whatever information Weiser got from Sassoonan, he must have informed the Proprietor that the Shawnees were not the sort of people to try to make fools of, and that, if any of them were to be dispossessed by the Walking Purchase, things had better be made right with them at once. It is probable that he visited Kakowatchiky for that purpose, and that his friendship for the old Shawnee chief, which was to last for many years, dates from that visit.

We can also understand why Conrad Weiser, in 1739 and 1740, all but severed himself from provincial affairs and devoted himself to the religious community at Ephrata. He must have been disgusted with the Penns. It took a personal visit from the new Governor, George Thomas, in 1741, after James Logan had retired from the presidency and Thomas Penn had left the country, to draw Conrad out of his retreat and back into the main current of Indian affairs.

But we have rested our case about the Wyoming journey too much upon conjecture. Here are the data:

James Steel to Conrad Weiser [26]

[Philadelphia, May 9, 1738]

My Friend Conrad Weiser

Our Prop^r being desirous of Speaking to thee about an Affair of Considerable importance whould desire thee to come as Soon as possible thou cans't. for that purpose to Philad^a where he will confer with thee Upon ye Occation of thy coming down to this place the Subject whereof will not I hope be disagreeable to thee . . .

Account of Indian Charges [27]

1738

June 6. [To Cash] p^d W Parsons to purchase sundrys
               for y^e Indians on his Journey to Wyoming   15 — —
               x   x   x   x   x

Oct. 6. D^o p^d d^o & C Weiser
               y^e Ball^e of their Account of Expences
               on their Journey to Wyoming . .   15 " 7 " 10½
               p^d Conrad Weiser for going s^d Journey 10 " = " —   25 " 7 " 10½

The fruits of the Wyoming journey are to be found in the terms of a treaty (noted by Richard Peters, August 1, 1739) between the Proprietors of Pennsylvania on behalf of King George of Great Britain, and the Shawnee nation:

That there shall be a firm Peace Amity and Concord held maintained cultivated and improved by and between the subjects of the said King of Great Britain inhabiting America and all the people of the said Shawonese Nation . . . while the Sun Moon and Stars endure.[28]

CHAPTER 12

... *Becomes a Priest After the Order of Melchizedeck*

EPHRATA in its early days was more than a system of beliefs, more even than a way of life: it was escape and fulfillment, a color of thought, a vision, a dream, an ideal. As such it had no existence except in the minds of its devotees, and to them it meant very many different things. To Peter Miller it was Jacob's Ladder, the rungs of which were faith, hope, charity, and the renunciation of self. To Weiser it was a dream of peace, a glimpse of paradise. To Conrad Beissel, on the other hand, despite all his jargon about the Virgin Sophia, it was the fulfillment of his ego, a celestial stage-set with the spotlight always on him. And to the Eckerling brothers— Emanuel (Brother Elimelech in the Kloster), Gabriel (Jotham), Israel (Onesimus), and Samuel (Jephune)—who were masters of political craft as well as of religious self-indulgence, Ephrata was a studio for the practice of their peculiar and complex art. They were spiritual aesthetes, romantics whose souls were stirred by strange, wild, melancholy rites, and by anything ancient and mysterious. At the same time they were ecclesiastical Iagos who loved secrecy and finesse for their own sakes. Under their influence Ephrata was transformed for a time into a secret society given to ghostly conjuring, the manufactory of charms, the unsheathing of the soul from the body, and all the arcana of a self-deceived religious sybaritism. It was also a hotbed of church politics.

They turned what had been a simple retreat of hermits into a strict monastic community, where the eye was held and the imagination stirred by fantastic buildings full of winding stairways, narrow passages, and gloomy cells; and they dreamed of erecting, beside the Cocalico, temples of stone to rival the works of ancient Egypt. They were all for ceremony and the practice of the occult. During their time of ascendancy, striking costumes were made for the Solitary, special forms prepared for their services. Strange music was composed, based on a new musical principle and chorused in an unearthly falsetto.

Beissel succumbed quickly to the new spirit, allowed himself to be called "Father," and let it be known how once on a sacred occasion the blood had gushed from his finger tips.[1] The cult of the miraculous spread like a plague. Prior Onesimus (Israel Eckerling) was rumored to have walked at midnight on the ceiling. The marks of his feet are still shown on the boards in the ceiling of the *Saal*.[2] Rosicrucian mysteries were explored, and experiments made with the *materia prima*, which first destroys flesh and then makes it immortal. Adepts held communion with the seven Archangels, Anaël, Michaël, Raphaël, Gabriël, Uriël, Zobadiël, Anachiël; and tried, through forty days and nights of sleepless watching, to win the seal of the sacred pentagon containing the Ineffable Name.[3] One man went mad in the ordeal and had to be flogged back to his senses. Unhappily the gravestones in the Kloster yard bear witness how difficult is this earthly immortality of attainment.[4]

For a time Weiser resisted the overspreading jungle of hocus pocus, and put himself behind the saner activities of the community. In 1738 he saved the publication of the *Zionitischer Weyrauchs Hügel* (*Zionitic Hill of Incense*) from disaster at the hands of Benjamin Franklin.[5] The *Hill of Incense* was a collection of 650 hymns designed for the use of the Separatists of the province, in the publication of which the community at Ephrata had joined with Christopher Saur of Germantown. Saur was to provide the type and ink; the Brethren were to assist in typesetting and the reading of proofs. When the type was set and the presses were ready, it was found that there was no paper on which to run off the 791 pages of print. Benjamin Franklin controlled the whole stock of printing paper in the province, and he demanded cash. He distrusted queer people. Saur did not have the ready money, and neither did the Solitary. Their funds (a good deal of money had come into their hands through the householders) had all been entrusted to Beissel, and he had given it away to beggars. So Conrad Weiser, whose credit as he said was good everywhere, undertook the journey to Philadelphia in summer to make the deal.

We find in Benjamin Franklin's Account Books the following:

Account with Conrad Weiser [6]

DR

1738
July 9 For 125 Reams paper . . . . £62 – 12 – 6
Sept. 8 For 52 Reams Genoa paper at 12/6 . . . . .   32 – 10 – 0
       For   1 Ream Post paper . . . .   1 – 10 – 0

Weiser "Settled & adjusted" the account with five payments spread over the following months.

In 1738 the Eckerlings were running strong, and it was difficult, even for Weiser, to resist being drawn into the whirlpool. That year they founded the Zionitic Brotherhood, of which Gabriel Eckerling (Brother Jotham) was the first "Perfect Master" or Prior. On the hill named Mount Sinai the three-story building Zion was erected.[7] On the first story was a large room, with adjoining pantries, known as the Refectory. On the second story was a circular chamber known as Ararat. This room was without windows. Its only light came from a lamp on a pedestal in the center, around which the votaries slept on pallets, arranged about the lamp like the spokes of a wheel. Upstairs was a room eighteen feet square, reached only by a trap door. It had four small windows, opening to the east, west, north, and south.[8]

This last room was reserved for the practice of the highest ritual and the great transformation. Here the chosen ones, by retiring during the full moon in May and immuring themselves for forty days and nights of prayer and study, by eating nothing but hard crust and drinking only rain water that had fallen during the month of May, by the letting of blood, by swallowing drops of a mysterious elixir, and toward the end by taking a few grains of the *materia prima* (the secret of which had been lost in the Garden of Eden)—by these preparations, and after losing the hair, teeth, skin, memory, and power of speech (all of which were later to be restored if the experiment was successful) they strove to reach a state of perfect communion with the archangels and to receive from them the limited "immortality" of 5,557 years.[9]

Out of the brain of Emanuel Eckerling (Elimelech) there sprang that same year, 1738, the ingenious concept of the Baptism of the Dead. Persons who had died without the grace of total immersion might yet be saved if they were baptized by proxy. Peter Miller, who never lost his head amid all these insinuating mummeries, was against it; but Beissel, ready as always to follow a religious will-o'-the-wisp, set the seal of his sanction upon it. Emanuel Eckerling was the first to receive baptism in this kind. In a pool of the Cocalico, under Beissel's hands, he was immersed on behalf of his departed mother.[10]

The principle once accepted, the thing became popular, and the next world must soon have been swarming with souls astonished to find themselves sainted by Cocalico immersion *in absentia*.

It was during this year also that another bold step was taken in the religious progress of the community: the apotheosis of Conrad Beissel. This came from the brain of Israel Eckerling (Onesimus). When it was announced, however, at a love-feast that Beissel had accepted the title "Father," [11] there was murmuring. At the best, it smacked of worldly priestcraft; at the worst, it was blasphemy: there is but one Father.

The serpent had been admitted to the garden. The Ephrata Confusion had begun. For the moment, a compromise was accepted. The householders (including Conrad Weiser) were permitted to call Father Friedsam (Conrad Beissel) merely "Brother." When that compromise broke down, Weiser spoke out; but what he said must be left to another chapter.

About this time, under pressure as usual from the Eckerlings, the tonsure was introduced.[12] Some special pledge, it was said, was needed to distinguish the Solitary from the Households. The matter was disputed hotly for three hours; but in the end the Prior knelt down and made a vow of perpetual chastity, after which, as the *Chronicon* tells us, Beissel cut a large bald spot on his head. Later all the Brethren knelt and were shorn in Zion, while the Spiritual Virgins had their crowns shorn in the Saal.

By this act the Solitary, both male and female, brought upon themselves the nickname of "croppies," applied by the unregenerate Scotch-Irish of the neighboring settlement of Donegal. These good Presbyterians scented Catholicism in the Cocalico wind, and the Prior did nothing to allay their fears when he had the Sisters make him a high priest's robe, and when he instituted night watches and torch-light processions. To the unbaptized, the valley of the Cocalico, whence came at midnight strange lights and strange sounds, was undoubtedly the Place of Serpents. Word flew around that it was a nest of Jesuit vipers.

Meanwhile in all this stir of mystical aestheticism Conrad Weiser held on to himself as well as he could. He had little in common with the Eckerlings beyond a growing dislike for Conrad Beissel. During the early days of Eckerling supremacy, he jogged along attending to the practical necessities of the community. Archangels, the *materia prima*, and the tonsure were out of his element. It was enough for him to grow a long beard. When we meet him in the records, it is, for the most part, in connection with matters of business. On August 9, 1739, he bought a sixteen-shilling dictionary from Benjamin Franklin for Peter Miller [13] (Brother Jabez). On August 13 of the same year he signed as one of the witnesses to a deed of conveyance made by Jan Meyle and Barbara his wife for 180 acres, covering the whole Ephrata settlement. Title was made over to Samuel Eckerling, Israel Eckerling, Emanuel Eckerling, and Jacob Gasz. What Eckerling craft there was in this transaction we need not stop here to consider; but Julius Sachse asks us to notice that "all parties to the conveyance, either as principals or as witnesses, were antagonistic to the Vorsteher." Beissel apparently knew nothing about this piece of business. Later, says Sachse, when it was found that Meyle and his wife Barbara had not owned the land after all, Israel Eckerling appealed to John Penn and got title from him.[14] There is record of quitrents paid to the Penns by "John Miley for y[e] Brethren of Euphrata," March 25, 1746/7.[15] But that was after Weiser's Cocalico race was run.

The community developed rapidly on a strict monastic pattern. In March 1739, Simeon Jacobs and his wife entered and at once separated, he going to Zion and she to Kedar.[16] In April, on the other hand, Ludwig Benter, having taken a wife with intent to "multiply in the flesh," was ejected from his cabin and sent out of the settlement.[17]

New buildings were going up. An elaborate Prayer House was built, with a huge hall to accommodate the congregation of both sexes, Householders as well as Solitary. At one end was a chancel, in front of which was a special place for the Father. The building was dedicated July 16, 1740, with, as tradition tells us, a flourish of mystic midnight rites—prayers, incantations, processions—stemming from the days of the Pharaohs.[18]

In the matter of the Prayer House, Beissel set his light, which had recently been hidden under the Eckerling bushel, on a hill. Shortly after the dedication, he condemned the new building and ordered the construction of another. "In this way," observes the *Chronicon* with an undertone that is not above the suspicion of raillery, "God kept the household in the Settlement in continual straits, in which all human reason was turned into folly." [19] Some house-fathers, offended by Beissel's arbitrary change of front, left the community. "Thus God ever purged the fold," adds the *Chronicon* demurely, "of such persons as loved their own life better than the leading of God." [20]

About this time James Logan wrote to Weiser asking him to come to

Philadelphia with some Indians who were expected in town. Weiser's reply may be guessed from Logan's letter of July 25, written after consultation with Thomas Penn: "I am Sorry it will not (tho' I hope it will) Suit thy affairs to accompany these people, for it would not only be a great ease to them and a Satisfaction to the Proprietor but in all respects convenient." [21] When the affairs of Zion were settled, Weiser did consent to come to town, where he served as interpreter in a conference with Shickellamy and Sassoonan commencing August 1.[22]

August was a busy month for Conrad, and one that tore his heart with strong and conflicting emotions. On August 11 Ann Eve gave birth to a boy whom, though he had been born in sinful wedlock, Conrad presumed to name Jabez after his Solitary friend Peter Miller at Ephrata. The child lived only seventeen days.[23] We do not know whether it was by mere coincidence, or whether it was in consequence of some burst of repentance at the birth of another child against his principles, but it is a fact that the same month that saw the birth and death of little Jabez saw also the culmination of Weiser's Ephrata career: his elevation to the priesthood.

Father Friedsam Gottrecht "in the presence of the whole congregation," as Sachse describes the scene, "solemnly consecrated Brother Onesimus (Israel Eckerling), Jabez (Peter Miller) and Enoch (Conrad Weiser) to the priesthood, by the laying on of hands; after which they were admitted to the ancient Order of Melchizedeck by having the degree conferred on them in ancient form." [24]

The Lord said unto my Lord, Sit thou at my right hand, until I make thine enemies thy footstool.

The Lord shall send the rod of thy strength out of Zion: rule thou in the midst of thine enemies. . . .

The Lord hath sworn, and will not repent, Thou art a priest for ever after the order of Melchizedek.

—PSALM CX

It was on this same occasion that Father Friedsam deposed Prior Jotham and elevated Israel Eckerling (Onesimus) to his place.

When Onesimus became Perfect Master, his pride knew no bounds. He made his enemies his footstool and his friends his enemies, till the burden of his discipline fell like a lash on all the Brotherhood. "Thus the Prior brought the Brotherhood into such thralldom," says the *Chronicon*, "that the only difference between a Brother of Zion and a negro was that the latter was a black and involuntary slave, while the former was a white and voluntary one." [25]

But there can be no doubt that Conrad Weiser, a stickler for independence, drew as much inspiration as did Israel Eckerling from Psalm CX.

The Lord shall send the rod of thy strength out of Zion.

It was not long before the rod of Weiser's strength went forth. The Perfect Master and the Father himself were to feel his stroke.

CHAPTER 13

. . . Leaves the Kloster

IN 1740 Conrad Weiser surrendered himself so completely to the spell of the new Ephrata that when in the same year the Hermit Order (that "angelic way of life" which Beissel had so highly commended in the past) was finally dissolved ("No hermit," said Beissel in a new revelation, "enters the kingdom of God"[1]), and conventual life was riveted in its place, Weiser left his wife and entered the Kloster. The name of Brother Enoch is listed in the *Chronicon* among the names of the Brethren "who at that time dwelt in Zion." [2]

But his days among the Seventh Day saints were numbered. The act of entering the Kloster was a surrender so complete, so convulsive, that it sated his emotional need; and the very violence of this spiritual orgasm provoked a correspondingly violent revulsion. The prevailing unreason about him, which he had before managed to endure, now put him in a paroxysm of wrath. All that was strongest in his nature rose in rebellion against the scandals, hypocrisy, and muddle-headedness that were fouling the clear springs of religion at Ephrata. Heaven was not to be found in the symbolism of doves and roses, nor in such rites as the Baptism of the Dead. Michael Welfare might preach his five-hour sermon and Conrad Beissel sing his forty-three-stanza hymn (as each of them did), but this was not the way to God's peace. No clouds of theosophical jargon could any longer hide from him the fact that Ephrata had dropped the substance of religion for its shadow. He had had enough of this Separatist Babel.

The dispute over Beissel's title ended, after a long debate, in an all but unanimous vote confirming him "Father."

"They attach to their Superintendent, whom they now call Father Friedsam," wrote the Moravian, Spangenberg, July 20, 1739, "the honor of being an intermediary between God and Man, so much so that one of them [was it Spangenberg's friend, Conrad Weiser?] declares no prayer can come before God that does not pass through the bishop's hand . . ." [3]

Even after the ending of this *casus belli* in the submission of the congregation ("Now everyone was diligent in a blind obedience" [4]), there was no peace. Israel Eckerling (Prior Onesimus), though he wrote books in praise of Beissel and addressed him as "Holy Father," [5] was plainly working with his three brothers in the flesh to bring him down. Even Sister Maria, the Prioress, had her knife in; "she sought," as the *Chronicon* says, "to further her own profit by stirring up differences between the Superintendent and the Prior." [6] On the other hand, "It was remarked that those Brethren fared best who kept on good terms with the Superintendent and maintained a constant strife with the Prior." [7]

Beissel was a born dictator. I quote the *Chronicon* again:

In the bestowal and withdrawal of his confidence he was immoderate. . . . In his intercourse he was not natural, and they who were nigh to him had to adapt themselves accordingly; wherefore no one could lay hold on him with his personality. Divine worship he appointed for the most inconvenient time, at midnight, and took special delight in the spirit if he could carry it on until daylight. If anyone offered him refreshment, he often said, "It gives me none," for his emaciated body was nourished by the Word that proceeded out of the mouth of God.[8]

His chief solace was in the Sisters' convent, a retreat which he entered at will and in which he heard soft voices calling to him out of every corner. "The young birds," he said, "have the same simplicity when their provider comes to feed them." [9]

Saur called Beissel a pope. The public thought him a wizard. A constable who saw him enter a certain house and followed to arrest him was willing to swear afterwards that he had the power to disappear when he pleased.[10] Weiser, who knew him better, thought his powers were of another sort: he had the power to appear where he should not be. The Sisters might chirp like birds in his presence, but behind his back they fought over him like wolves, and one of them invoked the law.[11]

At the moment when Weiser was waking from his dream to discover, like Titania, that he had been enamored of an ass, the government of Pennsylvania was devising means to bring their indispensable interpreter back into the provincial service. On May 12, 1741, the Delawares had written to Governor Thomas threatening to appeal the Walking Purchase to the Six Nations.[12] Indian affairs had reached another crisis. At all cost the Province Interpreter must be brought back into the world. How this was accomplished may best be told in the language of the *Chronicon*, where Peter Miller's flexible pen contrives good-naturedly to keep the Settlement's point of view without losing sight of Conrad Weiser's.

There are some things in the Superintendent's course which are specially remarkable and scarcely can be understood. Such is this, that people who at first exalted him to the heavens, afterwards became his worst opponents. In the preceding chapter we described the earnest conversion of a Brother, C. W. But as he did not keep watch over himself, there grew from the root of enmity to God within him, which had not been killed, an antagonism against the Superintendent, which was the cause of his renouncing the testimony of God again, and allowing himself to be taken up by the world. Since, however, God finally vindicated his glory in him, and through many circuitous by-ways brought him back to his first love and the wife of his youth, we do not hesitate to incorporate in this history so much as belongs here of the mistakes and circumstances of this remarkable man. As he possessed great natural talents in matters pertaining to the government of the land, and, besides, was Indian interpreter, having been adopted into their tribes, so that the country could neither wage war nor make peace with the Indians without him, everybody was sorry that so useful a man should have allowed himself to be fooled so. Wherefore Governor Th. who then was ruler, and who well understood the art of dissimulation, took measures to bring him over to his side again, to cope with which the good Brother was by no means competent. The former took hold of the matter very shrewdly, spoke in praise of the organization at Ephrata, and that he was not disinclined to come into closer relations with such a people. This he could well say, for he went to the trouble to visit the Settlement with a following of twenty horses and accompanied by many people of quality from Virginia and Maryland. He was worthily received by the Brethren, though the Superintendent and the Mother Superior of the Sisters held themselves aloof. He declared himself well pleased with the institution. But when he saw that the familites also had an own household in the Settlement, he wanted to know what the object of this was; and on being told that they too had entered the celibate state, he regarded it as something curious. Having made a favorable impression on the Brother (C. W.), he now tendered him the office of a justice of the peace, which the Brother would no doubt have gladly accepted if it were not against the principles of his people; he did so, however, only on condition that the congregation would permit it. Thereupon at his request a council was held to decide the question whether a Brother of this confession might be allowed to hold a governmental office. The fathers were of opinion that this could not be done. But the Superintendent thought differently, and asked them whether they had a right to restrict a Brother's conscience. And when he (C. W.) was asked about it, he declared that his conscience did not forbid him to accept; upon which full liberty was granted him. The Governor also gave him the privilege to withdraw from court whenever such matters should happen to come up as were against his conscience.

For a time favorable winds blew for him after this, and he could soon be seen as chief justice of court seated beneath the crown wearing his accustomed beard. At length, however, his office came to occupy him so much that he became estranged from his Brethren. He first and most severely took offense at his tried friend the Superintendent himself, of which the latter was himself the cause, for he loved the good Brother more than he could bear. He was indeed more than once repaid for his love in such coin, so that he used to say, that he trusted no one until he had been aggrieved by him. The occasion for his being offended C. W. took from a remark of the Superintendent, who told him that once, when he stood in the breach for a deceased Brother, the blood was forced from his finger nails; from which he inferred that the Superintendent must think himself to be Christ. Moreover, because the Superintendent on account of his office had to be in the Sisters' Convent a great deal, he forbade him this under penalty of severe punishment; because he took for granted that things were not as they should be. At length he was given an opportunity to carry out his purpose. It was thus: One of the first spiritual virgins [Anna Eicher] took the liberty to propose marriage to the Superintendent. And when he told her that if he were to do that he would have to deny God, she insisted on it no more; but still she thought he should allow her to assume his name. And when he declined this also, and when furthermore her younger sister after the flesh was preferred before her and appointed Mother Superior of the Sisters' Convent, her love changed to hatred, and she sought the Superintendent's life at the risk of her own. For she testified to the afore-mentioned C. W. that she and the Superintendent had made away with a bastard child. This he at once reported to the Governor. Just at the time when this was made known in the Settlement the Superintendent was in a sad condition, as the powers of darkness, whose lords rule the air, lay heavily upon him, in addition to which sickness came from without. For, though he lived an innocent life before God and men, yet this did not protect him against the tempter, in whose domain his natural body had grown up. Meanwhile two

Solitary Brethren [Peter Miller and Israel Eckerling] were sent to him (C. W.), who implored him for God's sake not to imbrue himself in innocent blood; to whom he also promised, if it were possible, to withdraw the matter. But the Governor wrote to him that he should give the witness another hearing, and then bring the case before the court at Lancaster. Thereupon he had another hearing of the witness in presence of a housefather, when she again confessed the whole thing; though soon after, when she heard that her own life was endangered, she took it all back, and confessed that her temptations had brought her to make the charge. And since she no longer had any guardian, she married. But just after she was wedded, and was about to retire to the bridal bed of old Adam, she was suddenly called into eternity; which we consider to have been a divine favor rather than a judgment.

As this attempt failed, he (C. W.) again sought out those who had been his acquaintances before his conversion, who rejoiced over him exceedingly, and in all things put him at the head; although there was little cause for rejoicing over one whose conversion had been such a failure. He may have formed many plans at that time to bring to naught the judgment of God against fallen man. Once he tried to prove in writing that Adam had been created for nothing higher than the natural life; that God had offered him a higher destiny under certain conditions, which was to be attained if these latter were fulfilled, but if not, then he would remain as he had been created. This effort, however, never saw the light of day, as no one gave any countenance to it.

Another incident concerning him must be mentioned. When he saw how heavily burdened the household of the congregation was, it did not seem right to him, and therefore he wrote the following letter to the organization:— "C. W., your former Brother, has the following to say to you in this writing, on behalf of the poor, sighing souls, of whom there are not a few among you, who are groaning day and night unto God because of the heavy Pharaohic and Egyptian bond-service with which the congregation is so heavily laden and burdened that it scarcely can endure it any longer. Besides which, this bond-service is much worse than the Egyptian; for the latter was for the payment of debts, but with that under which the congregation is in bondage no debts can be paid. Yea, what am I saying? Pay? The more one lets oneself come under this service, the more one sinks in debt. But they who withdraw from it, because they see that no debts can be paid with this bond-service, and that one cannot fulfill it so long as one lives, are refused fellowship as though they were evil-doers, and are even expelled from the congregation, etc." Moreover he advised that a reformation be commenced in the church which was very necessary, and said that if he were given word of it, he would come and help reform the church. The Superintendent made this letter known, but it was not taken into consideration, for every one knew that it had been written during temptation and with no good purpose.

After this all remembrance of him ceased in the Settlement, though various offices in the worldly life were heaped upon him. Meanwhile, however, God, in view of his earlier faithfulness in the work of God, bore him in mind, and opened the door of his long spiritual captivity, so that he visited first of all his old friend P. M. at the Settlement. And when he noticed that no one passed severe judgment upon him, he also hunted up the Superintendent, who soon became aware that the good once done for him had not been in vain, and received him with open arms of love, taking him into the Sisters' house, where his old acquaintances rejoiced with him that he had found again his piece of silver that had been lost. Soon after the congregation assembled for a love-feast, at which he by partaking of the holy sacraments, was reincorporated in the spiritual communion; although we willingly yield to his mother-church the honor of having garnered in his body.[13]

This last, a true *Chronicon* touch, was a slap at the Lutheran Church, with which Weiser, after some hesitation, had at length been reincorporated.

As we bring the narrative of this strangest of all Conrad's strange adventures to an end, it is well to take stock and see what Ephrata amounted to in the sum total of Weiser's life.

To begin with, we must admit that Conrad Weiser contributed little of permanance to the Kloster. Its development was not in the direction he had hoped for, and he was not strong enough to change it.

"Conrad Weiser has been in Zion," runs a curious memorandum preserved among Count Zinzendorf's papers at Herrnhut, "but has labored in vain. He says, he had to work on Stone without hands, except for the hand that came out of the wall." [14]

On the other hand, the Kloster contributed much to Conrad Weiser. The hope that had taken him into it, the dream of a simple faith wider than any sectarian bounds, remained with him long after his withdrawal and largely determined the somewhat tortuous course of his later church journey.

"These are my People," he wrote of the Ephrata Brotherhood as late as 1745.[15]

But this was not the only permanent influence the Kloster left on him. The six struggling years of what we might call imperfect celibacy left a deep mark on his character. I think it was this strange interlude in his career that finally cleared his mind of cant and vague idealism. He came to see the world for what it is: Adam created in God's image but clothed in a garment of clay. God made man flesh, and only a fool would try to approach Reality by denying the condition of his own existence. Conrad gave up trying to be a Böhmist, absorbed in God—trying to be God in fact. Henceforth he was content only to serve Him.

That was the turning point of his inner life. He had gone into the Kloster a fanatical idealist, threshing himself to pieces in ineffectual rebellion against a world that is full of paradox and compromise because men are not disembodied spirits. He had gone into it to seek peace in escape from such a world. He came out of it determined to seek peace in the only place it is worth looking for: in devotion to the world's work God had given him talents to perform. He would work in the vineyard. Ephrata, and Ann Eve, had taught him to accept the universe, and that was the prerequisite condition for the constructive work our world in America was waiting for him to do.

CHAPTER 14

. . . Enters Politics

DURING the autumn of 1741 Conrad Weiser took his first fly at provincial politics.

A French war was threatening. Pennsylvania's frontier was exposed. The Governor and Council were therefore perturbed at the pacifism of the Quaker Assembly. The Quakers constituted about one-third of the population, but they held two-thirds of the seats in the House. They even controlled the votes of the German population on the borders.

At this time the democratic movement in Pennsylvania, unlike that in Switzerland, had joined hands with pacifism, and there were forebodings that the offspring of this strange marriage might destroy both parents. With France entrenched in a line of forts beyond the Alleghenies, confining the English colonies to the seaboard and even threatening to dislodge them from that toe-hold, it was feared that a continuance of the Quaker hold on the legislative branch of the government might destroy the conditions under which democracy could survive. Under Quaker domination the province was incapable of resisting totalitarian France. Both self-interest and patriotism, therefore, impelled the proprietorial party to seek all aid in meeting this threat from within. Weiser's services were enlisted in an effort to relax the Quaker grip on the Assembly.

Of the constitutional problems involved in the democratic system already far advanced in Pennsylvania, Weiser had little understanding. But liberty he prized, and meant to keep it, if he could, both for himself and for his neighbors. He knew better than most men that freedom and justice are not things that come down the chimney at Christmas. They must be earned, even at the risk of one's life. Being, therefore, all for what we today call preparedness, he supported the Proprietors in their effort to stiffen the Assembly.

September 12, 1741, Thomas Cookson wrote to Weiser from Lancaster about the coming election. It seems that the death of Thomas Ewing had left a vacancy which James Blunston was campaigning to fill. Cookson asked Weiser to use his influence with his friends and acquaintances to help defeat Blunston and the "precious schemes" of him and his party, who were widening the breach between the executive and the legislative branches, and so paralyzing the government.

"Their main Argument with yᵉ Dutch," wrote Cookson about the Quaker party "are that if the Governors Party as they Call 'em prevail, They will be Assessed at a High Rate & obliged to Labour at erecting Forts &c & then putting them in mind of the Tyrrany of their Princes in Germanny Raise very Dreadful Ideas in yᵉ people." Descending to particulars, "wee think," he said, "James Smith woud make a good Comʳ" [1]

A call coming from James Logan about the same election business, Conrad Weiser went to town to consult with him. Between them they "cook'd up a L^{re}," as Richard Peters said,[2] the fruits of which came out of Tul-pehocken a few days later, where Weiser had done the actual writing. Conrad made a translation of this German manifesto, and sent a copy of it to Logan under the title, *A Serious and Seasonable Advice to our Country-men ye Germans in Pensilvania*. Logan proposed a few small changes, and on September 20 the printed circular was issued to the public under Con-rad Weiser's signature.

To whom credit should go for the "House divided in itself" passage, we cannot say for certain; but Weiser knew his Bible quite as well as Logan did, and the idiom in which the passage is couched is unmistakably Weiser's.

A Serious and Seasonable Advice
to our Countreymen ye Germans in Pensilvania [3]

Worthy Countreymen—

It is with great Concern I now Speak to you on the Occasian of the Ensuing Election of Assemblymen, the Importance of which is so great that it must Concern Every Inhabitant of this Province that possesses anything of temporal Goods, if it was no more but One's Own life if One Loves it. The thing itself is that Above a Year since a Difference happened about the Question. Whether it Was right to pay Tribute to Caesar or no? We the Germans in Particular have hitherto answered with No (to Judge according to Our Deeds) in Chusing such Assembly Men Once & Again who have been so far from Com-plying with our Gracious Sovereign about a Contribution towards his Wars, that they have Quarrelled with the Governour & not only not given one farthing to the War, but to the Govern^r not Even his usual Salary that has for above these twenty Years been allowed to the Governour for the time being.

Permit me to put you in mind that as We for the most part retired into this Countrey for Peace & Safetys Sake & to get Our living Easier then in Germany We not Only have obtained our Ends in all this, but We have also been well received and protected by the Govern^r of this Province Especially by the Present Govern^r; and it is not long since his majesty of great Brittain by an Act of his Parlement invested us protestants upon Very Easy terms with so many Priviledges & Libertys whatsoever that a Native born Englishman can Enjoy. Consider Whether all this should not move us to an Actual thankful-ness, & to answer the Abovementioned Question with *Yea*. When (without making reflection upon the favours we reesived) the Laws of God & men require it, & accordingly to Chuse such AssemblyMen which will no longer Oppose such reasonable Request, as the Present time requires it, for it is to be feared that if We, as Newly Come to this Country, & have received so many favours, do oppose the Governour any longer into his face under a pretence of Liberty it might not turn to our best, & may draw a particular displeasure upon us, as many of the Wisest of the Quakers themselves are afraid & show their dislike of the behaviour of the Assembly for this two Years past in their Opposition to ye Governour which whether or no it did not arise from a private Pique I Let the time itself & the Wiser Judge.

It is at this present time too more necessary to Elect another Assembly which may use their Endeavour to put a stop to the Differences betwixt the Governour & the Country and to think upon means which may restore peace & Unity to prevail amongst us since We are Every Day in Expectation of a

French War. The French Nation is many thousands strong in America, & possessed of Canada a large & Well fortified Countrey to the Northw^d of us & to the West of us they are Possessed of the Great River Messisippi which Extends in its several Parts far & wide   One Part of Ohio or Allegheny where Our traders go to deal with our Indians is within the bounds of Pensilvania, insomuch that between that & the West branch of Sasquehannah is but a short Land Carriage and all the Indians near the Waters of the Aforesaid great River are in league with the French, and it is an Easy matter for the French with the help of those Indians to Come this Road & lay this Province Waste in a few Days easier than any other neighbouring Province, & how Cruelly those Barbarians treat those whom they take for their Enemies is not to be Expressed in a few Words. I wish heartily We may never have the Experience of it. But on those Considerations if no other We ought all to be united as One People for *as We are told in the Gospel* a House divided in itself Cannot Stand. But in ord^r to divide us, many of you have been told it seems, that if you took not Care to Chuse Quakers you would be brought into the same Slavery you Came hither to avoid. It Grieves me to think that any should give themselves the Liberty to invent & propagate Such falsehoods. The Quakers are a Sober Industrious People & so far as they have been Concerned in Government We have shared in their Protection, but We see there are amongst them who shew they have the same Passions & give Way to them as much to the full as other Men, & We Want such as Will make up our Breaches and not Widen them, but as to the Slavery that has been mentioned you may be assured that whomsoever you shall Chuse by much the Greater part will be Englishmen, there is no Nation in the World more Jealous & Carefull of their Liberties than the English & therefore You may fully trust them. That You may be directed by Wisdom in your Choice & that Peace on Earth & GoodWill amongst Men may prevail is the hearty Prayer of

Your Friend
Conrad Weiser

Tulpehockin in Lancaster Co^{ty}
    the 20th Septr 1741
    [Endorsed] Conrad Weiser's Advice on ye Election 1741
                    in English translated by himself

This literary venture of Weiser's in the field of politics, like his other ventures in the same field, was a failure. Christopher Saur published a last-minute rebuttal, which was put into the hands of the German voters as they came to the polls. Weiser, translating Saur's circular for Logan's information, gathered such fury as he wrote that English words and English idiom failed him:

Translation of Dutch printed Paper
oct 1741 [4]

Worthy friends & Countrey people
  I of late Saw a writing where under Conrad Weisers name Stood, wherein he pretends to give you a Honest and well meaned direction how you ought to go on about the Ensuing Election but what I can See his intend is rather to Cheat and deceive you. therefore I thought it necessary to discover his Mistakes to you and to forwarn you that you may not be deceived of him to your own yea to the ruin of this happy Countrey

. . . Conrad Weiser is our Countreyman and of late is made a Justice of the peace and therefore he ought to have ben Carefull in this his first Exercise and ought to have Said nothing but what is the truth . . .

Out of this my dear Countrey people it is plain that Conrad Weiser is Cheated him Self (or which is more to be feared) that whereas he is latly made a Justice of the peace to please the Governor to keep him in Comission . . .

. . . as for the article of the danger of a War with france it is an unnecessary fear, the best and last Information Says that the princes of the Empire are inclined for peace and if it was not So, then Conrad Weiser Speaks not as one that trusts in Providens, by which we have ben protected hitherto and wy Should we be afaired now more then that he will frighen us with the french which are but a Handfull to us, and live a great way from us and have a very troublesome road to us, and must pass through Such warelike nations of Indians which are in Peace with us, and of whom they have ben afraid always in time of War.

Take therefore Care loving Countrey people that you may not be deceived & misleadit, one Single mistake in your Election is perhaps no more to be reformed, we See that the Governor is very Carefull in the lest thing in the government. If he don't like the Justices then he removes them—. . . I conclude with a hearty wish that you may be endued with understanding to See that Snare that is layd for you . . .

philadelphia the 29 of Septr 1741

Saur's roorback succeeded. The Quakers swept the field. The old Assembly was returned.

"I never knew," moaned Richard Peters in a letter to John Penn, October 20, 1741, "any good come to the honest & right side of a Question in this Province by Publick Papers." [5]

CHAPTER 15

. . . Welcomes the Moravians

IT IS A temptation to look on Weiser's dilemma, when he tried to play the part of Enoch and live in two worlds, as merely an amusing contradiction. But to do that is to overlook the fact that Weiser at Ephrata had set himself a lifelong and entirely sensible task: to reach a goal, a course to which has been charted not only by Böhme but also by Spinoza, Wordsworth, Matthew Arnold, and many others; a goal which, indeed, we still seek to attain today, and must continue to seek if we are not content to see our world collapse into rubble. Weiser was trying to achieve a harmony between the instinctive animal and the instinctive spiritual impulses of human nature, a harmony in which he should feel his oneness with the universal power that lay without as well as within himself—a power which Wordsworth called Nature and which we call God:

> *A motion and a spirit, that impels*
> *All thinking things, all objects of all thought,*
> *And rolls through all things.*

In his search Weiser had not found help among the quarreling sects at Tulpehocken. He had not found help in the midst of Beissel's fantasies at Ephrata. For a time, however, he did find help among the Moravians; and it is with this Moravian interlude in his career that this chapter concerns itself.

The Moravians were the least fanatical of all the German enthusiasts in the province. They had found peace within themselves, and they preached peace and union to the Christian sects without, through recognition of a common faith in the living Christ. Their leaders were educated men: well-informed, trained to think, and therefore not easily distracted by the excitement around them. Yet their learning had not left them a prey to dogmatic theology nor to a hesitating and arid intellectualism. Philosophy was their servant, not their master.

"My brother, my brother," said Peter Boehler to John Wesley, "that philosophy of yours must be purged away." [1]

The old Moravian Church (the *Unitas Fratrum* or United Brethren), which stems from John Huss and the teachings of John Wycliffe, had broken away from the Papacy as early as 1467, and by the beginning of the seventeenth century had become the most important Protestant group in Bohemia and Moravia. It was almost wiped out by the Thirty Years' War. But a small remnant—the "Hidden Seed"—continued for a hundred years to worship in secret in Moravia until, fresh persecution driving them out, they found refuge on the estate of the Lutheran pietist, Count Zinzendorf, at Herrnhut, Saxony. Here they recovered their strength under the Count's leadership. When persecution broke out against them in Saxony, a band of these "Herrnhuters" emigrated to America.

Their lives were simple and pure. Their objectives were the highest: peace on earth, goodwill toward men. But years of persecution had left a mark on them. In meeting intolerance, they had developed a quiet, stubborn bravery, and at the same time had accustomed themselves to say less than was in their minds. We cannot blame them if, under persecution, some of them had developed a habit of evasive speech, of verbal compliance, of doing good by stealth. Yet it was unfortunate, for it gave them a reputation for obliquity.

James Logan, disappointed at not receiving from Brother Pyrlaeus certain notes on the Six Nations language as promised, wrote to Weiser, "I am no Stranger to the uncertainty of that Sort of Gentry . . ." [2]

John Wesley, though his own spiritual life owed much to their influence, speaks repeatedly in his *Journal* of their "guile."

This reputation for indirectness preceded them to America and helped to defeat their campaign there for Christian unity. From the start they found themselves hated and feared like the Jesuits; and though, like the Jesuits, in the end they confounded their detractors by the single-hearted devotion of their missionary work among the Indians, for the first few years after their establishment in Pennsylvania they intensified the sectarian spirit they had come to destroy. When they poured oil on the Tulpehocken Confusion, the flames leaped higher.

Weiser's prime friend among the Moravians was Augustus Gottlieb Spangenberg ("Joseph" among the Brethren), whom he met in 1736. Spangenberg brought to America, when he first came in 1735, an A.M. from the University of Jena [3] and the experience of some six years of public lecturing and pastoral work among the students there. For a short time also he had been a professor at Halle. Then, his connection with the Herrnhuters, whose principles he espoused, having caused him to be expelled from that university, he went to the fountain head at Herrnhut and became Count Zinzendorf's most intimate friend. Thence he came to Georgia, where he established a Moravian colony. In 1736 he came up to Pennsylvania, where there were sympathizers though as yet no organized colony. He worked on the farm of Christopher Wiegner at Skippack, and when occasion offered preached among the German Lutherans and Reformed; for, though he had been "ordained a presbyter of the Moravian Church," [4] he recognized no denominational barriers sufficient to separate true Christians of one church from those of another.

A hymn he composed at Lancaster in 1745, expresses the principle on which he and his fellow Moravians worked among the different sects— drawing upon themselves, in consequence, the hostility of all the stiff-necked denominationalists in the province:

> The Church of Christ, which He hath hallowed here
> To be His house, is scattered far and near,
> In North, and South, and East, and West abroad;
> And yet in earth and heaven, through Christ, her Lord,
>   The Church is one.[5]

Spangenberg, who had something strong and massive about him, exerted at this time a healthy influence on Conrad Weiser. The man had gone to the very heart of religion, and stayed there. His mysticism led him into no hysteria, his philosophy into no labyrinths of theosophical speculation. He was, moreover, a man of affairs, a good organizer and leader. It was natural that Weiser should be drawn to him, and there ensued a friendship strong enough to survive a deal of disagreement.

It was through Spangenberg that Weiser made his first contribution to Moravian missions. In the Onondaga Journal of 1737, Weiser's description of the hopelessness then settling over the Indians, as they found themselves unable to resist the rot of the white man's vices, had touched Spangenberg. ". . . rum will kill us," the Indians at Otseninky had said, "and leave the land clear for the Europeans without strife and purchase."

Spangenberg wrote to Christian David at Herrnhut,[6] communicating Weiser's account of the story current among the Indians of God's message to an Indian seer: "I have driven the wild animals out of the country, for they are mine. If you will do good and cease from your sins I will bring them back; if not, I will destroy you from the face of the earth."

In Herrnhut, Spangenberg's letter moved the Brethren to organize an Indian mission. Christian Henry Rauch was sent out to look over the field. When he came to America, he received little encouragement from the white people, but he persisted, establishing himself at Shecomeco east of the Hudson River on the borders of New England; and thus began the saga of the Moravian missions among the Indians.

Rauch met every kind of obstruction. The Indians laughed at him, turned him from their cabins, even threatened his life; but he persevered with good words and good works until first the drunkard "Tschoop" (Job) and then other Indians became conscious of a new power working within them that brought hope back into their lives.

When Count Zinzendorf arrived in Pennsylvania in December 1741, he found his people already there in considerable force. Some had come up from the unsuccessful colony in Georgia, others had come directly from Europe. Pyrlaeus, Büttner, and Zander, newly arrived, were preparing for work among the Indians.

The headquarters of the Moravian colony at this time was a small log house on the Lehigh River, at the Forks of the Delaware. Count Zinzendorf, arriving here on Christmas Eve (New Style), and the company retiring to the adjoining stable, which was separated by a mere partition from the living room, to sing,

> *Not Jerusalem,—*
> *No, from Bethlehem*
> *We receive life and salvation . . . ,*[7]

the new settlement received the name of Bethlehem. Today on the Lehigh Hills the Star of Bethlehem still burns high at Christmas time to remind the great steel city of its origin.

Zinzendorf, who was always mapping large plans in his mind, dreamed for a time of establishing a corporate Christian state in America: "We must get a Proprietoryship in America *immediately from the Crown* . . . governed in the English manner, *but not in Warlike Manner, no Forts & no Harbours*," and not devoted to commerce lest it incur the jealousy of neighboring governments.[8] Not unnaturally the government at Philadelphia watched him with some anxiety. He had been exiled in 1736 from Saxony, and his church enemies were busy talking against him. He was known to be a good man, but said to be a dangerous one. Richard Peters sent a cautious report on him to the Proprietors, Dec. 4, 1741:

Count Zinzendorf arriv'd here yᵉ beginning of this Week & will probably cause large Quantitys of Land to be taken up by yᵉ Moravians in this Prov: He does not Propose to stay longer yⁿ yᵉ Winter his Intencion by this Voyage being only to view yᵉ Coʳʸ, cause some Houses to be built & some Lands to be taken up for yᵉ use of his Moravian Brethren & to try what Effect his Preaching will have.[9]

Weiser fround the Herrnhuters quite as earnest as the Ephrata people and much more sensible. They did not believe that mortification of the flesh provided a short cut to salvation. It was not their aim to escape from the world, but to walk with God in it. Matrimony they considered holy, and their young people lived normal and happy lives. When a party of Moravians visited the Solitary at Ephrata, Anna Nitschman left a flutter behind her among the Sisterhood in Kedar, and among the Brothers in Zion as well. Her views on matrimony caused her to be watched, and with reason. Not that Anna took advantage of the hospitality shown her; but a healthy mind in a healthy body is a powerful dissolvent of fanaticism. Weiser's friend Gottfried Haberecht, shortly after Anna's visit, left the Kloster and joined the Moravians; [10] and Anna was reported (at Ephrata) to have said that "most of the sisters in the settlement would like to throw off the yoke if they knew of another retreat." [11]

When Henry Antes, on behalf of Count Zinzendorf, issued a call to members of all denominations to attend a conference at Germantown "in order to treat peaceably concerning the most important articles of faith, and to ascertain how far all might agree in the most essential points, for the purpose of promoting mutual love and forbearance," [12] Weiser resolved to attend, and for the time being threw himself with all the ardor of his poetical nature into the Moravian campaign for Christian unity.

"Dear Church of God in Spirit," wrote Zinzendorf, versifying for the benefit of his followers a prayer to Jesus the Crucified:

> *We are thy own Inheritance*
> *The Purchase of thy bloody Pain*
> *This was the Fathers firm decree*
> *That we thy pure reward should be*

We must own that we know of no other foundation for our Salvation . . . but the *Wounds & Blood of the Lamb of God.* . . . we have a love for all the Children of God in the whole World and want to be united in Spirit to all of them tho they may differ from us in other matters.[13]

On New Year's Day, 1742, Conrad Weiser joined the Lutherans, Reformed, Moravians, Dunkers, hermits, and what-not who assembled at Theobald Endt's to explore the grounds of a common faith. Prior Onesimus was there with Peter Miller as part of the delegation from Ephrata, a delegation to which the Count is said to have paid special attention. Weiser's presence was also much marked. He was at that time the only German justice of the peace in the province, and already a man of some fame. His presence raised questions. Was he there in some official capacity (*als ein obrigkeitlich Person*)? So pressing were these questions that he found it necessary afterwards to declare that he had neither been invited nor sent to the conference, but had come as a *Privat Person* out of his own curiosity.[14]

Henry Antes opened the meeting, but Count Zinzendorf was soon in charge. His purpose, he explained, was "to enthrone the Lamb of God." Cavilers, of whom there were some even at this first conference which ended in apparent unity, whispered that the Count's object was to enthrone himself. A delegate from Ephrata remarked to Weiser that the Count had a big sack into which he intended to stick all the sects and separatists so that he could reign unchallenged.[15] This remark Weiser took amiss at the time; but afterwards, having quarreled in the meantime with the Count, he said that the later conferences showed the Brother from Ephrata to have been right.

"I attended the first Conference at German town from the beginning, but not to the End," writes Conrad, "and the one at Oley to the End, but not from the beginning." [16] So earnest was he at this time to promote Count Zinzendorf's work that he offered his own house at Tulpehocken for the fourth conference.

John de Türck's place at Oley, where the third conference was held, saw the first fruits of the Indian mission. Three of Brother Rauch's Indians from Shecomeco—Shebosh, Keim, and Kiop—were baptized in the barn and renamed Abraham, Isaac, and Jacob.[17]

But the harmony of the conference was disturbed when the *Siebentäger* (Seventh Dayers) from Ephrata, who were already regretting their involvement in the Count's proceedings,[18] presented a paper against matrimony, and a Scotch Presbyterian spoke up darkly about "the secret enemies of Jerusalem." [19] Harmony was temporarily restored by the departure of the *Siebentäger*, but the warning had been unmistakable. The demon of denominationalism, the pride of superior piety, was about to make all split.

In an effort to hold the crumbling edifice of church union together, an intricate device was concocted, based on the use of the lot (to which Zinzendorf was much addicted). There was selected, by repeated drawing of lots, a narrowing body of men: first thirty, then twenty, then ten, and at last five. These five elected three of their number to be trustees of the conference or Synod; and the three trustees were to select two devout men (their appointment to be confirmed by lot) to act as superintendents. The names of these two men were to be kept secret from all but the three trustees.[20]

This unfortunate device, with its dependence on the lot and its air of unnecessary mystery, was a contradiction of the very thing that had drawn many earnest Christians into the Moravian camp: their solid common sense. Immediately whole bodies of delegates withdrew. It was the last conference that Weiser attended. The next was held, not at Tulpehocken, but at Germantown again.

To all appearance the Synods were a failure. Zinzendorf had hoped to unite all German Christians in a kind of federated church, each branch retaining its own identity, but all members (of whatever communion) recognizing their spiritual unity in the central fact that Jesus Christ was their personal Savior. The movement was to be called "The Congregation of God in the Spirit."

We are one in faith in our Lord Jesus Christ, the incarnate Word of God. We are one in allegience to Him as Head of the Church, and as King of kings and Lord of lords. We are one in acknowledging that this allegiance takes precedence of any other allegiance that may make claims upon us.

This unity does not consist in the agreement of our minds or the consent of our wills. It is founded in Jesus Christ Himself, Who lived, died, and rose again to bring us to the Father, and Who through the Holy Spirit dwells in His Church. . . .

Our unity is of heart and spirit. We are divided in the outward forms of our life in Christ, because we understand differently His will for His Church. We believe, however, that a deeper understanding will lead us towards a united apprehension of the truth as it is in Jesus.

These words were not written by Count Zinzendorf. They are part of the *Affirmation of Unity* adopted by the Second World Conference on Faith and Order, held at Edinburgh, Scotland, in 1937. Count Zinzendorf was two hundred years ahead of his time.

Perhaps the objective was too high for the place and the time. The province was not ready for church union. The religious swamp had to be drained first into sectarian channels before its waters could be drawn into the sea of the Church Universal. John Wesley might say, "The world is my parish," but few persons in those days had a wider vision or broader sympathies than sufficed for the narrowest circle of loyalties. It was necessary for most people, if their faith was to survive at all, to pasture it in the narrow fields of church dogma. Over the fence they could see only a wilderness of unbelief.

Perhaps, on the other hand, the fault lay with Zinzendorf himself. He was a good man with a great vision, but he had no tact. Giving grounds of offense was his peculiar art. He had at the outset of his American mission committed the error of trying to divest himself of the name and title by which he was already well known in Europe—announcing himself, so Weiser tells us, variously as "Ludwig von Thürnstein, Ludwig Nitchman, item Siegfried von Thurnstein &c." [21] Besides, in failing to explain adequately the objectives of his movement, he had allowed the rumor to fly about that all his talk about union in the spirit was merely a preliminary softening of denominational bonds in order to make the easier proselytizing for the Moravian Church itself.

"Whether the Count's Conferences accomplished any real Good in Pennsylvania, I can't say," wrote Weiser, "the Day of Revelation must enlighten us. As far as we can see now, the coming of the Count and his Followers has produced one more sect, and the Conferences contributed to that end."

Weiser's interest in Count Zinzendorf did not, however, end with the conference at Oley. The private talk they had together, in which Zinzendorf spoke freely about himself, told of his studies at Halle, and praised the work of Professor Francke there, led Weiser to believe that the Count might help to heal the divisions in the Tulpehocken congregation.

He broached the matter and asked the Count's advice. How could they get a preacher from Halle?

There need be no trouble about that, responded Zinzendorf; he was himself in correspondence with Halle.[22]

After the conference, the Count (who once told Conrad that he had loved him from the moment he set eyes on him) [23] rode with Weiser to Tulpehocken to look the situation over, and he preached the Sunday following, February 14, in the Lutheran Church. He offered the services of Gottlieb Büttner for as long as the congregation desired, at least until a preacher could be brought over from Germany.

Büttner came, but he could not heal the rift. Zinzendorf withdrew him and, during Weiser's absence in Philadelphia with the Indians, appointed Philip Maurer in his place. Maurer was no more successful. It was observed that he followed the methods of Leutbecker, both in his style of preaching and in the form of church service he used. Most of the people adhered to Caspar Stoever. The Confusion crackled on.

Small wonder that, when a blazing comet appeared in the eastern sky on the night of February 22, some of those who watched it (especially at Ephrata, where Beissel had the alarm bell rung) thought they saw God's finger writing in the heavens a warning to unregenerate man.[24]

All this was disappointing, but Weiser was by this time becoming inured to religious disappointment and he did not as yet allow the sight of disagreeable particulars to spoil his vision of the Moravian work as a whole. For some years to come he threw himself whole-heartedly into the work of establishing the Brethren solidly in Pennsylvania. He helped them get land for settlement at Nazareth and for a road between Nazareth and Bethlehem; [25] he helped them to hold possession when "Captain John," "Deedamy," and other Indians disputed their title.[26] He took Brothers Pyrlaeus, Büttner, and Zander into his home to teach them the Mohawk language. He interested himself in the church confusion in Philadelphia (the Reformed had driven Pyrlaeus out of his pulpit). He sent his daughter Maria, with William Parsons' daughters, to Zinzendorf's home on Second Street, Philadelphia, for instruction.[27]

He visited Bethlehem frequently and, on occasion, Shecomeco. In the latter place he was deeply stirred by what he saw at the Indian mission.

"It was as if I beheld a little Flock of the First Christians together," he wrote to Büttner in 1743.

Their old people sat in the assembly some on Benches and others for Want of Room on the ground with great Gravity and devotion and hearkened to Brother P. as if they would hear the Words out of his very Heart. . . . The saying Jesus Christ the same yesterday today and Forever came quite fresh and alive in my Heart when I saw the Patriarchs of the American Church sitting there in a circle as so many witnesses to the Atonement of our Lord Jesus Christ.[28]

To Zinzendorf, during anxious days in the spring of 1742, Weiser confided his family troubles.

I must tell you [he wrote] that my Eldest daughter Magdalina has gone to Eternity,* I and my *Haussmutter* have god's comfort in the certainty that she has a part in the great propitiatory sacrifice *Jesu Christi* our Lord we had the greatest hopes for her recovery till within an hour of her departure, as she sat on a chair & talked with me, she asked me at length to help her back into bed, which when I did, she asked me to cover her well just than a brother from Ephrata who was present remarked a change. when I saw it was true she was dying, I helped my Wife from her room to her daughter, but she was no sooner come, for she too was very weak, and still is, than our very dear and dutiful daughter passed away, quite peacefully, without stirring a finger or making a sound, my other children are somewhat better except the Youngest Son, who I think has Intestinal gout, and may perhaps follow his sister.[29]

There was much exchange of letters, gifts, and information between Conrad, the Count, and the Count's followers, some of whom where struggling with Indian languages. "I have received a kind letter from br. *Pyrlaeum*," wrote Conrad to Zinzendorf in the spring of 1742, "but I can not answer it now, the word he wants is Ot thenuh-Quay iatsh (what is that)." [30] In June the Brethren listed Conrad Weiser as one of their flock at Tulpehocken.[31]

Even after Count Zinzendorf had left the province, Conrad continued for some years a warm correspondence with him.

> *To the Worthy*
> *Herr Ludwig von Thürnstein*
> *Somewhere in the World*
> *on his pilgrimage . . .*[32]
> Pensilvania Decʳ 1. 1745

Very dearly beloved and worthy friend and brother

I learned just an hour ago that Brother Kohn and his wife leave here tomorrow for philadelphia and sail thence for germany dec. fifth next. so I have an opportunity of sending you a few lines by him. . . .

* Anna Madlina died March 16, 1742.

I am still a good friend of the brethren in Bethlehem and love them, as they do me . . .

I continue to protest unceasingly against things at Ephrata. I mean against their teacher. Last summer I had another dispute with *Onesimo* and we exchanged letters, but he and his brother and Alexander Mack have left, bag and baggage Not, however, without bearing witness against Con. Beissel some others have gone off, even some of the sisters, it is a *Wunderlicher Krieg* & now that the hand of the Lord smites them so sorely I hope to god with prayer and heartfelt yearning that they may come to acknowledge Jesus of nazareth the crucified as the Christ and lord of all, they are still my People and I am still united in Heart with those whom I have found to be true. but I have nothing to do with their public worship which has become vain and denies Jesus the crucified . . .

I send kindest regards to you and the brethren with you & to my old friend gottlieb Haberecht. I should be heartily pleased to hear that you & yours are well and still more to see you. my wife sends her best regards I commit you to almighty god to whom be honor and praise in *Christo Jesu*. I am and remain your loving friend

CONRAD WEISER

CHAPTER 16

... Sees the Delawares
Taken by the Hair

I

THE drama of the Walking Purchase (with consequences yet hanging in the stars of Edward Braddock) moved into its second act when 160 Indians of the Six Nations appeared at Weiser's plantation in June 1742, on their way to the council fire at Philadelphia. Ostensibly they had come to receive further compensation in the way of looking glasses, shoe buckles, pots of vermilion, etc., for their release of the Susquehanna lands in 1736; in reality they had been brought down to deal summary justice on the Delawares at the Forks.

Nootamis, though he had signed the confirmation deed of 1737, now protested that the lands sold "as far as a man can walk in a day and a half" to William Penn by Mexkilikishi (deceased), had never been Mexkilikishi's to sell, but had belonged to Nootamis' grandfather, Tisherkum (also deceased), and that therefore the original deed was invalid and the land was Nootamis'.

Other Indians put in claims: Menakihikon (described variously as "an old King . . . beyond the great Mountains" and as "King of the Minisinks"), Moses Tattamy ("Deedamy"), and Joseph Peepy—the last a recent convert to Calvinism, whose natural disputatiousness had not been weakened by his change of faith. "Captain John," [1] a half-brother of the Teedyuscung who was to become famous thirteen years later, was disputing the ownership of the Nazareth tract, which the Proprietors were about to settle on Count Zindendorf's Moravian colony.

In a rambling petition dated November 21, 1740,[2] and sent to some Bucks County magistrates, the Delawares admitted the sale of certain pieces of land, for example "the Tract of Nicholas Dupuis" and "the Tract of old Weiser" (John Conrad); but they denied ever having sold to William Penn or his son Thomas ("he wearies us out of our Lives," they said) the bulk of the land taken in by the Walk. They threatened to remove intruders by force.

So it appeared that Yates, Jennings, and Marshal, far from disposing of the trouble at the Forks, had only extended it. Already Lappakoo had been killed for condoning the Walk, and a white man, William Webb, had been beaten to within an inch of his life [3]—only the skill of Dr. Graeme of Philadelphia, whose "vomits" were famous, had pulled him through. The white settlers on the Delaware River threatened to do themselves justice. Clearly the Indian war which the Walk had been contrived to avoid had been brought closer.

When the Six Nations Indians arrived at Tulpehocken, under the leader-

ship of Canasatego, a burly, bibulous chief whose oratory at the conference was to make history, Weiser was astonished at their numbers and
their condition. They were "almost famished," [4] and a number of them
were sick. Takareher died at Tulpehocken. Clearly they had come down
in such numbers not just for the sake of the purchase goods (fifty men
would have sufficed to carry these) but rather to escape the famine that
was sweeping the Indian country and to enjoy a few good meals in Philadelphia.

Weiser was even more concerned about those who had not come than
about those who had. There was no Seneca delegation. Since the Senecas
guarded the west door of the Six Nations and were therefore much exposed to French influence at Niagara and on the Allegheny (Ohio) River,
their absence was alarming. It was feared they might be turning to Father
Onontio.

"I . . . assure thee," wrote James Logan, whom Weiser kept informed
of every stage of the Iroquois progress, "that I long to See thy Self but
could wish thou hadst less company of Some Sorts & more of another, for
I cannot Sufficiently admire why there are no Sinnekas or Tsanundawanese
wth them   I expect y^{m} all here to dine about 2 or 3 in the Afternoon." [5]

The Indians, whose numbers grew as stragglers hooked on, moved like
an expanding cloud on Philadelphia. When they reached Logan's beautiful
home and garden at Stenton on June 29 (the sick in wagons, the hale on
foot) there were 188 of them, men, women, and children. After spending
a day with James Logan (consuming the better part of the twenty pounds
that the treaty cost him), they moved on in to the city, where they were
joined by Nootamis and his company from the Forks and by a party of
Conestogas and Nanticokes from the lower Susquehanna, bringing the
total number, according to Richard Peters' count, to well over 220. [6]

After their arrival, the visitors requested a few days of rest. The Governor and Council, thinking it wise to use this interval for a little diplomatic
reconnoitering to discover, as the Council Minutes record, "what depend-
ance we might have on them in Case their Aid should be wanted . . . at
this critical Time when we are in Daily Expectation of a ffrench
War . . . ," [7] treated the chiefs to what the Minutes describe as "An handsome Dinner" at the Proprietor's House. The food was "hearty" and the
drink heady: lime punch, with wine from Postlethwaite's. [8] Toasts were
drunk to the King, the Proprietors, and the Six Nations, after each of which
the chiefs responded with their solemn cry of approval. Then the Governor introduced the crucial question with what casualness he could.

Why had not the Senecas come down?

Canasatego, the Speaker—a stout man noted for effervescent spirits, who
often drank more and said more than was good for him—replied that "the
Senecas were in great Distress on account of a ffamine that raged in their
Country which had reduced them to such Want that a ffather had been
obliged to kill two of his Children to preserve his own & the rest of his
ffamily's Lives . . ." [9]

The Governor—"after a short respite," as the Minutes record, and (may we suppose?) fortified by a little something from Postlethwaite's—tried again. He asked if the French in Canada were making any warlike preparations.

The Indians answered, "Yes."

Then the Governor, "with a smiling Pleasant Countenance" (again the minutes), said to the chiefs, "I suppose if the ffrench should go to Warr with Us you'l join them."

The Indians were not taken off their guard. They saw at once that this was matter too dangerous to be left to the chance winds of after-dinner conversation. Whoever followed the Governor's lead must speak with the voice of the United Nations. "The Indians conferred together for some Time, and then Canassatego, in a chearful lively manner" (he was a match for anyone in the game of wine-glass diplomacy), made answer. It was all that Governor Thomas had hoped to hear:

We assure you the Governor of Canada pays our Nations great Court at this Time well knowing of what Consequence we are to the ffrench Interest He has already told Us he was uncovering the Hatchet and Sharpening it and hoped if he should be obliged to lift it Up against the English their Nations would remain Neuter and assist neither side—But we will now speak plainly to our Brethren—Why should We who are one fflesh with You refuse to help You whenever You want our Assistance—We have continued a Long Time in the strictest League of Amity and ffriendship with You And we shall be always faithful and True to you our Old and good Allies—The Governor of Canada talks a great deal but ten of his Words do not go so far as one of yours —We do not look towards them We look towards you and you may depend on our Assistance.[10]

The first public conference was held the next afternoon, July 6, at the meetinghouse. There, in a speech extolling the generosity of the Proprietors, the Governor presented the goods in payment for the lands west of the Susquehanna as far as "to the setting sun." The lands east of the river had been paid for in 1736. In this new dispensation, there were 45 guns, a quantity of lead and powder, 60 strowd matchcoats, 100 duffel matchcoats, 100 blankets, 60 kettles, 100 tobacco tongs, 120 combs, 2,000 needles, 24 dozen garters, 40 hats, 40 pairs of shoes, stockings, and buckles, 100 hatchets, 500 knives, 2 pounds of vermilion, 24 looking glasses, and so on.

It was a custom in Six Nations councils (as among those of Sir Thomas More's Utopians) not to discuss any important matter at the time it was first proposed. Canasatego deferred his acknowledgment of the powder and hats till the following day. Then, with Weiser's assistance as interpreter, he delivered himself of the following:

"Brethren We received from the Proprietors Yesterday some Goods in Consideration of our Release of the Lands on the West side of Sasquehannah— It is true we have the full Quantity according to Agreement but if the Proprietor had been here himself we think in regard of our Numbers and poverty he would have made an Addition to them—If the Goods were only to be divided amongst the Indians present a single Person would have had but a small Portion but if you consider what Numbers are left behind equally

intitled with Us to a Share there will be extremely little. We therefore desire,
if you have the Keys of the Proprietors Chest you will open it and take out a
little more for us.—

We know our Lands are now become more Valuable the white People
think we dont know their Value but we are sensible that the Land is Everlasting and the few Goods we receive for it are soon Worn out and gone for
the future we will sell no Lands but when Brother Onas is in the Country and
we will know before hand the Quantity of Goods we are to receive Besides
we are not well Used with respect to the Lands still unsold by Us—Your
People daily settle on these Lands and spoil our Hunting—We must insist on
your removing them as you know they have no right to the Northward of
Kittochtinny Hills—In particular we renew our Complaints against some
People who are settled at Juniata a Branch of Sasquahannah and all along the
Banks of that River as far as Mahaniay and desire they maybe forthwith made
to go off the Land for they do great Damage to our Cousins the Delawares.[11]

It was a good speech. It put Brother Onas on the defensive, and, since he
was about to ask the Six Nations for a favor (to adjudicate the quarrel with
the Delawares), it forced him to be open-hearted.

To the charge of trespassing, the Governor replied that magistrates had
already been sent to remove the settlers. The Indians retorted that the
magistrates did not do their duty; instead of removing trespassers, they
surveyed lands for themselves. "We desire more effectual Methods may
be used and honester persons employ'd." [12] The Governor promised to do
as they desired.

As for the purchase goods, the Proprietors, said he, "are all absent and
have taken the Keys of their Chest with them . . ." [13] It was impossible
on their behalf to raise the price of the land. But perhaps, he added, in view
of the Indians' poverty, the government might make them a present. Which
the government accordingly did, to the tune of £300: 24 guns, a further
quantity of lead and powder, 30 blankets, 24 tobacco tongs, 25 hats, 25
pairs of shoes, stockings, and buckles, 50 hatchets, 120 knives, and 5 lbs. of
vermilion.

From these proceedings we may gauge the quality of Canasatego. He
had a certain careless genius about him: easy manners, a flow of language,
and a sharp wit. He was quick to turn a phrase or a situation to his advantage. But he was more of a politician than a statesman. Pleasure-loving and
good-natured, he responded readily both to those who asked for and
those who offered gifts; and he had all the weaknesses of an over-ready
speaker. He was a wizard with words. He raised them, like ghosts; but he
could not lay them again—as the sequel to this conference will show. He
was trapped by his own rhetoric, and he allowed the borders to grow dull
in his mind between metaphor and fact.

On Thursday, July 8, the chiefs, dining again with the Governor, gave
their reply to a message that had been sent to them at Onondaga. It concerned the assault on William Webb at the Forks. Canasatego said that the
Six Nations had severely reproved the Indian involved, a Mohican named
Awannameak from Esopus; and he expressed the hope that, since Webb
had not died, the matter might now be allowed to rest. "The Indians know

no punishment but Death," he said; "they have no such thing as pecuniary Mulcts if a man be guilty of a Crime he is either put to Death or the fault is overlook'd." [14]

He returned the Governor's wampum, which had been delivered in connection with the Webb business, to signify that the matter was now closed.

II

The climax of the conference came next day, July 9. The Governor presented to the chiefs of the Six Nations, in the presence of Nootamis and the Forks Indians, a formal complaint against this "Branch of the Delawares" for their "Rudeness & ill Manners" in respect to the Walking Purchase. The Governor requested that the Six Nations, who had asked Brother Onas to turn off white trespassers from Indian lands, should now turn off these Indian trespassers from Brother Onas' land. A string of wampum served to point the request.

Conrad Weiser was instructed to interpret and explain to the Six Nations chiefs all the evidence in the case, from the transcript of the original deed of 1686 down to the recent abusive letters received from the Indians in the Forks. This took some time, as Conrad testified afterwards.[15] The Six Nations went about the business with deliberation. They heard the Delawares present their side of the case. Then they had the deeds interpreted to them, and examined the signers' names and their marks. Weiser explained the survey with the aid of a map.

Judgment was delivered at a council held in the Proprietor's house on July 12.

Canasatego lifted his tall, full-chested frame, opened his mouth, and let himself go. Justice may be blind, but certainly it was not, in the person of Canasatego, deaf. He loved to hear himself talk.

He addressed himself first to the Governor and Council.

Brethren . . . The other Day you informed Us of the Misbehaviour of our Cousins the Delawares with respect to their continuing to Claim and refusing to remove from some Land on the River Delaware notwithstanding their Ancestors had sold it by Deed under their Hands & Seals to the Proprietors for a valuable Consideration upwards of fifty Years ago and notwithstanding that they themselves had about —— Years ago after a long and full Examination ratified that Deed of their Ancestors and given a fresh one under their Hands and Seals and then you requested Us to remove them enforcing your Request with a String of Wampum Afterwards you laid on the Table by Conrad Weiser our own Letters—some of our Cousins' Letters and the several Writings to prove the Charge against our Cousins with a Draught of the Land in Dispute—We now tell you we have Perused all these several Papers We see with our own Eyes that they have been a very unruly People and are altogether in the Wrong in their Dealings with You—We have concluded to remove them and Oblige them to go over the River Delaware and to quit all Claim to any Lands on this side for the future since they have received Pay for them and it is gone through their Guts long ago—To confirm to You that we will see your Request Executed we lay down this string of Wampum in return for your's.[16]

Then Canasatego turned to the Delawares and, holding a belt of wampum in his hand, delivered his famous philippic. Conrad Weiser translated his words into English, and Cornelius Spring turned them into Delaware.

Cousins Let this Belt of Wampum serve to Chastize You you ought to be taken by the Hair of the Head and shak'd severely till you recover your Senses and become Sober you dont know what Ground you stand on nor what you are doing . . . We have seen with our Eyes a Deed signed by nine of your Ancestors above fifty Years ago for this very Land and a Release Sign'd not many Years since by some of your selves and Chiefs now living to the Number of 15 or Upwards—But how came you to take upon you to Sell Land at all We conquer'd You we made Women of you you know you are Women and can no more sell Land than Women Nor is it fit you should have the Power of Selling Lands since you would abuse it This Land that you Claim is gone through Your Guts You have been furnished with Cloaths and Meat and Drink by the Goods paid you for it and now you want it again like Children as you are—. . . You Act a dishonest part not only in this but in other Matters Your Ears are ever Open to slanderous Reports about our Brethren You receive them with as much greediness as Lewd Women receive the Embraces of Bad Men And for all these reasons we charge You to remove instantly We dont give You the liberty to think about it. You are Women take the Advice of a Wise Man and remove immediately. You may return to the other side of Delaware where you came from but we don't know whether Considering how you have demean'd your selves you will be permitted to live there or whether you have not swallowed that Land down your Throats as well as the Land on this side We therefore Assign you two Places to go either to Wyomin or Shamokin—You may go to either of these Places and then we shall have you more under our Eye and shall see how You behave—Dont deliberate but remove away and take this Belt of Wampum [17]

These words of Canasatego have been called by Daniel G. Brinton in *The Lenâpé and Their Legends* "braggart falsehoods." [18] It is only too clear that Canasatego understood rhetoric better than law or history. He had turned a judgment on a legal matter involving a few Indians at the Forks into an indictment of the whole Delaware nation; and, out of the question whether the Forks Indians had sold a particular tract of land to Brother Onas, he educed the principle that the Delawares had no right to sell land at all.

Canasatego was enjoying himself. Whether "the swats sae reamed" in his noddle that his figures of speech here took him a flight beyond his instructions (for he was speaking as the voice of the Six Nations) we cannot say for certain, but it would appear so. Such extensions of authority were a weakness of his. He was at one time suspected by his people of selling land privately to the Moravians. In 1749 he pushed a sale of Endless Mountains land at Brother Onas in Philadelphia (if we may trust the statement of Richard Peters), and went home to die under such circumstances as left at least a suspicion that the Six Nations had administered to him the only punishment they knew.[19]

One belt of wampum was not enough to exhaust the flow of Canasatego's hortations. He took up another belt and went on, still addressing the Delawares:

This string of Wampum serves to forbid You Your Children and Grand Children to the latest Posterity for ever medling in Land Affairs neither you nor any who shall descend from You are ever hereafter to presume to sell any Land for which Purpose you are to Preserve this string in Memory of what your Uncles have this Day given You in Charge—We have some other Business to transact with our Brethren and therefore depart the Council and consider what has been said to you—[20]

There is a tradition that as Canasatego gave the belt to the chief of the Delawares "he seized him by his long hair and pushed him out of the door of the council room!" [21]

The treaty ended on a Falstaffian note. Canasatego requested that, since the Indians had been "stinted in the Article of Rum in Town," Brother Onas should "open the Rum Bottle" on the road.[22] The Council responded by adding to the hundred pounds already set aside to defray Conrad Weiser's expenses with the Indians, going and coming, a further sum sufficient to buy twenty gallons of rum "to Comfort them upon the Road." [23]

III

This conference of 1742 at which, as Teedyuscung said years afterward (speaking as the voice of the Delawares) he had been taken by the hairs of his head and shaken,[24] has been regarded by most writers who have dealt with it as the turning point in Pennsylvania's Indian relations. Here, it is said, the government took sides with the Six Nations against the Delawares, dispossessed them of their lands, and even denied them the right to own land at all. In other words, for the benign policy of William Penn, there had now been substituted a policy of injustice and oppression which was soon to drench the province in blood. So at least some of the Quakers said in 1756 (after the event), and most historians have taken their cue from them.

As for the general principle of making the alliance with the Six Nations vital by recognizing their suzerainty over the Delawares, that was undoubtedly Pennsylvania's policy, and there can be little question of its wisdom. But to say that by this policy the Delawares were in 1742 deprived of their right to hold land, is to take literally an excited Indian orator's metaphor ("you can no more sell Land than Women") in the face of a great body of contrary evidence.

James Logan put no such construction on the expulsion of the Indians from the Forks. In telling Thomas Penn about this part of the treaty, he wrote as if the matter were a local one, concerning only "Nootamis & his Company, who complaining very heavily to their Uncles of their being cheated and abused, after a full hearing have this Day been commanded by them to quitt all that Tract intirely and to remove either over to Jersey again, or beyond the Hills." [25]

Neither Weiser nor anyone else at this conference supposed that Canasatego's rant had actually changed the relation between the Delawares and the Six Nations, or between the Delawares and Brother Onas. The Six Nations believed that the Delawares had no more lands left in Pennsylvania to sell. Therefore they forbade them to sell any.

But if there was no change in the status of the Delawares, there was a change in their temper. Their feeling of grievance had grown, and they were more open thereafter to the French agents operating through the Shawnees on the Ohio. The Six Nations had promised, when they "haled the Delawares over the mountain," that the lands at Wyoming should be held inviolate for their wards forever. When the Connecticut Yankees invaded the Wyoming Valley, the Delawares prepared for war.

CHAPTER 17

... *Draws Lots*
with Count Zinzendorf

COUNT ZINZENDORF was interested in all this stir among the Indians during the summer of 1742, especially since it brought to his hand the Six Nations, whose help he needed to extend his Indian missions. Before the conference, he had become acquainted with Coxhayion and his family, who lodged with him at his house in Philadelphia—to the considerable uneasiness of the Governor, who feared the Count might stint his liquor beyond the limits of Indian propriety or proprietorial interest.[1]

Weiser wrote roguishly to Zinzendorf about this last matter after having had a talk with Coxhayion on his return from Philadelphia:

About the Indian who lodged with you, he is entirely satisfied except that he was given no rum, which if he had been he says he could have joined in with greater heartiness at prayer time, he wondered how people could spend so much time in prayer which surely could have been put off to some future time, when there was nothing else to do, at the moment there were more agreeable things, like rum and such-like entertainments, he spoke very well of you and your company and said he had no doubt that when you came to know more about the nature of Indians, you would never speak to them on weighty matters without treating them to a good *trunk rum* [2]

After the conference, Count Zinzendorf himself called at Weiser's house in Tulpehocken (obeying a mysterious "call," as he tells us [3]—to the discomfiture of a cavalcade of Moravian followers who had been on their way through the woods with him to quite another destination) and found the Six Nations chiefs resting there before continuing their journey back to their own country. That was on August 3.

Zinzendorf saw in this meeting the hand of God. The Interpreter's house was to be the Moravian Gateway to the great Indian mission field.

The Count was greeted by Coxhayion and his wife and child. The child came running to clasp him round the neck. Nothing could have better suited his purposes, for the Indians were fond of their children and looked on this little incident as an omen.

He held a council with the chiefs, and presented the request that he and his Brethren be permitted to come into the Indian country bringing messages from the Great Spirit, with whom he was "specially and intimately acquainted." [4]

Coxhayion, Canasatego, Shickellamy, and the rest of the chiefs withdrew for an hour to discuss his proposal among themselves. Then, returning, they presented their formal reply:

Brother: you have journey a long way, from beyond the sea, in order to preach to the white people and the Indians. You did not know that we were here; we had no knowledge of your coming. The Great Spirit has brought us together. Come to our people. You shall be welcome. Take this fathom of wampum. It is a token that our words are true.[5]

"This," writes De Schweinitz in his life of the great missionary, David Zeisberger, "was the beginning of the friendship which existed for many years between the Moravians and the League of the Iroquois, and which gave the former standing among all other tribes." [6]

Weiser, too, saw the hand of God in this meeting, and he was determined to go with the Count as his guide into the Indian country, although Governor Thomas expressly asked him not to go at this time since he wanted him to do some fall electioneering against the Quaker party.

Weiser and Zinzendorf had been planning since the spring to make a trip together into the Indian country. The Count had expansive schemes, which he succeeded at least in getting down on paper: the route ("under the Lord's hand") was to be from Nazareth over the Blue Mountains to Esopus and Albany and thence back by way of the Susquehanna; the time, July, August, and September; the company, "Anton, Büttner, Rauch, Anna, Benigna and her Father [Zinzendorf himself] and lastly Conrad Weiser the Emperor of the 6 nations and a Christian of sorts (*etwa Christian*)." [7]

It was no delusion of grandeur that prompted the Count to call the man who was to be his guide through the woods the Emperor of the Six Nations, as though Conrad Weiser were the American Prester John. Zinzendorf was merely attempting to translate into terms understandable to his own mid-European mind the very remarkable name *Tarachiawagon*, which the Indians had lately given Weiser in substitution for his earlier name of Siguras. The significance of the new name will be explained in a later chapter.

Conrad's proposed itinerary was less ambitious than the Count's. In a letter of May 27 to his "Dear Brother Ludwig," he canvassed the whole situation, advised the Count to choose a time of year when the Indian corn was ripe lest he should find himself under the necessity of sharing his food and going hungry with the natives, and suggested that they go first to Shamokin, thence to Madame Montour's, fifty miles farther north on a branch of the Susquehanna, whence, as he said, "one can either go to the River Ohio, an arm of the famous Meshisippi river . . . or turn Northeast and go to the Shawannes who live at Scahantowahne." This latter place, he said,

. . . lies about 120 miles north of Philadelphia, according to an observation of the sun's altitude made by William Perassen [Parsons], a few years ago, when I and He were sent to this Place, on Land Business and Indian Affairs, but how far it is by land I cannot tell because of the . . . very many high Mountains, it cannot however be more than 100 Miles from Bethlehem . . . and an Indian Trail goes from here to Dorham probably by way of Bethlehem, but I have never been over it. . . . No European has ever come to any of the Indian Places I have mentioned preaching the Gospel.[8]

For a few weeks after the conference at Tulpehocken, Zinzendorf and Weiser were busy with other things. The Count made a journey to Shecomeco to visit the mission there; Weiser went to Shamokin to see Shickel-lamy about some trouble Maryland was having with the Nanticokes.

The Governor wrote to Weiser expressing his displeasure that he should propose to accompany the Count at a time when the "Peace & Welfare" of the province demanded his presence at home to prepare his countrymen "against the ensuing Election." [9] Weiser went ahead with his preparations notwithstanding.

It was well on in September before they got on to the trail. Conrad has left a written account of the journey, which provides as colorful a canvas as the times can show. Against a background of forest, mountain, river, and a mysterious silver mine, we see painted Indians, German missionaries, French half-breeds, and the always-busy interpreter shuttling back and forth between the settlements and the Indian mission field, trying to render dues to God and Caesar at the same time: electioneering, acting as secretary at a mission conference, saving the Count's life, quarreling with him over God's plan for their itinerary, and discussing religion with the Shawnee chief, Kakowatchiky, in the woods of the Wyoming Valley.

"In the year 1742 about the middle of September," he writes, "I set out from my house with the Count to visit the Indians living on the River Susquehanna. I kept no Diary, because I did not want to write anything in contradiction of those who did. The Count's travelling companions were First Anna Nitschmann, Martin Mack and his Wife, Peter Beler, Heinrigh Leimbach, and the two Indians from Shomokin." [10]

It was an interesting party. Martin Mack and his wife Jeanette were on their honeymoon. The spirited Anna Nitschman we have already met at Ephrata; she was later to become Zinzendorf's wife. Peter Boehler was the man who, on March 4, 1738, had brought about John Wesley's second conversion. The two Indians, Joshua and David, need no other introduction than as thorns in Zinzendorf's flesh, messengers from Satan sent to buffet him with their incessant grumbling.

They had saddle-horses and pack-horses, one of the latter loaded with the Count's books, for he intended to make the wilderness his library. The Count also brought along a large tent, capable of accommodating the whole party.

Of all the many traveling companions Weiser had in fifty years of jour-neying through the woods, Count Zinzendorf was the most interesting and at the same time the most trying. He was by nature a crusader, ever quarreling "in his Lordes war," and sacrificing both rank and fortune to his religious knight-errantry. If he had been uniformly as wise as he was worthy, he might have been more immediately successful, but he would surely have been less loved and he would certainly have accomplished less in the long run. He was a great-hearted child. His blunders were all gener-ous. They sprang from nothing mean or fanatical, but were the fruits of haste and warmth of spirit and a too ready surrender to the impulse of the moment.

This last was, indeed, a matter of principle with him. He was as sure that his promptings were divine as Joan of Arc was of the reality of her

Voices. He was a disciple of Jacob Böhme, and he followed the inner light
—though what he took for light seemed sometimes to others to be darkness.
He was an enigma: proud and passionate, a stickler for his own authority;
yet at the same time eager in submission to what he believed to be God's
will. Through all his self-contradictions, he was sincere. James Logan
described him as a religious Don Quixote, and noted (in an age of wigs)
that he wore his own hair.[11]

Everything was propitious for the journey except the mood in which the
Count undertook it. At Tulpehocken before starting out he had broken a
lance against the Confusion—or, as he put it, "had a slight contest with
Satan about the Sacraments." [12] He was dispirited and inclined to be severe.
Looking ahead, he was pained by what he expected to find among the
Indians. These descendants, as he believed them to be, of the Lost Ten
Tribes (mixed with Scythians) who had wandered "thro' yᵉ great Tar-
tarian wilderness" [13] and lay now in America under a curse, interested him
not primarily as fellow men, but as God's vineyard. He heartily disap-
proved of their persons.

"The indigestible Indian corn that constitutes their principal diet," he
wrote in his diary, "tends to thicken their blood and to stupefy their
mental faculties. . . . The Indians are averse to wearing breeches . . ." [14]

Even after the warm welcome the chiefs had given him at Weiser's, he
resolved not to visit the Six Nations country. The reason he gave himself
was not the obvious one that Weiser had not the time to spare for so long
an expedition. It was that he had been "unable to discern any promising
indications or signs of grace among them." [15] He complained of their
"indomitable pride." [16] He would therefore do as Weiser recommended:
he would visit the Delawares at Shamokin and the Shawnees at Skahan-
towano (Wyoming)—if it could be done, as he said, without exposing
himself rashly to dangers.

As it turned out, the only dangers to which he was to be exposed were
those he drew upon himself by his own indomitable pride.

It was to be an exciting journey. Weiser's passionate hero-worship coming into conflict with his equally passionate independence and self-reliance
was to lead him now (as it had led him before and would lead him again)
into the strangest of conflicts. He had defied the governor in Philadelphia
in order to go with Zinzendorf into the wilderness; and soon on the savage
banks of the Susquehanna he was to defy Zinzendorf in order to obey the
promptings of his own good sense.

To a man of such enthusiastic loyalty and combativeness as Weiser
possessed, Ludwig von Thürnstein, Count Zinzendorf, was a man whom it
was inevitable he should both follow and fight. Zinzendorf was a kind of
Christian mastodon, trampling ruthlessly over all obstacles that stood between him and the Lamb of God. He had enormous energy, grandiose
conceptions, a flaming poetical vision. He was always planning things on
a tremendous scale, and his mind leaped ahead defying time and space,
geography and enthnology, in the imagined accomplishment of his designs.
He placed the Wyoming Valley (which he visited) in Canada (which he

wanted to visit), and identified the Delawares with the Hurons. Not that there was anything weak about his mind. It was keen, penetrating, powerful. Some of his judgments show amazing insight. But his emotions were pinned to his purposes, and the intensity with which he concentrated on the latter so inflated the former that they overset the balance of his mind. He was like the Mikado: what he wanted to do was as good as done; therefore, it *was* done.

He read much, talked a great deal, and wrote prodigiously. Among his papers preserved at Herrnhut are quantities of journals, reports, hymns, satirical verses (e.g., on Conrad Beissel), odd sayings, letters—letters in English, German, French (to James Logan), and Latin (to "the Venerable Polycarp"), letters of rebuke, of admonition, of condolence, of direction, of announcement. He was a magnificent organizer on paper. He mapped out the mission field in America, divided it into districts, appointed apostles, and set down a *Hierarchia Pensylvania* with Spangenberg at the head and Conrad Weiser and Shickellamy somewhere down the line.[17]

He was generous, kind, considerate, for the most part, but almost insanely petulant and overbearing when he met with contradiction. He raged at trifles, yet he could keep his patience under really severe provocation. He replied coolly to a question put to him by Anna Eicher (the Ephrata Sister who charged Beissel with helping to murder her bastard child) by saying that he neither flirted nor whored with his Moravian Sisters and by God's grace he never would.[18] *Honi soit qui mal y pense*. Anna had fled to Beissel when he was a hermit; now, withering on the stalk, she despaired of Beissel's soul. No doubt she despaired also of Zinzendorf's.

Count Zinzendorf, like Conrad Weiser, was an original, and one of the best and most lovable men who ever set foot on American soil.

II

The Shamokin Trail had no surprises for Conrad Weiser, who already knew it as well as he knew the road to Philadelphia; but it was exciting enough to the Count and his charges, who were not accustomed to the wilderness. The route they took is today a familiar one to motorists, who follow its adventurous windings more or less closely by modern roads from Womelsdorf through Bethel over the Blue Mountain to Pine Grove, then through the Gaps in the Second Mountain, up the Broad Mountain to Joliet and Good Spring, off it again to Hegins, and so by way of Klingerstown at the old Double Eagle, past bucolic Urban in its nest of hills, past Fisher's Ferry on the Susquehanna, and so to Sunbury (the old Shamokin). But Zinzendorf, though he had an eye for natural beauty and speaks in his journal of the "lovely Susquehanna," was not on this journey disposed to be interested in scenery. He was concerned rather with the difficulties encountered in this "savage wilderness," such as rocks and stones and precipices (which were in 1742 not yet considered a proper part of scenery), and in particular with the ascent of the steep, stony, Broad Mountain (then unnamed, but which Conrad called Thürnstein in

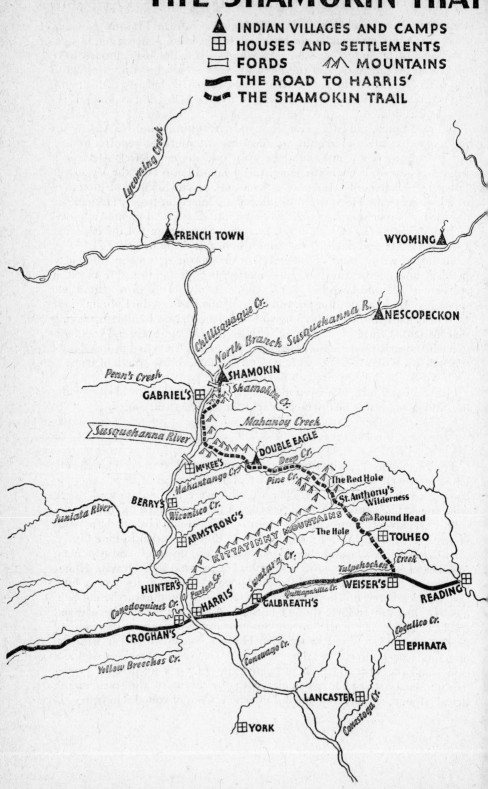

THE SHAMOKIN TRAIL

▲ INDIAN VILLAGES AND CAMPS
⊞ HOUSES AND SETTLEMENTS
▭ FORDS   ◁◁ MOUNTAINS
━━ THE ROAD TO HARRIS'
▰▰▰ THE SHAMOKIN TRAIL

Lycoming Creek

▲ FRENCH TOWN

WYOMING ▲

Chillisquaque Cr.

North Branch Susquehanna R.

▲ NESCOPECKON

Penn's Creek

▲ SHAMOKIN

Shamokin Cr.

GABRIEL'S ⊞

Mahanoy Creek

Susquehanna River

DOUBLE EAGLE

Deep Cr.

⊞ McKEE'S

Mahantango Cr.

Pine Cr.

The Red Hole

St. Anthony's Wilderness

BERRY'S

Wiconisco Cr.

Juniata River

◁◁ Round Head

⊞ ARMSTRONG'S

KITTATINNY MOUNTAINS

The Hole

⊞ TOLHEO

Swatara Cr.

Tulpehocken Creek

HUNTER'S ⊞

Paxton Cr.

Quittapahilla Cr.

WEISER'S ⊞

⊞ READING

HARRIS' ▭

GALBREATH'S ⊞

Conodoguinet Cr.

Cocalico Cr.

▭ CROGHAN'S

Yellow Breeches Cr.

Conewago Cr.

⊞ EPHRATA

LANCASTER ⊞

Conestoga Cr.

⊞ YORK

honor of the Count); and, five days later, for it took so long to cover the first eighty miles, with the descent in the late afternoon of the last mountain to Shamokin Creek—the members of the party hanging on to one another's coat tails. Zinzendorf has described the adventure:

Anna, who is the most courageous of our number, and a heroine, led in the descent. I took the train of her riding-habit in my hand to steady me in the saddle, Conrad held to the skirt of my overcoat, and Böhler to Conrad's. In this way we mutually supported each other, and the Saviour assisted us to descend the hill in safety.[19]

At Shamokin, which place Martin Mack described later as "the very seat of the Prince of Darkness," the Count spent only one day. He had some trouble getting the Delawares quiet while the party were at prayers.

Here they met Shickellamy, who came *to steal their mission*, as the Indian phrase ran; i.e., to learn the object of their journey. He brought also a message for Conrad Weiser from old Kakowatchiky in the Wyoming Valley, saying "that he wished to see him before he died." [20] The Count had a high regard for Shickellamy, but his design in this journey being rather to explore the mission field than to cultivate any single part of it, he was resolved to hurry on; he promised on his return to discourse more fully with the Shamokin Indians about his objectives.

On the morning of September 19, Shickellamy showed them the ford of the Susquehanna. Leaving Mack and his wife at Shamokin, they proceeded up the West Branch in the same leisurely fashion as before (having some trouble with strayed horses) and reached Ostonwakin (Montoursville) on September 21.

At Otstonuege [writes Weiser] we were remarkably well received. The Count had much discourse with an old Frenchwoman who had lived from youth among the Indians, and had fled with her relatives from Canada for I don't know what reasons. She spoke French with her children and was known to me for many years by the name of Madame Montour. She was a Roman Catholic and a very intelligent person, as were her children too.[21]

Her son Andrew, who at Weiser's request had met them on the trail (to help hunt for their horses), is worth stopping to look at. Zinzendorf wrote in his diary:

Andrew's cast of countenance is decidedly European, and had not his face been encircled with a broad band of paint, applied with bear's fat, I would certainly have taken him for one. He wore a broadcloth coat, a scarlet damasken lappel-waistcoat, breeches, over which his shirt hung, a black Cordovan neckerchief, decked with silver bugles, shoes and stockings, and a hat. His ears were hung with pendants of brass and other wires plaited together like the handle of a basket. He was very cordial, but on [my] adressing him in French, he, to my surprise, replied in English.[22]

Andrew later became an important figure in provincial affairs, and we shall meet him frequently zigzagging across Weiser's path.

Madame Montour brought two of her children to be baptized, but the

Count refused, explaining that it was the habit of the Brethren to baptize "only such persons as we thought we would have frequent opportunity of reminding of the significance of the rite." [23] He notes in his diary that Madame Montour was displeased.

Meantime Weiser had the election on his mind. Leaving the Count at Ostonwakin with the promise to meet him again in a few days at Wyoming, he returned with Peter Boehler in a hurry, stopping at Shamokin to send Martin Mack and the two Indians back to the Count, and made the remaining eighty miles of the trip to Tulpehocken in a day and a half, the Indian David on foot (by choice), using that peculiar cross between a glide and a shuffle with which the Indians eat up the miles with incredible patience on the trail. David made as much as twenty miles in one morning.[24]

In Weiser's absence, the Count grew more and more irritable. His journey from Ostonwakin into the Wyoming Valley was unpleasant enough, "over rocks and frightful mountains," [25] as the unpoetical Mack described it; but what followed when he reached the Shawnee country was much worse. Near the Indian town of Wyoming, his horse broke its girth at a ford, and the Count fell on his back in the water with the saddle on top of him. The Shawnees among whom he found himself were no chickens. Painted red and black, and carrying long knives,[26] they crowded about his tent, complaining that he had pitched it on an old Indian burial ground close to a silver mine which they had been settled there expressly to guard.

He tried to win their hearts by acts of generosity as extravagant as everything else he did. "The very clothes on his back were not spared," writes Martin Mack. "One shirt-button after another was given away, until all were gone, and likewise his shoe-buckles, so that we were obliged to fasten his under-clothes and tie his shoes with strings made of bast." [27]

Still the Shawnees were not satisfied. He informed them of his mission; but his arrogant manner spoiled everything he said. At last even his Indian guides and interpreters left him, and there is no telling what might have happened to him if Conrad Weiser had not turned up in time to stop the mischief.

A legend circulated later among the Brethren that Weiser's return was a miracle. It was said that Weiser, far beyond the ranges that hid Zinzendorf among the heathen, had received a message in the spirit that the Count's life was in danger, and that he had left his business unfinished and hurried back to save him.

Weiser himself is at hand, with a letter written to his friend the Reverend Mr. Brunnholtz of Philadelphia, to tell us what actually happened. He had finished his business at home, he says, and was ready to make a quick journey back into the woods to meet the Count at the time agreed on, when he was delayed by the coming of David Nitschman, Anton Seyffert, and Jacob Kühn from Bethlehem. They had been summoned by the Count to attend a missionary conference with him in the Wyoming Valley.

I set out from home again with this party [writes Weiser] and we were a week, as far as I can remember, before we reached the Count at Wajomak. Here we found everything in Confusion. The Count had pitched his tent about a mile away from the Indian village, or huts, on a hill where the Indians had always supposed a silver mine to be, though they kept it very secret. When I called on the Indians they were full of complaints against the Count. The three Indians who had accompanied him here from Otstonuage were particularly exasperated with him. They had, as a matter of fact, left him and were going home, I not having returned by the time agreed on, which, however, was not my fault but that of the party from Bethlehem. The burden ran that this man had not come among them for love, since he did not stay with them in their huts, but had pitched his tent at a distance from them there read his books (with which one horse had been packed) and no doubt had been calling on the spirits to tell him where their silver mine was, which he must have got wind of because he moved his tent from place to place till at last he came to the spot, as I saw, where the silver was. They added that his people had already been digging. In fine, the Count had made a complete mess of things, and I had all I could do to calm the turmoil in their wild and half-savage natures. I promised them to give the Count a talking to and punish him for his thoughtlessness. At the time I did not dare say a word on his behalf, but had to wait for a more favorable time. Meanwhile my fellow travellers went to the Count, who at once sent back to order me away from the Indians and to come and hear him first. I did what needed to be done first, however, and then I went to him. I received a curt welcome. If the Indians berated him, he berated them much more, particularly the three guides who he thought were not to be trusted. He accused me of deceiving him, sending him people like that who had given him no end of trouble. *Item* the natives had conducted themselves improperly towards him, showed no respect for his person, used to break wind in his presence in the tent, were always making fun of him, and smoked tobacco beyond all reason, etc. Certainly the poor Indians did not know how to behave with a Reichs Count, and if they had known they would have had no inclination thereto. Neither did the Count know how to behave with the Indians. He is pretty hot-headed and likes to give orders, the Indians on the other hand won't take orders in the least and consider a dictator nonsensical (*unsinnig*). So we went at each other hammer and tongs. My reason got the better of me and I told the Count that it would have been more fitting if he had made himself agreeable to the Indians and lodged with them, put up his tent by their Huts: I defended the Indians as well as I could and blamed him severely. But he flew into a rage, flung at me that I was a traitor and had deserted him in this savage place and as good as betrayed him. But his blood soon cooled again, when I pointed out the Dangers into which, out of ignorance to be sure, he had plunged himself and his followers. I believe all his companions knew me for a true and honest man, but they did not dare say anything. At last he and I came to a truce, and I managed to bring the Indians also round to a better frame of mind.[28]

III

Zinzendorf was always dramatic. He had set his heart on holding a great missionary conference here in the "wilderness" of Scahandowana. The Indians were to attend, and also the missionaries to whom the field was to be assigned. It had been revealed to him, said the Count, that this conference was to be held at Assarockne, a Mohican village some twelve miles farther up the Susquehanna. The Mohicans, we know, were at this time more subject to European influence than were the Shawnees; but unfortunately for Zinzendorf's plans, as Weiser was informed by his Indian friends, there were no Mohicans at Assarockne. The village was entirely deserted.

Nevertheless the Count [continues Weiser] was determined to go on to his goal; he suspected our informants of telling him Lies, said so openly. Now I thought it a piece of Foolishness, which we could never explain to the Indians, to go to a place, where they said there was not a living Soul, and so I opposed the Count's design. We went bravely at each other again (I and the Count, but we two alone, his followers were no better than his Domestics; their Silence showed they thought the same as I did, and that got them into his bad graces). However since the Count was a Foreigner I gave in to his whim though it went against all Reason, and consented. At once preparation was made for the journey, the Horses were saddled. Our Indian Guides were utterly against the business, and it seemed to the Indians a very odd thing to go looking for people where it was known in advance there were none to be found. The Count set off the same afternoon with some of his party, for Assarockne, I stayed behind with a couple of his people overnight among the Indians, in order to patch up a good Understanding with them again, in which I succeeded. Next day I travelled with those who had stayed with me, after the Count, expecting to meet him at the aforesaid place. A small Foot-path led there, and there were no Side Paths; when we had gone 3 or 4 Miles, we lost the Horse Tracks we had been following, we supposed from this, the Count must have got lost. I cannot recall now, whether there was an Indian with me. So we hunted left and right along the Trail, but found no Trace of Horse Tracks, so we had to ride back a piece, discovered at last that the Count had turned right and ridden off at right angles from the Trail. We followed the Tracks, which the Horses had made through high grass, at first through a Patch of Pine woods. When we emerged we saw distant Smoke and at length the Tent near the Susquehanna. On approaching him, I did not know what to say, and he did not know what to say to his people by way of excuse, for nobody could have missed the Trail. However, I could not contain myself, but said, I now saw well enough that he had brought me along to make a Fool of me, and that he must have quite other Projects in his Head than those he had ever told me. He snatched up the time-worn Weapon of the spirit: you are a *Rationalist,* and know nothing of the Savior's business: It is the Savior's will that the great Mission Conference shall be held here in this Place &c. and when that is done we go home. Seeing that in everything he did the Count hid behind the Savior, I kept quiet. I saw he was determined to be in the right, and as I had gone along as his guide, I did not want to oppose him any further. But the trouble I had in excusing the Count, to the Indians, (so that the Missionaries, who were to be sent out from Bethlehem, should not find the Lord's work hindered by all this commotion) I cannot describe. The great Mission Conference went ahead. We all had to go into the Tent. To begin with we sang a Couple of verses, had a prayer, and the Count made a short but pregnant speech, touching the matter in hand. The Count then asked: Brother Anton, will you take upon yourself the Lord's Work among the Heathen, and put your life to the hazard therefor? *Yes.* Brother Nitschman will you take this Nation under your care? *Yes.* Brother so and so &c, &c, &c, answered *Yes.* How exactly the Divisions went, and who was to serve what Nation, I really cannot say now. The Savior was consulted by the drawing of Lots, the Brethren had to give me their answer and it was all put down in the minutes: then a few verses were sung and the great mission Conference was over. It was for this that Bishop Nitschman, Anton Seifart and Jacob Kuhn had been brought from Bethlehem and had travelled 200 Miles, both coming and Going. They never returned to these Parts, but soon after went to Europe, except Martin Mack, who still sometimes makes a visit to the Susquehanna. By now we had to think about getting back. The Count asked the Savior by drawing Lots, whether we should go back the Way we had Come, or whether we should go to Bethlehem by way of Minessing on the Delaware River. The Savior wanted us (so the Count said) to go by Minessing and not by Shomokin. I protested on several grounds and said, I would not let myself be governed by lot, especially in Matters, in which common Sense could decide. Do you contradict the Savior again, and will you follow your own blind Reason and Caprice? I and my brethren will do, what the Savior says, and that is our Plan, said the Count to me in a rage. I retorted, I Knew No such Savior as told men to lie. What! Do you call the Savior a liar? *Answer: Yes*, if he told you not to go to Shomockin again on your Return. The Savior I Know and worship, he is the Truth itself. You promised the Indians at Shomokin, on your Return to tell them the Purpose of your Coming and so forth. If you do not keep your promise, what will the Indians say? Will they not take you for a Liar and Suspect the whole Business, and be offended with you, and so put Obstacles in the way of the Missionaries. Do what you will. I serve the Government of Pennsylvania as an ambassador to the Indians: up to now I have kept a good Name among them, and will not become a Liar now, but will rather go home alone by way of Shomockin and keep my word. But I shall report your Imprudence and Bad Temper to Brother Spangenberg, so he may know who has spoiled the Game. (*Nota* Mr Spangenberg had been put in charge of missions) (You must know that throughout the journey we spoke good brotherly *Pennsylvanisch* together, which tongue the Count understood as well as I) Well I must have been mistaken, responded the Count, we will ask the savior again, who is right, you or I and he handed me 2 Lots—little bits of paper, which I without thinking, took and turned up: There was a *Yes* on one, and a *No* on the other. Now, said the Count, draw. The Question is, whether we are to go back by way of Shomockin: and if you draw the *yes*, we shall. So then I handed the *No* back to him and kept the *Yes*, without thinking; and he took it without noticing anything amiss: for our Heads were full of Rats Nests. He told me to read mine and it said *Yes:* The rest of the Party, who were looking on, saw everything and smiled, but they kept still. So we went Back again to Wajomock, and from there Nitschmann, Mack and his Wife with Andreas, Madame Montour's Son as guide went by way of Minessing to Bethlehem, while we went with the Count to Shomockin. Before we separated, we had an interview with Kachhawatchiky, the chief of the Shawanos Indians. This man was already over 70 Years old, and during the Count's stay had been very kind and considerate to him, and had used his Authority so skilfully with his otherwise bloodthirsty people, that no Harm had come to the Count and his Party, else (humanly speaking) the Count would have lost his Life. All the same this old man on my Arrival, which he had long been waiting for, was the Count's chief accuser, thanks to my old Acquaintanceship with him he had confidence in me. The old chief came to the Count's Tent. He presented a dignified appearance, had his best Apparel on (which he wore only on state occasions)   The Conversation we had with him had to be translated by me into Mohawk for Andreas Montour, and by him into Shawanose for the old chief. It was a serious conversation, and might have been sufficient to give the Count a full understanding of the Indian attitude to the Christian Religion. I made no notes of it, because there was nothing new in it for me, but the Count took it all down assiduously. This I do remember, that the old chief said: He believed in God, who created the Indians as well as the Europeans, only there was this Difference, that the former were created Brown the latter White, the latter prayed with Words, the former in their Hearts, which God saw and was very kind to the Indians. He himself was an Indian of God's creation and he was satisfied with his condition had no wish to be a European, above all he was a subject of the Iroquois, it did not behoove him to take up new Things without their Advice or Example. If the Iroquois chose to become Europeans, and learned to pray like them: he would have nothing to say against it, but *as a matter of fact* there was not much behind the Prayers of Europeans. They were mostly bad People. He liked the Indian Way of Life. God had been very kind to him even in his old Age and would continue to look well after him. God was better pleased with the Indians, than with the Europeans. It was wonderful how much he helped them. He thanked the Count for his good intentions, but firmly declined his proposals though in the most courteous manner.[29]

Count Zinzendorf was furious. He rounded out his impressions of this missionary journey with a salvo of hymns, dated October 15, "from the tent . . . in the Wilderness of Skehandowana, in Canada." There, uncontradicted, he sang of "the bloody-minded Shawnees" and called their King (Kakowatchiky) "the Dragon"—Satan.[30]

CHAPTER 18

... *Reports on the*
Late Unhappy Skirmish in Virginia

I

THE year 1743 saw Conrad Weiser beginning to take charge of Indian affairs. He had, of course, for a long time been more than a mere "Province Interpreter," though curiously enough he was this year for the first time called by that title, which was the only official one he was ever to have in his Indian work. He had been for many years what he himself described as an "ambassador to the Indians";[1] but even in this capacity he had merely put into operation policies for which other men were responsible. Now he was himself given authority. As the aging James Logan retired more and more into the background, Philadelphia looked to Conrad Weiser to collect, digest, and interpret the Indian news from all over the borders, as well as to advise what should be done about these increasingly urgent Indian problems. The government looked to him also, as it had never done to James Logan, to act in time of emergency on his own initiative in the field.

The occasion that first presents him in this new rôle is the crisis developing out of an affair in the Shenandoah Valley, known in contemporary documents as "the late unhappy Skirmish in Virginia." The story of that crisis will serve to show not only Weiser's manner of handling the diplomatic problems of the frontier, but also the place he occupied in the governmental machinery of Pennsylvania.

The story begins on the banks of the Susquehanna a few miles above Madame Montour's place, when the wailing Indian call, "Que, Que, Que" —the Dead Cry, as Conrad calls it—was heard drifting across the water. What this meant, Thomas McKee explained to the Governor and Council in a deposition dated January 24, 1743.[2]

McKee was an Indian trader who had a store at a Shawnee town near the Big Island, some seventy miles above Shamokin on the West Branch of the Susquehanna. About seven o'clock in the morning of January 12 or 13 (he had lost any clear reckoning of time, having traveled through the woods since then in fear of his life for three days and nights without stopping) he was approached by some Indians at his store who said they had heard the "Dead Hollow." Soon after, hearing the same disturbing call himself, he took a canoe and paddled over to the island whence the sound had come. While crossing the water, he heard

... the Indians belonging to the Town call over to those on the Island and ask them what was the Matter to which they answerd that the White Men had killd some of their Men And on this Depon[ts] coming to them on the Island He saluted them according to the usual Way saying How do you do my

145

ffriends at which they shook their Heads and made no Answer But went over
to the Shawna's Town And this Deponent further Saith that there were ten
in Number of those Indians and that they belongd to the five Nations And on
their Coming to Town immediately a Council was called   And this Deponent
attended at the Council house and was Admitted And on opening the Council
The Chiefs of those ten Indians made a Speech to the Shawnas of the Town
Wherein he acquainted them that a Party of Indians of the five Nations to the
number of thirty (of which these ten were a part) sometime last ffall came
down Sasquehannah in their Canoes to John Harris's and from thence proposed to Travel thro' Pennsylvania and the back parts of Maryland and
Virginia against some Southern Indians . . .

The Indian speaker went on to say that in Virginia they had suffered
an unprovoked attack by a large body of white men in which a number of
their warriors had been killed, and that they, these ten, had been despatched
to the Six Nations to give notice of what had happened and to ask what
was to be done next.

McKee, seeing by the way this news was received that his own life was
in danger, explained that the people of Pennsylvania were in no way responsible for what had happened in Virginia, and appealed to the Six
Nations not to forget their treaty of peace with Pennsylvania but to
suffer him to remain unharmed among them.

Whereupon one of the Shawna's [continues the deposition] observed that
the white People are all of one Colour and as one Body and in Case of Warr
would Assist one another—That one of the Shawna's asking the Warriors if
they had met this Deponents Men who had been sent out to Chiniotta for
Skins was answer'd by another Shawna Indian that it could not be so for if
they had met them they would have Cut them off That on hearing these
Discourses this Deponent rose up and called out an Old Shawna Indian with
whom he was best acquainted and took him to his Store made him a present of
two or three twists of Tobacco and desired him to press to the Indians in
Council their Treaty of Peace with Pennsylvania and the ill Consequences of
breaking it in Cutting him off As this Deponent apprehended he had great
reason to fear they intended That some short Time after the same Indian
calld this Deponent from his Store and told him that he had offer'd in Council
what he had requested and it was approv'd tho' it seemd disagreeable to some
of the Shawna's And in a short Time after this Deponent was inform'd by
a white Woman who had been taken Prisoner by the Indians in their Carolina
Warr's That it was left to the Shawna's to deal with him As they pleased
And that they were gone to hold a Council concerning him at some distance
from the Town for privacy And that if he did not make his Escape he would
certainly be cut off Upon which last Information together with the Observations he had made of their Behaviour he thought it not safe to trust his Life
in their Hands and notwithstanding a considerable Quantity of Goods which
he had carry'd up there to Trade He determind to withdraw and leave his
Effects among them and accordingly Communicated his designs to his Man
and they came off privately travelling by Night & Day thro' the uninhabited
parts of the Countrey till they apprehended themselves to be out of Danger
being out three Days & three Nights And further this Deponent Saith not

To the Governor and Council this was no mere boys' tale of adventure. It was a warning of extreme danger to the province. It it were true, as the Iroquois contended, that the Virginians had fired the first shot, then the vengeance of the Six Nations might be expected to follow, in the course of which Pennsylvania would very likely be dragged down with her southern neighbor into the horrors of a frontier war. The immediate fear, however, was not of the Six Nations. They had reaffirmed their treaty of peace with Pennsylvania only a few months ago, and were known to be sticklers for their engagements. The fear was that the Shawnees, under cover of loyalty to the Six Nations but actually under the influence of the French to whose interest many of them were already attached, might commit murder, rouse the whites to retaliate indiscriminately on Indians of whatever tribe, and so precipitate the dreaded Indian war. What that would mean to the province is easily imagined. The pacifist Assembly had prepared no measures of defense, and among the back inhabitants not one family in ten had a gun.

The Governor prepared an urgent message, dated January 25, for the Assembly:

To prevent the flame from spreading Wider I propose to dispatch a Messenger to Conrad Weiser the Province Interpreter with Directions to proceed forthwith to Shamokin and there to take the most proper measures for giving the Indians of the six Nations and all others in Alliance with Us the Strongest Assurances in my Name of the Continuance of our ffriendship so long as they shall maintain it on their Parts tho' I confess it will be a very nice Affair should they in the prosecution of their Revenge attempt to pass thro' the inhabited Parts of this Province to make War on our fellow Subjects of Virginia —I doubt not of your giving the proper Orders to the Treasurer for defraying what Expences shall be incurr'd on this Occasion [3]

To this the Assembly replied, January 26:

We highly approve of the Measures the Governor is pleased to Inform us he proposes to take "to prevent the fflame from spreading wider by dispatching a Messenger to Conrad Weiser . . ." And if the Governor will also be pleased by the same Messenger to propose to them his good Offices to Mediate and obtain a reconciliation before any violent Methods are taken it may prevent future Bloodshed and divert those sudden Resolutions which on the first Hearing of this unhappy Affair they may have been prompted to take . . .

Whatever Sums of Money shall become necessary to expend to these good purposes we shall cheerfully pay and give the proper Orders to the Treasurer to this End [4]

On the same day the Governor, consulting with James Logan, who advised him to leave all to Weiser's "good judgment," prepared a letter of instructions, enclosing McKee's deposition, and informing the Interpreter of conflicting accounts given of the Virginian affair, each side, white and red, contending that the other had fired the first shot.

The Governor wrote:

I shall not take upon me to determine which of the Accounts is the truest but as I have received a short Letter from Shickcallamys Son desiring my Advice in the Case and it is my Duty not only to preserve peace in my own Government but to be the Instrument as far as lyes in my power of restore[g] it to any other of his Majesties Subjects I desire that you will forthwith proceed to Shamokin and there Concert Measures with Shick Calamy to inform the six Nations the Shawna's and all the other Indians that are in Alliance with Us that we shall continue to be faithful to our Treatys with them so long as they observe them on their parts that we are extremely sorry for the Accident that has happend that we Wish the six Nations would rather endeavour to accomodate the Matter with the Governor of Virginia in an Amicable Way than make the Breach wider by having recourse to Arms and that I shall be glad to contribute all I can to bring it about   These are my Sentiments but as you are well acquainted with Indian affairs in General and are now fully informed of this particular as I am I leave it to your own Judgment how far it may be proper for You as our Agent to proceed in it. . . . I do not doubt but our back Inhabitants are very much alarmed at the late unhappy Skirmish in Virginia and I am not without apprehensions of their falling upon some of the Indians as they did once before but it will be very much in your power to quiet their Minds by informing them of our late Treaty with the six Nations and that there is not the least reason to apprehend any Injury from them or any other Indians at this Time [5]

II

Weiser received the Governor's instructions on the evening of January 30, and on the 31st he set out for Shamokin "over Backstone"—i.e., by way of Paxton—in company with Thomas McKee. Weiser was soon made aware how serious things were. On the 3rd of February, at a trader's house about twenty-five miles this side of Shamokin, he met a band of Shawnees.

In his report to the Governor Weiser wrote:

. . . they ran into the House when they see Us come And sat down in the same Corner of the House where their Arms were   every one of them had a Cutlass besides their Guns and one of them who was a Brother of Cheekaqueton had a Pistol,   The Indian Traders Wife told Us while we lighted from our Horses that these Shawonese had ill Designs and talkd very unfriendly,   I went into the House first & shook Hands with them   their Hands trembled and none of them hardly lookd to my face till I sat down and began to talk to them in the Mohawks Language,   they said they could not understand me, By that Time McKee and one John . . . . . . (who was pleased to accompany me to Shamokin from Backstone) came in   I desired them to tell the Shawonese that I was sent by the Governor of Pensilvania with a Message both to the Indians at Shamokin and thereabout as also to the six Nations about the unhappy accident that happend lately in Virginia, They seemed to be well pleased with that . . . they accompanied us to Shamokin where we arrived that Day after sunset,   Shikellimo and Olumapies were very glad to see me . . .[6]

Next day Weiser formally presented the message from the Governor to a gathering of some twenty-five Indians, including Saghsidowa ("a Chief of the Tuscorara") and "Lapapeton of the Delawares." He addressed himself first to Shickellamy, who was in mourning for a cousin killed in the Virginia skirmish, and presented him with two blankets in order to comfort him and wipe the tears from his eyes. Then, reminding the Indians of their treaty with Pennsylvania by which there had been established a "Road from Philadelphia to the 6 Nations on which at any Time Conrad Weiser and Shikellimo may travel and carry Messages from one to the other," [7] he presented the Governor's request that Shickellamy should bear his offer of mediation between the Six Nations and Virginia.

To the Shawnees, Weiser made the request that the goods taken from Thomas McKee and other traders be restored:

it would be violating the Treaty of ffriendship if they should suffer by You And if in Case you do not like their Stages amonst You send them home regular and unmolested. I laid down a String of Wampum. Dixi. I have no more to Say.[8]

He did not forget to send also a "Strowd Match Coat" to Kakowatchiky, reminding him of their friendly conference the previous fall at Wyoming, and expressing the hope that, as he lived "about half Way from Philadelphia to the Six Nations," he would "take Care of the Chain of friendship betwixt the six Nations and Pennsilvania and never do nor suffer any of his People to do an injury to the said Chain of ffriendship and always observe the good Counsel of the six Nations and the Governor of Pennsylvania." [9]

Weiser, mindful as he always was of the courtesies, had other matchcoats to dispose of. He gave one to the old Delaware chief, Olumapies (Sassoonan), saying that "as he had been always a good ffriend and observer of Treaties, the Governor sent this to him to cover his old body." [10]

Another matchcoat was given to Saghsidowa "to make him shoes to travel to Onandago with Shikellimo and his Son." [11]

Before he left Shamokin, Conrad tried to get to the bottom of the conflicting stories about the Virginia skirmish, and he believed he succeeded. He was given a very clear narrative of the affair by "one who calls Shikellimo his Grandfather he was present in the Engagement in Virginia," said Weiser in his report, "and was strictly examined by Shikellimo and exhorted to tell the Truth. Shikellimo and Sagsidowa told me that I might assure their Brother the Governor that it was the Truth." [12]

Governor Thomas did in fact accept it as truth, and negotiations were undertaken by Virginia on that assumption.

"If the Inhabitants of the back Parts of Virginia have no more Truth and Honesty than some of ours," wrote Governor Thomas to Colonel Gooch, "I should make no Scruple to prefer an Iroquois Testimony to theirs." [13]

Conrad's official report on the Virginia skirmish is to be found in the Minutes of the Provincial Council (Provincial Record, Volume K, pages 678–679). Another version,[14] never printed, has in it a trifle more of Conrad's hurried succinctness and color, but it omits much significant material and its skirmishing orthography does not make for easy reading. I therefore lay aside what was evidently Conrad's first rough draught of the report, in which the Indians when attacked are represented as taking their "dam Hawks" into their hands, and present here the politely edited official version which gives them "Hatchetts" instead.

Here is Conrad's story of the late unhappy skirmish in Virginia:

The Young Man told Shikellimo his Grandfather that when they (22 Onondagoe Indians and 7 Oneidoes) got over Potomack River no body would give them a mouthful of Victuals   They wanted to go to some Justice to have their Pass renewed but could find none   They travelld along in great want of Victuals   There was no more Deer to be killed and they had been Starved to Death if they not killed a Hog now and then which they did at Jonontore [15] ["the great Hills"]   on the other side of the said Hills they Laid down their Bundles and sent three of them to look for the Road they must go . . . Some while after they came to a big House   the Indians observed a great Number of People in the House they were invited to come in   the main Body staid out some Distance from the House   some of the oldest went in but more & more white People gathering the Indians without Door called to their ffriends to come away   The white People would not permit them to go but sent out a Captain with a Sword on his side to bring the others in which they refused   In the Mean time those that were in the House thought proper to show their Pass which they obtaind in Pennsylvania   But the white Men told them they must not go any farther Upon which the Indians went out of the House   the Man with the Sword endeavourd to Stop them by force and drew his Sword when the others saw the naked Sword they made a field Cry and took up their Arms in order to defend themselves but were Commanded by their Captain to be quiet till they were hurt and to Let the white People begin Violence, the Indians did not mind the Man with the naked Sword but went away and took up their Bundles and travelled all night   they went on one side of the Road towards the Hills a Good way and Lodged there two Nights consulting what to do and some hunted for Deer,   They resolved to proceed on their Journey and set out in the Morning and travelled all Day peaceably and at Night went again toward the Hills for Lodging   Next morning early a white Man came to their ffires and counted them all   They asked where he was a going   he said a hunting   they mistrusted him very much when he went off toward the Hills after he got over a little Ridge of a Hill he went the other way and ran as fast as he could which one of the Indians that went after him as a Spy saw   The Indians hasted away and when they got into the Road again two Boys that were in the Rear heard a Great Talk & Noise of Horses and looked about and saw a Great number of white Men on horseback and they called to the foremost that there was the white Men a coming, who order'd them to come up, then the Boys ran and the white Men fir'd at them but missed them   The Captain of the Indians seeing the Boys receiv'd no hurt and a white Colour flying told the Indians to be quiet for that a white Colour was always a token of Peace with the white Men,   Whilst the Indians were laying down their Bundles and their Captain talk'd to them not to fire till the white Men had hurt them the white Men alighted from their Horses just by and fired the second Time and Killed two upon the Spott one of which was Shikellimo's Cousin   The Indians then made a field Cry and were commanded by their Captain to fight for Life who after he had fired off his Gun took to his Hatchett and exhorted the Stoutest to follow him and they ran in amongst the white People and did Execution with their Hatchetts which put the white Men to flight immediately But the Captain would not suffer them to pursue them, Told them they did not come to fight white Men but the Cawtabaws Upon which the Indians took up their Dead and wounded and went off about two Miles where they gave Physick to the wounded one of which died there and there remained four more wounded three of them not very dangerously but the fourth was very bad, they missed one out of their number A relation of him ran and looked for him, he was seen to pursue the white Men farther than the Rest, he was found shot through one of his ffeet and was brought up to the rest and is like to do well He said that he saw two white Men drop down not far from him and rise up again and drop down again and so on, That he had shot several Arrows into the white Mans back before he received that Shot Next morning the Captain sent some of the Indians to the Place where they had been engaged they found Eight white Men upon the spot whom they stripped and several Horses with some Provision grazing thereabouts they sat down for the sake of the Provision for which they stood in great Want The Indian Captn dispatched Ten of his Men to Onondagoe himself with the Rest and wounded went up along the River unto the Mountains to come home that Way The Action happen'd near the River called by the Indians Gahidoghson—[16]

III

There is appended to the unedited manuscript of the narrative a curious note that flashes a warm light on Conrad's personal relations with the Indians. It is this:

"memd. PS to buy a wooden pipe with a Civerin over it and the best I Can. to answer Saghsidowas dream" [17]

To answer Saghsidowa's dream! It was not uncommon among the Indians (who have an equally strong sense of propriety and humor) when they wanted to get something by the way of gift from a friend, not to ask for it outright but to say they had dreamed of receiving it, and confidently to await the issue.[18] There are numbers of instances of this dream diplomacy. Sometimes the dreams were reciprocal. Such an interchange is told of William Johnson and Chief Hendrick of the Mohawks. According to tradition, Hendrick dreamed that Johnson had given him a scarlet uniform. Johnson produced the uniform, and with it a dream of his own. He had dreamed that Hendrick had given him five hundred acres of good Mohawk land. The old chief did what was expected of him, but said to his friend, "I will never dream with you again." [19]

Oral tradition is not a safe guide to the truth. The Johnson-Hendricks tale is likely a local version of a stock joke circulated among Indian traders (like our modern "smoking-room stories") with variations attaching it to any famous names that came handy to the teller and gave it special point in a given locality. Pennsylvania has a variant of the dream story attached to the names of Conrad Weiser and Shickellamy.

A very old tradition is our sole authority for the statement that one day Shickellamy said to Conrad Weiser: "I have had a dream. I dreamed that Tarachiawagon gave me a new rifle."

Conrad, who owed much of his success to his strict observance of Indian etiquette, is said to have answered the dream with the rifle, and then to have spoken for himself.

"I, too, have had a dream," he said. "I dreamed that Shickellamy gave me an island in the Susquehanna," and he indicated the Island of Que at the mouth of Penn's Creek, on the site of what is now the town of Selinsgrove.

The old chief, we are told, matched Weiser's politeness, but, "Conrad," he said, "let us never dream again."

CHAPTER 19

... *Shows John Bartram*
the Remains of the Deluge

I

THE responsibility for peace or war between Virginia and the Six Nations was set squarely on the shoulders of Conrad Weiser.

On the 22nd of February, 1743, Governor Thomas wrote to him expressing the hope that he would not find it too difficult to persuade the Indians to lay aside all thought of vengeance now that Virginia showed herself disposed to a reconciliation. "I request," said the Governor, "that you will continue to take the most proper measures that shall occur to you for accomplishing So good a Work." [1]

Weiser let nothing slip. On the 9th of April, when Shickellamy with his son and Saghsidowa returned from Onondaga to Shamokin, the Interpreter was there to receive them. Next day the official message brought by them from the United Nations was delivered in open council.

The message, as Weiser records it, was stern but judicious.

"Brethren, the Shawonese," said Saghsidowa, speaking as the voice of the Six Nations: "You believe too many Lies and are too forward in Action You shall not pretend to Revenge our People that have been killed in Virginia, We are the Chief of all the Indians, Let your Ears and Eyes be open towards Us and order your Warriours to stay at home as we did ours

"Brother Onas," he continued, addressing Weiser as representing the Governor of Pennsylvania: "Your Back Inhabitants are people given to Lies and raising false Stories, Stop up their Mouths you can do it with one word, Let no false Stories be told It is dangerous to the Chain of ffriendship" [2]

The speaker thanked Brother Onas for his efforts at mediation, and assured him that the Six Nations would observe their ancient custom, which was not to avenge a first injury, however serious it might be, but to wait and leave an opening for peace; if, however, the injury was repeated, the United Nations would rise and knock their enemies down with a blow. "We have order'd our Warriours," said Saghsidowa, "with the strongest Words to sit down and not to revenge themselves Therefore Brother Onas go on with Courage in your Mediation." [3]

Shickellamy had brought strings of wampum from Onondaga to be sent to all the towns on the Susquehanna as a mandate to stop their warriors from going out against the people of Virginia.

From old Chief Kakowatchiky the speaker brought a personal message confirmed by four strings of wampum:

Brother the Governor of Pennsylvania

The Place where I live and the Neighbouring Country has been over-shadow'd of late by a very dark Cloud I looked with a pitiful Eye upon the poor Women and Children and then looked upon the Ground all along for Sorrow in a Miserable Condition because of the poor Women and Children In all that Dark Time a Message from You found the Way to Shamokin and when it was delivered to Us the Dark cloud was dispersed and the sun imediately began to Shine and I could see at a great Distance and saw your good Will and kind Love to the Indians & the white People I thank you therefore Brother Onas for your kind Message I am now able to Comfort the poor Women & Children.[4]

But the dark was not completely dispelled. Shickellamy was less hopeful than Kakowatchiky. He told Weiser in conversation that he believed there would be war after all, unless the government of Virginia were brought to undertake the proper steps for peace. There was a certain ceremonial to be observed. Since the Virginians had struck a hatchet into the head of the Six Nations, said Shickellamy,

The Governor of Virginia must wash off the Blood first and take the Hatchet out of their Head and Dress the Wound (according to Custom he that Struck first must do it) and the Council of the six Nations will speak to him & be reconciled to him and bury that affair in the Ground that it may never be seen nor heard of any more so long as the World stands.[5]

When Governor Thomas received Weiser's report, he sent it on to Colonel Gooch of Virginia with a covering letter in which he ventured to hint that there were two steps to be taken by Virginia in the interests of peace: One was to remove the hatchet that had been struck into the Six Nations' head; the other was to settle the land dispute that had been hanging fire since October 1736, when Weiser had drawn attention to it in a message dictated to him by the chiefs of the Six Nations.

A reply came quickly from Colonel Gooch in Virginia:

A journey to Albany at this Season to take the Hatchet out of their Heads is a Concession we would willingly avoid And therefore we request that You will be pleas'd to send your honest Interpreter once more to the Indian Chiefs and if Possible prevail with them to accept through Your Hands a Present from Us of £100 Sterl value in such Goods as you think proper as a token of our sincere Disposition to preserve Peace and friendship with them And as an Earnest that we will not fail to send Commissioners next Spring at the Time and to the place that shall be agreed upon to treat with them concerning the Lands in Dispute—[6]

It was on this embassy from Virginia that Conrad Weiser made his third journey to Onondaga.

II

He left home, July 5, with two companions, men whom the British authorities were encouraging to explore and report on this northern region on which the French were believed to be casting covetous eyes. These were John Bartram and Lewis Evans, who had arrived the day before from Philadelphia by way of "the Flying Hills" (the South Mountains near the Schuylkill), and had spent the night at Weiser's.

John Bartram was a Quaker farmer with a tireless mind and body and with a genius for botany. The place where he collected and grew plants from all over the world, is still, as he called it, a "Garden of Delight" to the many who visit it today in Philadelphia. Lewis Evans, the map-maker, was a less romantic figure: "an ingenious man," as Bartram was afterwards reported to have described him, but "not agreeable to the Indians nor Mr Weiser." Nevertheless Lewis Evans put "Wisors" on the first good map of Pennsylvania.

They were to pick up a man to help carry their provisions as far as Shamokin, but, finding him unable to get his horse shod that day, they rode over to William Parsons' plantation at Stonykill, not far from Round Head, and spent the night at his house.

Next morning they crossed the first ridge of the Blue Mountains, and "dined by a spruce swamp," as Evans tells us,[7] in the valley Count Zinzendorf had named Anton's Wilderness. Thence, following the Shamokin Trail, they passed through the two gaps of the Swatara and turned left up a "great ridge about a mile steep, and terrible stoney most of the way,"[8] where they had an adventure with "an enraged rattle snake."

They came down off the Broad Mountain by a steep path (near Good Spring) amidst "large craggy rocks,"[9] and camped that night by Laurel (now Pine) Creek. They slept little, being, as Bartram says, "grievously stung all night with small gnats."[10] In the morning they traveled more easily down a "pleasant and fruitful valley"[11] between two streams, where the trail kept a slight elevation—sufficient, as the Indians say, "to keep the moccasins dry." This valley, noted Evans, "would make a pretty settlement"—an estimate that time has confirmed, as the traveler today through the Lykens Valley will agree. They found a fishing place in the Gap where Pine Creek cuts through the Mahantango Mountain, and they dined a little farther on at the Double Eagle,[12] near the site of the modern Klingerstown. The afternoon was spent in a maze of valleys and uplands that has been described only confusedly by early travelers. At length they came to the top of a hill whence they "had a fair prospect of the river Susquehannah," and at night they slept beside the river near the mouth of Mahanoy Creek.

Next day, July 8, turning inland again, they came to the hill overlooking Shamokin, where Count Zinzendorf's United Brethren had descended holding to one another's coat tails a few months before. Now there was trouble again, this time with the pack horse.

"It was so steep," writes Lewis Evans, "we were obliged to hold the horse which carried our baggage both by the head and the tail, to prevent his stumbling headlong."[13]

When the travelers alighted from their horses at Shamokin (a town centering in some eight huts beside the Susquehanna, but with scattered settlements extending over seven or eight hundred acres between the river and the mountains) they were shown where to lay their baggage, and were at once given food: "a bowl of boiled squashes cold; this I thought poor entertainment," writes Bartram, "but before I came back I had learnt not to despise good *Indian* food. This hospitality is agreeable to the honest simplicity of ancient times, and is so punctually adhered to, that not only what is already dressed is immediately set before a traveller, but the most pressing business is postponed to prepare the best they can get for him, keeping it as a maxim that he must always be hungry . . ." [14]

On the 10th of July they set off again, accompanied now by Shickellamy and his son. The route they took was much the same as that followed by Weiser in 1737. Their worst enemy was rain, and from that the Indians protected them, when necessary, by peeling from the trees sheets of bark, seven feet long and three feet wide, setting four forked sticks in the ground, putting cross-poles on top of them, and laying the bark over all: making what Bartram calls "a good tight shelter in warm weather." [15]

On the morning of the 12th, not far beyond the site of the present town of Muncy, they met eight Shawnees on horseback, armed with rifles, pistols, and sabers, [16] traveling from Allegheny to Wyoming on important business. "We turned back with them," writes Bartram,

. . . to the adjacent wood, and sate down together under a shady oak; the *squaw* which they brought to wait upon them kindled a fire to light their pipes; our Interpreter and *Shickealamy* set down with them to smoke the customary civility when two parties meet; *Conrad Weiser* understanding they were some chiefs of the Shawanese, acquainted them with our business at *Onondaga*, a compliment they were so well pleased with, that they gave us the *Tobay*, a particular *Indian* expression of approbation, and which is very difficult for a white man to imitate well; after half an hour's grave discourse several of them went to catch the horses, and one of the principal men made a handsome speech, with a pleasant well composed countenance, to our interpreter, to the following effect: "That they were sensible with what an unwearied diligence he had hitherto been instrumental in preserving peace and good harmony between the *Indians* and the *White People*, and that as they could not but now commend the prudence and zeal with which he had effected this laudable purpose, so they earnestly entreated and sincerely hoped he would still persevere in the same endeavours and with the same success, and that his good offices may never be wanting on any future occasion." [17]

Taking leave of the Shawnees, Weiser's party rode on to Loyalsock Creek, on the far side of which they rode through the French Town, now deserted, where a few months before Weiser had introduced Count Zinzendorf to Madame Montour and her painted son Andrew. They camped that night on Lycoming Creek, fifty yards from a hunter's cabin in which lodged two Indian men, a squaw, and a child.

The severe test to which Conrad's tact was put that evening, is told by John Bartram:

. . . the men came to our fire and made us a present of some venison, and invited Mr *Weisar*, Shickcalamy and his son, to a feast at their cabin. It is incumbent on those who partake of a feast of this sort, to eat all that comes to their share or burn it: now *Weisar* being a traveller was intitled to a double share, but he not being very well, was forced to take the benefit of a liberty indulged him, of eating by proxy, and called me, but both being unable to cope with it, *Lewis* came in to our assistance, notwithstanding which we were hard set to get down the neck and throat, for these were allotted us; and now we had experienced the utmost bounds of their indulgence, for *Lewis* ignorant of the ceremony of throwing the bone to the dog, tho' hungry dogs are generally nimble, the *Indian* more nimble, laid hold of it first, and committed it to the fire, religiously covering it over with hot ashes. This seems to be a kind of offering, perhaps first fruits to the Almighty power to crave future success in the approaching hunting season, and was celebrated with as much decency and more silence, than many superstitious ceremonies . . .[18]

When they set off next day, the party was increased by the two men who had been their hosts the evening before, and who now accompanied them as far as the Indian town of Tioga (Athens), which they reached July 16. The greeting they received here was more than friendly. As they crossed the Cayuga Branch (now known as the Chemung River) to Tioga Point, they were welcomed by the beating of an Indian drum, and were escorted nearly a mile to the town with this sound pulsing in their ears. It did not cease till they had unsaddled their horses.

Their lodging for the night was a fine house, thirty feet long, its floors covered with long grass freshly cut and spread for their comfort. Visitors called, sat in polite silence, and smoked their pipes, "one of which was six foot long, the head of stone, the stem a reed." [19]

By this time the travelers had passed the most dreaded part of their journey, the "Dismal Wilderness" of the Lycoming Valley; but there were troubles enough ahead. North of Owego were mountains and swamps and thickets, cliffs to be skirted on the very edge of rushing waters, and streams to be forded "backwards and forwards," as Bartram puts it, with infinite weariness both to horses and to men. But when at last they had crossed the divide and had left behind them Gooseberry Hill, they dismounted from their horses and reveled in the feel of good, springy turf under foot, as they swung down the long, rolling hills that delighted the traveler then, as they delight the traveler now, approaching old Onondaga or modern Syracuse.

They passed the mountain on which, according to a legend, "religiously held for truth" among the Indians,[20] a maiden sent from heaven first planted corn, squashes, tobacco, and pumpkins, and showed a poor hunter where to find them and how to use them so that his starving people might have food and comfort.

The sudden change from rocky wilderness to the park-like country in which they now found themselves amazed them all.

. . . here we walked and looked about us, [writes Bartram] having not had such an opportunity for two days, during which time we had a fine prospect over the vale of the great mountain we had just crossed, and which differed so remarkably from all I had ever been upon before, in its easy and fruitful ascent and descent, in its great width, every where crowned with noble and lofty woods, but above all, in its being intirely free from naked rocks and steep precipices.

From these remarks, one might be naturally led to imagine, that the Waters at the flood gradually ebbed and retired on each side, towards the river *St. Lawrence* and *Susquenannah*, the very next ridges on either side being narrower, steeper, and some rocks washed bare, and so all the adjacent ridges the farther they are from this, appear to be more washed, more composed of great banks of craggy rocks and tremendous precipices, the soil more carried off, mighty rocks tumbled down, and those left appearing as if piled up in a pyramid and hereby preserved from a share in the awful ruin below among their fellows;   the soil being so perfectly washed from their root, as evidently no longer to support them. After having enjoyed this enchanting prospect and entertaining hypothesis, we descended easily for several miles over good land producing sugar-maples . . .[21]

Lewis Evans writes as warmly of this new land:

This country is varied with pleasant, swelling knolls, brooks and little lakes. In its vegitation it abounds with sweet-maple, linden, birch, elm, white pines in some places;   and with gooseberry under-woods on the north side of all the ridges.

Looking back on the desolate ranges which they had crossed, his mind was as much agitated as Bartram's by the problem of their origin:

They furnish endless Funds for Systems and Theories of the World, but the most obvious to me was, That this Earth was made of the Ruins of another, at the Creation. Bones and Shells which escaped the Fate of softer animal Substances, we find mixt with the old Materials and elegantly preserved in the loose Stones and rocky Bases of the highest of these Hills. These Mountains existed in their present elevated Height before the Deluge, but not so bare of Soil as now. The further Ridges which are much the largest and highest, proceeding from the Inclination of the whole toward the sea, are of very rich Land, even on the Tops;   while the very Vallies, on the hither side seem swept of all Soil. Their Height no doubt rendered them less exposed to that general Devastation, and preserved them unhurt, while the Soil and the loose Parts of lower Hills and Vallies, agitated by a greater Weight of water, were born away suspended in the dashing Waves, and thrown downwards in Seratas of different Kinds, as the Billows roll'd from different Parts: still obvious in our lower Lands Northward & Westward of Rariton and Delaware." [22]

Conrad Weiser and his party passed near a shallow lake (one of the Tully Lakes) on the east side of which Deganaweda is said to have shown the Onondagas by his bundle of sticks how the Five Nations could make themselves indestructible. In the midst of his demonstration (from which, as I was told a few years ago at Onondaga, it is a tradition that the actual founding of the League is to be dated), Deganaweda was disturbed by the noise of a great flock of geese on the water. He stopped for a moment and walked over to the bank.

"Go away," he said to the geese; "all of you, go."

At once the geese flew away; but in going they took so much water that the lake has been shallow ever since.[23]

The signs of cultivation that now appeared seemed to our travelers like glimpses of a golden age. Some of the maple trees had been tapped for syrup. Plum trees and apple trees, well laden with fruit, were ringed with bushes—planted there, so Bartram supposed, to keep little Onondaga boys and girls from eating the unripe fruit.[24]

The people among whom they soon found themselves, as they rode down into the "charming vale" of Onondaga, were what might have been expected of an Eden. The warm hand-clasps of the men, the modesty of the women, and above all the gentleness of men, women, and children (not a sign of quarreling, the travelers tell us, was seen on any side during all their stay) seemed to these pilgrims from the disturbed backwoods of Pennsylvania like some blessed glimpse of a Lost Horizon.

On the 21st of July they reached Cachiadachse, "the first town of the Onondagoes." [25]

Bartram writes:

> . . . here we halted and turned our horses to grass, while the inhabitants cleared a cabin for our reception;   they brought us victuals, and we dispatched a messenger immediately to *Onondago* to let them know how near we were, it being within 4 miles. All the *Indians*, men, women and children came to gaze at us and our horses, the little boys and girls climbed on the roofs of their cabins, about ten in number to enjoy a fuller view.[26]

See them there: black-haired, brown-skinned, clear-eyed, roly-poly Onondaga youngsters, two hundred years ago, clinging with bare feet to the bark of their fathers' houses to look at a better sight than any circus could give their descendants at Syracuse today. The travelers from Pennsylvania were indeed a sight worth climbing to the housetops to see. To these Indian children the sight of men with pale faces and peaked features was strange enough. But the best sight of all was Conrad Weiser.

His mere presence was interesting: the great peacemaker was already a legend among the people of the Six Nations. And the sharpest thrill of all (somewhat terrifying, as it appeared later) to children of a race whose men had hairless faces, came from the sight of Weiser's Ephrata beard, bobbing horrifically on his bosom as he moved. As late as 1755 King Hendrick's Mohawk counselors fled at the sight of Anabaptist long beards in Pennsylvania. But this day, in the year of grace 1743, at Onondaga, the children expected to be frightened—and to like it. Here was Tarachiawagon, as everyone knew, the god-man who was on earth but not quite of it; and Iroquois boys and girls, even the best among them, would have been disappointed if they had not felt terror mingled in due degree with the awe that seized them as they gazed upon the "Holder of the Heavens," swinging his beard (six years longer than it had been in 1737) through the trees.

CHAPTER 20

. . . *Takes the Hatchet out of the Head of the Six Nations*

I

THE messenger returned to say that the house of Annawaraogon, which was the Council House, had been appointed for their lodging. Accordingly they mounted their horses and set out again, riding by an easy descent into the Iroquois capital, Sagogsaanagechtheyky, which they found to be a town of some forty long houses scattered on either side of a creek for a distance of two or three miles, the bark "cabins" being separated by fields of corn and peas and squash. It was not so impressive as the walled town which Count Frontenac had destroyed near this site in 1696 (some of the posts of which were still standing), but it presented a welcome enough appearance to the travelers.

When they alighted at the Council House, they found the chiefs already gathered there to receive them, "which they did," writes Bartram, "with a grave chearful complaisance, according to their custom; they shew'd us where to lay our baggage, and repose ourselves during our stay with them; which was in the two end apartments of this large house. The *Indians* that came with us, were placed over against us: this cabin is about 80 feet long, and 17 broad, the common passage 6 feet wide; and the apartments on each side 5 feet, raised a foot above the passage" [1]—this by means of square-hewed timbers and joists. ". . . on these joists they lay large pieces of bark, and on extraordinary occasions spread matts made of rushes, this favour we had."

Boards or slabs of bark separated the apartments. There were shelves overhead where their bowls were set after they had eaten. Each apartment had its own fireplace, and above it a hole to let out the smoke. In rainy weather the hole could be covered with a piece of bark, which was easily moved into place or pushed aside again with a pole.

After the travelers had been refreshed with a dish of dried eels boiled in hominy, Canasatego, Caheshcarowano, and others came to smoke a pipe with them and inquire after their friends in Philadelphia.

At night, when they had lain down to sleep and their fire was almost burnt out, they were roused to enjoy the antics of an Indian comedian. A man in an odd dress and wearing a wooden false-face colored black came in and pranced about, shaking a rattle and braying like an ass.

"I asked *Conrad Weiser*," writes Bartram, "who as well as myself lay next the alley, what noise that was? and *Shickalamy* the *Indian* chief, our companion, who I supposed, thought me somewhat scared, called out, lye still *John*, I never heard him speak so much plain *English* before." [2]

By the light of their own fire, which an Indian boy accompanying the comedian had rekindled, they could see that the masker had a nose four or five inches long, a grinning mouth with long teeth, and eye circles ringed with brass and gleaming with white paint. From his crown hung strings of buffalo hair and ropes of plaited corn husks, which he brushed aside now and then to let his audience get a better view of his "ill-favoured phyz." For some time this "jackpudding" bounced about, striking "antick" postures and holding out his hand for gifts of tobacco; but when the boy attending him rapped on the floor in sign that the fun had gone on long enough, the hobgoblin sprang through the door and disappeared.

The next day being showery, Weiser and his party kept within doors and received callers. Tocanuntie came ("the black Prince of Onondago") and Caxhayion (Zinzendorf's friend), who expressed their satisfaction at Weiser's advent, since, they said, he never came without bringing good news from their brethren in Philadelphia.

Conrad smiled and observed that "it was enough to kill a Man to come such a Long & bad Road over Hills, Rocks, Old Trees, and Rivers, and to fight through a Cloud of Vermine, and all kinds of Poisen'd Worms and creeping things, besides being Loaded with a disagreeable Message." [3]

They laughed, enjoying a bit of friendly banter from one whom they had already come to look upon as "the Guardian of all the Indians." [4]

It was on this same day, to change the note for a moment, that a young Irish trader, William Johnson by name, living among the Six Nations farther east, was summoned for illicit trading in rum and strowds with the French and Indians. We shall hear more of this young gentleman's live-wire activities before we have done with Weiser's story.

On the following day, July 23, Bartram and Evans went off to see the famous salt spring, where the Indian women boiled the water down to salt (a pound to the gallon) and where the brine-covered bushes on the bank glittered in the sunshine "like flakes of Ice, or Snow." [5]

II

Meanwhile Weiser gave his attention to treaty business. He made an appointment with Canasatego to meet him in the woods, and there, taking the chief into his confidence and explaining all his wampum belts, he asked his advice on the best manner of presenting his affairs before the Great Council. Canasatego retired to consult with Caheshcarowano, the head chief of the Confederacy. In the afternoon Weiser and Shickellamy were summoned to meet Caheshcarowano. When they came, they were surprised to find themselves in the presence of all the chiefs of Onondago.

From this point on I shall quote extensively from Weiser's official Journal, which is valuable for the striking and intimate description it gives of the working of the League machinery, from the preparation of the agenda by a kind of permanent committee composed of all the chiefs at Onondaga, to the ritual and routine of the Great Council itself, called now into special session to consider the issue of peace or war with Virginia.

Tocanontie [writes Weiser] spoke to me after this Manner Brother the Chiefs of Onondago are all of one Body and Soul and of one Mind   therefore Canassatego and Caheshcarowano have acquainted us with the whole of what had passed betwixt You and Canassatego in the Bushes you have done very well and prudent to inform the Onondagoes of your Message before the rest of the Counsellors meet since it Concerns chiefly the Onondagoes and it will altogether be left to Us by the Council of the united Nations to answer your Message be therefore not surprized in seeing Us all Met in Council un-expectedly and explain the Paper to Us you have from our Brother the Governor of Pennsylvania which I did accordingly and acquainted them with the whole Message they seemed to be very well pleased and promised they would put every thing in such Posture that when the Council of the united Nations arrive I should have an Answer soon and such an one as they did not doubt would be satisfactory to the Governor of Pennsylvania and Assaryquoa [the Governor of Virginia] . . .[6]

On the 24th, the "Private Council," as Weiser calls it, sat again, and sent for Jonnhaty, "the Captain of the Unhappy Company that had the Skirmish last winter in Virginia . . . he was desired to tell the Story from the beginning how every thing happen'd which he did he seem'd to be a very thoughtful and honest Man and took a deal of Time in telling the Story . . . In the Evening the Cajuga Deputies arrived." [7]

The days of waiting while the deputies, summoned by runners, gathered in from the distant nations of the Confederacy, were filled with interest enough for Weiser. On the 25th Jonnhaty gave a feast, to which Conrad and Shickellamy were invited. The other guests were "the Chiefs of the Town about 18 in number the ffeast Consisted of a Cask of Rum of about two Gallons several Songs were sung before the ffeast begun in which they thanked Assaryquoa [Virginia, in the person of Weiser] for visiting them they also thanked Onas (the Governor of Pennsilvania) [in the person of Shickellamy] for conducting Assaryquoa and Showing him the Way to Onondago . . ." [8] Formal healths were drunk to the two English Governors, and responded to by Weiser, who wished long life to "the wise Councellors of the united Nations." After that "the Kettle was handed round with a wooden Spoon in it every one took so much as he pleased." [9]

On the 26th Weiser went to see some Nanticokes who had come to Onondaga on an embassy from their nation. Maryland had been complain-ing about a disturbance made by some of them at the instigation of the Shawnees. The Nanticokes had with them an interpreter who suffered under the handicap of being quite ignorant of any of the Six Nations lan-guages into which his people's message had to be translated. Weiser, how-ever, finding that the young man could speak some English, agreed to interpret for him before the Council.

The deputies from the Oneidas and Tuscaroras arrived on the 28th. Among them Weiser found an old chief, Aquoyiota, whom he describes as "an old Acquaintance of mine." Is it possible that this was the Caquayo-dighe from whom in 1723 young Conrad Weiser, Hans Lawyer, and Peter Wagoner had bought land on the border of the Oneida country?

The 29th The Onondago's held another Private Council and sent for me and Shikellimo every thing was discoursed over again and we agreed that Canassatego should speak in behalf of the Government of Virginia and the Wampums were divided into so many parts as there were Articles to be spoken of and the Goods were to be divided between the family's in Mourning and the Publick Council of the united Nations A Messenger was sent to hasten the Mohawks away from the Oneider Lake where it was supposed they tarried they arrived five in Number.[10]

What follows is of exceptional interest, giving as it does an eyewitness account, made by a sympathetic and understanding observer, of the ancient council ritual in its appropriate setting of national business.

The 30th about noon the Council then met at our Lodging and declared themselves compleat and a deal of Ceremonies Passed ffirst the Onondagoes rehearsed the begining of the Union of the five Nations Praised their Grand-fathers Wisdom in establishing the Union or Alliance by which they became a formidable Body that they (now living) were but ffools to their wise ffathers, yet protected and accompanied by their ffathers Spirit and then the discourse was directed to the Deputies of the several Nations and to the Messengers from Onas and Assaryquoa then to the Nanticokes to welcome them all to the Council ffire which was now kindled A String of Wampum was given by Tocanontie in behalf of the Onondagoes to wipe off the Sweat from their (the Deputies & Messenger's) Bodies and God, who had protected them all against the Evil Spirits in the Woods who were always doing mischief to people travelling to Onondago, was praised All this was done by way of a Song the Speaker walking up & down in the House [11] After this the Deputies & Messengers held a Conference by themselves and appointed Aquoyiota to return thanks for their kind reception with another String of Wampum Aquoyiota repeated all that was said in a Singing way walking up and down in the House added more in Praise of their wise ffathers and of the happy union repeated all the Names of those Ancient Chiefs that establish'd it they no Doubt said he are now God's and dwell in heaven then Proclamation was made that the Council was now Opened and Assaryquoa was to speak next morning in the same House and due Attendance should be given All those Indian Ceremonies took up that afternoon Jo-haas from every Nation was given—The 31st about Ten of the Clock the Council of the united Nations met and Zila Woolien gave me Notice that they were now ready to hear Onas and Assaryquoa Speak I called Canassatego and desired him to speak for me in Open Council as I would tell him Article by Article (according as to what was first agreed upon) which he Proclaim'd to the Council and they approv'd of it because they knew it required some Ceremonies with which I was not acquainted The Speaker then begun and made the following Narrative: "Brethren the United Nations you Togarg Hogon our Brother Nittaruntaquaa our Son also Sonnawantowano and Tuscaroro our Younger Sons you also our absent Brother Ounghcarrydawy dionen Horarrawe Know Ye. that what was transacted last Winter at this ffire by Us and our Brother Onas on behalf of our Brother the Governor of Virginia known to Us by the Name of Assaryquoa was all carefully put down in Writing and sent to Assaryquoa our Brother by our Brother Onas upon the Receipt whereof our Brother Assary-quoa wrote again to our Brother Onas and thank'd him kindly for his Mediation in healing the Breach occasion'd by the Late unhappy Skirmish and requested the Continuance of our Brother Onas's good Offices and that the Interpreter might be sent to Sagogsaanagechtheyky with such Instructions as Onas our Brother (who knowing the Nature Customs and the very Heart of his Brethren) shall think fit This is all what I have to say about what is past Now you will hear our Brother Assaryquoa himself who has been brought to our ffire by our Brother Onas—Then I took up a Belt of Wampum and told the Speaker Canassatego a few Words and he proceeded and Spoke in behalf of the Governor of Virginia as follows

—1.—Brethren The United Nations now met in Council at Sagoghsaanagechtheyky when I heard of the late unhappy Skirmish that happen'd in my Country between some of your Warriours and my People I was Surprized I could not account for it to my self why such a thing should happen between Brethren This Belt of Wampum therefore I give to the ffamilys in Mourning amongst You my Brethren at Sagoghsaanagechtheyky, to condole with them and moderate their Grief. The Belt was given and the usual Sound of Approbation was returned by the whole House—2.—Then I handed another Belt to the Speaker and Spoke to him he spoke much the same as before and desired that that Belt might be given to the ffamilys in Mourning at Niharuntaquoa or the Oneidos for the same Use Thanks was given again by the whole Assembly with the usual Sound then I handed a large Belt to the Speaker—3.—Brethren of the united Nations the Sun kept his Beams from Us and a dark Cloud overshadow'd us when the Late unhappy Skirmish happen'd between my People and Your Warriors My People are charged with having begun Hostilities I will not Dispute with You about it It is most certain that an Evil Spirit which governs in Darkness has been the Promoter of it for Brethren will never fall out without giving Ear to such Evil Spirits I and the Old and wise People of my Country highly Disapproved the Action I therefore came here to your ffire to fetch home the Hatchet from an Apprehension that it might have been unadvisedly made Use of by my People and I assure You by this Belt of Wampum that there shall be no more use made of it for the future but it shall be buried In Confirmation of what I say I give You this Belt of Wampum The solemn Cry by way of thanksgiving & Joy was repeated as many Times as there were Nations present Then the Speaker proceeded—4.—Brethren the united Nations this String of Wampum serves to bury all that unhappy Accident under the Ground and to Lay a heavy stone upon it to keep it under for Ever He laid down some Strings of Wampum The usual Cry was given—5.—Brethren the united Nations these Strings of Wampum serve to dispell the Dark Cloud that overshadowed Us for some Time that the Sun may shine again and we may be able to see one another with Pleasure He laid down som Strings of Wampum The usual Cry by way of Approbation & Thanks was given The Speaker proceeded—6.—Brethren the united Nations these Strings of Wampum serve to take away the Bitterness of your Spirit & to purge You from the abundance & overflow of your Gall All wise People judge it to be a dangerous Distemper when Men have too much of that it gives an Open Door to evil Spirits to enter in and I cannot help believing that my Brethren the united Nations are often sick of that Distemper he laid down four Rows of Wampum the usual Cry was given by way of Approbation the Speaker proceeded—7.—Brethren the united Nations this String of Wampum serves to mend the Chain of ffriendship again which was lately hurt and was in danger of being broke Let good understanding & true

ffriendship be restor'd and subsist among us for Ever   Layd four Rows of
Wampum   the usual Cry of Approbation was given and the Speaker
proceeded—8.—Brethren the United Nation The old and wise People of my
Country joined with me and we Lodged a fine present in the hands of your
Brother Onas for your Use as a token of my own and my Peoples sincere
Disposition to Preserve Peace and ffriendship with you   We will send Commissioners to you next Spring to treat with You about the Land now in Dispute and in the Possession of my People   Let the place and Time be appointed
for certain that we may not miss one another   Layd some Strings of Wampum
The usual Cry by every Nation in Particular was given by way of thanksgiving & Joy. the Speaker Concluded & said   Brethren I have no more to say
at present but only desire You to give me a Speedy Answer   I have been here
many Days.

All the Wampum were hung over a Stick laid across the House about six
ffoot from the Ground   several Kettles of Hominy boild   Indian Corn &
Bread was brought in by the Women the biggest of which was set before
Asariquoa by the Divider   all dined together there was about sixty People
After Dinner they walked out every Nations Deputies by themselves and soon
came in again and sat together for about two hours   then Zilla Woolie proclaimed that Assaryquoa was to have an Answer now imediately   Upon which
all the men in Town gather'd again and the House was full and many stood
out of Door (so it was in the forenoon when the Message was delivered to
them)   Zilla Woolie desired Assaryquoa to give Ear Tocanuntie being appointed for their Speaker Spoke to the following Purpose—1.—Brother
Assaryquoa the unhappy Skirmish which happend last Winter betwixt your
People and some of our Warriours was not less surprizing to us than to You
we were very sorry to hear it   all amongst us were surprized   a Smoke arose
from the bottomless Pitt and a dark Cloud overshadow'd us   the Chain of
ffriendship was indanger'd & disappeared and all was in a Confusion   We the
Chiefs of the united Nations took hold of the Chain with all our Strength
we were resolved not to let it slip before we received a deadly Blow   But to
our great Satisfaction in the Darkest Time our Brother Onas enter'd our Door
and Offer'd his Mediation   He judged very right to become Mediator betwixt
us   We were drunk on both sides and the overflow of our Galls and the Blood
that was shed had corrupted our Hearts both Yours and ours   You did very
well to come to our fire and Comfort the Mourning ffamilies We thank You
this Belt shall serve for the same Purpose to Comfort the ffamilyes in Mourning amongst You   Laid a Belt of Wampum—After I thank'd them their
Speaker proceeded—2.—Brother Assaryquoa you have healed the Wounds of
the Hearts of those ffamilys in Mourning both here & at Niharuntquoa   We
thank you kindly for your so doing   Let this Belt of Wampum have the same
Effect upon your People to heal the Wounds and Comfort them as yours had
upon ours   Laid a Belt of Wampum   the usual thanks was given & the Speaker
proceeded—3.—Brother Assaryquoa you judged very right in saying that an
evil Spirit was the promoter of the late unhappy Skirmish We do not doubt
but you have by this Time full Satisfaction from your own People besides
what You had from Us that your People had begun Hostilities   but let have
begun who will we assure You it was the Spirit that dwells amongst the
Catabaws and by which they are ruled that did it for Brethren will never treat
one another after this Manner without an Evil Spirit enters them   we agree
with you and your Counsellors the old and wise People of your Country and

disapprove the Action highly we thank You Brother Assaryquoa for removing your Hatchet and for burying it under a heavy Stone Let this Belt of Wampum serve to remove our Hatchet from You and not only bury it but we will fling it into the Bottomless Pitt into the Ocean there shall be no more Use made of it In Confirmation of what we say we give You this Belt of Wampum. after the usual Approbation was given the Speaker proceeded—4.— Brother Assaryquoa let this String of Wampum serve to heal the very mark of the Wounds so that nothing may be seen of it after this Day for it was done betwixt Brethren let no more mention be made of it hereafter for ever in Publick or Private Layd down four Strings of Wampum The usual Cry by way of Approbation was given and the Speaker proceeded—5.—Brother Assaryquoa this String of Wampum serves to return you our Thanks for dispelling the dark Cloud that overshadow'd Us for some Time Let the Sun shine again let us look upon one another with Pleasure and Joy Layd some Strings of Wampum The usual Aprobation was given and the Speaker proceeded—6.—Brother Assaryquo you have taken away the bitterness of our Spirit and purged us from the abundance and overflow of our Gall We judge with all the rest of the wise People that when Men have too much of that it is like a dangerous Distemper but it is not only your Brethren the united Nations that have too much Gall but the Europeans labour likewise under that Distemper in particular your back Inhabitants you did very well in taking away the overflow of Gall Let this String of Wampum serve to purge your People also from the overflow of their Gall and to remove the bitterness of their Spirit also we own it to be very necessary on both sides We thank You for the good advice Laid four Rows of Wampum the usual Approbation was given and the Speaker proceeded—7.—Brother Assaryquoa this String of Wampum serves to thank you for mending the Chain of ffriendship which was lately hurt and in danger we agree with you very readily Let good understanding & true ffriendship be restored and subsist among us for Ever Laid four Rows of Wampum The usual approbation was given and the Speaker proceeded—8.—Brother Assaryquoa we thank you kindly for the present you and the Old and Wise of your Country lodged in the Hands of our Brother Onas your good ffriend as a token of your sincere Disposition to preserve Peace and ffriendship with Us Let this String of Wampum serve to assure you of the like good Disposition towards you and your People and as an assurance that we will come down within the Borders of Pennsylvania to a place called Canadagueany next Spring and we will be very glad of seeing your Commissioners there we will treat them as becomes Brethren with good Chear and Pleasure we will set out from our several Towns after eight Moons are past by when the ninth just is to be seen this present Moon which is almost expired not to be reckoned Upon which You may Depend · in Confirmation whereof we give you this String of Wampum The usual Approbation being given the Speaker proceeded—Brother Assaryquoa we have no more to say at present but we will not permit you to Leave Us yet but stay a Day or two longer with us We have just now received Intelligence that the Jonontowas are on the Road with some of the Cherikees Deputies in order to strike a Peace with Us They the Cherikees hindred the Jonontowas from coming sooner And you will then hear the Particulars—Then the Speaker directed his Discourse to the Deputies of the Nanticokes who had been there all along present and said Brethren the Nanticokes we desire you will prepare for to morrow and deliver your Message to us and as you have neither the united

Nations their Tongue nor Ear we have thought fit to hear you speak with our English Ear and to speak to you with our English Tongue. There is the Man (pointing to me) who is the Guardian of all the Indians—I was desired to acquaint.the Nanticokes with it which I did and they were well pleased they could talk some English but not one word of the united Nations Language— The 1ˢᵗ of August the Nanticokes spoke and had their Answer the same Day the whole Day was spent about it—¹²

John Bartram, who had returned from a visit to Oswego in time for the main council events, was particularly interested in the colorful affairs of this day.

"The council met at 9 o'clock," he writes, "and the kettles of soop and a basket of dumplings were brought in for our dinner; after dinner the *Anticocques* delivered a belt and a string of *Wampum*, with a complaint that the *Marylanders* had deposed their king, and desired leave to chuse one for themselves; to this: as well as all the articles opened yesterday, the chiefs returned plausible but subtil answers. . . ."¹³

The 2ᵈ [continues Weiser's Journal] the Council of the united Nation met again and Zillawoolie desired me to give my Attendance and take Notice of what should be said to put it down in Writing imediately and with Particular Care he spoke as follows—Brother Onas Assaryquoa and the Governor of Maryland   we are ingaged in a Warr with the Catabaws which will last to the End of the World for they molest Us and speak Contemptuously of Us which our Warriours will not bear and they will soon go to War against them again it will be in vain for Us to diswade them from it we desire you by this String of Wampum to publish it amongst your back Inhabitants to be of good behaviour to our Warriours and look upon them as their Brethren that we may never have such a Dangerous Breach hereafter We give you the strongest Assurance that we will use our best Endeavour to perswade and charge them to be of good Behaviour every where amongst our Brethren the English with whom we are one body and Soul one Heart and one Head for what has happened is no more to be seen and no token or mark remains thereof Let the Spirit of the Catabaw's be banished away from Us which will set Brethren to fall out Let Treaties of ffriendship be observed and believe no Lies Our Brother Onas knows very well that some Years ago we made a new Road on the outside of your Inhabitants tho' they had seated themselves down upon our Land now your People seated themselves down again upon the new Road and shut it up and there is no more room for a new Road because of the Terrible Mountains full of Stones and no game there so that the Road cannot be removed To inforce this upon You we give you this String of Wampum which serves likewise for an Assurance that we will observe Treaties of ffriendship with You and believe no Lies and will perswade our Warriours to behave well every where amongst your People our Brethren —Laid a String of Wampum of three Rows they desired that this might be sent to Maryland and Virginia immediately from Philadelphia—Brother Onas this String of Wampum serves to return you our Hearty thanks for your Kind Mediation We thank our Brother Assaryquoa for the Kind visit Let good ffriendship and Peace be amongst Us to the End of the World—After all was over according to the Ancient Custom of that ffire a Song of ffriendship and Joy was sung by the Chiefs after this the Council ffire on their side was put out   I with the same Ceremonee put out the ffire on behalf of Assaryquoa & Onas and they departed—The 3ᵈ of August I put down in the Morning the Speech of the Nanticokes and visited Tocanuntie   All the Chiefs of the Onondagoes came to see Us   took my Leave of them   set out about nine and departed from Onondago.[14]

Bartram notes that, when they took their leave, the chiefs "bid us adieu by shaking hands very kindly, and seemingly with much affection." [15]

"They desired," writes Weiser in conclusion, "to be remembred to their Brethren in Philadelphia in Particular to the Governor and James Logan— The time that We staid at Onondagoe we were well entertain'd with Hominy Venison Dryed Eels Squashes and Indian Corn bread   They gave Us provision on the Road homeward so much as we wanted [two bags, says Bartram, of parched meal]."

III

They returned by the way they had come. At Cachiadachse they took their leave of the boys and girls, to whom, no doubt, Conrad managed to slip some little present, as was his custom with Indian children. At Owego a squaw at whose cabin they stopped set before them a bowl of huckleberries and "a large kettle full of small homony boil'd in strong venison broth," which Bartram found "noble entertainment."

"I heartily pitied the poor *Squaw*," writes John, "for I believed she had dressed it for herself and several children: she also obliged us to accept of a fine piece of venison to carry away." [16]

Between Owego and Tioga, the Nanticoke interpreter, who had attached himself to Weiser's party, strayed from the trail to hunt and got lost. He wound up at an Indian village some three miles up the Chemung River. Here he quickly made himself at home, for, though deficient in tongues, he was well versed in the universal language of the eye. When he turned up at Tioga later in the day, he was found to have attached to himself a Mohican squaw. The two lodged that night in a corner of Brother Enoch's cabin. *Lente lente currite noctis equi.* It was the Nanticoke's intention to take his "occasional wife" with him to Maryland, but Conrad Weiser's vexation was an obstacle not to be overcome. It was explained to the Nanticoke next morning that the lady's company would be contrary to the best principles of economy: she would have to be fed out of the common store. Her escort was constrained to agree; and so, when the travelers came to Tioga Point and crossed the river, the Nanticoke Leander left his Hero behind him on the shore, taking leave of her with a farewell shout across the water. There is no record that he ever saw her again.

On the 10th of August the Nanticoke, who had a genius for errantry of one sort and another, wounded an elk and pursued it for hours while Weiser's party waited impatiently for him at the Licking Place. He left them at eight o'clock and turned up at two. When at last they made camp in the evening, John Bartram expended his accumulated energy by climbing up a rocky hill and rolling loose stones down behind him as he went.

"This I found the *Indians* much disturbed at," he notes, "for they said it would infallibly produce rain the next day." [17]

On the 11th Weiser tried a short cut, such as he had taken perforce in 1737. Leaving the dismal hemlock thickets of the Lycoming Valley and striking south (very likely at what is now Fields Station on the map), he took his party up a high, bare hill, and soon involved them in a tedious country full of flat stones on which the horses had difficulty keeping their feet. They stopped for a while to rest the animals, amusing themselves with gathering huckleberries. At night they dined on fresh venison, and listened to the singing of "the great green grass-hopper . . . (Catedidist)," which Bartram says was the first he had heard that year.

In the morning before daybreak it began to rain, the shower lasting an hour. The Indians insisted that Bartram was responsible: he had rolled stones down the mountain. John retorted that if their theory was right it should have rained the day before. To which the Nanticoke interpreter "cunningly" replied with a hit at the white man's almanacs, in which the prognostications, he intimated, often had to be allowed as much as a two days margin of error. Perhaps he had been reading *Poor Richard*. Franklin had written in his almanac of 1737, "We modestly desire only the favourable allowance of a day or two before and a day or two after the precise day against which the weather is set."

They came down off the mountains to Loyalsock Creek in time to have their noon meal at the deserted French Town. A heavy squall of rain overtook them there, in the midst of which, writes Bartram, "about half a score of the 5 *Nations*, who had been on the back of *S. Carolina* to fight the Catawba's, passed very fast through the town with one poor female prisoner, they shouted couragiously, but we learnt no particulars of this great enterprize . . ." [18]

They reached Shamokin at 11 o'clock in the morning of the 14th, ate a meal of boiled dumplings with watermelon, and stayed the night. Setting out again the next morning, they made good time over the Shamokin Trail. On the 16th they crossed the Broad Mountain, dined in St. Anthony's Wilderness, and climbed the last ridge of the Blue Mountains. By this time their horses were covered with sweat, although, as Bartram tells us, that day they led them most of the way for twenty miles. They stopped to rest on the summit, enjoying the "fine prospect of the great and fertile valley of *Tulpihocken*." [19] Descending, they spent the night at a comfortable house, two miles beyond the mountain, where they had clean straw and slept late, "free from fleas."

In the morning Bartram's mare was lame, and they could scarcely get her to move; but, the energetic Quaker carrying her load a good part of the way on his own back, they managed to reach Weiser's house by noon. When the mare came into the pasture, says Bartram, "she stretched herself at full length and rose no more for 24 hours." The tireless botanist himself went up Eagle Peak—"Mr. *Weisar's* high hill"—and spent the afternoon there collecting seeds.

We are not told what reception Conrad received from Ann Eve and

the family on his return, that 17th day of August, 1743. We do not know
what the Governor said to him a few days later in Philadelphia, when he
turned up there with his report of successful peace negotiations at Onondaga. But we do know that on September 16, 1743, Christopher Saur's semi-
monthly newspaper, *Der Hoch-Deutsch Pensylvanische Geschichte-
Schreiber, Oder: Sammlung Wichtiger Nachrichten aus dem Natur-und
Kirchen-Reich*, carried the following item:

We are reliably informed that the Breach, which was caused by the Skirmish
last Winter, between the *Virginians* and the *6 Nations Indians* has now been
peacefully ended, through the Mediation of our Governor;   on July 31 some
Belts and Strings of *Wambum* were exchanged to this effect at Onontage between *Conrad Weiser* Esq; representing Virginia, and the great *Council* of
these *Nations;* So that all differences (as the Indians say) have been sunk in
the sea, never to be seen nor thought of again.

CHAPTER 21

. . . *Cuts His Beard*

I

WHEN Conrad Weiser came to Philadelphia with his report on the
negotiations at Onondaga, he stopped at Benjamin Franklin's shop
and bought a copy of Samuel Butler's *Hudibras* for seven shillings and sixpence.[1] What prompted him to buy this famous satire on the Puritans we
do not know. The suggestion may have come from Benjamin Franklin himself, who must have loved it. Ben had as little regard as Butler for the
quarreling sects who

> . . . *prove their doctrine orthodox*
> *By apostolic blows and knocks,*

and persons who take their theology more seriously than their virtue. He
knew a good many of the Ephrata Brotherhood (Weiser, Miller, the Eckerlings, etc.), and he may have welcomed the sly means Butler's book gave
him of letting his friend Conrad see how the world regarded saints like
Beissel who were in all things

> *Still so perverse and opposite*
> *As if they worshipped God for spite.*

Certainly there are many passages in the book startlingly apposite to
the Solitary at Ephrata, to Justice Weiser himself, and even to his late
negotiations at Onondaga. Weiser would see himself in the lines describing
Hudibras as a man

> *Great on the bench, great in the saddle,*

and one whose "hairy meteor" of a beard

> . . . *was canonic and did grow*
> *In holy orders by strict vow.*

There were lines, too, that fitted the Onondaga journey as closely as did
Saur's news item of September 16:

> *We that are wisely mounted higher*
> *Than constables in curule wit,* . . .
> *Quantum in nobis, have thought good*
> *To save th' expense of Christian blood,*
> *And try if we, by mediation*
> *Of treaty, and accommodation,*
> *Can end the quarrel, and compose*
> *The bloody duel without blows.*

Hudibras is a witty, biting, partisan book in which there was much to
offend the tenacious godliness of Conrad Weiser. But there was much in

it also to flatter his common sense. Conrad's own wit was keen enough, and his religion genuine enough, to see that the object of Butler's bombing couplets was not religion but the fools and hypocrites who abused it; and Conrad would, moreover, delight to find in it encouragement of his own revulsion against certain Hudibrastic elements that had crept in among the Seventh Day German Baptists at Ephrata—

> *A sect, whose chief devotion lies*
> *In odd perverse antipathies . . .*
> *That with more care keep holy-day*
> *The wrong than others the right way—*

Dunker disciples of Jakob Böhme (or Behmen), who follow

> *. . . a dark lantern of the spirit*
> *Which none can see but those who bear it . . .*
> *An* ignis fatuus *that bewitches,*
> *And leads men into pools and ditches . . .*
> *To dive, like wild-fowl for salvation,*
> *And fish to catch regeneration.*

There were lines also that echoed Conrad's detestation of Father Friedsam, who had to sustain a character suitable to the author of *Ninety-Nine Mystical Sayings* and *The Penitentiary of Carnal Man*, and to reconcile it with a reputation for tippling and worse,

> *As if hypocrisy and nonsense*
> *Had got the advowson of his conscience.*

The knight's squire, Ralph, was described in terms equally apposite to certain of the Zionitic Brotherhood, the Eckerlings in particular, who had a taste for astrological hieroglyphs and Rosicrucianism:

> *For mystic learning wondrous able*
> *In magic, talisman, and cabal . . .*
> *He Anthroposophus and Floud,*
> *And Jacob Behmen, understood;*
> *Knew many an amulet and charm,*
> *That would do neither good nor harm;*
> *In Rosicrucian lore as learned,*
> *As he that* Verè adeptus *earned.*

Surely it is more than a coincidence that on September 3, five days after the purchase, Conrad Weiser wrote a blistering letter of farewell to Beissel and the Brethren. We are entitled to believe that *Hudibras* helped him to make up his mind.

> *Worthy and Dear Friends and Brethren.*

It cannot be denied at Ephrata that I and several other members of the community, partly gone to their rest, partly still living, were compelled to protest for a considerable time against the domination of conscience, the suppression of innocent minds, against the prevailing pomp and luxury, both in dress and magnificent buildings, but we achieved about as much as nothing; on the contrary, in spite of all protests, this practice was still more eagerly continued, and following the manner of the world, the attempt was made to cover such pride and luxury with the name of God. It was most zealously defended, so that for years nothing has been heard in public assemblies but the boast: *There the work stands; it is the work of God,* as if it were the first Babylonian masterpiece. Whole assemblies were held in honor of this loathsome idolatry, while the leaders have indulged in the most fulsome self-praise by all kinds of fictitious stories.

For these and other reasons, which I reserve for myself to state them at a fitting opportunity, I take leave of your young, but already decrepit sect, and I desire henceforth to be treated as a stranger, especially by you, the presiding officers (superintendents), whenever I should come to Ephrata because of business or other personal inclinations, or should meet you somewhere else. You will no doubt know how to instruct, as usual, the other, partly innocent, minds, as to what they have to consider me. I make a distinction between them and you, and hope the time will come when they shall be liberated from their physical and spiritual bondage, as also from the thraldom of conscience, under which they are groaning. I protest once more against you, the overseers, who feed yourselves and do not spare the flock, but scatter and devour them . . . . I hope the end is near and deliverance has come. Of course I know beforehand that you will not consider my words, especially since I am not the son of a prophet or a prophet myself. Nor do I appeal to a spirit in my head or body as the cause of this letter, but my conclusions are founded upon the eternal truth and the reasonableness of the thing itself. I am in earnest; you may ridicule me as much as you please.

Herewith I conclude and live in hope that the time will come when all knees shall bow before the name of Jesus, even those of such proud saints who publicly declare rather to burn in hell than bow before Him.

Why doest thou extol thyself, O poor earth? The judgment of God can humble thee in a moment. Do it rather willingly; it is no disgrace, for the heathen are his inheritance and the uttermost parts of the earth his possession. He is the King of all kings and a Lord of all lords. Worship, majesty and power belong to Him, for the Father has made all things subject to Him. He will give His honor to no other, nor His glory to the mighty. He is the Lord, and beside Him there is no Savior.

If there is any one not satisfied with my statement, let him convince me of the contrary. Victory belongs to truth. The authority of man has no power. To be silent is good at times, but in this case it would be bad. If you have anything to say in your defence, or undertaken a reformation, let me know, for I shall be glad to hear it.

Finally, I remain a friend of truth and sincerity, and of all those who love them, but a sworn enemy of all lies and hypocrisy. Farewell [*Vale*].

September 3, 1743.   CONRAD WEISER [2]

Of this incident Weiser wrote a few weeks later to Count Zinzendorf:

I have recently taken leave by letter of the teachers and elders at Ephrata. It seems to me they are in a great hurry to come to an End of Their work and now give clear evidence of what they are and what they are after, They are destroying the community itself and seeking to establish a Cloister and to give your Conrad Beissel a place in the Calendar of saints. ludwig Blum has recently left them, whether from Pride or from Wickedness I do not yet know. likewise the so-called Swiss Baby [*die sogenannte Schweitzer Beby*] has left the *Jungfrau Kloster* from scruples of conscience—[3]

Ludwig Blum was the master-singer who had organized the soon-to-be famous singing school at Ephrata, but had been discharged—Beissel taking the school over himself at the request of his enamored female songsters.

The scruples of the "so-called Swiss Baby," who may have been Anna Thoma (Sister Tabea) from Viedendorf, Canton of Basel, Switzerland,[4] seem to have been in relation to a promise she had given Daniel Scheibly, after a secret courtship, to marry him. But in this matter the Superintendent was to have the last word. When on the appointed day she stood up with her bridegroom to be married, Conrad Beissel called her aside and in a few minutes won her again for the Virgin Sophia. She went back into the Sisters' House.[5]

Among the papers of Count Zindendorf, preserved at Herrnhut, we find the following verses. It is difficult to think they were not inspired by Conrad Beissel, Dictator of the Cocalico, Father of Lies (for whom the Count shared with Weiser a robust and commendable contempt), and addressed to Beissel's flock. Beissel speaking:

> *Pour des Parrots qui ne sont qu'un Jeu,*
> *Vous avez tort d'Etre en colere,*
> *Il est vrai que j'y ments un peu;*
> *Mais au lieu de vous mettre en feu,*
> *Ce mensonge auroit du vous plaire:*
> *Que diable auroit-ce donc été,*
> *Si jaurois dit la Vérité?*
> *Dun Homme qui se veut dire Sacrée.*[6]

I am willing to believe that the impulsive Count Zinzendorf did, on occasion, feel disposed to "say Damn." His pacifism was a matter of principle, but it had not dulled his God-given capacity to hate evil.

II

Was it also in consequence of reading *Hudibras* that Conrad condemned his beard "to submit to fatal steel"? We do not have his barber's account, and so we can give no dates; but we do know that before the Six Nations chiefs visited Lancaster next spring Conrad Weiser had cut his beard—cut it in half.

If the shearing was intended to make an irrevocable break with his past, like the burning of the Books, Weiser was bound to be disappointed. Conrad Beissel was too near a neighbor to be put so easily out of mind.

There is a story that Weiser, soon after leaving Ephrata and entering upon his duties as a justice of the peace for Lancaster County, one day saw Conrad Beissel approaching on horseback.

As Father Friedsam drew level, Weiser expressed surprise at seeing him riding a horse when an ass was good enough for his Master.

"Ah," said Beissel, "but the asses have all been made justices of the peace."

CHAPTER 22

... *Investigates the Murder of*
John Armstrong

T HE Black Prince had said at Onondaga, July 31, 1743: "We will set
out from our several Towns after eight Moons are past by when the
ninth just is to be seen   this present Moon which is almost expired not to
be reckoned." [1]

The eight moons were now past, and Conrad Weiser was awaiting news
of the Indian ambassadors. The Governor and Council in Philadelphia were
uneasy. No word had come recently from the north. It was feared, by
those who did not understand the Six Nations, that a people who reckoned
time by moons might be inconstant in their agreements. The government
was concerned lest something might have intervened to cause the Six Nations to change their minds, or to turn their deputies back before they had
completed the long journey to Philadelphia.

There was good reason for alarm. Saur's newspaper of April 16 printed
a rumor that the Indians of Pennsylvania had gone over to the French.
Whatever was back of this particular rumor, the danger of disaffection was
real. The Delawares had grievances. France and England were at war.
Pennsylvania was in no position to resist a squeeze from the west if made
by the French and Indians together.

It was of the last importance, therefore, that all causes of friction between
the Six Nations and the southern colonies should be removed, and that
Pennsylvania's Indian policy should be made continental in scope so as
to interpose the Great Confederacy between the English colonies and the
French.

All depended on the success of the Lancaster Conference.

That is why the murder of John Armstrong at the Narrows of the Juniata
(ever since called Jack's Narrows) provided more than a tale for the campfire. It gave the government in Philadelphia weeks of grave concern. If it
had not been for Weiser's investigation of the case and the judicious advice
he offered the Governor in connection with it, Jack Armstrong's bones
might have risen to wreck the conference and all that hinged on it.

There was enough mystery and horror about the story to haunt the trail
through Jack's Narrows for all the years it was subsequently used by the
Indian traders. Even now, as we turn over the pages of old documents in
the archives at Harrisburg and Philadelphia containing the letters, journals,
and depositions of men who saw the crime or took part in its uncovering,
the imagination is seized and we are apt to forget that today in the Juniata
Valley one hears the whistle of the Chicago-Washington express and the
whir of New York-to-Pittsburgh motor traffic. As we read, two pictures
take shape in our minds: one is of an Indian, whose face was streaked with

black paint, footing it grimly over the Old Allegheny Trail; the other is of eagles and vultures circling lazily above a rock beside the river.

One day early in April 1744, when Conrad Weiser returned home from Philadelphia, where he had just become a naturalized British citizen, he found a letter waiting for him which four Indians had brought down from Shamokin. It contained a message from Shickellamy asking him to come at once: there was trouble stirring among the Delawares.

Shickellamy gave no particulars, but Conrad must have known it was the Armstrong business, rumors of which had reached him before he left home. For reasons that he explained afterwards, Conrad decided to do nothing for the moment, but to stay at home and let matters take their course. His part in the drama was to be played efficiently enough two weeks later.

Meanwhile agitation had developed among the whites along the Susquehanna River. Jack had disappeared some time about the middle of February, and suspicion was approaching certainty that he had been killed on the trail. Alexander Armstrong, his brother, had evidence that the crime had been committed at the Juniata Narrows. He gathered a body of men and set off into the woods to find the body.

The story of their adventures—as thrilling in its way as anything Fenimore Cooper gave us in our boyhood—is contained in a deposition made before Justice James Armstrong at Paxton, April 19, 1744. To paraphrase this deposition would destroy the folk flavor. I present it, therefore, in the form in which Alexander Armstrong, Thomas McKee, and the rest of them signed it.

The Deposition of the Subscribers Testifieth & Saith, that the Subscribers having a Suspicion that John Armstrong, Trader, Together with his Men, James Smith & Woodworth Arnold, were Murther'd by yᵉ Indians. They met at the House of Joseph Charmbers in Paxton, and there Consulted to go to Samokin, To Consult with the Delaware King & Secalima & their Council, what they Should do Concerning the Affaire. Whereupon the King & Councel Ordered Eight of their men to go with the Depᵗˢ to the House of James Berry, in Order to go in Quest of the Murther'd persons; but that Night they Came to said Berry's House, three of the Eight Indians ran Away, And the Next Morning, these Depᵗˢ, Together wᵗʰ yᵉ five Indians that remain'd, Set on their Journey Peaceably to the last Supposed sleeping place of the Deceased, and upon their Arrival these Depᵗˢ dispersed themselves in Order to find out the Corps of the deceased, & one of the Depᵗˢ Named James Berry, a Small Distance from the aforesᵈ sleeping Place Came, came [*sic*] to a White Oak Tree which had three Knotches on it, & Close by sᵈ Tree he found a Shoulder Bone, (which these Depᵗˢ does Supose to be John Armstrongs, And that he himself was Eating by the Indians) which he Carried to the Aforesᵈ sleeping place & Shewed to his Companions, one of which handed it to the sᵈ five Indians to Know what bone it was, & they, after passing different Sentiments upon it handed it, to a Delaware Indian, who was Suspected by the Depᵗˢ, and they Testify & Say, that as Soon as the sᵈ Indian took the bone in his hand, his Nose Gushed out with Blood, & he directly handed it to Another, from whence these Depᵗˢ Steered along a Path About three or four Miles to the Narrows of Juniata, where they Suspected the s^d Murther to be Comited, & where the Allegany Road Crosses the Creek. These Dep^ts Sat Down in Order to Consult on what Measures to take in Order to proceed on a Discovery, Whereupon most of the White Men, These Dep^ts Cros't the Creek again, And went down the Creek & Crost into an Island where these Dep^ts had had Inteligence the Corps had been Throwne; And There they Met the rest of the White Men & Indians who was in Company, & there Consulted to go further down the Creek in Quest of the Corps, & These Dep^ts Further Saith, they Ordered the Indians to go down the Creek on the Other side, but they all Followed these dep^ts at a Small distance, Except one Indian who Cros't the Creek Again, & Soon After these dep^ts Seeing Some Bawld Eagles & Other Fowles, Suspected the Corps to be thereab^ts, And thereab^ts lost Sight of the Indians, & Imediately found one of the Corps, wch these dep^ts Says was the Corps of James Smith, one of s^d Armstrongs Men, And Directly upon finding the Corps, these Dep^ts heard three Shotts of Guns, which they had great Reason to Think was the Indians, their Companions, who had deserted from them, and in order to let him know they had found the Corps, these dep^ts fired three Guns, but to no purpose, for they Never Saw the Indians any More, and Ab^t Quarter of a Mile farther down the Creek, they Saw More Bawled Eagles, whereupon they made down towards the Place, where they found another Corps, (being the Corps of Woodworth Arnold, and the other Servt of s^d John Armstrong) lying on a Rock, and then Went to the Former Sleeping place, where they had Appointed to meet the Indians, but Saw No Indians, Only that the Indians had been there & Cooked Some Victuals for themselves and had gone off. And that Night these Dep^ts further Says they had great Reason to Suspect that the Indians was then Therab^ts, and Intended to do them some Damages, for a Dog these Dep^ts had with them Barking that Night, which was remarkable, for the s^d Dog had not Bark't all the time they was Out till that Night, nor Never Since, which Occasioned these Dep^ts to Stand upon their Guard behind Trees, with their Guns Cock't that Night. Next Morning these Dep^ts went back to the Corps, which they Found to be Barbarously and Inhumanly Murthered by Very Gastly & deep Cuts on their Heads with a Tomahawk, or Such Like Weapon, which had Sunk into their Sculs & Brains, & in one of s^d Corps there Appeared a hole in his Scul near the Cut, which was Suposed to be with a Tomahawk, which these Dep^ts does believe to be a Bullet hole. And these Dep^ts, after taking a Particular a View of the Corps as Their Melancholy Condition would Admit, they Buried them as decently as their Circumstances would Allow, and returned home to Paxton, the Allegany road to John Harris^s, Thinking it Dangerous to return the Same Way they went Out: and Further These Deponents Saith not.[2]

One fact had now been established: Jack Armstrong and his two men had been murdered. But who had killed them? On the solution of this further mystery rested the peace of the Indian border.

The danger was that an attempt on the part of the Indians to conceal the murderer would provoke an explosion of race hatred, and no one cared to think where that would lead to. Shickellamy and Olumapies were thoroughly alive to the danger and set about to remove it. They acted with such vigor that when Weiser wrote from home to Richard Peters on April 26 the case seemed to be closed.

"Just now I heard that Olumapies & ShiKelimo had Sent a delaware Indian to prison for having Killed an Indian trader." [3]

But in the meantime the captured Indian, Mushemeelin by name, had accused another Indian of sharing the crime with him. The arrest and subsequent escape of this second man, "John, a Son of Neshalleeny," provided a further complication that once more threatened to provoke violence on the frontier.

Thomas Cookson to Governor Thomas [4]

[Lancaster, April 22, 1744]

Hon^d Sir

Just now is brought to this place Jno Mussemeelin a Delaware Indian who having Confessed the Murder of John Armstrong & Woodward Arnold one of his Men and that John a Son of Neshalleeny another of the Delawares Killed James Smith another of J. Armstrongs Men was (after a Council held by Shickalamy & ye other Indians, at Shamokin) Adjudged Guilty of ye s^d Murders And was Sent down with ye s^d Indian John by Shicallamys Sons & some other Indians, into the Settlements   But on their Coming to James Berrys ab^t forty Miles above John Harris's on Sasquehanna Shicallamys Sons apprehensive of the resentment of Neshalleenys Friends ag^t their Father for thus delivering up the Young Man who was in great Esteem with them thought it most prudent to release him & deliver up Mussemeelin only, for ye present, in Order to be Secured & Receive his Punishm^t . . . I shall Order him to be kept Safe in Our Goal [sic] here till Your Honour shall be pleased to give Some Orders about him, He expects to be kept till the Indians Come down to ye Treaty   That he may be executed in their way—He thinks it very hard that the other Indian shou'd be released & that the reason assigned by Shicallamys Sons was not ye true reason . . .

The escape of Neshalleeny's son so inflamed Alexander Armstrong that he dashed off a letter to Olumapies threatening "war."

Alexander Armstrong to Olumapies [5]

To Alimoppus King of the Delawares

Great Sir. as a parcel of your men have murdered my brother and two of his men, I write to you, knowing you to be a king of Justice that you will send us in all the murderers and the men that was with them. as I looked for the Corps of my murdered brother, for that reason your men threaten my life, and I cannot live in my house. now as we have no inclination or mind to go to war with you our friends, as a friend I desire that you will keep your men from doing me harm and also send the murderers and the Companions I Expect an Answer and am your much hurted friend and brother

Ap^l ye 25th 1744   ALEXANDER ARMSTRONG
we have sent
   John Mashamelon
   to Goal

To Shickellamy, "the great Councellor for the Mingoes," Armstrong wrote also, appealing to him to send in "all your men that are guilty of the murder." [6] The letter throws a flash of light on the character of

Mushemeelin (or *Musham y Hillin*, as Weiser spells the name), who, says Armstrong, "is not willing to die till all the rest are brought in to him." [7] This sturdy exponent of elementary justice (no one had much good to say of Jack Armstrong) faced his end stoically, but, like Shakespeare's Barnardine in *Measure for Measure*, would not consent to die except on terms of his own choosing. He never quite forfeits our respect.

What provocation Mushemeelin had had, how the murder was committed, and how the several mysteries connected with it were solved, form the theme of Conrad Weiser's report of May 2. For the Council at Philadelphia, taking a grave view of the whole situation, had sent urgent instructions to him to go to Shamokin and clear things up. His report from that place provides us with so dramatic an evocation of the spirit of the old frontier that I present it in full. Its moving narrative, quick dialogue, and flashes of characterization, all set in a style crisp and rhythmic as a woodsman's axe, bring us the feel of the forest as closely as we can recapture it from those days before the French and Indian War.

Trader and Indian, greed and revenge. The force of tradition and their own native good humor still held the Indians for the most part in check; but at the same time as we read we feel the drifting fog of suspense that was to hang about the woods wherever white men passed until at last the war cry was heard on the Susquehanna in 1755.

The narrative is here printed as it appears in the *Minutes of the Provincial Council of Pennsylvania*,[8] with certain variations (indicated by brackets) introduced from Conrad Weiser's original, unedited manuscript.[9]

Conrad Weiser—his Report of his Journey to shamokin

Shamokin May 2ᵈ 1744

This day I delivered the Governor's Message to Olumapies the Delaware Chief and the rest of Delaware Indians in the presence of Shick Calamy and a few more of the Six Nations; The purport of which was That I was sent Express by the Governor and Council to demand those that had been concerned with Mussemeelin in Murdering John Armstrong, Woodward Arnold and James Smith; That their Bodies might be searched for and decently buried; That the Goods be likewise found and restored without fraud—. It was delivered to them by me in the Mohawck Language, and interpretred into Delaware by Andrew, Madam Montures Son.

In the afternoon Olumapies in the presence of the aforesaid Indians made the following Answer;

Brother the Governor.

It is true that we the Delaware Indians, by the Instigation of the Evil Spirit have Murdered James Armstrong and his Men; We have transgressed, and we are ashamed to look up; We have taken the Murderer and delivered him to the Relations of the Deceased, to be dealt with according to his works.

Brother the Governor.

Your demand for the goods is very just; We have gathered some of them; We will do the utmost of what we can to find them all; We do not doubt but we can find out the most part and whatever is wanting we will make up in Skins, which is what the Goods are sent for to the Woods.

Brother the Governor.

        The dead Bodies are Buried; it is certain that John Armstrong was buried by the Murderer, and the other two by those that searched for them. Our Hearts are in Mourning, and we are in a dismal condition, and cannot say any thing [more] at present

Then Shick Calamy with the rest of the Indians of the Six Nations there present say'd, Brother the Governor, We have been all missinformed on both sides about the unhappy accident. Mussemeelin has certainly Murdered the three White men himself, and upon his bare Accusation of Neshaleeny's Son, which was nothing but spite, the said Neshaleeny's son was Seized, and made a Prisoner. Our Cousins, the Delaware Indians, being then Drunk, in particular Olumapies, never Examined things, but made an Innocent person Prisoner, which gave a great deal of Disturbance amongst us. Hower the two Prisoners were sent, and by the way in going down the River they stopped at the House of James Berry, James told the Young man, "I am sorry to see you in such a Condition, I have known you from a Boy, and always loved you." Then the Young man seemed to be very much struck to the Heart, and say'd, I have said nothing yet, but now I will tell all, let all the Indians come in and the White people also, they shall hear it. And then told Mussemeelin in the presence of all the people.

Now I am going to Dye for your Wickedness; You have killed all the three Whitemen; I never did intend to kill any of them. Then Mussemeelin in anger say'd, It is true I have killed them; I am a Man, You are a Coward; it is a Great satisfaction to me to have killed them; I will Dye with Joy for having killed a Great Rogue and his Companions—Upon which the Young Man was set at liberty by the Indians—We desire therefore our Brother the Governor will not insist to have either of the two Young Men in Prison or Condemned to Dye; It is not with Indians as with White people, to put People in Prison on Suspicion or for Trifles; Indians must be first found Guilty of a Crime, then Judgement is given and immediately Executed. We will give you faithfully all the particulars; and at the ensueing Treaty entirely satisfie you; in the mean time We desire that good friendship and Harmony may continue; and that we may live long together, is the Hearty desire of your Brethren the Indians of the United Six Nations present at Shamokin.

The following is what Shick Calamy declared to be the Truth of the Story, concerning the Murder of John Armstrong, Woodward Arnold and James Smith from the beginning to the end. to wit.

That Mussemeelin owing some Skins to John Armstrong, the said Armstrong Seized a Horse of the said Mussemeelin and a riffled Gun, the Gun was taken by James Smith deceased. Sometime last Winter Mussemeelin met Armstrong on the River Juniata, and paid to about Twenty shillings, for which he offered a neck-belt in Pawn to Armstrong, and demanded his Horse, and James Armstrong refused it, and would not deliver up the Horse, but enlarged the Debt, as his usual custom was, and after some Quarrel the Indian went away in great Anger without his Horse to his Hunting Cabin. Sometime after this Armstrong with his two Companions in their way to Ohio passed by the said Mussemeelin's Hunting Cabin, his Wife, only being at home, demanded the Horse of Armstrong, because he was her proper Goods, but did not get him (Armstrong had by this time sold or lent the Horse to James Berry) after Mussemeelin came from Hunting, his Wife told him that Armstrong was gone by, and that She had demanded the Horse of him, but did not get him, (and as is thought pressed him to pursue and take Revenge of Armstrong) The third day in the Morning after [Armstrong] was gone by, Mussemeelin said to the two Young men that Hunted with him,   Come let us go towards the Great Hills to Hunt Bears,   accordingly they went all three in Company; After they had gone a good way Mussemeelin who was foremost was told by the two Young men that they were out of their Course. Come you along said Mussemeelin, and they accordingly follow'd him till they came to the Path that leads to Ohio. Then Mussemeelin told them he had a good mind to go and fetch his Horse back from Armstrong, and desired the two Young men to come along, accordingly they went. It was then almost Night and [they traveld all night. Next morning] Mussemeelin say'd, now they are not far off. We will make Ourselves black, then they will be frightned and will deliver up the Horse immediately, and I will tell Jack that if he dont give me the Horse, I will kill him, and when he say'd so, he laughed; The Young Men thought he Joaked as he used to do. They did not blacken themselves, but he did. When the Sun was above the Trees (or about an hour high) they all came to the fire, Where they found James Smith sitting, and they sat also down, Mussemeelin asked where Jack was,   Smith told him that he was gone to clear the Road a little. Mussemeelin say'd he wanted to speak with him, and went that way, and after he had gone a little Distance from the fire, he say'd something and looked back [and laughed], but he having a thick throat, and his Speech being very bad, and their talking with Smith hindred them from understanding what he Said; they did not mind it. They being hungrey Smith told them to kill some [turkis], of which [there] were plenty and [he] would make some bread, and by and by they would all eat together,   While they were a talking they heard a Gun go off not far off, at which time Wood-ward Arnold was killed as they learned afterwards. Soon after Mussemeelin came back and say'd Why did [not] you two kill that White man according as I bid you,   I have laid the other two down; at this they were Surprised, and one of the Young men commonly called [Jamy] run away to the River side. Mussemeelin say'd to the other, How will you do to kill Catabaws if you cannot kill [a white man]. You Coward Ill shew you how you must do, and then taking up the English Ax that lay there, he Struck it three times into Smith's Head before he died,   Smith never stirred,   then he told the Young Indian to call the other, but he was so terrify'd he could not call; Musse-meelin then went and fetched him and say'd to him that two of the Whitemen were killed, he must now go and kill the third, and then each of them would have killed one;   But neither of them dare venture to talk any thing about it. Then he pressed them to [Come] along with him, he went foremost,   then one of the young men told the other as they went along, My Friend don't you kill any of the White People, let him do what he will, I have not killed Smith, he [Killed him] himself, we have no need to do such a Barbarous thing, Mussemeelin being then a good way before them in a hurry, they soon saw John Armstrong sitting upon an old Log, Mussemeelin Spoke to him and Say'd, Where is my Horse? Armstrong made answer and say'd he will come by and by; you shall have him, I want him now said Mussemeelin; Armstrong answer'd you shall have him. Come let us go to that Fire (which was at some distance from the place where Armstrong sat) and let us Smoke and talk together; Go along then sayd Mussemeelin, I am coming said Arm-strong do you go before; Mussemeelin [Said] do you go foremost, Arm-strong looked then like a Dead Man, and went towards the Fire, and was immediately shot in his Back by Mussemeelin and fell [down.] Mussemeelin then took his Hatchet and Struck it into Armstrong's head, and say'd, Give

me my Horse I tell you. By this time one of the Young men had fled again
that had gone away before, [after a while he Came up again.] Mussemeelin
then told the Young men, they must not [tell a word about this or they Should
not live], but they must help him to bury Jack, and the other two were to be
throw'd into the River. After that was done, Mussemeelin ordered them to
load the Horses and follow him towards the Hill where they intended to
hide the Goods, accordingly they did, and as they were going Mussemeelin
told them that as there were a great many Indians hunting about that place,
if they should happen to meet with any, they must be killed to prevent their
Betraying them—As they went along Mussemeelin going before, the two
Young Men agreed to run away [So Soon as they Should happen to met any
Indian], and not to hurt any body. They came to the desired place, the Horses
were unloaded, and Mussemeelin opened the Bundles, and offered the two
Young Men Each a Parcell of Goods. They told him that as they had already
sold their Skins, and everyBody knew they had nothing, they would certainly
be charged with a black Action were they to bring any Goods to the Town,
and therefore they would not accept of any; but promised nevertheless not
to betray him; Now says Mussemeelin I know what you were talking about
when you stay'd so far behind; You have agreed to betray me, but you shall
fare like the White men if you intend to hurt me. The two Young Men being
[a feared of their own lifes (as they had ben all that day)] accepted of what
he offered to them, and the Rest of the Goods they put in a heap and covered
them from the Rain, and then went to their Hunting Cabin; Mussemeelin
unexpectedly finding two or three more Indians there, laid down his Goods
and sayed he had killed Jack Armstrong and taken pay for his Horse, and
should any of them discover it, that person he would likewise kill; but
otherwise they might all take a part of the Goods. The Young man called
Jemmey went away to Shamokin, after Mussemeelin was gone to bury the
Goods with three more Indians with whom he had prevailed; one of them
was Neshaleeny's Son, whom he had ordered to kill James Smith, but those
Indians would not have any of the Goods.

Sometime after the Young Indian had been in Shamokin, it was whispered
about that some of the Delaware Indians had killed Armstrong and his Men. A
Drunken Indian came to one of the Tudolous Houses at Night and told the
Man of the House that he could tell him a piece of bad News, What is that
said the other? the Drunken man said, Some of our Delaware Indians have
killed Armstrong and his Men, which, if our Chiefs [dont] resent and take
them up, I will kill them my self to prevent a Disturbance between us and the
White People our Brethren. [next Morning very Early this Tudolow Indian
Came to Shikelimo. and told him what he had heard last night—Shikelimo
went Imediately to Olumpies the delaware Chief and told him, and pressed
upon him to make Imediatly inquiry and find out the murderers] Shick
Calamy, and some other Indians of the Delawares were called to assist
Olumapies in Council; Then Shick Calamy and Olumapies got one of the
[tudolow] Indians to write a Letter to me to desire me to come to Shamokin
in all haste; that the Indians were much dissatisfyed in mind. This Letter
was brought to my House by four Delaware Indians sent Express; but I was
then in Philadelphia, and when I came home and found no particulars
mentioned in the Letter, and that none of the Indians of the Six Nations had
been down, I did not care to medle with Delaware Indian affairs, and stayd at
home till I received the Governor's Orders to go (which was about two
Weeks after). Olumapies was advised by his Council to employ a Conjuror

(or [Seer] as they call it) to find out the Murderer[s], accordingly he did, and the Indians met; the Seer being busy all Night told them in the morning to Examine such and such a one, they were present when Armstrong was killed; naming the two young men, (Mussemeelin was then present) accordingly Olumapies, [Quithey-yquont] and Thomas Greene an Indian, went to him that fled first and Examined him; he told the whole story very freely; then they went to the other but he would not say a word, but went away and left them. The three Indians returned to ShickCalamy and informed them of what Discovery they had made, When it was agreed to Secure the Murderers and deliver them up to the White People. Then a great Noise arose among the Delaware Indians and some were afraid of their Lives and went into the Woods; [Every one was afeared] to meddle with Mussemeelin and the other that [would not Say anything], because of the Resentment of their families; but they being Pressed by Shick Calamy's Sons to Secure the Murderers, otherwise they would be cut off from the Chain of Friendship, four or five of the Delawares made Mussemeelin and the other Young man Prisoners and tyed them both. They lay twenty-four Hours and none would venture to conduct them down, because of the Great Division among the Delaware Indians; and Olumapies in danger of being killed, fled to Shick Calamy and begged his Protection. At last Shick Calamy's Son [Jak] went to the Delawares, most of them being Drunk, as they had been for Several Days, and told them to Deliver the Prisoners to Alexander Armstrong, and if they were afraid to do it, they might separate their Heads from their Bodies, and lay them in the Canoe, and carry them to Alexander to Roast and eat them, that would satisfy his Revenge as he wants to eat Indians; they prevailed with the said [Jak] to assist them, and accordingly he and his Brother and some of the Delawares went with two Canoes and carry'd them off.

[I left the delawares in great Confusion among themselves ShiKelimo told me the old people wer inclined to make Every thing Easy but they had no Comand at all over their yong man. if it Should happen that Some of them that Seized Mushamy Hillin would be Hurted, there would be sat work and may perhaps agree in Nothing then to do Mischief to the bake Inhabitants of this province. ShiKelimo also Sent a Message to met the deputies of the Six nation in their way to pensilvania, to let them Know that if they should happen to hear of this noise not to be discouraged to Come, but to Come along, and take no Notice of the Storrys that would be industrously Spread among the Indians by the delawares about this affair]

Mushemeelin was removed to Philadelphia before the Six Nations reached Lancaster. There was some little discussion of the affair at the conference, but no unpleasantness. The Indians were invited to send representatives to the trial.

Weiser was present a few months later when the case came up in court. Benjamin Franklin's *Gazette* of November 8, 1744, gives it a brief notice:

Monday last [November 5], at the Court of Oyer and Terminer held here, the Indian, Mushemelon, who murdered Armstrong the Trader, and his two Men, received Sentence of Death, having confessed the Fact.

On November 15, William Bradford's *Pennsylvania Journal, or Weekly Advertiser* noted that "Yesterday the Indian who kill'd Armstrong and his Men, was hang'd."

CHAPTER 23

... *Signs the Lancaster Treaty*

I

THE spring of 1744 was a bleak time for the English colonies. They were at odds among themselves, quarreling about their boundaries. In the west, Indian trouble was brewing. The Shawnees were fractious. Chief Kakowatchiky was faithful to his engagements, both to the Six Nations and to the English; but he was old, and the hot-heads among his people did not listen to him. They listened to Peter Chartier out on the Ohio who was all for the French. Chartier's Indians were trying to get the Delawares to come west and put themselves under French protection; and the Delawares, at Shamokin especially where some of them had settled after being haled out of the Forks in 1742, were inclined to go. The unrest at Shamokin had come to a head, as we have seen, in the murder of John Armstrong.

The one thing more needed to demonstrate the importance of friendship with the Six Nations was the outbreak of a war with France, and that came in due time. In March, France declared war on England; and on June 11 the Governor in Philadelphia presented to his Council "His Majesty's Declaration of War against the French King."

Meanwhile arrangements went ahead in Maryland, Virginia, and Pennsylvania for the "grand Treaty" with the Six Nations at Lancaster. Conrad Weiser, on advice from Richard Peters, had a long conversation with John Kinsey,[1] Speaker of the House, in which he convinced him of the necessity of having Governor Thomas present at the treaty in order to keep things running smoothly, the southern commissioners being ignorant of Indian customs and inclined to be supercilious with "savages." Kinsey assured Weiser the Assembly would engage the Governor to be present if either the Indians or the southern commissioners invited him (which was a foregone conclusion) and would pay the piper.

By the beginning of June all three governments were anxiously awaiting the Six Nations deputies. If the Indians had set out when eight moons were past, as the Black Prince had promised, they should have arrived long before the middle of June. The Virginia delegation, consisting of two commissioners ("Col⁰ Lee a high Man in his own Country & Col Beverley") with "seven Flaming fine Gentlⁿ"[2] whose narrowness, haughtiness, and ignorance of Indians affairs, thought Richard Peters, made poor prospects for the treaty, were waiting testily in Philadelphia. They were much dissatisfied, and thought Conrad Weiser should be got rid of as interpreter—which would have been a disaster, as Governor Thomas of Pennsylvania very well knew. "It is my Opinion," he had written to Governor Gooch of Virginia, "that neither your Government nor that of Maryland will be able to carry on the Treaty without him."[3]

Conrad himself, waiting uneasily at Heidelberg for news of the Indians, was taken ill.

Richard Peters to Conrad Weiser [4]

Philad^a. 4. June 1744

Sir

I am favour'd with yours by your Son & am truly in great concern at the ill State of your health—Dr Grame sends you a Vomit gentle and easy, just to clean your Stomach and some Papers of Bark which if taken according to his directions will relieve you imediately and bring your Strength again in a very quick and surprising manner   as you are a man of sense you will not be against proper remedies and the Governor orders me to tell you that he has taken the same things in such a disorder as yours is & has been relieved by the Bark as if it was a Charm—and I do not doubt but you will recover your Strength instantly if you take them according to the Doctors Prescription.

The Governor gives me further in charge to desire you will have a man & horse ready to send to Annapolis, the moment you hear from Shamokin that the Onontagos Senekas & Cayugas are arriv'd there & that you will in your Letter press the Governor or his Commissioners to set out imediately on the Receit of your Letter & not to stay a moment if they can avoid it but to be as expeditious in their Journy to Lancaster as possible.

I hope Mr Cookson has bespoke Bread Beer and Butchers Meat and will have a large and commodious place for the Indians to be together in—. . .

Your sincere friend
RICHARD PETERS

You will let us know when the Indians will be at Lancaster & when you would have the Governor be there—

It was not till June 13 that Weiser heard from Shamokin of the approach of the deputies. At once couriers were despatched with the news to Annapolis and Philadelphia, and Weiser himself set out for the Susquehanna to bring the Indians down.

Looking back on the Lancaster Treaty from the vantage point of today, we see it to have been a turning point in our colonial history. The "chain of friendship" there made, which extended Pennsylvania's Indian policy to Maryland and Virginia, was the first great setback to the French in the West, and it prepared the way for the downfall of France in America. The treaty gave the English colonies as far south as Virginia an Indian ally capable of protecting their borders. More than that, since this ally held suzerainty over many of the Indians in the West, nominally under French influence, it made an actual break in the chain of settlements and protectorates by which France designed to lock the English colonies in between the mountains and the sea.

To avoid a picturesque and popular misunderstanding that has grown up concerning this treaty, it is as well to say at the outset that it was the Iroquois alliance, not the cession of Iroquois lands, that gave the Lancaster Treaty its importance. It is true that the release given by the Six Nations to Virginia of lands within that province "to the setting of the sun" was used later as legal foundation (by a dubious interpretation) for our claim to the Northwest—a territory comprising the present states of Ohio, Kentucky, Indiana, Illinois, Michigan, and Wisconsin. But it is not true that the Iroquois were cajoled by Virginia into selling that vast country for the £200 in coin and the like sum in knives, kettles, jews'-harps, and other perishables that changed hands at Lancaster. The Iroquois had not come south to dicker over kettles and jews'-harps.

It was an honest treaty. To the Six Nations it was as great a triumph as it was to Maryland and Virginia. In return for lands to which they held only a nominal title (by right of conquest over tribes that had long since been dispersed) they had gained the right of free passage through Virginia for their warriors: i.e., the use of the "Virginia road." They had gained also new allies. Their prestige was thereby heightened among their tributaries and their power increased both with the English, who had been brought to acknowledge dependence on them, and with the French, who feared the new Onondaga-Williamsburg axis. In consequence this gallant little nation, whose whole population at the time amounted to no more than fifteen thousand, was enabled for a few years longer to hold the balance of power between France and England in America, and to determine the course of continental history during the most crucial years of our national minority.

II

To pick up the narrative where we left it: Conrad Weiser, "fortunately reliev'd by Dr Grame's Prescriptions," [5] was able to meet the Indians on the 15th at "James parrys, about 20 Miles above John Harris." [6] There he did the honors: "Killed a Stier for them," and bought "200 hundred weight of flower." There were 245 men, women, and children to be fed.

He found many old friends among them. There was Canasatego, in age "now inclining to three score," whose girth and wit still expanded readily under the influence of the white man's liquor. There was the thoughtful Jonnhaty, captain of the company that had had the late unhappy Skirmish in Virginia, and to whom the present conference was just one stage on the way south again with another war party against the Catawbas. There was Tocanuntie, the Black Prince, tall, thin, black-chested—whose name Loskiel derives from the designs tattooed into the skin of his chest with gunpowder. Tocanuntie, at sixty, was already become a name, a legend of Homeric proportions. He was reputed on one occasion to have broken into a stockaded castle, scalped his enemies, and escaped unhurt.[7] Witham Marshe calls him "One of the greatest warriors that ever the Five Nations produced." [8]

The *Memorandum of the Indian Expences* [9] that Conrad Weiser submitted to the Government of Maryland contains a virtual diary of the journey with his Iroquis friends to Lancaster. On the 16th he bought three hundredweight of flour from Joseph Chambers and "five Shillings worth of Bread and Milk of Simon girty"—father of the good-natured Simon Girty whom legend has evolved into the ogre of Revolutionary tradition.

The Indians lodged that night with a settlement of Nanticokes on the Juniata to discuss the Maryland trouble. Next morning Weiser received a request from the chiefs for more provisions, since they found it necessary to stay two or three days with their wards. He sent them five hundred-weight of flour and nine loaves of bread.

the 19 in the Evening they arrived
    at Joseph Chambers Said they were
    very Hungry I bought a Stier for them
    of Jos. Chambers at 4   00   00
    gave them 300 weight of flower 1   1   00
    treated the Chiefs & others with a
    glass of Rum   8   00
    ten pound of tobacco   5   00
the 20 they being very desireous in the morning to
    have one dram more which I Could
    not deny them   8
    by the way as we Came to John Harris
    two Sheeps 40 loaves of Bread Several
    Beals full of Midling Bear all amounted to .... 2—13— 8
             x   x   x
the 21 at Thomas Harris for diner .... —16— 3
    at our lodging at Samuel Scot they
    having had allmost nothing that day
    I bought four Sheeps at .... 2—00—00
    250 lb flower ....   17— 6
    —Bread & other necessaries ....00 15—00
    paid to a waggener for Carreing
    7 or Eight disabled Indians that day ....00—12—00
    I also paid 12/ to a special Messenger
    from Joseph chambers to lancester with
    Information of the Indians Coming 00 12

Some of the women and children rode into town on horseback, but the twenty-four chiefs and most of the company were afoot. They marched in, equipped with "fire arms and bows and arrows, as well as tomahawks," on Friday, June 22, "in very good order," as an eyewitness, Witham Marshe, records,

. . . with Cannasateego, one of the Onondaga chiefs, at their head, who, when he came near to the Court House, wherein we were dining, sung, in the Indian language, a song inviting us to a renewal of all treaties heretofore made and that now to be made.
Mr. Weiser, the interpreter, who is highly esteemed by the Indians, and is one of their council of state (though a German by birth) conducted them to some vacant lots in the back part of the town, where sundry poles and boards were placed. Of these, and some boughs of trees from the woods, the Indians made wigwams or cabins, wherein they resided during the treaty; they will not, on any occasion whatsoever, dwell, or even stay, in houses built by white people.
They placed their cabins according to the rank each nation of them holds

in their grand council. The Onondagoes nation was placed on the right hand, and at the upper end were the others, according to their several dignities.

After dining, and drinking the loyal healths, all the younger gentleman of Virginia, Maryland and Pennsylvania went with Mr. Conrad Weiser to the Indian camp, where they had erected their several cabins. We viewed them all, and heartily welcomed Cannasateego and Tachanuntie, (alias the Black Prince) two chiefs of the Onondagoes, to town. They shaked us by the hands and seemed very well pleased with us. I gave them some snuff, for which they returned me thanks in their language.[10]

The author of this journal was a well-connected young Englishman who had come out to Maryland in 1737 and was now secretary to the commissioners from that province. Bred in the aristocratic traditions of his time and class, he wrote an observant but unflattering account of the conference, which is valuable because it is candid.

He visited the "wigwam" of Madame Montour, whom he found "genteel and of polite address," though her surroundings depressed him.

The Indians in general were poorly dressed, having old match-coats and those ragged, few or no shirts and those they had as black as the Scotchman made the Jamaicans when he wrote in his letter they were as black as that ● blot.

When they had rested some little space of time several of them began to paint themselves with divers sorts of colors, which rendered them frightful. Some of the others rubbed bear's grease on their faces and then laid upon that a white paint.[11]

The sixteen-year-old town of Lancaster was not at that time, as it has since become, the center of the hearty, busy, house-proud, and hospitable Pennsylvania Dutch community. It was, if we are to believe the fastidious Witham Marshe, a well-laid-out but ill-inhabited settlement of High Dutch, Scotch-Irish, English, and Israelitish people, most of them "sluts and slovens." He found the place detestable for its hot sandy winds, hard water, and "Dutch fleas." The prevailing two-story frame houses, each with its pile of filth beside the door, did not impress him, though he found the Lutheran church (of stone) and the Court House (of brick) "spacious."

It was to the large hall in the latter building that Conrad Weiser took the chiefs, between five and six o'clock on the evening of their arrival, to receive the official welcome that Indian etiquette prescribed. After a round of handshaking, the Indians seated themselves in proper order on the steps flanking the judge's bench. The Governor of Pennsylvania occupied the judicial seat, with the southern commissioners beside him: Col. Thomas Lee and Col. William Beverley of Virginia on his right, and the Hon. Edmund Jennings and the Hon. Philip Thomas of Maryland on his left. The secretaries sat at a half-oval table below the railed bench, William Black of Virginia on the right, Witham Marshe of Maryland on the left, and William Peters of Pennsylvania in the center. Short speeches of welcome and acknowledgment were exchanged; wine, punch, and pipes of tobacco were passed to the chiefs; and healths were drunk on both sides. Then the

Indians retired, with an invitation to return on Monday, after enjoying the decent interval of rest that Indian etiquette again prescribed, to hear the Governor of Pennsylvania formally open the conference.

For the next two weeks we find Conrad Weiser acting as the Indians' unofficial host. He escorted them about and looked after their comfort. He bought tobacco for them by the hundredweight, cracked jokes with Canasatego, bought "two Hates" at Bond's [12] for Onichnayqua, interpreted, advised with all parties to the treaty, composed differences (without yielding rights), and in general maintained throughout the long proceedings an atmosphere of friendly understanding without which the conference would have been a failure even if the chiefs had deeded the moon to Virginia.

For all that, the Indians at Lancaster did not find the idyllic reception that Weiser, Bartram, and Evans had enjoyed at Onondaga. For one thing, they were crowded. Weiser tells us that there were not enough wooden shelters for them. For another, the Southerners were at first determined to take a high tone with "savages." The Virginia commissioners, in particular, had the notion that they could frighten the Indians out of their claims.[13] Governor Thomas of Pennsylvania found it necessary at the outset to warn Lee, Jennings, and the rest that a war with the Six Nations could be nothing but an expensive blunder: even a victory over them would be a disaster to the English, since to crush these people would be to destroy their own barriers against the French.

At first the conference seemed headed for a breakdown. Conrad Weiser, "being told of the Jealousy which Col° Lee had entertain'd of him" [14] (Richard Peters, who is our informant on this matter, was no doubt also Conrad's, Peters being the most assiduous tale-bearer in the colony) determined to leave Lee to his own devices, and absented himself from the Indian councils. His Iroquois friends were perplexed at this change in his behavior and quite at a loss without his advice. Canasatego announced that "they had a Right to one half of him," [15] and sent for him through the Provincial Secretary, enforcing the invitation with a bundle of skins. In the end Conrad accepted, notes Mr. Peters, "& promis'd to act as he us'd to do." [16]

Another shadow that lay on the conference was the disposition of the young blades who attended the southern commissioners to make fun of the Indians. Weiser was alive to the danger, and took quick means to meet it. When these fine gentlemen made their first visit to the Indian encampment, he gave them instructions in good manners, which Marshe faithfully records:

Our interpreter, Mr. Weiser, desired us, whilst we were here, not to talk much of the Indians, nor to laugh at their dress, or make any remarks on their behavior; if we did it would be very much resented by them, and might cause some differences to arise betwixt the white people and them. Besides, most of them understood English, though they will not speak it when they are in treaty.[17]

III

At 10 o'clock on the morning of Monday, June 22, the chiefs reassembled in the Lancaster Court House and the negotiations began.

It was an Iroquois conference. Governor Thomas presided, but he observed the forms of Iroquois ritual. Brother Onas was host at Lancaster, but only in the provincial sense: in a larger sense Pennsylvania and the other English colonies were guests of the Six Nations. The English were come from across the sea, but the Six Nations had come out of this ground.

It was an inflexible law of Iroquois decorum that the party who had called a conference should lead off with a statement of its purpose. Therefore, although the Six Nations had brought to Lancaster well-considered proposals of their own, they observed the strict forms of courtesy and left it to Maryland, on whose particular invitation they were come, to open the discussion.

This was a stumbling-block to Virginia and led to a diplomatic tangle. Col. Lee, a stranger to Six Nations character and unwilling to see English notions of propriety surrendered to those of the Iroquois, balked at this initial procedure and attempted to teach the savages their place. In return for which instruction they paid him by teaching him his.

When Lee observed "that the Indians gave the Precedency to Maryland as being the Government who first invited them, he sent for Conrad & presented him with thirty Pistoles to influence the Indians to give Virginia the preference before Maryland and to tell them that as they were the oldest Colony, they had a right to have the precedency." [18]

The Indians replied that "it was nothing to them who was the oldest Colony." [19] They had come on Maryland's invitation, and Maryland should speak first. If their host, Brother Onas, wished to change the order of ceremony, that was his affair; but of themselves they would never put such an affront on the Annapolis government.

Brother Onas declined to intervene. The Indians stood firm. Maryland spoke first. And Lee was man enough to think more highly thereafter both of the Six Nations and of Conrad Weiser.

The debate that followed Maryland's speech, in which that province (supported by Virginia) contended that the Six Nations had no right to any lands within their borders, but at the same time offered to make compensation if any such rights could be proved, affords one of the best examples of the literature of the Indian treaties—which Lawrence C. Wroth calls the only indigenous literary form produced in America.[20] It is to be noted that literary merit attaches chiefly to the presentation of the Indian case, through Conrad Weiser's translation.

Since possession is nine points of the law, the colonies had an initial advantage in the argument; but Canasatego, Tocanuntie, and Gachradodow, having been trained among a people who had raised statecraft and public debate to the highest art, handled their points with a precision, energy, and imagination that left their antagonists nowhere.

". . . ye Indians really appear superior to ye Comiss^rs in point of Sense & Argum^t," [21] said Richard Peters.

Canasatego picked up the ball from Maryland. Letting his thoughts spring naturally from the words of the Maryland speaker, he gave an excellent history of the problem:

When you mentioned the affair of the Land Yesterday, you went back to old Times, and told us you had been in Posession of the Province of Maryland above One hundred Years, but what is One hundred Years in comparison to the length of Time since our Claim began? Since we came out of this Ground? For we must tell you, that long before One hundred years Our Ancestors came out of this very Ground, and their Children have remained here ever since; you came out of the Ground in a Country that lyes beyond Seas, there you may have a just Claim, but here you must allow Us to be your elder Brethren and the Lands belong to Us long before you knew any thing of them. It is true that above One hundred Years ago the Dutch came here in a Ship and brought with them several Goods such as Awls, Knives, Hatchets, Guns and many other particulars which they gave Us, and when they had taught Us how to Use their things, and we saw what sort of People they were, we were so well pleased with them that we tyed their Ship to the Bushes on the Shoar, and afterwards likeing them still better the longer they stayd with Us, and thinking the Bushes to Slender, we removed the Rope and tyed it to the Trees, and as the Trees were lyable to be blown down by high Winds, or to decay of themselves, We, from the affection We bore them, again removed the Rope, and tyed it to a Strong and big Rock [Here the Interpreter said they mean the Oneido Country] and not content with this, for its further Security We removed the Rope to the Big-Mountain [Here the Interpreter says they mean the Onondago Country] and there we tyed it very fast and rowled Wampum about it, and to make it still more Secure We stood upon the Wampum and sat down upon it, to defend it, to prevent any hurt coming to it, and did our Best endeavours that it might remain uninjured for ever.—During all this Time the Newcomers the Dutch acknowledged Our Rights to the Lands, and Sollicited us from time to time to grant them Parts of Our Country, and to enter into League and Covenant with Us, and to become one People with Us.

After this the English came into the Country, and, as we were told, became one People with the Dutch. about two years after the Arrival of the English, an English Governor came to Albany, and finding what great friendship subsisted between Us and the Dutch he approved it mightily, and desired to make as Strong a League and to be upon as good Terms with us as the Dutch were, with whom he was United, and to become one People with Us, and by his further care in looking what had passed between Us he found that the Rope which tyed the Ship to the Great Mountain was only fastened with Wampum which was lyable to break and rot and to perish in a Course of Years, He therefore told us that he would give us a Silver Chain, which would be much stronger and last for Ever. This we Accepted, and fastned the Ship with it and it has lasted ever since. Indeed we have had some small Differences with the English, and during these misunderstandings, some of their Young men, would, by way of Reproach, be every now and then telling us, that we should have perished if they had not come into the Country and furnished us with Strowds and Hatchets and Guns and other things necessary

for the Support of Life, But we always gave them to understand that they
were mistaken, that we lived before they came amongst us, and as well or
better, if we may believe what Our Forefathers have told Us. We had then
room enough and Plenty of Deer, which was easily caught, and tho' we had
not Knives, Hatchets, or Guns such as we have now, yet we had Knives of
Stone and Hatchets of Stone, and Bows and Arrows—and these Served Our
Uses as well then, as the English ones do now. We are now Straitned and
sometimes in want of Deer, and lyable to many other Inconveniences since
the English came among Us, and particularly from that Pen and Ink work, that
is going on at the Table.[22]

Pointing to the secretaries, he proceeded to give an instance of this "Pen
and Ink work": the Dongan Deed of 1786, when the Six Nations gave their
Susquehanna lands to the Governor of New York to hold for them in
trust—only to find later that he had gone to England "and carryed Our
Land with him, and then Sold it . . ."
So much for the general background. But Canasatego did not allow himself to become lost in generalities:

We now come nearer home. We have had your Deeds Interpreted to Us,
and we acknowledge them to be good and valid, and that the Conestogoe or
Sasquehannah Indians had a Right to sell those Lands unto you, for they were
then theirs; but since that time We have Conquered them, and their Country
now belongs to Us, and the Lands we demanded satisfaction for, are no part
of the Lands comprized in those Deeds; they are the Cohongoroutas Lands.
Those we are sure you have not possessed One hundred Years; No, nor
above Ten years. And we made our Demand so soon as we knew your People
were Settled in those Parts. These have never been sold, but remain still to be
disposed of; And we are well pleased to hear you are Provided with Goods,
and do assure you of Our Willingness to Treat with You for those unpurchased Lands. In confirmation whereof We present you with this Belt of
Wampum.[23]

When later the commissioners of Virginia in their turn declared that "the
Great King holds Virginia by Right of Conquest, and the Bounds of that
Conquest to the Westward is the Great Sea," [24] Gachradodow replied with
a dignity of manner that gave his irony double force:

The World at the first was made on the other side of the Great water
different from what it is on this side, as may be known from the different
Colour of Our Skin and of Our Flesh, and that which you call Justice may not
be so amongst us; You have your Laws and Customs and so have we. The
Great King might send you over to Conquer the Indians, but looks to Us,
that God did not approve of it, if he had, he would not have Placed the
Sea where it is, as the Limits between us and you.[25]

Witham Marshe was not a man to overestimate his fellow creatures,
especially if they lacked clean linen; but his description of Gachradodow,
whom he heard wind up the debate, would have pleased Rousseau:

This Gachradodon is a very celebrated warrior, and one of the Cahuga
chiefs, about forty years of age, tall, straight-limbed, and a graceful person,

but not so fat as Cannasateego. His action, when he spoke, was certainly the most graceful, as well as bold, that any person ever saw; without the buf-foonery of the French, or over-solemn deportment of the haughty Spaniards. When he made the complimentary speech on the occasion of giving Lord Baltimore the name of Tocary-ho-gon, he was complimented by the Governor, who said "that he would have made a good figure in the forum of old Rome." And Mr. Commissioner Jenings declared, "that he had never seen so just an action in any of the most celebrated orators he had heard speak." [26]

"You know very well," said Gachradodow, "when the White People came first here, they were poor; but now they have got our Lands, and are by them become Rich, and we are Now poor; What little we had for the Land goes soon away, but the Land lasts forever." [27]

If it is true that the importance of the treaty lay not in its pen-and-ink work (of which the Indians had so lively and well-founded a distrust) but in the friendly atmosphere that was built up during the proceedings and united all parties in the end, then its proper climax is to be found in the great dinner given by the commissioners of Maryland to the twenty-four chiefs, Governor Thomas, and "a great many gentlemen of two or three British colonies." Witham Marshe is our guide again to this lively scene in the Court House.

We had five tables, great variety of dishes, and served up in very good order. The sachems sat at two separate tables; at the head of one, the famous orator, Canasateego, sat, and the others were placed according to their rank. As the Indians are not accustomed to eat in the same manner as the English, or other polite nations do, we who were secretaries on this affair, with Mr. Thomas Cookson, prothonotary of Lancaster county, William Logan, esq., son of Mr. President Logan, and Mr. Nathaniel Rigbie, of Baltimore county, in Maryland, carved the meat for them, served them with cider and wine, mixed with water, and regulated the economy of the two tables. The chiefs seemed prodigiously pleased with their feast, for they fed lustily, drank heartily, and were very greasy before they finished their dinner, for, by-the-by, they make no use of their forks.

The interpreter, Mr. Weiser, stood betwixt the tables, where the Governor sat, and that, at which the sachems were placed, who, by order of his Honour, was desired to inform the Indians he drank their healths, which he did; whereupon they gave the usual cry of approbation, and returned the compli-ment by drinking health to his Honour and the several Commissioners. [28]

IV

The treaty came to an end on July 4 in great good humor. Canasatego made a speech in which he promised aid to his English brethren against the French. The Six Nations, he said, would use their authority over many nations in alliance with the French, especially the Praying Indians "who stand in the very gates of the French"; and would see to it that these tribes remained neutral. Further, the Six Nations would forbid the French to pass through any part of their dominions to hurt the English.

He praised Conrad Weiser: "We hope Tarachawagon will be preserved by the Good Spirit to a good old age; when he is gone under Ground, it will be then time enough to look out for another; . . . while he lives there is no room to complain." [29]

Canasatego proposed that a health be drunk in rum out of the booty the English had supposedly taken from the French in a recent engagement —but not drunk out of the small "French glasses" the company had used the day before. Accordingly the Governor circulated larger glasses which he said were English and therefore more generous. All drank the health of King George and of the Six Nations, and the treaty ended with three British cheers.

The commissioners of Virginia, on taking their leave, presented Canasatego with "a Scarlet Camblet Coat," and the commissioners of Maryland gave Gachradodow "a Broad Gold-Laced Hat." [30] Virginia's written promise to put in a good word for the Six Nations with the Great King across the water for "his further Grace and favour to the Said Six Nations," [31] was left by the chiefs with Conrad Weiser for safe keeping.

In the evening, when Governor Thomas visited the Indians to take his leave of them, he brought up the matter of Conrad Weiser's beard. Presenting his guests with a string of wampum, "he told them, that was in return for theirs, praying him, that as they had taken away one Part of Conrad Weiser's Beard, which frightned their Children, he would please to take away the other, which he had ordered to be done." [32]

Whether the Indians wished the famous beard to submit again to fatal steel, it is impossible from that brief record to determine. It may be that the councilors merely intended to say, in their humorous, allegorical way, that as their business had already drawn Weiser in good part from his seclusion at Ephrata, they hoped the Governor would see to it that he should emerge wholly and devote himself exclusively to "council affairs." Or it may be that they were only having a last joke with Brother Enoch. The final word has not yet been said about the mystery of Conrad Weiser's beard.

If the colonies had good reason to be satisfied with the treaty, so had the Six Nations. It had strengthened their hand with the French, the French Indians, the Catawbas, the Delawares, and the Jack-in-the-box Shawnees. To Weiser, who had shaped this triumph for them, they paid the unusual compliment of asking him to sign his name to the Maryland deed, as representing the Mohawk nation which had sent no deputies. And he was to sign his new name, Tarachiawagon, the Holder of the Heavens.

The use of the name Tarachiawagon (Tarughia Waggon, Tarenyawagon, Tarachawagon, etc., are all attempts to render in English spelling the same Indian sound) was in itself an unparalleled honor. The name comes from the old Iroquois pantheon, in which Tarachiawagon, the Holder of the Heavens, was chief. He was, says Horatio Hale,

. . . the Master of Life. He declared his will . . . in dreams, and in like manner disclosed future events, particularly such as were important to the public welfare. He was, in fact, the national god of the Iroquois. It was he who guided their fathers in their early wanderings, when they were seeking for a place of abode. He visited them from time to time, in person, to protect them from their enemies and to instruct them in useful arts. . . . this deity, who is certainly, in character and attributes, one of the noblest creations of the North American mythologies, dates from the era of the confederacy, when he became more especially the chief divinity and protector of the Kanonsionni.[33]

About this time the mythical Tarachiawagon was becoming confused in the minds of story-tellers with the historical Hiawatha. According to "Governor Blacksnake" (a Seneca chief who was born shortly before the Lancaster Treaty, became a friend of George Washington, and died at a ripe age in 1859) it was Tarachiawagon who, seeing the distresses of mankind, took upon himself a human form and came down to earth in a white stone canoe. Here, as Hiawatha, he formed the Great League and established peace.[34]

Tarachiawagon-Hiawatha, the god-man: Holder of the Heavens and founder of the United Nations.

That is what Count Zinzendorf had in mind when, in letter after letter, he referred to Conrad Weiser as the "Emperor of the 6 Nations" or "Emperor of the Nations." [35] That is what he had in mind when, in the early spring of 1742, he wrote to the "Venerable Polycarp" about the journey he proposed to make *inter populorum Sex*, Onondagum *patres conscriptos, cum imperator illorum Conrado Weiser, patre gentium* [36]—a visit to the Senators of the Six Nations at Onondago, in company with their emperor Conrad Weiser, Father of the Peoples.

That also is what William Johnson had in mind when, jealous of his rival, he forbade the Mohawks to call Conrad Weiser *Tarachiawagon*, that being, as he said, too high a name for any man.[37]

And that, it may even be, is what the Zionitic Brotherhood at Ephrata had had in mind when they gave Conrad Weiser the name of Enoch on his entrance into Zion; for that name is as close a one as could be found in Biblical lore and rabbinical tradition to the blended Tarachiawagon and Hiawatha. Enoch, the father of Methusaleh, did indeed live in two worlds. Tradition tells us that he was taken from earth to heaven, where he was called the "Prince of God's Face," and where he was appointed the guardian of the celestial treasures as well as chief of the archangels; and upon earth (to which he returned for a space of 243 years) he was a king who brought peace to his people.

And now Conrad Weiser, "the guardian of all the Indians," [38] *pater gentium*, who here at Lancaster had raised Hiawatha's and Deganaweda's League to its last peak of greatness, was asked to sign the treaty with the name of the Confederacy's ancient founder and protector.

But this affectionate apotheosis did not save Weiser from the distresses that flesh is heir to. At the end of his account of *Indian Expences in June 1744*, he scribbled a note which is here translated from the German:

Memorandum [39]
Mad. Montur's fever medicine
a good thimbleful tied in a rag and
dissolve it in a half pint of water
and throw away what is left over
it melts like salt little crystals
remain which are to be thrown away
when the fever comes on the half pint
of water to be given the patient
to drink and repeat if it returns
(for a Child in proportion)

CHAPTER 24

... Corresponds with
Thomas Lee of Virginia

ONE of the best things that came out of the Lancaster Treaty was the friendship between Conrad Weiser and Thomas Lee.

A portrait of Thomas Lee in his wig and crimson gown of office used to hang for many years in Stratford Hall. One cannot look at that portrait and not love the man. We need not feel, as his grandson Thomas Lee Shippen felt, a disposition to kneel before it; but at least we cannot fail to recognize what the painter has so well conveyed on canvas: a blend of nobility and gentleness that is altogether irresistible. Not that there is anything abstract about the picture. The face is highly individual. It shows spirit and determination, as we should expect of the President of the Council, Commander in Chief, and Acting Governor of Virginia. But it is also open and friendly. It is not at all a typical eighteenth-century face. There is a suggestion of Elizabethan dash and "magnanimity" about it, together with a strain of chivalry, a touch of mild Puritanism, and even something of Poor Richard's shrewdness and humor. It belongs less to his time than to his nation. It is an American face.

It was natural that Weiser should be drawn to such a man, and that Lee should be drawn to Weiser. More than political expediency (though there was that, too) went into the expressions of friendship that passed between them. There was a real community of mind, which differences in origin, language, and education could not hide.

Burton J. Hendrick, in *The Lees of Virginia*, writes of Thomas Lee's "deep religious feeling, his sense of paternal responsibility, devotion to friends, dislike of cheap ostentation, directness of purpose . . . decision of character and imperiousness." [1] Every word might have been written of Conrad Weiser. In a passage intended to show how much Thomas Lee had in common with George Washington, Mr. Hendrick again uses terms that bring Conrad Weiser before our minds. Lee was an "outdoor" man. He "loved to watch his crops develop"; he was impelled by "a constant reaching out into new fields"; he was "an impassioned American . . . imaginatively spellbound by the future of the continent"; and his eyes "saw beyond the Blue Ridge hills, beyond the Alleghenies." [2]

There was, it must be admitted, another side to Thomas Lee's character which rendered him not too attractive to official Pennsylvania. He was sometimes careless about the methods he used in reaching out into new (and perhaps other men's) fields, so that he impressed himself upon James Hamilton of Pennsylvania as "a haughty overbearing Virginian . . . as full of Cavil and Chicanery as an Attorney." [3]

Weiser had early run into this least amiable of Thomas Lee's moods and, on contact, had reacted with his usual explosive warmth, as we have seen. Lee harbored no resentment for the correction he received at Lancaster, and treated Weiser thereafter with respect and consideration. Lee interested himself in the things in which Weiser was interested and could instruct him. In so doing Lee showed himself to be both the patriot and the gentleman. He put Weiser at his ease and so won his coöperation in the play then beginning in the Old Dominion for the stakes of western empire.

Thomas Lee was a grandson of the Richard Lee who had come from England, established the family, and begun the saga of the Lees of Virginia. Thomas had dreams of English expansion into the Great West. In Weiser he recognized another man of vision, and from him he learned that the necessary preliminary to any such expansion was an understanding of the race that had "come out of this ground."

In the early correspondence between the two, the religion, social customs, and polity of the Six Nations was the principal theme. Thomas Lee asked the questions, and Conrad Weiser answered them with generous takings from his own store of experience. No man was better qualified than he to discuss the Six Nations. He had known them intimately from boyhood, and wrote not from hearsay but from observation. At the same time, no man was better able to interpret them, because, not having lived with them uninterruptedly, he had never lost his perspective. They were not mere "redskins" to him. He felt their common humanity. But he thought of them always in comparison with the whites, and so gave his readers the touchstone of dramatic sympathy.

To Weiser, who was rebellious against the complacent hypocrisies of the social system to which he was bound, the Indians seemed to be in many ways better men than the whites. Especially among the Six Nations at Onondaga he had found the simple virtues that the Christian world appeared to have thrown away as relics of a barbarous age. But there was another side to the picture, and Weiser was too honest to overlook it. He was no sentimentalist writing advance notices for Rousseau. He did not idealize his brown brethren. He saw their faults and talked about them —sometimes to their faces. His description of Indian customs is, therefore, dispassionate. But though he is honest, he is never dry or disquisitional. In the letters that follow, he is writing about people, not ethnology: while discussing institutions he never steps far beyond his own observation and experience. He is *at home* with these people, having shared in their amusements, their council business, their family griefs, and their national pride.

The correspondence opens with a letter from Colonel Lee about the Virginia Road.

Thomas Lee to Conrad Weiser [4]

Stratford Augt 30. 1744

Sir
     the 26th of this month I rec'd your letter of the 16th of July with the names of the Cheifs our friends: which I thank you for. Imediately we had the Indian roads printed as you will see in the print inclosed, with a written form

of a pass. you may assure our Brethren y[t] every thing we promis[d] shall be done, I have a great deal of Good will for them, and will be their friend to the utmost of my power. the roads were printed y[t] none of our people might pretend Ignorance. you have soe . . . much trouble in these affairs, and have done the King & the three Colonys soe much service, with faithfulness to the trust the Six nations have in you y[t] I think you ought to have a pension for life.

I shall be obliged to you to give me as full an acc[t] as you can of the religion and Government of these our brethren how many fighting men in each Nation how many they have tributarys, and allies, and how farr each of y[e] Six Nations are from Lancaster.

I order the postage to be p[d] to Philadelphia & recom[d] it to the Postmasters care. my Son returns you his service & thanks for your kindness to him, and I assure you I am very Sincerely & with much Friendship

your very hu[ble] Serv[t]
THOMAS LEE

If we can persuade the Cawtabas
   they shall come to you to be conducted
    in safety—

The letter Weiser sent in response is not at hand, but it is known what he wrote. He used his first letter to Lee, and a second that followed, to satisfy the inquiries of others, notably Edmund Jennings and Christopher Saur. The letter to Saur was widely circulated and has been preserved for us in several early transcripts, in the printed pages of Saur's newspaper and almanac, and also (in part) in a pamphlet published by Benjamin Franklin. It is from the Saur letter that we take what may be safely regarded as the gist of Weiser's reply to Thomas Lee.

Conrad Weiser to Thomas Lee [5]

Of what is generally called a Religion, vix., a person openly contracting or uniting himself to God, and acting according to his prescribed laws and commands, either through fear or love, they have certainly . . . no outward form; therefore they have neither preacher nor meeting, no Formal Doctrine, no Formal Prayers; but when occasion offers we see that some confess and worship the Creator of all Things; they have usually a quantity of superstitions; if some of them are argued with, and such truths presented which they cannot deny, they apparently acknowledge and do not Contradict them; but perhaps a few minutes afterwards they will make a laughing-stock of them and scorn them. And they sometimes ask very foolish questions, for they have many silly fancies about spirits, about their dreams, and their sorceries; they believe that there are spirits in everything, in stones, rivers, trees, mountains, roads, &c. with which their old men can talk; sometimes they make offerings to these spirits, to incline them to protect them, and give them good luck in hunting and in battle.

A certain Indian was on a long journey through the bush with a German, and one evening, as a very heavy rain was coming on, they were building a hut; the Indian wanted to drive stakes into the ground; but, as the ground was stony, and the stakes would not go in, he began to speak to the spirits in the stones, telling them they must give way, so that he could drive the stakes into the ground, or he would force them to yield; presently he entreated them, saying, "My Friend! I and my companion want to stay here to-night, and you must let me drive these stakes into the ground; so give way a little, or I will dig you out of the ground and throw you into the fire." And thereupon he worked hard, every now and then speaking harshly, as if he were striving or fighting with some one. The German laughed at him; but he said, "You see that I am beating, for the stones are giving way on one side. We poor Indians cannot use iron instruments like you Europeans; but we have other means, which we have learned from our Grandfathers, and we have it much easier if we talk to the spirits, and call them friends, and mingle threats therewith, then we succeed." . . .

There is very little to say about their government or manner of governing and justice, excepting what pertains to their transactions and demeanour with other nations, for in that respect they take great pains: Each nation of the six tribes sends Deputies to the great Council at Onontago once or twice a year to confer with each other; they are very slow in coming to a decision in the Council, and have good rules which are looked to and kept inviolably . . .

. . . When any one has done anything that is considered worthy of death, the most eminent men of the nation meet and examine into it, whether the charge is true or false; for no one is charged with or accused of anything among them except of murder or robbery. If it is found to be true, the friends of the guilty person try to appease the injured party with gifts, and then they are present at the tribunal. When the crime is too great, and the guilty person is a notorious murderer or thief, that is, has been guilty several times before, then they counsel his own tribe to kill him, his tribe advise his own family to tell him the sentence, and then his nearest friend, and very seldom any one else, kills him.

The criminal is made drunk, and perhaps a quarrel is begun with him by the one who is appointed to do it, who then charges him with his offence, and at the same time informs him of the cause of his death. And in the ensuing quarrel he is killed, and the rum bears the blame, so that the avenger of blood has no power over the doer of the deed. . . .

Concerning their Warriors. We cannot say with certainty concerning their number and the number of their warriors, for they are very much scattered about the streams which flow into the Mississippi, and around the Lakes or Seas of Canada and among the French.

The Maquaische are considered to have about 100 warriors at home.

The Oneider perhaps as many.

The Tuscarrora have about 150.

The Onontager not many over 200.

The Cayjucker about 500.

The Sinicker about 700 at home, or not far from home.

The Six Nations live about 400 miles from Lancaster; if we could go there in a straight line, it would be much nearer; but we cannot travel directly there on account of lofty mountains. . . .

Concerning their Allies and Friends, we have heard from a trustworthy Indian, who has travelled a great deal, that of them there are as follows:—

(1st) The Zis-a-gech-Roonu, who live in three great cities on the eastern side of Huron's Lake, have of warriors about 2400

(2nd) The Unich-Kalliagon have of warriors 3000

These live on the west side of Lake Erie, and onward to the strait of Huron's Lake.

(3rd) The Runada-Wadeeny are the next mentioned neighbors. Their warriors are about 400

(4th) The Oyjachdanich-Roonu live near the Black River, and have of warriors about 1000

(5th) The Towwichtowich-Roonu, on the Thunackgi River have 300

(6th) The Gechdagech-Roonu, on the great River Mississippi 500

(7th) The Ofkuniagis, on an arm of the Ohio towards the west 1000

(8th) The Karbaguch-Roonu (in German wild people) dwell and are to the north of Huron's Lake; they do not sow, but journey from one place to another; their number is uncertain. It is said they are more numerous than all the rest in alliance with the Iroquois.

(9th) the Schawanös, on the River Ohio, have of warriors 200

(10th) The Dellewar, in Pennsylvania and Ohio 200

(11th) The Mohickander, which are scattered along Hudson River and in New England, not fewer than 300

Thus in all such as bear arms in war there are 9300

The art of war they understand extremely well, particularly in the wilderness, for it is their occupation from their youth up. Indeed, they seek no other honor or happiness than to be good warriors. The parents do everything in their power to make their sons brave heroes; they frequently send them into battle when they are only 12 or 15 years old, but under the control of good officers. They are light on their feet, can endure hunger three to four days, indeed, if it is necessary, even longer, and at the same time march every day thirty, forty, to fifty English miles and attack their enemy. In war they are a crafty, cruel, and daring people. A European who wishes to stand well with them, must practise well the three following virtues: They are—

(1) Speak the truth;

(2) Give the best that he has;

(3) Show himself not a coward, but courageous in all cases.

They believe that when the soul of a person leaves the body, it takes a long journey to a happy land, where there are quantities of fat game, and everything grows luxuriantly. There the huckleberries are as large as a man's fist, and the strawberries are equally as large, and their taste is much better than ours. There a man can lie in the shade the whole day, and the most beautiful maidens wait upon him. There no one grows old. Those who have been the best and most heroic warriors here, there have the pre-eminence, and rule over the good women. No bad people come to this place, but if a common man got there, he must be the servant of the others for many a year. . . .

I have been at their burials; there we see everything that the dead man owned brought to the burying place, and as soon as he is buried, everything is divided; among others, everything is put in the box with the dead; but they always give him bows and arrows, hatchets, kettles, and a dressed skin for shoes, so that he is provided for in the long journey until he reaches the pleasant land of souls, where they hope to meet with their fathers and grandfathers, and other good friends in a blissful life.

When a chaste wife has lost her husband, she is not married again until a winter and a summer have passed, and then she must be urged to it by her friends. During this time she should rather lose her life than do anything dishonorable. And so, too, with an honorable man; they mourn a long time, and at first go to the grave almost every morning, afterwards every month, and make their lamentations very mournfully and sorrowfully to inspire one with pity; they allow no grass to grow on the grave, but scrape the ground daily with their hands, so that it looks as if it had been made yesterday.

When the time of mourning is over, the friends come and bring gifts to wipe away the tears from the sorrowing eyes. In the mean time, the deceased has arrived in the land of souls, and the friends give a feast. No one dare mention the name of the dead person after he is buried; if any one does it ignorantly, he commits a misdeed; but if some one does it in defiance, they often avenge it with death to cool their anger, etc. . . .

I am your devoted
CONRAD WEISER

Thomas Lee to Conrad Weiser [6]

Stratford Dec[r] 28, 1744

M[r] Weiser

I recd your letter with the acc[t] of our Friends the Six Nations and I must Own my self very much Obliged for that curious account. I tho't by what I had seen in some of their treatys, y[t] they had both believed in, and Worship[d] a supreme being, and I wish I had not been mistaken   we have some among those y[t] have had the light of revelation, y[t] Scoff at religion almost in the Indian manner, and yet have the folly with Shekellemy to believe what cannot possibly be true.

What more you may recollect be soe kind to write me   I shall not be weary of corresponding with you. what is marriage, have they more wives than one, does y[e] marriage last for life. is chastity a virtue among them. doe the children inherit any thing from their parents, or are they when grown, left to make their way, without any further care of their parents, pray doe, tell me all you know about these extraordinary people and don't be niggardly in your information.

I have done you Justice here and at London, and you may be sure of any thing I can doe for you

I am

Your friend and humble Servant
THOMAS LEE

the Gov[r] will write you ab[t] the Cataubas.

Conrad Weiser to Thomas Lee [7]

. . . If, by the Word Religion, People mean an Assent to certain Creeds, or the Observance of a Sett of religious Duties, as appointed Prayers, Singing, Preaching, Baptism, &c. or even heathenish Worship, then it may be said, the *Five Nations*, nor their Neighbors, have no Religion. But if by Religion we mean an Attraction of the Soul to God, or an Union of the Soul with God, from which proceeds a Confidence in, and Hunger after, the Knowledge of him, then these People must be allowed to have some Religion amongst them, notwithstanding their sometime savage Deportment: For we find amongst them some Traces of a Confidence in God alone; and even sometimes (though but seldom) a vocal Calling upon him.—I shall give one or two Instances of what fell under my own Observation. . . .

The two instances are from the Onondaga journey of 1737, and in both Shickellamy is the principal figure. It will be recalled that on March 25, while the party was climbing along the snow-crusted mountainside to escape the floods in the Lycoming Valley, Shickellamy slipped and would have fallen over a cliff if his pack had not caught in a small tree and held him. When he got down off the mountain and looked up at the cliff over which he had so nearly fallen, he "was astonished, and turned quite pale; then, with outstretched Arms, and great Earnestness, spoke these Words; 'I thank thee, great Lord and Governor of this World, in that thou hast had Mercy on me, and hath been willing that I should live longer.'"

On the following 8th of April, 1737, Conrad had been so worn out with cold, hunger, and floundering through snow in the "terrible forest" north of Otseninky, that his spirit broke. Turning aside from the trail, he sank down trembling and prepared to die. His companions soon missing him came back and found him sitting there.

He declared that he was unable to go on. "Here will I die," he said.

The Indians were silent for a moment. Then an old man among them spoke. "My dear Companion," he said, "thou hast hitherto encouraged us; wilt thou now quite give up? Remember that evil Days are better than good; for when we suffer much, we do not sin; and Sin will be drove out of us by Suffering: But good Days cause Men to sin, and God cannot extend his Mercy to them; but, contrariwise, when it goes evil with us, God has Compassion upon us." [8]

Conrad got up and went on his journey.

Conrad Weiser to Thomas Lee (continued) [9]

As for Betrothal and marriage among the Indians, that according to ancient custom is a Contract made by the parents of the two young people. What brings them together as a rule is the love and respect their parents have for each other but though the parents have arranged the match and advised the young people the latter are left free to accept or not as they please · the young man or his parents give presents to the promised bride the value depending either on what they can give or on what she is worth: her father takes charge of the presents: She has nothing to do, except now and then bring her fiancé some Indian corn-bread or carry a load of wood to his home and sit down beside him for maybe an hour, or longer: she does not say a word to him, nor he to her, both look very serious and if they did not behave so it would be frowned on as a breach of wedlock. There is no wedding ceremony except a banquet which their friends celebrate with them. When the wedding is over each of the parties usually goes back to his own house and they do not at first live together. however, as soon as the wedding feast is over the bride claims the presents that had been given for her: if however she takes an aversion to him and refuses to receive him or likes another man better then she must follow the established custom and take back the presents to him herself.

It happens now and then that some old fellow bespeaks a beautiful young girl and brings her parents many gifts of deerskins etc. looks after her and becomes her protector or guardian until such time as her mother pronounces her ready for marriage, and they consider such an arrangement no discredit to the girl, on the contrary she is proud of the fact that her maidenhood is so highly esteemed: but once she is old enough to marry if she finds herself more attracted to another man, she has only to say she will not have him.

Their marriages are binding only so long as both parties desire it; if either the man or the woman is no longer content to live with the other, and simply says: I will go away and leave you, then the other says: All right! and that is the end of the marriage.

They never engage to live together for life. They say such a promise would be foolish: for certainly no one can say how long a couple will be at one.

A man seldom has more than one wife: but if he has two, each of them must remain in her own cabin till he visits one or the other.

If they have children and are divorced, the woman keeps them: but when once they have 3 or 4 children they seldom separate.

When the man takes a distant journey, or goes off on a long hunt, and his wife is with child or is otherwise prevented from going, she does not get angry if he takes another woman along to look after him, and when he comes back she returns to her cabin and he to his: the women do not quarrel about it, but are friendly with one another.

Chastity is a virtue with them: when a virgin has such a reputation (as indeed there are many among them who deserve the name) she is respected by everyone, the bravest warriors and the best hunters seek her in marriage. When such women go out, they cover their faces with a veil, and speak to no man on the way, except their husband, or father or brother: it is a crime for them to speak to anyone else: And it is the same with a man who meets a woman. No one among them would accost a woman except lewd fellows, of whom there are some among them though they are not nearly so common among them as among the Christians

If a woman desires a man in marriage, she goes into his cabin and lies down at his feet: when he asks her what she wants, she says, she wants to marry him. If he likes her, no further ceremony is necessary. In the morning at sunrise she goes home, bakes a basketfull of Indian corn-bread: if however she has no corn, nor her friends either, she fetches a load of wood to the bridegroom's house, as a service to the good women of the house: then a feast is held by the bridegroom's friends.

But if a woman has thus laid herself at the feet of a man as described and he does not want to marry her, he speaks kindly to her and lets her go home again: or if she stays overnight, she does it only to try the persuasion of friendly words: if she is a modest woman, she will not allow herself to be touched, and it would be a great crime on his part to think of molesting her, he would lose all reputation. . . .

The children inherit no property from their parents; when the old people die, they leave their property to others, it generally remains with their friends; the oldest man of the family makes a present out of it at his pleasure, the children very seldom receive any of it, even though they desire it; if they are grown up they must take care of themselves.

If a young man is a good hunter, he is in no want, his wife or her mother, or his mother, if he is not married, is master of his deerskins; but he is well clothed, and everything necessary is given to him that he may live like a gentleman of his kind. . . .

There is a bit at the end of the Saur letter which, though no part of the original correspondence with Lee, is too rich to be passed over, exhibiting as it does the essential conflict between Conrad Weiser and the world of wigs, powders, and pomades.

He observed that he liked the language of the Six Nations because it recognized no social distinctions. Its pronoun *isë*—"thou" or "you"—was used for everybody, high or low. This lingustic brotherliness (corresponding with the broad use of the friendly *du* among the Pennsylvania Germans)

he contrasted with the snobbery of proud persons who employed the High German *Sie* for respectable address, and reserved *du* for God, or people one disliked, or the dog.

He contrasted also the Christlikeness of the Indians, who shared everything they had and coveted no titles, with the grabbing and place-hunting that infested the Christian community. If the Indians ever became Christians, he remarked slyly, they would have one advantage over the rest of us: they would never have to off-hat to anyone, since they had no hats to begin with.

From this it will be seen that at heart Conrad Weiser was still one of the "Plain People." He was not at home with periwigged Christianity. He hated the whole glittering show of eighteenth-century gentility, with its brittle-minded people wearing peach- and plum- and cherry-colored satins, bowing and scraping and uttering such a deal of "pickled-herring compliments" (*Bickel-herrings Complimenten*) as put the honest interpreter off his feed.

CHAPTER 25

... *Receives Henry Muhlenberg into the Family**

THE closing entry in Weiser's autobiography was made when his last child, Benjamin, was born. That was at Heidelberg on August 12, 1744. By good fortune Conrad was able to be at home, as far as I can learn, for that event. But within a day or two of Benjamin's arrival, Shickellamy and some thirty Delaware Indians, bringing with them the two young men whom Mushemeelin had demanded should be brought in before he would consent to die, turned up at the house, where they stayed "3 days and nights." Then they took Conrad along with them to Philadelphia, arriving there on the 18th, to help "Clear the Air that was rendred foul and Corrupted" by the murder of John Armstrong. Conrad Weiser, as interpreter for Shickellamy, removed the hatchet that had been struck into Brother Onas' head, and buried it "deep under Ground, that it may never be seen more, nor remember'd by Us nor those who are under the Ground to the latest Posterity." [1]

In September he took eight young men up the trail with him to build a "locke house" for Shickellamy. This log house was a handsome affair, "49½ foot long, and 17½ wide," [2] its floor raised high above the ground so that the old chief's last years might be lived in peace—out of reach of the drunken Indians whom he abominated, being himself a teetotaler.

Conrad was in Philadelphia again for a couple of weeks in October, taking part as interpreter in the trial of Mushemeelin. The story of this sturdy Indian was drawing to a close. He had said, it may be recalled, that he would die gladly for having killed a great rogue and his companions; but he had no intention of dying before his time. On August 21, 1744, Shickellamy warned Governor Thomas that that night Mushemeelin intended to break prison with the help of "the Black Art," of which he was a master. [3] The Governor, who had enough faith in Indian art to accept Indian herb remedies for his own apparently incurable disease, took Shickellamy's warning seriously and had the prisoner put in irons. In due time Mushemeelin was tried, condemned, and hanged. The two young men, whom Weiser's report from Shamokin had exonerated, were allowed to go free.

It was probably this same autumn of 1744 that gave birth to the legend about the Hains boys and the prank they played on the Provincial Interpreter. According to a tradition current in the Hains family, some of Conrad's neighbors found him too "high hat" for their taste, and determined

* Acknowledgment is made to the editors of the *Historical Review of Berks County* for permission to reprint parts of an article entitled "Conrad Weiser's Son-in-Law," contributed by the author to the issue of July 1939.

to have a little sport with his dignity. One night the Hains boys put straw up in a tree near his house and set fire to it while he and his family were sleeping in the attic. When the blaze brought out the Justice, *coram populo,* in his nightgown, he was greeted with a shout, in good *Pensylvanisch: De King's Bull iss verreckt. Mir müssen celebriren!*—"The King's bull is dead. We must celebrate!" The legend has it that the Interpreter, incensed at this interruption of his Provincial Slumbers, haled the Hains into court— and there suffered the further indignity of having the case against his puck-ish neighbors dismissed.

I should like to think this story true, and not a mere dilution, as I fear it is, of an exceedingly ugly crime that came near to wiping out the whole Weiser family.

The facts are these: The Heidelberg community in 1744 was terrorized by the doings of some of the less amiable members of the Hains family, whose misdemeanors ranged somewhat too freely over the ground covered by the Ten Commandments. Already law-abiding members of the commu-nity were thinking of moving away for better safety, when Conrad Weiser, compelled as a justice of the peace to take notice of "Adam & George Heans Cow & sheep Stealing," ordered the arrest of Adam Hains and refused to be bribed off.[4] When the Hains brothers found it impossible to "fix" the judge, they determined to get rid of him, and set about it on the night of November 15, 1744.

The Rev. H. M. Muhlenberg's account of that night's happenings may be read in the *Hallesche Nachrichten,*[5] but a better account is to be found in a letter written by Conrad himself to his Moravian friend Pyrlaeus, who had spent three months at Weiser's the year before studying Mohawk.

Conrad Weiser to Christopher Pyrlaeus[6]

[Tulpehocken, November 23, 1744]

Dear Pyrlaeus
   . . . I must tell you, that in the Night between the 15 and 16 November my House was set on Fire in the Roof just over the Door, and the Door was fastened on the outside with a stout Rope to one of the Roof Posts so that we should all have been burned if it had gone according to the Will of the enemy. But the so faithful Father-heart of Almighty God had mercy on us. The flames were already shooting up 7 or 8 feet high in the attic when my Children (Philip in particular) were wakened by the smoke, and so the Alarm was given but they could hardly get downstairs because of the flames. They had already torn the Door open (I still cannot understand how they managed to do this it was so strongly fastened) [Muhlenberg says the boys had got out of the window] before I was awake. I cannot describe how the shrieking of my wife and children, O Father the House is on fire, affected me. But divine Providence kept me from losing my head, However dreadful the fire might be I knew with God's help we could put it out the Children brought water and in a minute or two the fire was out. The Lord be praised. I am tired—thinking about it So will say no more about it. It is a sign that Satan the ancient foe is threatening my destruction and his dear faithful ones stand ready to do his will. But, though they take our life. Goods Honor Child & Wife, Yet is their profit small. these things shall vanish all. The kingdom ours remaineth. Who

know how near we all are to Salvation. For the whole creation longs with us
to be released from the service of this transitory Life. God will hear us at
last. To him be Honor & Praise. Majesty & power and Thanksgiving from
Everlasting to Everlasting Amen. Hearty greetings to you and to your
Susana. Give my regards to the Brethren especially to good old Camely I
close and remain in bonds of love

Your friend & Brother
CONRAD WEISER

This attack on his family (all but two of whom were in the house at
the time, including three-months-old Benjamin) made Weiser reluctant to
leave home on the long trips he had been accustomed to make on government business, at least as long as the Hainses were at large. When the Governor asked him a few weeks later to go with a message to Onondaga, he
replied that he did not know whether he dared leave his wife and children.
The Hainses were "worse then any french or Indians." If the Hainses had
had their due, they would have "ben out of the world." [7]

The Governor took the matter into his own hands and published in
German and in English a reward for the capture of Adam Hains, the ring-
leader. The *Pennsylvania Gazette* of December 18 announced: "We hear
that the Persons suspected to have set Fire to Mr. Weiser's House, are apprehended and committed to Prison." It was difficult, however, to pin
the crime on Adam for lack of witnesses; but his record gave the law other
holds on him. In the minutes of the Court of General Sessions, Lancaster,
August 6, 1746, it is recorded that Adam Hains was on that day convicted
of fornication and bastardy, and also of the "felonious stealing one Cow,
the property of Philip Phittsmire." [8] His sentence included twenty-one
lashes on his bare back at the whipping post.

Meanwhile Weiser had been busy with a host of other things. Toward
the end of the year 1744, Philip, the eldest son, had been sent to Virginia
after one of his father's "Honest Debters." [9] The January following one of
the boys was sent to Philadelphia "with an order to Mr Shippen" for goods
suitable for a condolence present for Shickellamy, whose son "unhappy
Jake" had been killed in the Catawba War.[10] Toward the end of the
month Conrad scalded his foot and had to see a doctor. The accident left
him lame for some weeks, but it did not prevent his attendance early in
February at court in Lancaster, where, as he tells us, "there was a deal of
Buisness to be done under a great deal of noise," [11] and where, by the way,
we find him judged as well as judging. He was sued by Thomas Rouse and
defended by William Peters, brother of the Provincial Secretary; judgment
for fifty shillings without costs being filed against him in the May court.[12]
Later in February his foot was well enough for him to make the eighty-
mile journey to Shamokin with the present for Shickellamy. On March 26
we find him back in Lancaster at the Orphans Court. Other duties in
plenty held his attention. There was the farm to attend to, and he kept the
pound for the neighborhood. The *Pennsylvania Gazette* often published
notices, such as this of March 26, 1745, to the effect that Conrad Weiser,
"Ranger of the North-East Corner of Lancaster County, has in his hands

the following Strays . . ." Sometimes his own strays figured in the *Gazette,* from which we learn that his brand was ^C_W.

The early spring months of 1745 were filled with disturbing news from the West, where the Shawnee half-breed, Peter Chartier, was flirting with the French. There was better news from the south: the Catawbas were at last ready to make peace with the Six Nations. It was proposed in government circles that Conrad Weiser should make another trip to Onondaga, on Virginia's behalf, to arrange for a peace conference. Governor Thomas' formal instructions to that effect were signed on April 24. By May 19 he was on his way. But before he left there had occurred at Heidelberg an event of importance to the Weiser family, to Conrad himself, and to the Lutheran Church in America. That was the marriage, on Friday, April 22, 1745, of his eldest daughter, Maria, to the Reverend Henry Melchior Muhlenberg of New Providence.

This young gentleman, who was to exert such a profound influence on Weiser's religious life (winning him—though somewhat incompletely—away from the Moravians, and certainly turning him into the most prominent Lutheran layman of his time in America) must be given a little space here for himself.

Henry Muhlenberg was born September 6, 1711, at Einbeck, Hanover. An earnest, bookish, though very active boy, he early came under the influence of the Pietists, studied at Göttingen, Jena, and Halle, and taught in the Orphan House at the latter place. He at one time expected to go as a missionary to East India, but, receiving through the Reverend Dr. Francke at Halle a call to Pennsylvania, he devoted his missionary zeal to organizing the dispersed German congregations in that colony.

His early experiences in Pennsylvania were not of a kind to make him soft. He met challenge at every step. Some districts to which he came were without either churches or preachers; others were the scene of violent church feuds. Here and there were union churches, such as those at Tulpehocken and Lancaster, where the contributing parties locked the church doors against each other and fought it in the courts for possession of the key. A number of religious adventurers roamed the countryside preaching, though like Chaucer's Pardoner they had no more aptitude for the clerical profession than a neat gift in taking up a collection. When Muhlenberg arrived, these saintly pirates set upon him with bluff, intimidation, and cooked-up scandal to drive him out. But he kept his head, drove his enemies out into the open, and there demolished them.

During this time the Moravians were working in the same territories, and even in the same congregations, with as fervent a zeal as his own to bring light out of darkness. Conrad Weiser was much drawn to them as a people who had touched the inner heart of religion; but Muhlenberg fought them as threatening the corporate life of the Lutheran Church.

All this was crude warfare, but from it Muhlenberg emerged a hero of real stature—perhaps a little hard, rigoristic, unbending, but a man to trust one's soul to in an emergency. He possessed, moreover, some of the magnetic qualities of leadership. He had a principle to fight for, a clear gospel to preach; and he had at his command the resources of good sense, quick wit, a genius for organization, and the power of quickly adapting himself to strange circumstances and people. He soon made himself at home in democratic Pennsylvania.

He was sympathetic to the pietism of Halle. At the same time he was well aware of the necessity, especially in pioneer communities, of a strong church organization and strong leadership to control the jealousies and the hysteria of a scattered flock. He had something solid, uncompromising about him, such as was necessary for a man who would tame a religious jungle. At the same time there was a warmth in him that responded to what he calls the enthusiasm and "poetical ardor" of Conrad Weiser.

The Tulpehocken Confusion brought the two men together in 1743. The young pastor, who had crossed the Schuylkill in response to an invitation from some members of the divided church community, was at first interested in the Indian Interpreter chiefly as a possible ally in the denominational struggle; but the friendship that sprang up between them was based on something deeper than church politics. They shared common ground in character and religious experience. They were both products of the new evangelical movement. They were both active men, open in their methods, and pugnacious. They both hated confusion and loved order. They both liked music (at Weiser's Muhlenberg sang the Halle hymns and played his own accompaniment on the little house organ). They had both quarreled with Count Zinzendorf and been called liars.

And there was Anna Maria.

We have no documents recording Anna Maria's secret thought when the handsome, broad-shouldered young clergyman came courting—if we may employ so worldly a term to one who spent his life in rooting out the primitive in man; but, knowing as we do her age and inexperience, and knowing also something of Muhlenberg's character and of his recent encounters with the world, we may be certain that he presented a dashing appearance to the eyes of Weiser's sixteen-year-old daughter—"a maiden never bold."

Henry Muhlenberg was not at a loss in conversation, and, to judge from his early diaries, he knew how to tell a good story about himself. He had plenty to talk about when the Weisers gathered round their fireplace in the evening and listened to the cultivated voice of the young gentleman from overseas. He had known many interesting people. He was a friend of Herr von Munchausen (High Sheriff of Hanover), of Count Wernigerode, Count Reuss, Baroness Gersdorf, and Dr. Ziegenhagen (the Court Pastor in London). He knew all about the orphans at Halle. He could talk about his travels—best of all about his voyage across the ocean (again we judge from what he had written not long before in his journal): How the supply of fresh water ran short and what torments were suffered by all on board; how the ship's passengers drank rainwater from off the sails and decks; how even the rats in the hold, driven to the ingenuity of despair, bit the corks out of vinegar bottles, dipped in their tails, and drew them out to lick.[13]

This last story, it must be admitted, sounds a trifle unclerical. Though it is found in Muhlenberg's journal, it savors rather of Baron Munchausen than of the Patriarch of the Lutheran Church. In fairness to Muhlenberg, however, it should be said that the sporting Baron (Munchausen of Boden-werder, not Hanover) whom the rascally Raspe of the Göttingen library has made famous, was himself not much older than Anna Maria and certainly, at this time, not yet advanced to years of mendacity.

When Muhlenberg went on to tell, as his journal leads us to suppose he did, how one day the smell of gunpowder (arms having been got ready to repel a suspicious-looking Spanish merchantman—which in the end turned out to be no pirate after all) freshened him up, "so that in the evening," as he says, "I could for the first time in a week eat a bit with an appetite" [14]—it was Othello and Desdemona all over again, but this time with a happy ending. The lady lived to marvel, years afterwards, at the exploits of her famous son, General John Peter Gabriel Muhlenberg of George Washington's staff, who did something more than smell powder at Brandywine, Germantown, Monmouth, Stony Point, and Yorktown.

The report Henry Muhlenberg sent to Halle concerning his marriage, which took place at Christ Church, Tulpehocken, Pastor Wagner officiating, is interesting for the glimpse it gives us of Anna Maria, and also for the sidelight it throws on the character of the earnest young clergyman himself.

It was in keeping with the spirit of the time that the man who had known Herr von Munchausen, Count Wernigerode, Baroness Gersdorf (Zinzendorf's aunt) and the rest should feel it necessary to explain a connection made on the frontiers of Pennsylvania with the family of an Indian interpreter. Muhlenberg tried to make himself believe that the marriage was what we might call one of holy convenience. It did, in fact, offer him a way out of some of the difficulties that beset him in his church work. Bachelors under the best of circumstances are a natural prey to gossip. His situation was unusually embarrassing since he was almost without salary and therefore dependent on the charity of good householders who expected him to acknowledge their kindness by marrying one of their daughters. Anna Maria delivered him from further anxiety on that score, as he takes pains to say. Nevertheless, his report is too naively triumphant over the success of his suit to have had much likelihood of convincing the Fathers at Halle that his sole motive in choosing a wife was the advancement of the Kingdom. He was in love.

Henry Muhlenberg to the Fathers at Halle [15]

[New Providence, December 12, 1745]

. . . As to the principle of selection I considered nothing [more] than sincere piety as requisite, such as might be "convenable" both for myself and for my work. The Lord also regarded my prayers and granted me a young woman who is pure of heart, pious, unpretentious, meek and active. My wife's parents are Lutherans by descent, but as religious affairs were in such confusion in this country, my father-in-law has had a very varied experience in that respect. He was first awakened by the reading of the church-postils of the sainted Prof. Francke. Afterwards he had some connection with the so-called Sabbath Friends, who insisted so much upon the matter of self-denial and at first had a great following. At the beginning he thought well of them, because they made such diligent use of the writings of the fathers at Halle. This, however, did not last long; then came the followers of Dippel, disseminating his writings also, and the result was that people began to reject Jesus Christ. So my father-in-law left them at once. When Count Zinzendorf appeared and presented the doctrine of atonement through the Redeemer so prominently, he thought he had found the truth at last. The Count paid him great attention at once, for he supposed that by my father-in-law's influence he might find his way open to reach the wild Indians. Indeed, the Count prevailed upon him to teach several persons the Indian language. He made extraordinary efforts to secure this man and his family for his cause. Whenever in the conferences held by the Count any reference is made to a personage of official rank, that personage always is Conrad Weiser. However, he has a wise head and does not commit himself, and as he would not adopt all their plans, the Count said that he was too much of a rationalist [*er hätte zu viel Vernunft*], and that was the reason why he could not go the whole length with them. Whilst the matter above spoken of was yet in progress, the Moravian preacher, Pyrlaeus, entered his complaints and said that it was not at all right for him to give me his daughter to wife, for the child could have been married to such greater advantage amongst them. *Caetera transeant.* The whole affair was the occasion of much talk and gossiping, *pro and con.* But my congregation are well satisfied, and extend to my wife many proofs of their regard and love. . . .

Conrad Weiser's account of the affair was succinct. "My daughter Maria," he wrote to Count Zinzendorf, December 1, 1745, "has been married to Pastor Muhlenberg. She had my consent." [16]

The marriage was a success, as we all know; and their country is grateful to Anna Maria and Henry Muhlenberg for the leaders they presented to the nation soon to come into being: General John Peter Muhlenberg; the Rev. Dr. Henry Ernest Muhlenberg, botanist and educator, first president of Franklin College (the Franklin and Marshall of today); and Frederick Augustus Conrad Muhlenberg, a delegate to the Continental Congress and the first speaker of the United States House of Representatives.

The two families, Weiser's and Muhlenberg's, held well together. They often exchanged visits, especially on such occasions as marriages and christenings. The elder man's influence in the community was turned to the service of his son-in-law's church.

When Henry was so borne down by the pressure of the "confusions" about him and a sense of his own shortcomings as to feel himself to be "of no more use in the world," he found relief through taking his "Beloved Father" into his confidence. [17] As time went on, he entreated his father and "dear Mother" to visit their grandchildren when health and weather permitted. When the young pastor and pater found himself in straits for money, Conrad Weiser was at hand with a lift. Sometimes Henry sent his father-in-law books to help while away the long winter evenings at Heidelberg.

The two men did not, of course, see eye to eye in everything. As the years passed, Muhlenberg, who was always very much the church promoter, found Weiser not as "churchly" as might have been desired. He even went so far as to express regret that Indian affairs and the duties of a justice of the peace left Conrad Weiser too little time for "meditation, self-searching, and prayer." [18]

But these differences in denominational intensity did not dry up the springs of family affection, as the story that follows will show.

Part III

WEAK LINKS

CHAPTER 26

... Inquires into the Strange Alarm among the Mohawks

I

CONRAD WEISER'S journey to Onondaga in 1745 failed of its prime purpose, which was to end the Catawba War; but it was so important in its consequences to Conrad himself that it may be called the turning point in his public career. It brought him for the first time into contact with the main forces that were henceforth to be opposed to him, French intrigue and New York politics; and it set him off on a long trail of international adventures that shaped his career to a climax during the last round of the struggle between the French and English in America.

Pleased with his late achievements at Onondaga, Shamokin, and Lancaster, Weiser entered the conflict very sure of himself. When Governor Thomas, in a letter of January 31, 1745, proposed the Onondaga journey to him and added in a postscript the caution, "You are to consider whether you run any risque of being made a Prisoner by the French," [1] Weiser replied confidently:

I shall hardly met any Frenchman in Onontago but a Messenger or two perhaps which Can not hurt me and if there are more I think they will have more to fear from me then I from them. The Counsel of the Six nations have allways looked upon me as their friend and one of their own nation It will be dangerous for a few French man to medle with me amongst the Indians they will Soon find their mistakes . . .[2]

He soon found his. The French never attempted to meddle with him among the Indians. They did not need to. They went to work a better way. Understanding the precarious situation of the Six Nations spread thinly across northern New York from Albany to Niagara, the French managed to apply different kinds of pressure to the different parts of the Confederacy so as to confuse the Indian councils, stir up a conflict of interests within the Long House, and thus destroy the power of the Onondaga Council which, by the unwritten constitution of the League, could act as a unit only on the unanimous decision of the member nations.

The journey to Onondaga was undertaken at the instance of Governor Gooch of Virginia, to whom the King of the Catawbas had proposed that Conrad Weiser go as a peace emissary to the Six Nations.[3] Gooch sent the Catawba letter to Governor Thomas of Pennsylvania, who in turn sent it to Conrad Weiser. "With a little of your good Management," wrote Thomas, "I do not doubt but the Six Nations may be brought to send Deputies to meet some from the Catawbas at a third place. Let me know what you think of Williamsburgh in Virginia for the Place and whether you will undertake another Journey to Onontago this Spring, to put the finishing hand to so good a Work . . ." [4]

Weiser was willing enough to undertake the journey for the general good, but he had no great liking for the Catawbas, and suspected their motives. "The Catawbaws are known to be a very Broud people," he wrote to the Governor,

and have at Several treatys they had with the CheroKees used high Expressions and thought them Self stout warriors for having deceived Garontowano (the Captain of that Company that was So treacherously Killed) . . . the Catawbas are also Know to be an Irregular people. they have no Counsel. the richest or greatest amongst them Calles him Self a King with the Consent of his Brothers. Gousins or wifes, and proofes often the greatest full, acts all what he does as an arbitrator, the rest dont mind him and after all Sends him to the grave with a Broken head. . . .

I should be well pleased if the Six nation would make Williamsburgh the place of Congress. but question very much whether they will not think of given up to much or Submit to much to the Cawtabaw to agree to that place. as to Send Messengers or deputies to the Catabaws they the Six nations will refuse at once and therefore that point must be given up . . .

as for the time to Set out for onontago I think it allmost Impracticable before the Midle of May because for the Creeks and for food in the woods for the Horses. . . . I should have liked it much better they had Sent two or three old men as deputies, I would have traveld with them to the MohoKes Country by way of albany and having got the Opinion of the Counsel of the MohoKes I would have acted accordingly without any danger to the Catabaws. I intent to go Round by albany now if I do go.—[5]

Before he set out, news came from the West that changed his embassy from a humane gesture on behalf of Virginia to an act of self-defense on the part of Pennsylvania. Peter Chartier and his Shawnees had gone over to the French, and a band of French and Indians had robbed some English traders. Peter Tostee, James Dinnen, and George Croghan, according to their affidavit made in Philadelphia on May 14,[6] had lost some thousands of bear, beaver, raccoon, and deer skins.

After such a notorious breach of Faith, [wrote the Governor to Weiser] it will be neither honourable nor safe to send any Messenger from hence to the Shawnese; therefore you must lay the whole matter before the Council of the Six Nations at Onontago, and press them, as far as is consistent with prudence, to demand Restitution, in my behalf, of the Shawnese for the Goods taken, and that they deliver up Peter Chartier to me forthwith, as the King of Great Britain's Subject, now in open Rebellion against him.

As this is an Affair of some Delicacy, much must be left to your own Discretion; but as the Interest & Quiet of this province will greatly depend upon your Success with regard to Chartier, I must press you to use the most effectual Instances to perswade the Six Nations to apprehend him & to deliver him up to me if he can be taken alive, that he may receive the Punishment due to his Villainy. I once more wish you a prosperous Journey . . .[7]

It had from the first been Weiser's intention to visit the Mohawks' country, which he had not seen since he left the Schoharie in 1729. Before he set out, there came from Governor Clinton of New York a message that served to give his visit an official character. Clinton requested Thomas to instruct Weiser to go among the Mohawks and

. . . make a Strict Enquiry amongst y^m concerning the Cause of ye Dissatisfaction conceiv'd by y^m last Winter ag^t the Inhabitants of N. York Governm^t & what could be the Occasion of ye Strange Alarm amongst them & who were the Reporters of that Surprising Surmise, Th^t ye English or White people, intended to destroy the Mohawks. That if possible the authors of this Mischief might be detected & punished.[8]

It seems that about the middle of January five or six Indians coming home from Schenectady in the dead of night had alarmed their "castle" with news that the white men were coming in force to cut them to pieces. The Indians fled to the woods. A missionary, Mr. Barclay, persuaded the Mohawks of the lower town that the rumor was groundless; but "the Upper Town," as he writes, "was all in a Flame, Threatening to Murder the Inhabitants setled about them, And had Sent Expresses to All the Six Nations." [9] Barclay was sure the French were at the bottom of the business. Chief Hendrick accused a Frenchman, Joncaire; but the evidence was shaky. In the uncertainty the government, fearing French intrigue, had an attack of the jitters. It was hoped that Weiser, through his intimacy with the Mohawks, might lay bare the plot if there was one.

II

Weiser set out with the peace of three colonies in his hands: Virginia, Pennsylvania, and New York. He left Tulpehocken on May 19, accompanied by his sons Philip and Frederick. The boys looked after the pack-horses, which were laden with "Bread Rice Rum and Sugar," as well as with "several Pieces of Ribbons, Ferret, Knives Scizzars & Vermillion" which he had bought of William Parsons "to serve as Money." [10] He stopped at his brother Christopher's house a few miles out to pick up a party of Moravians headed by August Gottlieb Spangenberg who were going to Onondaga to seek permission from the Great Council to remove their Mohican converts from the exposed mission at Shecomeco to Wyoming. With Spangenberg, who was an old friend of Weiser's, were John Joseph Bull ("John Jacob" to the Moravians, and *Shebosch* or Running Water to the Indians), and David Zeisberger, the latter of whom was to become one of the great missionaries of the continent.

Reaching Shamokin on the 21st, Weiser sent a messenger on horseback after Shickellamy, who had ridden off some forty miles to Chambers' Mill. While awaiting his return, they crossed the water to call on Madame Montour, now in this neighborhood; and they paid a visit also to Olumapies, the Delaware chief, whom they found lying on a bearskin, blind and destitute. They gave him a present of tobacco.

Shickellamy returned on the 25th. He consented to act as guide. Andrew Montour and Shebosch went across the Susquehanna to get some fresh horses (Philip and Frederick having already started back for the Tulpehocken), and on the 27th the party set out again, with Shickellamy, his son James Logan (though lame, "the most martial figure of an Indian that I had ever seen," [11] as David McClure once said of him), and Andrew Montour added to their number.

The first night out from Shamokin, they were joined by a footsore Indian named Anontagketa returning from an expedition against the Catawbas in which he had lost everything but his life. He had no shoes, no stockings, no shirt, no gun, no hatchet, no fire-flint, no knife—nothing but an old torn blanket and some rags. He was on his way to Onondaga.

I knew him, [writes Weiser] and asked, how he could undertake to go a Journey of Three Hundred Miles so naked and unprovided, having no Provisions, nor any Arms to kill Creatures for his Sustenance? . . . he told me very chearfully, that God fed every Thing which had Life, even the Rattlesnake itself, though it was a bad Creature; and that God would also provide in such a Manner, that he should arrive at *Onondago;* . . . that it was visible God was with the *Indians* in the Wilderness, because they always cast their Care upon him; but that, contrary to this, the *Europeans* always carried Bread with them.[12]

The Limping Messenger, as Spangenberg called him, responded to the comfort of Weiser's kettle and campfire, which he shared for two nights, by hurrying ahead (equipped with shoes, flint, tinder, knife, and hatchet) to announce Tarachiawagon's coming.

Weiser and his party followed the familiar route through the Lycoming Valley, which Spangenberg, like others of that day, found *grausam;* the forest being so dense, he writes, "that one does not see the sun all day long . . . sometimes one can hardly see twenty paces ahead"; the mountains, all cone-shaped, resembling ant hills, and "so high that we could scarcely see to the summit." [13] Swamps and tangled windfall made it next to impossible to get the horses through. But when they emerged, they found a warm welcome waiting for them at Tioga, where the kettle had been hung over the fire in preparation for their arrival.

Weiser has left no record of the trail and little of his conversation with his companions. But the Indian, James Logan (named after Shickellamy's friend, the Provincial Secretary) provides us with a glimpse of Conrad Weiser. James Logan had never, so he is reported as saying afterwards to Bishop Cammerhof, traveled with such a good man as Spangenberg before; but Weiser "was by far not so good, he always quarreled." [14] Nevertheless Weiser was good enough to enjoy the company of Spangenberg, which, as Conrad tells us, he found "at all times very agreeable and edifying." [15]

The opening sentence of Weiser's official report takes us in one leap from Heidelberg to Onondaga, without mention of the Warriors' Camp, the "Coffee House," the Bear's Claws Camp, the painted posts round which the

Indians danced, or the stocks in which their prisoners were secured at night.

The Limping Messenger made good time and reached Onondaga three days ahead of Weiser—in time to catch the chiefs when they were on the point of setting out for Canada on invitation of the French Governor. They deferred their journey and sent runners to the outlying nations to summon the members of the Great Council to come and hear what Tarachiawagon had to say.

Weiser's advent was celebrated with a parade, accompanied by the music of violins, flutes, and a drum. He confided his business to Canasatego and Caheshcarowano, who agreed to assist him. On June 9 he addressed the Council, inviting his "Brethren, the Six United Nations now met at Council Fire at Onontago," to send deputies to a peace conference with the Catawbas at Williamsburg. In confirmation he laid down a large belt of wampum, which was received with the ceremonial *Jo-ha*. Announcement that presents would be given at Williamsburg evoked "Shouts of Joy" from the younger Indians.

He turned to the Ohio matter:

The Shawnese are in your Power and so is Peter Chartier, who is turned from a Subject of the King of Great Britain a Rebel against him—You will therefore see your Brother the Governor of Pennsylvania Justice done against that Rebel Peter Chartier and compell the Shawonese to make restitution of the Goods and Prisoners taken by them—To enforce this upon you I am ordered by the Governor of Pennsylvania to lay this Belt of Wampum before his Brethren the Council of the Six Nations—[16]

Next day the Council made answer. It deferred taking action on the Catawbas' invitation until after the return of the embassy from Canada. "Your Request is of very great Importance," said the Black Prince, their Speaker, "and which concerns our Allies as well as Us, and the Deputies now met at this Council Fire cannot take upon them to give a positive Answer to it—The Warriors must be Consulted about it, and all the Cheifs of the Six United Nations together with the Captains of War must Meet and Consult together before a firm and lasting Peace can be made with the Catawbas . . . In the meantime we will keep our Warriors at home . . ." [17] Under any circumstances, they said, it would not be to their credit to go as far as Williamsburg to meet the Catawbas, especially since none of the preliminary ceremonies had been undertaken to render it suitable for their reception: "no Council Fire is yet kindled there, neither is there any Road clear'd to that Place." [18] Philadelphia would be more proper, and they might be expected to send deputies in the spring.

They were less evasive about the Shawnee matter.

Brother Onas, [said the Black Prince] We are sorry to hear what has happened to Your Traders at Ohio by that treacherous man Peter Chartier through the Influence of the French—we go now to Canada and shall take your Belt of Wampum with us—we look upon what has happened to your Traders as an open Breach of the Peace on the side of the French against us and the Blow that is given as if it were given to our head—depend upon it that the French shall make restitution of Men and Goods if it be their doings, otherwise the Shawonese shall—we are very glad that this News has reach'd our Council Fire before we set out for Canada—after our Return you will have a full answer to this Affair, and no doubt but a satisfactory one—we have no more to say—[19]

The council ended with a feast, Tarachiawagon and his friends from Pennsylvania being served first with a kettleful of food, after which all present, councilors and onlookers as well, received each his portion. "Whatever was left over," observed Spangenberg, "each had to take along to his home. On that occasion they returned to Conrad the Belt or String of Wampum which he had given the Limping Messenger as a sign that he would surely come. In the evening the Indians had another dance of three hours length." [20]

III

After the conference Weiser visited Oswego, the English trading post and fort that lay twenty-five miles to the north of Onondaga and directly across Lake Ontario from Fort Frontenac. Oswego was an irritating rival to the French trading posts at Frontenac and Toronto, and a tempting object for attack, especially since it lay so close to the spinal cord of the Six Nations.

Weiser had recently heard a good deal about the place from Shickellamy. According to advices received at Shamokin through Jonnhaty, the French Governor had "sent an embassy to Onontago . . . to let the Council of the 6 Nations know that the French had made warr against the English, whome they would soon Beat . . . and as the English traders had run away from Oswego, Cowards as they were, Onontio would take the house of Oswego to himself . . ." According to the same advices, "the Council of the united nations had agreed to send some of their Chief to Catarochkon (ford frontiniac,) to let their father Onontio know, that his children the united nations, did not approoff of his Intention to take the house at Oswego to himself, which could not be done without Blood shet, and as there were allways some of the united nations with their Brethren the English at Osswego, it might probably fall out so, that some of them would be sprinkled with Blood, which would rise the Spirit of Revenge." [21]

In company with Spangenberg, Weiser left for Oswego on June 11. Joining a party of chiefs with their followers, in all a hundred or more Indians (men, women, and children), who were setting out for Canada in six canoes on the muddy Oswego Creek, they ran the rapids, portaged round the falls, and reached the fort at the creek's mouth on June 13.

That part of Weiser's journal describing his visit to Oswego and afterwards to the Mohawk country is not to be found in Pennsylvania's archives. It was confidential and contained too much political dynamite to be put into the public records. Fortunately the journal has been preserved in a signed transcript, sworn to by Weiser himself before Daniel Horsmanden of New York, leader of the opposition to Governor Clinton in that province.

It should be remembered as we read that the French fortress of Louisbourg, key to the St. Lawrence, had fallen on June 6, the day of Weiser's entrance into Onondaga, though the news of its capture by the New Englanders had not yet reached Oswego when Weiser was there.

Extract of the Subscribers Journal,[22]

taken New York July ye 15th 1745.

. . . The 13th About 8 o'Clock in the Morning, arrived at Oswego: The Indians at a Distance Saluted the *Fort* with the Discharge of their Guns a 2^d time, & were answered by the Fort, wth the Discharge of some Guns. After we landed, the Officers of the Fort, came down to receive us kindly; invited me to the Fort, & I went accordingly wth them. Soon after, the Onontago's, with others of the Six united Nations, came to the Fort to visit the Officers: They were served with a Dram round. The Black Prince, asked for another to drink the Kings health, which they had, & afterwards, the said Indian, at a 2^d Visit asked for a 3^d to drink the Governour of N. York's health, which they had also. Whilst they sat with us, & smoked a Pipe, They asked several Questions, about the War between England & France. Complained that their Brethⁿ the Commiss^{rs} of Indian Affairs in Albany, never told them the Truth, how the War goes on; sometimes they would tell how many Ships the English took of their Enemy, but never of the Loss they sustained; When on the other Side, the French would always tell them, whether they had lost or gained, & would never hide anything from the Indians. They desired to know every thing in particular, & as they were now going to Canada, for the Publick Good, & for the Preservation of their house at Oswego, it was Sufficient [proper] they should know.—They gave all the Assurance that could be expected from an Indian Council, That their Intent was good, & that the Governour of Canada, would never prevail upon them in any thing hurtful, to their Brethren the English, who they knew did not like their going to Canada, which did only arrive [arise] from the Mistrust they put in [had of] their Brethren, the Six united Nations. That their Brother, the Governour of New York & the Commiss^{rs} of Indian Affairs in Albany desired them to Stay at home, Yet they were resolved to go to confense [convince] their Brethren, that their Mistrust is groundless.

They said further, That on their Return from Canada, their Brother The Governour of N—Y. Shall know all what passed between them & ye Governour of Canada, which they assured, & pointed with their Finger to above, & said, That God heard them now Speak, who would punish them certainly, if they told any Lies in that affair, which was of such great Importance.

After they had done, I advised, that the Officers might go into a Room by themselves, & agree upon an Answer, which was done immediately, & the Indians were told by me, with the approbation of the Officers, as follows.
Brethren of the United Six Nations, And You Deputys of said Nations, now
    in your way to Canada, Hear me.

When the King of France about 12 months ago, first proclaim'd War against Your Brethren the English, This people, immediately cut off a little Town upon the Borders of New England, which was Setled with Plowmen, Women, & Children, who knew nothing of the War, & the French carried off some prisoners to an Island near the Mouth of St Lawrence's River, where they have a Strong Town with many hundreds of Soldiers, besides the Inhabitants: The New England people therefore, made themselves ready to return ye Hatchet & went with several hundreds of their people to take that Town, & some of the Great King's Ships of War, went with them to assist them in their Undertaking, & they will, if possible, make that Town, & the whole Island, Subject to the Great King George over the Water; and we have had Letters, which Say, That your Brethren, the English, have taken several Great Guns, & a strong Fortification already, & are in hopes to be Masters of the Chief Town, & whole Island, in a few weeks, But that this News must be confirm'd before we take it for Truth.

As to the taking, & loosing of Ships: When any are taken from the French in North America, they are brought into the Ports of Boston, New York, Philadelphia &c, & we Seldom hear of them, 'til after a 12 month, And therefore the Commissioners could not give a certain Account of them, 'till Some time after—Besides, the taking or loosing of a Ship, was no more looked upon than to hear of the Death of a Horse, or a Cow, since so many have been taken on both sides; But according to the Calculation made by wise men, the English got the better by a great deal, considering, they got the most money, which was what the Europeans fight for.

As for their going to *Canada*.

(There was at this time no stopping of them)

We believ'd what they said, to be the Truth, & that it was for the publick Good, & for the preservation of their house at Oswego: wisht them a good Journey, & safe Return, & concluded that I would inform the *Governour* of N— York, & Pensylvania of the *promise* they had made, with which they were pleased.

The Indians desired, that their Brethren might give them a Meal of Victuals, according to what poor Indians do to the Council of the united Nations, on their Travels, & to the White People y^{m}selves; But the Officers had been at some Charge already: A Gallon of Rum is 12 ^{s} at Oswego, & four or five Gallons had been spent to serve all the Indians going to Canada with two Drams each. They were at a Loss how to do, but gathered about 3 Baggs of Pease, about 30 Pound of Porke & four or five Loaves of Bread, & gave it to the Indians: They return'd Thanks, & were well pleased; But it was not Sufficient for One Quarter part of them, to serve for One Meal. They complained to me of the Covetousness of their Brethren of Albany, That they reaped a great profit of Thousands of Pounds at the House of Oswego, but never would give them a Meal of Victuals at Oswego.

The 14th [June] The Indians came again to the Fort.—I treated them with a Dram, & gave them a 2 Gallon Cask of Rum on their Journey, to drink the *King* of Great Brittain's health in Montreal after their Arrival, presented ye Speaker with a Match Coat, Shirt, & a pair of Stockings.

Having seen the Indians off on their journey across "the Lake of Frontinace," Weiser prepared to return. He bought four pounds, thirteen shillings worth of provisions and hired three militiamen to take him and his party by water to Onondaga.[23]

The 15th I set out again from Oswego, for Onontago, where I arrived the 16th—

The 17th I spent one Day with Cathkerrowano and Canasatego, the very Chiefs of that Nation, who staid at home *to meet the Governour of N—York in Albany (as they said) some time this Fall.*

This may very likely have been the day when Conrad Weiser received, in private conversation with "one of the most politick of their Sachims," as Governor Thomas told his Assembly, an analysis of Six Nations policy in relation to the Balance of Power in America.

However meanly they may be thought of [said the Chief] they were not unacquainted with their own true Interests, and therefore would not join with either Nation in the War unless compelled to it for their own preservation; . . . hitherto, from their Situation and Alliances, they had been courted by both, but should either prevail so far as to drive the other out of the Country they should be no longer considered, Presents would be no longer made to them, and in the End they should be obliged to submit to such Laws as the Conquerors should think fit to impose on them.[24]

This may also have been the time when Conrad Weiser and Canasatego held the conversation that Benjamin Franklin described (sketching from memory nearly forty years later) in his *Remarks concerning the savages of North America.*

The same Hospitality, esteem'd among them as a principal Virtue, is practis'd by private Persons; of which Conrad Weiser, our Interpreter, gave me the following Instance. . . . In going thro' the Indian Country, to carry a Message from our Governor to the Council at Onondaga, he call'd at the Habitation of Canassatego, an old Acquaintance, who embrac'd him, spread Furs for him to sit on, plac'd before him some Boil'd Beans and Venison, and mix'd some Rum and Water for his Drink. When he was well refresh'd, and had lit his Pipe, Canassatego began to converse with him; ask'd how he had far'd the many Years since they had seen each other; whence he then came; what occasion'd the Journey, &c. Conrad answered all his Questions; and when the Discourse began to flag, the Indian, to continue it, said, "Conrad, you have lived long among the white People, and know something of their Customs; I have been sometimes at Albany, and have observed, that once in Seven Days they shut up their Shops, and assemble all in the great House; tell me what it is for? what do they do there?" "They meet there," says Conrad, "to hear and learn *good Things.*" "I do not doubt," says the Indian, "that they tell you so; they have told me the same; but I doubt the Truth of what they say, and I will tell you my Reasons. I went lately to Albany to sell my Skins and buy Blankets, Knives, Powder, Rum, &c. You know I us'd generally to deal with Hans Hanson; but I was a little inclin'd this time to try some other Merchant. However, I call'd first upon Hans, and asked him what he would give for Beaver. He said he could not give more than four Shillings a Pound; "but," says he, "I cannot talk on Business now; this is the Day when we meet together to learn *Good Things,* and I am going to the Meeting." So I thought to myself, "Since we cannot do any Business to-day, I may as well go to the meeting too," and I went with him. There stood up a Man in Black, and began to talk to the People very angrily. I did not understand what he said; but, perceiving that he look'd much at me and at Hanson, I imagin'd he was angry at seeing me there; so I went out, sat down near the House, struck Fire, and lit my Pipe, waiting till the Meeting should break up. I thought too, that the Man had mention'd something of Beaver, and I suspected it might be the Subject of their Meeting. So, when they came out, I accosted my Merchant. "Well, Hans," says I, "I hope you have agreed to give more than four Shillings a Pound." "No," says he, "I cannot give so much; I cannot give more than three shillings and sixpence." I then spoke to several other Dealers, but they all sung the same song,—Three and sixpence,—Three and sixpence. This made it clear to me, that my Suspicion was right; and, that whatever they pretended of meeting to learn *good Things*, the real purpose was to consult how to cheat Indians in the Price of Beaver. Consider but a little, Conrad, and you must be of my Opinion. If they met so often to learn *good Things*, they would certainly have learnt some before this time. But they are still ignorant. You know our Practice. If a white Man, in travelling thro' our Country, enters one of our Cabins, we all treat him as I treat you; we dry him if he is wet, we warm him if he is cold, we give him Meat and Drink, that he may allay his Thirst and Hunger; and we spread soft Furs for him to rest and sleep on; we demand nothing in return. But, if I go into a white Man's House at Albany, and ask for Victuals and Drink, they say, "Where is your Money?" and if I have none, they say, "Get out, you Indian Dog." You see they have not yet learned those little *Good Things*, that we need no Meetings to be instructed in, because our Mothers taught them to us when we were Children; and therefore it is impossible their Meetings should be, as they say, for any such purpose, or have any such Effect; they are only to contrive *the Cheating of Indians in the Price of Beaver*.[25]

Conrad Weiser's Journal (continued)

The 18th set out for the Mohawks Countrey, pass'd through the Tuscaroro & Oneida Countreys, & arrived at Canachocany.

The 24th had a ffriendly Conference with Dyionogon [Hendrick], Abraham, & Arughiadekka, Chiefs of that Town. They were extreamly pleased to see me. At their Request, inform'd them of my Transaction at Onontago, & what I had in Charge from the Govr of N— York concerning the late Alarm; desired to know the Reason, the Author, & how things now stand; Whether every thing was setled; assured them of the Govr of N— York's good Disposition, & Love towards them.

After a Short Consultation amongst ymselves, the aforesaid Dyionogon in presence of the rest, made Answer to the purport following.
Brother.

We are Sensible, that Our Brethren the English (named the Govr of N York, Boston Philadelphia) intended no hurt against Us, & always were kind to Us,—But Albany People did intend to hurt us,—& have in a manner ruined us, & would prevail upon the foresaid Governours, to destroy us if they could —They have cheated us out of our Land,—Bribed our Chiefs to sign Deeds for them—They treat us as Slaves—Did not suffer the *Bostoniers* to come to Us last Spring—and compelled us in a manner, to give the *Bostoniers* such an Answer, as they pleased, Some Weeks ago To conceal their Knavery, they will never Suffer Us to go to Boston, Philadelphia, or any where else, Upon Invitation of Our Brethren:—Last Spring they stopt the Bostoniers for 10 Days, would not suffer them to come to Our Towns; and after all They would not suffer the Bostoniers to speak to us, without it be in their Presence,

& great many Instances could be given, ffor which Reason the Indians would no more look upon *the Commiss*[rs] as their true ffriends, and went to Canada on the Invitation of the ffrench Governour, to Show Albany People, that they would be no more advised, nor ruled by them.—We are heartily inclined to y[e] *English* Interest,—But Albany People are not.—*They have sold many Barrells of Gunpowder, last Fall to the French, fetched by Some of the Praying Indians* [26] *gone up y[e] Mohawks River, & a great deal by Surractoga, which enabled the French to fight against the English.* . . .

(How true this is, I must leave to be further Examined.)

We could see Albany burnt to the Ground, or every Soul taken away by the Great King, & other people planted there—We desire you to call upon The Governour of New York, & let him know all this, And that the Quarrel with Albany will never be made up—They had in a manner made it up by word of Mouth, but on both Sides, only the Tongue Spoke, & not the heart, & we will never be ffriends again with Albany People.

I tried to make them sensible of the good Will, & kind Disposition of all the English, & in particular of the *Governours* of N— York who had it in Charge from the Great King over the Water, to see the Ind[ns] Justice done.—They thanked me for my good Office, & said that they were sensible of what I said to be the Truth. But Albany people had ruined them now, by cheating them out of their Lands & wisht for nothing [more] than the Destruction of the Mohawck Nation.

I inquired for the Chiefs names at *Dyiontorogon*, the lower Castle of the *Mohawcks:* I was told that Aaron was y[e] Chief, & Brant, & Thomas; But the two latter being Jealous of Albany people, no manner of *Notice was* to be given, to what they said.—Old Cajendarunggo, a Chief above 80 years of age, sent for me, desired to Speak to me—I went to see him: He made the same Complaint against Albany people as the afores[d] did, but said he beleiv'd nothing of the Alarm, That the Ind[ns] were to be cut off by the White people. Told me the Treatys of ffriendship subsisting between the Indians, & the White people. Desired me to live & dye a ffriend of the Indians, to keep a good Correspondence, between both Indians & White people. Assured me of his good Will, & Fidelity, to the great King & his people.

The 27th arrived at *Dyiondarogon*, or Fort Hunter,—was received kindly by the Chiefs of that Town. They made a ffriendly Speech to me. Desired to know my Business at Onontago, & whether I had any thing to them in particular, being I had not been in their Town for many Years.

I answered, That I would Speak to them at a Day they sho[d] appoint; I lookt upon myself to be at home with them, & was not in a Hurry; (I had my own Reasons to Stay Some Days in their Town)

The 29th The Indian Council met to hear of me what is said before. I told them all what was transacted at Onontago, & desired to know how the Alarm begun last Winter, Who was the Author And how things are now, & assured them of the Gov[r] of New Yorks good Will, & kind Disposition towards the Indians, & that he was Surprised to hear of such an Alarm, at a time when he thought there was a very good Understanding, & Brotherly Correspondence, between the English people & the Indians.—In the Afternoon They made me an Answer to the following purport, directing their Speech to the Governour of N. York & said,

Brother the Governour of New York.

We the Chiefs of the Mohawks Town called Dyiondorogon return You Thanks for your kind Messages. It was a very great Alarm indeed, but is all

made up: Our Brethren of Albany came to us last Winter, & all was thrown
into the Bottomless Pit never to be thought on more, neither by us, nor by
Our Posterity; no further Search for the Author ought to be made: It is
agreed by the United Six Nations, *That* the Author Shall not be discovered
for Spies are of use, & if they fail sometimes in their Information, they ought
not to be discouraged: We had great Reason to believe that the people of
Albany intended to hurt us, & will now tell you some particulars.

Last Fall, Albany People (as we have been told) agreed to kill us or drive
us away from Our Lands, *which they Covet;* and got Shenectady people, *to
Sign the Conclusion;*   and it was agreed, That by the first Snow, Ammunition
& Guns should be carried to Fort Hunter, to destroy us after we were all met.
Soon after, Powder & Balls were brought to the Fort, & *a private Message
arrived,* from Our ffriends among the White people, & to give us warning to
take Care of our Lives.—Two Days after, another of our people arrived in
time of Night, & said that the White people of Albany, were a coming with
Drums & Trumpets with several hundreds to kill the Mohawks. Then we fled,
some ran up to the upper Nations, to alarm them, & all was in a Confusion.
The dead Cry was heard everywhere, Que, Que, Que.

Brother the Governour of New York.

We are now reconciled with our Brethren, in Albany, & it was agreed,
that *no further Enquiry should be made,* nor any Resentment shown for, & to
the persons, that *sent us Warning:* But our Brethren in Albany stil continue
to make Enquiry, and threaten the person if they could find them out. We
therefore desire You will order the Commissioners, Our Brethren, to make no
further Inquiry for that person that gave us Warning;   To signify Our Request we lay before You this String of Wampum.

Aaron Asarageghty, Speaker

A few Days after, the said Aaron & another of the s^d people informed me,
That the matter with Albany people *was not made* up, but only by words of
Mouth: Their Brethren never Spoke from their heart to them, And there-
fore They (the Indians) could do no otherways but Speak with their Mouth
only in the last Council. *The ffriends of Albany carried the Day:* But the old
Cause, That we have been cheated out of Our Lands, stil remains unsetled.

CONRAD WEISER, Interpreter.

Weiser's report was frank. It was unexpected. What Governor Clinton
had wanted was a scapegoat. What he got was an indictment of himself,
his policy, and his people. New York never forgave Honest Conrad, as
the sequel will show.

CHAPTER 27

. . . Finds Everything in Confusion
at Albany

WHEN Weiser went back to Albany in October, he found that the
Governor and the Albany traders had it in for him.

"The 5th," he writes, "I was sent for by Governor Clinton's Secretary
who informed me that the Indians seem'd to deny what they had told me
last Summer in the Mohocks Country concerning the People of Albany,
& that the Albany People were not pleased with my Coming. I answer'd
that the first I did not believe but the second I did." [1]

The conference he had now come north for was a piece of hasty im-
provisation on the part of the New York authorities. Late in the summer
a rumor had been brought to Albany by "a trusty Mohawk Indian" to the
effect that at Montreal the Six Nations deputies (from whom Conrad
Weiser had parted at Oswego on June 15) had accepted the French hatchet.
The Indian commissioners of New York thereupon appealed to Governor
Clinton to call a conference of the neighboring provinces to consider the
emergency. Clinton sent letters to Pennsylvania, Massachusetts, Connecticut, and the Six Nations, inviting them to meet him at Albany, October 4.

The Six Nations, on receipt of the Governor's invitation, raked out their
fire, as they said, and came to listen to their Brother Corlaer. It was a
courteous gesture on their part, for they left behind them business of
importance: the Catawba peace overtures, the Shawnee trouble in the
West, and the report of their own deputies returned from Canada. But these
things they laid aside on New York's behalf, expecting in return to find
hospitality at Albany and reasonable despatch in the conduct of business.

They found neither. The conference was a bungle of cross-purposes,
bad temper, and incompetence. It had been called by Clinton to combat
French influence with the Six Nations and to impress the latter with the
power of the united English colonies. It ended with an exhortation from
Canasatego to his English brethren to pull themselves together and "be all
one mind one heart & one body" so that their enemies might be afraid of
them.

The colonies had split over the question of Six Nations neutrality. New
York and New England were sure the Indians would soon be drawn into
the war on one side or the other, and thought the best way to prevent their
going in with the French was to commit them to an early declaration for
the English. The Pennsylvania commissioners, two of whom were members of the Assembly, professed religious scruples against engaging the
Indians in any war at all.

On this matter of Iroquois neutrality Conrad Weiser had no fixed
opinion. He inclined to the policy of the Pennsylvania commissioners

(whom he attended as interpreter); but he had no religious scruples, and he was not a doctrinaire. He saw too deeply into the Indian situation to confuse a point of tactics with a principle of strategy. His strategy was to keep the Six Nations strong. Whether it was good tactics to use the war hatchet or the peace belt to that end, the exigencies of a developing situation would have to determine.

He knew the danger of a split in the Onondaga Council, which the French were working to bring about. He therefore deprecated the truculence of New England and New York, and the haste with which they sought to bring the Mohawks into a war that other parts of the Confederacy could not support. The Senecas in the West were as inevitably drawn toward the French, who overlooked them at Niagara, as the Mohawks in the East were drawn toward the English; while the Onondagas, Cayugas, and Oneidas in the center were trying to control these centrifugal forces by urging a policy of neutrality upon all.

Conrad Weiser was for conserving the authority of the Onondaga Council as long as possible, and for the time being he favored neutrality as a means to that end.

At Albany in October Weiser was no ambassador plenipotentiary, as he had been at Onondaga in June, but a mere interpreter attached to the Pennsylvania commissioners and borrowed from them by the Governor of New York. He writes, therefore, only as an observer, expressing no opinions of his own. But his report of the Albany Conference [2] is like a night flare dropped over enemy lines. It throws a momentary daylight over what Pennsylvania's neighbors would rather have kept hidden, giving so sensational a picture of New York's conduct of Indian affairs and making so dangerous an exposure of colonial disunity (dangerous if hostile eyes ever scanned it) that when it was sent overseas for information of the ministry in England the sealed document was endorsed by the Provincial Secretary of Pennsylvania, *to be Sunk in case of an Enemy*.[3]

It reveals, among other things, the "Weakness, Sottishness & Dishonesty of the G— of Y" (a description attributed by Governor Thomas to James Logan's pen).[4] Pictures such as these stand out from its pages: Governor Clinton damning the Indians to their faces; Governor Clinton disputing with Conrad Weiser and damning him also (by proxy; the Governor damned his secretary for letting him know that Conrad Weiser was right and the Governor wrong); Governor Clinton nagging at the Indians about the "late Alarm among the Mohawks"; Chief Hendrick interrupting him and speaking "very bold and rude" until Conrad Weiser took the Governor's wampum belt into his own hand and told Hendrick to "forbear and hold his tongue"; Governor Clinton declaring war "in the name of God" against the French, and throwing down a belt of black wampum with a war hatchet inworked; the old chiefs restraining their young men (who wanted to dance the war dance at once), and telling the Governor they would hide his hatchet in their bosom until the ways of peace had been tried further; Governor Clinton giving the Indians a present that had somehow dwindled in value from the £1,000 set aside for it by his assembly to what Weiser estimated to be a mere £300 worth of goods; a party of Mohicans waiting on the Governor with a present of venison and being damned by his secretary and dismissed without seeing him.

"Every thing was by this time in Confusion," writes Weiser. ". . . The Governor begun to hurry away & the Indians asked him for a Barrel of Beer to drink, he damn'd them and sayd he gave them some the other day and order'd them a Barrel of Beer." [5]

Such were Conrad Weiser's chief impressions of the conference. Governor Clinton ("That Monster of a Man," as Conrad called him privately) [6] in the end flounced off without attending to what the Indians had been given to understand was to be the main business.

"The Governor of New York went away without fulfilling his Promise to remove the Indians Grievances about Lands & otherwise at which the Indians were intirely displeas'd and told me Now you see yourself how we are treated." [7]

Certainly the Albany Conference cast "No light, but rather darkness visible" upon the deepening tangle of Pennsylvania's Indian affairs.

Governor Thomas to Thomas Penn [8]

Dʳ Sir   Philadᵃ Decᵇʳ 11ᵗʰ 1745

. . . Peters has my Directions to send you Conrad's Minutes of what passed at Albany, distinct from the Transactions of our Commissioners with the Indians. The Six Nations will undoubtedly take up Arms against the Enemy, if they can be assured of being well supported. The G—— of Y—— will promise much, but how much will be perform'd, I will not say. You know as well as I, what our People will do. I wish the poor honest Creatures may not be given up as a Sacrifice in the end—Nothing but an Act of Parliament setting the Quotas of the several Provinces can render us formidable; and if that were done, & Matters put into honest Hands, we might soon drive the French out of Canada. But these are things rather to be wish't for, than expected. . . .

CHAPTER 28

...*Keeps an Eye on the Canada Expedition*

I

THOUGH Governor Thomas informed John Penn in a letter of November 5, 1745, that "The Province is now in a state of Tranquility beyond what has been known by the oldest in it,"[1] government circles were soon on the verge of panic. On November 29 James Logan sent Weiser news that "a party of the Enemy or ffrench Indians had on Saturday night the 16th Surpriz'd and burn'd the Fort and Village of Saraghtoga . . . I must request thy thoughts of it," continued Logan, "if thou art not immediately coming down, for I doubt not but thou art very well acquainted with the place, as of what Size was the Fort, what number of Guns in it, what Garrison to defend it what or whereabouts at a Guess, ye number of Inhabitants, and what its real distance from Albany?"[2]

The news depressed Weiser, and, as he searched in his memory for answers to Logan's questions, he set to brooding on the future of his country. He understood the significance of the incident and had a prevision of what was to come. The massacre at Saratoga was a lever used by the French against the Six Nations. It helped to bring the Mohawks into a war to which the Senecas were known to be averse. Henceforth the Six Nations were united in name only. The disintegration of the Confederacy had begun; and, as Weiser feared, in the *melée* that followed, the relations between Indians and whites so deteriorated that in the end it became a war, not between two white nations with their strings of Indian allies, but between two races, the white and the red.

The Conspiracy of Pontiac was born at Saratoga.

In a letter to Count Zinzendorf about the Saratoga affair, Weiser dashed off a sketch of the continental scene so startlingly prophetic that it demands consideration here for the new light it throws on the power of Weiser's mind. We have already seen how keenly he grasped the detail of Indian diplomacy. In this letter we are shown how well fitted he was with the stateman's ability to see things as a whole, to grasp the outlines of a general situation—in this case of such a situation as Pennsylvania's Indian policy had been intended to forestall. He foresaw what to us is plain history: the years of confused Indian warfare on the borders, ending in the flame of Pontiac's and Tecumseh's great schemes for marshaling all the red peoples against the white men and restoring the continent to its aboriginal owners.

Conrad Weiser to Count Zinzendorf[3]

Pensilvania Decr 1. 1745

. . . Today I received the depressing news that the french and Their Indians

232

had burned a village 30 English miles from albany called Sarachdogon. and
struck down women and children without mercy, the people were attacked
before they knew there was an enemy within 100 Miles of them and some 30
families sadly murdered the consequences will be that now the *Iroquois* and
all other Indians in north *America* will be drawn into the War. The English
Governments have been content that the Indians should remain *neutral*, which
was what the french also asked of the Indians, now however, the latter have
broken it in a barbarous manner. So from now on there will be no end to the
killing of farmers on both sides all along our borders from the northern part
of new England to the maryland border there are over 1000 English miles
without fortifications nothing but farmsteads. On the french side it is not
much better. They have of course the advantage that they have only a head
but no bread a house and a mob of beggars the Indians on both sides have
an Understanding with each other to let each other pass, and on both sides
they watch the growth of the Europeans in America with jealous eyes, and
now that they go to war it is as if we had put sword and fire into their Hands
to kill the Europeans . . . without mercy and root them out of this land . . .

                                                          CONRAD WEISER

On the 17th of December, Governor Thomas addressed a letter to "Conrad Weiser Esq[r] Captain of y[e] Heidleberg Company," retailing a wild
rumor "that the French and French Indians living at a Town or Fort on
a Branch of the River Mississippi, have made a large House full of Snow
Shoes, in order, so soon as the Snow shall fall, to Attack Albany, Sopes,
and the back parts of Jersey and Pennsylvania. . . . You are therefore
hereby ordered to give notice of this Intelligence to the Company under
your Command, that they may have their Arms and a sufficient Quantity
of Ammunition in readiness to repell the Enemy in case they should make
any Attempts upon the Inhabitants of the West Side of Sasquahanna." [4]

The Governor wrote him another letter on the same day asking him to
organize an intelligence service. "I think," he said, "what we were talking
of relating to Spys ought to be forthwith carryed into Execution; therefore
employ three or four young sensible Indian Men to observe every thing
that passes in the back parts of the Country & to give you notice, that you
may transmit what appears any ways material to me." [5]

This was the beginning of the Indian secret service, directed by Weiser,
which was to provide so much drama during the French and Indian War.

Conrad refused to share the nervousness of the capital over the snowshoe rumor. Two weeks later (December 31), the Governor wrote to
persuade him to go to Shamokin and do something with the Indians there
before it was too late.[6] Weiser took his own time. The weather was bad,
and he did not set out until January 16. Then he went up with one of his
boys by way of Paxton (his usual route when the trail was bad), reaching
Shamokin on the evening of the 18th.

He found the Indians there much excited, not over the snowshoe rumor
(Shickellamy laughed at that) but over news that had been brought down
by a succession of messengers from the north, the last directly from the
Onondaga Council itself, to the effect, as Conrad reported, "that the french
Governor in Canada had not only threatend the Six Nations with Warr

but had actually begune Hostility and proclaimed Warr against the Six Nations and their allies . . . and that it was now High time to Sharpen the arrows and puting on new Strengs on their Bows to fight the french as becometh noble Warriors." [7]

The French, he learned, had already brought over to their side two powerful western nations; and it was feared that Peter Chartier ("a great Cowart himself," but "very wicked and proud") "would not fail to do Some act to make him selfe great among the french If possible." [8] It was thought a blow would be struck against the back parts of the province in the spring.

Weiser gave Shickellamy a store of powder and lead to be distributed among such Indian scouts as Shickellamy and Olumapies should think fit to employ. Leaving Shamokin in deep snow on Monday the 20th, he returned by way of Paxton, where he saw Captains Armstrong and McKee muster their companies, and reached home on Thursday.

II

The expected blow in the spring never came, and for some months after this Shamokin journey we find Weiser attending to his civil duties as farmer, county ranger, judge, and churchman. Not that there was perfect peace on the home front. On the contrary. Both as judge and as churchman he was dragged through the sulphurous fumes of the Lancaster Confusion. In the Lutheran Church at Lancaster, two parties were at each other's throats struggling for possession of the property. The strict Lutherans, whom Henry Muhlenberg (just up from Providence to settle the matter amicably if he could) designates "the 70," picketed the church and kept Pastor Nyberg (a Moravian itinerant) and his followers out of it. Whereupon Pastor Nyberg had nine of "the 70" arrested "for hindering the worship of God allmighty." [9]

On Thursday, February 6, two women appeared in court to testify that Christopher Frantz had been beaten up in front of the church. These witnesses refused to take the oath; but Pastor Nyberg and some of his friends, less squeamish about their yeas and nays, swore that "the 9" had broken the King's peace. When the jury brought in a verdict of "not guilty," Nyberg's lawyers fought for the retention of "the 9" till the next court; but "the Bench said unanimously," as Muhlenberg reports, "let the people be discharged, and so they were."

Conrad Weiser ("the *Mine*," Spangenberg calls him, "which he [Muhlenberg] intended to spring if need arose" [10]) next day, supported by a companion on the Bench, Sebastian Zimmerman, went privately to Pastor Nyberg with peace proposals. Why should not the parties use the church for morning worship on alternate Sundays, and so with the afternoon services? They might thus worship separately, and neither have precedence over the other—the deed to the church property being kept in a chest in the sacristy as belonging to both parties alike. Muhlenberg carried the same proposal to the 70. On Friday all seemed well. The parties were agreeable.

But by Saturday the devil was in it again. On Sunday the church was locked. Pastor Muhlenberg preached in the Court House and left town. Weiser went home in disgust. "The method made use of in preaching the gospel in our day to the white people," he wrote to Brownfield, "has only divided them more into parties and sects without any reformation, in my judgment. Every party has given sufficient proof that it seeks its own, and not the interest of Christ Jesus." [11]

In time Nyberg and his people built their own church in Lancaster, and had a deed to the property.[12] But in the meantime the Bethlehemites back of him had conceived a strong dislike to Justice Weiser. Spangenberg, after sneering at Conrad (formerly acclaimed by Zinzendorf a "doughty worker" [13] for the Lord) for his decline in religion, observed: "Nevertheless he has expressed himself very freely in the Quarrel between Muhlberg & Nyberg & waxed most poetical over his Son-in-Law." [14]

Though Weiser's relations with the Moravians had been strained by his encounters with Zinzendorf and his connection with Muhlenberg, he still interested himself in their work. In March of this year he was instrumental in freeing David Zeisberger and Frederick Post from the New York prison in which their enthusiasm for the conversion of the Mohawks (incomprehensible to the nervous New York authorities) had landed them. At a meeting of the Governor's Council held in the City of New York, March 20, 1746, this note was made:

The Petition of David Zeisberger & Christian Frederick Post having been Presented to his Excellency & read desiring to be free'd from their Confinem^t & to have leave to return home, & a Certificate of Conradt Weiser Esqr one of his Majesties Justices of the Peace for the County of Lancaster to the said Petition annexed being also Read:
Ordered that the said David Zeisberger & Christian Frederick Post be released from their Confinement Paying their Fees. [15]

But Weiser opposed the establishment of a Moravian smithy at Shamokin (the Indians had asked for it, Shickellamy especially; and they offered to give the smith a house and to bring his goods up the Susquehanna by canoe).[16] On April 24, 1746, Spangenberg wrote coldly of Conrad Weiser in his journal. We let him alone, he said contemptuously: "he is a *politicus* & now a war-*Captain*." [17] The good bishop repeated the charge of *Politicus* in a letter of May 29, and added thereto: "He makes now no parade of *Religion*." [18] The United Brethren were no longer broad enough to include in their brotherhood Tarachiawagon, the "Father of the Peoples."

III

During this year Weiser carried on a vigorous correspondence with Thomas Lee of Virginia. Lee had written on January 9 proposing that another effort be made to bring about a peace between the Catawbas and the Six Nations, and that Weiser should invite the Six Nations to meet Catawba deputies at Fredericksburg, Va. In a postscript Lee added a personal request that was to run like a thread through their correspondence for nearly two years.

"I shall be Obliged," he said, "if you can among the Germans near Lancaster get me ab^t 20 Young true Rhenish Vines in a Tubb in Earth directed to Mr Baxter at the Principio Works   I will pay the charge thankfully" [19]

Conrad Weiser to Thomas Lee [20]

Philadelphia. April the 15th 1746

Honoured Sir

I am Sorry to hear since I came to this town that my Letter to you is gone but a few Days agoe and as my friend tells me no vines were to be had which occassioned the Delay of my Letter I went therefore to Charles Brokdon myself Imediatly he told me as he Did my friend that he had hisen all Cut down Last fall but next Spring he would be able to send you a thousand   one Stephen Beneset who has of the same sort if not better Removed Last fall with hisen from Phil^a to germantown   I can get of him as much as you will want but not this Season my Living a great way from Phil^a has been a disapointment to Several times I shall from hence forth Direct my Letters Directly to the Post office and not Stay for a private opportunity

I Let your honour know that I Intend to Set out for Shomokin some time next week to learn what Passes among the Indians more Especially among our friends the Six Nations   the new yorker are very much Concerned for their fidelity and Doubt whether the will Stand alltogether Our friends   I for my Part allways thought it would be a very Difficult for us to Engage them against the french in this war but much more Difficult for the French to Engage them against us   they seem to be absolutely resolved to Stand newter but as we Live in a age where the Stedfastness of mankind is not to be Depended on and most all nations are guided by Self-Interest It would not be a great wonder If the poor Indians would look out for gain and more so as the french are for Ever Busy about them to keep them their freinds Cost what it will and their known Experience and Crafteness in Indians affairs often getts the better of us   I will let you know what passes among the Indians on my Return and what Shickelimy says to our proposals on the affair with the Catawbas   Shickelimy is to be depended on very much in Indian affairs   I Conclude and am

Sir
your obedient and humble Servant
C: W:

Lee replied from Williamsburg, April 22, thanking Weiser for his peace efforts:

Take ye best method you can, it is left to you . . . When we went from Lancaster to Visit your Friends I was shew^d on ye Road a Vineyard of ye Rhenish Grapes which I tho't was conv^t to you   tis ye true sort y^t Grows near where your family came from   y^t I want & no other, Mr Baxter at ye Principio Works will take care of y^m   if they are direct^d for me   I shall be very glad to see you at Stratford where you may be sure of a hearty welcome . . .[21]

IV

For the next few months Weiser's chief interest was in the expedition being organized by the united English colonies against Canada, and in the conference being held with the Six Nations at Albany in the hope of winning their support for British arms.

Of the key position held by Conrad Weiser in the struggle, now approaching its crisis, between France and England for control of the American continent, no more concise and illuminating statement has come down to us from a contemporary than one dropped from the grudging pen of Bishop Spangenberg. All the English provinces, he writes (Bethlehem, July 23, 1746), are, by order of the king, recruiting. "They intend to take Canada. The Indians are to help them in it. Cunr. Weiser is their *tool* to *effectuate* it." [22]

Governor Thomas at Philadelphia issued a proclamation (which Conrad Weiser was asked to translate into "High Dutch") [23] announcing "His Majestie's Gracious Intentions" to raise troops "for the immediate Reduction of Canada." Officers and men, the proclamation ran, "shall come in for a share of any Booty to be taken from the Enemy, and be sent back to their respective Habitations when this service shall be over, unless any of them shall desire to settle Elsewhere; which unquestionable they will be encourag'd to do by Grants of the Conquor'd Lands in preference to all other persons." [24]

Weiser was offered a captain's commission, but after some delay declined it. The Governor, as we have noted, had addressed a letter as early as December 17, 1745, to "Conrad Weiser Esq[r] Captain of y[e] Heidleberg Company"; and in another letter of the same date had given him these instructions: "You will communicate the Letter directed to you as an Officer to all your Brethren Officers within Your Reach." [25] Again, on December 31, the Governor had written him: "I have signed Commissions for all the Persons recommended in your last Letter, and I suppose M[r] Peters will send them by the first Opportunity." [26] In 1748 Bishop Cammerhof wrote to Zinzendorf: "Two years ago he [Conrad Weiser] was commissioned a captain and then recruited actively for the Canada expedition." [27] James Logan, when Weiser was preparing for the Ohio Journey of 1748, entreated him "to put the people of Tulpehockin, as thou art their Captain before thou goes in a good posture of Defence." [28]

But Logan must have used "captain" figuratively, or as a courtesy title only, for Weiser himself, in a letter to Thomas Lee of July 5, 1746, said positively, "Governor Thomas has been pleased to offer me a Captains Commission in the Expedition to Canada but Some of my friends and other Circumstances prevented my accepting thereof." [29]

He was not to be "a Captain of Warriors" yet.

Nevertheless he planned to go to Albany to meet the Indians and look things over: that is, as he said, if Governor Thomas went—or perhaps even if he didn't. "If he dont go I have a great Inclination to go out of my own accord and for my own Satisfaction." [30]

He soon learned that Governor Thomas would not go. The pains in the breast that had been tormenting him ever since the Lancaster Conference, though allayed for a time by the help of Indian remedies, had now returned with prostrating intensity.

"Our Governor sinks under his Pains," wrote Richard Peters (who attributed His Excellency's illness to his drinking no wine), "& cannot be persuaded to go to Albany & tho I have taken great Pains to bring this about yet all my Skill has failed—I asked him what Commands he had for you & he said none— Also what will become of the Indian Treaty at Albany— None going from Pennsylvania will it is feared give Suspicion to the Six Nations: & how is it to be avoided? Can a man of your Interest & warm heart sit still at Tulpyhocken & what pretence can you have for going?" [31]

Even the news that "The Rebels are defeated and . . . there is reason to think y^t Pretender Charles is fallen" [32] (news which Philadelphia folk next day celebrated with bonfires, house illuminations, and the breaking of Quakers' windows) [33] failed to dispel the Reverend Richard's gloom. "You & I have seen so much of Life," he said, "y^t nothing better is to be expected than a mixture of good and Evil—"; and he closed with a snuffle about "these Troubles," the present "very hot Spell of wheather," and his own tolerable health.

Conrad Weiser rode to New York, and there took passage in a sloop for Albany.

Conrad Weiser to Richard Peters [34]

Albany the 27 of Sept^{br} 1746

Dear Sir

I arrived in this toun in good Health the day before yesterday. I wish I was able to write an agreeable letter to you, but I find nothing at all agreeable in the affair of the Expedition (and Else where). It appears to me very dismal. our friends the Six nation have promised to fight but a friend of mine of that people with whom I Spent an Hour or two yesterday Confesed it was only their lippes that spoke and not their Heart. So many accident happened which are looked upon by the Indians as bad omens. first when they Came to town they wer soon Catched by the Small Box and the other distemper Called the long feaver both distempers Curried of above 200 of Albany people and makes sad work among the Indian most of them fell Sick before they Came home and a great many died.

Two of the Said Indians were lately Surrounded near Crown point by some french Indians and made prisoners and brought to Crown point, one of which was well Cloathed and very Kindly used and Sent to his home at the Mohocks Country with a Message or proposition. the other was Sent to Montreal where he was Kindly used and Sent to Onontago with some presents and an other proposition in which the french promise to re Call their forces from the frontiers of new york Government and not do any more damage there, but only to New England where they must revenge Cape Britton. the six Nations wer desired not to Engage ag^t the french but to advise the french what they must do.

Some more of the Mohocks have ben taken by the french Indians and Sent home with presents   in Short every thing runs ag^t us. two french Indians have been Killed Some time ago both appeared to belong to the Six Nations one a Oneider who was gone over to the french two years ago. the other a Cayucker gone over at the Same time, thus far Indian affairs   I Intent a Journey to the Mohocks Country next week.

Now for our own people. A Set of Men that Can damn Curs and Swear are at the head of the affair who Suffer no Body about them that does not agree with them, and the very Counselers of the King who understand or ought at least to under Stand the present affair are not heard, every Body that has any thing to loose here is in danger to loose it every day the soldiers that are quartered on both Sides the revir up and down, Killed many Cattle. and Sheep, and play the mis Chief with other things the officiers from the highest to lowest Excepting a few drinks and damns and the misery Albany labours under is unExpressable and No Expedition is Expected nor Intented by, G. C. who is made a Colonel If he Can help it this fall. Waggens ar now making to Carry the Canons and orders will be Sent to M^r livingston's furnis to run Some Canon Balls. every week two or three Expreses goes to Newyork for fresh limes, etc at least it is the Comon report so and I belief it to be true.

the four pensilvany Companies are posted about 13 miles above albany on the West Shoer at a place Called the half moon. they have no Blankits yet no great Coat their Stokings hangs over their Shoes of Some of them, received no pay as yet nor are the likly to receive any Soon and Cold Wheather is a Coming on. I advised Capt diemer yesterday. to go to the Governor for Some plankits and be bold for Several pieces Came up to Albany in the Same Slope I Came, he went accordingly and got the Gov^{rs} word for them. Governor Clinton is Much pleased with pensil^{la} Companies and Showed the officiers a good deal of respect and invited them to dine with him. Capt diemers Company got the praise above all. Capt^s diener [sic] and Shanon are here for provisions with an Escort of their men.

Colonel Waldo of Boston is Expected here to day or to Morrow to Comand the forces as General If he brings no money (let him be as prudent as he will) a Mutiny will ensue the dissertion is now great and Ill language every where among the Soldiers Some of them have Cocked their Musquet ag^t their officiers and Swore by their maker they will rather be hanged then go without pay and other necessarys; we hear 2500 men from New England will join our forces next week about the first Carring place or below.

here is a distemper Called the long feaver besides the Smal Box which makes the place unhappy and disagreeable   most in every house some is Sick I hope divine providents will protect me. I will now Conclude this Confuse letter and leave you to Judge what you please. It is Certain that things looke so in my Eies, but will Expect some thing better when General Waldo Comes. I likewise leave to you If you thing proper to Inform our Honourable Governor of my Information   who am

Sir
your humble Servant
CONRAD WEISER

p.s. pray Sir Excuse this bad writing. a Slope is Just now going to newyork I have not time to write it over again and mend it.

In the end nothing better for the English colonies came out of the Canada Expedition than a lowered prestige among the Six Nations.

"How is it possible that you cou'd be beat before you fought?" said the Cayugas, as reported by Shickellamy to Weiser. ". . . We once more must return your Hatchet to You & desire you to fight like Men." [35]

v

This same year, 1746, brings to a close the story of the elder John Conrad Weiser. The stormy-natured old Swabian (Burgher, Baker, corporal in the Württemberg Blue Dragoons), who had brought his family to the New World, and had there felled trees, ploughed land, drilled soldiers, and fought furiously with governors, proprietors, and the members of his own family, now turned his face south from the disturbed borders of New York and sought peace among his children and grandchildren in Pennsylvania.

Conrad had lost touch with his father for years, but in 1742 he heard of him from the three Mohican converts, Abraham, Isaac, and Jacob, whom Brother Rauch baptized in John de Türck's barn at Oley. They said they had been acquainted with old John Conrad Weiser in the neighborhood of Shecomeco.[36] John Conrad had settled east of the Hudson, a day's journey behind the old East Camp at Livingston Manor. The Indians had not seen him lately, and did not know whether he was alive or dead.

Conrad sent him a letter through Rauch at Shecomeco, but had no reply. He tried again to reach him, this time through Count Zinzendorf, having heard that an Indian from Nösting (in the neighborhood of Shecomeco) was with the Count. "Be so good," said Conrad, "as to find out from the Indian whether old Conrad Weiser or as he used to be called Captain Weiser is still alive in that same region, he will doubtless know him." [37]

Word soon came from his father (Zinzendorf at Shecomeco had given instructions to have him looked up) and in May 1743, Conrad paid him a visit.[38] For a time the old man, now in his eighties, was content to remain where he was among these quiet hills. But after the Saratoga disaster this part of the country was infested with French scalping parties.

"The latest news from Schecomeko is that all is in alarm," wrote Spangenberg at Bethlehem. "The French Indians have scalped, burned, and murdered as far as *Kinderhook*. That is only about a Day's travel from Checkomeko. Everywhere the call to arms." [39]

Conrad sent two of his boys to Shecomeco in May 1746,[40] and they brought their grandfather down out of danger to Pennsylvania.

"He was so worn out by his long journey," writes Henry Muhlenberg, at whose home in Providence John Conrad stopped to rest,

that he was carried into my house almost dead. After he had lain in bed for 24 hours and had taken some nourishment, he came to himself again and began repeating in broken words the hymn: *Schwing dich auf zu deinem Gott*, &c. . . . His eyes were almost dark and his hearing gone, so that I could not converse with him. But I could not withhold my tears when I heard him repeating over and over the great texts relating to the blessed atonement in Christ, such as: *Himself took our infirmities* &c. . . . to which he added companion texts, such as: *Come unto me all ye that labor and are heavy laden. . . .*

My father-in-law meanwhile sent a wagon with a bed, and had him brought fifty miles farther to his home, and when he had given us his blessing, had with great difficulty reached his destination, and had lived for a short space longer with his Joseph in Goshen, he fell asleep at last amid the heartfelt prayers and tears of the children and grandchildren who stood round him, after having been between eighty and ninety years on his pilgrimage.[41]

Old John Conrad Weiser planted a strong seed in America. There are said to be over ten thousand of his descendants now living in the United States, spread across the continent from New York, Pennsylvania, and Virginia (where a strong branch grew) to California. He was independent, fearless, and God-fearing. He deserves our grateful remembrance as one of the race of colonial frontiersmen who cast this country in the mold of freedom and religion.

In the schoolhouse at Middleburgh (once Weisersdorf) beside the Schoharie this tablet has been erected:

IN MEMORY OF
Johann Conrad Weiser

———————

Palatine Pioneer, Leader, Diplomat,
Soldier and Magistrate
and
Founder of Middleburgh (Weiser's Dorf)
1713
Born in Germany 1660
Arrived in New York 1710
Captain in Canadian Expedition 1711
Palatine delegate to London and
Imprisoned in Tower 1719
Returned to Schoharie 1723
Died and buried in Tulpehocken, Pa., 1746
Father of Col. Conrad Weiser
Distinguished Indian Interpreter

Erected by village of Middleburgh
and the state of New York 1933

CHAPTER 29

... *Puts an End*
to the Tulpehocken Confusion

ON SUNDAY morning, January 11, 1747, Weiser and Pastor Kurtz
(who had succeeded Tobias Wagner at Tulpehocken's Christ Church,
Lutheran) attended service with the Moravians, and left the same evening
for Philadelphia.[1] Late on Monday evening they reached Henry Muhlenberg's house at Providence and broke their journey there. They arrived
in Philadelphia on Wednesday.

While Weiser was in town, it seems he called on Pastor Brunnholtz (one
of the many Evangelical Lutheran clergymen who came out from Halle
to work under Muhlenberg's leadership in Pennsylvania), and discussed
with him the ever-simmering quarrel between the orthodox Lutherans
and the followers of Count Zinzendorf. On January 20, after Weiser had
gone back to Heidelberg, Brunnholtz wrote him a letter that pulled him
head over heels into the ecclesiastical cauldron. The letter proposed nine
pointed questions about Zinzendorf's activities in Pennsylvania, and asked
what Weiser knew about them.

Weiser began his *Responsum* by saying that he did not wish to get mixed
up in a church row, and then plunged in headlong. He shot back flaming
answers that sent discretion gibbering off among the shades. In reply to
Brunnholtz's request for a general estimate of the Count, Weiser struck
off this silhouette:

I take him to be a man who in his youth had the great misfortune never to
have his strong will broken: in his college years, to be sure, he was diligent,
and sought the truth, and he was visited in his time by the light of God's
grace, for which he, being a high-born count, was much admired and praised.
But . . . he never had his fingers properly rapped, instead he was always
treated as the high-born count, and in short seems to have come out of the
oven with too little baking to make a Reformer of the Church of Christ. He
likes to command and dictate. . . . His ideas came in flashes, and were often
good, he confirmed them by drawing lots. His flock had to swallow them;
They called submission to his dictates "Giving up one's will." . . . In attaining
his ends, the Count was bound by no law, human or divine. He held that
whatever served his flock was right however much falsehood might be involved in it. . . . He is very hot but soon cools again. He holds no grudges.
. . . I cannot separate his qualities, I mean the good from the bad. Certainly
both are intermixed in him. And I doubt if he by himself, however much he
tried, could ever get free from this tangle without the help of God's strong
hand: for it is his very life. I hope his enemies, who *bombard* him without
cause, or out of sectarian jealousy, may not read these words. . . .[2]

This extraordinary letter, from which considerable quotation has already
been made in the chapter entitled . . . *Draws Lots with Count Zinzen-*

dorf, tells us almost as much, between the lines, about Conrad Weiser as it does about the Count. Conrad's mind was active, observant, imaginative, but he looked outward rather than inward. Though pleased with his own success in the world of affairs, he was not much interested in himself as an object of contemplation. To him, almost literally, all the world was a stage, and he took his chief pleasure in watching the drama unroll. His letters and journals are rich in human comedy. Whether he is talking about "the green Gentelman" [3] from Maryland or the "Swiss *Beby*" at Ephrata, he makes drama of everything. He has a feeling for character, color, irony; and with it he has the gift of swift, expressive speech: original, unspoilt, unselfconscious.

The letter for Brunnholtz was taken to Philadelphia by Weiser's second son, Frederick,[4] who took with him also a letter for James Logan containing the news that all was quiet at Shamokin,[5] and another for Richard Peters containing a reference to the eighth chapter of Romans—which commended itself to the new Provincial Secretary as evincing (so the Reverend Richard said) a "strong and lively sense of Religion on your mind—" [6]

Frederick missed Henry Muhlenberg as he passed through Providence on his way to town, but Henry sent his father-in-law a delightful letter [7] a few days later, opening with a cautious reference to the explosive nature of the Brunnholtz missive (which he was evidently expecting), expressing the hope that it was written *cum Judicio et grano salis*, since *was geschrieben das bleibet*, and closing with the request that Mother Weiser should send them some wolfs' teeth for John Peter, who would soon be teething.[8] This was the John Peter Gabriel Muhlenberg, Weiser's first grandchild, who had entered the world five months before on the first of October, and who was, all in good time, to run away to join the British army in Europe and later to fight it in America as a member of George Washington's staff.

During March, April, and May there were many secular activities to attend to: the plantation at Heidelberg, Quarter Sessions at Lancaster, the purchase of 116 acres of land (April 18, 1747) from John Thomas of New Britain,[9] a petition for a highway from Dietrich Six's farm at Round Head to the Philadelphia Road at Kobel's Mill,[10] the duties of a road viewer in the same connection,[11] and so forth.

Meanwhile the Moravian-Lutheran pot was stewing over a brisk fire. The Lutherans under Pastor Kurtz of Christ Church, Tulpehocken, had appealed to Weiser as a Justice of the Peace to get the old Rieth Church back out of the hands of the Moravians. Weiser advised them to ask for the key. They asked for it, but did not get it. Then Weiser himself wrote to Bethlehem.

"Conrad Weiser has become a Zealot for the Lutheran Church and its uniformity," wrote Bishop Cammerhof to Zinzendorf. "He dislikes us because of our success with the Indians, thinking he may be the loser thereby. This is causa occulta of his attitude.[12] . . . He blames us for having deceived or cheated the Lutherans out of their church. I will go soon again to talk the matter over." [13]

The Bishop went, and on May 15 Weiser and he sat down together at Tulpehocken to sip the piping-hot brew of church controversy. Their tongues were soon raw.

Before we listen to their conversation, it will be well to look into the background for a moment to see what kept alive these bickerings between the Lutherans and the Moravians all over the province.

The followers of Count Zinzendorf (the Count, it will be remembered, had given refuge to the persecuted Moravians at Herrnhut in Saxony and had made himself their leader but insisted that he was nevertheless a Lutheran) had established themselves in a half-communistic Christian settlement at Bethlehem and thence sent out missionaries and preachers throughout the country. The Bethlehem brotherhood was one of the noblest religious experiments ever undertaken in this country, and is to be credited, in any far view, with a great enrichment of Pennsylvania's religious life; but, like most departures from conventional ways, it at first evoked bitter opposition—so bitter that the "Bethlehemites" or "Zinzendorfers" (as they were often called) were driven out of many communities.

The popular distrust that beset these good people was in large measure due to a conflict of ideals in their own councils. Those who held, with Count Zinzendorf, to the principles of the *Diaspora* (I Peter, I, 1) sought not to make converts for their own church but to pour fresh streams of spiritual energy into other churches. There were, however, some among them who aimed primarily at extending the membership of their own church. So it came about that while certain of the preachers from Bethlehem gave themselves out to be Moravians, others claimed to be Lutherans or Reformed.

What had drawn Weiser originally to the Moravians was, among other things, their catholicity—their abjuration of sectarianism and their sense of the unity of all followers of Christ, in whatever church they might be found. To a man like Weiser, so far in advance of his time as to worship freely with Protestants of many denominations and also (if tradition is to be credited) with Catholics and Jews, nothing could have been more attractive than the simple, devout lives of these modern followers of Huss and Wycliffe, brethren whom no rigid forms or narrow dogmas separated from others who had felt the presence of Christ in their hearts.

"We are a communion without a Name," said Cammerhof, "consisting of Moravians, Lutherans, Reformed, etc." [14]

But that was exactly where the hitch lay. Weiser, always impulsive and too easily disillusioned in matters religious, was torn by a suspicion that the brethren were just another sect after all, and that their preachers called themselves Lutherans or Reformed or what-not in order to insinuate themselves the more readily into other communions whence they could draw converts to swell their own ranks.

There was some frank speaking when the Justice and the Bishop sat down to discuss the twenty-year-old Rieth Church—first built by the Lutherans but later torn down by the Moravians (the congregation having split into factions) who erected a new church of stone.

"Weiser was angry, Cammerhof sharp," wrote the Bishop in his dairy, which he sent to Zinzendorf. Weiser, he said,

"began his story with what had occurred in Leibecker's and in Stieber's times, that he had always sought to cement the unity of all Lutherans. For this purpose he had asked Zinzendorf for one preacher for all. Hereupon several, such as Caspar Reith, Michael Schaefer, Michael Reith and others went and got a deed for the land on which the old church stood, demolished it and built a new one. These were the only ones we had given a pastor. The other Lutherans had borne this long in quiet, but would bear it no longer, and now would institute suit for possession of the church, and he continued with *right*, for it belonged to them as they had built and worshipp'd in the old church, before the land had been bought or taken up. He called the former pirates and robbers! [15]

At this point we turn to Conrad Weiser's version of the conversation, which he set down next day as meticulously as if he were his own Boswell.

Dear Conrad! [protested Cammerhof] you are prejudiced against us. We love you much, remain our friend, as you have always been.
I replied: I have never been your enemy;   I have served the Brethren in Bethlehem, wherever I could, and will continue to do so;   but I hate your deviousness, your ambiguous way of speaking and interference with other people's rights. . . .
Finally he asked me, if I could not believe, that the Community at Bethlehem was innocent of the present church quarrel. I answered: No! on the contrary I considered them the authors of the quarrel and would continue to think so of the Bethlehemites, who had seized property that did not belong to them, till they had given it back again; for it was plain Church Robbery . . . .[16]

In the end the Lutherans "recaptured the land of their fathers," as Weiser expressed it. They appealed again to Justice Weiser, and again he advised them to ask for the key. They did so, "but," as Pastor Kurtz wrote in his diary, "they were given a flat No. Thereupon Mr. Weiser told them to inform my congregation that they might take back the church as their own property." [17]
Accordingly two men were appointed to break open the church, remove the Moravian lock, and put a new one of their own in its place. The Lutherans would then have and hold the key.
Weiser wrote an account of this religious foray ("full of lies," was Cammerhof's comment [18]) for Saur's newspaper, the *Pensylvanische Berichte*, where it appeared, October 16, 1747:

They let the Zinzendorfers know in advance the day they intended to do it. Some of the Zinzendorfers looked on. They had a chattering female there who took liberties with the 9th Commandment, but nobody paid any attention to her.[19]

Weiser himself and Pastor Kurtz stayed away.
"The church now stands empty," wrote Bishop Cammerhof to Zinzendorf. "Our friends will not fight, but let the church go." [20]

"There is no longer any preacher of the Brethren here," reported Pastor Kurtz to Halle, ". . . and all but one of their adherents have left and most of them have come back into the fold and I now preach regularly in this church once every three weeks. For the two churches are only two miles apart." [21]

Following Weiser's report in the *Pensylvanische Berichte*, Christopher Saur (whose wife, it will be remembered, had run away from him and gone to Ephrata) inserted the sly comment, "As usual, two wrangling factions in the one religion."

If it was not specifically of these people, it was perhaps of their brothers under the skin that Bishop Spangenberg wrote in his *Life of Zinzendorf*, "It had become proverbial, respecting any one who cared not for God and his word, that 'he was of the Pennsylvanian religion.' " [22]

CHAPTER 30

... *Finds Johnson in the Saddle*

SEVENTEEN forty-seven. By the latter part of May the season had opened again for Indian affairs, and Conrad Weiser turned his attention to the Onondaga confusion. The methods of summary justice could not be used here. New York was in the saddle. Conrad Weiser had no authority within Governor Clinton's jurisdiction.

Clinton himself, drunken and unscrupulous but in his own inscrutable way earnest for the good of the colony, was aware that things were not drifting in the right direction. Trade, politics, and corruption bedeviled Indian affairs. To correct the situation that he and his Assembly between them had allowed to develop, he put William Johnson, a young Irish trader, nephew of Sir Peter Warren, who had led the British fleet at the taking of Louisburg, in command of Indian affairs.

The emergence of Johnson from the murk was like nothing so much as one of the *Arabian Nights* genii taking form out of smoke. Young Johnson was a product of his surroundings, a politician who worked best in the half-light. But he was a good man for the job. Dark ways and subterfuges did not bother him as they bothered Weiser: his eyes were accustomed to darkness. He did not look far ahead, and we lack in him the bold and penetrating vision of Weiser and James Logan; but he mastered the cross-currents of political intrigue, turned them to his own benefit, and in the end made his own interests serve the interests of the state. He became a good servant of the Crown and the greatest Indian agent (as distinct from an Indian ambassador) that the English colonies ever produced.

Johnson is remembered today as one of the great eighteenth-century empire builders. But when Weiser first knew him he was only in chrysalis. The grub of the Indian trader had not completed its transformation into the public servant. He was an opportunist, easy-going in his morals, and quite uninhibited by anything like "meditation, self-searching, and prayer." With breezy energy he was entering upon courses which were later to bring the colonies and himself a world of trouble.

Johnson had a social gift amounting to genius. His influence among the Indians was soon supreme—within the range, that is, of his hand and voice. He danced the war dance with the Mohawks, filled his speeches with Indian metaphor, and made Molly Brant the mistress of his household. He loved the forest, and adapted the freedom of its ways to his own convenience, "scattering his Maker's image o'er the land" in the grand manner of the eighteenth century and leaving something like a hundred such likenesses (according to tradition) in the long houses of the Mohawk Valley. With all his flame and dash, he had also something of the *grand seigneur* about him. At Fort Johnson and later at Johnson Hall he kept *salon* in the wilderness.

The Pennsylvania authorities soon found they had no reason to like him. He was knocking the props out from under their Indian policy. James Logan, Weiser, Shickellamy, and Thomas Penn in England (who, despite his distance from the American scene, showed a remarkable understanding of the Indian situation) all knew that the vital question in Indian relations was not how soon the Six Nations could be brought into the war with France, but how long their Confederacy could be held intact. Whether as allies of the English or as neutrals ("I Never was afeard of the Six Nations Engageing against the English," said Weiser [1]) the Six Nations were a barrier against France. Their importance to the English colonies as a whole lay, not in the number of their warriors (which Weiser estimated to be less than two thousand) but in the network of allied or dependent nations, five times as numerous in fighting men, whose policy the Six Nations controlled. Since this control was exercised from Onondaga, it seemed only reasonable to Pennsylvania that the authority of the Onondaga Council should be upheld.

New York looked at it differently. Remembering Saratoga, the New Yorkers thought the important thing was to get as many Indians of whatever kind into the provincial forces at once, with or without the approval of Onondaga. An Indian in the bush was worth two at the council fire. The war was on New York's doorstep and her militia needed stiffening.

A letter of Weiser's is illuminating on this latter point:

ShicKelimy further Informs that a party of Albany men with about 30 of Indians of the MohocKs & Oneiders in all about 130 men had fell in with a french party of about the Same Number all french man who had but one Indian with them as their guid. an Engagement inSued. the Indians Stood Neuter and looKed at it. the Engagement lasted till Night and begun again in the Morning. then the Indians Said to albany people Brethren Stand Still and look at us and learn how to fight. we will now Engage the french, which accordingly they did. the Indians then Came near the french behind the Bushes & trees and fired one Sally and then tooKe to their hatchits and put the french to flight Imediatly . . ." [2]

New York was glad to take the Indians as they came. The Mohawks were the most handy (Fort Johnson near the mouth of the Schoharie was in the midst of them), and their young braves, excited by Johnson's war dance, were received without too much examination of their credentials. What this meant to the Onondaga Council, New York did not seem to know or care. William Johnson, a newcomer on the Indian scene, had as yet little understanding of the significance of the Great Council. The tradition of Hiawatha and Deganaweda meant nothing to him. The Confederacy was only a name. To him the Indians of the Six Nations were like fish in the sea. He threw in his net and took what came: they were all fish. If ten Mohawks and one Cayuga danced the war dance with him—then "the Six Nations" had danced it. The idea of a Six Nations soul—a mystic presence residing in the traditions and ritual of the Onondaga Council— was unintelligible to him. At least it was in 1747.

To Weiser, on the other hand, who had "Conversed with Indians," as he tells us, "and with the most politest of them above 33 years now," [3] the tradition of the Council, half-religious and half-political, was a live thing, as it was to the best part of the Indians themselves. It therefore puzzled and angered him to see Johnson playing tricks with Onondaga—in a word, destroying the Ark of the Convenant.

Johnson had an agent in the Indian trade who needs an introduction here. We shall meet him often enough in Weiser's story. This was John Henry Lydius, a trader, born in Albany of Dutch parents. He had worked in New England for a time and, before we meet him, had lived for some years among the French in Canada, where he had married an Indian woman of the Roman Catholic faith. He was a slippery scoundrel who apparently played the secret agent game from both ends. In Canada he had been caught tampering with the Indians, pronounced "a very dangerous man," [4] and banished from the colony. "There is no fear that he will return to New England," wrote Beauharnois and Hocquart to the Count de Maurepas in Paris, "where, we understand, he has been bankrupt and has been obliged to abscond in order to hide himself from the suits of his creditors." [5]

He came back to the English colonies nevertheless—for reasons that perhaps the Count de Maurepas might have explained to us. His track has not been followed throughout its course, but, wherever we cross it, we find a scent that is strong and not sweet.

It was evident enough, when Johnson employed him, that Lydius was a man who needed watching. During King George's War he acted as an Indian agent for the British, and nothing that he touched seemed to prosper —for the British. In 1746 the New York authorities accused him of having correspondence with the Governor of Canada. But Johnson was having a good time in the woods, making a name and money for himself, and John Henry Lydius helped him to it.

"I am Glad to Hear from your welfare," wrote Lydius to Johnson (Albany, September 17, 1746). ". . . Tenks be to God I am at present in a Parfect Helt . . . You left me no order to sell any of Your Bever or Skins But Judging them for Sale I have Sold for £190, 6 for Which I have the Cass." [6]

Cash: "A comfortable doctrine, and much may be said of it." Lydius had enough soul for Johnson's purposes.

I have told enough to explain why the Council in Philadelphia asked insistently for Conrad Weiser's estimate of these two men and their work, and why Conrad was willing to oblige.

In a letter of June 15, 1747, he reported that Johnson and Lydius had engaged only the Mohawks in the French war, though with the addition of a few unauthorized stragglers from the other nations.

"I would say if I could without words," he added, "that Mr Lydius Can not be ruined he has nothing to loose—but Col^l Johnson may; but he has Neither wife nor Children and admiral Warren is his oncle." [7]

"As to the Treaty of Col. Johnson and M^r lydius with the Mohocks," he wrote again a week later,[8] "I dislike it, and the Six Nations are offended . . ."

He warned Pennsylvania, in a letter of July 20, not to 'believe Col. Johnson and Mr John Lydias their Report, that the Six Nations have Engaged in the warr against the French." If Johnson and Lydias, he went on, had not known better and had merely been too credulous, which he was apt to believe "for Charities sake," they showed that their judgment was "under age"; but if, he concluded, "they knew better. and with Design gave a false Information, I have Nothing to Say to them. . . ." [9]

Weiser's analysis of the Indian situation in New York was reported to Governor Clinton, who contradicted it flatly. "In my meetings," he wrote to the President of the Pennsylvania Council, "with Several of the Nations of Indians, as well far Nations as Mohawks, when at Albany, I could not perceive any dissatisfaction . . . so that I must think Mr. Weiser must be imposed on in his information." [10]

Disgusted as he was with the turn Indian affairs had taken in New York, Weiser was no less disturbed by what was going on in Pennsylvania. The Indian traders on her frontier had forgotten the eagles in Jack's Narrows.

"I have Informed the Government Several times," wrote Weiser in his letter to Peters of June 21, "of the Mischief Some of our people from time to time. did to the poor Indians. but I dont remember that ever any thing Effectualy was done for relief   I desire you will press it on the Counsel in the best manner you can to order the Indians Justice done in their Complaint. that they may be Satisfied of our true and upright heart towards them, according to what we promise in public treaties. I shall be Sick of Indian affairs If no Medium is found to do them Justice. It may happen that Some of our people may be Served as J. A. was which is the only resentment the Indians use. when once Satisfied they have to deal with a rogue. and Cant get other Satisfaction" [11]

"The Indians must have Satisfaction made for private Injuries," he said again in his letter of July 20. ". . . I own it will be a Difficult matter to Come to the truth in private quarrels between the white and the brown People for the former will out swear the very Devil and the Latter oath is not Good in our Laws." [12]

In August Weiser received a happy letter from Henry Muhlenberg, thanking him for his interest in the Lutheran flock, and telling him the latest news about the family. He with Maria and "little John Peter" had been to Philadelphia, where the pastor had bought some good books, as appears from an entry in Benjamin Franklin's ledger dated July 25, 1747:

> Revd Muhlinburg Dutch Parson   Dr
> Watts Serms II   Dickinson's Vindn &c 1/ " 12 " —[13]

From Thomas Lee came a letter about the Rhenish vines.

Thomas Lee to Conrad Weiser [14]

Stratford Aug. 10. 1747

Sir
I have not heard from you of a long time, the last was wth the Vine pl[ants] which I thank you for & am ready to pay ye charge . . . we hear the Six

Nations have told Govr Clinton they must make peace with the French,   this should be prevented,   I shoud be glad you woud write me y^r thots of their intentions and how they may be kept firm to us. Admiral Anson has taken a great convoy of Arms & Amunition designd from old France to Canada; . . . the Dutch privateers will help us to destroy the Enemys trade, in all places, & will I hope soon put an end to the Warr to our advantage . . .

> I am truly
> Sir
> Your affectionate
> friend & Servant
> THOMAS LEE

It was a hot summer, and a malignant fever was raging in Philadelphia. In the woods the flies were intolerable. No doubt Weiser was glad to have some relief from Indian business. For a few weeks during August and September the records do not mention him in this connection. Indeed, the first official record of him again is in a council minute of October 3 to the effect that "as no Letter is yet come to hand from Weiser in answer to the Secretaries Letter the Council postpon'd the Consideration of Indian Affairs to another Day." [15] The Secretary's letter referred to had been written September 26, asking Weiser to employ his thoughts on how best "to give the Indians satisfaction on their Complaints," and concluded with an acknowledgment of the dependence of Indian affairs upon the seasons: "There are many more things necessary at this Season to be thought of in order to be put in execution before the severe Wheather setts in, that will occur to You tho' they don't to me. Consider therefore very seriously & give Your Sentiments fully that the Council may do all in their Power." [16]

Weiser, meanwhile, had been engaging in provincial politics. He had run for the Assembly. On Wednesday, September 30, he rode over to Lancaster with Pastor Kurtz [17] and there awaited the outcome of the election. Bishop Cammerhof was there, too, and noted the election results in his diary next day with some satisfaction: "Election for the Assembly is held over the Province. Weiser wished to be elected and the Lutherans all electioneered for him and he canvassed for himself. But he received only 400 votes and lost the election. Two Quakers got in." [18]

Bad news came from Shamokin. Shickellamy was ill. Olumapies was dead. The old Delaware chief had left the bearskin on which he had lain for so long, and been buried with his face to the west, according to Delaware custom, so that he might on rising follow the sun. He cannot have been greatly mourned, for he had long been an imbecile. Shickellamy would not have him at the council fire, his habits there were so disgusting. Conrad Weiser had written of him only a few weeks before:

Olumapies would have Resigned his Crown before now but as he had the Keeping of the public treasure (that is to say the Counsel Bagg) Consisting of Belts of wampum for which he buys Liquor and has been Drunk for this two or three years allmost Constantly and it is thought he wont Die so long as there is one Single wampum Left in the Bagg.[19]

But the fall of royalty makes a great crack. Repercussions were heard at Onondaga and Philadelphia. Both capitals were concerned about his successor.

Lapapitton [wrote Weiser] is the most Fitest Person to be Successer, he is an Honest true hearted man and has very Good Natural Sence he is also a Sober man Between 40 or 50 years of age he is well Esteemed among his Country people and others, but whether or no he will trouble himself with public affairs is a Great Question, he has Lived Retired for this several years with his Family.[20]

Weiser wrote to James Logan, September 27, to tell him he was going to Shamokin to visit Shickellamy.[21]

Logan replied at once,[22] urging Weiser to use his "utmost endeavors" to see that at least Pisquetomen (brother of "Shingas the Terrible" who was soon to write Pennsylvania's history in blood) should not succeed Olumapies, sending his "kind Love to Shekallemy," and recommending "the Bark called Jesuits" (which he hoped was to be found at Tulpehocken) as a cure for the old chief's Ague—"(not ego)," wrote Logan, with an eye to Conrad's spelling.

Bad weather delayed the visit, but on October 9 Weiser arrived at Shamokin with medicine for Shickellamy, "a good Quantity of Barks & Vomits & Rhubarb," etc., from Dr. Graeme. The old chief being ill and almost destitute ("he had *verdoctert* almost all his clothes"[23]), Weiser lodged at the Moravian house, where he was given a friendly reception, as Alexander Mack reported to the Brethren at Bethlehem.[24]

Conrad Weiser to Richard Peters [25]

Tulpehocken, October 15, 1747

. . . I was Surprised to see Shickelimy in such a miserable Condition as Ever my Eies beheld he was hardly to stretch forth his hand to bid me wellcome, in the Same Condition was his wife his three Sons not quite So bad but very poorly, also one of his Daughters and two or three of his Grand Children all had the feaver; there was three Burried out of the family a few Days before, to wit, Cajadies, Shickelimy's Son in Law, that had been Married to his Daughter above 15 years, and Reckoned the best Hunter among all the Indians, Item. his Eldest Sons wife and a Grand Child, Next Morning I administred the Medecins to Shickelimy and one of his Sons, Under the Direction of Doctor Greams which had a very Good Effect upon both, Next Morning I gave the Same Medecine to two more (who would not Venture at first) it had the Same Effect and the four Persons thought themselves as Good as Recover'd, but above all Shickelimy was able to walk about with me with a Stick in his hand before I left Shomokin which was on the 12th in the Afternoon . . .

On my Return about three miles this Side Shomokin I met elleven onontagers coming from Warr, they with some of the Cajuckers in all 25 men, had an Engagement with the Catabaws in which five of the Cajuckers were Killed the onontagers Said the Catabaws were 200 men I sat Down and Smoked a pipe with them I had Some tobacco and a little Rum Left with which I treated them and we Discoursed about the warrs their Captain was a very Intelligible man I told him before we parted that we their Brethren of pensilvania long to hear of the Six Nations How things go Cocerning the warr with the french whether or no they had Engaged in it, that If they had we were Desirous our Brethren the Counsel of Onontago would let us know, If they have not we had Nothing to Say to them, well knowing that our Brethren the Six Nations were a people of understanding and Experenced in the Warr we therefore leave that Intirely to them only we wanted now and then to Receive a message from them in these Criticall times and to hear of their wellfare I gave the Captain a piece of Eight to Remember what has been Said to the Counsel at onontago . . .

I must at the Conclusion of this Recommend Shickelimy as a proper object of Charity he is Extreamly poor in his Sickness the horses has Eat all his Corn his Cloaths he gave to Indian Doctors to Cure him and his family but all in vain he has no Body to hunt for him and I cannot See how the poor old man Can Live he has been a true Servant to the Government and may perhaps Still be, if he lives to do well again, as the winter is Coming on I think It would not be amiss to Send him a few Blankits or Matchcoats and a little powder and Led, If the Government would be pleased to Do it and you Could Send it up Soon I would Send my Sons with it to Shomokin before the Cold weather Comes

Olumapies is Dead Iapaghpitton is allowed to be the fitest man to Succeed him, but he Declines, he is afraid he will be Envy'd and Consequently be-witched by Some of the Indians However, this must lie still till next Spring according to what Shickelimy Says

. . . I arrived this Day about 12 of the Clock at my house in good Health, and I hope this will find you in perfect Health and profound peace of Mind who am

Sir
Your ever Dutiful
C   W

On receipt of Weiser's letter, the Council instructed James Logan to prepare a suitable present to the value of fifteen pounds for the old Oneida gentleman at Shamokin. Accordingly Logan sent word, October 20,[26] that he was sending:

> 5. MatchCoat Strowds
> 4 White Duffell MatchCoats
> 1 p^r Blue Halfthicks
> One Quarter Cask of Gun Powder
> $\frac{1}{2}$ cwt of Barr Lead &
> 1 doz^n Knives

Conrad Weiser to James Logan [27]

Tulpehokin October the 23 1747

Respected freind

I Received yours of the 20 Instant and it Gave me a Deal of Satisfaction to understand that the Councel is pleased with my Services in Indian affairs, I must let you know that Since my Return from Shomokin (on the 17) I have been taken Sick and obliged to keep my bed Ever Since, this morning I feele myself Some thing better, I got up to write to you if I can. I was taken with a feaver which allthough is not very voilent, yet put my head in Confusion particularly at nights. I was for the most time light headed alltogether. the feaver followed the flux and a voilent Cough which was worse then all, the Day before yesterday I ventured and took a Vomit which Did me a great Deal of Good, and I hope by the further assistance of God I shall Do well. my Son that accompanied me to Shomokin is also very bad much the Same (Excepting the flux) as my Distember,   Just now I have been to See him and find he has the Mazzels, and is Extreamly weak   the Cough most Ruined him.

Instead of the Strowed, I wish you would Send So many plankits or So many more Duffels Matchcoats   all the Rest is very well, but Now I do not know how to Send them things Now to Shickelimy   I must Leave them till I Can think about it. . . .

CHAPTER 31

... *Takes Communion with the Lutherans*

ONE day in November 1748, Shickellamy called at Heidelberg on his way to Bethlehem with a party of Moravians. Finding that Weiser was not at home, Shickellamy went on. When Weiser returned shortly after and learned that his old friend had been so unmindful of Indian etiquette as not to wait an hour or two for his return, he was offended and blamed the Moravians.

"I hear he is made a Convert of," he wrote to Richard Peters, November 21; "I wish a true Christian, but I Expect nothing but mischief by them people." [1]

If he had known what had just been said of him at Bethlehem, he might have had the more reason for his expectations. The Brethren had told Shickellamy that Conrad Weiser had not wished Brother Johanan (Count Zinzendorf) to present the gospel to him at Shamokin. The new convert said he knew this to be true, "for," as the Bethlehem Diary records, "Conr. Weiser followed the evil Spirit . . ." [2]

Ever since the Tulpehocken Lutherans, on Justice Weiser's advice, had taken the Moravian lock off Rieth's church and put on one of their own, there had been war between Weiser and the Brethren. The latter thought Weiser was at the bottom of the Tulpehocken Confusion, perhaps even at the bottom of the Muddy Creek trouble as well. They sent deputies to expostulate with him.

Conrad Weiser to Bishop Spangenberg [3]

Dear Spangenberg

a few days ago Christian Rauch and another brother came to me from Bethlehem said they were sent by the community with a commission when I asked about this commission Christian began to speak but the commission stuck in his throat and when I saw that under their clothes they had anti-christian or murderous weapons I snatched them out of their hands so they might do no harm with them for their intent was evil enough when I finally insisted on knowing their commission they said that herewith the congregation at Bethlehem gave notice that our friendship was at an end. They regarded me as an enemy (that is they declared war on me) though they hedged on that last. This is therefore sent to you so you can let me know what was intended whether you really consider me an enemy or not if I have done wrong I will give satisfaction but if right and justice are on my side I have no fear though a great army were against me I belong to the Lord of Lords and shall meet the enemies of my Lord like a Christian and a man as long as there is a heartbeat in me the Lord be judge who is terrible I do not pass judgment I am no Searcher of Hearts neither are you Watch out what you do you have plenty of people in your own community who sing with tears before the Lord of Hosts the 59th chapter of Isaiah against you and your co-regents do no more wrong   God's justice might overtake you before you make amends or perhaps even before you have time to repent   make no mistake God is not mocked   I am under the Lord in some authority and am assured of his protection and wish no harm to you nor any man   I remain the servant of my Lord and the friend of his friends and children

Heidelberg the 13 February   CONRAD WEISER
      1748 [4]

After that letter was despatched, word got around that the Moravians were out to pray Conrad Weiser to death. His family were anxious. By the middle of April they were terrified. April 13, a large comet was seen in the sky.[5] By April 18 Conrad Weiser was given up for lost.

It came about in this way: [6] On Sunday, April 17, Conrad Weiser and his family rode to church, accompanied by Henry Muhlenberg and several other Lutheran clergymen who were staying at Weiser's on a visit. Pastor Handschuh preached at Christ Church, Tulpehocken, on Matthew V, 6: "Blessed are they which do hunger and thirst after righteousness: for they shall be filled." The congregation celebrated the Holy Communion. It was noticed by the visiting ministers that, while Weiser's family partook, he himself abstained: "For," writes Pastor Kurtz, "since his rebaptism by the Ephrata people his association with the Lutherans had not been fully restored."

In the afternoon they rode together to Rieth's church, two miles away, where Kurtz preached. "After the sermon," says Kurtz, "we rode back with Mr. Conrad Weiser to his house, with great satisfaction, where he told me all the circumstances relating to the fore-mentioned church [Rieth's] and read us his correspondence with the Moravian Brethren at Bethlehem and especially with Spangenberg, and also [recounted] some conversation he had had with 2 of their deputies and with Cammerhof about the same church."

They all retired at midnight. But they were no sooner in bed than Conrad Weiser, who had taken a chill, was seized with a violent spasm of sickness. Muhlenberg, who stayed up with him all night, has left a vivid account of what happened:

It began with severe vomiting and within an hour he was cold and numb almost all over and then a cold sweat broke out on the upper part of his body. As far as one could tell from the *Symptoma* it was probably the *Colica pituitosa*. Nature turned all her energies to expelling the malignancy, so that he complained of the most excruciating pains around the navel, he was quite sure he was going to die . . . it looked as if each moment would be the last. I was very much disturbed at this, because among other things the Moravians had recently had the effrontery to tell him in no uncertain terms that they intended to pray him to death. They certainly had desired his death and said, they had the power and would bring it about, because he stood in their way. But his piety put me in hopes, for, as well as one can judge from the fruits, he is strong in the faith that conquers through love, and he seeks through daily intercession to find expiation for his sins and frailties. We had no medicine and there was no doctor near. I asked my colleagues to join in prayer to God through Christ for his life and health. Which they most willingly did; . . . and meanwhile I made a poultice, for he had nothing else in the house, not even an enema-syringe. We sent 9 miles for the nearest doctor, a man who in Germany had once been a servant to Dr. Conradi, the Rev. Mr. Struensen's father-in-law, and who was practising here. He came at daybreak, boiled camomile blossoms in wine and also used some powder, which had a good effect. But the prayers had the best effect.

Pastor Kurtz came on the scene some time during the day. He writes:

I found him very ill, so ill that they had expected him to die during the night. We bowed our knees in silence before God and begged Him to let us have our friend a little longer, if it was His will; afterwards we all gathered about his bed and some questions were asked him about what he believed and then about his dealings with the Moravian Brethren, in the matter of the local church, whether he had gone too far with them . . .

Henry Muhlenberg was particularly insistent in his questioning, the man's soul being at stake. "I asked him again," writes Muhlenberg in the journal he afterwards sent to Halle, "whether his conscience pricked him, for behaving so and not otherwise with the Herrnhuters? He replied, that he had acted in God's sight to the best of his own knowledge and conscience and felt no qualms about the matter."

We turn again to Kurtz's journal:

Finally [we asked him] whether, if he got better again, he would not join with other Christians in full communion with Jesus Christ. Whereupon he asked if it could not be done at once, in that very room: Here is water, why should I not be baptized? We did what he wished immediately. He proceeded to give various reasons, why he had gone off with the Ephrata people. Now, he said, I see that God is bringing his Evangelical flock out of the mire and is taking care of it. He said many other things, all edifying and affecting. We knelt as penitents before God. he did not want to remain in bed while he partook of the Holy Communion; we had to help him out, we sang a few verses, he made his penitential prayer with tears, which at length Pastor Handschuh brought to an end with sighs. As Pastor Brunnholtz spoke the words: Adorn thyself, O beloved soul—and came to the following: came on foot to the bright light, he sang out clearly—; then he got up by himself from his chair and Pastor Handschuh led him to the table and so he partook of the body and blood of Jesus Christ in the bread and wine. We all received it together. That was a joyful hour.

In such manner was Conrad Weiser received again into the bosom of the Lutheran Church.

CHAPTER 32

... *Sets up a Flag on the Ohio*

I

ON HIS way to Shamokin in October 1747, Conrad Weiser had seen a French scalp at the house of Thomas McKee, and had met the Indian from the Ohio who had brought it there. The Indian, reported Weiser,

pressed very hard upon me to receive the Scalp for the Government of Pennsylvania, in who's favour the Scalp was taken . . . I told him that I had been concern'd in Indian Affairs these many Years, but I never knew the Government of Pennsylvania had given the Hatchet or employ'd any body to kill French Men, . . . and therefore I cou'd not receive the Scalp, . . . and as my Commission for the Transaction of Indian Affairs did not extend to Ohio . . . but reached only to the Six Nations I must leave that Affair to those that had Correspondents that way to inform the Government of it and receive an answer, I hoped he wou'd excuse me, and so we parted in Friendship.[1]

The government at Philadelphia, meanwhile, had been informed by George Croghan (an Irish trader who is suspected of having incited the western Indians against the French in order to secure the Ohio fur trade for himself and Pennsylvania) "that the Indians on Lake Erie were making War very briskly against the French but were very impatient to hear from their Brethren the English, expecting a Present of Powder & Lead which if they do not get he is of opinion they will turn to the French." [2] Whereupon the Council sent for Conrad Weiser to advise them what was best to be done.

Such was Conrad Weiser's introduction to the Ohio affair—one of the most important episodes in his career, for his journey to Logstown in 1748 laid a train of gunpowder that exploded the mine of the French and Indian War, and at the same time opened the way for British America's expansion into the West.

To most Pennsylvanians at that time the Ohio was *Ultima Thule*. The word "Ohio" was not merely the name of a great and beautiful river (*La Belle Rivière* of the French) which included in its course what is now known as the Allegheny River as well as the Ohio proper, and which swept down from its source near Lake Erie through the mountains past Venango, Kittanning, and Logstown to the great plains where it joined the Mississippi. It denoted also an ill-defined and mysterious region to which no English except the fur traders had access: peopled by a mixed race of Shawnees, Delawares, Wyandots, and émigrés from the Iroquois Long House in New York; and bordered on the west by strange tribes like the Twightwees (or "Naked Indians") who were on the distant fringe of the Six Nations' circle of alliances.

The Iroquois settled on the Ohio were for the most part young people who had recently come west to find better hunting than their native lands could afford them in these days of white encroachment, and liked the country so well that they remained and established homes. Here the Indian way of life could be maintained a little longer against the pressure of the whites. Soon great men were to come out of the Ohio country. Joseph Brant and Tecumseh were both born there.

It was evident to the sachems of the Six Nations that the growth of this colony threatened the integrity of the Great League. To meet this danger they appointed, about 1747, a vice-regent or "half king" (like Shickellamy at Shamokin) whose duty it was to maintain the authority of the Onondaga Council over the Ohio territory. The move was necessary. The Ohio colony, though it acknowledged the suzerainty of the Six Nations, did so grudgingly and pulled at the leash, just as the English colonies on the seaboard were doing with England.

The significance of this Indian colonial problem was not at first realized in Pennsylvania. More easily understood were the possibilities the Ohio offered for the extension of the fur trade. Pennsylvania traders were already out there in large numbers, and, by virtue of the superior quality and the greater cheapness of their goods (an advantage the British navy gave them over the French), they were driving the French traders out of the field.

To the romantic Thomas Lee, who described the boundaries of Virginia as "on the west, the Great South Sea [i.e., the Pacific], including California," [3] which he took to be an island, the Ohio was a Gate of Horn opening on vast dreamlands of empire that beckoned seductively to the Old Dominion.

To Conrad Weiser also the distance beckoned, but his visions were less grandiose. He looked on the Ohio country with the eyes of a diplomat. He saw it as an empty square on the American chessboard on which England and France were playing the game of empire. It was an important square, for not only was this valley on the main line of communications between Canada and Louisiana, but it was also the key to the West. Why not move his knight and call "Check"?

James Logan was another man interested in the Ohio. He had investments in the Indian trade. More than that, he was alive to the imperial issues involved. He wrote to Weiser, October 20, 1747, informing him that two hundred pounds had been laid out for a present to the Indians on Lake Erie, and requesting his presence in town to consult with the President and Council about "the Proper Method of dividing the Present to Each Nation." [4]

Weiser was too ill to come at once, having picked up a fever at Shamokin. In a few days he was in the saddle again, but before he ventured on the long journey to Philadelphia he rode to Lancaster to attend the Quarter Sessions. In Lancaster he met ten Indian deputies on their way to Philadelphia from the Ohio.

They were headed by Scaroyady (another "very inteligible man," [5] who was to play an important part in Weiser's further story), and they confided to him enough of their errand to convince him that their embassy was of the greatest importance to the province. They told him privately of developments on the Ohio, and asked him whether he thought the Pennsylvania government would approve of what the young warriors out there proposed to do: "to erect a Council Fire" in the spring. They added that already "all the Indians on Lake Erie & round about them to a great distance had consented to come to that Fire." [6]

Weiser put the Ohio deputation under the care of Justice Schwoope, who conducted them to the city. We find Weiser himself in Philadelphia a few days later (though he was "Still troubled with the Cough" and uneasy about his sick children) [7] assisting as Province Interpreter in what was to prove one of the most important Indian conferences ever held in that city.

The Indians from the Ohio declared that, though the old men at Onondaga were for neutrality in the present war with France, the young warriors were resolved to lay their old people aside and to take up the English hatchet; "and we are now come to tell You," said their speaker, "that the French have hard Heads, and that we have nothing strong enough to break them— We have only little Sticks & Hickeries, and such things, that will do little or no Service against the hard Heads of the French: We therefore present this Belt to desire that we may be furnished with better Weapons, such as will knock the French down . . ." [8]

The issue had been clearly presented. Pennsylvania had to decide whether to deal separately with the Ohio colonists, or to refer them to Onondaga. James Logan and the provincial Council, fearful of causing any infringement of the prerogatives of the Great Council, "was at first of Opinion that they should be told this governm^t never advis'd them to take up the Hatchet, that there was no Kettle hung on in this Province, that they were out of their Road & shou'd have gone to Albany." [9] But Weiser, who was called in, offered contrary advice. He told of the strength of the Indians in the Ohio region, and, declaring that "he thought Providence had furnished this Province with a fine opportunity of making all the Indians about the Lakes their Friends, & warm Friends too," [10] he proposed that they approve of the Indians' taking up the Hatchet; and that, in acknowledgment of their "seasonable declaration" in favor of the English, the province should give them a small present at once and should send a large one to the Ohio in the summer. "And tho' he had never been in those Parts," so runs the Council minute of November 16, "yet he judg'd the attaching these Indians and their Friends to the English Cause to be so necessary, that he wou'd, if the Council pleased, & his Health shou'd permit, go with the Present himself, and see with his own Eyes what number of Indians were there, & in what disposition." [11]

The Council followed his advice. For the province, it was a significant decision. For two years her Indian policy had been in the doldrums, owing to the confusion at Albany. Now it was moving again and, as a result, Pennsylvania was first among the English colonies to advance into the Ohio Valley.

For Conrad Weiser it was no less significant. The Ohio venture was the first major decision in Indian policy for which Conrad was singly responsible. One result of these two years of uncertainty, disillusionment, and exasperation (three steps on the road to decision) had been to make him more self-dependent in the formation of Indian policy.

The wisdom of the Ohio decision was made apparent next July, when deputies from the Twightwees, a great nation of twenty towns on the river Wabash, whose principal chief was called La Demoiselle by the French and Old Briton by the English, came to Lancaster to enter the English orbit by way of Pennsylvania. The Twightwees presented thirty beaver skins and a Calumet Pipe "with a long Stem, curiously wrought, & wrapp'd round with Wampum of several Colours," [12] which both parties to the treaty smoked; and they prayed that they might be admitted to the English chain of friendship, announcing at the same time that twelve other nations were only waiting to hear of the success of the Twightwees' "Application" before making the same advances to the English.

Scaroyady had accompanied the embassy to act as their speaker; but he had had a fall and lay ill for ten days (attended by his wife and child) under shelter in Weiser's orchard—which suffered considerable damage in consequence.[13] The treaty was interrupted for a day and a half while Weiser and Montour rode over to the plantation to get particulars from him about the Shawnees on the Ohio, who were said to have repented and to desire to be taken back into English favor. Scaroyady said it was true. At a meeting held by Kakowatchiky (now living on the Ohio) and other chiefs, the Shawnees had asked the Delawares and the Six Nations to intercede for them. "We the Shawonese have been misled," they said.

. . . We travell'd secretly through the bushes to Canada, and the French promised us great Things, but we find ourselves deceived. We are sorry that we had any thing to do with them: We now find that we cou'd not see, altho' the Sun did shine;—We earnestly desire you wou'd intercede with our Brethren the English for us who are left at Ohio, that we may be permitted to be restored to the Chain of Friendship, and be looked upon as heretofore the same Flesh with them.[14]

This last request, when presented to the Commissioners, was granted, with conditions. Kakowatchiky, who had not wavered in his fidelity, would ever be remembered by the English with gratitude. On the other hand, "Neucheconno and his Party" ought to be chastised by the Six Nations "in such Terms as shall carry a proper Severity with them." [15] After that, the English would forget what was past. In token of which a belt of wampum was laid down, and a promise was made that Conrad Weiser should take a "Present of Goods" to the Shawnees when he made his trip to the Ohio.

II

Preparations for the Ohio journey were long and complicated. The strain of them, spread over months, tore down Weiser's health. He had two serious illnesses in nine months, gave himself no time for convalescence, and felt the effects for the rest of his life. After this summer, he was never long in good health.

On the part of the government, there were many hesitations and post-ponements. The necessary funds had to be voted, appropriate goods bought, transportation arranged for, and time-tables made to synchronize Weiser's flickering movements with the peregrinations of various Indian delegations heading from distant places through the woods to Philadelphia.

The coöperation of Maryland and Virginia was invited. After long delay Virginia contributed two hundred pounds. Maryland was unable to give anything.

Thomas Lee was easily interested: he was already casting eyes on Ohio real estate.

Thomas Lee to Conrad Weiser [16]

Stratford Feb^ry 13. 1747/8

Sir

. . . our Gover^t is extending our Frontier by large grants of land as farr as Ohio, and I am concerned in one, which when we begin to settle I shall hope for your help to make it agreeable to the Indians   the vines you were soe kind to send me I have sav^d ab^t 10 of the plants, which I will cultivate as fast as I can, and you shall be sure of an invitation to the first Vintage. I am glad you have not forgot the Indian Songs which I long to see. I hope you have success in your good natured application for poor Shikallemy. his son Jack was kill^d ab^t 2 years agoe, by a Catawba boy, who Observing Jack to lye behind a log, when he lifted his head to fire into the Cabbin, shot him dead with a pistole. I wish you health and prosperity with all my heart, being very truly.

Your affectionate & humble Servant

THOMAS LEE

I am glad to hear y^t Canasategoe is well

Twice during these anxious and exciting months of preparation Conrad Weiser himself came near to letting the expedition down: once when he was taken ill (and "lik'd to have Dyed . . . & if he had what must have become of Indian Affairs," said Richard Peters [17]); once when, on receiving a disturbing report from Shickellamy advising against the Ohio treaty,[18] he hesitated about the wisdom of the whole proceeding. Shickellamy said he had information that the western Iroquois had not taken up the hatchet against the French as reported. Only the Zis-a-gech-roona (the Missi-saugas) had done so. The Ohio Indians would do nothing without instructions from Onondaga. Apparently the old chief feared Pennsylvania's separate dealings with Ohio might undermine the Onondaga Council.

When word of Weiser's hesitation reached Philadelphia, he and Shickellamy were both sent for. They came in haste, on the way popping in for a meal at Muhlenberg's and surprising the Rev. Mr. Handschuh, newly arrived from Halle, who noted in his diary of April 19: "At dinner, Mr. Conrad Weiser came with an Indian king and his son. After dinner these persons left for Philadelphia on business." [19]

For a month before he set out, Conrad was near distraction. He had enough to worry him. It was a bad season for the crops. The weather was hot. Indian affairs were unusually trying. Shickellamy wanted him to come to Shamokin to hear the latest reports from the Six Nations. The government wanted him to go to Shamokin with complaints from South Carolina against the Senecas, who had kidnapped Captain Haig. Weiser sent word to both he would not go: he was setting out from George Croghan's on July 18 for the Ohio. Croghan was waiting impatiently with his pack horses.

On Sunday, July 10, Weiser was at Heidelberg, wondering what had become of the Twightwee deputies Andrew Montour was supposed to be bringing east for a treaty. On Tuesday he rode to Lancaster to settle some affairs of his own. On Thursday George Croghan turned up with news that the "Towick Towicks" had passed John Harris' Ferry and would be in Lancaster next day. Weiser rushed back to Heidelberg to find Andrew Montour, who had gone there to find him, and there on Saturday he met William Franklin, who had brought a letter from the Provincial Secretary containing instructions for the Ohio journey. On Sunday he went back to Lancaster for the treaty, the Indians being afraid to go on to Philadelphia because of the sickness there. On Tuesday morning the treaty began. In the afternoon he hurried back to Heidelberg to interview Scaroyady. On Wednesday he returned to Lancaster with his report. On Thursday the treaty was resumed, Weiser interpreting for the Six Nations as Montour did for the Twightwees.[20]

The natural annoyances of treaty business were intensified by what Peters calls "the heats of the Season and the Fatigues of restless Nights occasioned by unclean Beds." [21] A weight of nagging details, including the distribution of presents in such a way as to awaken no jealousies, fell on Weiser. There were only a few Indians from the West: "two towick towicks, three shawonese two head men of the Six nations, with Some others . . . including a Cuple of womens." [22] The difficulty was not with these. It was with a flock of Nanticokes, the fellow tribesmen of the interpreter who had distinguished himself for his ignorance of languages at Onondaga in 1743.

Conrad Weiser to Richard Peters [23]

Lancester August the 4. 1748

Sir

    . . . The NontiKook Ind^s have ben very troublesome to us, they where like so many wolfs and I had no Influence on them upon no account there Came but 18 persons from Ohio. and with the Said Nontikooks. and a few Canastoge Indians. the number of Indians here in Lancester present at the last treaty amounted to 55. persons. among whom were 4 Sick which gave particular trouble and Charges. the Twicktwees I left in very good thoughts of the English. and I am for my part Satisfied they are Sincere in our Interest. and within a year or two you will See a good many of the farr Ind^s in Pensylvania be it Warr or peace. I have given every one of the Indians Such present as I was ordered by the Comissioners. that is to Say to the twicktwees. to the others that Conducted them down. I gave to Each of them a Strowd Match Coat, a Shirt, a pair of Indian Stocking a Knife and a ½ Barrel of powder and 100 lb. of let, one lb. of vermilion betwixt them all. this last I took out of the General present the NontiKooks Stood and looked very dull because they got nothing. I was quit out of Humour with them for the disorder the occasioned. yet upon a Second thought I gave them 25 lb. of powder and 50 lb. of let out of the General present rather to please the Indians from ohio (that they might Keep what little they had received) then the said Nontikooks with which they went of glad to have Some thing. I had told them that they were very indiscreet people to hunt the Stranger all along without any order or request from the Governor of Pensilvania or these people themselves Except two or three of them.

     . . . I Should think meselve happy If I had nothing to do in public affairs and Could turn a farmer intirely. at present I leave you but Shall take my fare-well at George Croghans from whence I will write to you again. I remain Sir your obedient

                                                                          CONRAD WEISER

P S. I gave my account against the Government to Mr Kinsey. but as for my last Services I have Sent no account. You know I have ben twice in Philada Since last Spring per order of the Council. the first Journey 11 days. the Second 12. from home. beside my Services at the last treaty being in that time 18 days in the Governments Service. all this I leave to your Care

     The letter Peters sent with the government's instructions had not been of a kind to soothe a harassed temper.

                    Richard Peters to Conrad Weiser [24]

                                                        Philada 14th July 1748
Sir
     . . . I have no money to send you to bear your Expences my own Treasure is exhausted & I am considerably in advance—The Provincial Treas[urer] has no money & I do not care to apply to Mr Kinsey—so Mr Croghan & You must beg borrow or steal as much as is necessary to take with you. . . .
     I most heartily wish you a good Journy & am

                                                        Sir
                                                        Your most humble
I do not now send up ye   Servant
   little Flagg—   RICHARD PETERS

                                         III

     At last, on the 11th of August, Conrad Weiser set out from his house for the Ohio. He was accompanied by William Franklin (son of the Post-master General) who, though only nineteen years of age, had already had a taste of campaigning, having been an ensign on the Canada Expedition. George Croghan had been sent ahead with twenty horses carrying seven hundred pounds worth of goods.

     They took an old trail known as the Allegheny or Frankstown Path. The motorist of today may follow its course fairly closely without ever leaving hard-surfaced roads. Towns and farmsteads have tamed some of

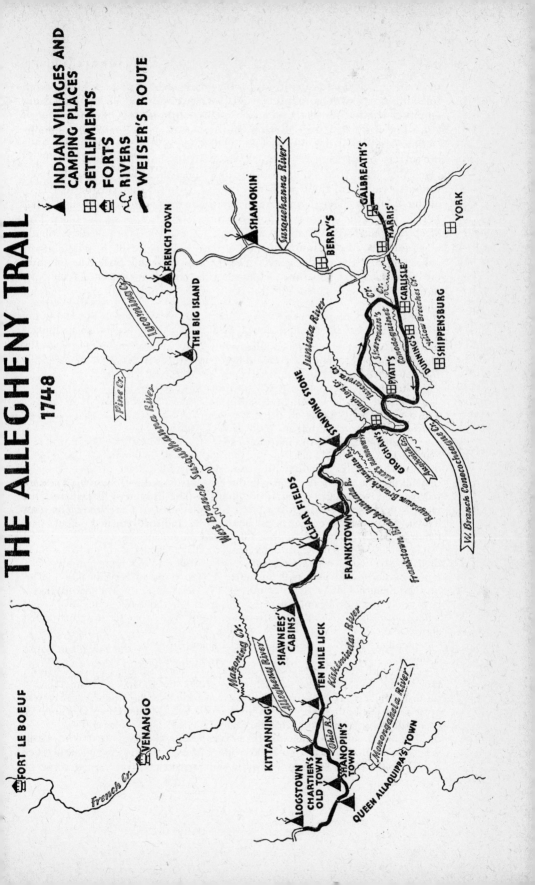

THE ALLEGHENY TRAIL

1748

INDIAN VILLAGES AND CAMPING PLACES
SETTLEMENTS
FORTS
RIVERS
WEISER'S ROUTE

FORT LE BOEUF

VENANGO

French Cr.

Mahoning Cr.

Allegheny River

KITTANNING

LOGSTOWN
CHARTIER'S OLD TOWN
SHANOPIN'S TOWN
QUEEN ALLAQUIPA'S TOWN

Ohio R.

Kiskiminetas River

Monongahela River

SHAWNEES' CABINS

TEN MILE LICK

FRANKSTOWN

Frankstown Branch Juniata R.

CLEAR FIELDS

Raystown Branch Juniata R.

STANDING STONE

GROGHAN'S

Black Log Cr.

Aughwick Cr.

Tuscarora Cr.

Juniata River

West Branch Susquehanna River

Pine Cr.

Lycoming Cr.

THE BIG ISLAND

FRENCH TOWN

SHAMOKIN

Susquehanna River

BERRY'S

Sherman's Cr.

Conococheague Cr.

PYATT'S

CARLISLE

DUNNING'S

Yellow Breeches Cr.

SHIPPENSBURG

Wt. Branch Conococheague Cr.

HARRIS'

GALBREATH'S

YORK

the valleys, but the mountains are still as they were in Weiser's day: bold, forbidding, and yet enticing. Heavy forests cover the slopes, stretching on either hand as far as the eye can reach along interminable ridges, with a sky-line flat as the sea's horizon, and range succeeds range in seemingly endless parallels of diminishing blue. There are no peaks to arrest the eye, no turrets or precipices to break the flowing line. But there are half-concealed gaps through which streams burst their way, escaping from valley to valley till they reach the Juniata River or the Allegheny. Many of the old names have disappeared from the maps, but others remain. What Weiser called the *Tuscarora Path*, the *Shades of Death*, and the *Black Log Sleeping Place* are remembered today in the names Path Valley, Shade Gap, and Black Log Mountain and Creek.

Except for "Rainy Wheather," which compelled the travelers to "lay by" on some days and lose time drying clothes on others, there were no unpleasant interruptions to the journey—unless it be the finding of John Quen's body.

24th Found a Dead Man on the Road who had killed himself by Drinking too much Whiskey; the Place being very stony we cou'd not dig a Grave— He smelling very strong we covered him with Stones & Wood & went on our Journey—came to the 10 Mile Lick......32 Miles

25th Crossed Kiskeminetoes Creek, & came to Ohio that Day. . . . 26

26th Hired a Cannoe—paid 1000 Black Wampum for the loan of it to Logs Town—our Horses being all tyred we went by Water, & came that Night to a Delaware Town; the Indians used us very kindly.

27th Sett off again in the morning early—Rainy Wheather—We dined in a Seneka Town [at the Forks of the Ohio, the modern Pittsburgh], where an old Seneka Woman Reigns with great Authority, we dined at her House, & they all used us very well   at this & the Last mentioned Delaware Town; they received us by firing a great many Guns, especially at this last Place; we saluted the Town by firing off 4 pair of Pistols—arrived that Evening at Logs Town, & Saluted the Town as before—the Indians returned about One hundred Guns—Great Joy appear'd in their Countenances—. . .

The Indian Council met this Evening to shake Hands with me & to shew their Satisfaction at my safe arrival . . .

30th I went to Beavers Creek an Indian Town [home of King Beaver and his brother Shingas] about 8 Miles off chiefly Delawares, the rest Mohawks to have some Belts of Wampum made [he used ten thousand grains, black and white, during the treaty]   this afternoon Rainy Wheather set in which lasted above a Week—. . .

September 2d Rain continued—the Indians brought in a good deal of Venison.

3d Set up the Union Flagg on a long Pole—treated all the Company with a Dram of Rum—The King's Health was drank by Indians & White men— towards Night a great many Indians arrived to attend the Council—there was great firing on both sides,   the Strangers first Saluted the Town at a quarter of a Mile distance, and at their Entry the Towns People return'd the fire, also the English Traders, of whom there were above twenty,   At Night, being very sick of the Cholick, I got bled.

4th Was oblig'd to keep my bed all Day, being very weak.

5th I found myself better; Scaiohady came to see me; had some discourse with him about the ensuing Council.[25]

On the 8th, Weiser held a council with the Wyandots (Hurons). These Indians, though their nation had been all but destroyed when the Iroquois raided their Georgian Bay settlements in 1649, had for many years been on good terms with their conquerors and, as they told Weiser, "were now one People with them."

I treated them [continues the journal] with a Quart of Whisky & a Roll of Tobacco, they expressed their good Wishes to King George & all his People and were mightily pleas'd that I look'd upon them as Brethren of the English. . . .
10th . . . This Day I made a Present to the old Shawonese Chief, Cacka-watcheky of a Stroud, a Blanket, a Match Coat, a Shirt, a Pair of Stockings, & a large twist of Tobacco & told him that the President & Council of Philadelphia remember'd their Love to him as to their old & true Friend, & wou'd Cloath his Body once more & wished he might weare them out so as to give them an opportunity to cloath him again—There was a great many Indians present, two of which were the big Hominy & the Pride those that went off with Chartier, but protested against his proceedings against our Traders—Catchawatcheky return'd thanks & some of the Six Nations did the same, & express'd their Satisfaction to see a true man taken Notice of, altho' he was now grown Childish.[26]

Despite his infirmities, Kakowatchiky had not lost the spirit he had shown forty years earlier when, a party of Shawnees having had a brush with some Pennsylvanians, he wrote his letter to the governor demanding the return of the gun one of his warriors had lost on the field. The year after Weiser's treaty at Logstown, when Céloron de Blainville came from Canada demanding the expulsion of all Englishmen from the Ohio country, "Old Cackewatcheka," according to Richard Peters, ". . . was so exasperated at the Pride & Insolence of the French pretending to say that the Indian's land belonged to them that while he was in the midst of his Speech, the old King being blind and unable to stand without somebody to support him said in a low voice to those who sat next to him Why dont you shoot this French Fellow—Shoot him—shoot him." [27] The officer, says Peters, broke off, and the French left hurriedly in their canoes.

Weiser's task at Logstown was a difficult one. He had to conciliate a scattered crowd of Iroquois, Delawares, Shawnees, Mohicans, Wyandots, and Zisagechroonas, bound together by no common traditions, language, or loyalties. "I found the Indians very Jealous at one another," he wrote to James Logan when he got home, "they being of So many different nations   Each of them pretending to have as Wise people as the rest. and in General they are a people of very litle or few Morals exept the Wantats [Wyandots] and Shawanos." [28] But Weiser's skill was never better displayed. He made friends all round. He was patient, considerate, reasonable, yet by no means mealy mouthed. He was there to demand justice as well as to give presents, and they respected him the more for it.

He asked the Senecas to give up the Englishmen they had taken in South Carolina. Captain Haig, he learned, had been murdered, but his man, Brown, was alive and at hand. Thanayieson, speaker for the Senecas, expressed regret for the blood that had been shed, took the remaining prisoner by the hand, and, laying down "a String of Wampum, mostly black," delivered him safe to Conrad Weiser.

What was to be done about liquor? A certain Henry Noland had brought thirty gallons of whisky to Logstown. In Philadelphia Scaroyady had complained about English traders debauching the Indians with rum. Weiser showed a recent proclamation issued by the Governor forbidding traders to bring rum to Indian conferences. To show that the Governor's words were not idle, Weiser and Croghan staved in one of Noland's eight-gallon kegs. But, said Weiser, the Indians themselves were much to blame, and the government could not stop the traffic without their coöperation.

You send down your own Skins by the Traders to buy Rum for you; You go yourselves & fetch Horse loads of strong Liquor—But the other Day an Indian came to this Town out of Maryland with 3 Horse loads of Liquor; so that it appears you love it so well that you cannot be without it. You know very well that the Country near the endless Mountain affords strong Liquor, & the moment the Traders buy it they are gone out of the Inhabitants, & are travelling to the Place without being discover'd, besides this you never agree about it; one will have it, the other won't (tho' very few), a third says we will have it cheaper; this last we believe is spoken from your Hearts (here they Laughed), Your Brethren therefore have order'd that every . . . of Whisky shall be sold to You for 5 Bucks in your Town, & if a Trader offers to sell Whisky to You and will not let you have it at that Price, you may take it from him & drink it for nothing.[29]

On the 17th of September he arranged the presents in separate piles, corresponding in size with the numbers and influence of the various tribes that were to receive them.

Brethren [he said] Some of You have been in Philadelphia last Fall and acquainted us that You had taken up the English Hatchet and that You had already made use of it against the French and that the French had very hard heads, & your Country afforded nothing but Sticks & Hickorys which was not sufficient to break them, you desir'd your Brethren wou'd assist You with some Weapons sufficient to do it—Your Brethren, the Presid[t] & Council, promis'd you then to send something to You next Spring by Tharachiawagon . . . and here are the Goods before your Eyes, which I have, by your Brethrens Order divided into 5 Shares & laid in 5 different heaps . . . ; & as you are all of the same Nations with whom we the English have been in League of Friendship, nothing need be said more than this, that the President & Council & Assaraquoa [Virginia] have sent You this Present to serve to strengthen the Chain of Friendship between us the English & the several Nations of Indians to which You belong—[30]

Before Weiser left, the Half King (Tanacharison) with some others in authority came to Tarachiawagon, explaining the difficulties of their position and asking him to hold up the sky for them. They "inform'd me," said Weiser,

that they often must send Messengers to Indian Towns & Nations, & had nothing in their Council Bag, as they were new beginners, either to recompense a Messenger or to get Wampum to do the business, & begged I wou'd assist them with something. I had saved a Piece of Stroud, an half Barrell of Powder, 100 lbs. of Lead, 10 Shirts, 6 Knives & 1 lb. of Vermillion, & gave it to them for the aforesaid use; they return'd many thanks, & were mightily pleased.[31]

Allaquippa, "the old Sinicker Queen" (she had met William Penn way back in 1699 or 1700, and it was at her house that Conrad had dined a few days before) came to Logstown to talk with Tarachiawagon about getting "a cask of powder and some small shot to enable her to send out the Indian boys to kill turkeys & other fowls for her, whilst the men are gone to war against the French, that they may not be starved." Weiser expressed regret that he had already given away all his powder and lead, but promised to represent her case when he got back to the white settlements.

"She seemed," he writes, "to have taken a little Affront because I took not sufficient notice of her in coming down."

The interpreter, upset by the "Wheather" and "Cholick," was in no mood to take a reprimand even from a queen. "I told her," he notes, "she acted very imprudently not to let me know by some of her friends who she was, as she knew very well I could not know by myself. She was Satisfied & went away with a deal of kind expressions."

The same day (September 19), "about 12 of the clock," he "set out for Pennsylvania in Rainy Weather, and arrived at George Croghans on the 28th Instant."

So ends the official journal presented to the Council and Assembly at Philadelphia. There is another version, transcribed by a descendant, Hiester Muhlenberg, which adds a little more detail about the homeward journey.

The 22d, the weather cleared up; we travelled this day about 35 miles, came by the place where we had buried the body of John Quen, but found the bears had pulled him out and left nothing of him but a few naked bones and some old rags. . . .

The 1st of October reached the heads of the Tulpenhocken.

The 2nd I arrived safe at my house.[32]

Richard Peters to Thomas Penn [33]

Philadelphia 24th Octr 1748

Honourd Sir

Mr Weiser being in Town when I went to Newcastle it was agreed between him & me that he shoud write to you a full Account of all Indian matters and send you a Copy of his Journal to Ohio and his proceedings there and that therefore I shoud not write any thing about those Matters by this Conveyance but supply his Defects by the next. Instead of that he was sent for as I understand by a Sister of his in Jersey & left his Journal behind him without a single Line, owing I suppose to some unavoidable call, I send it you as it is, ill

formd & ill spelld, rather as a piece of Intelligence yⁿ as a formal Report tho it
was read in this Dress both in Council & Assembly. The Indians are numerous
in those parts, but yᵉ Scum of the Earth the Ouandaets [Wyandots] &
Twightwees excepted, yet tho they are of this mixd dirty sort of people they
are of great consequence & may be made extremely useful to the Trade & security of this Province. One of the most important Discoveries made by Mʳ
Weiser is this that the Moment you leave the last ridge of Hills the Lands are
exceeding good & continue so interruptedly, he says what I cant believe that
the Body of the Lands for many miles together Sixty or Seventy at least is as
good as Conestogo Lands—he talks in Raptures about the Soil & Waters,
Surely then you will give Orders that ye Virginians or Marylanders be prevented from selling any Lands within this Province. What measures ought to
be taken for this purpose you will best judge of shoud not some of your
Friends, Mʳ Hockley for instance & some others that you coud depend on men
of Weight & Authority, to counter ballance the great men of the other
Colonies be employd imediately in the Indian Trade.

Pennsylvania traders swarmed into the Ohio Valley by the hundreds.
Richard Peters, among others, was seized with the speculative fever and
invested heavily in the Indian trade. The rush for the West had begun.

Conrad Weiser had set in train a movement by which France in a few
years was to lose her American colonies. Conrad Weiser—Céloron de
Bienville—George Washington—Fort Le Boeuf—Fort Necessity—Fort
Duquesne: these are the successive steps on the road that led from Logs-
town to Quebec and ended on the Plains of Abraham within a year of
Weiser's death.

Meanwhile Weiser's sister, Anna Margaret, in New Jersey, had died
before Richard Peters wrote his letter. On October 22 Joseph Scatter-
good, Surrogate, had received "from Conrad Weiser Esqʳ Administrator
of all & Singular the Goods Rights & Credits of Margaret Weiser Deceased
the sum of Thirty Shillings in full for Letters of Administration on the
Deceaseds Estate." [34]

When Weiser returned from New Jersey he tinkered with, but did not
complete, the description of the Ohio country he had started to write for
Thomas Penn. A fragment, however, has been preserved (undated) among
his papers. I quote it as evidence of Weiser's eye for the present and his
vision for the future.

Private Sentements of Ohio [35]

. . . The River of Ohio is a very fine River and from its rise it begins to
be navigable for Canoes & Batoes to its mouth where it runs into the Great
River Misisippy It must be by all accounts near a tousand Mile long it differs
from all the rivers in North america for its Smootness Considering its lenght.
[Weiser's footnote: the traders and Indians in going down the river they
Boil their victuals a litle before night and go into their Canoes again and they
tie 3 or 4 Canoes together and let them drive all night and they lie themselves
down to Sleep and there is not the least danger of overseting] the lands on
both Sides are very good and a great deal of it Extraordinary rich. and between the Said river and the lake Erie the greatest part is good land White oak

Blake oak & Spanish oak is the timber that grows on it, it is by the timber what the Indians tells me grows on it I think the Indians themselves Can not Judge of the land itself only of the low lands & plans of which is so much that one thinks it a tousand pity that Such a large and good Country Should be unsetled or fall into the hand of the french who have allready made Some Setlements below or on the river Comonly Called Wappash a Branch of Ohio. this fall the high Ground about ohio was all Covered with acorns. a midling good Hunter among the Indian of ohio Killes for his Share in one fall 150. 200 dears the pensilvania traders had all the Skins this 2 or 3 years. the Erecting of a good Corespondents and a Regular trade with the Indians on ohio would Secure that fine and large Country to the English nation, a good beginning is made by the last present from the Governt of pen. that I Caried there. the trade itself If but in Regulation will ansr all the Cost of Keeping Such Corespondents and Consequently the land will fall at last into the English hands. the westerly bounds of pensilvania must reach Some of the Eastern Branches of ohio If not the river itself in Some places and the lands on the road that leads to ohio from pensilvania is good So that If their Honours the proprietors of pensilvania purchase that part of their province from the Indians I dare say within 10 years after the purchas is made, the land will be Setled to within 50 miles of ohio.

He includes a word of advice which, if it had been taken in time, might have saved the life of General Braddock:

persuade the 6 nation to take of the petticoat from the delewares and give them a Breech Cloath to wear and Call them for the futter their Brethren or Children and leave out the word Cousin (because in the Indian linguage at Signifies a Subject or one that is under Comand) which the Government may do.

CHAPTER 33

... Condoles with the Children and Grandchildren of Shickellamy

SHICKELLAMY'S journey to Bethlehem in November had been made at the invitation of the Moravians.

The old chief at Shamokin had little in common with most of the Indians around him, who were an easy prey to the rum traders and spent their evenings drinking and howling. For friendship he turned to the little group of Brethren living in the neighborhood. The Moravians had established a smithy at Shamokin, to which the Indians came from a distance to have their hatchets mended; and they grew turnips, for which the Indians had a great taste.

"Shikillmy is always delighted when he receives a present of turnips," wrote Bishop Cammerhof on his visit to Shamokin in January 1748. "He also treats the Brethren to venison. He places great confidence in them, brings his harness and other things to them to keep for them, so that when he needs them, he can quickly get them, for in his house there is the greatest confusion." [1]

Since the Bishop's Journal gives us the best picture available of the courteous old Oneida gentleman and his family circle during his last days, I continue to quote from it.

Shikillmy's youngest son's (Logan) wife is a Mohican . . . She is a relative of our Abraham (Mohican) She had a daughter four years old. Last November she took it with her on the annual hunt, when it died, bewitched by a Delaware sorcerer. The Mother brought the body back and had it buried in Shikillmy's ancestral burying ground. She came to our house and asked Sr. Mack for a few nails and wood to make a coffin. There she related that the child before it died had said: "Mother, I will soon die—greet the white people and tell them I never stole any turnips; that they should not suspect her of such a theft, for I always asked when I wanted one." . . . "Do you think my child will go to your God?" she inquired. Sr. Mack told her she thought it would, and spoke of the love of God for children. . . .

Our brethren attended the funeral of the child. Its mother showed them the child in the coffin with its presents viz: a blanket, several pairs of moccasins, buckskin for new ones, needle and thread, a Kettle, two hatchets—one large and one smaller—to cut kindling wood, flint, steel and tinder, so that on its arrival in the new country, it could at once go to housekeeping. Besides, it was beautifully painted and had a supply of beans, corn and a calabash. The Indians thought it was cruel in us not to have supplied Hagen [the smith, who had died in the 1747 epidemic] with all these things, but we told them that as soon as we came to the Saviour, he would supply us with all we needed. Then the mother sat aside of the child and sang and wept—"Wake up, my child, arise and eat, for five days you have tasted no food." When we reached the grave, the mother kneel'd and wept and sang: "The sorcerer killed my child! This, my child, was killed by the sorcerer!" This was the burden of her wail, in which she was joined by another squaw. After the funeral she came to our house, with a quart tin which she gave to Sr. Mack, saying: "This had been my daughter's—keep it in remembrance of her." It is an Indian custom, that when one dies, not all the effects are buried with it, but that some are reserved for distribution among the deceased ones friends. I think we will gain this Mohican woman for the Lord—perhaps the first fruits of Shikillmy's family—

All the family think very highly of us. . . . On Sunday evening with Mack I visited Shikillmy and his family. Last Fall many of his family died viz: his wife, his oldest sons wife and five children, his son-in-law and some of his children. The mother was still in mourning, sitting in the ashes with an old torn blanket about her. Logan also lost three of his children. Shikillmy was also sick unto death.[2]

Shickellamy apologized to the Bishop for his neglect of the white people.

"My brother!" he said, "don't take it amiss, that the smith at Shamokin up to this time has had not much to eat. I have been sick and so have my sons and their children, and many of them died. We have been mourning and unable to go to the chase. When better, we will hunt, and then the smith and his wife shall have more to eat."

"Shikillmy, my brother!" replied Cammerhof: "My brother the smith and his family at Shamokin, are not dissatisfied. They had as much meat as was necessary; and T'girhitonti [Spangenberg] and his brethren are also not dissatisfied, but are glad of your kindness to the smith." [3]

In October Bishop John de Watteville came, bringing to Shickellamy a gift from Count Zinzendorf: a silver knife, fork, and spoon, and an ivory drinking cup. He brought also from the Count a message, which Zeisberger translated, bidding him remember "the Gospel which he had heard from his lips." [4]

The friendly consideration shown him by the Moravians touched the old chief. These were dark days. He was grieving for the loss of wife, children, and grandchildren. He was bothered by the conflicting reports of war and neutrality and alliances which came through the woods and which his old brain could no longer master and bring to any reasonable shape or conclusion. He was oppressed by the meanness and wickedness of the Pennsylvania traders, a thieving lot of men for the most part, whose chief commodity, rum, was ruining half the Indian population. Shickellamy turned to the Brethren from Bethlehem who traded in nothing but God's love.

Their religion was not new to him. He had breathed it in the woods: the spirit of the Great Father who is present in cloud and tree and river. But the story of the incarnation and the doctrine of the atonement brought religion home with new force to a man whose failing senses could no longer, as in his youth, apprehend God in the scent of the pine woods and the sound of the cataract. His eyes were dim and his mind was bewildered. In these days when Indian customs and traditions were losing their sanction, when old loyalties were undermined and even the authority of the Onondaga Council—till then the axis round which his world had revolved—was shaken, he turned to the Moravians for reassurance. There was peace in their faces. In the midst of war, pestilence, and famine, they were undisturbed. His world was breaking up. Their world still had a center. Could he reach over from his world into theirs and find in the Christ of whom they spoke a new sense of significance in life which his strained nerves had lost?

Shickellamy came to Bethlehem to learn more about Jesus. He received daily instruction; and there, among the Lehigh Hills, his heart opened completely to the God made manifest in the man from Bethlehem of Judaea.

The Moravians did not baptize him, for he told them he had been baptized as an infant by a priest in Canada; but, in token of his new entry into the Christian communion, he was persuaded to throw away the "manitou" he wore around his neck as a charm to keep off sickness.

On his way home he was taken ill at Tulpehocken, and had barely strength, with the aid of David Zeisberger, to reach his home in Shamokin. There, as De Schweinitz writes in his life of Zeisberger, "the old chief stretched himself on his mat, and never rose again." [5]

He died on Tuesday, December 6, in the presence of his daughter, some other members of his family, and David Zeisberger. The daughter had come for David about noon, saying that her father was "going home." [6] David came, and found the old chief's family (children and grandchildren) gathered round him in a tumult of weeping. Shickellamy could no longer speak, but he acknowledged David's presence with friendly eyes, smiled, and passed away contentedly. [7]

The Moravians were confident that all was well with him.

But all was not well with the people he had shepherded for so many years. With the death of Shickellamy, "Our Enlightener," a lamp went out that left the Indians at Shamokin in darkness.

"Now our uncle has passed away," runs the Iroquois ritual of condolence—the Mourning Ceremony:

he who used to work for all, that they might see the brighter days to come, for the whole body of warriors, and also for the whole body of women, and also for the children that were running around, and also for the little ones creeping on the ground, and also those that are tied to the cradleboards: for all these he used to work that they might see the bright days to come . . . He who has worked for us has gone afar off. [8]

His three sons were away at the time of his death. Runners were despatched for them. The lame son, James Logan, who had been out hunting, arrived on Thursday. [9] Meanwhile Shickellamy's daughter, with the help of Henry Fry, had made him a coffin. In it were placed the things his family thought he would need on the long journey into the Spirit Land: two new blankets, a loaf of bread, a tobacco pipe, a quantity of tobacco, flint and tinder, etc. [10]

On Friday he was buried (quietly: no shots were fired), all Shamokin attending, in the old Indian burying ground near the Susquehanna River, within the boundaries of the present city of Sunbury. A natural monument overlooks the grave from across the river: a rocky cliff on which may be seen an Indian profile—"Shickellamy's Face."

Tah-gah-jute (James Logan) asked David Zeisberger to write a letter to Weiser informing him of the chief's death.[11] Weiser reported the news to the government in Philadelphia. Official condolences were sent, after some delay, to the sons of Shickellamy at Shamokin.

Conrad Weiser to Richard Peters [12]

[Heidelberg, April 22, 1749]

Sir

By these lines I let you Know that I returned from ShomoKin on the 18 of this Instant. I happened to meet the Eldest and youngest Son of ShicKelimy at the trading house of Thomas McKee about 20 miles this Side of Shomokin by whom I was informed that all the Indians had left ShomoKin for this present time because for want of provision, So I thought best to deliver my message there to the Sons of ShicKelimy. there was three more of the Six nation Indians one of them was *Toyanogon* a noted man among the CayucKers. all what I had to do was to let the Children and grand Children of our deceased friend ShicKelimy Know that the Governor of pensilvania & his Counsel Condoled with them for the death of their father which I did accordingly and gave them a Small present in order to wipe off their tears according to the Custom of the Indians. the present Consisted of Six Strowd Matchcoats and Seven Shirts, with a Streng of Wampum. after this was over, I gave another streng of Wampum to *Taghneghdoarus* [13] ShicKelimy Eldest Son and desired him to take upon him the Care of a Chief in the Stead of his deceased father and to be our true Correspondent untill there Should be a meeting between the Governor of pensilvania and Some of the Six nation Chief. and then he Should be recomended by the Governor to the Six nation Chiefs and Confirmed If he would folow the foot Steps of his deceased father He accepted thereof and I Sent a Streng of Wampum by Toyanogon (who was then Seting out for CayucKquo) to onantago to let the Counsel of the Six nation Know of Shickelimys death and my transaction by order of the Governor. . . .

Sir
your very obedient
CONRAD WEISER

The cleared land has become a thicket.
    Woe! Woe!
The clear places are deserted.
    Woe!
They are in their graves—
They who established it—
    Woe!
The Great League. . . .
Their work has grown old.
    Woe!
Thus are we become miserable.
    —The Iroquois Mourning Ceremony [14]

The death of Shickellamy marks the end of an epoch. He was the last of an imperial line of Iroquois statesmen with continental vision, upholding the tradition of Deganaweda and Hiawatha.

"He was truly an excellent man," wrote Count Zinzendorf, "laying claims to refinement and intelligence. He was possessed of great dignity, sobriety and prudence, and was particularly noted for his extreme kindness to the inhabitants with whom he came in contact." [15]

This last trait he passed down in full to his son, James Logan, who is remembered in tradition as the Indian who warned the settlers of the impending massacre of Wyoming. But Logan's kindness to white men was thrown away. A gang of murdering land-grabbers and rum-sellers wiped out his whole family and turned Shickellamy's son into a vengeful savage. At the Battle of Mount Pleasant in "Cresap's War" he is said to have taken thirty scalps with his own hand. The message he sent to Lord Dunmore of Virginia—spoken by Logan to Simon Girty and repeated by Simon Girty to John Gibson, who wrote it down—closes the story of the Shickellamies in words that sum up the tragedy of the dispossessed Indian race.

I appeal to any white man to say, if ever he entered Logan's cabin hungry, and he gave him not meat; if ever he came cold and naked, and he cloathed him not. During the course of the last long and bloody war Logan remained idle in his cabin an advocate for peace. Such was my love for the whites, that my countrymen pointed as they passed, and said, "Logan is the friend of white men." I had even thought to have lived with you, but for the injuries of one man. Colonel Cresap,[16] the last spring, in cold blood, and unprovoked, murdered all the relations of Logan, not sparing even my women and children. There runs not a drop of my blood in the veins of any living creature. This called on me for revenge. I have sought it: I have killed many. I have glutted my vengeance: for my country I rejoice at the beams of peace. But do not harbour a thought that mine is the joy of fear. Logan never felt fear. Logan will not turn on his heel to save his life. Who is there to mourn for Logan?—Not one!

> —Thomas Jefferson's version of "Logan's Lament" [17]

Now listen, ye who established the
Great League. Now it has become old.
Now there is nothing but a wilderness.
Ye are in your graves who established it.
Ye have taken it with you and have placed
it under you, and there is nothing left
but a desert.

> —The Canienga Book of Rites [18]

CHAPTER 34

. . . *Grows Tired of Indians*

THE DEATH of Shickellamy changed the whole tenor of Indian affairs in Pennsylvania. Anthony Palmer had once described the old chief as "a Person of Character at Shamokin." [1] He was precisely that. Weiser had depended on him for advice, and blundered dangerously when he first found himself without it. The Indians on the Susquehanna never got over his loss. His presence had given them cohesion and a sense of importance. Even the deputies from the Onondaga Council in 1749, when they passed through Shamokin without him, seemed a mere rabble that Conrad Weiser could do no good with.

Before we get into the tragi-comic story of the Indian conferences in 1749, which resulted in the purchase by Pennsylvania of the first ranges of the Endless Mountains, we must look back for a moment on Conrad Weiser's Ohio journey, because the idea of the purchase was Conrad Weiser's from first to last, and because it had been suggested to him by something he had seen on the Allegheny Trail.

When Weiser set out for Logstown, he carried instructions to turn off any white men found settling on unpurchased Indian lands. From the Tuscarora Path (Path Valley), near what is now Powell's Mill, he wrote on August 15, 1748, about the difficulties he found in the way of these turnings off. The problem was not as simple as it had appeared in Philadelphia. It was to be taken for granted, of course, that, if the government allowed white settlers to occupy Indian lands, the resentment of the distant Six Nations would be incurred, with the risk of reprisals and war. To turn these poor settlers off, on the other hand, was to risk the resentment of the Indians on the spot. Indians, of whatever tribe, were a warm-hearted people whose sympathies were quickly roused at the sight of anyone in distress, white or brown.

Scaroyiaty [wrote Weiser] with a few more of the Indians that attended the last treaty . . . had ben Informed that the people here were to be turned off by the Govern^t and I Suppose the people used them well on their Coming by and Informed them of the design, they the Indian asked me about them, and desired that at least two family to wit Abraham Shlechl and another might Stay that they the Said Indians had given them liberty and that they thought it was in their power to give liberty to Such as the licked. . . . the Indians have desired me not to join to turn off the people till I Came from ohio. I promised I would not . . .[2]

That was one side of the picture. The other side is shown in a letter of April 22, 1749, written to Richard Peters, the Provincial Secretary, shortly after his meeting with the sons of Shickellamy at McKee's:

The Indians are very unEasy about the white peoples Setling beyond the Endless mountains on Joniady. on Shermans Creek and Else where. they tell

me that above 30 familys are Setled upon the Indians land this spring and
dayly more goes to setle thereon Some have Setled all most to the heads of
Joniady River along the path that leads to ohio. the Indian Says (and that with
truth) that that Country is their only Hunting ground for dears because
further to the nord there was nothing but Spruce woods and the ground
Covered with palm prushes not a Single dear Could be found or Killed there,
they asked me very Seriously whether their Brother Onas had given the people
leave to Setle there.[3]

Peters wrote to say that the governor intended to send "the Sheriff and
some of the most prudent & intrepid Magistrates to remove them"; [4] but
that he feared it might not be in the power of the government "to prevent
these mutinous Spirits from settling those lands."

Conrad was more afraid of the government's precipitate zeal than he
was of any immediate disturbance from the Indians, and he advised against
evicting the settlers "till Some of the Six Nations Chiefs Come down." [5]
He was not speaking from any sentimental awe of the Great Council. He
recognized the government's difficulty, which was briefly this: To restrain
or dispossess the squatters on Indian lands might cause disturbance not
only on the frontier but also in Philadelphia, where the Assembly was
inclined to take the side of the settlers; on the other hand, not to restrain
them would be to commit an injustice against the Six Nations which the
latter might be tempted to avenge.

Weiser not only saw the difficulty; he saw a way through it. Having
heard from the Shickellamies that a deputation from the Onondaga Council
was coming to Philadelphia to discuss the matter of peace with the Catawbas, he proposed that the government keep quiet about the western settlers
until after the Six Nations chiefs, who, as they came down the Susquehanna,
could not fail to take notice of the movement across the river, had themselves made a complaint. Then the Assembly and all the people of Pennsylvania would see the necessity of removing the new settlers.[6] This public
complaint should provide the groundwork for a proclamation against settlement over the Susquehanna, a proclamation that would have ten times the
effect it would have had if the first motion had not been made by the Indians. At the same time everyone would see the need of a new purchase.

Up to a certain point the plan worked out precisely as Weiser expected.
Deputies from the Seneca nation (who came alone, having failed to meet
the deputies from the other United Nations at the appointed rendezvous
in the woods) reached Weiser's house on June 22,[7] and, fortified with
420 pounds of beef and two gallons of rum, proceeded under Weiser's
escort to Philadelphia, where their complaint was duly made in public
conference.

Whereupon, as Richard Peters wrote to the Penns,[8]

. . . all Persons mouths were full of the necessity of an Indian Purchase, and
indeed all sorts of Persons saw clearly that unless one was made it wou'd be
impossible to preserve the Peace of the Province, for the lower sort of People
who are exceeding Loose & ungovernable from the mildness of the Constitution & the pacifick principles of yᵉ Friends wou'd go over in spite of all

measures & probably quarrel with the Indians: but Mr Weiser apprehends a worse Effect, that is that they will become tributary to the Indians & pay them yearly Sums for their Lycense to be there. he says positively that they are got into this way on the East side of Sasquehanna' beyond the Hills & receive acknowledgments & are easy about those Lands, and that if they do the same on the West side of that River the Proprietaries will not only have all the abandon'd People of the Province to deal with but the Indians too & that they will mutually support each other & do a vast deal of Mischief.[9]

The Governor, now assured that the people were behind him, gave Weiser private instructions "to send a message by the Senekas to the Council at Onontago" (it is Richard Peters writing) "to know if they wou'd sell any & what Lands to the Proprietors." [10]

Weiser proposed that the new purchase should be "all the Lands on the Waters of Juniata," even to the heads of the creeks that fed it, which meant a vast tract extending nearly to "the Waters of Allegheny." [11]

Though this particular part of Weiser's plan was not to be fulfilled— not, at least, for some years to come—an odd turn of the cards put an ace into his hand that turned the trick before the Penns in England even heard that a purchase was in the air. Early in August Canasatego turned up at Tulpehocken with a mob of 279 hungry Indians counting on their Falstaf- fian chief to give them a good time in Philadelphia. The connection between this incident and the Purchase of 1749 will be explained in the narrative that follows.

Canasatego was unwanted. The Governor, through Weiser, had given what Richard Peters calls "peremptory Orders" to the Seneca deputies, if on their return they met the tardy deputies of the other nations, which it was supposed they might do at Shamokin, to tell them not to proceed to Philadelphia, the business there having been completed and the Governor being now intent on other things.

But Canasatego, unwanted, was the more determined. He and his as- sociates tossed aside the Governor's commands, and "in very wantonness" (so moaned the Penns' "Dutiful Servant," Richard Peters) [12] "press'd into their Company most of the Shamokin Indians, Nantycokes, Tutelas & Delawares," and came down like thunder over the Shamokin Trail.

When Weiser got home from the Lancaster Court on the evening of August 4, he found four Indians awaiting him with news that the deputies of the Six Nations had lodged the night before at Justice Galbrecht's (the modern Hershey), and desired Conrad to meet them with a wagon and provisions, since they were "most Starved (their usual Complaint)," as Weiser writes,[13] "for want of victuals, they being So numerous that four or five houses Could not afford victuals enough for them."

Weiser was more than exasperated. He had been dashing about for some days, trying to attend to his own business and also to accommodate these Indians by meeting them at a given time at their own designated rendezvous, "the witow Chambers." Not finding them there, after three days waiting, he had persuaded himself that they had thought better of their visit and were not coming. Now he learned they were coming after all—coming in swarms, deputies of the Great Council with no one knew how many "old womens" and children in their train.

What was to be done with them? They must be met and provisioned, of course. And of course they must be entertained on his plantation. What would happen to his fruit trees? Would the government defray the cost? How many mouths would there be to feed that night? Turning over such thoughts in his mind, he mounted his horse again and rode to "the upper end of Tulpehockin," where he bought a bull and "30 Bigg loaves of Bread for their Supper." [14]

They astonished Weiser when they came at last, astonished him for their numbers: between two and three hundred pouring down the road, dirty, tired, and footsore, the lame ones in a wagon. It was more than Weiser's patience could stand. He had thought Canasatego would have had more sense than to come, more courtesy than to come with such a crowd.

Instead of greeting them with outstretched hand as was his custom, Conrad stood at a distance like a stranger, as he tells us, for above a quarter of an hour, to signify that he was not well pleased; and, when he did at last unbend, it was to shake hands grudgingly with but a few.

At length he sat down with Canasatego beside the creek where the Indians were encamped, and began a salty conversation of which he has left us a record.

"Where are you going with such a great number of Indians?" asked Conrad.

"You know where I am going," retorted Canasatego, "by the message I sent you."

"When you sent the message," said Conrad, "you had not then met with the Seneca chiefs who had been in Philadelphia lately and did the business that was to be done."

"I did meet the said Indians at Shamokin and brought them back. Not all was done what ought to have been done. As I had come so far with the rest of all the deputies of every nation of the Six United Nations, I could not return before I been in Philadelphia."

"You might have left the Shamokin Indians and the rest of the Susquehanna Indians behind," persisted Conrad.

"Everyone is at liberty to come along or stay at home on such occasions," responded Canasatego. "I and the rest of the deputies signified to them that their company was disagreeable by not giving them share of our provision. Some of them came along for all that, but the greatest part have returned home."

No arguments having availed to dissuade Canasatego from pursuing his journey to Philadelphia, next day the wagon jolted its load of lame Indians, and the road vomited its horde of hale ones, on to Weiser's plantation. Irritably the Interpreter wrote to Richard Peters, asking for instructions. What was he to do? Was he to go with Canasatego and his flock to Philadelphia, buying victuals by the way? If so, it would come to a great sum of money, for which (though, as he said, his credit was good where his money was short) he had no assurance of being paid, since the visit was against the Governor's wishes. Or should he stay at home—and by so doing offend the Indians, disoblige the Governor, and perhaps cause disturbance among the back inhabitants since hungry Indians take what they want by force?

"I declare," he wrote, "I wish I had gone out of the way into a neighboring province, I am altogether tired of Indians, my patience with their behaviour is wore out ! . . ."

They had of late grown insolent and haughty because, so it appeared to him, the English and the French had spoiled them, courting their favor from both sides during the last war.

"I Belief I must have a very Smart Conference with them before they leave my house," said Conrad.

And a very smart conference he had, in which, as he candidly confessed afterwards, he offended Canasatego, though he succeeded also in putting into the chief's mind the germ of the purchase idea.

"I thought it imprudent," so Conrad reported his remarks to Canasatego and others,

for them to go to phil^{ia} with Such a great number of people that had no Buisness there at all. then only to get drunk etc. and as their number was So great, they Could not Expect to get all Victuals Enough that among white people every thing was Sold and the Money wherewith their provisions was bought was a free gift by the inhabitants—and as the Sinicker deputies had ben down with a good number of other Indians not long ago. and had Cost a great deal of money. I imagined their going was needless or at least they must not Expect any presents without they had Some thing Else to do that perhaps I did not Know. that they remembered very well when they were down formerly. they were sent for. and when they Received large presents it was for Some land; and then the proprietors paid. that their Case was otherways now and that they ought to Know that the great number of good for no thing people. makes their Case worse.[15]

That blast coming from the Holder of the Heavens shook the Indians so severely that, as John Shickellamy reported afterward to Weiser, some of them proposed to go back—but not Canasatego; controversy sobered him, and he preserved his dignity even in anger. Following the good custom of the Six Nations (which corresponded with that of More's Utopians, who would "dispute or reason of no matter the same day that it is first proposed"), he withheld his formal retort till the morrow. Weiser made a careful report of it when it came, even though it was to his own disadvantage.

Memorandum, August 7,[16] of "a discourse with the Indian Counsel at my own house"

Canasatego, Speaker   about 38 Indians

Brother Tharagh^n you told us last night that you looked upon our going to phil^{ia} to be imprudent and you Said that we brought too many of our allies & Cousins with us. and so forth.

we let you Know that when ever we the Chiefes of the united nation goes to our Brethren the White people we allways invide them to accompany us and take Share with us be it no thing or Some thing and we have allways done So when we went to phil^ia and never have been reprimanded for it after this manner   perhaps it is because you got all our lands that you wanted from us and you dont like to See us any more and Consequently our fate is the Same as our Cousins the delawares & Mohickans. we asked for no thing but you Say we must not Expect presents: no not our Belly full of victuals because we are So Numerious. We therefore will return to our own Country and give over going to philadelphia. and We Will not trouble our Brethren in philad^ia nor you again   as part with our Cousins and allies the Shawanos delawares & Nontikooks also the Tutalous we Can not now Since they Came so farr. Consider therefore and let us know what you think of the whole . . . is what you Said to us according to the Instruction you have from the Governor & our Brethren in philadelphia you need Say no more. or is it you own thoughts as words of advice then Say . . .

By this time Weiser had come some distance on the way back to diplomatic poise and calm judgment. Harm had been done that could not be undone: he had insulted the Six Nations. But he could divert their anger from Brother Onas to himself and so save the province.

The Memorandum continues:

I made ans^r that it was my own thoughts as a Word of advise to them, and that I had received no Instruction as yet from their Brethren in philadelphia that this was not the first time I advised them   If they approved of my advise well & good   If not it was well and good again as to what belong to me

The continuation of our narrative is found in a letter from

Conrad Weiser to Richard Peters [17]

Madetchy at the house of
Rudolf Bonner. august the
12. 1749

Sir

As to What passed between me and the Indians before I left my house with them, which was on the Eight of this Instant I must reffer till I See you. I am So farr reconciled with them that they own their fault in Coming with Such a number but they between them Self have had high words. Canasatego is Blamed very much for inviding Some of them to Come down that had no Buisness here at all, to wit Mohikans, delawares NonticocKs. & ShomoKin Indians   he finding his mistake traveld behind all along and for the most part of the time Kept drunk he paying for ligquor to Some of the hungry tavern Keepers. as to what I said about the ohio Indians must have ben a mistake. Some of the Gang about me now, being behind then Came up to my house on the 7 of this Instant, which made the whole number amount to 260. I Counted them meselve but there is only 250 with me now, 10 of them being Marodows [marauders] stayd at my house to give my family trouble till the rest Comes back from philadelphia, we traveld the first day from my house to Wm Hartelys, where the Indians encamped out of door   it rained very hard all night the poor Creaturs most perished. I was oblidged to give them a dram all round next morning. which I never did before or after, we where oblidged to lay by next day because for the rain. on the 10 we traveld all day in the rain and Came to Manuatany, the neighbourhood Complained very much about the Indians taking of the Bark of all the Wall nut trees about Reading town. but I Belief for the most part from the proprietors land, from all other timber they Could not take of the Bark it being out of Season and in Short they made Sad work about the Indian Corn fields. their alowance being but So & So as you will See by my account. yesterday morning we had a great dispute one of the drunken Indian haveing Struck a White man with his Hatchit and offered to Stick a Nother with his Knife. I demanded Satisfaction and told them that they Came without any invidation and where Suplied with victuals not with Standing their great number, and they ought to behave as becometh or Else I would not pay any more victuals for them. I insisted upon to bring up the felow that did the Mischief. Canasatego Seconded me and said let him be of what Nation he will all his Company Shall return home (he Knew it was a NontiKook) and So Shall those that Says any thing in his behalf. but it appeared that the Indian was So well paid by Some of our people that Came to the assistance of the white man. that he Could hardly walk. and I drapt the Case. in the mean time Canasatego & Saristaquo the Chief of the onoyiuds had a quarrle. Sarristaquo resolved thereupon to go back with his people to wit all the onoyiudes and Tuscarrorows and Mohickans. I being a feared of Mischief to be done in their return, and haveing receivᵈ your letter by Valatine Herchelroad that morning about 3 of the Cloke. I told them that I had informed the government of what passed between me & them at my house about their Number and had received in answer that Since they Came so farr they must proceed to the City of philadelphia and not part from one another and So they Came along. I am now Easy in my mind let things go as they can go nothing Shall for this Journey trouble me any more. but I can not Come to philadelphia before next Sunday with this people Some of them did not Come up this night nor the night before last. So that I wonᵗ get farther to day then to White Mash to Christopher Robes. This time I Belief I must not trouble Mʳ logan. this is all at present. from

Sir
Your very obedient
CONRAD WEISER

P.S. If I Said any thing in my former unbecoming me, pray put the best Construction upon it   I was So out of Humour with every Body because I thought every thing was against me, and the Indians drunk & Sober gave me So much trouble and I had not assistance about me. every thing about my house was destroyed

Next day Conrad and his crew made port in the city. "They write from Philadelphia," said the November 1749 issue of a London periodical, *The Universal Magazine of Knowledge and Pleasure*, "that on the 13th of August last, arrived there Conrad Weiser, Esq., and with him the deputies of eleven different nations of Indians in order to transact some affairs with the government, Senecas, Mohawks, Cayugas, Oneidas, Tuscaroras, Shawonese, Nanticokes, Delawares, Mohigans and Tuteloes. The whole number amounting to 260 Persons."

The best account we have of the Philadelphia conference, with its climax in the purchase, is found in a letter from Richard Peters to Thomas Penn.

The Indians, wrote Peters,

. . . came to Town in number 290, behaving very rudely on the Road—Indeed to my great Mortification I found the Indians another sort of People & Canassatego no better than the rest, they had in the course of the War been so imprudently manag'd by the Governor of New York that they were grown as irregular & dishonest in Council as out of Council, & wou'd you believe that Canassatego mistrusting that as they had no Business they wou'd receive no Presents shou'd move in Council that the Proprietaries shou'd be ask'd to give them another Present for the Lands already sold, tho' they had been well paid for them under pretence that the Consideration was but trifling & brought the Proprietaries more in one Year than they had for the Fee Simple of the whole. On this unexpected piece of Knavery Mr Weiser broke from them & wou'd not be prevail'd on to sit any Longer in Council—On this they trump'd up a Speech, the best they cou'd without Conrad's assistance; & for fear Least the Government shou'd give them no Present they of their own head propos'd to sell some Lands to the East side of Sasquehanna' as far as Thomas McGee's House which is about ten Miles from the Blue Hills, and Left to the Governor to say what he wou'd give for those Lands—. . . tho' the Council were unanimous & pressing that the Purchase shou'd be made and the Proprietaries give 500, yet the Governor hesitated a long while till Mr Weiser giving it as his opinion that if they did not accept this, bad as it was, or something like it, it might be exceeding difficult to bring about another Indian Purchase, & besides wou'd furnish both Indians and White People with good reasons for receiving and paying tribute nor cou'd the good Lands on the West side of Sasquehanna' be procur'd unless the People might have Liberty to settle on the East side—Mr Weiser I say being sanguine as well from the regard he had, as he said, for the Proprietors as the Country . . . the Governor perfectly agreeing with me in Judgment order'd Mr Weiser to make this Offer, That the Governor for the Proprietors wou'd treat with the Indians for that Tract of Land which lay between Shamokin & the Blue Hills & between Sasquehanna' and Delaware, . . . that is to say, that the North Boundary shou'd be a straight Line from Shamokin to the Mouth of the Lechawachsein on Delaware —This they absolutely refus'd, whereupon at Last it was agreed on both sides to accept a North boundary to begin at the North side of a Hill near Mahoniaghy called Moxunay in the Map, & from thence by a straight Line to the North Bank of the Mouth of Lechawachsein on Delaware.[18]

This innocent "straight line" was the one piece of crookedness in the treaty. Brother Onas was somewhat less than candid. The Six Nations were determined to keep inviolate the famous Wyoming Valley, to which, it will be remembered, they had in 1742 haled the Delawares by the hair. The Mahanoy Mountain was far enough away from the North Branch of the Susquehanna at Shamokin, but the straight line to Lechawachsein ran close to Wyoming itself, since the river bends down a little here.

The extent of the Land purchas'd is Laid down in a Map herewith sent [continues the pious Peters] which is an exact Copy of one annexed to the Indian Deed, save in this, Sasquehanna' is Laid down beyond Wyomin, but in that annex'd to the Indian Deed it is broke off just about Shamokin & the reason was Sasquehanna' after you come to Shamokin tends so much Easterly that Mr Weiser was apprehensive on the Indians seeing the Course of the River & how near the Land sold went to Wyomin they wou'd not have ratifyed their Contract. The £500 was paid at the request of the Indians in pieces of Eight amounting to 1,333/3 One thousand was distributed in Publick & the other 333 went to the private Purse of Canasatego, Shickalamy's Sons, Nutimus and some other particular Persons according as Mr Weiser thought proper.

The Indians left town on the 25th, many of them drunk. Weiser got no farther with them that day than Whitemarsh, where he was obliged to wait for the stragglers to come up.[19] It took four days to reach Reading, and even at that rate the journey was too much for some of them. He had to hire wagons.

"The Old Six Nations," said Peters, "lose their Influence every day & grow contemptible." [20]

Where should the blame for this Indian fiasco rest? Was Peters right—were the Six Nations become degenerate? Thomas Penn, as shrewd a student of the Indian situation as we can find, laid the blame flatly on Richard Peters and the rest of the authorities in Pennsylvania. "As to the Indians," he wrote, February 13, 1750,

I think you went too far in pressing them not to come down, and should another time not treat with a part of a Deputation, and give them presents, but only entertain them 'til the others arrive. I do not wonder at their improper behaviour after being so ill treated, and fear it will be long remembered, I am satisfied they never were so slighted since my Father Setled the Country, and desire great care may be taken that they shal not be so for the future.[21]

CHAPTER 35

... *Crosses Richard Peters*

I

DURING 1748–49 Weiser was exposed to the fever of land speculation, of which there was an epidemic in the colonies, and went down with a mild attack. It was difficult to avoid infection. Albany land sharks were thrusting into the Mohawk country by means of rum-bought signatures and false entries. In Virginia the Ohio Company, with Thomas Lee at the head of it, was preparing the bold stroke of planting settlements on the Ohio, unfrightened by the threat of trouble with the French, the Indians, and Pennsylvania.

Conrad Weiser was a patriotic Pennsylvanian. The Ohio journey had stirred in him visions of empire for his province. I do not think Lee's letter to him of Dec. 11, 1748, was any too well received, though events for a time led Weiser to take an interest in Virginia's plans. Lee wrote:

> I send you a small Sketch of our frontiers, you remember by the treaty of Lancaster the frontiers of Virginia were to be extended at the King's pleasure. Soe all without the Pennsylvᵃ Grant is our frontier. we propose to settle a trade on the branches of the Missisippi and to make our Settlement at the Mouth of Mohongala, and we have the leave of the Indians, but if yᵉ Governᵗ of Pennsylvᵃ don't regulate their traders, the rascally fellows yᵗ goe among the Indians by lyes & treachery will be Authors of much blood shed and in consequence give the french posession of the trade. . . . I depend on yʳ friendship & assistance, as I have a very great Opinion of your honesty, I recommend you heartily to our Governʳ . . .[1]

Weiser's concern with land matters was not all a matter of provincial patriotism. He wanted land for his family. The small plantation on the slopes of Eagle Peak was not enough to provide for Philip, Frederick, Sammy, Peter, Benjamin, Maria, and Margaret. If it was in the power of the Indians to give lands on the Juniata to such white men "as they liked," surely it was also in their power to give lands on the Susquehanna to the white man they liked best of all. Conrad Weiser accepted from the Shickellamies a gift of several hundred acres at Shamokin, and hoped that the Proprietors of Pennsylvania would, in good time, grant him legal possession.

If we are disposed to share Thomas Penn's indignation at this transaction, we should remind ourselves of Conrad Weiser's circumstances. The illnesses and rushings-about of the preceding year had left him weak in body, nervous, and apprehensive of the future—apprehensive particularly for his family. He knew he might not be with them much longer, and he was fearful of what might happen to them after he was gone (Muhlenberg's letter of January 24, 1780, to Ann Eve,[2] who had been found by her grandson, General John Peter, almost destitute in Reading, shows us that Conrad's fears had not been idle). Is it any wonder that for a time his temper became short and his judgment hasty, and that he came to concern himself more insistently than his critics think proper with the principal commodity in which the continent was rich—arable land?

Certainly Thomas Penn had not overpaid him for his services. When Weiser asked for the addition to his plantation of some land on the slopes of Eagle Peak, Richard Peters advised Penn to indulge his request since it was poor land and nobody else would want it. Peters suggested further that the loyalty of the province to the proprietaries would be encouraged by so gracious an exhibition of interest in Conrad Weiser's "little country affairs." [3] Thomas Penn accordingly gave Weiser patent to the land, at the usual quitrent. The Shickellamies were more generous. When they acknowledged the debt of all the Indians to Tarachiawagon, they did it whole-heartedly with the best thing they had to offer—a good slice of Shamokin land in outright gift.

II

The years 1749 and 1750 were uneasy ones for the Governor and Council in Philadelphia. There were rumors, all too well founded, that Canada was sending "an Army of a thousand French" (Peters, July 5) [4] to descend the Ohio and undo Weiser's work at Logstown. George Croghan was despatched to the Ohio to discover what truth lay behind the rumor. The formation of the Ohio Company in Virginia was only a little less disturbing to the authorities of Pennsylvania, who feared that the Company's grants from the King infringed upon Pennsylvania's bounds. Representations were made through Thomas Penn in England. And there was the still unsolved problem of the settlers on Indian lands.

It was not for nothing that Conrad Weiser ran a tannery and set up his son Peter as a saddler. Conrad knew the use of saddle leather as well as any man of his day. Between November 1749 and November 1750 he was, except for a few weeks at home during the winter, almost constantly in the saddle on government business. From Heidelberg he rode to Shamokin, to Reading, to Lancaster and Ephrata, to Philadelphia. He crossed the Susquehanna River, rode over the Tuscarora Mountains, visited the settlements on Sherman's Creek and the Juniata River, visited Shippensburg. He rode to Bethlehem—Esopus (Kingston)—Albany—Onondaga, and returned by way of the Catskills and the city of New York.

There were private matters also to attend to. He rode to Providence and was a guest of the Muhlenbergs when his second grandson was born there on January 1, 1750. [5] He was present at the baptism on the 15th, [6] when the boy was named Frederick Augustus Conrad—after Dr. Frederick Ziegenhagen (Court Pastor in London), Dr. Augustus Francke of Halle, and his grandfather Conrad Weiser.

Leaving the farm to others to attend to, Conrad Weiser threw himself into Indian affairs, church affairs, court affairs. He was interested in Benjamin Franklin's Academy for the Improvement of Youth, interested in getting the new county of Berks erected, interested in laying out the town of Reading and speeding the building of houses there (he hoped as many as twelve good stone or brick houses might be put up during the summer).[7] As nursing mother to the new town he mounted his horse and went over the lands of Justice Francis Parvin, whose "Obstinacy & Stiffneckedness"[8] had precipitated a dispute with Richard Peters and the proprietaries. This dispute Weiser tried to mediate. He reported in Parvin's favor, told Peters the land in question was not worth a fight, and proposed that Parvin be given his way for the good of the town.[9]

"in Some of my last letters you was Informed of Reading affairs," he wrote to Governor Hamilton, May 4, 1750, "and that we got water at 52, or 3 feet I hope you will Come that way. and be at my house on Saturday night the 12 of this Instant and I will maKe as Well Come as I Can. and maKe you Governor of my place as long as you will please to Stay with us"[10]

It was well that Weiser was busy with so many different things. It would have been unhealthy to ponder long over any one of them, so much was going wrong. The Indian policy was cracking, his friends were disappearing, his position in the province was being undermined.

The Reverend Richard Peters, astute and acidulous, was beginning to find Honest Conrad getting on his nerves. It was not that the Reverend Richard failed to recognize Weiser's merits. These were plain enough; that, indeed, was the trouble. Peters, being a snob, wanted to despise Weiser, but was too clear-headed to be able to. Compared with the interpreter, the Provincial Secretary did not shine in the public eye with the superior luster his rank entitled him to. The rough diamond somehow caught more light than tarnished brass. In revenge, Peters tried to put the Proprietaries (who could break Weiser with a stroke of the pen) into the same discomfort as his own: to make them feel dependent on a mere backwoods pioneer. He managed (all too well for his own peace of mind, for he really loved the province) to make the impressionable Thomas Penn tired of Honest Conrad as Conrad had been tired of Canasatego's Indians.

Peters was too ingenious to damn Weiser with faint praise. He damned him with overpraise. In letters to the Penns he coupled regrets about Weiser's avarice with praise so high of his services to the province as to make it appear that the Proprietaries had been trapped by the man's indispensability into condoning low practices no family like the Penns could tolerate.

Peters chose as his point of attack Weiser's request for the Mahanoy lands which the Secretary himself had said Weiser richly deserved.[11] The sons of Shickellamy, as already noted, had granted Weiser some hundreds of acres of land at Shamokin. Private grants from Indians were not valid in Pennsylvania law, but it was Weiser's hope that the Proprietaries would either make good this grant by patent of their own or give him the equivalent in land elsewhere in the province. Since the purchase of 1749 did not include the Shamokin lands, and these were not, therefore, the Penns' to dispose of, it was proposed by the Indians as well as by Weiser that the Penns should grant him, in substitution, lands at the mouth of Mahanoy Creek.

Accordingly, on instructions from the Provincial Secretary, William Parsons and Edward Scull in October

. . . Surveyed to Conrad Weiser Esqʳ Two Tracts of Land situate at Mahoniay One of them Containing Three hundred & nine Acres and the other Sixty Six Acres And also Three Islands in the River Susquehannah opposite thereto One of them Containing Two hundred & Seventy three Acres Another Containing Two hundred & four Acres and the other Fourteen Acres Being in the whole Eight hundred Sixty Six Acres and the usual Allowance of six Acres Per Cent for Roads &c.[12]

There ensued a spirited exchange of letters between Philadelphia and London that has a double interest for us. It shows what sort of people Weiser had to deal with, and it shows his preponderant influence in Indian affairs.

"The new Purchase turns out to be very bad land as was expected," wrote Peters to Penn, Feb. 16, 1750, about this great anthracite region.

you will observe in the Draught which I believe is a very faithful one that there is a Tract of Land surveyed together with two Islands in Sasquehannah marked C. Weiser and amounting to the Quantity of   [sic] This Mʳ Weiser pitches upon in lieu of his Land at Shamokin and expects the Proprietaries will be pleased to order him a Warrant for it, and hopes they will put no other price upon it than the common Quit Rent and I will freely give my Judgment that Mʳ Weiser is not at this time to be disobliged—he is appointed with Mʳ Parsons to reconnoitre the Bounds of the Province a very troublesome and fatiguing work which must take him all the next summer—he has undertaken to bring the Indians into a humour to sell the Lands on the West of Susquehannah and to educate a Son to succeed him—All these are great matters and require high Rewards, Mʳ Weiser like other people as he advances in years thinks more than he used to do of an Estate to leave his Children and sets a value on his Services higher in his own thoughts than when I first knew him. I dont say this to prejudice Mʳ Weiser for he has at the same time a real Love for the Proprietaries and cordially and industriously consults their Interest and will spare no pains to advance it—these things considered be pleased to order a Warrant for the Land tho it be a great Quantity and very valuable I suppose worth now £ 40 Per hundred and I desire Mʳ Thomas Penn will inform me of Mʳ Weisers Claims to the Land at Shamokin as I imagine from what I have heard him say that Mʳ Penn gave him some Promises.[13]

Thomas Penn took the matter up directly with the Governor.

I find Conrad Weyser sets a very high value on his Services [he wrote, May 5] so as to desire impropper gratifications; . . . 800 Acres . . . a gratuity much too large for such a purchase as the last of perfect Rocks . . . I desire you will acquaint Conrad I am not well pleased with this request of his, for tho' Mʳ Peters writes me Conrad is not to be disobliged now, I shal never submit to be made the property of those I imploy any more, and discard him without hesitation the moment he ceases to act such a part as I think he ought to do.[14]

Meanwhile Richard Peters continued to press the sore place with judicious fingers—hard, but not too hard, lest he cause the painful tumor to break.

Your Sentiments about Mr Weiser's conduct perfectly agrees wth the Governors and my own [he wrote to Penn] and when this years work is done he must in the properest manner be made sensible of what your thoughts about this manner of acting; but I dare not risque the Consequence of speaking openly to him yet—for shoud he as he is heartily tired wth Indian Affairs throw up it woud put the Government into a bad plight especially shoud the French attempt ye removal of the Indian Traders from Ohio . . .[15]

Thomas Penn dangled with obliging snobbery on the Reverend Richard's hook. Peters was indeed a fisher of men. The bait, of course, was the Penn Family Pride; the hook was the Family Purse. He wrote:

You say Conrad Weiser must have the Land he applys for granted him & is not to be disoblig'd. I may consent to his having the Land, but I know no honest Man wou'd desire to have so large a Front on the River for so small a piece of Land . . . In your Letter of the 16th of February you write that Conrad Weiser takes this in Lieu of the Shamokin Land, & at the end of the same Paragraph say I have given him expectations of the Shamokin Land— Does he want this besides? Let me know what you mean, but you shall not grant him this now Survey'd 'till he has deliver'd up the Deed given him by the Indians then you may give him a Patent at the same time telling him from me that I am much surpriz'd he could ask for Land Survey'd so very much to the disadvantage of my Family . . .
I think Conrad has been a serviceable Man, & I think he has been well paid for a Man in his Station, & I would continue to make him an handsome allowance, but as I do not take his Indian Claim at Shamokin to be anything, on the contrary admire he has the assurance to name it, I think for the last Indian Purchase he will be paid more than three times the value of what he should have for coming down with them. in short I shall never esteem him or desire his Service if he insists on so injurious a Survey, & do not desire he should make any Interest with the Indians to induce them to another Sale 'till he is sent positively to do it, and then he shall do it as he is instructed, for I will not have any more of his great Services.[16]

Richard Peters played his fish lingeringly and well; it was the sport he enjoyed, not the kill, and in the end he would toss his victim back into the stream.

Conrad but too much deserves your Censure [he wrote, September 28, 1750] & is really grown avaritious, nor did I ever nor can I justify him, but then I cannot help saying that if in your absence & whilst Indian matters are in so uncertain & precarious a Condition, & before any other person be fitted to succeed him, he shoud be so far disobliged as to lay down, He will put the Governor & your Officers into such difficulties as will be intolerable, and woud draw on the Proprietaries an Expence of ten times the value of his demand

tho' unreasonable, for if the Assembly would give nothing, or nothing considerable pretending that they coud not confide in any but Conrad, must not
the Proprietaries give? and suppose either the Indians or Assembly or both be
disobligd at Conrads laying down where will this fall? . . . No notwithstanding all Conrads faults which I take purely to arise from a growing avarice he
is honest & well inclind to the Proprietaries & of Talents infinitely superior to
any other y^t can be got   I verily believe it is in his power to turn the Indian
Councils which way he pleases & y^t they absolutely rely on his Judgment . . .
It was really the Virginians that spoild Conrad for as he keeps a close Correspondence with Col^l Lee he sends him every now and then for what I cannot say, a Bill of Exchange of £ 30 or £ 40 Sterl^g. I mention this with no other
view than to let you see what has alterd Conrad & what an Estimate he now
thinks he ought to make of his Services on a Comparison with the Generosity
extended to him by the other Governments. So far I believe may be said with
truth, y^t if that Treaty had never been held at Lancaster Conrad would never
have thought of asking for nine hundred Acres of Land in so fine a Situation
& of so good Quality.[17]

Gently he removed the hook from Penn's jaws and threw him back in:

Conrad does not want any Land at Shamokin nor any other Land,   if you
thought so it must be owing to my dark manner of Expressing myself.

The lands at Mahanoy Creek, islands and all, were patented to Conrad
Weiser, October 17, 1750.[18]

Time and the salve which Richard Peters knew how to administer to
those above him in worldly station healed the Penns' pride. In the spring of
1751 Thomas Penn wrote to Peters:

We are glad to find Conrad thinks so propperly about the gratification he has
received and I dare Say wee shal have no further difference in Sentiment as I
shal always desire to be kind & generous to him as far as prudently I can.[19]

To show that the breach was really healed, Magnanimous Thomas authorized the surveying for Honest Conrad of a tract of wild land adjoining
his plantation, a tract that the Reverend Richard assured the Proprietor
was not much good, it being "rather taken up to keep out bad neighbours
or for range than for any culture." [20]

II

It is impossible to say at what point Weiser became aware of the web
Peters was spinning about him; but it was apparently not later than June
1750, if the flare-up that came during that month is any indication.

Peters' over-ingenious plans for the reconnoitering of the province provided the occasion. It came about in this way. In consequence of the
boundary dispute with Maryland and Virginia, and in consequence also
of the desire to expand Pennsylvania's trade in the Indian country, the
Penns wanted a secret reconnaissance to be made of the western and northern bounds of the province. Thomas Penn desired Bartram and Evans (the
botanist and the map-maker) to be appointed to this service; but Peters,
knowing how difficult Evans was to get along with, took it upon himself

to engage in his stead William Parsons and asked him to approach his friend Conrad Weiser, whose presence on the expedition was considered indispensable to its success.

William Parsons reported that, upon his opening the affair to Mr. Weiser,

. . . it affected him pretty much, as he looked upon it a Matter of great Importance, but did not hesitate Obedience. He is entirely of Opinion that it will be best to proceed from South to North, and that it will be impracticable to prosecute the Business till some time in August next, as well upon Account of Subsistence, which will not be to be met with in those parts before that Time, as upon Account of the Gnats, Musketoes, flies and other vermin which are intollerable in the Summer Season, and especially to Horses.[21]

Richard Peters' mind was exercised with difficulties other than those pertaining to the season of the year—though whether the scheme he confided to Thomas Penn was designed to fool the Indians or to disgrace Weiser it is impossible to say. Peters, by his "dark manner" of expressing himself in a letter to Penn of May 5, 1750, allowed it to be inferred that this elaborate deception was hatched in conference with Weiser himself, although Weiser at the time knew nothing about it.

John Bartram [he wrote] . . . sayd . . . That in his opinion M[r] Weiser must make one and must have a Message to deliver to the Indians, and as he was the known Interpreter he & he only coud cover such a design he added that Lewis Evans tho an ingenious man was not agreeable to the Indians nor to M[r] Weiser; and that therefore somebody else shoud be appealed to who coud do Evans's part. On these reasonings W[m] Parsons was thought of and he & M[r] Weiser consulted on the Occasion—and when this was done, it was thought that considering the present posture of Affairs at Ohio, a Message to the Indians as well settled there as to the Six Nation Indians might with great propriety and use be drawn up & given in charge to M[r] Weiser with Strings of Wampum and then he might as usual pretend a Visit to his Relations among the Mohocks & so carry the whole affair thro without the least Suspicion— And as the Cover entirely depended on M[r] Weisers publick Character and the Importance of his Errand it was thought unnecessary to clogg the thing with any more Persons—Indians were to be provided in order to carry the Luggage who would still further confirm the Embassy & give an Air of publick business to it—[22]

When Weiser learned of this scheme—which, if carried out, would have destroyed all his influence with the Indians—he wrote a vigorous letter to the Governor proposing that the journey be put off until such time as it might be made openly. To read this letter, after coming through the close, humid, disease-laden air of Richard Peters' correspondence, is like suddenly feeling on one's face a wind off the mountains.

Conrad Weiser to Governor Hamilton [23]

[Heidelberg, June 30, 1750]

Honoured Sir
    Notwithstanding my obligations to the Honourable proprietors and my good will to serve them on all occasions, and my late promises to reconnoitre

the province with W. P. I am very Scrupulous in my mind and find great difficulty to perform, because I Know I Can not do it with [out] giving great offence to the Six nations of Indians and to their Chiefs in particular. they are a very Jealous people and too Cunning to be Satisfied with a triffling Excuse that I might alledge which would only make my Case worse   Suppose I was Seting out with my Comp. from Geo Croghons towards ohio I would meet Several Indians on the way and the news of my Coming would be Carried before me to the Indians on ohio, and the would Expect me in their towns with Some affairs of Some moment, and after I Came to ohio I should Steer West toward the lake Erie and from thence north to the Sinicker Country over Mountains & brocken ground rocks and thickets without haveing a frequented path, what will the Indians on ohio say when they hear of this. what Shall I Say to the Sinickers. Cayugers. and onontagers. I can not pretent to be an ambassador,   Such men must travle not only the frequented Roads but the usual Road that ambassadors travles   I[n] Short I fear it will be of no good Consequences. in the first place they would mistrust me for the further, and they would Certainly Suspect the Governor of pensilvania of haveing Some thing in view to their detriment in under takeing Such a thing without leave from the Counsel of onontago and their Special Safe guard. It is true I Could get Andrew Montour and Tachnechdoras Shickelimys son to go long but they would Shelter behind me as well as John Bartram and lewis Evans and say you are a great man among the Six nations and you know what you do we leave you to answer for the whole;   we folow you as a Member of the Counsel of the Six nations. and they would Set themselves against me If things would turn out wrong and lay all the Blame on me. I beg of your Honour to weigh what I here Submit to your Judgment and I[f] possible let the Journey be postponed till things are Clearer or leave obtained from the Six nations which I will under take to do If your Honour Approves of It. I ask pardon for my being troublesom. I am

> Honoured Sir
> Your v. ob. & h Serv.
> CONRAD WEISER

The matter ended as Weiser hoped it would end. The Governor, on instructions from Thomas Penn, called off the reconnaissance.[24]

CHAPTER 36

... *Turns the Settlers Off*

"THE Dutchman at Scokooniady [Juniata]," said Saghsidowa to Conrad Weiser at Shamokin, April 10, 1743, "claims a Right to the Land merely because he gave a little victuals to our Warriors . . . this String of Wampum serves . . . to take the Dutchman by the Arm and to throw him over the big Mountains within your Borders" [1]

By this metaphor the Six Nations signified their intention to keep the lands west of the Susquehanna inviolate from the white man's axe. They had given the Juniata River, they said, as a hunting place to their cousins the Delawares and their brethren the Shawnees, and they desired, therefore, that Brother Onas should remove all white men settling there.

This the government in Philadelphia promised to do, and tried to keep its word. Ever since 1721, indeed, when the first proclamation against settlement on the west side of the Susquehanna had been issued, the government had been trying. But settlers continued to flood in. The Indians were angry, but they were not unreasonable. Canasatego in 1749, recognizing, as he said, that Brother Onas had no more control over his frontier people than the Six Nations had over theirs, had proposed a way to settle the difficulty. He sold a strip of land east of the Susquehanna in order to accommodate the evicted settlers. It now remained for Brother Onas to do his part by clearing out the settlers from the unpurchased lands west of the river.

In May 1750, accordingly, Richard Peters and Conrad Weiser were sent to do this. Equipped with authority to summon local magistrates to do the actual evicting, they set out from Weiser's house on Tuesday, May 15. On Wednesday they found assembled at John Harris' a number of magistrates [2] who all volunteered their services—to the evident distress of Peters, who feared to give local offense by refusing the services of any of them, and at the same time feared to give offense to the Penns in England by paying for all of them. George Croghan, the trader, cheerfully offered to supply "Rum Whisky Bread & salt Provisions" [3] sufficient for the needs of a party swelled to some size by the addition of Indian onlookers or inspectors—a party that was to travel over mountainous country offering no other civilized subsistence than milk and butter, and that to be had only from settlers whom the magistrates were come to drive off. Croghan's offer was accepted, and the whole party crossed the river to his place at Pennsboro.

They held a conference at Croghan's with the Indians on Thursday. Tachnechdorus (John Shickellamy) and his brother were there, with Saiuchtowano ("a man of note" among the Six Nations), Catardirha, and Tohomady Huntha ("a Mohock from Ohio" who had come east with Andrew Montour).

Saiuchtowano opened the proceedings. He laid down a string of wampum to comfort the Governor's heart and wipe the tears from his eyes for the loss of his Chief Justice, John Kinsey. He commended the Governor's intention to turn the settlers off. "But," he continued, "We are afraid, notwithstanding the Care of the Governor, that this may prove like many former Attempts; the People will be put off now, and come next Year again, and if so, the Six Nations will no longer bear it, but do themselves Justice. . . ." [4]

From Croghan's the party struck north by a short cut over the Tuscarora Mountains, which Peters found astonishingly steep and high,[5] to the chief settlement on the Juniata near the site of the present Thompsontown. Here they arrested some "trespassers" and burned two cabins, on the advice of Conrad Weiser, who observed that if the white men did not do it now the Indians would do it later and murder the inhabitants into the bargain.

For several days the officers moved about the countryside, evicting squatters, burning cabins, arresting such as offered to resist (Andrew Lycon on the Juniata offered to shoot when Weiser, Peters, and the rest approached). Simon Girty, who had recently pushed west from Chamber's Mill (where Weiser had bought bread and milk from him for Canasatego's Indians in 1744) was turned off from his new place on Sherman's Creek. His seven-or-eight-years-old son, Simon (the ogre of later legend), was perhaps by this incident first turned against the white men, who must certainly have seemed to him at the time both unjust and cruel.

On Monday the 28th the expedition, which had divided into several parties in order to cover a wide area with speed, reassembled according to plan at a public house in Shippensburg, and lay by for a few days "in Gusty and rainy Wheather" [6] before proceeding to the burning of cabins in Path Valley (where the town of Burnt Cabins is today's memorial of the expedition), Tuscarora Gap, and the more extensive and valuable settlements of the Conollaways and the Big and Little Cove beyond the "Temporary Line" on the disputed border with Maryland. Here Peters was to find himself in difficulties, since Pennsylvania had encouraged settlers to enter these districts in order to forestall Colonel Cresap and the Marylanders. The settlers, on Peters' arrival, presented a petition reminding him of this fact. But the problem was Peters' and need not detain us here. Weiser had washed his hands of it. He had left the party in the wind and rain at Shippensburg and gone home.

The question why he did so has stirred up a kettleful of speculation among biographers. Joseph S. Walton, in *Conrad Weiser and the Indian Policy of Colonial Pennsylvania*, suggests that Weiser's retirement from the expedition may have been because he saw that his influence with the Indians might be jeopardized by the further use of force against the settlers. "He well knew the changeableness of the Indian heart and recognized that if a squatter was hardly used, there were Indians to sympathize with him and hold with him a semi-smothered sense of revenge against the perpetrators." [7] The subsequent story of Simon Girty comes to Walton's mind in this connection. Walton suggests also another explanation: that Weiser feared his position as Indian interpreter for the government of Maryland, which he had exercised on occasion, might be injured if he tampered with the boundary dispute between that province and Pennsylvania.

If biographers are permitted to indulge in such unsupported "may-have-beens," I may perhaps be forgiven for suggesting an explanation that at least fits the character of the two chief actors. Richard Peters, whose amiability was not to be relied on except in the presence of his superiors or inferiors (and Weiser was neither), had no doubt been tried severely at Shippensburg by the nasal constrictions with which wet weather afflicted him, and he may have at last dared to "risque the Consequence of speaking openly" to Weiser (see his letter of May 5 to Thomas Penn, on page 290). We know that Conrad, in wet weather or dry, would receive the kind of insult Peters had been itching to give him with about as much complacency as a tank of gasoline receives a lighted match. If the time of Weiser's sudden withdrawal from the expedition is noted in connection with the dates of the letters contained in the last chapter, it will be seen that there is some reason to suppose an explosion had occurred at Shippensburg—an explosion of a kind neither man would care to put into the official correspondence on which we are dependent for our evidence.

Peters' report certainly does not help us in our speculations. He dismisses the episode (Weiser's sudden departure from Shippensburg) with a word, and Weiser, who affirmed Peters' report to be "a just and true Account" and desired "it might be received as his own in the several Transactions wherein he was personally concerned," [8] adds no further light.

This is what Peters wrote for the Council: "Mr Weiser most earnestly pressed, that he might be excused any further Attendance, having Abundance of necessary Business to do at Home; and the other Magistrates, tho' with much Reluctance, at last consenting, he left us." [9]

What this necessary business was, the records do not say. For more than a month ensuing there is no record at all of his activities. Perhaps, after all, the underlying (and sound) reason for his withdrawal was that he foresaw what was to happen and declined to be a party to it. The evictions broke down. The magistrates, as they went on half-heartedly with their work, discovered that more complex and more dangerous issues were involved than had at first been apparent. There was, on the one hand, the danger of not keeping faith with the Six Nations; on the other hand, the danger of provoking civil war among the whites. These were the horns of the dilemma. The magistrates, endeavoring to do justice to the Indians, were attempting to put the clock of history back. They were at Shippensburg confronted with one of the great popular movements of modern times: the expansion of English civilization into the country beyond the Alleghenies.

Did Weiser see in a flash that to turn off these large bodies of settlers at the instance of the Six Nations was equivalent to inciting the whites to a war of extermination against the Indians? Did he see, further, that the problem of the relations between Pennsylvania and the Six Nations could not be isolated; that not two but three races (French, English, and

Indian) were to settle their American destinies here on the western borders of Pennsylvania? And did he decide, on behalf of his brown friends, to postpone the showdown as long as might be?

Peters himself soon gave up. He informed the petitioners from the Little Cove and the Big and Little Conollaways that he would for the present "decline their removal & consult the Governors further pleasure." [10] He saw as well as anyone else that the push of population into the American west was more than government proclamations, under-sheriffs, and the burning of cabins could stop. He returned to Philadelphia.

"The People over the Hills," he wrote to Weiser, October 3, "are combin'd against the Government, are putting in new Cropps & bid us Defiance." [11]

CHAPTER 37

. . . Accepts Mr. Lee's Invitation

THOMAS LEE, the so-called "President of Virginia," entertained a vast design of uniting the English colonies "from Nova Scotia to Georgia" in a common alliance with the Six Nations. To this end he proposed that Conrad Weiser invite the Onondaga Council to send deputies to meet representatives of the colonies at Fredericksburg.

In the correspondence that developed between Lee and Weiser on this subject we find ourselves far removed from the petulant higgling of Richard Peters, to which the last chapters have accustomed us, and entering once again, in the spirit of the Lancaster treaty, on a discussion of the bold outlines of a national policy. "We are all one people," said Thomas Lee, who with reason has been called one of the first Americans, an honor that he shares with Conrad Weiser.

The letters are here printed in full, as many of them as could be found, to serve as an example of Weiser's diplomatic correspondence, and to show the intimacy that subsisted between Weiser and the first of the great Lees of Virginia.

Thomas Lee to Conrad Weiser [1]

Stratford Feb. 27. 1749/50

Sir

I have the favour of your letter of the 11th of December, and thank you [for] the assurances you give me, which I relye on, for ever since I have [know]n you, I have found you a very honest man, and that you have [made] use of that influence you have with the Indians for the good of His Majestyes Subjects, as well as for the Indians whose real interest it is to be friends with us. and there is noe man that I know of, yt can doe soe much good in these matters as you can, and in this light I have constantly represented you to this Governt.

I remember the promise to the Six Nations at Lancaster, and I have accordingly procured them Several presents since. I expect soon to [have] his Majestyes order to appoint a treaty with them . . . next Summer; and to have an order to make them a present [upon] their comg for we are to have the goods directly from London. [I] shall relye on you to bring the Indians there, and to assist me as Interpreter &c, for which you will be amply Satisfyed.

Soe soon as I hear wt his majestyes pleasure is, I shall send you notice soe in the spring, I hope you will not be farr out of the Way.

The Grant to the Ohio Company is Imediately from the King, for the public service and the Governmt here is directed to support the Company. The public good and the Kings service I have chiefly in View, to make a strong settlement and carry on a fair and extensive trade by these means to gain the Indians to ye Brittish interest, notwithstanding the Craft of our rivals the French I intend to hold the treaty at Fredericksburg by the falls of Rappah[annock] where the Indians may be well accomodated and is as near you . . . [as] any we have. I propose to treat with them in General for the Bri[tish] subjects, both with respect to trade, and settlement, we are all one people, and shoud have noe selfish ends, where the public is soe greatly concernd, this I assure you is the principle I shall be governed by and because you have the same way of thinking, I have the Greater Esteem for you

  I have sent Mr Parker to you with a letter he is a sensible and by w^t I have Observed an honest man, he will acq^t you who of ye trad[ers] we have reason to suspect, for we hope we shall have noe re[ason to] complain of any Gentlemen, even as encouragen of their f . . .

  I wish you long life, health and quiet, and I am truly

Your affectionate

I take notice of w^t you say
relat^g to the Catawbas danger

friend and humble Servt
THOMAS LEE

Conrad Weiser to Thomas Lee [2]

[Heidelberg, April 20, 1750]

Honoured Sir

  This day Mr Parker delivered me yours of the 16 of January last. but was favoured by a letter of yours Sent Express by M^r paxter before to which I thought no Imediate answer was required, but Having ben up at Shomokin a few days ago at the request of the Indians there to Setle Some differences between the Six Nation Indians liveing there, and the delawares I tooke that opportunity to Comunicate to the Sons of Shickelimy deceased the Substance of your last letter and desired them to be about Home because I belieft the King had ordered the Governor of virginia to have a Meeting with the Chiefes of the Six Nations of Indians and that I Belieft it was a thing of great Moment and that a Message Must be Sent to onondago Some time this Sumer. They all three promised both Secrecy & integrity and I have no reason to doubt, they are Satisfied of my good Will towards them, in particular Since their fathers dead, this My last Journey was at their request, and to Serve them. they have ben the occassion of the death of a delaware Indians who was charged to have killed Several Indians by Conjuring and was at last Killed by Some of the Six nations by advise of Shickelimys Sons. but now every thing is made up amicably by my means. I dont incline to trouble your Honour with many words but hope by the first opportunity to make it appear that I am in truth

Sir

Heidleberg in
  Lancaster County
  April the 20
  1750

your very obedient and
humble Servant
CONRAD WEISER

PS. a Message was Sent by the Six Nations to the Indians on SusqueHana with a large Streng of Wampum to let them Know that the french will remove the English traders from ohio, and If the Indians will not give them up and move away they must be treated as Enemies according to what the french had declared. whether this is fact or not time will Show. However their Expedition against the Catabaws is layd aside by it and the Indians Expects warr with their father onontio.

Thomas Lee to Conrad Weiser [3]

Stratford June 21. 1750

Sir

I recd yours of the 12th Instant this day. I am much disappointed that the Indians cannot be bro't to Fredericksburg this summer, as the Kings present is now there and the woolens may be spoiled, and powder is a dangerous article to keep.

I am the more concerned that this cannot be done, from what I hear from Gov[r] Clinton of the intrigues of the French with the Ohio and other Indians, and of the probabillity of their bribeing or frightening them into their measures w[ch] may be of pernicious consequence to these Colonys, and I did not doubt you woud be able to have prevailed on them to have made a brisker motion to receive the Kings present, the Goods were bo't by the Kings order in London, and in consequence of the treaty of Lancaster, in order to seat these back lands, west of our Mount[ns] and as the present is more y[n] they ever had at one time, I hoped to have had an op[ty] to satisfye them, y[t] it was their interest to keep firm to the Brittish interest, which I intend to inculcate to them; to be the same from Nova Scotia to Georgia. I have noe partial Views, the peace of the Colonys was w[t] I proposed and to doe Justice to the Indians. and this they shall find in all my actions. to be sure I invite them by my Royal Masters command, and it will look like slighting the King's favour I have invited the Catawbas there to Confirm the Peace which mention or not as you see proper, while they are at Warr our frontiers will be disturbed. I have a great Opinion of the Six Nations, and they may depend I will doe all I can for them, this you may assure them. I can attend at Frederick all September, not later, and pray forward it all you can I woud have all the Govern[ts] see the Sincerity of my behaviour, and therefore, I have desired the Gov[r] of N. York to send an interpreter, you will be there, as a friend to truth, the King, and your fellow Subjects; and Pensylv[ia] will be out of doubt when you report w[t] is proposed, the Carolinas and Maryland will have notice

The thing is of Great Consequence

As to the Ohio Company they are encouraged by His Majesty . . . and if their trade succeeds soe will all others and the Indians being fully supplyed; will be the most Effectuall way to disengage them from the French and fix them in the Brittish interest, soe y[e] Ohio Indians must be there to settle the whole business I greatly relye on you, and your Friendship for the Indians is what I like, for as far as I can Judge, they ought to be used Justly and Kindly and that as Brittish subjects we ought to be tender of their lives and Safetys Cresap had noe directions from me to act y[e] part, for as to Indian affairs I shall make use of noe other whilst I can have your honest assistance

I order [all] under my directions to use them kindly and even where they are to blame, as by some late acc[ts], to let the matters rest, to have what is necessary setled at the treaty Amicably. you can say nothing to the Indians for me that I ought to doe, but I will doe. give me constant Intelligence from time to time by the post & hasten the busines all you can and endeavour that the Six Nations And those at Ohio meet at the time appointed, and come all together, y[t] there be noe disappointment nor occasion for Jealousy. I wish you health to goe thro this fatigue and remain truly

Sir

I write this in great   Your sincere fr[d] and humble Serv[t]
hurry. soe don't expose it   THOMAS LEE

James Glen, Governor of South Carolina, wrote also to Weiser, entreating him to use his good offices in halting the Catawba War.

The Governor of South Carolina to the Governor of Pennsylvania [4]
for the Use of Conrad Weiser Esquire

S° Carolina 7th July 1750.

Sir

There is a Nation of Indians called the Catawbas, who have been always firmly attached to this Government, and tho they are a very brave People, yet there seems to be a great Danger of their being totally destroyed, as many Nations of Indians far Superior to them in Number have for some time past carried on a War against them; those Nations pass under the general name of Nottaweegas, and they are sometimes called Senecas, but it is certain that besides the Five Nations, there are the Delawares and some of the Indians on the Ohio, as well as the Susquehannah and the Virginia Indians, united in this War. There is the greatest Reason to think that these Indians are set upon the Catawbas by the French, who weaken the British Interest by making our Friends destroy one another but besides the Loss of such Faithful Allies as the Catawbas who have always proved an Excellent Barrier to the Province the Incursions of these Northward Indians is attended with other bad Effects, for under Pretence of going to War against them they spread themselves over the whole Province and wherever they can find any Indians as there are many who live quietly among Us in our Plantations not being at War nor expecting War from any other Indians, they knock them on the Head. they being also to attack and rob our White People as well as Negroes, and it may be difficult to determine where these Practices may end if longer permitted. I therefore hope that you will endeavour to dissuade any of the Indians in Friendship with your Government and all such as you have any Influence over from coming to War against the Creeks and Catawbas who are equally the Friends of the English and the Children of the same Great King with our Indians.

I am

Sir

Your most obedient
and most humble Servant
JAMES GLEN

Thomas Lee to Conrad Weiser [5]

Williamsburg 11 July 1750

Sir

I wrote you a particular Answer to your Letter by my Express, Since which we are alarm'd with an Account of the French with 15 Castles of the Ottawawas marching to Exterpate the Indians on the Ohio, and then the Six Nations, The Affection and firmness that these our Friends have Shewn to the British Interest makes us greatly Concern'd for them, and resolved to give them any assistance in our power; We hope the Northern Governm^{ts} have taken proper Measures to prevent any Mischief for the present, and before the Enimy can form any other designs Mischievious to our Friends, we shall have timely Notice, so that we may prevent the execution of them; I desire you to make a full Inquirey into this Affair, and give me a particular Account of it by the Post, or if the Case is Urgent, by an Express, which I will pay for; and if you find it Necessary and it will be of Use to Our Friends the Six

Nations, and Necessary for their Preservation, you may apply to Cap^n Beverley Robinson at New York, on whom I have given you a Credit of two hundred & fifty pounds Sterling to be laid out by you in Arms and Ammunition to enable our Friends the Six Nations to repel the force of their Enimys, and this we desire you to make a proper use of, that they may be Convinc'd how Sincerely we are their Friends, and wish their Preservation, and besides this You may take Occasion to Convince them of the Kings Affection to them by sending them the Present which I am to deliver them when you can bring them to Fredericksburg,   I need not add any perswasive to you, as you know the Necessity, and how much it is for the Service of His Majesty, and all his Subjects here, and how much it will Oblige

Sir
Your Sincere Friend & humble Servt
THOMAS LEE

Seal Capt Robinson's Letter
before you give it him

Conrad Weiser to Thomas Lee [6]

[Heidelberg, July 25, 1750]

Honored Sir
   I was favoured with your on the 11. of this inst by your Express but your Answer to my letter by your former express is not com to Hand yet what concerns the french their Desing [sic] against the Ohio Indians and the Six Nations I've heard of early in the Spring and gave the Governour of Pens: Notice thereof It seeming to me when I was told the Story as if the french had a Mind to drive away the English Traders from Ohio by force and had declared that if the Indians on Ohio would offer to defend the said traders they would use them all a like they proposed the destruction of the 6 Nations, and some of the Chief of the Ottawawees in Counsel att Montriel or Quibek but no sooner the Ottawawees came to the Lake of Frontinac (, or Ontario.) they send words to Onontago, and lett them know all what had passed, However I shall inform my self fully when I come to Onontago, where I will go my self, and not send Indians, I intend to Set out by the 13 or 14th of next Month by the Way of Albany, I shall make propre use of the Credit you give me on Captain Beverly Robinson if necessary, other ways till your further Ordre Delay of giving the Indians any thing I was ordered by the governour of Pensylv: to inquire into the Truth of Alarm of the french against the Indians but could find no more when I was at Jamokin a little while ago then the before mentioned, and I believe that is all I have at present, not further to trouble you with, but assure your Honour again of my firm Resolution to execuite Your Comand in the best Manner I am capable of, who am—
   Sir,

Your most obedient
and very humble Sv^t
CONRAD WEISER

   Meanwhile, before accepting Virginia's overtures, Weiser had discussed the matter frankly with the Governor of Pennsylvania. He showed him Lee's letter (probably that of June 21) and asked for advice, saying that if the Governor disapproved of his undertaking the Fredericksburg treaty he would give it up. Weiser's frankness put Hamilton in a dilemma. He was suspicious of Virginia, jealous of the Ohio Company (whose traders were already the cause of dispute between the provinces), and afraid that permitting Weiser to engage in the Virginia affair might advance the rival company's interests. At the same time he was afraid of disappointing Weiser (whose motives he affected to believe were purely mercenary) by a blunt refusal. He therefore declined to offer advice, but said he left the decision to Weiser's own discretion—with what result we know.

"He is to go this fall to Onondago," reported the Governor to Penn, July 10, "to invite the Six Nations with those of Ohio to meet him in Virginia the next summer . . ." [7]

Thomas Penn was not pleased, but he made the best of it. "I wish Conrad Weiser had not been so forward in accepting Mr Lees Invitation," he wrote, August 27, 1750, "tho' I think it better he should be imployed than a Stranger, as I think he will not suggest any thing to the Indians in prejudice to our Country." [8]

CHAPTER 38

... Finds Great Changes at Onondaga

I

Thomas Lee to the Board of Trade [1]

Williamsburg, June 12, 1750

My Lords:

. . . I have received his Majesty's present for the Indians of the Six Nations, . . . and have taken the best methods I could think of, to bring those Nations to Fredericksburg in this Colony, and I have invited the Catawbas to meet them and make a peace personally, which has never been done yet . . .

Richard Peters to the Penns [2]

[Philadelphia, July 12, 1750]

Honour'd Proprietaries

. . . Mr Weiser has engagd in his Journy to Onondago to promote a Purchase of Lands for the Propty & to endeavour to obtain from the Indians their Consent to the Erection of a Trading House for Pennsylvania on the Waters of the Ohio or on Lake Erie or both places as shall on due Examination of the places be thought best he has likewise engagd to carry his Son into the Indian Country & leave him there for suitable Instructions.

NOT one of the ends for which Conrad Weiser undertook his journey to Onondaga in 1750 was achieved. The Six Nations declined to attend Virginia's conference at Fredericksburg; William Johnson took the Catawba negotiations out of Weiser's hands; the changed atmosphere at Onondaga made it inexpedient to propose any fresh purchase of lands or the building of a fort in the Ohio country; and Sammy did not go along at all.

Yet the journey stands out as one of the most interesting in Weiser's career, and the accounts of it gathered from several sources give as vivid a backdrop as one could wish to have of the colonial life against which all his adventures were played.

A rare company of early Americans was grouped about him at every stage of the journey. Accompanying him was Daniel Claus, a quiet-spoken, attractive young Württemberger of family and education, whom Weiser a few months before had found stranded in Philadelphia waiting for a ship on which, with borrowed money, he proposed to escape from the New World in which he had been so badly taken in. He had lost all his money in a tobacco swindle engineered by one of his fellow countrymen. [3] Weiser's intervention saved him for a distinguished career in the colonial Indian service under William Johnson and, as it turned out through his association with Joseph Brant, to the ultimate shaping of a national life for Canada.

Weiser and Claus set out from Heidelberg on the afternoon of Wednesday, August 15.[4] At Bethlehem on Friday they picked up Henry Melchior Muhlenberg,[5] who was to go along with them as Weiser's guest as far as Rhinebeck on the Hudson. Henry, when they met him, was "a sight to dream of, not to tell," and he felt as wretched as he looked. It was not merely that a bad catarrh had taken away his voice, leaving him unable to preach, as he confided to his journal. That meant suffering for the inner man; the outer man was no better off. One of his hands was swollen and painful, for Anna Maria, his wife, in bleeding him a few days before, had cut too deeply into the vein. All in all, Henry Muhlenberg, with a voice like a seal's and a hand like a boxing glove, perched on top of an old, stiff horse (which a few days later he gave away for nothing, at the same time taking a price for his saddle), was feeling both sore and ridiculous.

At Bethlehem they had coffee with Bishop Cammerhof,[6] who looked after them handsomely, showing them the community buildings laid out where the Lehigh River meets the mountains, accompanying them over the ten miles of new road to the colony at Nazareth, and telling Weiser about his visit with David Zeisberger earlier in the year at Onondaga.[7]

After an early start next morning, they crossed the Blue Mountains by a rocky pass (probably Tat's Gap) [8] over which they had to lead their horses; and then, leaving the Pocono Mountains on the left, they proceeded to the house of Nicholas DuPuy (grandson of a Huguenot refugee who had come to New Amsterdam in 1662) who put them up for the night. DuPuy was an old friend of Weiser's. He had bought three thousand acres from the Minisink Indians in 1727, and it is not unlikely that Conrad may have stopped here (the modern Shawnee, Pa.) on his journey with the family to the Tulpehocken in 1729. DuPuy had at one time been a justice of the peace, but he was now retired. Being neither well versed in English law nor in touch with those who were, it had been DuPuy's way to advise parties who brought their disputes before him to go out into the yard and settle things there by the law of Fist-Right—a method of dispensing the King's justice, observes Muhlenberg, that caused him in the end to lose his position and withdraw from the world. But he was a good Christian. Muhlenberg notes that his prayers (before meals, after meals, and on going to bed) were impressive and that his conversation was edifying. The catarrh kept Muhlenberg himself from conversing with the old gentleman, but his father-in-law had a good talk.

On the 19th they crossed the Delaware near DuPuy's house and traveled for two days along the east side of the river, having a noon meal and a long chat on the second day with another Justice, former acquaintance of Weiser's, and DuPuy. This was Major DuPuy. In the evening of that day they found themselves still in the forest. They saw a bear, which took flight at their appearance, and they met a party of Indians, with whom Weiser stopped to speak. At night they found no better accommodation than that provided by Emanuel Paschal, nicknamed "the Spaniard" because his father had come to this country a Spanish prisoner. His mother was a Hollander.

Muhlenberg found nothing edifying about this old fellow. "Spanish gravity and Dutch boorishness were united in the man," he wrote.

He would give us no supper and told us haughtily to lie on the straw, seated himself with great solemnity in his arm-chair and had his six grown sons sit round him, smoking tobacco with their father and demonstrating that they were all apples off the same tree. Throughout the journey Weiser's name was held in high esteem, but this Spaniard had no mind beyond the wilderness he lived in, and his sons, and was interested in nobody but himself.[9]

They did not sleep late on the Spaniard's straw, but rose early and set out for Kingston. They were now on the old mine road, one of the oldest highways in the country, the Rondout-Neversink Road by which the Dutch had brought ore from the copper mine near the Delaware River to the Hudson at Esopus (Kingston). The travelers rode all day through the heat, enjoyed a meal of raccoons and pumpkins at an inn by the way, and came in the evening to Kingston after covering a distance, by Conrad's reckoning, of forty-four miles.

They were very tired, having come two hundred miles in five days, and were glad enough next day to find that heavy rains gave them an excuse for lying still. They were now within sight of Muhlenberg's destination, Rhinebeck, just across the river. Rhinebeck was on the site of the old East Camp at which the Weisers had had their first home in America in 1710. It was now the home (or should one say the arena?) of Muhlenberg's friend, Pastor Hartwick, who found himself in the center of a "Confusion" which Muhlenberg had come hoping to help him settle.

On Thursday, August 23, they embarked, men and horses, in a small boat and crossed the river: "for the sake of a better road," [10] wrote Weiser in his official report; "to see his old home and good friends," [11] wrote Muhlenberg in his private journal.

There was a warm greeting from these same friends, after which Weiser rode on with Claus, Muhlenberg, and Hartwick to Livingston Manor, where they were received by Robert Livingston, son of the Patrone who had provided the early Palatines with salt meat and bad beer.

From Robert Livingston Weiser heard a disturbing report that the French from Canada had won over most of the Six Nations; "which news," observed Muhlenberg, "made Weiser uneasy." He would have been still more uneasy if he had known the circumstances under which he was to enter Onondaga a few days later.

Muhlenberg and Hartwick rode back to the Camp that evening, but Weiser spent the night at Livingston Manor and next day went on to Albany. The 26th being Sunday, he "Lay still" and talked with Indian friends,[12] among them Henry Peters. This was the famous "King Hendrick" of the Mohawks who had visited London in 1710 and was afterwards said to have offered Queen Anne the Schoharie lands for the Palatines. Henry, though now an old man, "grey headed as Silver" [13] (White Face Mountain in the Adirondacks is said to have been named after him), was still a warrior, a politician, and a pleasure-seeker who was to make a deeper impression on American history in the years that remained to him than in those that lay behind. He was to set his mark to a vile document that was to plunge his people into war, and he was to make expiation for that fault by his own death on the field of battle.

With Hendrick were Nickas and eight more Mohawks. Nickas, a warrior of note, had much to tell. He and two others of the company had just come from Canada, where they had been held prisoners, suffering harsh treatment because they had fought for the English during the last war at a time when the Six Nations Confederacy was officially neutral.

"I spent the Evening with them," wrote Weiser, "in a publick house and treated them with several Bottles of Wine."

He was with them again in the morning, conferring about his journey to Onondaga. They warned him. Most of the Onondagas had gone over to the French and had, so they said, even accepted "the French religion."

They told him also

. . . that Colonel W. Johnson had a Commission from the Governor of Carolina . . . to bring about a Peace between the Six Nations and the Catawbas, and had actually made Proposition to the Six Nations about the Affair. Henry told me privately that he did not believe Colonel Johnson could bring the thing about; but if the Governor of Carolina would make him, Henry, a handsome Present, or pay him well for his trouble, he could bring about a Peace between the Six Nations and the Catawbas.

In the afternoon, Weiser and Claus set off for the "Schohairee where Mr. Weiser first lived & learned the 6 Natⁿ Language," as Daniel Claus writes. They probably went by the familiar way over the Helleberg and down Fox Creek, a route that Weiser had used more than thirty years before to bring supplies to the starving people of Weisersdorf. They reached Schoharie Creek on Tuesday, August 28.

the Twenty Ninth [writes Weiser] Took a Ride to a small Mohocks Indian Town about eight miles Southwards and conferred with the Indians there, they being my old acquaintance as I had lived from the Year 1714 till the Year 1729 within two miles of their Town, they were very glad to see me, and acquainted me with every thing I desired to know of them, and told me of the bad circumstances with the Six Nations, and that the Onondagers, Cayugers, and Seneca's were turned Frenchmen, and that some of the Oneiders inclined that way, and that they abused the Mohocks and used them ill for being true to the English, and that the Indian Affairs lay neglected, and no body minded them, and that since the Peace with the French, the Governor of New York never spoke to the Indians, nor offered them any thing, and that the Mohocks themselves who had fought against the French with the loss of much blood received no thanks for their good service.

the Thirtieth Was spent with my old Friends and Acquaintance at the aforesaid Place.

The Thirty First I set out through the Woods for the Mohocks Country, it rained most of the day, having but a very blind Indian Path was lost, but met accidentally two Indians, who accompanied me to the Mohocks Country where we arrived about an hour after dark, came that day about twenty five miles.

September the First Had a Conference with some of the Chiefs of the Mohocks that live near Fort Hunter, among whom was Brand and Seth, they wanted to know what the Governor of Virginia had to say to the Six Nations of Indians, whether it was anything about the Catawbas. I told them that I was sure, that the Invitation was in consequence of the Treaty of Lancaster held six Years ago, that according to that Treaty the Government of Virginia had recommended the Case of the Six Nations to the King of Great Britain, and that accordingly the King had sent a fine and large Present to be given to the Six Nations. After several other Discourses, I went to Colonel William Johnson, about three miles from Fort Hunter, where I arrived about eleven of the Clock before noon, and was kindly received and hospitably entertained by the Colonel, he is the only and sole Commissioner of Indian Affairs in that Government. I staid twenty four Hours with him, and acquainted him with my Business at Onondago, we had a great deal of discourse about Indian Affairs, he showed me among other Papers relating to Indian Affairs, a Copy of a Letter, the Governor of South Carolina wrote to the Governor of New York, wherein the Governor of New York was desired to bring about a Peace between the Six Nations and the Catawbas, which Affair the Governor of New York had left to Colonel Johnson, who told me that he had already begun his Negociation, and was in hopes to succeed; the Mohocks having promised him their assistance, that he had undertaken to bring Five, Six, or Ten of the Catawbas to the Mohocks Country or Fort Hunter to speak to the Mohocks first, and to obtain their Safeguard or Protection to travel through the united Nations to Onondago. We both agreed, that it was best for me, not to say any thing about the Catawba's, because he had made, as is to be hoped, a good Beginning.[14]

There is no need to condemn Weiser, as some have done, for surrendering to Johnson his commission from South Carolina. The blame should rest with Governor Glen for duplicating the commission. Under the circumstances Weiser did the right thing. He refrained from interfering with negotiations already under way and apparently in responsible hands. Any other course would not only have prejudiced his position as a Pennsylvania agent operating in New York territory, but also have given the Indians fresh cause, when they had too much already, to think the councils of the English childishly divided.

Next morning Weiser and Claus, "about ten of the Clock," left Johnson to his house-building (he was finishing what Claus calls "his Seat on the Moh^k River of a large Stone House with two Wings," afterwards known as Fort Johnson) and proceeded by the Ambassadors' Road toward Onondaga. They had five bad days on the trail before they reached the principal town of the Oneidas—five days of discomfort and misadventure. Their horses went lame. They had to leave them and take others. Beyond George Cost's ("the last Settlement of White people on the Mohocks River") the trail was "very blind" and full of mud holes. "at the last Settlement," writes Claus, "they hired a Man & horse to carry some Refreshments thro' the Ind^n Country but Col. Weiser according to Indian

Hospitality wch he was no stranger to, always shared with the people of the House he put up at, whenever he took a meal." [15]

On September 6, after spending eleven hours that day in the saddle, they reached the Indian town of Oneida "a little before dark in rainy weather." The chiefs of the Oneidas, being as it happened all at home, called a council in Weiser's honor for the following morning.

> The Seventh [writes Weiser], The Council met and let me know that if I had any thing to say to them, they were ready to hear me, I went to the House, where they met with the Messenger that came for me, and acquainted them with what I had in charge from the Governor of Virginia, and desired them to send their Deputies with me to Onondago, to meet the Council of the Six united Nations, which they agreed to do, I desired them to send a Messenger before me to Onondago to acquaint the Onondagers of my coming, with a Message from their Brother Assariquoah, and that I desired they might kindle their Council Fire, I gave a String of Wampum to the Messenger that went to Onondago to be sent to the Cayugers and Sinickers, the Messenger set off immediately, the Oneiders desired me to spend that day with them and said, as the Message was gone I had time enough the Council could not meet in less than six or seven days; I agreed to stay with them, the whole day was spent with some of their Chiefs, discoursing about State Affairs . . .[16]

They talked about the Catawbas. The Oneidas said the English were mistaken in supposing the Catawbas really wanted peace: "they had declared to the Tutulows and Cherekees they would never sue for a Peace with the Six United Nations, that they would fight against them whilst there was one of them alive, and that after their Death their very Bones shall fight the Six Nations . . ."

They told him what he had already heard many times in the last few days: that the Onondagas had gone over to the French. They lamented the divisions that had grown up among the whites no less than among the Indians.

> . . . the Head of the Oneiders Disononto by name, a Man of above seventy Years of Age, but yet strong and nimble, asked me several times, whether I knew the reason of the Governor of New York, and the Great Men of that Province (the Assembly) disagreeing, I told him I did not, and ask'd several other Questions about Publick Affairs that I could not answer. This Disononto fought under Colonel Schyler, when the Mohocks Towns were burnt, and were taken Captives by the French in the former Century, and is a man of exceeding great Parts, I sat up with him in my Lodging till almost midnight.[17]

On his way to the Tuscarora town of Canachsoragy next day, Weiser met a messenger from Onondaga.

> . . . the Onondagers did let me know that they were sorry to acquaint me, that Canassatego their Chief, died the night before last, and that in consequence thereof, there could be no Council summon'd, and they were sorry I came so far, because of the present melancholy time.
> NB. It is to be known, that the Six Nations don't meet in Council, when they are in mourning, till some of their Friends or Neighbours, wipe off their

Tears, and comfort their Heart, it is a certain ceremony, and if they appear in Council without that Ceremony being performed, the dead Person was of no Credit or Esteem, and it is a certain affront to the deceased's Friends, if he has any.

About an hour after my arrival at Canasoragy, another Messenger arrived from Onondago, to let me know, that notwithstanding the melancholy Event that befel Onondago, the Council had upon a second thought resolved to hear me, because I came such a great way, though contrary to their ancient custom, they desired I would proceed on my Journey, and that a Council of the Six Nations was accordingly summon'd.

the Ninth, I set out from Canachsoragy, and arrived after eight hours Ride at Onondago, took up my Lodging as usual, with Tohashwuchdioony, a House which now stood by itself, the Rest of the Onondagers having moved over the Creek, some a mile, two miles, three miles off, Saristaquoah came to see me, so did Hatachsogo, two Chiefs; an old man, and a Member of the Council, came with me from Canasoragy, he begun to sing a Lamentation Song, just when we set out, to signify to me in an allegorical way, that the Town where I was going to was no more inhabited by such good Friends as formerly, and now more especially since the *Word* died, meaning Canassatego, the evil Spirits would reign, and bring forth Thorns and Briars out of the Earth, his name is Gechdachery a Brother of Soterwanachty deceased—at the resting Place I treated him with a Dram of good Rum, and told him, that nothing was certain in the World, and that the great Being, that had created the World knew how to govern it, that I believed he would order every thing well, to which he said Amen in his way.

The Tenth, Saristaquoah, came again to see me, the Rest of the Chiefs being in Mourning did not appear; the Indians seemed to be much affected with the Death of Canassatego, as they have lost several of their Head Men in a short time, three noted Men died in their Journey to and from Philadelphia, to wit, Tocanihan, Caxhayion, and Soterwanachty a Chief.

The Eleventh, Nothing was done, and no Deputies arrived: In my going up, I was told by Mr Livingstone at his Manor, and Colonel Johnson in the Mohocks Country, that the French had erected a new Fort at St Lawrence River, at a Place called Swegatsy, not far from the Lake Frontinac, for the Indians; and that a certain French Priest was there to instruct the Indians in the French Religion, and that he cloathed all the Indians that came to live there, and built Houses, and cleared Land for them at his own, or at the French King's Cost, and that one half of the Onondagers had actually begun to live there. Of all this I was confirmed when I came to Onondago, by several creditable Persons, and by the Council of Onondago itself, with this Addition, that the French Priest at Swegatsy had made about a hundred Converts among the Onondagers, Men, Women and Children that came to live at Swegatsy last Spring, and that the aforesaid French Priest had cloathed them all in very fine Cloathes laced with Silver and Gold and took them down, and presented them to the French Governor at Montreal, who had received them very kindly, and made them large Presents. Several of the said Converts, came back to Onondago, and drank away their fine Cloathes, and reported that the French Priest at Swegatsy was not good, and endeavoured to make Slaves of the Indians, notwithstanding his fine Speeches he makes to the Indians, that in one of them he had told them Onontiquoah the French King did look upon the Indians as his own Children, and would take care, that they should not want, nor no body should hurt them, that he would appoint a great man as a Guardian over them, whom he hoped his Children the Indians would obey as their Father Onontioquoa himself in every respect, and that the new Converts should not mind what the unconverted Indians said in their foolish Council, that their Father Onontioquoah would find everything for them, and protect them against all Nations, so that they had no need of Indian Government— this they interpret that the French want to make Slaves of them, and in a mocking way tell one another—Go and get baptized again by your Father, and bring home fine Cloathes that we may get some drink. No, said another, still joking, he will be hanged now, if he goes again for fine Cloathes, his Father is angry, because his holy water is of no force with the Indians; many such discourses I have heard, by which I saw plain, that they do not pay any respect to any Religion let it come from where it will, if they do not get by it.[18]

II

There was no man in all America whom the English had greater reason to fear than Canasatego's successor. This was Tohashwuchdioony, *The Belt of Wampum*, with whom Weiser lodged at Onondaga. Tohashwuchdioony was a Roman Catholic convert, pro-French in his politics. He was in a position to do the English colonies much harm, being now the chief sachem of the Iroquois. But Tohashwuchdioony treated Weiser with all the courtesy to be expected of the head man of a people still proud of the traditions, political and ethical, derived from Hiawatha and Deganaweda. *The Belt* was considerate and gentle with his guests, entertaining them with that earnest, humorous, friendly conversation of which the people of his race are such unqualified masters when they find themselves among friends.

I know of no more delightful scene preserved for us out of the haze of those last years of Iroquois supremacy (when, holding the balance of power between the English and the French, the Six Nations still controlled the destinies of America with their council fires and belts of wampum) than that of which Conrad Weiser has left a written account (kept for nearly two centuries among the papers of the Penn family) describing a conversation between his Indian friends Tohashwuchdioony and Ganach- quaieson, in which they threaded the mazes of religious controversy with- out generating the slightest heat.

Count Zinzendorf while in America once wrote down a brief analysis of the mind of the Iroquois, examining their susceptibility, nation by na- tion, to Christian preaching. The Mohawks, he said, attend Presbyterian churches for the most part; the Oneidas, Cayugas, and Tuscaroras have a feeling that all is not well with them—that they are miserable lost crea- tures; the Onondagas have the same knowledge of themselves, but there is something so *heroisch und philosophisch* about them that they are more likely to recommend the Gospel to others than to accept it at once for themselves.[19] The conversation at Tohashwuchdioony's house gives some color to Zinzendorf's judgment.

One Evening whilst I was [at] Onontago [writes Weiser] I heard a friendly Dispute between Ganachquaieson, a protestant Convert and one of the

Deputies of Oneido. And the good Man of the House where we lodged. Tahashwuchdioony by name. a professed Roman, he is at the Head of Affairs in Onontago Since the Death of Canasatego.

Tahashwuchdioony asked Canachquaieson, whether it was true, that such a one, (naming an Oneido Indian) said in a desperate way that he must go to Hell after he dies, and live with the Devils?

Ganachquaieson answered! Yes the Man said so, but he was very Sik when he said so, and was in great Trouble because he had been true, according to the Pact of his Baptism;

Tahashwuchdioony said, if you must go to Hell, after you are baptised, what signifys your Baptism? then we that are baptised by the French priests, can never be damned, we very seldom or never are true to our Baptism pact, but the Fathers tell us that they pray for us, and after we are death, they can fetch us from Hell by their prayers, and we have in our Choice to go to the place, where the french Fathers goes, with the Rest of good people, or whether we will go to the place where the foreFathers of the Indians go to, the french priests can obtain either for us.

Ganachquarieson! what you say of the power and Strenght of your Fathers prayers, and the Choice you have, to go to where you will, is a Mistake of yours, your Fathers deceive you, it is made manifest by the Creator of Heaven & Earth, that the good people only shall dwell with him after their Live, and the evil Doers shall dwell with the Devils, and without Repentance and Faith in Jesus Christ, there no Salvation for an evil Doer, let your french Fathers say what they will.

Tahashwuchdioony! perhaps both, your, and our Fathers are in the Right, as they are of different Nations, and Languages, they understood the Creator in a different Way; Our french Fathers tells us, that they can Speack with those happy Souls, that dwells in Heaven now, and learn any thing from them, and your Fathers say, they have a Booke wrote by the Creator himself, but our Fathers denies that and say, that they got the Original of that Book, and yours have only a Copy of it, made by one that did not understand it.

Ganachquajeson! The Book we speak of, is the same among all Nations, and our Fathers have the same, what your Fathers have, that is what they all allow, that the Book is the same; But your Fathers tells you, that they can speak, with the happy Souls that dwells in Heaven, it is they, that makes the Mischief, for they tell us Stories contrary to the Things wrote in that Book by the Hand of the Creator, and this is the Reason that your french fathers will not allow common people, to have such Books, for fear their *Deceit* will be found out:

Tahaswuchdioony! I'm Satisfied, that the french Fathers tells us Lies sometimes, I asked once a french Father whether or no we could be forced to go to Heaven, where the french Fathers and all good people went? he told me no, I desired an other to make Inquiry in Heaven, whether or no my Grandfather, (named him) was there, he promised he would, next Day he told me that he saw him there, I asked how he came there, because he mortally hated the Fathers & their Religion and he took once a Father prisoner, and brought him to Onontago, and had burned him there to Ashes, & he charged his Children, and grandchildren, to hate and kill the french Fathers, whenever they had them in their power. The french Father made answer, that perhaps he mistooke the person, and said he would looke again, and told me some Days after, when I went to see him, that he certainly made a mistake, that the person he saw in Heaven, and mistooke for my grandfather, was my Fathers grandfather, and that my Grandfather was in Hell, I told him that he was a Liar, and that I was Sure, my Grandfather was gone to the plentifull Country, where the forefathers of the Indians goes; And it is to that place, that I will go, and no other we are cheated by the white people in this World, and If we don't stand clear of them, the will cheat us in the other and make Slaves of us

Ganachquajeson; Since I can not well inform you of the Truth of Things, according to the Doctrine of our Fathers, I'm well pleased, that you choose to go to our Indian Forefathers rather, then to the place where the French Fathers go.[20]

III

The 12th of September came, and still no deputies. Weiser heard disturbing news from the Ohio.

I heard [he writes] that Ontachsina (Jean Coeur or some such name) the French Interpreter who resided in the Sinicker Country, during the late War, was going through the Sinicker Country in his Way to Ohio, with Merchant Goods, and five or six Frenchmen with him, and told the Sinickers that he had orders from the Governor of Canada to drive away the English Traders from Ohio, with the Assistance of the Indians.[21]

Tohashwuchdioony, who, as his conversation revealed, had an ancestral bias against missionaries, had no good report to make of the visit Cammerhof and Zeisberger had paid to Onondaga earlier in the summer. These two men on their return to Bethlehem reported that the decision of the chiefs on their proposal to establish two missionaries at Onondaga or elsewhere in the Six Nations country had been delayed day after day and week after week because the savages were too drunk to do business. Tohashwuchdioony attributed the delay to quite other causes, as is seen in Weiser's *Memorandum taken at Onondaga the 12th Septr, 1750:* [22]

Tohaswuchdioony my LandLord, now Chief of Onontago, and Saristaquoh a Chief of the Oneiders, told me that some time this Summer two Men of the people that lives in the forks of Delaware to wit Camerhoff and David Zeisberger came to their town at Onontago, and did not take up Lodging in pensylvania House, but went by it to lodge with Canasatego since deceased, which my LandLord did not take well, the Deputies of other Nations then meet at Onontago upon some Bussiness of their own, send Word to the two Men that came from Pensylvania, to let them know that if they had anything to say to the Counsel now Sitting and just ready to break up, they must appear now, and they should be heard, the Pensylvaniers sent words that they had nothing to say to the Counsel, after the Deputies from other Nations being gone, the two above named and some others to wit Sequarissery Arhounta, Anuharishon Ascotacks, a Sinicker, Dyaoneshserisha, Toowatsjarany and Hatasoqua, Sent for Mr Camerhoff and David Zeisberger to hold a privat Conference with them they having been informed that they had several private Conferences with Canasatego in the Bushes; Camerhoff and Zeisberger appeared they spoke to them by Saristaquoh to the following purport;

"Brethren, we find that you love to speak in the Bushes we therefore send for you to meet us in the Bushes, we desire to know of you, how much & what you have brought from Pensylvania for Canasatego, we know what passed between you and him we only try your Honesty and will hear it from your own Mouth."

Mr Camerhoff made answer that he gave to Canasatego 16 Silver armbands to wear above the Elbow and 17 dito to wear under the Elbow about the Wrest, a quantity of Silver Rings Several Silver N[eck] Cloath, two broad pieces of wrote [wrought] Silver to be divided among the Indians as Canasatego pleased; The Indians reprimanded Mr Camerhoff for so doing and said, he should have given his Presents in open Counsel; Camerhoff said that he had something to say in Counsel also, the Indians desired to know what Camerhoff by his Interpreter Zeisberger said, that he had it in Charge from the King of Great Brittain, to forewarn the Indians, not to let to much of their Lands be Settled by the white people, which would make them poor and would ruin the Trade with them, and desired them by a Streng of Wampum, to take Notice of this Caution.

By an other Streng of Wampum he desired Leave to erect a Smith Shop on Scahantawano (Wojamock) then by a large Belt of Wampum he desired Leave to send two of his Men to Onontago to live two years there to learn the Indian Language perfectly and promised that they shall take Care of the Indian affair; The Indians wanted to know of Mr Camerhoff what was the reason, that Tharaghiawagon did not come with that Message, Camerhoff answered Tharaghiawagon was an other Sort of people and no more in Favour with the Goverment of pensylvania and after our People can Speak your Language perfectly he will have nothing more to do with Indian affairs Hereupon my Landlord said he lied and said all what you have told us is your Invention our Brother Onas nor the Chief men of Philadelphia knows nothing of your Coming here; you'll find that Tharaghiawagon will be the same till he dies as he is now, you can not hurt his Caracter;

Mr Camerhoff made answer that he was send by several great Men of Pensylvania to wit Tagerhidonty and Caniadarechion &tc: the Indians did remember the other names, upon this my LandLord bid him to take up all his Wampum and be gone with it, that he should never have an answer, and that he was an Imposter, and not sent by an authority;

Mr Camerhof told them, they might keep the Wampum gratis, they informed me further that Mr Camerhoff went from Onontago, to the Cajuger & Sinicker Country and told the Indians there that he had bought a great piece of Land of Canasatego and paid him with Silver Ornaments (I doubt the Truth of this Last article and beliefe it was invented to blaken Canasatego Caracter) but it was currently reported at Onontago, and perhaps occasioned his Canasategos Death.

The sequel to this *Memorandum* is to be found in the Herrnhut Archives.[23] On June 17, 1752, Spangenberg and two of his associates presented themselves before Governor James Hamilton of Pennsylvania to offer a defense of Cammerhof's transactions at Onondaga in 1750. Cammerhof himself having meanwhile died, it was left to Joseph Spangenberg to be "bold and affirm that all these Accusations were intirely groundless. . . . It might possibly be," suggested Brother Joseph, "that Mr Conrad Weiser had some such kind of Jealousy, with respect to the Publick Affairs of the Indians."

The Governor, reports Spangenberg, said he did not remember the details, but he recalled that in speaking with Mr. Cammerhof, "he found things to have been very much misrepresented, tho' he thought upon the Whole, he might have acted a little more cautiously."

There followed some correspondence between Weiser and the Brethren; and on April 12, 1753, Spangenberg issued a very sensible "Instruction to our Brethren, who have dealings with the Indians," reminding them that they had no other business to attend to among the Indians than the saving of men's souls.[24]

IV

When at last, on the 13th, the deputies arrived (the Cayugas and Senecas having sent word that they could not come, the Cayugas empowering the Oneidas to act on their behalf) the Great Council assembled about noon. Everything was transacted with the usual decorum.

Ganachquayieson opened the Council [writes Weiser] and desired to be heard as soon as the Council pleased, he was answered that they were ready to hear him immediately—After a short pause, he begun to speak, and directed his Discourse to the Onondagers, and said,

"*Father* (so the Oneiders, Caiugers and Tuscoraros stile or address the Onondagers, Sinickers and Mohocks), We your Sons, the Oneiders, Cayugers and Tuscoraros, jointly with your Brother Assaryquoah entred your door, in a very melancholy time, when your Eyes were almost blind with the Tears you shed, and when your Heart is sorrowful to the highest degree, for the Death of that great Man our Word, who died but the other day (a dead man's name must not be mentioned among those People) we your Sons and your Brother before named, make bold to come near you, in order to comfort you in your trouble and to wipe off the Tears from your Eyes, and to clean your Throat, to enable you to see about you, and to speak again, we also clean the Place where you sit from any deadly Distemper that may remain on it, and might perhaps have been the occasion of the great Man's Death—Here the Speaker gave a String of Wampum of Three Rows, in Behalf of the Oneiders, Cayugers and Tuscoraros—I gave another of the same size, with a Belt of Wampum to cover the Grave of the deceased—After a short pause I desired to be heard, to which they answered they were ready to hear me. Then I said, "*Brethren*, the United Six Nations, to wit, Togarihoan, Sagosanagechteront, Dyionenhogaron, Neharontoquoah, Sanonowantowano and Tuscoraro I am sent to your Council Fire, by your Brother Assaryquoah, and what I am going to say to you is according to his Request—I gave a String of Wampum—and proceeded—*Brethren*, the Governor of Virginia desires that you will come to Fredericksburg, a Town a little way from Cachwangarodon (Patowmec) to a Publick Treaty, and to receive such Presents as the King of Great Britain your Father has ordered to be given to you by the Governor of Virginia, in Consequence of the Treaty of Lancaster, held about Six Years ago—, I gave a large String of Wampum—and proceeded—"*Brethren*, the Governor of Virginia will kindle a Council Fire at Fredericksburg in Virginia where you may sit in Safety, as under the Shadow of a great Tree, as at your own Fire at Onondago, to hear what your Brother the Governor of Virginia will say to You, by the Direction of the King of Great Britain, your Father, the things that will be said to You will be of Importance, and altogether for the Good of the

Publick, especially of the Six United Nations, tending entirely to their Preservation—for the Confirmation of what I have now said to you, your Brother Assaryquoah, the Governor of Virginia gives you this Belt of Wampum'—Here I gave a large Belt of Wampum.

I concluded, and desired to have their answer that night if possible, I was told, that I should have their answer on the morrow.

By Sun set the Onondagers gave thanks for the Condolement, and returned the Compliment by a long Oration, made by Tahashwuchdiony and gave a String of Wampum of three Rows to the Oneiders, Cayugers and Tuscoraros, and one to me, and desired that we may be comforted over the Death of the Great Man.

September the Fifteenth, The Indians being in Council all Day, in the evening I was told by three of them that were sent to me, that I should have my Answer, at the Oneider Town on my Return, which they hoped would be satisfactory.

The Sixteenth, According to Custom, I put out the present Council Fire, which was kindled by me, and took my Leave of the Onondagers, and came with the Deputies of the Oneiders and Tuscoraros to Canasoragy before night —I bought a Quart of Rum here for me and my Companions to drink at six Shillings, but the Company being too great, I was obliged to buy two other Quarts.

The Seventeenth, Arrived by rainy weather at Oneido, about two o'Clock in the Afternoon, the Oneiders met immediately in Council, and after about two hours Consultation by themselves, they sent for me, and told me that they were ready to give me an answer, and desired me to hear—I told them I was ready to hear—The Speaker directed his Discourse to the Governor of Virginia and said.

Brother Assaryquoah, We take your Invitation very kindly, and return you our hearty thanks, we would be very glad to see you, but every time that we have been down with our Brother *Onas* in Philadelphia, we lost so many men, and last Year we lost Twenty, among which Number were several of our Chiefs—the evil Spirits that dwell among the White People, are against us and kill us, and we are now in a manner like Orphans, all our great and wise men are dead, and as you live so much deeper within the Settlements of the White People, the evil Spirits must needs be more numerous, and of course, will be more destructive to us. We therefore desire, that you will move your Council Fire to Albany, and kindle it there, which can be but very little or no trouble to you, since you have Vessels to come by Water, and at Albany we will gladly hear you, and receive the Presents sent by the Great King over the Waters, for the Lands, some of our former Deputies assigned to You, we desire that you will take our answer in good Part, and come to Albany, to meet us at our Council Fire there burning—the Speaker gave me a large Belt of Wampum.

Brother Assaryquoah, the Belt of Wampum you gave us, concerning your Council Fire, we will answer and exchange, when we shall have the Pleasure to see you in Albany, we will do all that is in our Power to please you—pray consider well our circumstances, and you will then do the just thing—The Speaker gave another smaller String of Wampum.[25]

Though the embassy had failed in its original purpose, the time spent on it had not been wasted. Weiser's private conversations with the chiefs

at Albany, Canajoharie (the Upper Mohawk Castle), Onondaga, and
Oneida, had dispelled the fog of rumor and uncertainty that had blurred
his course in Indian affairs for the past few years. He had learned the extent and something of the cause of the great change that had come over
the disposition of the Six Nations toward the English. The Iroquois had
no natural love for the French, but they had been slighted, cheated, and
insulted by the New Yorkers until they had become suspicious of almost
everything that emanated from the English provinces. Governor Clinton
was openly contemptuous of them. Albany traders kidnapped their children to hold as security for their debts [26]—and drove a trade in these same
children as servants or slaves. It can be no wonder that the Six Nations
Indians were distrustful of New Yorkers and that they extended their distrust even to the soft-spoken missionaries from Pennsylvania. They observed that the white men who now came to Onondaga, though they
might travel by the Ambassadors' Road, spoke not as ambassadors of a
united English people but as representatives of private trading companies
or of religious sects or of political parties. They suspected even Cammerhof
because he spoke too much in the bushes.

Yet they listened to Cammerhof seriously enough on one subject: his
warning against selling more land to the English. This last part at least of
his message they had taken to heart, and Weiser found it inopportune to
broach the matter of a new purchase, however much it might be to the
ultimate advantage of the Six Nations as well as of Pennsylvania, since to
talk of land matters now would only serve to fix more firmly in their minds
their suspicions of the English and to destroy what little influence Brother
Onas still had with them.

If Weiser saw clearly what had gone wrong with the Indian policy, he
saw as clearly what was needed to restore it. The Six Nations must be
made to feel again, as they had felt at Philadelphia in 1736 and at Lancaster
in 1744, that Brother Onas found his welfare in theirs, and that he desired to strengthen their authority. Weiser saw, too, that there was one
place in which the old Logan-Weiser-Shickellamy policy could still be
made effective: in the matter of the Iroquois colony on the Ohio.

From the chiefs at Oneida he drew a statement that was to serve as a
compass for him during the Ohio negotiations of the next few years.

After some pause I told them, that I believ'd the Governor of Virginia could
not come to Albany, and would perhaps give the Presents to the Indians at
Ohio, as the Ohio Indians were one and the same with the Six United Nations,
and of their own Blood—they made answer that the Ohio Indians were but
Hunters and no Counsellors or Chief Men, and they had no Right to receive
Presents that was due to the Six Nations, although they might expect to have
a Share, but that Share they must receive from the Six Nation Chiefs, under
whom they belong.

I took my Leave and told them, what I had said last was my own thought,
and I would let their Brother Assaryquoah know, what had passed as soon as
I came home.[27]

V

The death of Canasatego, since it required Weiser "to go thro a formal Ceremony of Condolence before he could proceed upon his other Businiss," as Daniel Claus tells us, put too great a strain on the commissariat, and "their stores were consumed before the Bus⁵ was half finished and they obliged to depend upon an Indian Diet of Indⁿ Corn, Squashes, Entrails of Deer &c. which altho no hardship for Mʳ Weiser who experienced the life before, was a great one for Mʳ Claus who never saw such eatables made use of before by Mankind, and was pretty well pinched with Hunger before he could persuade himself to taste them . . ." [28]

That the diet, however, was not uninvigorating is shown by the speed they made on their return journey. On September 20, Weiser and Claus reached the Upper Castle of the Mohawks. From there, avoiding Albany, they struck across to Schoharie by a "blind" Indian trail, passed through what had once been known as Weisersdorf, and crossed the mountains to Catskill—"by a small Indian Path much a nearer way than I went," as he writes—"and arrived at my House on the first Day of October in perfect health." [29]

But not, I think, in perfect conscience. The narrative that leaps from Catskill to Heidelberg in so summary a fashion has left something out that Weiser thought unnecessary to insert in an official journal that he knew would find its way into the minutes of the Governor's Council. Perhaps Muhlenberg's journal can help us.

Muhlenberg was at Kingston (just a few miles below Catskill on the Hudson) on September 22, and at eight o'clock that evening went on board a vessel to join the "honorable ship's-company" for which he offered his thanks to God.[30] If Weiser was on board that same vessel which next day, Sunday, at four o'clock in the afternoon brought them to the Fort at New York, we can understand his reference in a letter of November 27, 1752 [31] (addressed to Albinus in London), to a visit he had made to New York "two years ago."

He can have spent only two or three days in the city, but he had time for a talk with the Lutherans there (Muhlenberg was investigating another Confusion), and then hurried home by way of Bethlehem.

From Bethlehem he despatched a note to Secretary Peters: "I believe that the English Interest among the Six Nations can be of no Consideration any more, the Indians speak with Contempt of the New-Yorkers & Albany People, and much the same of the rest of the English Colonies." [32]

From his home, a few days later, he wrote a letter to President Lee.

Conrad Weiser to Thomas Lee [33]

Heidelberg in Lancaster County,
October the 4ᵗʰ 1750

Honoured Sir.

By these Lines I lett you know, that I am Safely retourned from Onontago, on the first on this Instant; And how things are at Onontago, you will See

by the Copy of my Journal, hereby send, I found things altered very much
at Onontago; The friends of the English among the Counsel are dead, and
those that are at the Head of affairs now, are devout to the French, and confess it freely, and it is my Opinion, that the Onontagers, Cayiugers and
Sinickers are tourned entirely from the English to French, some of the
Oneiders are the same, but most of them with the Mohocks, may be yet in our
Interest though divided in their Counsel. They complain very much of the
bad Management of the English in general, especially in a Neighbouring Government and say that Since the Peace they have never been Spoke to; The
Oneiders and Mohocks, are at a Lost, what to do if a War Should break out,
between us and the French, their Case would be desperate, but not so bad as
ours, because they may Shelter under other Nation of Indians, and do, as they
do; The french Indians are thick at Onontago, there came 8. or 9. to see
me, and owned they came from Canada to see their Friends of Onontago,
behaved otherwise very civil;

The Counsel gave their Reason as you will see in my Journal, but they
reserved one Reason, why they would not come to Frideriksburg in Virginia
viz: they belieft that your Honour send for them to Virginia to meet the
Catabaws, and make a peace with them, which they thought would be to their
Dishonor, to meet a most conquered Enemy so far, it would looke, as they, the
6. united Nations sued for a Peace; I could not remove that Thought, or get
it out of their Heads, I never mentioned a Word to them about the Catabaws,
as I told you Honour before in one of my Letters, I was satisfied, it would not
be proper but they had heard of my Coming and it was Said for that Purpose;
Be that as it will, they have often been told, by the former Commissioners in
Albany, to desist from their going to the Southern Governments, but stick to
their Fire in Albany because Albany Commissioners, and perhaps the governor
of New York, judge that Indian affairs, could be better transacted at one place
and jointly by all the Governours of the neighboring Provinces, they have
told me so much, some years ago, and are perhaps in the Right; I find that the
bad Circumstances of our Indian affairs, requires a very able Counsel and
Unity among the English Colonies in North America, for the French have
very far overcome us, among the Indians, and that, since the last War broke
out between the two Nations. Herein inclosed is your Honours Letter to
Capt: Robinson, I think I had no Reason to make Use of it, but safe till a
better Oportunity will offer, I also inclosed an account of my Expences, not
to press for the payment, but to clear up every thing that it may be known,
how things are. I can think of nothing now worth to trouble you with, till I
shall know your further Ordres; I remain
Sir

Your very obedient Servant
Conrad Weiser

Thomas Lee, in a letter of November 6, 1750, informed the Board of
Trade in London that he had sent a messenger to the Six Nations at Onondaga, "a very knowing Interpreter . . . a Man that is perfectly acquainted
with them and their Designs," who reported that he found the Six Nations
quite altered from their former way of thinking, having left the British
interest and gone over to the French. "I will try to secure the Ohio Indians," wrote Lee, "who are increased to near 2000 fighting men . . ." [34]

Thomas Lee died within a few days of the despatch of that letter. But the problem he had posed remained for some years one of the gravest confronting the English colonies: What was to be done with those distant Fires on the banks of the Ohio?

CHAPTER 39

. . . *Leaves Sammy among the Mohawks*

A SHARP division of opinion followed on Weiser's return from Onondaga. It seemed to most observers that the Onondaga Council was now as good as lost to the English, and that Pennsylvania, therefore, had better tend her own garden and cultivate the Ohio Indians. Those of this opinion, of whom George Croghan was one, were for dealing directly with the Ohio Indians (instead of approaching them through the Onondaga Council)—as "all the Indians of the Six Nations setled at Ohio"[1] had requested earlier in the summer.

But there were others who looked more keenly into the future. They saw that the Six Nations were still a great people, that they could weight the scales decisively either way, for England or for France. They might yet save the English. Conrad Weiser, while at Onondaga, had been kindly treated even by their Roman Catholic, pro-French head chief. They responded as ever to courtesy and fair dealing. The cause of their defection from the English interest was known to be the neglect in which Governor Clinton's colony had left them after the peace of Aix la Chapelle. They must not be further alienated. It must even be attempted, by a strong resumption of the Logan-Weiser-Shickellamy policy of raising the authority of the Onondaga Council, to recover their friendship. If the Six Nations could still be made to feel that the prestige of their confederacy was a point of English policy, they might be persuaded to return to that benevolent neutrality which had in the past been the mainstay of the English colonies.

Those of this opinion thought it best to treat the Ohio Indians as a colony, and to deal with them only through the Great Council, as members of the Council had proposed to Weiser at Onondaga. This had been Thomas Penn's opinion from the first. As early as October 1748, Penn had said that to treat the Ohio Indians as a separate people would be to strike a body blow at the Six Nations Confederacy, and that such action must, if possible, be avoided.[2]

But was it possible to avoid it? A test was already at hand. Presents were to be distributed by Pennsylvania among the western nations, Twightwees, Wyandots, etc., allies of the Six Nations, when they assembled on the Ohio in the summer of 1751. Would it be politic to allow such of the Six Nations as lived there to stand by and receive nothing?—to tell them that they might expect to receive later such share of a present to be given the Onondaga Council as that body might think fit to send them?

The government at Philadelphia made up its mind: the Ohio Indians were to have an independent present, and Conrad Weiser was to give it to them, May 15, at Logstown. It was too delicate a matter to entrust to anyone else. On this the Governor and the Assembly were agreed. It was expected that Weiser would return from this conference in time to attend another at Albany, to which Governor Clinton had asked all the English colonies to send representatives for the purpose of concerting common measures for the conduct of Indian affairs.

> . . . your Presence is absolutely necessary at Albany [wrote Peters, April 13] . . . this is of more consequence than the Journey to Ohio as you may in conjunction with Coll Johnson to whom you have wrote on the subject suggest good Councils to Governor Clinton on which the whole depends since all the Western Indians will take their measures from the Six Nations who are to be fixed for the English at Albany.[3]

Weiser in his reply excused himself from undertaking the Ohio journey on the ground that he could not handle the business properly at Logstown and get back in time to go to Albany. The treaty goods could not possibly reach Logstown by May 15, and it would be impolitic to assemble the Indians before the goods were there, "because this is a hungry time with the Indians," and "it would create Discontent and ill Will by many of the Deputies, to wait with an empty Belly for the Goods of which they might after all Share but little." [4] He therefore recommended that George Croghan and Andrew Montour were "every way qualified to do that Business," since there was no particular treaty to be held at Ohio, be despatched in his place.

Weiser's advice was followed. Croghan and Montour went to Logstown, carrying with them minute instructions that had first been submitted by the Governor to Weiser for his approval. Even the speeches which were finally delivered to the Indians on May 28 at Logstown had been written by Weiser.[5]

Meanwhile the Assembly of Pennsylvania, suspicious of any proposals emanating from New York, declined to take part in Clinton's treaty. They requested, however, that Governor Thomas should "direct Conrad Weiser to meet the Six Nations there with the small Present provided for them, and a Message of Condolence on the Death of Canassatego and their other chiefs who were our steady Friends . . ." [6] The interests of the province were thus left in the hands of Conrad Weiser alone.

Accordingly on June 10, 1751, Weiser left for Philadelphia, where he received his instructions from the Governor, and set out again by way of New York for Albany. With him went his son, Sammy.

Ever since Weiser's illness in May 1748, when Richard Peters had written of "the dreadful Situation this Province will be in for want of an Indian Interpreter to succeed Mr Weiser in case of his Death," [7] the government at Philadelphia had been casting about to find someone who could be trained to succeed him. The name of Andrew Montour had been suggested and rejected. ". . . he has a good Character among the Indians," wrote Peters, "but he is untractable & extravagant & keeps low Company . . ." [8]

There was also George Croghan. "Conrad Weiser has frequently told me," wrote Peters to Thomas Penn, February 15, 1750, "that Croghans Interest with the Indians is next to his own, and shoud he dropp Croghan is the fittest Man to succeed him." [9] But Croghan's honesty, loyalty, and intelligence were all under question. At best, he and Montour could serve only in a mean capacity. For the general conduct of Indian affairs, Richard Peters rather fancied himself. "I have . . . at no small Expence & with an unwearied assiduity," said the reverend gentleman, "endeavour'd to gain the Esteem of the Indians, & I am told by Mr Weiser that I have succeeded so far as to be consider'd as a young Logan . . ." [10]

In the end Conrad Weiser, though he had always "been obstinately determined that none of his Children shoud learn Indian," [11] and had at the Upper Mohawk Castle in 1750 made tentative arrangements to have his sister's son (who lived within a mile of the Castle) educated as an interpreter,[12] was persuaded "with ye greatest difficulty" [13] to let his son Sammy go among the Mohawks to learn their language.

As Sammy's tutor, Daniel Claus went along—"a pretty young Gentleman, and very fit for the employment," as ex-Governor Hamilton described him.[14]

Weiser has left us several accounts of this journey. One is found in the Council Minutes of August 12, 1751.[15] It tells briefly of the condolence business transacted at Albany. A fragment from a fuller journal has been preserved among Weiser's personal papers.[16] This second narrative gives more background, telling of the protest the Six Nations reported themselves as having made to the French against the latter's building a fort at Niagara, and describing the Catawba peace embassy which Weiser took under his wing when their speaker lost his nerve and forgot his words on finding himself in the presence of "the very chiefs" of the fabled Onondaga Council. Still a third journal has been preserved in the Du Simitière Collection of the Library Company of Philadelphia. This one is full of the liveliest personal detail in which Weiser once more appears as the sharp-eyed, warm-hearted, keen-witted spectator of the scenes in which he played a part. He presents so lively a picture of the time when, for a brief interval, white man and brown man met on nearly equal terms in America, that it is a little classic of its kind. It is especially interesting to the biographer, since Conrad Weiser is far from leaving himself out of the picture. The third journal is here presented, with a few interweavings, indicated by brackets, from the second:—

A Journal of the proceedings of Conrad Weiser in his Journey to Albany with a Message from the Governor of pensilvania to the Six Nations of Indians. annod: 1751 [17]

1751
June the 10   Set out from my house in lancaster County—
     the 11   arrived in philadia and received my Instructions from his Honour the Governor
     the 14   left philadelphia and went by Burdenton [Bordentown] & Amboy to new-york.

the 17   arrived in new york and waited on Governor Clinton with a letter from Governor Hamilton, I tooke the Same apportunity to ask leave of Governor Clinton to put my Son Samy into the mohoKs Country to learn the Indian language, the Governor was pleased to Say he would lay my request before the Counsel and I Should have his answer to-morrow by Eleven of the Clock

the 18   at the appointed Hour went to the fort, the Governor Sent Word to me that I must Call again the next day. Waited on Mr Bull

the 19   Went again to the fort, Governor Clinton Sent word by Mr Edward Holland, that I was Wellcome to put my Son in the mohocKs Country. I visited the Catabaws, one of them Spoke the onontago very well, he being a prisoner Some time ago in that Country, the Catabaw King being Informed that I was an Interpreter to the Six united nations, and in good Esteem with them, he told me by his Indian Interpreter, that he was Invited by the Governor of South Carolina, to Come to the treaty at Albany, and that out of Respect and Brotherly love to the English he Consented to Come, in order to make peace with the Six united nations of the Northern Indians, upon Equal terms but would not Sue for it, his people would rather spend the last drop of Blood in the Warr then to Sue for peace. Notwithstanding he desired me to use my Endeavour with my friends to bring about a peace between the Northern and the Southern Indians, he said further that he was tired of the Warr, and wished that those what are now Born might live in peace and die of age. I promised to do all what was in my power, to bring about a peace and that I had ben Employed Several times by the Governor of virginia, but without any Sensible Success. only that the Six united nation in the year 1736 had agreed to a Cessiation of arms and performed it. but the Catabaws not Coming to the place of Congress appointed by the Said nations. (to wit Albany or Philadelphia) all Came to Nothing; and that the 6 nation charged the Catabaws with Treachery and that their word of Honour was nothing. the Catabaw King reply'd that he was Sensible that If all old Storries would be told over again there Could be no peace made he on his part would never repeat any, though he might repeat Some. among other things King Nap-Keehee * asked me whether I thought it Safe for him to be in Albany, Supposing the Six nation would Come to no termes, I told him yes it was, for the Governor of New-york would take Care of them, If any danger appeared, but I was Satisfied the 6 nations would not hurt them, provided they the Catawbas would take advise. I told NapKeehee further, that If nothing Can be done towards a peace. the 6 nation Counsel will tell you to go home in peace and that they will Send after You and Kill you in your own Country. This was the Substance of my discourse with the Catawba King during our stay at n-york of which I thought proper to make but one paragraph.

* the name
of the
Catabaw King

During my Stay in new-york I dined Several times with M[r] Bull the Comissioner from South Carolina, and we had Several Serious discourse about the affair of the peace between the northern and Southern Indians. I told M[r] Bull that I thought the Catabaw King was a litle to Haughty in his mind, and that I was afeared all would turn into Smook, without he Could be brought to make a more humbler and indeed a more Reasonable speech to the 6 nation, then what he gave me to understand, M[r] Bull told me it was more the desire of the Government of S Carolina then the Catabaws to have a peace between the said Indians, because their back Setlers Suffered a great deal & etc. M[r] Bull had the thing very Much at heart and Seamed to me to be an Experienced man in Indian affair, and a Gentleman of a free and open Conversation, he desired I would assist him in the affair with what lay in my power, which I promised to do. no vesel went off to Albany this week all were taKen up by Some Gentlemen in order to folow Governor Clinton to Albany to be present and see the treaty

the 20   M[r] Bull made a diner for the Catabaws and desired my Company. I Complied with his request, the Catabaw King Signified to me that it was a very great Satisfaction to him to get acquainted with me. & etc. the Catabaws being well cloathed in Blue, and the King wore red Breeches.

the 22   Governor Clinton let me Know by M[r] Holland that he was Informed all Albany Shloops wer taKen up, and that I Could get no passage I should be Wellcome to go in one of his vesels, I returned his Excellency thanks and let him Know I took passage for meselve & Companions in M[r] Beckmans:

the 24   found the M[r] Beckmans vesel to full took passage with M[r] Egberty who had the Catabaws and other passengers from Albany on Bord, this afternoon by four of the Cloke Gov[r] Clinton went under Sail with a fair Wind the rest of the vesels folowed him

the 27   we arrived in Albany, but found the Indians were not arrived as yet, I tooke up lodging at M[r] Rosebooms a private house

the 30   the Indians arrived but not in Such great number as formerly on Such occasion, there was but a few of the SinicKers & of the CajucKers, and not many of the onontagers. most of them were Mohocks. oneidos. & Tuscarroros, five of the mohocK Chiefes Came to see me that Evening, they thought I had Brought the Catabaws with me to make a peace for them with the Six nations, I told them that I accidentally meet them in new-york, and got acquainted with them and for want of a better oppurtunity I Came in the Same vesel with them from new-york. they Seamed to be well inclined for a peace with the Catabaws and wished the Catabaws would make a Sutable Speech to the Counsel of the Six nations. they asKed whether the Governor of pensil[ia] or any Commissioner was Come I told them no. but that I was Sent with a Message from the Governor of pensilvania to the Six nation to be deliverd to them after the Governor of new-york had done with them.

after they being gone they Sent one of them back to let me Know, that It was unsafe for the Catabaws to be Seen by the Six nation of Indians before a Speech was made, nothwithstanding Some might be inclined for peace as well as the MohocKs, yet others might offer to Cut their throats upon the first Sight. I acquainted Mr Bull with this, and a Centry was ordered before the Catabaws door, and they wer ordered to Keep above Stairs

I visited Brand a Chief of the mohocks and told him that I brought one of my Sons in order to put him in the Mohocks Country to learn the language and If they (that is Brand and his wife She being present) would receive him I was inclined to leave him with them. both Brand and his wife appeared to be very glad, and Embraced my Son Samy with tears in their Eies, and Said they would receive him as their own Child, If I would leave him with them. they haveing but one Child and Just then brought him to Albany to put him into an English Shool to learn English. Brands wifes family is the family in which I was Adopted as a Son, . . . in the year 1714

July the first   Several of the Chiefes of the oneiders Came to See me and discoursed with me about Several things . . .

the 2   this day above twenthy Canoes arrived with french Indians they Came loaded with Beavers. they the french Indians went and paid their Compliment to Govr Clinton, as did the Chiefes of the Six nations afterwards. Dyion nen ho carrow a SinicKer Chiefe Came to Salut me very friendly, he is one of them that Came to philadelphia when the proprietor Mr Thomas penn first Came in, also the Shochary Indians Came to See me. I was obliged to receive a good many visits. Spent the Evening with Mr Stevens the provincial Interpreter and Some of the Chiefes of the mohocks, to wit Heinry. Nickes. Abram & others. they asked what Buisness the french Indians had in Albany at this time and said that the Govr of Canada would not Suffer the MohocKs in Canada, he would tell them to be gone by Such an Hour or Suffer Imprisement, they Said further that they Could not open their heart to the Govr of n-york in the presence of those Indians, but it is well Known that the french praying Indians are all or Most all Mohocks and are allways Kindly received in the mohocKs Country

the Indians Spoke in publice to the Governor and Condoled with him over the death of the Kings Eldest Son and gave a Bundle of Skins . . .

the 5   the Chiefes of the oneiders & Tuscarrorows Came to return a Belt & a Streng of Wampum that remained un Exchanged at oneido last year about the virginia affair . . .

the 6   Governor Clinton Spoke to the Indians. . . . the Governors Speech was Interpreted by Mr Holland into low dutch for the Interpreter to the Indians. and by him into MohocKs. . . .

the 8   the Indians gave their answer. I was present and assisted in the Interpretation.

after the Indians had gone Mr Bull Spoke to them. Captain

Callick the Interpreter from Baston was prevailed upon to Interpret for Mr Bull.

the 8   the Interpreter Arend Stevens desired to be Excused, he did Expect that Mr Bull Should have offered him pay for his trouble. I assisted Captain Callick. Mr Bull delivered a letter from the Governor of South Carolina under the Broad Seal of the province which I at the request of Callick Explained to the Indians. after Mr Bull had done the Catabaws were Sent for at the request of the mohocKs as well as the govern^r I went to meet them and Conducted them to their proper place they Came along Singing with their Collabashes dressed with feders in their hands, they Continued Singing for a while after the Sat down. in the mean time. the Calmet pipe was offered by the Catabaw King to all the Chiefes and old people of the Six nations, and after this another Calmet was offered by one of the Warriours of the Catabaws, and the Six Nations Indians Smooked out of Both. then the Catabaw King Stood up & Spoke, but appeared to be very Much daunted and Could make no hand of it. It was a very difficult matter for Mr Tooll. the Interpreter that Came with the Catabaws to English it, Captain Callick had obliged himself to Interpret, but Could not go through with it. though he spoke the MohocKs a great deal better then I, and so the Indians were at a last [loss]. they desired me to let them Know the Substance of what was said. Which I did, to their Satisfaction.

[the purport of the speach was as folowes Brethren the united nation of the north we Came a great way to meet you here at the Counsel fire of which the Govr of N-York has Kindled We had it in our thoughts last year to have Come but Sickness prevented us we long wish^d to have had a Opportunity to see you and now we are very glad to See you we are desireous to treat with you upon peace we are weary of the warr let those that are now Born grow up in peace and die upon their Beds of age this is the advise of our Brethren the English with which we very heartely Comply and Came to your Counsel fire for that purport to Establish a lasting peace. gave a large Belt of Wampum and Some Indian pipes & the feders! that was died to a post after done Singing]

the 6 nations made answer by Acquyioda an oneider Chief as folowes. We are glad to See the Catabaws at our Counsel fire in Albany, we thank them for their Kind Speech and after we have Considered and diliberated together about the thing, we will give them their answer which probably will be To morrow. the Catabaws for this time took their leave and Shoke hands with most all the Six Nation Indians that were present, [and their King lay his hands about Heinrys Body and Impraced him] and the Six Nation Indians Espeically the Chiefes appeared very Cordially to them. the meeting which had lasted Several Hours Broke up now.

towards the Evening the Carolina Interpreter desired me to Come and See his Indians and Smooke a pipe with them, when I Came there, the Catabaw King Stood up with his Companions and ShaKed hands with me and thanked 'me for my Interpretation of his Speech, he told me that his friend him that was prisoner at onontago had told him that I helped his Speech and put it in good order for him and that he would remember my Kindness as long as he lived

the 9   being Informed that the Governor had Sent to the Butcher and BacKer for their Bills and was preparing to go off. I waited on him to get leave to deliver my message but was told by his Exellency that as Soon as Mr Bull and the Catabaws had their answer I Should deliver my message.—

everything Seamed to be in a Confusion the Indians found Some hard Expressions in Mr Bulls Speech, which Sounded very rash by the Interpretation of Capt: Callick. they were also unEasy about the Governors presents, they haveing ben told that after they had given their answer to Mr Bull & the Catabaws they Should receive them, the Indian Counsel Sat all day. they Sent for Arend Stevens Capt: Callick and me. to repeat to them what was Said by Mr Bull and the Catabaws which we did haveing a Copy of Mr Bulls Speech with us

the 10   the Indian Counsel Sat again till most noone then they Came and gave their answer to Mr Bull . . . [and the Catawbas had also a friendly answer as folowes

Brethren the Catabaws

We are glad to See you at our Counsel fire at Albany and we thank you for the kind Speach you made to us. we give you this Belt of Wampum to wear about your neck as a token that you are our friends that have ben at our Counsel fire.

we give you another Belt of Wampum to make you more powerfull and so on. (the Indian Said to make you Hornes) and the next time you Come again you must bring the prisoners you have of our with you for this is the Custom among all the Indians when they Come to make peace to bring the prisoners with them which is allways taken as a Sure token of their Sincerity of which Custom you might have be unacquainted we therefor Insist upon that the next time you Come you bring at least of our people that are prisoners amongst you with you and we will Set the prisoners we have of you then at liberty a tocken of your Sincerity will be if you Come to our town in the North Country within 12 months

the Catabaws answer

Brethren we thank you for your Kind Speech. we will & see you again in a very short time & If you would be so good to send 2 or 3 or More of your people with us to our Country we will take good Care of them and Come with them back to your Country and bring the prisoners with us.

the 6 nation ansd Brethren this is never done that we send of our people with messengers of peace that Come the first time but when they Come here the 2 or 3 time we send people with them and so we will do with you.

the 10   Brethren the Catabaws as there is a great number of Indians
in treaty with us it will take Some time before we Can give
them all notice of what is here passed. We must desire that
the next time you Come again. you will Come again by Water
for fear that the Indians you will meet with by the way will
kill you for all the Indian back of virginia Maryland & pensil^{ia}
are in league with us. we must further desire you to bring a
guid with you from your Brethren of S. Carolina to Certify
that you are the Same people.]

Mr Bull gave the Indians a Barrle of Bear to drink with the
Catabaws. and the Governor ordered his presents to be delivered to the Indians as did Mr Bull.

the Governor Called me into his house and told me in the
presence of doctor Goldin that I was now at liberty to deliver
my message when I pleased, provided I had nothing Else to
Say then what was Mentioned in Governor Hamiltons letter
to me, I told him that I had not, So he Called for a Glass
of wine and drunk Governor Hamiltons good Health and he
ordered the Glass to be filled for me, I wished his Excellency
a good Voyage to new-york he haveing Said that he was Just
a going. accordingly he went off. the Indians being very Much
exasperated, because they being all by ye door and the presents
lieing there undivided and his Exellency went off without taK-
ing Some of them by the hand or Saying So Much as farewell. besides the Indians had not done Speaking with him. they
wanted Some provisions on their return, & etc. but his
Excellency Expected (as Mr Bull told me) that the Comissioners of Boston Mr Bull and meself Should not provide for the
Indians.

I Informed the Indians that all the vesels were going of that
Evening and I Could get no passage to new-york perhaps in
ten days, I would therefore desire them to Come and receive
the Message I had from the Governor of pensilvania that after-
noone. accordingly between five & Six of the Cloke they Came
to my lodging, to the number of thirty & upwards Some of the
Chiefes of Each nation among them and as Such Message
required a good deal of Sermonies, which no European Can
perform I folowed the Example of Governor Clinton and
hired an Indian (to wit Canachqua-ieson a Chief of the
oneiders) to Serve me on that occasion after the Indians were
all Seated down, I ordered them some drink. in the mean time
Canaque-ieson walKed up and down the room and Sung
lamentation Songs over the death of Canasatego & others,
named all the Chiefes that died of late which lasted about a
quarter of an Hour, and then he Sat down, and after a Short
paus he Stood up, and Said Brethren the united Six nations.
the Governor of pensilvania has Sent Tharachia Wagon with
a message to you. you are desired to hear attentively. the
Speaker gave a Streng of Wampum and proceeded

Brethren. The Governor of pensilvania was but last year
Informed of the death of Several of the Chiefes of the Six

nations died on their way homewards from Philadelphia, and that after their arrival in their own towns his good friend[s] Canasatego & Sit Ko wan aghty & etc. have also died, the Governor and the people of pensylvania are very Sorry to hear of the death of those their good friends and Brethren, and have therefore Immediately ordered Tharachiawagon to your towns with a present to Signify to the relations of the deceased and to the Council that the Governor & people of pensilvania Condole with you on the loss of Such valuable persons, and to Wipe of the tears of your Eies.

the 10   Brethren the winter being so near at hand, when Tharachia-wagon was Charged with this Message, that he would not venture to travle and therefore delayd till now. A Streng of Wampum was given and ten pieces of Strowts delivered to them. and they were told that one piece thereof was given in particular on the death of Canasatego to wip of the tears of his relations, and to Cover his Grave. the piece of Strowt being layd by itself when brought into the room. there was another piece of Strowt layd by itself, and they were told that. that was given on the death of Gunjaquoh an old Mohock Warrior who died in his Majestys Services in the last Warr as he Served as an outSkout, and was Killed by the french. and on the death of a Son of Cayen quarachton [18] a SinicKer Chief who was also Killed by the Comon Enemy in the last Warr. they were told that that piece of Strowt Served to Cover the Graves of these two warriors. Honourably, and wipe of the tears of their Relations. as they had Sacrified their live for the good of the Comon Cause in obedience to his Majesty King George—

After the message was delivered to them, they Sat a good while and Wispering to one another. about a Small present that they ought to have Sent to the Governor of pensilvania, but they had parted with the few SKins they brought on other occasions, Abram a Chief of the Mohock acquainted me with their Concern, I gave him to understand that they need not Stand for that at present that I would Excuse them in the best manner I Could with the Governor and people of pensilvania, Abram then went again to his place and after a Short Con-sultation with the rest of the Chiefes he Stood up and Said

Brother Tharachiawagon. the Message you delivered to us Just now from our Brethren the Governor & people of pensil[ia] gives us a great deal of Satisfaction. it is the largest that every we received on Such occassion, and we take it as a fresh toKen of the Brotherly love of the Governor and people of pensil-vania towards us. We desire you by this Streng of Wampum to return thanKs in our name. to our Brethren the Governor and people of pensilvania in the best manner you are Capable of. the Speaker gave me a Streng of Wampum.—

After a Short pause. I told them that I had Some thing else to Say to them, about an affair of my own. and Said Brethren I have Brought one of my Sons with me to put him into the mohocks Country among my relations and in the Same family in which I was Adopted as a Son 37 years ago, to learn the mohock language to enable him to Serve as an Interpreter between the people of pensilvania and the Six united nations, I begine to grow old and must give over traveling into the Indian Country before long. I must therefore recomend my Son into Your Care, in hopes that you will do all what lies in your power both for his Safety, as Instruction in your linguage. particularly in Council affair. gave them a Streng of Wampum

After a Short Consultation they had together Abram Spoke & Said. Brother Tharachiawagon we are glad to See your Son, and more So because you brought him to leave him with us, you did very well in bringing your Son to the place of your Birth and to your family, we looKe upon him as our own Child, and We will use our best Endeavour to learn him Speak well, and to maKe a man of him. in Confirmation Whereof he gave me a Streng of Wampum. and the Indians all Shaked hands with Samy

As the Hour was approaching for the vesel that Stayed for me to go off (She was the only one left) I told the Indians So, haveing Some drink ready for them, we dranK together and then took our leave of one another, it being passed ten of the Cloke at night, my Son Samy & daniel Claus his tutor folowed me to the water side, where I gave them the last Charge and bid them fare well.—

the 11   we Came to an anchor about 12 miles this Side of Albany (there being four Sloops in Company) Col¹ peter Shuyller invided me to Come on Bord of his Sloop and dine with him, which I did, and Soon after a Strong North wind sprung up, and Mʳ Shuyller would have me stay on Bord of him. with which I readely Complyd our Sloope being Too full.

the 12.   about Eleven of the Cloke arrived in new-york with the rest of the vesels, in one of which was Governor Clinton. but the Sloop in which my things was, and the yong man that accompanied daniel Claus to Albany, Came to an anchor at Soppus (or Kings town) and lost thereby the appurtunity of the fair wind, did not arrive till

the 16.   in the Evening we Could get no passage then, till

the 19   we left new-york and arrived in philadelphia the 22

the 22.   waited on the Governor and made Hast to get home finding meselfe unwell. being taKen with a feaver.—

the 23   I left philadelphia, was taken very Ill that day Stayd at Rudolph Boners,[19] two nights & two days doctor diemer attending me with visick

the 27   arrived at my house in a very weak Condition but the feaver haveing left me, I soon recovered.—

Heidleberg the Second day   CONRAD WEISER
of August. 1751   Interpreter

The Albany Conference of 1751, like that of 1745, was a Clinton fizzle. Nobody got anything out of it but William Johnson.

It had been called "to defeat the Designs and intrigues of the French" [20] by renewing the "Old Covenant Chain" [21] between the Six Nations and all the English colonies from New Hampshire to South Carolina. Pennsylvania had hoped Weiser and Johnson together might lay the foundation of a common Indian policy. But all hopes were soon lost. Hardly any of the colonies sent representatives. Johnson, who had lately resigned his management of Indian affairs for New York (ostensibly over the nonsettlement of his accounts) had to be coaxed to attend. King Hendrick, speaking for the Six Nations, said that without the Colonel's Large Ears and Large Eyes (to hear and see for the Indians) their interest must decline, and he sent a messenger for him "sooner [i.e., faster] than a Horse." [22] Johnson came and, with ears cocked and eyes wide open to his own advantage, enlarging on "the uncommon and great Sufferings" he had had in his "Zealous Service of the Crown," [23] consented to assist in the treaty; but it was no part of his political scheme to concert measures of Indian policy with his rival, Conrad Weiser.

When the conference was over, when the last beer barrel had been broached and the last sloop had sailed away, there was nothing to show for the cause of colonial unity. There had been the usual speeches, compliments, presents, and condolences. The Catawba King's peace overtures left a pleasant taste in the mouth, Governor Clinton's boorishness a sour taste, and Johnson's syncopations an uncertain taste. But for Pennsylvania there had come out of the conference little more positive than a confirmed distrust of the New York government, which had taken so high a hand with her Indian ambassador.

To Conrad Weiser the journey to Albany had piled fresh anxieties upon an over-burdened mind. To the perplexities of Indian affairs there was now added a new family worry. Sammy, never very robust of body and somewhat too yielding in character, had been left to grow up among a people who had not changed for the better since Conrad himself had first fled from them when they became drunken and violent thirty-eight years before. Weiser's uneasiness was not lessened when Sammy himself ran away and, "without acquainting his parents," [24] returned to Pennsylvania. Conrad had entered into an engagement regarding his son with the government of Pennsylvania. He sent Sammy back to the Mohawks.

CHAPTER 40

. . . Tells Virginia to
Knock the French on the Head

I

EVERYONE could see that France and England were moving toward a showdown in the Ohio Valley. But the approaches to war were devious and confused. The years 1752–55 were lived in an atmosphere of uncertainty, hesitation, and suspicion not unlike the years between Hitler's accession to power in Germany and the outbreak of war in 1939. Weiser's correspondence shows a growing strain and irritation. He liked to have things clear and explicit, as they seldom are in the shadow of war.

The story of his life at this time must show something of the mounting tension in his mind, which betrayed itself in indecision: his accepting and then resigning a commission from Virginia to conduct a treaty on the Ohio; his opposing and then supporting a show of force in that valley; his recalling Sammy from among the Mohawks; his outburst against Andrew Montour at the Carlisle treaty; and finally, the blaze of exasperation at the hesitancy of Pennsylvania to build a fort, send troops, or in any material way encourage the resistance of the Indians to French penetration in the Ohio Valley—exasperation in which he dashed off a letter advising Virginia to go in and knock the French on the head.

The death of Thomas Lee had not been allowed to sever Virginia's relations with Conrad Weiser. The Old Dominion took steps to keep Conrad's interest in her Indian problems alive.

Lewis Burrwell to Conrad Weiser [1]

Virginia Feb: 11th 1750/1

Sir
This serves to inclose to you a Sett of Bills of Exchange on Messrs John and Capel Hanbury, Merchants in London, for thirty pounds sterling; which was design'd to have been sent long ago to you, by the late President, Thos Lee Esqr but was unhappily prevented by his sudden death: & as Mr Robinson designs to pass thro' Philadelphia, in his way to New York from this Colony; I make use of the Opportunity, of transmitting the Bills of Exchange to you, which are design'd as a reward, for some of your Services to this Colony, & so I bid you heartily farewell and am

Your Loving Freind
LEWIS BURRWELL

As the Negotiation of Indian Affairs have been transacted cheifly by you; I must desire the favour of you whenever there is Occasion, to give me such Intelligence of those Affairs, as you shall think will be conducive to his Majesties' Interest.

333

In the spring of 1752 Governor Dinwiddie of Virginia sent an express to Weiser with the request that he go to Logstown in May as interpreter at a treaty in which presents were to be given to the Six Nations Indians living in the Ohio Valley. Colonel Thomas Cresap, who forwarded the letter to Weiser, added his own request that Weiser get wampum for the treaty and inform the Colonel "what Quantity of Liquor or any other necessarys may be proper to be provided . . ."[2]

Weiser sent the correspondence to Governor Hamilton in Philadelphia, asking that, if he were permitted to accept the Virginia commission, he might also be permitted to bring Sammy down from New York and take him along to improve the boy's knowledge of Indian affairs. The Governor granted both requests.[3]

I was very willing to give him leave to go [wrote Hamilton to the Penns] since I think the Virginian present coming so soon after ours cannot fail to have a good effect upon the Minds of those people, and by the means of Conrad, I shall be better inform'd, than I could otherways be, what the designs of the Virginians tend to. I do, intend to instruct Conrad that if he finds the Virginians desirous to Obtain leave from the Indians to build a Fort in any convenient place, to assist them with all the Intrest of this Government, as being a thing that would be greatly serviceable to the English in General, and particularly to our Province, as it would at least serve to divide the Expense with us of retaining those people in our Interest, which, tho inconsiderable when compard with that of some other Colonies, yet is sufficient to keep our Assembly allways grumbling.[4]

Arrangements went rapidly forward. On April 1, Thomas Cresap wrote to invite Weiser to join the Virginia commissioners, on their way to Logstown, at his house on or about April 25.[5]

Meanwhile there had been unpleasant developments in the West. From George Croghan came a letter (dated February 8, 1752) enclosing a message from the Shawnees. The latter informed the Governor that the French had killed thirty of the Twightwees, and asked him to assist the Ohio Indians against the French, who, they said, "directed by the Evil Spirit, and not God, trouble us much . . . and . . . threaten to cut us off."[6]

Governor Hamilton found himself on the horns of a dilemma. He did not wish to offend the Shawnees by declining to give aid. At the same time, knowing the pacifist sentiments of his Assembly, he did not wish to make engagements which he could not fulfill. He therefore tossed the ball to Virginia. Writing to the Shawnees in reference to the treaty at Logstown, which he understood all the Indians were to attend, he said, "I think the Counsellors and Commissioners for Virginia will be better enabled on the spot to judge of what shall be proper for you and the other Indian Nations to do, and will, I doubt not, give you good and faithful advice."[7]

The situation was rendered still more delicate by the ambiguous relationship of the Ohio Indians (Shawnees, Six Nations, Delawares, and what not) to the Onondaga Council. Indeed, the message from the Shawnees seemed to have put Pennsylvania on the spot—to the great advantage of the French. Pennsylvania, if she supported the Ohio Indians in war against the French, risked the anger of the Six Nations, who claimed the sole right to determine the issues of peace and war among the Indians in that valley. But, if she failed to support the Ohio Indians, she risked losing them to the enemy, since they would be driven under any wing that offered protection. Under the circumstances, the easiest course for Pennsylvania to pursue was to slip out from under by referring the Indians to Virginia. Yet if the Virginia treaty was conducted by Conrad Weiser, Pennsylvania's foremost Indian ambassador, it would be impossible to slip out from under. Whatever Weiser's formal status at the treaty might be, the Indians would look on him as the official representative of Pennsylvania.

This dilemma may explain why Conrad Weiser did not, in the end, go to the Ohio. Some time in April he hurried to Williamsburg to excuse himself, "and with great difficulty obtained his discharge." [8]

The thinness of the records at this point leaves us in some doubt as to the full and final cause of his change of mind. Mr. Peters had a simple enough explanation. When Conrad Weiser was at Onondaga in 1750, wrote the Secretary to Thomas Penn, he found that the Council there "entered a sort of a Caveat" against giving presents to the Ohio Indians.

M[r] Weiser forgetting this did in the Spring of this Year with the Consent of your governor, accept the Office of Interpreter and Distributer of this very Present among the Ohio Indians, but recollecting himself before the time appointed to go, he, by the Advice of the Governor, went to Williamsburg, shewd his Reasons to Governor Dinwiddy and got excused.[9]

Though Mr. Peters protested that "this was truly the Cause, and no other," of Weiser's resigning the Virginia service, it is difficult to believe that there was not something more in the background. Peters usually told the truth, but not always the whole of it. It is improbable that Weiser should have been so forgetful of a cardinal point in the policy of the Six Nations, especially after the Indians themselves had drawn his attention to it. No doubt if he had gone with the presents to the Ohio, he could still have reconciled this action with the wishes of the Onondaga Council by representing (as he now advised Virginia to do) [10] the presents as coming from the Six Nations themselves.

A contributing, perhaps even a determining, cause of the change in his plans may have been the discovery that George Croghan was taking too active a hand in the game—and pulling something out of his sleeve. That Croghan inspired as well as drafted the Shawnee message asking for help against the French, cannot be said with certainty. But it is certain that Weiser at this time was coming to suspect the "Prince of Traders," [11] whom he had at one time described as honest and fit to succeed him,[12] of being the "vile Rascal" [13] Richard Peters pronounced him.

Weiser had for some months past been keeping an eye on Croghan. He believed him to have misrepresented the wishes of the Six Nations on the Ohio in 1751, when he reported them as begging Pennsylvania to build a fort there. This report created a stir in government circles, and both Croghan and Weiser were in consequence called before the Assembly to explain themselves. From that time on suspicion mounted to certainty among those who had to do with Croghan that he was not merely "a man illiterate, impudent, and ill-bred, who subverts the purposes of government," [14] as Colonel Bouquet came to describe him; but also, as Governor Hamilton said, "an Intriguing, Disaffected Person" [15] whom it was " . . . highly necessary to keep a watchful Eye upon." [16] John Langdale called him "the most implacable Enemy to ye Province." [17] Israel Pemberton, Quaker, said he was "as vile a wretch as could be pick'd up." [18]

II

It is not to be supposed that the moves on the continental chessboard absorbed all of Conrad Weiser's attention. Much of his time still went into the affairs of his local community: laying out country roads, selling lots in Reading, attending court sessions, erecting the new county of Berks. In this last business alone he spent thirty-three days during the months of January and February 1752, with such success that the new county was at last created out of parts of the counties of Lancaster and Philadelphia. "It is my opinion," wrote Secretary Peters to the Proprietors, "that Conrad Weiser has teased the Assembly into the Erection of the County of Berks—had John Kinsey been alive, we shoud have had no County—." [19]

He put punch also into the building of the town of Reading. It may be said (after Dickens) that he brought up the young town by hand. The Secretary wrote, March 16, 1752:

Reading is a most surprising Place, one hundred well built houses many with costly decorations in Front rear their heads on high to the admiration of all who behold the Sight—and another hundred will I am perswaded be built this next Year, It was very lucky that I gave the management of that Town to Conrad, whose Imperiousness has been of great Service, for they build regularly, and if they dont, or are any way abusive, Conrad deals about his Blows without any Ceremony, and down drops the Man that dares to resist his ponderous Arm—but withal I must say that it is guided by good Sense and a necessary fortitude—[20]

"Down drops the Man." Conrad's fortitude, thus described, was perhaps not intended to please the genteel Thomas Penn; and it is not surprising to find that the said Thomas, while delighted at the progress his town of Reading was making (in the July 2 issue of Franklin's *Gazette* it was reported that 208 houses had been counted, "all built since the Beginning of June, 1750"), was not amused at the means by which that progress had been attained. "We . . . do not much approve," wrote Penn to Peters, "of Conrad Weiser's method of enforcing his orders." [21]

It took fortitude of mind as well as muscle to lay the foundations of the new county seat. The Reverend Richard Peters, who had Large Ears for "polite scandal" (he expressed regret to Margaret Freame that he had not more of this commodity on tap) and Large Eyes for the spot where the truth should make his neighbors smart, wrote engagingly to Weiser, July 28, 1752:

I hear that there are some people underhand making Observations on your Conduct, and that they intend (one & all I suppose of the mad disappointed people) to throw together abundance of Aspersions against you and lay the Paper before the Governor. Poor people they will not nor cannot do any thing themselves & yet are extremely angry that there is a man of better Sense & more Spirit than them selves. . . .

I wish you perfect health & perfect Patience & good humour.

I am wth abundance of true respect

Sir

Your affectionate

humble Servant

RICHARD PETERS [22]

He might have added a tag from Shakespeare's *Henry IV*:

> *. . . my love to ye*
> *Shall show itself more openly hereafter.*

But that would have been to anticipate the dénouement by five years.

Through all his dizzy whirl of activities (besides the affairs of county, town, and colony already noticed, he was running the farm and tannery, administering the Freame tract for the Proprietors, sitting as President Judge of Berks County, and driving his own lawsuits, of which he had many, through the courts against defaulting debtors), he did not forget the church. And here it must be said that Weiser, though deeply religious and possessed of a mystic sense of contact with the Eternal, had neither taste nor leisure for metaphysical discussion. He was more interested in works than doctrine. The religion of his mature years was not fed on dialectic, nor did he, like some of the Puritans, spend his time scratching for spiritual fleas. He worshipped God by doing a good job in the Indian service, by wielding a ponderous arm at Reading, and by helping the poor Pennsylvania preachers. When Gotthilf August Francke wrote to him from Halle, May 1, 1751, it was to thank him for the valuable beaver coat Weiser had sent him as a gift, and to thank him also for the help he had been giving to "the workers in the Lord's vineyard among the Pennsylvania congregations." [23]

III

Sammy came down for the Logstown journey and then, his father having decided not to go, stayed on so long at home that Philadelphia officialdom grew querulous.

"I am repeatedly commanded by the Governor," wrote Peters, July 11, "to desire you would not fail to send your Son Sammy to his Indian Residence as soon as the hot season abates—As his Honour is frequently expressing some doubts about your own heartiness on this Occasion and as Sammy likes yᵉ thing well & will certainly improve I hope you will not give the Governor Room to complain." [24]

Sammy was a worry to Conrad and Ann Eve no less than to His Excellency. The boy was never strong, and his father, much as he loved the people of the Mohawk Valley, knew too much of their weaknesses to be happy about Sammy's residence among them. ". . . pray desire Mʳˢ Weiser from me not to be so anxious about Sammy," [25] wrote Peters; "he may lay the foundation of an hardy strong habit of Body, & his mind will be the better for comparing the Inconveniences of an Indian Cabbin with the Elegancies & Plenty of a full Plantation."

Sammy and Mr. Claus returned to the Mohawk country in August and resumed their life with the Brants. This was the time of the great ginseng boom.

Daniel Claus to Conrad Weiser [26]

Fort William, Augᵗ 23ᵈ 1752

Most highly honored Herr Weiser

On the 10ᵗʰ last past of this month we all arrived here safe and Brand brought Us over in his Wagon from Sceneckdady as we had written asking him to do He was very glad to see Samuel again Samʸ gave him the 10 Pounds in your letter . . . we found things on the whole not as we had been informed in the letters from Albany . . . in general things are better than we thought But I cannot adequately describe what a Furore there is round here over the famous Roots Coll Johnson has already bought over 1600 Bushels, and for 3 weeks has been paying 40/: for the green and £ 4 for the dried, most of the good people of Albany are laying out money and goods in speculation in the stuff and many of them don't know where to send it; as I hear Coll: Johnⁿ sends his to London and from there it is sent on to China where it is bought as the greatest rarity; In Canada this Root Business is said to be much bigger because the french Indians in Oswego give 1 lb of beaver for every Pound of green Roots the Indians call it Ochdéra I wonder if the same is to be found in Pennsylvania Samy and I were out with brand helping him look for the stuff he is at it all day long, it makes the Mohawk River quite Rich since a child can earn 10/ a Day, Coll: Johnson has sent Belts of Wampum to the United 5 Nations to collect the stuff for him, and he is the originator of this trade, which makes him very popular; . . .

We hear the Catawbas sent 4. Deputies to confirm the peace proposed last Summer in Albany, in which they were successful and a few [Indians] from here accompanied Them home I enclose a true Copy of Arent Stevens letter to Wᵐ Bull you will be able to gather from it what the Author was trying to say; . . .

I shall lodge this time with brand's Son Thomas

I have nothing more of consequence to tell you I remain with affectionate greetings to your dear Wife and . . . family ever

your

Obedient humble servant

DAN: CLAUS

Brant wished me to write the enclosed P: Sᵗ to you

It would certainly do no harm to write a letter to Coll Johnson, Capᵗ Buttler seems very much pleased to have had your Letter.

Brant's postscript, beginning, "I caress you, my brother!" offered greetings, told something about the family, and mentioned the Catawbas (the peace with whom was more than a nine days' wonder):

Brant to Conrad Weiser [27]

Watkanochrochquania Diatatégo!

Sego Deddenonhe akwego ethioagóa Oni Wagatsanóni gaady Sackeyatgachths Decanachquachse, Soziziowano, akquach z'yoyennere Zikanochtonnio Yochníro nówa Agenigoora, Yowéso Sane Ziyaguéntero Yéteron Akonhechty Yockhiatsteristha yackguax;

Niho S'attóndeck Diatatego Aniyuch Carich wio Wakantarichróna Catawba, Agonochsaguégs

Kadinówese Igéchre;

HANAKARADON

This idyllic picture of Sammy among the Mohawks, roaming the forest in search of ginseng for William Johnson's drug trade with the Orient, did not close Conrad Weiser's eyes to the fact that all was not well with Claus, Sammy, and "Brand their Indian Tutar." [28] There were goings on at the Lower Mohawk Castle that disturbed him.

Conrad Weiser to Richard Peters [29]

[Reading, April 24, 1753]

Sir

yours of the   of this Instant I received from the hands of Mr Read. with the letter of daniel Claus directed to you and also a packet of letters from my Son Samuel and the said Clause, they wrote to me for money,   what they did with what the received of me and out of the proprietary Cassa I do not know, they had about ten pound from me. which I thought was well Enough with a letter of Credit I then gave them, besides what they received of you, I have ordered Samy to Come home and bring me an account Mr Clause may Chuse for himself, either to Stay or Come. . . .

CONRAD WEISER

Weiser's fears were well enough grounded. A few months later Daniel Claus, explaining to Governor Hamilton his reasons for taking up his residence with William Johnson, observed that his Indian landlord, Brant, had "ruined himself by marriage, & was forced to leave his place & move 20 miles higher . . ." [30]

Conrad paid a visit to the Mohawks country that summer, and visited Brant to size things up for himself. Finding him "debauched," [31] he removed Sammy and brought him home.

IV

It was Andrew Montour who put into Richard Peters' head the idea of sending Weiser to Onondaga in 1753. Peters had found himself obliged to rescue the "unintelligible" [32] Andrew from jail by paying out of his own pocket the sum of fifty pounds in discharge of the debt for which

Andrew had been arrested. Andrew, it seems, was going to Onondaga with a commission from Virginia. He had, moreover, lately been "chosen a Member of the Onondaga Council for the Ohio Indians." Under the circumstances it seemed to Peters "dangerous to the Publick to suffer him to be imprisoned." [33]

But it was also dangerous to the public to let him be at large. It was suspected that in his journey to Onondaga he would try to feather his own nest by getting "a Grant of Juniata Lands from the Council." [34] He had for years been trying to worm himself into possession of land "over the hills," fancying himself in the rôle of a great landlord drawing rents from the settlers on his domain.[35] To offset his designs, which were against the best interests of the province, the Secretary proposed that Weiser should go to Onondaga and keep an eye on his activities. Such a journey could easily be explained to the Indians, said the ever-ingenious Peters, as a visit of "pure Affection." [36]

Conrad Weiser had come to have no liking for Andrew, whom he suspected of wishing him to death in order "to have the Management of Indian affairs all to himself." [37] Montour's successes had gone to his painted head. But he was not dangerous. His great pride, Weiser thought, would "soon render him odious to the onontago Counsil." [38]

"I think it is best to give him rope," said Conrad Weiser.

A journey at this time to Onondaga on Andrew's trail would have been a blunder.

I question very much [wrote Weiser] whether my makeing a Journey to onontago . . . would do any good. because then I Could not Sumons a Counsil haveing nothing of public affairs to Lay before them, and my not Sumonsing (or requiring a Counsel to be Sumonsed) would render the onontagers Suspected by the other nations, and myself to the onontagers as a Spie because they know I wont Come without haveing Some thing of Importants to lay before them [39]

It would be better, he suggested, to send one of the Shickellamies. But before this could be attended to a crisis intervened that made Montour's peccadilloes seem unimportant.

While Andrew was at Onondaga, seven French Indians arrived there with a belt of black wampum (the war symbol) six feet long and twelve grains wide, to inform the Six Nations that 250 Frenchmen, to be followed by six thousand more with large numbers of Indians, were descending the Ohio to build a fort at the forks of the Monongahela and drive the English traders out of the Ohio Valley.[40]

Tohashwuchdioony (head chief of the Iroquois and Weiser's theologically inclined host of 1750) was said to have sent back word to Onontio from the Six Nations to the effect that the Ohio lands were theirs and they would keep them; and, as a warning that the Six Nations meant what they said, he declined to accept the belt of black wampum and sent it back to the sender.

Governor Hamilton, on receiving this news, sent for Weiser "to consult what Steps it may be proper for us to take at this Juncture . . ." [41] These were anxious times, and Weiser's services were never more in demand. Indian affairs, wrote Governor Hamilton to Thomas Penn that year, "take up more time, and give more trouble to a Government, than Allmost all other Business put together . . ." [42]

From the Shickellamies, meanwhile, Weiser had heard even more alarming news:

. . . that the Council at onontago had sent two large Belts of Wampum by him [Montour], one to the Governor of pensil[1a] and the other to the Governor of virginia to desire the said Governor to Call home their traders from the waters of Ohio, and not to suffer them to go again on their (the traders) peril.[43]

If this report were true, and if it meant that the Six Nations had taken sides with the French, Pennsylvania's frontier was in extremest danger. But was it true? It was vital to Pennsylvania to find out, and the job was too important to be given to anyone but Conrad Weiser.

Accordingly, on July 28, with fifty pounds from the Receiver General on his person together with a paper of instructions, Conrad Weiser set out for Onondaga.

MEMORANDUM [44]
for Conrad Weiser Esquire
delivered Saturday the twenty eighth Day of July 1753

1. You are to enquire among the Six Nations, whether the Report that We had from Ohio, to wit, that the French were building Forts there was true, and whether They, the French, had Leave from the Six Nations.
2. Whether the Six Nations are in fear of being hurt by the French, if they dont comply with their Desires.
3. Whether it be true, that the Six Nations in earnest require that the English Traders shall be removed from Ohio.
4. And upon the whole, How They, the Six Nations stand at present as to the Chain of Friendship between Them and the English.
5. And to assure them, that the Government of Pennsylvania will do all that can be in Reason expected, as to furnish Cloathing and so forth, if the French should attack Them, the Six Nations.
6. Whether, in Case the Proceedings of the French be disagreeable to the Six Nations, they intend to oppose them, and in what manner, and whether they expect any Assistance from this Government, and of what Sort?

Not mentioned in these instructions were two other pieces of business that Conrad Weiser had on his mind: [45] first, "the conduct of the Virginian Affairs," namely, the purchase of land on the Monongahela and Youghioghaney, with permission to build a trading post out there; second, the purchase for Pennsylvania of land west of the Susquehanna River.

Weiser and Sammy (the latter having been brought home from the Mohawks to give an account of himself and his expenditures) took "the Stage Boat for Bordentown," [46] and on Wednesday, August 1, reached New York. There Conrad, being ill, rested for a day or two, sending

Sammy to Flushing with a letter for Governor Clinton from Governor Hamilton. Sammy, finding that His Excellency was not at home (he had gone to the Plains), "left the Letter with his Lady" and returned.

The Weisers waited for a response till August 4, and then, not having received any, took a sloop for Albany, which they reached on the 7th. After a day there spent in assisting the New York commissioners at an Indian conference in which the return of some white prisoners held by the French Indians was discussed, they set out "with a Schenectady Waggon for the Mohock's Country."

Meanwhile Governor Clinton had come home to his Lady, and, hearing that Weiser was in New York, had sent him a summons to appear before him and receive instructions. When he learned that Pennsylvania's ambassador had already left for Albany, Clinton ("that Monster of a man") sent a scorching letter after him, instructing him to consult with William Johnson, who was himself going to Onondaga, and to transact no Indian business except "with the Consent and Approbation of that Gentleman, and in his Presence." [47]

It was as well that Weiser did not receive Clinton's letter as he went up country or he would have blistered the trees as he passed. Nothing could have been more insulting to Weiser or more insulting to the province he represented. Fortunately the wagoner who should have delivered the letter put it in his coat pocket and then, as he explained afterward, left his coat at home.[48] The purport of the message, however, reached Weiser soon enough, though its impact was tempered by the soft palm of William Johnson. That gentleman showed him the door out of the province with so charming an air that for the life of him Conrad Weiser could not lose his temper. "the Coll. has been very kind to me," wrote Conrad, "and entertained me and my Son very handsomely during my Stay, and was open and free in all Discourse to me, and would have me to change now and then a Letter with him, and whenever I came to the Mohocks Country to make his House my Home." But the said gentleman made it abundantly clear that he did not want Weiser's company to Onondaga. To avoid stirring up heat between the provinces, Weiser "thought it was best," as he says, "not to proceed any farther at this time but to return." [49]

Before he left the neighborhood, he held a meeting with the Mohawks and learned that it was true that the French had passed Oswego with a large army and "some great Guns," and that they planned to descend the Ohio, building forts as they went, "and so take Possession quite down till they met the French coming from below . . ." [50] His best source of information was Abraham (brother of Hendrick), whom he described as "an old Acquaintance of mine, and is looked upon to be the most sincere Indian of that Nation." [51]

He told me by Way of Discourse [runs Weiser's report] that the Six Nations were afraid of the French, because They the Indians being so divided and the French Alliance among the Indians so strong, that the Six Nations could not prevent the French in their Undertakings. That the English had lost Ground among the Indians in the Time of the last War. That altho the English their Brethren shoud supply them with Ammunition and Cloathing, they could not resist the French without a numerous Body of English Men that would and could fight. That the French were now about taking Possession of Ohio, against the Will of the Six Nations, but they could not resist. That he was well assured, that as soon as the French had Possession of Ohio and built Strong Houses there, they would send their Indian Allies against the Southern Indians in League with the English, to wit, the Catawbas, Cherokees, Cawidas &cᵃ to force them the said Indians to sue for Peace, and to acknowledge Onontio for their Father, and so make himself Master of all the Indians and their Lands.[52]

In all his public career Conrad Weiser received no greater affront than the one Governor Clinton put upon him when their paths crossed for a last time on Conrad's return. He writes:

18th I left Albany, arrived in New York on the twenty third in the Night.

24th Waited on Edward Holland one of the Council to know whether Governor Clinton was expected in Town. He did not know, I went to wait on Mr Kennedy for the same Purpose, who told me that his Excellency was very ill, and he Mr Kennedy would go to Flushing to morrow to see him, and would inform his Excellency of my Return from the Mohawk's Country, and that he would be back again the same day.

25th I waited on him again in the Evening, but Mr Kennedy told me that all the Horses and Chairs over the River were employed, and that he could get none, which prevented his going to Flushing.

26th Being Sunday.

27th I went to Flushing on Long Island Seventeen Miles from New York to wait on Governor Clinton, he happened to be from home but came in by one o'Clock. I paid him my Compliments at his Door, he called me in and asked me how far I had been, and signified to me that it was a wrong Step in me to proceed to Albany before I had his Directions. I asked Pardon and told him my Reason why I proceeded, his Excellency said it was well, he did not disapprove so much of my Proceeding as of my Son's not staying for an Answer, his Excellency seemed well enough pleased with my Return, and of my not proceeding to Onondago, and was pleased to tell me, that he intended to be in New York next Wednesday, and would then have me to wait on him and take a Letter to Governor Hamilton and so dismissed me, but would have me stay and eat a Bit of Victuals first, and ordered his Attendance accordingly to get it for me and my Companion; after Dinner I left Flushing and arrived in New York the same Evening.

Augt 29th His Excellency arrived in New York in the Evening.

30th By seven o'Clock a Packet of Letters directed to Governor Hamilton was sent to my Lodging, by one of Governor Clinton's Attendance, who told my Landlord (I being gone to take a Walk and to inform myself if Governor Clinton came to Town last night) that his Excellency Governor Clinton wished me a good Journey to Pennsylvania, and desired to mention his Compliments to Governor Hamilton, and deliver that Packet of Letters to him. I being not altogether pleased with this Message, went about nine o'Clock to the Governor's House in the Fort, and one Mr. Askue went up to tell the Governor that I wanted to see him, and take my Leave of him. Mr Askue came down again, and told me that the Governor sent his Compliments to me and wished me a good Journey to Philadelphia, and desired I would mention his Compliments to Governor Hamilton. I left New York the same Day by

Twelve o'Clock and arrived in Philadelphia on the second Day of September by Seven o'clock in the Morning.[53]

The Governor's letter of August 8 had meanwhile left its repose in the wagoner's coat pocket and followed the Weisers back to New York, where it was finally delivered by the hand of the Deputy Postmaster, Mr. Alexander Colden,[54] to Sammy and by him to his father, affording Pennsylvania's snubbed ambassador something to grit his teeth on during the tedious journey back to Philadelphia.

When news of Weiser's rebuff reached England, Thomas Penn went furiously into action. He had interviews and expressed opinions. Clinton he despised. Johnson he knew to be an abler man, but thought him interested solely in perpetuating his own authority. "I . . . desire Conrad will be very much upon his Guard against Coll⁰ Johnson," he wrote to Peters, November 16, 1753; and he added: "I have communicated his [Conrad's] Journal to some of the Ministers and you will have heard before this time what orders are given from hence on these affairs. nothing but the former behaviour of Mʳ Clinton could make one believe he would send his orders for Officers of an independent Government." [55]

The "indecent Repulse," [56] as Peters called it, which Conrad Weiser had received at the hands of Governor Clinton, did not go unanswered. The Crown no less than the colonies desired unity along the Atlantic seaboard in the face of a common enemy. The bungling George Clinton, who had tried to snatch the Six Nations out of Conrad Weiser's hand, was recalled. An opening more suited to his capacities was found for him in the governorship of Chelsea Hospital, the veterans' home on the Thames, built with bricks supplied by the author of *Robinson Crusoe*.

But the removal of incompetents was not enough. London wanted action. New York and Pennsylvania were for the moment crippled, the one with politics and the other with pacifism; but gallant Virginia was ready for a tilt. England encouraged the Ohio Company to be stiff. Accordingly young George Washington was sent into the Ohio Valley to give the French defiance.

Conrad Weiser's journal, though it brought no honors to its author, had given the signal for a clean-up in American colonial affairs.

v

It was the Carlisle conference of 1753 that finally convinced Conrad Weiser that the time had come for action and that Virginia was the colony to undertake it. Since the death of Thomas Lee, Weiser had had little confidence in Virginia's diplomacy, but he had never doubted her spirit.

Scarcely was Weiser returned from the Mohawks country when Governor Hamilton called on him to accompany Isaac Norris (Speaker of the Assembly), Benjamin Franklin, and Richard Peters to Carlisle, where they were to meet a deputation of Ohio Indians on Saturday, September 22. Everything was done in a haste comporting with the urgency of the time.

On Thursday, September 20, the Governor had received his first notification that the Indians were coming—that, in fact, they expected to reach Carlisle the next evening. Hamilton "commissionated" Norris, Franklin, and Peters to proceed immediately across the Susquehanna to meet them.[57]

Weiser at Heidelberg received his instructions on Saturday.[58] On Monday Franklin and the other commissioners arrived at his place. On Tuesday they all set out, with Sammy added to their number, and, making all speed, reached Carlisle on Wednesday.[59] They found the Indians just arrived, in company with George Croghan and Andrew Montour.

The latter, "a dull stupid Creature," as Mr. Peters describes him, "growing jealous of Mr Weiser and his Son, openly quarrelled with him, and we had enough to do to reconcile them." [60] Further amenities of the sort were exchanged between the commissioners and Andrew's brother, Tan Weson, "a perfect French Man," to quote again from Peters, "having resided during the War in Canada—this man had the Imprudence to come to visit Andrew at the time we were in Treaty with the Indians at Carlisle, which Andrew resented so much as to desist further interpreting, but this was at length likewise got over." [61]

The conference was conducted in a bad atmosphere from beginning to end. Fine speeches did not conceal a mutual distrust. The situation was not improved by the fact that the commissioners had arrived empty-handed. Their haste to reach Carlisle had resulted in their outstripping the wagons containing the indispensable adjuncts to a treaty—presents. Since proceedings could not be opened without the due formalities, including condolences for the death of great men (the Wyandots had recently lost all their chiefs), and since it was the judgment of Scaroyady, who had been appealed to on this point, that "the Condolances could not be accepted, unless the Goods intended to cover the Graves, were actually spread on the Ground before them," [62] the conference was delayed for five days awaiting the arrival of the wagons.

Meanwhile the commissioners consulted with Scaroyady and others on the state of the Ohio country. They learned (with the help of Weiser and Montour, who interpreted respectively for the Six Nations and for the Algonquin tribes) that the Ohio Indians had by their Half King or Viceroy, Tanacharison, served notice three times on the French to turn back to the place whence they came—three times, as Scaroyady explained, because "the great Being who lives above, has ordered Us to send Three Messages of Peace before We make War . . ." [63] What had come of the Half King's warning was not yet known.

"Conrad Weiser," runs the report of the commissioners,

to whom it was earnestly recommended . . . to procure all the Information possible from the Indians of his Acquaintance, touching their Condition and Disposition, and the real Designs of the French did likewise acquaint Us, that all Persons at Ohio would have their Eyes on the Reception of those Indians, now at Carlisle, and judge of the Affection of this Province by their Treatment of them; and that as the intended Present was no Secret to those Indians, it was his Opinion, that the Whole should at this time, be distributed;

for if anything can, such a generous Donation must needs attach the Indians entirely to the English.[64]

While they were engaged in these private conferences, word came that the Half King's three notices had been rejected contemptuously, that the French threatened to throw Brothers Onas and Assaryquoah over the hills, and that the Half King, in tears, warned English traders not to pass the Ohio because the French would certainly hurt them.

Amid these gloomy warnings of approaching danger, the conference opened on October 1. The commissioners associated themselves with the Six Nations in wiping the tears from the eyes of those whose chiefs had lately died, and in wrapping (figuratively) the bones of the deceased in a number of real Philadelphia blankets. The chain of friendship with the Twightwees was renewed; the old fire was rekindled and fresh fuel was put on.

These preliminaries occupied the first day of conference. The second was devoted to the formal distribution of presents. On the third Scaroyady spoke, requesting the better regulation of the fur trade on the Ohio: the concentration of the traders in a few places only, so that the Indians could protect them; and the restriction of the rum trade. "The Rum ruins Us," he said. ". . . We desire it may be forbidden." [65] Various asseverations were made of the unity of all peoples represented at the conference. Scaroyady spoke on behalf of the Shawnees (some of whom, it will be remembered, under Peter Chartier's leadership had formerly gone over to the French), recommending them to the English "as a People who have seen their Error, and are their and our very good Friends."

The Twightwees, calling themselves "an unhappy People" because some Englishmen had been killed or captured in their town when the French attacked them, appealed to Brother Onas to continue to look on them as brethren.

"Brother Onas," said their speaker:

Hearken to what I have to say to the Six Nations, Delawares, Shawonese, and English.
The French have struck us; but though We have been hurt, it is but on one Side; the other Side is safe. Our Arm on that Side is entire; and with it We laid hold on our Pipe, and have brought it along with Us, to shew You it as good as ever: and We shall leave it with You that it may be always ready for Us and our Brethren to smoke in when We meet together.[66]

The speaker delivered a calumet decorated with feathers, and continued.

Brother Onas, We have a single Heart. We have but one Heart. Our Heart is green, and good, and sound: This Shell painted Green on its hollow Side, is a Resemblance of it.
The Country beyond Us, towards the Setting of the Sun, where the French live, is all in Darkness; We can see no Light there: But towards Sun-rising, where the English live, We see Light; and that is the Way We turn our Faces. Consider Us your fast Friends, and good Brethren.[67]

There came a message, confirmed with four strings of wampum, black and white, from the wife of the great Twightwee chief (of the Piankashaw tribe), called Old Briton by the English and La Demoiselle by the French. Old Briton had been killed at Pickawillany by the French Indians, who had thereupon boiled and eaten his body within sight of his own people. The message was addressed to the Shawnees, Delaware, Six Nations, and English.

Remember, Brethren, that my Husband took a fast Hold of the Chain of Friendship subsisting between your Nations: Therefore I now deliver up his Child into your Care and Protection, and desire You would take Care of him; and remember the Alliance his Father was in with You, and not forget his Friendship, but continue kind to his Child.[68]

Then Scaroyady, representing the Six Nations in the Ohio country, stood up and said:

Brother Onas, The Shawonese and Delawares delivered this Speech to the Six Nations, and desired they would deliver it to the English, and now I deliver it on their Behalf.

Brethren, We acquaint You, that as the Wife of the Piankasha King delivered his Child to all the Nations, to be taken Care of, they desire that those Nations may be interceded with, to take care that the said Child may be placed in his Father's Seat, when he comes to be a man, to rule their People. And the Six Nations now, in behalf of the whole, request that this Petition may not be forgot by the English, but that they would see the Request fulfilled.[69]

In response, the commissioners sent "two Strouds to the Young King as an acknowledgment of our Affectionate Remembrance of his Father's Love to Us and of our good will to him." And to the late king's wife they sent two handkerchiefs to wipe the tears from her eyes.

Despite these assurances of friendship and unity, when the conference ended (in haste, owing to the gravity of the news from the West) the commissioners came away with a feeling of foreboding. ". . . it appears to me that the Ohio Indians are a debauched People," wrote Peters to Penn, November 6, "and several of them will go over to the French notwithstanding their warm Professions . . ."[70]

Who could blame them? The French were attacking Pennsylvania's Indian allies in the west, yet Pennsylvania offered them no military support. The principal commodity with which the Quaker province supplied her forest friends was rum—and this in such quantities that the Indians were become "dissolute, enfeebled and indolent when Sober, and untractable and mischievous in their Liquor, always quarreling, and often murdering one another." And, added the commissioners,

the Traders . . . by their own Intemperance, unfair Dealings, and Irregularities, will, it is to be feared, entirely estrange the Affections of the Indians from the English; deprive them of their natural Strength and Activity, and oblige them either to abandon their Country or submit to any Terms, be they ever so unreasonable, from the French.[71]

Weiser had had unusual opportunities to probe behind the rhetoric into the real mind of the Indians, for his Mohawk brother, Jonathan Cayenquiloquoa, was there. Jonathan, though Weiser at this time in a special report to the governor listed him as pro-French,[72] was nevertheless loyal to Tarachiawagon and was later to do the English great service.

Weiser learned that the Ohio Indians thought pacifist Pennsylvania, though she might be generous enough with handkerchiefs and Philadelphia blankets, was letting them down in an emergency that called for men, guns, and powder.

During the weeks following the conference, Weiser turned things over in his mind, corresponded with the authorities in Philadelphia, sent his sons Frederick and Sammy to Shamokin, and at length, blazing with an anger that could find no outlet through the medium of action in his own province, and that was not allayed by "the bad Cold and Cough"[73] from which he was suffering, sent a letter to Virginia (probably to Col. Taylor, "a principal member of the ohio Company,"[74] though the scribbled fragments that have come down to us in Weiser's hand are without address, date, or signature), proposing a course of action.

Conrad Weiser to Colonel Taylor[75]

Kind Sir
. . . We have had a visit from the ohio Indians last october they Sent very Boldly to our Governor to Come and meet them at Carlile in Cumberland County. . . . We have ben told a great many lies by the Said Indians they were Supported by Andrew Montour and Some of our traders . . . In Short we have ben imposed upon, by the said Indians and our own people. they Cost this Government about a tousand pounds and after all they forwarned our people to Come away from the other Side the Allegeeny hills, Charged you Commissioners that they gave occasion in the 1752 by asking leave of the ohio Indian to Build a ford on ohio. for the french to Come & take possion of the land. I was very angry and told the Indians in the presence of And Montour and others that If the Virginians asked Such leave of the ohio Indians. It was a weakness in them for that the Govern^t of Virginia had bought all the land in their Charter at treaty of lancaster from the Chiefes of the Six Nation and for that reason had no had to ask leave of the Indian on ohio to Build forts on their own land. Andrew Montour denied that and Said the Indians never Sold nor released it If they did they were imposed upon by the Interpreter. This he Said in the presence of our Comissioners I told him in plan words that he was an Impudent felow to Say So in Short he wants your govern^t to puy the land from the ohio Indian and yet not Setle it. I am Sorry that ever I recomended him to this and to your Government in the least thing
If the french are Suffered by the English to take and keep possesion of ohio as they now have of Some part to wit about 100 Miles above logs town a place called Win incko. they will be very troublesome neighbours to us. they will get Setler out of Pensil^{la} in great Number for here are a great many of the King of french Subjects out of Elsase lorain &etc a good many of them would never as yet naturalise under the Crown of England and our people Connives at them. If they Should hear that the french King would give them land on

ohio for a litle or nothing and tollerate them in Their Religious persuasion it is my opinion Several hundreds If not tousands would Steal away (which they can very Easely do) and go over to the french to ohio and provide them with Cows and Horses and plowman—to Say nothing of Rogues and villans that would fly from Justice and run over the hills to them. what the french and the ohio and other Indians would be to us in time of Warr I leave to you and other Gentemen to Judge I can not think on Such a time but with Terror. as to their Number the best account that I Could get of them was that they were about 1000 men french and Indians. but the latter allmost all left them and went back again unwilling to assist the french in taking possesion of ohio. I think it highly necessary for this Colonies to raise about 2000 men and take possion of ohio by force Build fords and Speak Boldly to the Indian but with prudence—and If the time of peeace will admit knock every french men on ohio that wont run to the head and If we dont do now we never again shall be So able to it. and our posterity will Condemn us for our neglect.

CHAPTER 41

... *Makes a New Indian Purchase*

I

THERE was one theme that set the hearts of Richard Peters and Conrad Weiser beating in unison: the preposterousness of William Johnson. Peters, who was himself a master of irony, knew how to appreciate Weiser's sarcasm when it was directed, as in the following letter, at Sir Peter Warren's nephew, playboy of the Mohawk Valley, envoy extraordinary to the Onondaga Council.

Conrad Weiser to Richard Peters [1]

Heidelberg in the County of Bercks
January the 28 1754

Sir

I was favoured with yours of the 14 of this Instant with a packet of M[r] levers, and a Copy of Col[l] Johnson Treaty at onontago last September, of which you require my remarks and you also desired me to deal Candidly and fully with it, I have read it twice over and am Surprized that nothing was Said to the Indians of the true occasion of Coll: Johnsons going up to onontago, when as you know, Heinry the Mohock Chief Came to new-york last Sumer with Some other Indians and in a maner proclaimed Warr or at least alarmed Governor Clinton, his Counsel and Assembly, to Such degree that allmost every Body was afeared of an Indian Warr, and Coll: Johnson received his Majestys Comission to repair forwith to onontago and Setle every thing &c. It looks very Strenge to me that when the Coll: Came to onontago he dreshed the old Straw over again [condoling for the death of Canasatego, three years in his grave], and did nothing else—but (as he thought) adding two nation of Indians to the Six nation in order to make them more formidable, the Tedarighroano are the Tutulows that left Shomockin about two years ago, and went up the river towards CayiuKqus, they are but a few familys not ten I am assure, and as good for nothing people as any among the Indians, they left upon the river of SusqueHana many years and the Six nations minds them no more than the English do the nigers, the Shaniadara-dighroanos are our NontiKooks that Came from Maryland Some years ago, and Setled on the mouth of Joniady, and from there went higher up the river SusqueHana and no doubt the Indians of the Six nation had recomended them as two powerful nations that Came from the South in order to get larger presents from the English, I am tired all ready of making remarks you are able to Judge your Self, the whole puts me in mind of what I have read about the Election time in franckfurt on the Mayn in Germ[y] when Carl Albrecht Bavarus was Choosen Emperor of Germany when Marshal Beleisle was stiled by one of Bavarian Ministers "Seine Exellenz Herr Carl ludwig august fouquet. Graff von Belleisle. Marshall von franck reich, Ritter der orden des Konigs Governator der Stadt and Citadelle Metz, der länder Messin und verdun, ObristerComendant der dreyen Bisthumer Metz Toul & Verdun, der provints de la Sarra auf den gräntzen von luxemburg, von der Herrshaft

Sedan, Monzon, Mezieres, Karen, Charleville auf den grantzen von Champagne, Comendant der Koniglichen Truppen in lothringen, und auserordentlicher abgesandter von Seiner Allerchristlichen Majestäte in Teutshland." after the Bavarian Minister had don with this title which made him Sweat, he had but Just time left to get drunk and go home, and what Could Coll: Johnson do more, he was Satisfied before he went that the Six Nations knew nothing of all the above mentioned alarm and that for that purpose no embassy need to have ben Sent to onontago, and Something he Must Say and what Could he have said better, If what he said to the Indians did no good, it did no harm,—

Indian Affairs are what I Shall not trouble my head any longer after I had the Satisfaction to make another Stout purchase of the Indians for the Honourable the Proprietors, there is now so many Cooks in that Kitchen that the brothe is allready Spoiled . . .

Sir

Your Most obedient
CONRAD WEISER

He was right about the broth. By 1754 Pennsylvania's Indian relations were all in confusion. The clear pattern that James Logan, Shickellamy, and Conrad Weiser had traced and that Thomas Lee had approved, was now all splotched with blood and bile: the death of Logan, Shickellamy, and Lee, the jealousy of New York, the break-up of the Six Nations politically and morally, war, intrigue, rum, French missionaries, Clinton, Johnson, Lydius, Croghan, Montour, settlers on the Juniata, boundary disputes with Maryland and Virginia, Le Gardeur de St. Pierre on the Ohio, Connecticut's grab at the Wyoming Valley. Everything was crisscross and Weiser was frankly at a loss. "I am perplects with Indian affairs," he wrote, "and Can not say such or such is best." [2]

But through all the murk about him he saw two things clearly: first, a western purchase must be made for Pennsylvania; and, second, the Connecticut purchase of the Wyoming Valley must be blocked.

The western purchase was something he had long been angling for, not only because of the enrichment it would bring to the province, but also because of the good effect it would have on Indian relations. The encroachment of white settlers on Indian territory was something that could not be stopped; but it could be legalized by purchasing the land. This was the only way left to allay Indian resentment against the white squatters.

Weiser would have pressed such a purchase at Onondaga in 1750 if the time had been propitious. He would have proposed it again in 1753 if Johnson had not blocked his way. Now the pressure of the French on the Ohio had increased tenfold the need of a purchase—as a war measure if nothing else. In defending her western lands, it was not enough for Pennsylvania to say that the Six Nations had promised not to sell them to anyone but Brother Onas. It was necessary to say that the Indians had actually sold them to him.

There was trouble stirring in the Wyoming Valley (in the neighborhood of the present Wilkes-Barre). The new Susquehanna Company claimed to have bought these lands from the Mohawks, and to have authority from the governor of Connecticut to settle them as being within the bounds of the Connecticut charter, which was older than the Pennsylvania charter. The government in Philadelphia resented this as an infringement on the rights of the proprietaries of Pennsylvania.

Richard Peters (who was, to borrow some phrases from Rudyard Kipling, an astute fish, but a creature whose infinite resource was not matched by commensurate sagacity) proposed to Conrad Weiser that he should "get some Peaceable Persons to live on Weyomink, to take Possession in the Name of the Proprietors of Pensilvania." [3] Weiser, accordingly, invited the Moravians to undertake the venture of thus forestalling Connecticut; but he was not at all easy about this business that Peters was pushing him into—a business "so extraordinarily important that it is better to be attended to by word of mouth than put down in writing," [4] as Weiser wrote dubiously to Bethlehem.

Having made the proposal to the Brethren, Weiser was content to let the matter ride. He knew that more was involved in the Wyoming affair than the boundaries of Pennsylvania. He knew that if the Wyoming Valley were sold for settlement—the valley to which the Six Nations had removed the Forks Delawares in 1742 with the assurance that the land should be held inviolate for them for ever—there would be an Indian war. This would be bad enough in itself. Linked with a French war it might be fatal.

It was suspected that William Johnson was secretly working on behalf of the Susquehanna Company. It was known for a certainty that John Henry Lydius was. The government in Philadelphia kept in close touch with Conrad Weiser to concert means of obstructing the deal. Thinking Weiser's authority in Indian affairs might have weight in high places, they proposed sending him, accompanied by the Surveyor General, William Parsons, with a personal appeal to the governor of Connecticut.

To this last proposal, however, Weiser was averse. "I can not see," he wrote, "what good I Could do with the Governor of Connecticut that Could not as well be done by letters from this government but as I dont understand State affairs, I will obey the Governors orders, and go with Mr Parsons If required." [5]

Weiser's advice was taken, and Governor Hamilton contented himself with writing a letter to Governor Wolcott of Connecticut, in which he stated the case both for the Proprietors and for the Indians. The keen knowledge of Indian affairs disclosed by the letter, and the intimate detail used to show the unwisdom of setting up a "Difference between the Mohocks and the Rest of the Six Nations, between whom there is an Agreement that the Mohocks shall have nothing to do with the Lands in Pennsylvania, nor take any Part of the Presents received for them," [6] shows that Governor Hamilton had consulted with Conrad Weiser before the letter was drafted.

In order to put the Six Nations on their guard against the agents of Connecticut, Governor Hamilton proposed that Conrad Weiser should go to Onondaga—by the Susquehanna route so as to avoid New York and William Johnson. A letter to this effect (delivered by the hand of Andrew Montour) provoked a spirited reply.

"Sir," wrote Weiser to Peters, March 15, 1754,[7]

I am greatly surprized with your Proposal of my making a Journey to Onontago this ensuing Spring Season, pleased to let me tell you at once, that is
impossible for me to perform it, for the following reasons. First, it is impossible
to me to walk a Foot from Shomockin to onontago, 2ᵈ It is also impossible to
get along with a Horse, because for the many Branches of Susquehana River
which are now full of Water, and will continue so till about the middle of
May, and there is neither Boat, Canoe or Ferry, or any Soul living nigh them,
Excepting the Branch Tyiaogon. It is true I travel'd to Onontago a Foot in
the Year 1736 at the Request of Mʳ Thomas Penn. I set out from my House
the 27ᵗʰ Day of February Winter was over then with us, and the Ground dry
and the Rivalets Shallow, but I did not find it so above Shomokin where in
stead of Rain, that fell with us that Winter, there fell Snow and lasted till the
middle of April. I arrived at the head Town of Onontago the 11ᵗʰ of April
following, almost starved by misrys and Famine I suffered, and Andrew
Montour suffered Extramly last year about this time in his Journey to Onontago by Land, and he is a Young Man and in the best of his time, when I am
old and Infirm. I could seek nor Expect nothing from a Journey to Onontago
now than my Grave, or feeding the Wolves and Bears with my Body.

He proposed that the Onondaga journey be postponed till after the
coming Albany conference.

As for the western purchase,

I may perhaps fall in with some greedy fellows for Money, that will undertake
to bring things about to Our wishes. I have very good grounds that C. J.
[Colonel Johnson] is in Our way as to Land Affairs, and has to this Day our
large Belt which we sent to Onontago by Canasatego in the Year 1749, for
obtaining the Lands on Juniata &cᵃ in his House, upon no other Condition than
that the Indians will not or shall not part with any Lands without his consent;
I am confirmed in my notion by what I heard from Andrew . . . everything
lies in such a Confusion, that I am quite Perplexed in my Mind, and do not
know how to act in Indian Affairs any more. they are apostates as to their Old
Natural principal of Honesty, and become Drunkards, Rogues, Thieves and
Liars . . .
    . . . most certain it is that I am tire'd of Business, and things begin to go
against me; but patience for a little while, It won't be long before we will
both be Sumon'd I hope to a better place. rest before labour is nonsense.
pardon my Scribling who am, etc.

Governor Hamilton read that letter and replied to it himself,[8] expressing
agreement with Weiser's estimate of Johnson ("you are perfectly right
in your Opinion Concerning that Gentleman"), and going on to say that
he had heard the Connecticut people planned to ask Johnson's assistance
("and would no doubt pay him handsomely for his Interest") in promoting their purchase of the Wyoming Valley. For this reason, said Hamilton,
he had been obliged to send an express to Johnson with the request that
he keep his hands off.

The upshot of the visit paid by Weiser soon after to the Governor was,
as stated in the minutes of the Council, a decision to send Weiser "to
Shamokin & to the Susquehannah Indians in order to apprize them of the
Intentions of the Connecticut People," [9] and also to get what news he could

of the attitude of the Indians toward France's undeclared war in the Ohio Valley.

Conrad Weiser to Richard Peters [10]

Heidelberg in Bercks Aprill
the 17. 1754 in the morning

Sir

Just as I was ready to mount my horse to proceed on my Journey to Woyomock I have an oppurtunity to write a few lines to you. I arrived from philadelphia but last Tuesday a week and then before I Could get every thing in Readenness Easter day was at hand and Some bad Weather. I hope I Shall make a Satisfactory Journey, no news Stirrs here but what we make our Selves, and so not worth to trouble you with, however 10000 french men are at ohio. with as many tousands of Indians and at least 50 great Canons and pensilvania is gone to the french, and do not know what Else—If weather Continues good as it now is I hope to be at Shomockin the 20th of this Instant or before and presently after my return from Woyomack I will Send an Express to philadelphia. I have nothing to add but am

Sir
your most humble Servant
CONRAD WEISER

He set off with Sammy and Michael Bauer, packer, the latter "Carrying a Horse Load of Provision" which included twenty-five pounds of bacon, twenty pounds of dried beef, fifty pounds of biscuit, and "6 Gallings of Rum @ 5/ Per Galling." [11]

At Shamokin Weiser picked up this news from the west:

. . . that a large Belt of Wampum one End black and the other White was sent by the Shawonese and Delawares on Ohio to Onondago, with the following Speech, by the black Part the Shawonese spoke. "Brethren the United Nations, hear Us; The French your Fathers Hatchet is just over our Heads, and We expect to be struck with it every moment; make haste therefore and come to our assistance as soon as possible, for if You stay till we are killed, You wont live much longer afterwards, but if You come soon, we shall be able to fight and conquer the French our Enemy." The Delawares said by the white Part, "Uncles the United Nations, We expect to be killed by the French your Father, We desire therefore that You will take off our Petticoat, that We may fight for Ourselves, our Wives and Children: in the Condition We are in You know we can do nothing." [12]

On this trip Weiser set in motion the machinery (conforming to an old Indian custom that antedates our congressional lobby) for bringing about the new purchase.

Conrad Weiser to Richard Peters [13]

[Heidelberg, May 2, 1754]

Sir

. . . I arrived at Shomokin (as I have told the Governor) on the twentieth of April, and found of the Shick Calamys only James Logan at home, almost naked, and after my Inquiry where his Brothers were, he told me they had left the Place, and went up to the Creek called Canasoragy, and I presently perceived that they were not in Amity with one another. I told him with some Gravity and Earnestness, that "I came to Shamokin with a Message of Importance from the Governor of Pennsylvania, and the Proprietors, and I was resolved to employ them, the Shick Calamys, in the Service of the Government Jointly, and not at all separately, and if they could agree together and be of one mind, they might now render themselves useful, and get something to relieve them from their Poverty, and make themselves esteemed, but if they would not be of one mind, and not take heed what I now said to him, and had to say when they met, I must lay them aside entirely and not so much as mention their Name again in the Presence of the Governor of Pennsylvania, that I knew where to apply to upon such an Occasion, but their former Promise (to be of one mind and as true and good Friends as their Father was) gave me yet some Hopes that they would be advised by me, and agree together, and be of as much Service as they could." Upon this the lame one, James Logan as he is called, made Answer, and said, that he would send for his Brothers immediately, and desired me that I would say the same to them all, when they should meet, which accordingly I did at their meeting by a String of Wampum, and I hope it had the Effect wished for.

I engaged them in a Journey to the Cayugers or the Oneiders wch they should think best, to try to bring about an Indian Purchase for the whole Province.

With meticulous precision Weiser listed the seven points he had impressed upon the Shickellamies for the furtherance of their embassy.

1.) I told them if they did not now stir, Others would bring it about, and they would then be obliged to sit and kill Lice and Fleas, and repent their Backwardness and Folly. I told them what Col. Johnson had said in New York, to wit, that it was out of the Power of any Body to make Indian Purchases without him, and that he would undertake to get Wyomink for the New England People, and the Rest for himself, and Others of his Friends in New York and Albany.

2.) That the Ohio Indians had offered to sell the Lands to the Proprietaries of Pennsylvania, but the Proprietaries would not accept of it, but perhaps they might if the Six Nations contrary to their Agreement (which I then shewed) should offer to sell to any other People.

3.) That Andrew Montour had already sold some of the Land on Sherman's Creek or Juniata, which the Indians of Ohio gave him, and had settled several Others upon it as his Tenants.

4.) That the Chiefs of the Six Nations had agreed to sell to their Brother Onas, and to no body else, and I gave them the Copy of the Agreement, and read the Names to them. They desired me to let them have it for their use with the Six Nations, which I did, and told them to get Col. Johnson to read it to the Indians as of their own Accord.

5.) That they should promise Kachradodon one hundred Pieces of Spaniards, if he assists and bring about such a Purchase.

6.) That They themselves should be well paid for their Trouble, and each of them, to wit, John and James, that is the two Eldest to have every Year Ten Pounds a Piece as a Pension.

7.) That certain Districts shall be reserved for the Indians where they now live, and not included in the Purchase, and hereafter bought by the Proprietaries, when the Indians want to sell them, otherwise the Indians to live upon them forever. . . .

John Shick Calamy and James Logan are very hearty in the thing, and in great earnest about it; they came down with me to Thomas McKees, where I furnished them with necessaries for their Journey, they will set out by Water in a few Days, with an hired Hand along with them, I left them what Provision I had to spare, they will come back by Albany and be at the Treaty by the 13th or 14th of June precisely. . . .

I am

Sir

Your very humble Servant
CONRAD WEISER

What the quarrel was among the Shickellamies is not known, but some cause of the dissension may be guessed from a letter of Weiser's written earlier in the spring:

Some time ago Shickelimys daughter was down here with her Children and a few more Wimens, for Some provision the man being gone over SusqueHana to hunt and left them Some where this side in the new purchase, without provision, She told me that her Brothers are under Allegeny hills to hunt, and her husban died a while ago with the Small Box, for whom She was in Mourning, also for her Son. and her Sisters Son who have both ben Killed in the Catabaw Country last fall, I told her that it was the hand of the most high that fights now against those that went against the Catabaws after they had made a public and firm peace with them, She Said She had told her Son so before he went, but her Brother John petty the youngest of Shickelimys Sons, prevailed on her Son and Cousin, and took them with him, however he Came back Safe, and is Much perplexed and ashamed because for his folly.[14]

II

There was to be no rest for Weiser this summer. He was still busy with Reading lots (he got a patent for land in town for the Lutherans on May 2,[15] and helped Dr. Busse get a lot [16]). He had court business. He had recently been appointed a trustee of the free schools [17] that were being organized for the benefit of the Germans in the province. But these affairs, as well as those of his farm and family, he had to forsake at the Governor's call to attend the Indian conference at Albany.

Richard Peters to Conrad Weiser [18]

[Philadelphia, May 24, 1754]

Dear Sir

The Commissioners set out on Friday next for New York and desire you will be in Town the Thursday that is the thirtieth day of May, in order to proceed with us for New York.

The Governor orders me to write this to You that he may confer with you before he gives the Commission.

I shall expect to see you here on Thursday the Thirtieth day of this Instant with your Son Sammy.

I am

Sir

your affectionate

humble Servant

RICHARD PETERS

Col[1] Johnson has actually refused to be concerned for Connecticut & has wrote a charming Leter to our Gov[r] on the Subject.

Johnson had a way with him that few persons could resist. Even Weiser could not dislike him *while in his presence*. Thomas Penn, on the other hand, residing at a safe distance, seemed to be immune to Johnson's charm. "Coll[o]. Johnson's behaviour," he wrote to Peters, June 10, 1754, "is that of a Man who expects to be courted, but I expected to find him a Person of a more Gentlemanlike Turn than I conceive from his Letter." [19]

When Weiser received instructions from the Governor to do all in his power to assist the commissioners from Pennsylvania (John Penn, Richard Peters, Isaac Norris, Benjamin Franklin) he accepted, but with a curious proviso which the Governor was constrained to insert in his letter of instructions to the commissioners:

. . . that he may not be made Use of as a principal Interpreter, inasmuch as from a Disuse of the Language He is no longer Master of that Fluency he formerly had, and finding himself at a Loss for proper Terms to express him-self is frequently obliged to make Use of Circumlocution, which would picque his Pride in the View of so considerable an Audience. He says he understands the Language perfectly when he hears it spoken, and will at all Times attend and Use his Endeavours that whatever is said by the Indians be truly inter-preted to the Gentlemen; and in this Respect I really think You may securely rely on his good Sense and Integrity.[20]

Weiser and the commissioners set out from Philadelphia on Monday, June 3, and, traveling by way of Kingston [21] and Brunswick, reached New York on Wednesday afternoon. Crossing the Bay in an hour and a quarter from Staten Island Point, they waited on Governor Delancey at Mr. Watts', and retired at night to a coffee house and tavern. On Thursday Weiser helped the commissioners decide on the list of Indian presents to be bought. The party dined with the Governor at Willet's. On Sunday they boarded a sloop and sailed up the Hudson, reaching Albany on Mon-day the 17th.

No Indians had arrived yet, but on Wednesday John Shickellamy turned up with the Cayuga chief Gachradodow, whom he introduced to Weiser as a man who was "hearty for the Proprietaries" [22] (*Pieces of eight! pieces of eight!*) and who would confer with him about the proposed Indian pur-chase. Next day Gachradodow, visiting Weiser at his lodging, undertook to act as his private counselor "and direct what Measures to take to engage the Indians for a Sale." [23] We learn from Weiser's account of charges, sub-mitted to the Proprietaries, that Gachradodow received the promised hundred pieces of eight (worth forty pounds, New York money). Incidentally, Weiser borrowed "2 pieces" of Mr. Franklin.[24]

Bribery and corruption? Conrad Weiser, when the Quakers hinted at this interpretation of his activities at Albany, defended himself by citing the universality of this way of doing business with the Indians—a way to which the Quakers themselves subscribed by a plentiful distribution of "Silver Ware" at subsequent treaties.

> Whoever is acquainted with the Nature of an Indian [wrote Weiser] knows that they have their Hands and Eyes open, to receive at all Times; be the Thing ever so just, that is required of them, they want some Present before they consent to it; and look upon us that we have enough to give, and that we dig Silver & Gold out of the Mountains as plenty as other Stones, & they stick at nothing, where they can get any Thing.[25]

The main efforts of the commissioners were devoted to placating the Six Nations, whose feelings had been rasped to the limit of endurance by the land sharks of Albany and by His Insolence, Governor Clinton. Hendrick spoke bitterly of the neglect in which the English had left his people. Taking a stick and throwing it behind his back, "You have thus thrown Us behind your Backs," he said, "and disregarded Us, whereas the French are a subtle and Vigilant People, ever using their utmost Endeavours to seduce and bring our People over to them." [26]

Benjamin Franklin, whose plan of union proposed at Albany is a milepost on this country's road to nationhood, has done most to make the conference remembered. But it was Conrad Weiser who made it possible for the conference to achieve its original purpose: the brightening of the covenant chain which bound the Six Nations to the English colonies. Conrad, though ranking only as an interpreter, was the soul of this conference as he had been of the conference at Lancaster ten years before. He interpreted, helped the commissioners draft their speeches, conferred with the Indians (at their request) to smooth out difficulties, made a public speech of his own in rebuttal of Hendrick's attack on Virginia and Pennsylvania, and outmaneuvered the same irascible chief when he tried to block Pennsylvania's western purchase after the other Indians present had shown a disposition to agree to it.[27]

Weiser suspected Lydius and a certain Mr. Woodbridge (who kept an Indian school in New England),[28] both of whom were intimate with Hendrick, to be responsible for the dissensions that arose among the Indians and for the niggardliness of their offer when it came to the disposal of the western lands. They proposed to sell a tract extending no farther than the Allegheny Mountains. The Ohio was not for sale. Weiser said flatly from the commissioners that the offer was not acceptable, and that it looked as if the Six Nations "were under Contract with the French for the Ohio lands." He snubbed Hendrick, expressing astonishment that the opinion of one of the Mohawks (a people who had never had any claim to these lands, since it was not they but the Cayugas and Oneidas who had conquered them from the Susquehannocks) should be seriously considered

on this matter. But with his genius for Indian tact, he asked Hendrick
to deliver the curt answer of the commissioners to the chiefs, thereby serving the double purpose of complimenting Hendrick and of putting him
in his place.

Weiser's management was successful. Hendrick reported the commissioners' displeasure to the Indian council, "and then in a pathetic Speech,"
as Weiser learned,

in which he set forth the constant good Usage of the Province of Pennsylvania,
and their affectionate and generous Usage of the Indians, he advised them to
take the Frowns off from the Brow of their Brethren, and to grant them the
Lands according to the Western Bounds of the Province, which he had enquired of, and was told by the Interpreter extended beyond the Ohio, and
took in the Eastern Part of Lake Erie.[29]

Weiser was then called to the Indian council. They told him they would
not let the commissioners part from them in anger. He and the chiefs together settled the bounds of the purchase.

Accordingly on Saturday, July 6, in a great council held at James
Stephenson's and attended by the representatives of the two races, Hendrick took the frown off Brother Onas' brow, assured the commissioners
that the Six Nations were not in collusion with France, and offered to
sell lands west of the Susquehanna and south of the West Branch "to the
North of the West as far as your Province extends, let it reach beyond the
River Ohio and to Lake Erie wherever it will. . . . make out your Deed,"
he said, "and be not long about it." [30]

The famous deed of 1754 "from the Six Nations to the Proprietaries"
was signed by Hendrick, Abraham his brother, Brant, John Shickellamy,
Tagashata, and a number of other chiefs of the Mohawks, Oneidas, Onondagas, Cayugas, Senecas, and Tuscaroras—representing the Great Council;
and thus, for the sum of four hundred pounds, with another four hundred
to be paid "whenever the Lands over the Apalacian Hills should be settled,"
an Indian empire passed into the hands of Brother Onas, with all the "Rights
Privileges Hereditaments and Appurtenances whatsoever thereunto belonging or in any wise appertaining"—with this *proviso:* "that notwithstanding any Sales of Lands which the Indians now make or hereafter shall
make to the said Proprietaries or their Successors there shall ever subsist
and mutually be preserved between both the said Parties and their Children and Childrens Children to the latest Posterity the same Love Friendship and kind Treatment that hath all along subsisted and does now subsist
between them . . ." [31]

The fact that four years later Pennsylvania considered it the part of
wisdom to give back these lands to the Six Nations, naturally raises the
question in our minds: Had the purchase been a wise measure at the time
of its making? The Quakers answered, No. This hasty bargain (they said),
driven through in the space of a week, frightened the Ohio Indians, who
owned the land by grant from the Senecas (the Quakers still speaking)
but were not even consulted in the purchase—frightened them into the

arms of the French; it antagonized the warriors of the Six Nations, who were opposed to any such purchase; and it was, moreover, illegal, since it had not been made in accordance with the established usage of the Onondaga Council, but had been managed in the bushes instead of in the open. In short, it "ruined our Interest with the *Indians*." So wrote Charles Thomson five years after the event.[32]

"This is a Notorious lie," responded Conrad Weiser when he read Thomson's attack on him and the purchase he had fathered.

The Governor of New York, and Sir William Johnson both knew & approved of it. The People of Credit in Albany assisted, the Deed was signed openly. Mr. Isaac Norris & Mr. Benjᵃ Franklin Commissioners for Pennsᵃ are witnesses to it, with many other Gentlemen. Had the Proprietor of Pennaᵃ not bought that Land, the People of Connecticult would have bought either that or other Land on Susquehannah. Some other Reasons why such a large Purchase was made must still be in the Memory of some Gentlemen not concerned for the Proprietaries of Pennsylvania.[33]

As for the charge that the Six Nations warriors condemned the purchase, Weiser retorted that "A great Number of them were Present, they never complained to us; tho' allways had a free Access." Nickas, the Mohawk, who was present at Albany, told Weiser afterwards that he "was an Entire Stranger to that complaint." [34]

The ohio Indians had no Buisness at that Treaty [continues Weiser], and the Six Nations allways declared them Hunters, and no owners of Land, but in Conjunction with the Six Nations. The Author is much mistaken that it was only a Weeks Work to make & Confirm the Purchase, the Thing was moved to the Six Nations in their Counsel at Onontago, some years ago, with a large Belt of Wampum. The Chiefs consulted Sir William Johnson about it, and if he had not then approved of the Thing, they would not have executed the Deed. . . .[35]

The Author tells another Lye; in saying that the Shawanose were deprived of their Hunting Ground, on Juniata by that Purchase.

The Shawanose and Delawares, were then gone to Ohio, and not one Family of either of them lived there when the Purchase was made, and neither of these Nations, had any Right to the Land, but had it only as their Hunting Ground upon Sufferings of the Six Nations. and left it contrary to the Advice of the Six Nations & went to Ohio, and would not return on the repeated Request of the Six Nations; These Latter sold it the rather.[36]

To the charge that the purchase had been made without the sanction of the Onondaga Council, Weiser replied bluntly:

It is a notorious Lye, that the Person known to have a considerable Influence among the Indians [i.e., Conrad Weiser himself], made the Indians Sign a Release contrary to the Established Costum, and Usage of the Six Nations; I say the Author of the Pamphlet is a Scoundrel & an Ignorant fellow in Indian Affairs.[37]

III

Weiser's success at the Albany treaty seemed to be complete. He had brought about the western purchase for Pennsylvania, and he had apparently saved the Wyoming Valley from Connecticut. Mr. Woodbridge and other agents of Connecticut, being shown the treaty of 1736 in which the Six Nations had promised to sell no lands *except to the Proprietors* within the limits of the royal grant to Pennsylvania, agreed to drop the Connecticut project.

But, as the conference broke up and the Indians dispersed, John Henry Lydius, French agent (as Weiser and the commissioners were convinced), played the sharpest trick of his career. He got Hendrick and a few other chiefs into his house, made them drunk, and caused them to put their marks to the Wyoming deed—the vilest of all the land frauds practised on the Indians and one in retribution for which blood flowed for a generation.

"That man sitting there is a Devil," said an Oneida sachem some time afterwards, pointing to Col. Lydius during a conference at Mount Johnson, "and has stole our lands, he takes the Indians slyly by the Blanket one at a time, and when they are drunk, puts some money in their Bosoms, and persuades them to sign deeds for our lands upon the Susquehanna which we will not ratify nor suffer to be settled by any man." [38]

Lydius worked hard with the deed, trying to make the signatures appear as fully representative of the Six Nations as he could. Some Indians he got to sign at the break-up of the conference. Others he invited down from the Indian country afterwards to visit him at Albany. He took a ride up the Mohawk Valley, and at the Lower and Upper Castles he got more signatures.[39] The news leaked out to Johnson, who told it to Claus, who passed it on to Governor Hamilton.

What was to be done? Weiser was appealed to by the government in Philadelphia. Lydius had worked secretly, and no one seemed to know exactly how much harm had been done. Weiser advised sending at once for Hendrick. He if anyone would know who had had a hand in the business. Were the signatures sufficient to give an appearance of authority from the Onondaga Council, which alone had the right to dispose of Indian lands? The province must act with speed and, for the moment, in silence. Daniel Claus might bring Hendrick down by way of the Schoharie-Catskill trail, avoiding Albany. Claus knew this trail, having come that way with Weiser in 1750.

If he Henrick [wrote Weiser] refuses to Come he might be Suspected to have a hand in it, and we Must then act by the Shickelimys & Jonathan and as Secretly as possible otherways lydias & that Wicked priest at Canohackquagy [the Reverend Gideon Hawley, a Presbyterian missionary from Connecticut, working among the Six Nations Indians on the upper Susquehanna] will defeat our designs I would in the mean time advise to have Belts of Wampum provided and two or three large Belts all Blake. you will want a Couple to Send to the South before long, and one must be made use of to demolish lydias^s proceedings I had a touch of the Gravel so that I Could not venture so farr otherways I would have Come to philadelphia on this occassion.[40]

Conrad Weiser to Richard Peters [41]

[Heidelberg, October 27, 1754]

Sir

Yours of the 21 of this Instant by peter Spicker is Come to hand but last night, because the great Rain that fell last week prevented the bearers Coming up Sooner.

I am at a lost what to writ to Heinry the mohock Chief either in the Governors yours or my Name, you dont want a dictator However (As to the Connecticut Affair, I am Clear of opinion that by order of the Governor You Should write to him Hendrick, puting him in mind of his promise made to the Comissioners of this province in Albany when he said that he would Come down to us upon any occassion to advise with the Governor *as in the presence of the most high* this last may be left out, and that the Governor wants to see him now to Consult with him in this Critical time about matters of moment & c.) there you have my opinion whether you wanted or not. as to daniel Claus I prescribed the road (that they are to take) in my last, (and for him to Keep every thing relating to this affair as a Secret and to Search very diligently whether Heinry had no hand in Signing the deed to the Conecticut people. If he has not we will Succeed without doubt. he must have the liberty to bring one more Indian with him.

If all wont do that Heinry would not Come, we must send to Onontago next Spring &ec. I should be Sorry If the Conect^t people Should Countenance the deed that lydias So feloniously got. If they do and Setle upon the land there will Certainly be blood Shet, for the Indians allways Said they Would never Suffer any white people to Setle Woyamock or higher up, and If an Indian or french warr Should break out the Consequence of the Conecticut people Setling there, would be bad on the English side, because the Indian would then be oblidge to move away, and to where Can they move too. only to Ohio and there they would be under the Influence of the french and in their Interest, as the Sinickers and Onontagers now are, and perhaps the rest of the Six Nation dont think themselve Safe without Creeping under the wings of their father Onontio). . . .

CONRAD WEISER

Richard Peters had a consultation about Weiser's letter with Governor Hamilton and William Allen, the Chief Justice. It seemed to them that Colonel Johnson "should have the Conduct of this Affair." Otherwise, when news reached him of what was going on (as it certainly would, since Hendrick would go to him for advice), he might take offense and block the whole scheme. Johnson, they assured themselves, would "be very hearty & bring everything we ask to bear." [42]

In a measure, as it turned out, they were right. Colonel Johnson spoke heartily enough against the Connecticut purchase. "Inside the court room," writes his biographer, Arthur Pound, "Colonel Johnson might report sagely on a just Indian jolicy; but outside, his former agent, Col. Lydius, guilefully swung the infamous purchase of the Wyoming Valley for the Connecticut company." [43]

Johnson was to earn a reputation for integrity before he died, but there were no signs of dissolution upon him yet.

The sale had no validity in Indian law, since it was not made openly by the Onondaga Council or its instructed representatives. The Connecticut people, nevertheless, took possession, and the protests of Pennsylvania were allowed to be lost in the complexities of intercolonial law. In the end the deed proved valid enough to bring on the Delaware War, to cause war between Pennsylvania and Connecticut, and to precipitate the Massacre of Wyoming in 1778.

John Henry Lydius lived to a great age and died in his bed.

CHAPTER 42

... *Makes the Best of Fort Necessity*

THE commissioners at Albany prepared a Representation to be submitted to His Majesty's government in England. One section of it belongs to our story:

That it is the evident Design of the French to surround the British Colonies, to fortify themselves on the Back thereof, to take and keep Possession of the Heads of all the important Rivers, to draw over the Indians to their Interest, and with the Help of such Indians, added to such Forces as are already arrived and may be hereafter sent from Europe, to be in a Capacity of making a general Attack upon the several Governments. And if at the same Time a strong Naval Force be sent from France, there is the utmost Danger that the whole Continent will be subjected to that Crown.[1]

The commissioners did not know, while they were considering the Representation "Paragraph by Paragraph"[2] on Tuesday, July 9, that on the preceding Wednesday, at eight o'clock in the evening, Major George Washington had signed articles of capitulation at Fort Necessity.

This was the end of Virginia's first attempt to "knock the French on the head." George Washington, it will be remembered, had been sent by Governor Dinwiddie in the fall of 1753 to summon the French to leave the Ohio Valley. Accompanied by a party of woodsmen and Conrad Weiser's old acquaintance, Tanacharison, the Half King, Washington had pushed through the snow to Fort Le Boeuf, where he confronted Le Gardeur de St. Pierre with the summons. The elderly commander received his young antagonist with all the distinction an old-world courtesy could achieve in this log fort set on a river bank in the midst of a frozen forest. But to Virginia's summons, he replied that he thought himself "not obliged to obey it,"[3] since he held command under other authority. He assured his guest, however, that he would send Dinwiddie's letter to the Marquis Duquesne and await his instructions.

When Washington returned to Virginia, the Old Dominion resolved to match fort with fort, and sent a small detachment of the Virginia regiment to construct defenses at the Forks of the Ohio. But they were too late. St. Pierre had sent north the promised communication, and the reply was swift and decisive. As soon as the spring break-up freed the rivers of ice, a French force of nearly a thousand men, with cannon, came down to the Forks, dislodged the Virginians who were just getting to work on the erection of a fort there, and proceeded to put up their own more formidable Fort Duquesne to checkmate the English in the Ohio Valley. George Washington brought his detachment buzzing round the French force like a swarm of bees around a bear. The Virginians would have done well to keep on buzzing, but they settled down behind earthworks on the Great Meadows (George Croghan had let them down in the matter of transport and supply), and the bear lifted its paw at Fort Necessity.

Washington's defeat was a small enough matter if one considers only the number of troops engaged; actually it was a colossal disaster. It showed the Ohio Indians, as Thomas McKee said, that the English were a weak reed to hold to.[4] "The Unlucky defeat of our Troops Commanded by Major Washington," wrote William Johnson, July 29, "gave me the utmost Concern. . . . this will not only animate the French, & their Indians, but stagger the resolution of those inclined to Us, if not effectually draw them from our Interest. . . . I wish Washington had acted with prudence & circumspection requisite in an officer of his Rank . . . he should rather have avoided an Engagement until our Troops were all Assembled." [5]

What made it doubly serious was that Washington's inexperience with the Indians and their "Phantastical" ways (the word is Weiser's), and his unwillingness to take advice from grizzled warriors like Tanacharison and Scaroyady, had alienated his brown allies. Not an Indian was with him at the final engagement. If Pennsylvania and Virginia had lost their protective screen of friendly Indians, anything might happen. "You may expect to hear of nothing but continual Murders committed by the French Indians who may be immediately expected down upon the back Inhabitants," wrote William Trent, who had been at the Great Meadows with Washington; "the French sent me word they intended to come & see me soon they make no doubt of being Masters of all America." [6]

Wild rumors were circulating. Captain Robert Stobo, taken to Fort Duquesne as a hostage after Washington's capitulation, managed to smuggle out two letters, one of which was carried by Delaware George and the other by Moses, the Song (brother of Conrad Weiser and brother-in-law of Scaroyady).[7] This is the same dashing Stobo who, escaping from Quebec, whither he had been taken from Fort Duquesne, gave the English a sketch of the town and its environs, and suggested to Wolfe the landing at the Cove and the scaling of the heights to the Plains of Abraham. The Song brought from Stobo a rumor that the Half King and Scaroyady had both been killed, and that their wives and children had been distributed among the Catawbas and Cherokees. If the rumor were true, wrote Stobo, there would be no further dependence on the Ohio Indians. "The Shawonese, Picts, and Delawares" had been having a conference. What they had decided, he did not know; but certainly "a Present well-timed now" would be of great service to the English cause.[8]

Both letters came eventually to George Croghan at Aughwick (now Shirleysburg), where he had a trading post. With Delaware George's letter, which arrived first (and which Croghan opened, sending on a copy to Governor Hamilton; somehow the French learned of Stobo's writing and punished him) Croghan sent a message of his own to Philadelphia, informing the Governor that the Half King, Scaroyady, and many other Indians had fled with their wives and families to Aughwick.

The Half King [he wrote] has sent Three Men off for Shingass and the Delawares and the Shawonese to bring them here in ten Days, and has ordered me

to write to your Honour to meet or send one to meet them here in Ten
Days; . . . it is my Opinion this Meeting will determine the Ohio Indians
either in Favour of the English or the French.[9]

Events moved rapidly. Croghan's letter, written August 16, reached
Philadelphia on the 20th. The Governor laid it before the Council, which
took action at once: Weiser must go to Aughwick for the Indian conference. As it happened, Weiser was in town attending a meeting of the
trustees of the German Free Schools.[10] He received his instructions on
Saturday the 24th, and set off the same evening with three hundred pounds
of government money in his possession and authority to spend it as he
thought best for the service of his province. A messenger was sent ahead
to announce his approach—"which," said Croghan when he heard of it,
"was a very agreable piece of news to the Indians in general." [11]
But the letter from Governor Hamilton to George Croghan containing
that agreeable piece of news contained also a paragraph that was ominous,
showing as it did the rift between the Governor and his Assembly, a rift
that was to paralyze Pennsylvania for a long time to come:

That the Indians may not be discouraged, or imagine Us wanting in a just
Sense of their and our Danger, or in an hearty Disposition to oppose and repel
the French, Mr Weiser has my Instructions to acquaint them, that notwithstanding the present Appearances of great Backwardness in our Inhabitants,
yet it is entirely owing to an unfortunate Disagreement between me and the
Assembly about the Mode of raising the Money—But as the time fixed by me
for my Administration draws to a Period, and a new Governor is hourly
expected to arrive, We entertain good hopes that this Difference will no longer
continue, but give Way to a perfect Harmony, and that fitting Supplies will
be immediately raised, and this Province concur with Virginia in vigorous
Efforts to repel the common Invader.[12]

Journal of the Proceedings of Conrad Weiser in his
way to and at Auchwick by order of His Honour Governor
Hamilton, in the Year 1754. in August and September.[13]

On the 24th of August, I Received the Governors Instructions left Philadelphia that Evening, the wheather being exessive hot I arrived at my House
in Heidleberg on the 27th and Rested the 28th the wheather being Altered I sot
out for Auchwick
  the 29th of August left my House and Arrived at James Galbrechts that Day.
  30th Arrived early in the Morning at John Harris's Ferry and heard that the
Half King had been arrived on the River about 4 days ago, and was now down
the River at one Tafes House, I sent my Son down to him with a String of
Wampum, to invite him to come up to me, and Accordingly he came within
a few Hours, and after some friendly discourses, he agreed to set out with me
next Morning to Auchwick he being a little in Liquor, some Gentleman
from Philadelphia met him at the said Tafe's and were glad to see him, and
gave him Plentifull of Drink—
  31st The Half-King according to appointment came early in the morning to
see me, and told me what he knew of the last engagement of Major Washington and the French near Menongehela, and before we had our breakfeast some

Indians hollowed over the River, and soon after we saw it was Andrew Montour, Nicklas Quibeck, and others, and by their comeing I was Obliged to stay till after Dinner in order to talk over Measures about my Message, they, the last mentioned informed me that a great Meeting is appointed at Auchwick, wherein the Indians from Ohio and those on the River of Susquehannah would be present, and that the meeting would be about the 4ᵗʰ of September next, I desired Andrew Montour to Accompany me to Auchwick, so did the Half King towards the Evening we sot off and got but to Tobias Hendricks

Septʳ 1ˢᵗ I thought best to alter my Rout and not go along the Great Road for some Particular Reasons, took therefore the Road to George Croghan's Cape, and Sheremans Creek, and arrived that Day at Andrew Montours, accompanied by himself, the Half King, and another Indian, & my Son, I found at Andrew Montours, about 15 Indians, men women, and Children, and more had been there but were now gone, Andrew's Wife had killed a Sheep for them some days ago, she complained that the had done great Damage to the Indian-Corn, which was now fit to Roast, and I found that there were most every Day Indians of those that came from Ohio with some Errand or another which always wanted some Victuals in the Bargain, I gave him Ten Pounds of the Governments Money.—

the 2ᵈ We sot out from Andrew Montours without any Provision because he told me we would be at Auchwick before Night, we rid 6 Hours before noon and 3 Hours after, took up Lodging in the Woods

the 3ᵈ We sot out by 6 o'Clock, and by 8 we came to the Trough Spring, by 9 to the Shadow of Death by 11 to the Black Logg, and by 12 Arrived at Auchwick. the Indians fired off many Guns to make me welcome, according to their Custom. By the Way, Thanachrishon otherwise called the Half King, complained very much of the Behaviour of Coll. Washington to him (though in a very Moderate way Saying the Coll. was a good-natured man but had no Experience) saying that he took upon him to Command the Indians as his Slaves, and would have them every Day upon the out-Scout, and Attack the Enemy by themselves, and that he would by no Means take advise from the Indians, that he lay at one Place from full moon to the other and make no Fortifications at all, but that little thing upon the Meadow, where he thought the French would come up to him in open Field. that had he taken the Half Kings advise, and make such Fortifications as the Half King had advis'd him to make, he would Certainly have beat the French off, that the French had acted as great Cowards and the English as Fools in that Engagement, that he (the Half King) had carryed off his Wife and Children, so did the other Indians, before the Battle begun, because Coll. Washington would never listen to them, but always driving them on to fight by his Directions.

When Weiser arrived at Aughwick, the Indians came to his house and presented him with a string of wampum to wash the sweat from his face and the dust from his eyes. What his eyes saw, thus cleansed, was interesting enough. There were two hundred Indians at Aughwick: Six Nations, Delawares, Shawnees. Among the Six Nations, besides the Half King there were Scaroyady, Seneca George, and Moses Contjochqua, the Song. Chief among the Delawares was the Beaver (brother of Shingas). Catousima was there, grandson of Weiser's old friend Chief Kakowatchiky of the Shawnees.

More than twenty Indian cabins had been set up near Croghan's house, and others were scattered about the neighborhood for a distance of two or three miles. Croghan had fed the refugees. He had twenty-five or thirty acres of the best Indian corn Weiser had ever seen, but the corn was fast disappearing and so were his squashes and pumpkins. Besides, Croghan had been supplying the crowd with butter and milk. Weiser made all right with him, and commissioned him further to buy for the Indians five hundred bushels of wheat. Among other expenditures, Weiser paid for messengers, wampum, powder and lead for the hunt, flour for the family of Kissakoch- quilla deceased, and provisions and a brass kettle for the Half King's family. He sent a dollar to his brother "Jonathan Cayenquiliquo," through Jonathan's daughter. Jonathan, who had fled from the Ohio and was now living on the Big Island on the West Branch of the Susquehanna, turned up with some five of his friends a few days after Weiser's arrival. They were all destitute and did not even have the necessaries for hunting. Weiser gave them twenty-five pounds of powder, twenty-four pounds of lead, a dozen knives, thirty yards of linen, and a "side of leather."

A war refugee camp is never lovely. Sickness had got among the Indians, "the Bloody Flux." There was also a flux of liquor.

Lewis Montour [wrote Weiser to the Governor], Andrew's brother, disturbs them often by bringing strong Liquor to them, they cannot help buying and drinking it when it is so near, and Lewis sells it very dear to them, and pre- tends that his Wife which is an ugly Indian Squa, does it he sends Indians to the Inhabitants to fetch it for him, and Mr Croghan can by no means pre- vent it because they keep it in the Woods about or within a mile from his House, and there the Indians will go (after having Notice) and drink their Cloathing and so come back to George Croghan's drunk and naked. It is a surprizing thing that no means can be found to prevent the Inhabitants in Cumberland County from selling strong Liquor to the Indians, I am credibly informed, that some of the Magistrates of that County sells the most. Mr Smith was at Aucquick, I suppose to gather some Money for Liquor he sent, he is an old Hypocrite, told me that the Governor ought not to suffer any strong Liquor to come to Aucquick; I asked him whether he would have the Governor come Up with his Sword and Pistol to prevent it, no said he, well then says I, there is no other way for the Governor than to break You all and put others in Commission that are no Whiskey Traders, and will exercise their Authority.[14]

About noon on September 4, the Delawares and Shawnees summoned Weiser to their cabin, where, addressing him as the Governor of Pennsyl- vania, whom he represented, they wiped the tears from his eyes and assured him of their friendship. Weiser responded by condoling with them for the death of Lawachkamicky (the Bride, a great warrior) and Chief Kissa- kochquilla.

On this same day Weiser delivered the Governor's formal message to all the Indians, Six Nations, Delawares, and Shawnees. He welcomed them to Aughwick, commended them for placing themselves under the protec- tion of the Pennsylvania government, urged them to stay quiet and "mind nothing but Counsel affairs till You see Us first stir," and encouraged their young men to "run to Ohio now and then" to get news of "the Proceedings of the French."

At still another meeting on the same day, as Weiser's Journal informs us,

. . . the Beaver, the Speaker of the Delawares stood up and directed his Discourse to the 6 Nations and Said.

Oncle I still remember the time when you first Conquered us, and made Women of us and told us that you took us under your Protection, and that we must not Mettle with Warrs, but stay in the House and mind Counsel affair, we have hitherto followed your directions, and Lived very easy under your Protection, and no high wind did Blow to make us uneasy. but now things seem to take another turn, and a high Wind is arising, we desire you therefore Uncle to have your Eyes open, and be Watchful over us your Cousins, as you have always been heretofore
Gave several Strings of Wampum

Then the same Speaker directed his Discourse to the Governor of Pensilvania and said.

Brother. the Governor of Pensilvania by your Speech just now made to us, you Comforted our Hearts and you removed all doubts and Jelousy, it is what you said to us like the Morning Sun, we see now Clear your kindness and good will to us and our Allies. we will make it known to all, we are Extremly pleased to hear you Speak so Sincerely and so agreeable to us we thank you kindly for your good will
gave a String

Brother. the Governor of Pensilvania I must now go into the Depth and put you in Mind of old Histories and our first Acquaintance with you, when William Penn first appeared in his Ship on our Lands we looked in his Face and judged him to be our Brother, and gave him a fast hold to tie his ship to. and we told him that a Powerful People called the 5 united nations had placed us here, and established a fire and lasting Friendship with us and that he the said William Penn and his People shall be welcome to be one of us. and in the same union, to which he and his People agreed, and we then erected an everlasting Friendship with William Penn and his People, which we on our side so well as you have observd as much as Possible to this day, we always looked upon you to be one Flesh and Blood with us, we desire you will look upon us in the same Light, and let that Treaty of Friendship made by our fore-Fathers on both sides subsist, and be in force from Generation to Generation. both our Lives, our wife and Childrens Life and those as yet unborn depends upon it. Pray Brother consider well what we say and let it be so.
A large Belt. . . .

the 5th In the Morning I answered the Shawanose and the Delawares first Speech, in the following Manner.

Brethern, the Shawanose, . . . I have it in Charge from the Governor of Pensilvania to let you know, that he Aproves of your Proceedings. & desires you will always act agreeable to his Advise in everything and in so doing you will do well
gave a String . . .

Brethern the Delawares it is true you are one People with us, for you sprung out of the same spot of Ground with us, and are therefore our Country Men, and Older Inhabitants then we are, as to your Present Habitation on Ohio we look upon as your hunting Cabin Only for here is your Mother-Country and we look upon you as ourselves, we therefore take the Recomendation well, and are glad that you and your Grand-Children the Sawanose are of one Mind, we believe that what they said came from the Bottom of their Heart. and there remains no doubt with us, we thank you both for your kind Speeches

gave a String

Then I took up the Big Belt that the Delawares gave me yesterday & said

Brethern, by this Belt you was pleased to put the Governor of Pensilvania in Mind, of the first Treaties of Friend-Ship and acquaintance with the People of Pensilvania, when the great William Penn first Arrived on your land and you repeated over what then Passed, bettwen your forefathers and the said William Penn & his People, I must tell you Brethern, that, that is too weighty a Matter for me to give you an Answer upon it or to Exchange the Belt, I will therefore take it with me to Philadelphia and lay it before the Governor and he will lay it before his Counsel, and all the old and wise People of Pensilvania they are only able to Consider this, and make a Suitable Answer, I am too mean a Man and no way Impowred nor Capeable to answer it, but can only say that I am very well Pleased with what you said, and am glad to carry this Belt to Philadelphia

> The Indians in General as well those of the Six Nations as Delewares & Shawanose appeared to be extreamly pleased with what I told them & gave their Approbation in the Usual sound. . . .

the 6th this Day & at their Own Request I informed them of what Passed in Albany at the last Treaty, and of the Purchase of the Land that was made there, they seemed not to be very well Pleased at first when they heard of it, because of such a Large Tract that the Six Nations had released to the Proprietaries of Pensilvania, but when they were Informed of the New England Peoples design, and the French taking the Ohio lands in Possession, which they might look upon as lost to them, they were Content, but would have been more so if the had received a part of the Consideration.

This Evening I let them know that, as now all Publick Buissness was over I would set off to morrow Morning they to wit Thanachrishon, & Scarujady desired me to stay longer with them, to Discourse over some Private Affairs, as they had hitherto no time, to which I Consented. but they got Liquor that Evening and all got Drunk, however I stayd, and in the afternoon Thanachrishon & S[carujady] got sober and I learned from them in a Private Discourse, first, that the Senecas from time to time had sent Messages by Belts and Strings of Wampum to the Indians on Ohio to order them not to Meddle with the French, neither in one way nor an other, but stand Neuter and keep their Ears and Eies towards the Six United Nations

Secondly that the Twichtwees had sent Severall of their Head Men this Summer to the Lower Shawano-Town with a Messuage, the Purport ware as follows

Brethern, the Shawanose, you know that the French has invaded our Country on all sides, why do you set so still, will you be slaves to the French, and suffer them to be masters of all the Land and all the Game, raise up and take the Hatchit and follow our Example we have killed not long ago fifty frenchmen, all Warriors and in one day five other Nations have Joined us and if you and your Grand fathers the Delawares. will but stir the French will soon be forced to fly

this Article is Confirmed [by] Mosses, otherways Called the Song a Mohawk Indian who was Present. at the Delivery of the Message.

To which the Shawanose made answer

Brethern the Twichtwees, we are supprized at your request. the Six United Nations have desired us to sit still and not mind the French and that we must keep our Ears and Eies to the Six United Nations so does our Grand father the Delaware, we desire you spare us, and leave our Town, before the French hear of you, and come and kill you here, and plunge us into the Warr before the 6 united Nations begin it

The Twichtwees Accordingly went home in Disgust. and Thanachrishon and Scarujady are out of Humer with the Shawanose for not consulting them about an answer to the Twichtwees.

The following article I was Charged to keep to myself, to wit.

Thirdly, that they, to wit Tanachrishon, and Scarujady were Creditable Informed that the Mohawks, Oneiders and Tuscarrors would Assist the English against the French, as soon as the English gave prooff of their being in Earnest

Fourthly, Scarujade is going to Oneido Soon, (it is his Native Country) to inform himself of the minds of the Six United Nations, and to use his Endeavours to bring them to side with the English, against the French.

Fivthly, I found that the Shawanose and Delawares are very strictly United together, and that the French made them large Presents, desiring them to stand their Friends or Neuter. they the Shawanose and Delawares, made them no answer at all, but sent these men about 12 in Number to see their Brethern the English (:and I suppose to learn what they are about:) and to renew their Friendship with them. . . .[15]

Conrad Weiser to Richard Peters [16]

Heidelberg in the County of Bercks
September the 13. 1754

Sir

By this few lines I let you know that I am Safe arrived from Achwick yesterday. I need not repeat anything here of my transactions there, because you will have an opportunity to See my Journal herewith Sent to his Honour the Governor. I am well pleased with the Journey though it is further then I thought it was, the way I went through Shirmans Valley and And^w Montours house I made it 130 Miles going round by the great Hill this Side Achwick otherways 15 Miles less—I must Say Some thing to you about And^w M: not to ridicule him but to Inform you how to act with him. in the first place when he meet me at John Harris he Called for So much punch that himself the half King & other Indians got drunk. the Same at Tobias Hendricks I bought 2 quarts of Rum there to use on our Journey but he drunk most all the first day. he abused me very much Corsed & Swore and asked pardon when he got Sober. did the Same again when he was drunk again. damned me more then hundred times so he did the governor & M^r peters for not paying him for his trouble & Expences, he is vexed at the new purchase told me I Cheated the Indians, he Says he will now Kill any white men that will pretent to Setle on his Creek, and that the Governor and M^r peters told him So much Saying *he* was *a Warrior*

how he *Could Suffer the Irrish* to *encroach upon him* he would now act according to advise and kill some of them. I reprimanded him when sober he begged pardon, desired me not to Mention it to you, but did the same again at another drunken frolick. I left him drunk at Achwick, on one legg he had a Stocking and no Shoe on the other a Shoe and no Stocking. from 6 of the

Cloke till past nine I begged him to go with me but to no purpose, he Swore
terrible when he Saw me mount my horse. I went that day over Tuscaroro
Hill to Jacob Piat in a very great rain (the 8th last past) and over Kitidany
Hill the next day to James duning on the 10th by 9 of the Clok in the morning I Came to Carlisle light at Willm Buhanons where I found Andw M: he
wellcomed me with Shaking hands Called me a one Side Asked pardon for
offences given. he was arrived there the day before he never stopt at his own
house but for an Hour for fear of failing in Meeting me. he is now gone to
Virginia. he was Scares of pocket Money I paid him forty Shillings for his
trouble in this last Service and tooke his receipt in order to Save the Governor
trouble, notwithstanding what I Said here I dont take him to be in himself
an Ill Natured felow. but it is rather a habit he took from the Indians and
Indian traders, he is allways Extreemly good Natured to me when he is
Sober, and allways will act according to my advice. I desire you will take no
notice of this letter without it be to Governor Hamilton.
    . . . to Conclude I assure you the Indians at Achwick are our good friends
and will be advised by pensilvania I am

Sir
your humble Servant
CONRAD WEISER

Despite the assurance contained in the concluding sentence, the news
from the west was ominous. Near midnight of September 20, there came
to Aughwick a friendly Indian who had traveled night and day to give
the English warning that three hundred French Indians were setting out
to harry their back inhabitants. Croghan sent word a few days later that
the French intended to have him killed that fall, and with him Scaroyady
and Andrew Montour.[17] Friendly Indians were uneasy, seeing no sign of
English preparations. Some were leaving and going back to the Six Nations
country. Those who remained, Croghan feared, would be obliged to fall
in with the French.

The government in Philadelphia was incredibly apathetic. It showed
no interest in continuing the negotiations that had been started at Aughwick.

Conrad Weiser to Richard Peters [18]

[Heidelberg, October 27, 1754]

Sir
    . . . By my Journal to Achweek you will See that Some thing ought to be
said to the Indians there, who Stayd for the new Governor, and news from
the King
    the Belt the delawares then Sent by me to the Government is of Importance
wont It be Considered, is there not an answer due to it
    the Shawanose made a Speech though it was only an answer and by no
means of the Same Importance with the former, yet the Meaning is the Same
and are one people with the delawares a Smal Belt as a token of the kind
reception of their answer, would be very proper, there is not allways need
of presents, but a Kind Corespondents is allways needfull, even at a time when
we dont want their aid
    the Governors arrival Should have ben Notifyd to the Indian at & about

Shomockin, If they find themselves neglected they ar untractable when you want any thing of them, I desire you not to think that I want Buisness, I am heartely tired I assure you, any Body may do this So Can my Son Samy If ordered to do it

I am Sensible I Should have waited on the Governor before now, but I have realy ben unwell Since my return from Shomockin, riding does not agree with me very well at least I would not venture as farr as philad^{ia} for fear of the return of the Gravel, pray Sir If you See Cause remember me in the best manner you Can to his Honour . . .

CONRAD WEISER

The neglect of Indian business brought danger not only to Pennsylvania. It imperiled the whole system of Indian alliances on which the safety of the English colonies depended. Daniel Claus wrote anxiously from Canajoharie, the Mohawk Upper Castle:

. . . they say there was never the like seen how quick the Nations turnd, after Col¹ Washingtons Defeat, . . . I dare say if the s^d Nations were properly managed so that they might be acquainted of the forces the English have & assured of being assisted by them in Case of Need, such defections to the french would never take place [19]

William Johnson warned that, if Indian affairs were neglected, all the Six Nations would be lost, "and with them everry other Indian in the country." [20]

CHAPTER 43

... Gathers Indians for
Braddock's Army

I

BETWEEN the time of the conference at Aughwick and Braddock's conference at Alexandria, Conrad Weiser was in an Irish stew of activity. In September he took six workmen to Shamokin to build a house for the Shickellamies. He was away from home sixteen days, using part of his time to run the boundary line of the last purchase.[1] In this latter undertaking he was stopped by the Shickellamies, who saw that the line, if it followed the courses laid down in the deed, would cross the West Branch of the Susquehanna below the Big Island. This was not according to the bargain, said the Shickellamies, and Weiser agreed with them. The purchasers at Albany, depending upon Lewis Evans' map, had assured the Indians that the northwest line, following a course agreed upon, would not touch the river. Weiser stopped the survey and wrote to the government, urging them to play fair with the Indians, the letter of the deed notwithstanding. It was a policy of enlightened self-interest. Weiser explained to the Secretary that, if white people settled on the river, the Indians were resolved to kill first the cattle, as a warning, and then "the Folks." [2]

While Weiser was at Shamokin, the Half King, Tanacharison, died at Paxton—"I suppose by his hard drinking," said Conrad; "most every Body treated him." [3] John Harris buried him well. This was gratifying to his friends and relatives, but the Indians in general were much alarmed. A medicine man who attended him at the end said the French had killed him by witchcraft in revenge for his striking them.[4] He had assisted George Washington on the Ohio. Scaroyady pressed Harris to inform the governors of Pennsylvania and Viriginia. An urgent message was sent to Conrad Weiser.

This last marks the beginning of a short but interesting connection between Weiser and the John Harris who is commonly known as the founder of Harrisburg. For a few months the two were in frequent contact, especially during the feverish weeks between Braddock's defeat and the organization of the Pennsylvania army. Conrad Weiser was the hub of the provincial intelligence service, and John Harris was one of the spokes in the wheel. Evidence of this is seen in the fact that when Harris once wrote directly to the Governor, imparting news of the Penn's Creek massacre, the Governor expressed his dissatisfaction at Harris' not sending the intelligence through the proper channels, that is, through Conrad Weiser.[5]

When Weiser came home from Shamokin in October, he found Jonathan and his family waiting to see him. Conrad told his Mohawk brother of the proceedings of Lydius. Jonathan said the purchase would never stand.

I asked him [reported Weiser] what he thought if the Govern.^r of Pensilvania should send for the six Nations to come down early in the Spring, he approved of it, and thought it was the best thing we could do, he left my House this Day [October 12] and is going a Hunting, and told me the Place where he could be found, because I told him perhaps he would be sent, as John Shickelemy had a sore Leg, and his Brother a lame one, I question whether any of them can be sent but I would send them rather, because they are Cayuckers and I find that none of the Cayukers are mentioned in Claus's Letter to have signed, and they Claim the Lands on Susquehannah, with your Approbation I will send Samy to Shamokin to call the Shikelmys down to consult with them.[6]

A visit to William Parsons, who was at his "favorite Mansion house"[7] on the plantation known as Stonykill under the Blue Mountain near Round Head, to discuss the Wyoming Purchase, was a foretaste of the close collaboration soon to come between these two men during the dark years after Braddock's defeat. In November, when Parsons stopped for two rainy days at Weiser's and discussed the Connecticut affair again, the two agreed that a treaty with the Six Nations, held in the Wyoming Valley, would be the best way to discourage the New Englanders. Parsons, enthusiastic, proposed ordering one hundred pounds of corn at once from DuPuy, at the current low price, for delivery at Wyoming in the spring.[8]

During November and December Weiser kept closely in touch with the government. The new governor, Robert Hunter Morris, seemed promising. He cleared up two pieces of Indian business that had been dragging dangerously for months. He let Weiser write a speech for him, to be presented to the Indians at Aughwick, announcing his arrival and promising them his protection. "I can assure you," the new governor was to say (we have it all in Weiser's handwriting),

that after the King of great Britain has tried all the fair means to remove the French from the new fords they Build on Ohio and the french remain obstinate he will take them by the arm and fling them a Cross the lake of CataroghKy to the place where they Came from, and protect his Indian Children, and more to If they desire it of him in a Suitable way
here give a Belt [9]

The speech was sent by messenger to George Croghan, who delivered it to the Indians at Aughwick amid great satisfaction.

The Governor also sent an invitation to "the Politician Hendrick," inviting him to come in all haste to Philadelphia, there to consult on matters affecting "the safety of the Indians and his Majesty's Colonies." [10]

In December Weiser made a journey to Philadelphia, discussed the Indian situation with the Governor, and helped him draw up another speech for the Indians at Aughwick.[11] This month Scaroyady, who had succeeded Tanacharison in the conduct of Six Nations affairs in the West, was engaged to go to Onondaga and lay the whole matter of the Connecticut Purchase

before the Great Council. Scaroyady assured the Governor that, with the
sad vision before his eyes of multitudes of skulls and dry bones (those
who animated them having been destroyed by their enemies), he would
urge the Six Nations to join in assisting their brethren the English against
the French, whom they hated. In good time Scaroyady made his report
to Onondaga, and received from the Great Council there assurance that
the Wyoming deed would be invalidated in open council and a protest
sent to the governor of Connecticut.

King Hendrick came down to Philadelphia under conduct of Daniel
Claus. Chief Hendrick was attended by Brant (Conagaratuchqua), Brant's
son Nicholas, Seth (the principal chief of the Schoharie Mohawks),[12] and
a number of other personages. On his arrival, January 7, 1755, he was
greeted by members of Council and escorted by the town militia, amid
"Acclamations of Huzza" [13] to the State House, where the Governor received him. Afterwards he was "elegantly entertained by the Mayor." [14]
Conrad Weiser, notified by an express,[15] came to town as interpreter. A
conference was held, lasting several days, at the State House, attended by
the Governor, members of the Provincial Council, Conrad Weiser, the
Mohawks, and twelve Cherokees who had recently escaped from captivity
in Canada and were on their way home to the South. Special constables
were hired for the occasion.

Hendrick was affable and communicative. He paid the government "an
elegant Compliment" [16] for the compassionate treatment given the Cherokees, who were provided with shirts, passports, guides, letters of recommendation, and Sammy Weiser as an escort as far as John Harris'.[17] Hendrick complained of the deceit of the people of New York, who granted
away the very castles the Mohawks lived in without their knowledge
(Philip Livingston had somehow got a patent for the Upper Mohawk
Castle, Canajoharie, and the lands adjacent); [18] and he inveighed against
the rudeness of Governor Clinton, who had broken his promises and run
away to England. He agreed with Brother Onas that the Connecticut deed
should be destroyed—but in due form, through joint action taken in conference by the Six Nations and Pennsylvania. He agreed further that the
Six Nations should execute a conveyance to the Proprietaries of all lands
lying within their grant from the King of Great Britain, so as to put it out
of the power of men like Lydius in the future to disturb the peace of the
province by their frauds.

The conference ended in high good humor. Pieces of eight were distributed to all Hendrick's retinue, and special presents were given to "the
more considerable Indians." Hendrick got a saddle and bridle; Brant's son
got a suit of clothes; and a present was sent through Daniel Claus to Brant's
wife in the Mohawk Valley.[19]

Weiser wrote a tactful letter to William Johnson: [20]

[Philadelphia, January 23, 1755]
Kind Sir
    I take this Opportunity to trouble You with a few Lines, having read the
Secretary's Mr Peters, to You, dated either the 21st or 22d of this Instant;   I

since thought, upon reflecting on it, that something about the ensuing Treaty with some of the Deputies of the Six Nations at Mount Johnson required a little more Explanation, whether I am wrong or right, You will be best able to judge, when You compare mine and Mr Peters's together.

First, Henry, Brandt and Seth, undertook to assist in the Affair against the Connecticut People, in making that Deed obtained by Lydius from the Six, or some of the Six, Nations, void, as it was obtained in a very wicked manner.

Secondly, That they would secure Things concerning the Land in Mr Penn's Grant so sure to the Proprietaries of Pennsylvania, as to put it out of any such as Lydius their Power to do any more Mischief.

Thirdly, That in all this they will consult with You about every thing, and proceed according to your Advice.

Fourthly, When the Time is fixed that the Treaty shall be, to give Mr Peters Notice as soon as possible, so that the Treaty be early in the Spring; the Notice is meant to come from your Honour.

In my humble Opinion, the more secret this can be carried on the better, let Mr Claus be sent to Onondago with some one or two of Henry's Friends; by what I can learn the Indians are sorry for what happened, and will be very glad to see the Things put upon such a Footing; that the Proprietaries of Pennsylvania shall have what the King has granted them, and that the Indians may come off as blameless as possible, and the wickedness of Lydius be exposed —I believe I have no need to trouble You with more Words, knowing that Mr Peters wrote a long Letter to You.

I wish you Health and Happiness, and am

> Sir
> Your most humble Servant
> CONRAD WEISER

The aftermath of the conference was not so pleasant for Weiser himself. One could change the Cherokees' shirts, but not their skins, which were soon so tight with liquor that the Governor asked Weiser not to leave town till they did, and then to conduct them at least as far as Germantown on their way.[21] Sammy needed backing.

II

With all these comings and goings on state affairs, Conrad Weiser still had time left for other business, public and private. He attended to his court hearings; he opened a new school at Tulpehocken ("Mr. George Davies from Ireland, Master");[22] and he made considerable additions to his lands.

In October Thomas Penn had written to Peters expressing his satisfaction with the Albany Purchase. He desired Weiser and Peters to receive for their services in this matter "two Tracts of two thousand Acres each, of good Land, and well situated."[23] Warrants were taken out for Weiser's land "in any part of the New Purchase," January 21, 1755;[24] and next day Nicholas Scull, the Surveyor General, appointed Sammy to make the survey. In the spring Sammy and several of his brothers went out into the woods looking for likely land, which they found on the bank of the Susquehanna opposite Weiser's Mahanoy holdings and beyond this about forty miles west of George Gabriel's place at the mouth of Penn's Creek.[25] The trouble was that squatters were found everywhere, some willing to go off for a price, and some not. Mr. Armstrong, surveying in Cumberland County, warned Sammy that it was "absolutely necessary to bring 3 or 4 Indians along for fear of being Stopt by the Irish with guns." [26] "If this be realy the Case," wrote Weiser to Peters,

as (I Belief it is) I will lay aside all thought of haveing any lands in the new purchase for I will not venture my own nor take other Mens life to get the lands the proprietors gave, I Know what the Consequence would be If I should go there with Indians, I rather forbear or give all over, I find that dame fortune Gradually (a favour She is not used to Show to all her favourits) begines to leave me . . .[27]

The upshot was that Weiser contented himself for the time being with having Sammy survey for him a tract of 305 acres on the east bank of the Susquehanna, north of the Mahanoy Mountain, together with an island of fifty acres lying opposite.[28] Apparently other tracts, much larger, were selected on the west bank soon after, one stretching from Penn's Creek to Middle Creek, though it was not surveyed till after Weiser's death.[29]

Richard Peters had particularly requested Weiser to get him land adjoining his own, but to keep his name out of the affair, especially since there was danger of dispute. "If I coud gain the Universe," he wrote to Weiser, "I will not hold lands where any other man has the least Pretensions. the poorer the man the more unfit is it for me to distress him." [30] Besides, Peters did not like entrusting the business to so young a person as Sammy, since the wild Irish settlers were combining "in knots." But on second thoughts, since Weiser had already published Peters' name, he supposed it "better and more consistent to put my name in the Warrant along with yours that all may know I am concerned and that there be no room for any charge of hypocrisy or double dealing, which I abhor." [31]

When avarice struggles with sanctimony, they usually end by going to bed together, and their offspring is mischief. It proved so in the heart of Richard Peters. He wrote a letter to Thomas Penn designed to stir up that gentleman's sensibilities against Honest Conrad. "I am sorry," replied Penn, "to hear that Conrad Weiser acts so unreasonable a part as to desire to Survey Lands fixed upon by others, and be angry because you cannot quarrel with the whole Country for him. . . . He is no doubt a very valuable man, but ought to show some Modesty in his demands." [32]

Deep in his heart, the Reverend Richard was saying, "How long, O Lord, how long?"

It was to be several years yet.

III

Much of Weiser's time was taken up with caring for the Indian refugees whom the affair at Fort Necessity had thrown upon the province. For the death of the Half King, he gave a condolence present to Johnny, the

Half King's son. A present was also given to Aroas, or Silver Heels, a noted Seneca warrior. He arranged for the distribution of food among the Indians at Aughwick, John Harris', and Shamokin. He entertained refugees frequently at his own plantation at Heidelberg. One party, headed by Weiser's brother, Jonathan Cayenquiloquoa, presented Conrad with a string of wampum to be sent to Philadelphia with the request that the Governor send "Some of your Industrious people up next Spring to fence in a Small piece of ground for a Cornfield for us," the new settlement to be established on the Susquehanna at Otstuagy or French Town, where Madame Montour had once lived.

With Jonathan's belt Weiser sent a warning to the Governor about the situation in the Wyoming Valley.

Conrad Weiser to Governor Morris [33]

[Heidelberg, March 1, 1755]

Honoured Sir

. . . I take this oppurtunity of Informing your Honour that when Tachnechdorus the Chief of ShomocKin of the CayiuKer nation, was down here in the beginning of the winter, he told me that the Indians about ShomoKen & otsinachson had ben Informed that a Set of people from New England had formed themselves into a Body to Setle the lands on SusqueHana and Especially Scahantowano (WoyumocK) and that against the advise of their Superiors and asked me whether it was true what they had heard. I told him it was true, as to their Intention (to Setle that land) but whether with, or without the advise of their Supperiors, I Could not tell, but that I was persuaded by Some letters I Saw last fall in philadelphia, It was against the advise of the Supperiors of that Country. the said Chief then desired to make it Known. "That whosoever of the white Should venture to Setle any land on WoyumocK or thereabout belonging hitherto to the Indians will have his Creatures killed first, and then If they did not desist they them Self would be Killed, without distinction, let the Consequences be what it would." I found he had Inteligence from the Indians up the river, that Some of the new England people had ben there Spying the lands. I found this a difficult matter, and was no ways inclined to make it Known. to Keep off trouble from meself, but the last visitors Insinated the Same thing, So I resolved to acquaint your Honour with it who is best able to Judge, what must be done to prevent Blood Shet. among us by the Indians who would then certainly (If they Should do Such a thing as I fear they will) out of a gilty Conscience Submit themselves to the Protection of the french, the Consequence of that would be very disagreeable to the English in General in this and Neighbouring Colony. I have nothing else to trouble your Honour with at present, but with a great deal of pleasure Subscribe me Self

Honoured Sir
your most obedient & humble
Servant
CONRAD WEISER

Conrad maintained the warmest relations with his Mohawk brother. Jonathan, though well on in years, did excellent work for Conrad and his government, making difficult journeys through the woods on their behalf.

Conrad, for his part, sent Jonathan's two sons to Philadelphia for an education, proposing that they be lodged for a time in the home of his married daughter, Margaret.

Conrad Weiser to Richard Peters [34]

[Heidelberg, May 19, 1755]

Sir,

My Son Sammy is coming to you with two Indian Boys, the Sons of Jonathan Gayienquiligoa, a noted Mohawk, that can Read and write in his Language, well known to you; he is Poor and Prays that you with the Gentlemen Managers of the Academy will teach them to Read and write in English; and to provide Necessaries of Life for them, during their Stay in Philadelphia; which will be as long as it will require Time to teach them! That the bigest of them is a very Intelligible Boy and good Natured; the other is not so, but more of an Indian, and something cross as his Father says. If you could prevail with Mr Heintzelmann my Son in Law, for a few Weeks to Bord with him, it would be agreeable to the Lads; because my Daughter is some-what used to the Indians, and understands here & there a Word: then afterwards, you can put them where you Please. The bigest his Name is Jonathan and the others Name is Philip: I believe their Father will let them stay long enough to learn the English to Perfection, provided, proper Care is taken of them, which I hope wont be Wanting.

Jonathan wanted me to go to Philadelphia with the Boys, but I thought Sammy could do as well. The Indians on Susquehannah are starving, and have almost nothing to Eat, because the Deers are Scarce. He thought to have had an answer before now, concerning their Petition to the Governor for some Provision, and the Fencing in of a Corn-Field.

French Margret with some of her Family is gone to the English Camp in Virginia, and her Son Nicklaus is gone to Ohio, to the French Fort. I suppose they want to join the strongest Party, and are gone for Information. "The Indians that are with the French on Ohio are chiefly AnaKunKis, Neighbours to New-England, and neither they nor the Rest (I cant learn their Number) will be true to the French, as they give out to our Indians! The other Indians on Ohio think our Troops march too slow! They say they will be glad to see the French drove away from Ohio." This Report was brought by one of Jonathan's Sons from Ohio; he was not in the French Fort; he was afraid of coming nigh it, but the Indians thereabout have told him so.

I wrote to the Governor last week about the Indians Petition; I hope he has received my Letter! The Indians should have an Answer. what can I say to them without having it from the Governor or Assembly? and they are continually plagueing me for an Answer, which I hope you will send, if you can, by this Oppurtunity. I have nothing to add, but am

Sir

Your most humble Servant

CONRAD WEISER

PS. Tachnechdorus Sent word by Jonathan for me to Come up to Shomoc-Kin that the Indians had Some thing of Importance to lay before me

I understood Since by Jonathan that Several Messages had arrived at OtsuacKy from the English army or virginia (as was Said) with Strengs of Wampum to forwarn the Indians on SusqueHana, not to Come nigh the army for fear of being taKen for french Indians and to Stay where they are

Governor Morris himself replied to this letter in Peters' absence, saying that the Indian boys had arrived, and that he had recommended them to Mr. Allen and Mr. Franklin; "and you may assure Jonathan," he continued, "that they will be taken all imaginable care of, not only as to their learning but their Morrals." He sent fifty pounds from the Assembly to buy provisions for the Indian refugees. "As to the Cornfield," he added, "it is left to your Judgment to do what you shall think best." [35]

Jonathan's boys remained several years at the Academy (progenitor of the University of Pennsylvania), where they were reported by the Reverend William Smith, in a letter to Lord Oxford, November 1, 1756, to be doing well, having learned to read and write English.

IV

Meantime General Braddock was growling and grumbling his way toward the Monongahela: moving like a tortoise, said the Indians, which falls over on its back at every obstacle. "The Governor has laid before the Assembly a most alarming Letter from General Braddock," wrote Edward Shippen to his father at Lancaster,

which charges him in strong Terms with Faction and Disaffection, and assures them That as the assigning Quarters for the Army is his Province, He shall take due Care to burthen those Colonies the most that shew the least Loyalty to his Majesty, And lets them know That he is determined to obtain by unpleasant Methods what it is their Duty to contribute with the utmost Chearfulness. The Assembly know not how to stomach this military Address, but 'tis thought it will frighten them to some reasonable Measures, as it must be a vain Thing to contend with a General at the Head of an Army, tho he should act in an arbitrary part, especially as in all probability he will be supported in every Thing at home.[36]

One of Braddock's first acts of authority on arrival in the colonies was to give William Johnson "the sole Management & direction of the Affairs of the Six Nations of Indians & their Allies," and to require all other persons whatsoever "to cease & forbear acting or intermeddling therein." [37] This plain disaster for Pennsylvania was confirmed by his successor, Lord Loudoun. How Pennsylvania got around this obstacle and managed, through Conrad Weiser, to save something out of the wreck of her Indian policy, is matter for another chapter.

Braddock dealt his orders and curses about him like blows. Unprepared for the jealousies and fretful pacifism of the colonies, he became suspicious of everyone around him. From Fort Cumberland he wrote to Governor Morris about the folly of Mr. Dinwiddie, the roguery of his Assembly, the disaffectedness of "a fellow at Connegogee one Cressap"; concluding with the remark that, except in the contract for the Pennsylvania wagons, he had everywhere met with nothing "but lies & villany." [38]

"He looks upon the country, I believe," wrote Washington, "as void of honor or honesty." [39]

As the weeks and months dragged on, and Braddock's column moved slowly in the wake of the axemen over the forest-clad ranges toward Fort Duquesne, it became evident that his peremptory manner was losing for the army one of the most necessary adjuncts to such a campaign, Indian scouts. Braddock had a contempt for Indians as well as for colonials. He snubbed them and ordered them about. He told the chiefs in what manner they and their braves were to fight. Shickellamy reported to Weiser at Tulpehocken that the General would not let them take French scalps; that many Indians had therefore left him; that they appealed to the Governor and wanted to know whether this was peace or war.[40] The chiefs knew better than Braddock how to lead their men in battle. Killing is an ugly business—and being killed. The Indians knew fear as well as the whites did. Honor led them on, and the insignia of honor were human scalps.

George Croghan tells us that he brought some fifty Indians to Braddock at Fort Cumberland, but the General, on the advice of Colonel Innes, ordered all but eight or nine of them off as likely to be troublesome on the march.[41] Among the few that remained and took part in the battle at the Monongahela were Silver Heels, Johnny the Half King's son, Tohash-wuchtonionty or the Belt, and a son of Queen Allaquippa named Kanuk-susy.

Meanwhile French Indians scouted about the neighborhood of fort and army and picked off soldiers and inhabitants at will. John Harris wrote to tell Weiser of scalps taken and throats cut in great numbers, and to express the fear that if these murders were not stopped the back inhabitants would all flee and leave their crops.[42] July 8, Edward Shippen wrote from Shippensburg to James Burd:

John Harris says that he has an account of 30 Cannoes of our friend Indians (if we have a friend among them which I much doubt) coming to his house for Provisions for themselves, & families; & that our Government has sent Mr Weiser to meet them & to buy the flour for Them; but can any MORTALMAN tell me why these Indians are not with our Noble General? [43]

That Weiser felt as Shippen did, and was prepared to do something about it, is shown by the next letter.

Conrad Weiser to Governor Morris [44]

> [John Harris's Ferry, July the 9th
> 1755. At 11 'oClock]

Honoured Sir,
According to your Order, I came to this Place last Monday, and found the Indians waiting for Me. Yesterday I distributed about 200 Bushels of Meal among them; after that was over, they enquired how Things stood as to the War: I told them what had happened to some of the Back Inhabitants; And that the ffrench Indians were like to do a great deal of Mischief & c^a They seem'd to be very much concerned; There was about 30 of them, out of which Number, 9 offered themselves to go with Me, or my Son Sammy, to Wills's Creek, and serve as Outscouts against the French and their Indians, and to protect the poor People settled about them parts; And It was agreed that they shou'd meet me, or my Son, at this Place in Ten days hence; And

that in the mean Time I was to obtain your Honour's Leave; and a proper Pass. This morn^g Captain Glassier, Express from the East arrived at this Place, with the agreable News of the Defeat of the French at Nova Scotia; and the taking of the ffrench Men of War, by Admiral Boscawen. I read and explain'd the printed Paper to the Indians; and they expressed a good deal of Satisfaction & pleasure with the News. Capt Glassier gave me to understand, that He shou'd be very glad if some of these Indians wou'd accompany him to the Enlish Camp, with the Dispatches He had for the General, in this dangerous Time. I proposed it to the Indians; they approved of the thing; But, having Intelligence of your Honour's coming up, and that you wou'd be in Lancaster this Day, they wou'd hear, and receive your Approbation; And have accordingly desired me to stay with them, at this Place, till your Honour's Arrival; which I have promised to do; and have sent the Bearer hereof Express to let your Honour know of this, and to receive further Order. I am, Sir,

Your very Obed^t hble Servt

CONRAD WEISER

P.S. Capt Glassier is in a great Hurry, and if it is not convenient for y^r Honour to be up here, in such Time as is expected, let your Order and Passport, for this End, come.

On that same day, July 9, Braddock met Dumas at the crossing of the Monongahela.

CHAPTER 44

. . . *Gives Bed Lace to the Wyandots*

THE story of Braddock's defeat is familiar to every schoolboy, but there are some circumstances connected with the engagement that are not commonly known and that are necessary to the understanding of Conrad Weiser's story.

If it had not been for one very brave man that day, we should now be talking about Braddock's victory. There was no ambush at the Mononga-hela. The French had prepared no trap. Both forces reached the ford at about the same time. The French were beaten before the battle was fairly begun, and routed almost immediately.

There had been little spirit among the French troops before the engagement. Fort Duquesne was in bad condition and almost defenseless. Provisions were low, the men were ill, and most of the garrison had been recalled to Canada. The Indians of the neighborhood held aloof. Only some bands of France's traditional allies, brought from a distance, were to be depended on. Contrecoeur, commander of the fort, had little hope of success when he sent out Beaujeu and Dumas with a small body of men to meet the English and see if anything could be done.

When Beaujeu's small force met Braddock's large one, the French were smashed at once by Braddock's massed volleys; their commander was killed, and the white troops together with their Indian allies took to flight.

But there was a man of genius among the French whom the fortunes of war now placed in command. When Beaujeu fell, Dumas took his place. Dumas (remembered today in French Canada as "The Hero of the Mo-nongahela" [1]) rallied his men, posted them in the woods, and settled them down behind trees to pick off the English at leisure. These were tactics the Indians understood. Pontiac with his Ottawas, and other bands of Indians, from this point on gave Dumas excellent support.

It was then that Braddock made his mistake. The character of the battle had changed. The advantages of the initial shock were past. But Braddock persisted in holding to the mass formation that had won him the first round. If he had died, like Beaujeu, at the opening of the battle, all might have been well. George Washington and the Virginians could have met the French and Indians at their own game and beaten them. But Braddock lived long enough to snub the colonials and see his army disintegrate into a mob hurtling back against its supports and infecting them also with panic. Wagon trains were abandoned, powder kegs destroyed, packs dumped on the road, and a hopelessly beaten army fled back into Fort Cumberland.

Even that was not the worst of the disaster. Braddock had made a brave and not dishonorable error in judgment; but Dunbar, now in command of a large army still intact and under the shelter of Fort Cumberland, began a cowardly and senseless retreat. Against every law of manhood and good soldiering, and in defiance of explicit orders, he withdrew his army in haste across the mountains, leaving the settlements uncovered and Braddock's new road undefended in his rear, thus facilitating pursuit and the devastation of the frontier by the enemy.

"We have lost a number of brave men," wrote Benjamin Franklin, "and all our credit with the Indians." [2]

The Indians were the nub of French policy. The French themselves were in no condition to do what Dunbar feared: to march in force against an army at Fort Cumberland. But Braddock's defeat enabled them to carry out other plans which had long been maturing. They handed the hatchet to the Delawares and Shawnees.

Dumas, who replaced Contrecoeur [3] in command at Fort Duquesne, understood as well as Weiser did the power held by the Six Nations over the Delawares; but that power he now set himself to break. The Connecticut Purchase of the Wyoming Valley from the Six Nations had given him a lever, and with it he set about inciting the Delawares to turn against their Uncles and assert their independence. He went farther. Just as it had been Weiser's policy to keep the Delawares in fear of the Six Nations, it became Dumas' policy to put the Six Nations in fear of the Delawares. How well he succeeded may be seen in a letter of his written from Fort Duquesne, July 24, 1756.

Dumas to the Minister [4]

. . . Since last year, Monseigneur, it has been my honor to command here with much greater success than might have been expected. I have succeeded in setting against the English all the tribes of this region who had been their most faithful allies. . . .

May I also, Monseigneur, congratulate myself on having largely determined the policy of the Five Nations, setting those of this river in defiance of them and stopping parties from the five towns who pass here on their way to attack distant tribes; I have succeeded in making almost all of them attack the English, and if any of them resisted I have always managed to destroy them, so that I have put the Iroquois in fear of the Delawares and Shawnees unless they follow their example; and since the war-parties I have intercepted here have taken scalps and prisoners back to their towns, they find themselves engaged in the war, so to speak, in spite of themselves. . . .

But we are getting ahead of our story, and must return to the days immediately following Braddock's defeat.

For nearly a week no news of the disaster got through to the Susquehanna. The Governor came from Lancaster to John Harris' and went on to Carlisle. From Carlisle Captain Glasier took his leave of the Governor and set out with his despatches for General Braddock. [5] Captain Glasier had not gone more than a day's journey when he met three wagoners, deserters, bringing the first news from the Monongahela. Whether Weiser and his Indians were with Glasier at this time (taking the place of a regular military escort, which the Governor had been unable to provide), and whether it was the Berks County Justice who, turning back while Glasier hurried on with the despatches, brought the wagoners to Carlisle on

Tuesday, July 15,[6] for questioning by the Governor, is matter for conjecture. A cloud settles over the records at this point, since the Governor tried to suppress the bad news and ordered those who knew of it to say nothing.

There is evidence that Weiser knew what was in Captain Glasier's letter.

Captain Glasier to Governor Morris [7]

Sir,

There are three Men belonging to the Waggons who have made their Escape from Camp, who say, that there hath been an Engagement last Wednesday between the General with an advance Party of Fifteen Hundred Men, within 5 Miles of Fort Du Quesne, in which General Braddock was killed, and the Party defeated; And that they saw Sr John Sinclair brought back, by a Party of Soldiers, wounded to Colonl Dunbar's, who was left with his Regiment, with all the Baggage; and several Soldiers coming from the defeated Party running in every Moment; And that Colonl Dunbar's Regiment was alarmed immediately, and beat to Arms; And it was more than the Centry's cou'd do to keep the Officers, and Soldiers from running away from His Party. This they seem all to agree in, and offer to make Oath to. I thought proper you shod know to Night, I am, Sir,

> Your most humble
> and most obedt Servt
> B. GLASIER

Weiser did not go to Fort Cumberland. We find him at John Harris' with the Governor on the 18th and 19th.[8] For a few days thereafter Weiser preserved silence; and then he wrote to the Governor, who had left for Philadelphia, a letter which betrays a discreet impatience at the withholding of the news from the public.[9] It put him in an awkward position with the Indians, in particular with John Shickellamy and Jonathan, who wanted to be off, but whom Weiser thought it inadvisable to let slip back into the woods before the facts about Braddock were established.

Conrad Weiser to Governor Morris [10]

[Heidelberg, July 21, 1755]

Hond Sir

I must inform you that on the same Day you left John Harris's, about Twenty Five Indian Women and Children arrived from Achweek, only one Old Man wth 'em. They say that it was agreed upon, when their Husbands and Young Men went to the English Army under General Braddock, they shou'd come down to the inhabited Parts, where they shou'd be provided for; And as they had no Body to hunt for them, they cod not live without being some how assisted by their Brethren the English; And that a good many more were on their way coming down. I bought 500 Weight of Flower and gave it to them; and gave Orders to John Harris, that when the rest arrived to give them some Flower also, 'till the Governor's Pleasure shou'd be known, wch I desire your Honour will signify to me, or John Harris as soon as possible.

Jonathan, and John Shickalamy will stay among the Inhabitants, 'till they hear from your Honour concerning the English Army and Genl Braddock.

Our People are very malicious against our Indians, they curse, & damn 'em to their Faces, and say, "must we feed You, and your Husbands fight in the mean Time for the French, &ca. I am

Your Honour's
Most obliged and
faithful Hble Servt
CONRAD WEISER

It is difficult for a world grown used to the radio to understand how such news could be kept hidden for so long, but it is not difficult to understand that even persons who had the news failed to credit it. As late as July 22 (nearly two weeks after the battle), Armstrong could write to Weiser from Carlisle as though the facts had only just emerged from the fog of rumor. "Our bad News is now too true," he said, "being confirm'd beyond all doubt." [11]

It was all so incredible, as John Bartram expressed it, that it seemed more like a dream than a fact. "But I doubt," he added, "ye dreadful consequences will soon convince us that it is too true!" [12]

The condition of the border, and Weiser's position in relation to it, are seen mirrored in two letters from Shippensburg.

Charles Swaine to Governor Morris [13]

Shippensburgh 20th July 1755.

May it please your Honour

I have first to inform you, that two Indians came here, One named Cherigea, and the other called the Song, to see if they cou'd have any Assistance, and Provisions, is their Message; They have left behind Five Wyondotts, and two others of the 5 Nations, who did not chuse to come along with these, who were to return to them in Two Days, to the Place where they left them, ffourteen or Fifteen Miles beyond the Hills in Tuscarora Path. I have given them Entertainment, also a Pass, and forwarded em to Conrad Weiser; I send enclosed an Affidivit, from three Persons come from the Road; a Defeat, I believe, is beyond all doubt; Mr Burd is gone to Fort Cumberland. . . .

Charles Swaine to Governor Morris [14]

[Shippensburg, July 23, 1755]

Sir

. . . Yesterday the two Indians mentioned in my Last returned from Carlisle, could not proceed after Mr Weiser whom they heard was gone to Philadelphia, by reason they were to return to the Owendats and the Five Nation Indians who were waiting for them at Pyatts, and who were so afraid of the Inhabitants, as they would not come on, and if not joined by these Messengers Yesterday Evening were to make the best of their Way under a Notion that the Messengers were either secured or killed. One of the Indians had tired his Horse, and as I could not get one here, let him have mine, that they might join those at Pyatts at the appointed time, and expect them with the other Indians to return here tomorrow in their Way down the Road. I entertained these two Indians and their Interpreter and tho' I had no Order in this respect, hope I have acted in a manner, which your Honour will approve of.

The unfortunate General Braddock is dead and buried near the Great

Meadows, he met with a complete Defeat, a great Loss of Men and Artillery. . . .

When the Governor received word of the two Indians from the Ohio, he communicated instantly with Weiser, asking him to bring them to town. Conrad, being ill when the message arrived, sent Sammy, who found himself obliged to go as far as Carlisle to find them, since Jagrea, the Song, and the Wyandots were afraid to come any deeper into the settlements without a Weiser escort.[15]

The strain under which Conrad was living (he was ill and he was still unsure of what had happened to Braddock's army but fearful of what might even now be happening nearer at hand) was too much for him and he could not restrain his anxiety. Before Sammy had time to get back, his father sent enquiries about him to Richard Peters.

Conrad Weiser to Richard Peters [16]

Heidelberg July the 31 1755

Sir

I have heard nothing of Samy and the Indians, they must have ben gone down by lancaster, or are not Come yet to John Harrises, Jonathan was here to visit me and is gone to John Harris^s again, the day before yesterday perhaps he will Come down with Zigerea, order Samy to write to me If he is in philadelphia, I have no particulars of the unhappy fate of our army under General Braddock. as to my Illness I hope I am on the mending hand, I hear every day of the Confusion of the people about Joniady & etc. they are in a dismal fear.—

I am Sir your very humble Servant

CONRAD WEISER

The Indians turned up with Sammy at Heidelberg a few days later, and Conrad, by now recovered, came down with them himself to Philadelphia.

Conrad Weiser to Richard Peters [17]

Sir

I arrived Just now in this place and prevailed on the bearer Adam Torrance who Came with the Indian from beyond Carlile to Carry this, in order to be Informed where I must bring the Indians I shall wait for him Just a litle a this Side the town of philad^{ia} under the Green trees with your orders. who am

Sir

German town at   your h^e Servant
10 of the Clock   CONRAD WEISER
August the 7. 1755
at peter Smiths

The Governor did the handsome thing. He sent first the Provincial Secretary with a string of wampum to bid the Indians welcome, and then, as the Council minutes tell us, "About two hours afterwards the Governor in person with some of his Council paid his Compliment to them and invited them to Dinner." [18] After dinner there was a short conference (Weiser interpreting), at which the Mohawk Jagrea (Zigerea) introduced the Wyandots, and the Governor invited them all to another conference to be held in a few days when Scaroyady and some others had come to town.

Scaroyady arrived on the 13th, accompanied by Andrew Montour and some famous warriors of the Six Nations. On the 15th the conference was held. The hearty thanks of the government were extended to the Wyandots for their visit and to the Six Nations warriors for the valor they had displayed at the battle of the Monongahela. But Scaroyady, Silver Heels, the Belt, and the other warriors who received these compliments, wanted more than words of praise. They had made a dangerous journey from the Ohio to get men and munitions. Scaroyady told Weiser privately that all was at stake on the decisions now made. If the Wyandots were sent back to their people without positive assurance of support in the war, they would be forced to go over to the French. And not only the Wyandots, but also the Delawares, Shawnees, and Ohio Mingoes (Six Nations Indians). Scaroyady knew exactly what was going on among the Indians under his supervision on the Ohio, where Dumas was trying, as yet not quite successfully, to turn them away from the English. "You can't live in the woods and stay neutral," said Scaroyady. The Delawares knew that the French would protect them against the English. Would the English protect them against the French?

The Governor and the Quaker Assembly were snarled in a tangle of pacifism and privilege. The Assembly had passed a bill for defense entailing the taxation of the proprietorial estates. The Governor, having signed a bond to the Penns requiring him to allow no such thing, could do nothing but veto the bill. Both parties found the emergency a convenient political weapon to force the other to yield. The Indians waited impatiently, the alliance of a dozen nations at stake.

More Indians came down, demanding action: Jonathan, John Shickellamy, and others. The Wyandots, having waited ten days and received no satisfaction, made up their minds to go home. Weiser found them in a temper and reported this fact to the Governor and the Speaker of the House. The latter agreed that a present should be given them at once. Accordingly Weiser and Peters ordered goods to the value of fifty-seven pounds, five shillings, and sixpence, to be sent to the Governor's house and delivered to the Wyandots after dinner: an assortment of bed lace, morris bells, "Cuttoe Knives," "sorted Rings," awl blades, vermilion, scarlet garters, white half-thicks, blue strowds, blankets, lead, guns, powder, tobacco, long pipes, "2 Pieces Garlich," etc.[19]

"We cannot give you the Hatchet," said the Governor with an eye to the Quaker Assembly, "but we depend on the continuance of your Friendship"; and with that he gave the disgruntled Wyandots a belt of wampum.[20]

The Wyandots concealed their thoughts. They had wanted an army and they got bed lace and morris bells. Politely, in a speech made two days later, they expressed their thanks and affirmed their friendship with Pennsylvania, adding with an irony that Weiser could appreciate (he understood

Indian humor): "We live on this side Lake Erie at a place called Deonandady, If you should get the better of the French and come into our parts, You will find us your Friends, and we will join you." [21]

Scaroyady, meanwhile, was bent on rousing the English to a sense of what was at stake. He went to Weiser's lodging, and there, in a private conference (being determined that nothing of what he had to say should reach the ears of the Wyandots, whom he distrusted), made representations of such importance that Weiser took them down and presented them afterwards to the Governor in Council, August 22, with Scaroyady himself and several other Indians attending.

Brother, the Governor of Pennsylvania & all the English on this Continent It is now well known to You how unhappily we have been defeated by the French near Minongelo. We must let you know that it was the pride and Ignorance of that great General that came from England; He is now dead; but he was a bad man when he was alive, he looked upon us as dogs and would never hear any thing what was said to him, We often endeavoured to advise him, and to tell him of the danger he was in with his Soldiers, but he never appeared pleased with us & that was the reason that a great many of our Warriors left him & would not be under his Command.

Brethren, We would advise You, not to give up the Point though we have in a manner been chastised from above, but let us unite our Strength, You are very numerous & all the English Governors along your Sea Shore can raise men enough, dont let those that come from over the great Seas be concerned any more, they are unfit to fight in the Woods, let us go ourselves, we that came out of this Ground We may be assured to Conquer the French.

Gave a String of Wampum & desired that the
English would consider the matter well.

Brethren the English, We let you know that our Cousins the Delawares as well as our Brethren the Nanticokes have assured me, that they were never asked to go to War against the French in the late Expedition but promised in the strongest Terms that if their Brethren the English, (especially those of Pennsylvania) will give them their Hatchett they wou'd make use of it, & wou'd join with their Uncles against the French. So we assure you by this belt of Wampum that we will gather all our Allies to assist the English in another Expedition. One word of Yours will bring the Delawares to join You . . .[22]

"One word of yours." The Governor did not speak that word. He played safe. He was having trouble with his Assembly, and besides, His Majesty had not declared war on the French. What reply should he give to Scaroyady? He asked for Weiser's advice. Weiser thought it best, under the circumstances, to give a general answer and suggest that the Delawares await the determination of the Six Nations. This the Governor did, adding the fatuous hope that the Delawares would "continue their friendship."

To soften the rebuff to Scaroyady, a condolence present, consisting of a saddle and "a new Castor Hatt," was given him for the death of his son.[23] Even this gesture was spoiled, however, by the requirement laid upon the poor father to testify under oath to his son's death [24]—which had come about through a wretched blunder committed by an English sentry who shot him by mistake two days before the action at the Monongahela.

Other presents were given to show Pennsylvania's Large Heart (in lieu of Large Eyes to look out for her own interest or that of her wards). Johnny, the Half King's son, got another condolence present for the death of his father.[25] Rewards were given to Silver Heels, Davison, the Belt, Kanuksusy, and others who had been in the action with Braddock; and Kanuksusy, son of old Queen Allaquippa (now living near Rays- town) was given a new name, *Newcastle*, because, as the Governor said, "in 1701 I am informed that your Parents presented You to the late Mr William Penn at Newcastle." [26]

Even these last efforts to cover up the fatal lethargy of the province were botched. "The Guns which the Indians Received as Presents," runs a *Memo* of Conrad Weiser's dated August 23, "proved very bad. They ware alowed to return them to the Secretary or Conrad Weiser, and re- cieve 25/ for each in Money, that Sum being the first Cost. They re- turned 12 . . ." [27]

In such manner Pennsylvania kicked away the loyalty of her Indian allies.

"I am heartily Sick of our present Situation," wrote Benjamin Franklin to Peter Collinson;

I like neither the Governor's Conduct nor the Assembly's . . . The Assembly ride restive, and the Governor, tho' he spurs with both Heels, at the same time reins in with both Hands, so that the Publick Business can never move for- ward, and he remains like St. George in the Sign, always a Horseback, & never going on [28]

At Fort Duquesne, Dumas was using the argument of powder and lead to persuade the Ohio Indians to follow him.

Part IV

BLACK WAMPUM

CHAPTER 45

... *Raises an Army by Three O'Clock at Benjamin Spycker's*

DUMAS at Fort Duquesne was all too successful with his Indians.

> . . . I have succeeded, [he wrote to the Minister, July 24, 1756,] in ruining the three adjacent provinces, Pennsylvania, Maryland, and Virginia, driving off the inhabitants, and totally destroying the settlements over a tract of country thirty leagues wide, reckoning from the line of Fort Cumberland. M. de Contrecoeur had not been gone a week before I had six or seven different war-parties in the field at once, always accompanied by Frenchmen. Thus far, we have lost only two officers and a few soldiers; but the Indian villages are full of prisoners of every age and sex. The enemy has lost far more since the battle than on the day of his defeat.[1]

Now if ever Pennsylvania needed the help of the Six Nations.

On October 1 there came to see Weiser at Heidelberg Tohashwughtonionty or the Belt,[2] a Seneca warrior who had fought under Braddock —not to be confused with Tohashwuchdioony, the Belt, of Onondaga. "Tohashwughtonionty (the Belt)," Weiser had written some days before on meeting him at John Harris', "is a man of very good understanding, has a good Countenance, speaks well and is reckoned amongst the greatest Warriors among the Six Nations.—I esteem him much." [3] With him were Jonathan, James Logan, and Jagrea.

The Belt delivered a speech to the Governor through Conrad Weiser.

> Brother Onas. . . . We have agreed among ourselves to settle at Shamokin, and to summons and exort all our Indian Brethren, to come and settle there, and live and die with us.
>
> We therefore desire you to supply us with Provision, Powder, Lead, Tobacco and Vermillion, and as it is most certain by the last Message we received a few days ago from Oneido, that Warr is proclaimed between the Six United Nations and the French and their Allies, those of the Six Nations that have French hearts may go to their wicked Father Onontio (we hope a very few will) the Six united Nations with their Allies will certainly Chastize Onontio for his Wickedness. We pray Brother Onas & the people of Pennsylvania not to leave us in the lurch, but so supply us with necessaries to enable us to fight the French.[4]

Weiser despatched this message to Philadelphia. Two weeks later Richard Peters wrote to say that the Governor had not presented it to the Assembly for fear of subjecting himself to further insult.[5]

While the good people of Philadelphia played politics—comfortably assured that other men's bodies stood between them and the scalping knife

—the tomahawk was carried deep into the province. On the evening of October 17 a woman of the Penn's Creek district (near the present town of Selinsgrove) called at a neighbor's house and found two persons lying dead and scalped beside the door. She gave the alarm.[6] It was found that some fourteen persons had been killed and eleven carried away.

The survivors in the settlement petitioned the Governor for help in the defense of their land.

. . . we are not able of ourselves to defend it [they wrote] for want of Guns and Ammunition . . . We therefore humbly desire y^t your Honour would take the same into your great Consideration and order some speedy relief for the safety of these back Settlements, and be pleased to give us speedy order what to do . . .[7]

A report of these murders was sent to Philadelphia by John Harris. The friendly Indians at his place, said Harris, sent wampum to the Governor: two white strings from the men and a black string from the women, "both requesting that you'l lay by all your Council Pipes immediately and open all your Eyes and Ears to view your Slain People in this Land . . . Any Delay," added Harris, "of our acting vigorously now at this time will be the loss of all Indian Interest . . ."[8]

The Governor tried again to suppress the news. In Philadelphia that was possible, but not at Heidelberg. The Penn's Creek massacre brought the war close to Conrad Weiser. He had a nephew living up there, and sent his sons Frederick and Peter to bring him and his family down—though that Heidelberg itself could be considered safe, Conrad Weiser was not at all sure. "the people down here seem to be senseless," he wrote to the Governor, "and say the Indians will never come this side Susquehannah River but I fear they will, since they meet with no opposition no where."[9]

It was difficult for quiet, peaceable Pennsylvanians to conceive of danger as something threatening themselves. Christopher Saur in his newspaper of September 16 had said that Pennsylvania had nothing to fear: for seventy years no one had been captured or robbed by Indians. Governor Morris knew better, but he put his head under the pillow. The Assembly behaved like schoolboys watching a fire in the next block. Only those who had smelt burned flesh and seen torn scalps seemed to be concerned about what was going on along the frontier.

"How long," wrote William Trent, "will those in power by their Quarrels suffer us to be massacred?"[10]

John Harris, like Weiser, was restive at inaction. Spurred by the news from Penn's Creek, he took a body of forty-nine men with him up the river to reconnoitre, and reached Shamokin on Friday, October 24.[11] The day before, there had arrived an Indian messenger from the West Branch of the Susquehanna with news which Andrew Montour passed on to him: more than fifteen hundred French and Indians had left Fort Duquesne some sixteen days before, intending to burn all before them. "Carlisle and my house is two appointed places," reported Harris, "and the whole of Cumberland County if they can Effect it which in the Situation we are in may be easily done and I think we are in as much danger as can be imagined from such Enemies." [12]

Shamokin had an ugly look. There were too many canoes coming and going, and too many strange Indians about, "all painted Black which gave suspicion." Andrew Montour was painted like the others, a circumstance that did not recommend him to the confidence of Harris' party. When Andrew advised them to avoid the west bank on their return and go down by the more difficult east side of the river, they suspected a trap and did just what Andrew had warned them not to do. They crossed the river, on October 25, at what is now known as Shamokin Dam, reaching the west bank above George Gabriel's, and prepared to go down to the ford at the Mahanoy, where they would cross the Susquehanna again as usual.

They did not get so far. ". . . when they Came to John penns Creek," wrote Weiser a few days later, ". . . Just as they entered the Creek they were fired upon from the other Side by Indians and Some dropt which put them in Confusion Some Cried let us fly, others Stand your Ground . . ." [13] The "shooting and hideous hallowing" of the Indians, as Harris himself tells the story, frightened the main body of his men away, and they turned and galloped back to the ford of the Susquehanna. Harris himself with about fifteen men "took to Trees and Attacked the Villains, kill'd four of them on the Spot and lost but three Men Retreating about half a mile through Woods and crossing Sasquehanna one of which was shot from off a horse Riding behind my self through the River   my horse before was wounded and failing in the River I was oblig'd to quit him and swim part of the Way   4 or 5 of our Men was drowned Crossing the River,   I hope our Journey tho' with Fatigue and the loss of our Substance and some of our Lives will be of Service to our Country by discovering our Enemies who will be our Ruin if not timely Prevented . . ." [14]

When the news reached Shamokin, the Indians there made up a party of twenty-nine armed men and set out at once for the scene of the skirmish. Among them were the three Shickellamies (John, James Logan, and John Petty), Andrew Montour, Jagrea, and Tohashwughtonionty. Weiser heard afterwards that "The Old Belt at the head of them cry'd like a Child." [15] No doubt he saw his world tumbling into ruin. The French Indians had struck at the English. Would not the English in revenge soon look upon all Indians of whatever nation as their enemies?

There was nothing to be done. The enemy had slipped back into the bushes and disappeared. Next morning the Shawnee chief, Paxinosa, visited the scene with some young men. They found several bodies, as David Zeisberger reported after talking with Paxinosa, "a Suit of Womens Cloaths with new Shoes lying near the River," and "a bloody Glove lying by a Tree which had been very much Shot . . ."—property, as it turned out, of Thomas McKee, the Indian trader, who had been wounded in the hand. Paxinosa found a track and followed it into the woods,

. . . where the s^d Chief spied a Sapling cut down & a little further a Grub twisted, then he call'd his Company & told them this betokend something, and upon search they found a Parcel of Leaves raked together which upon removing they found a Grave, & an Indian well dress'd who had been shot lay there whom they discover'd by the Hairs of his Head being pull'd out excepting a Tufft on his Crown to be a French Mohack Indian they Strip'd & Scalp'd him.[16]

Before the news of this latest disaster at Penn's Creek reached Weiser, Frederick and Peter had returned to Heidelberg with news that their father thought grave enough to be put into a despatch for the Governor and taken to town express by Sammy. Sammy was to get as far as Reading that night, where he would find a bed at the house of his brother Peter, the saddler.[17]

The news that Sammy carried was this: While the boys were at George Gabriel's house (burned a night or two later while the French Indians danced round it in the light of the flames) a messenger had arrived from James Logan and the Delaware Capachpitton with word that a large body of French and Indians had been seen on this side of the Allegheny Hills. The Shamokin region was in danger, but the Indians there were loyal.

. . . if the White people will come up to Shamokin and assist [wrote Weiser], they will stand the French and fight them. They said that now they want to see their Brethren's faces, and well armed with smooth Guns, no rifled Guns which requires too much cleaning. . . . I pray good Sir dont slight it—The lives of many thousands are in the utmost Danger. It is no false alarm.[18]

That was written on Sunday, "at 5 o'Clock in the Evening."

Meantime, following the affair at Penn's Creek, the wildest rumors spread through the woods. It was said that the main force of French and Indians was already on the east side of the Susquehanna, that they were laying all waste, and that they had already killed a great many people from Thomas McKee's at the Mahanoy down to Hunter's Mill near John Harris'. It was also said that Lancaster had been burned to the ground.[19]

On Sunday, October 26, the Reverend John Elder of Paxton heard the first of these rumors and sent it up country to another Presbyterian minister, whose congregation, assembled for evening service near Adam Read's (a little south of Indian Town Gap) broke meeting to make preparations for defense. Messengers were sent to Conrad Weiser, who received "the Melancholly news" at about 10 o'clock on Sunday night.[20]

That hour marked his entrance upon a military career. He went into action with an explosion of his old-time energy that affords one of the most dramatic episodes in Pennsylvania's colonial history. It was an hour of conversion. He had never had any desire for soldiering. He had declined a commission during King George's War. He had prayed that an Indian war might be averted. But, like his famous grandson, General (the Reverend) John Peter Gabriel Muhlenberg, he believed that there is a time to pray and a time to fight—and that this was the time to fight.

Little John Peter (the General to be) was visiting his grandparents on the farm at Heidelberg, and that night he had his first taste of war.

Within an hour of receiving the news from the Susquehanna, Weiser's plans, which must have been simmering long in his mind in anticipation of such an emergency, were in full operation. It was a large task Weiser had undertaken: to comb several hundred square miles of its manpower and make an army out of the findings overnight. The settlers had to be roused, assembled, armed, officered, and set in motion—all before the enemy had time to move up the valley. His servants were sent out as couriers. The men of Heidelberg were to meet by daybreak at Weiser's, and those of Tulpehocken Township at Benjamin Spycker's where Weiser and his Heidelberg contingent would later join them.[21]

These dispositions made, he wrote at 11 o'clock at night to James Read in Reading, telling him what he had done. "for Gods sake," he said, "let us stand together, and do what we can and trust to the hand of Providence, . . . I pray beware of Confusion be calm you and Mr Seely and act the part as fathers of the people." [22]

There was no calmness in the Tulpehocken Valley that night. Messengers were flying about from farm to farm. Horses galloped up the road between Heidelberg and Reading. Sammy had gone that way earlier in the evening. James Read saw Sammy before six in the morning and gave him a fresh despatch for the Governor. Read did not take the time to write a letter of his own, but sent on the letter he had received from Weiser, adding to it his own postscript at "6 A.M.": "I shall raise our Town in an hour . . . I could wish your Honour could order us two or three Swivel Guns and Blunderbusses with a few Muskets and some Powder Swan Shot." [23]

In Philadelphia the calm of a Quaker Sunday had melted into the dawn of Monday's political stalemate. Colonial officialdom awoke and addressed itself to the task of correspondence. Both the Governor and the Secretary took up their quills to communicate with Thomas Penn. Governor Morris told about the unpleasantness at Penn's Creek—the first murders. His letter leaves us with the impression that he thought something should be done about it, some time. He had written, he said, to General Shirley asking him to send down some troops from Albany, and expressed the hope that they might arrive that winter. "But if," he added, "the season should prevent the removal of these Troops The People must make the best shift they can for I have no reason to expect anything from the Assembly." [24]

Richard Peters, seated at his walnut desk, expressed concern about Conrad Weiser, who, it appeared, was fading out of the colonial picture: "Mr Weiser grows every day more & more tired wth Indian Business . . . Conrad will still give advice & may attend the Call of ye Governmt but he grows too unwieldy for fatigues & Journys." [25]

While Peters sat at his desk day-dreaming about Weiser's incapacity, Weiser himself, after a night of alarms at Heidelberg, was in the saddle, organizing an army, and preparing to lead it himself against the enemy.

Conrad Weiser to Governor Morris [26]

[Reading, October 30, 1755]

May it please the Governor,

. . . After I had received the news that Paxton People above Hunters Mill had been murdered I immediately sent my Servants to alarm the Neighbourhood. The people came to my house by break of Day. I informed them of the Melancholy news and how I came by it, &c[a] They unanimously agreed to stand by one another and march to meet the Enemy, if I would go with them. I told them not only myself but my Sons and Servants should go; they put themselves under my direction: I gave orders to them to go home and fetch their Arms whether Guns, Swords, Pitchforks, Axes or whatsoever might be of use against the Enemy and for three days provision in their Knapsacks and meet me at Benjamin Spickers at three of the Clock that afternoon about six Miles above my House in Tulpohoccon Township, where I had sent word for Tulpohoccon also to meet. I immediately mounted my Horse and went up to Benjamin Spickers where I found about one hundred people who had met before I came there; and after I had informed them of the Intelligence I had and promised to go with them as a common Soldier and to be commanded by such officers and leading men whatever they might call them as they should chuse, they unanimously agreed to join Heidleberg People and accordingly they went home to fetch their Arms and Provisions for three days and came again at 3 o'Clock, all this was punctually performed and about two hundred men were at Benjamin Spickers by two of the Clock. I made the necessary disposition and the people were divided into Companys of thirty men each Company, they chosed their Officers, that is a Captain over each Company and three inferiors under him each to take care of ten men and lead them on or fire as the Captain should direct, I sent privately for M[r] Kurtz the Lutheran Minister who lived about a Mile off, who came and gave an Exhortation to the men and made a Prayer suitable to the time and then we marched towards Sasquehannah having first sent about fifty men to Tolheo in order to possess themselves of the Capes or Narrows of Swahatawro where we expected the Enemy would come through with a Letter to M[r] Parsons who happened to be at his Plantation. . . .

These tactical dispositions were sound. In marching down the valley toward Paxton, his force was protected on the flank by the mountains, unless the enemy came over the Shamokin Trail. It was to meet this threat that he despatched the fifty men, the number being increased later to about one hundred, under William Parsons, with orders to occupy the "Capes" or upper Gaps of the Swatara (above the site of the modern town of Pine Grove), where the trail threaded a wild and narrow pass through the Second Mountain.[27] If Weiser's instructions had been followed, if breast-works had been erected to supplement the natural defenses of the place and the enemy had found himself vigorously opposed there, the tragedy that occurred a few days later in St. Anthony's Wilderness might have been prevented. As it was, Parsons' men, in the absence of their commander who had gone to Tulpehocken (whence he sent an express to Lancaster) in search of ammunition, went no farther than the top of the first mountain. There they put up some defenses near Pilger Ruh, spent the night, and returned home next day—firing their guns as they went to keep them dry in the rain, and by so doing spreading panic among the people who heard them in the valley and set in motion a train of the wildest rumors. A few days later a small band of Indians came through the Gaps, unopposed and unobserved, and carved a bloody trail into the county.

Weiser's main force, meanwhile, went on its way to head off the enemy supposed to be approaching from the Susquehanna. Weiser was on horseback. The contingent that followed him was like a frothy brown stream born of one of the cloudbursts that deluge this region, overflowing the furrows of the road that ran along by the foot of the Blue Mountains. The men were fitted with every variety of weapon, of clothing, of beard. There were men of the Plain Sects among them, pacifists by principle, who would fight, nevertheless, to save their homes.

"I had two or three long Beards in my Company," wrote Weiser, "one a Menonist who declared he would live and die with his neighbours; he had a good gun with him." [28]

Conrad Weiser to Governor Morris (continued)

. . . We marched about ten Miles that evening; my Company was now increased to upwards of Three hundred men mostly well armed, tho' about twenty men had nothing but Axes and Pitchforks, all unanimously agreed to die together and engage the Enemy, wherever they should meet with them, never to enquire the number but fight them & so obstruct their Marching further into the Inhabited parts, till others of our Brethren should come up and do the same and so save the Lives of our Wives & Children. This night the Powder and Lead came up that I sent for early in the Morning from Reading; & I ordered it to the care of the Officers to divide it among those that wanted it most. On the 28 by break of Day we marched; our Company encreasing all along. We arrived at Adam Reads Esqr in Hanover Township Lancaster County, about 10 o'Clock, there we stoped and rested till all came up. Mr Read had just then received intelligence from Sasquehanna by Express . . .

For the first time now Weiser received particulars of what had really happened on the Susquehanna—the story of the skirmish at Penn's Creek, which need not be rehearsed here. The rumor of an enemy in great force at the mouth of Lebanon Valley was dissipated.

. . . Upon this we had a Consultation, and as we did not come up to serve as Guards to Paxton people but to fight the Enemy, if they were come so far as we first heard, we thought best to return and take care of our own Townships—After I had given the necessary caution to the People to hold themselves in readiness as the Enemy was certainly in the Country, so keep their Arms in good order and so on, I discharged them and so we marched back with the Approbation of Mr Read. by the way we were alarmed with a Report that above Five hundred Indians had come over the Mountain at Tolheo to this side and had already killed a number of People. We stopt and sent a few men to discover the Enemy, but on their return it proved to be a false Alarm occasioned by that Company I had sent that way the day before whose Guns getting wet, they fired them off, which was the Case of my Company on their Returning they fired off their Guns not considering the ill Consequence, and the whole Township through which we marched were very much alarmed. In going back I met several Messengers from other Townships about Conestogo who came for intelligence and to ask me where their Assistance was necessary promising that they would come to the place where I should direct. I met also at Tulpehoccon above one hundred men well armed as to Fire Arms ready to follow me, so that there were in the whole about 500 men in Arms that day all marching up towards Sasquehannah. I and Mr Adam Read counted those that were with me, We found 320.

I cannot send any further account being uncommonly fatigued, I should not forget however to inform Your Honour that Mr Read has engaged to keep proper Persons riding between his House and Sasquehannah, and if anything material Shall occur he will send me Tidings at Heidleburgh or here, which I shall take care to dispatch to you. I find that great care has been taken at Reading to get people together and near two hundred were here Yesterday Morning; but upon hearing that the People attending me were discharged the people from the Country went off without consulting what should be done for the future thro' the Indiscretion of a Person who was with them and wanted to go home, and near the Town they meet a large Company coming up and gave such accounts as would do their Duty, but without some Military Regulations, we shall never be able to defend the Province. I am sure we are in great Danger, and by an Enemy that can travel as Indians do we may be surprized when it would be impossible to collect any number of men together to defend themselves, and then the Country would be laid waste. I am quite tired, and cannot say more than that

I am,
Your Honours,
most Obedient Servant
CONRAD WEISER

CHAPTER 46

. . . Is a Colonel Without a Regiment

I

CONFUSION and panic swept the frontier. It was every man for himself. John Harris loop-holed his house on the Susquehanna.[1] Weiser distributed arms at Reading.[2] But there was no cohesion anywhere and no spirit among the people. Without an army to stiffen them or a blockhouse to fall back on, the mass of the people fluctuated between terror and apathy. The justices of the peace did what they could, but the people would take no orders. In Tulpehocken, Weiser appealed to the parsons, but their influence availed little in the emergency. The Indians were allowed to cross the Blue Mountains all along the line between the Susquehanna and the Delaware. Soon the sky was filled with the smoke of burning houses and barns.

What gave the invasion a peculiar pall of horror was that local Indians —inoffensive, shiftless, companionable fellows as they had seemed a few weeks before—were among the scalping parties. The back inhabitants reported, according to John Bartram, that

. . . most of yᵉ Indians which are so cruel are such as was allmost dayly familiar at thair houses eate drank & swore together was even intimate play mates & now without any provokation destroyeth all before them with fire ball & tomahawk they commonly now shoot with rifles with which they will at A great distance from behind A tree fence ditch or rock or under yᵉ covert of leaves take such sure aim as seldom miseth thair mark if thay attack A house that is pretty well maned thay creep behind some fence or hedge or tree & shoot red hot iron slugs or punk into yᵉ roof & fires yᵉ house over thair heads & if thay run out thay are sure to be shot at & most or all of them killed if thay come to A house where yᵉ most of yᵉ family is women & children thay break into it kills them all plunders yᵉ house & burns it with yᵉ dead in it or if any escaped out thay pursueth & kills them if yᵉ cattle is in yᵉ stable thay fire it & burns yᵉ cattle if thay are out thay are shot & yᵉ barn burnt [3]

Nothing could better show the vigor of Conrad's mind than the letters he wrote during the black days at the end of October and the beginning of November. He was, of course, impressionable enough to feel something of the common fear that surrounded him, and he signed his name along with others to a wild appeal to the Governor dated at "Reading, October 31ˢᵗ 1755 8 o'Clock at night":

We are all in Uproar, all in Disorder, all willing to do and have little in our power, . . . If we are not immediately supported, we must not be sacrificed, and therefore are determined to go down with all that will follow us to Philadelphia, & Quarter ourselves on it's Inhabitants, and wait our Fate with them.[4]

But Conrad kept his wits about him. His vision was not blurred, and his letters, though they are excited, give an undistorted picture of the situation as it developed hour by hour.

On Hallowe'en he was in Reading, gathering information, writing letters, conferring with local leaders, and distributing arms. Shortly before noon his son Frederick hurried in from the farm at Heidelberg relaying news from Shamokin brought by one Charles Williams, who had been in the engagement at Penn's Creek. The Indian James Logan had told Williams that a party of the enemy, under command of the well-known Delaware Pesquitomen, was then only six miles from Shamokin, and that a body of fifteen hundred French and Indians from the Ohio (how that false rumor persisted!) was only a day's journey behind them. Despite the news about Pisquetomen, Weiser refused to give up the Susquehanna Indians as lost to the English cause. He understood their dilemma and was determined to help them if he could. He knew that they were in fear of both the French and of the English. The latter threatened them to their faces. Weiser called for volunteers to go to Shamokin *without arms* and invite all Indians who found themselves in danger to come down into the settlements with their wives and children.[5] Twenty-five men offered to go—if they might take arms; but Weiser, knowing that such a party would more likely precipitate bloodshed than save it, would not have them. At length George Gabriel, turning up in town opportunely, accepted fifty pounds to go with two of his hands, unarmed, carrying the message to Shamokin.[6] Weiser found them horses and sent them off. He himself rode out to the farm at Heidelberg to see what he could do there to organize the people.

At night a neighbor brought him a letter torn to pieces by the many hands through which it had passed—a letter signed by James Galbreath, Barney Hughes, Robert Wallace, John Harris, and others, dated "Paxton October 31st 1755 From John Harris's at 12 a Clock at Night," addressed "To all his Majesties Subjects in the Province of Pennsylvania, or elsewhere."[7] It contained a deposition to the effect that Andrew Montour, the Belt of Wampum, Scaroyady (*alias* Monecatootha), two Mohawks, and some other Indians had brought word from Shamokin that the enemy was "actually encamped on this side George Gabriels near Sasquehannah and that we may expect an attack in three days at farthest and a French Fort to be begun at Shamokin in ten days hence." Appeal was made to the settlers to march against them at once. Galbreath added in a postscript that Scaroyady, the Belt, and others of the Indians insisted "upon Mr Weiser's coming immediately here to John Harris's with his Men, and to Council with the Indians"

Confronted with this fresh news of the enemy, Weiser "sent after George Gabriel to call him back,"[8] had a copy made of the Paxton letter (the original being too badly torn to send to the Governor), enclosed it in a letter to James Read at Reading, and sent Sammy off with it express. "God help us, our Cause is desperate," wrote Weiser, "and the People are hardened and without feeling. I am tired to speak to them any longer though willing to do what I can . . . I wish you would send a few Gunns and some powder and lead—to my house here." [9] The letter, as it has come down to us, has a few lines added by Sammy: "Father ordered me to mention that the within inclosed Copy ought to be forwarded."

Conrad Weiser was more nearly distracted at this time than at any other point in his tumultuous career. He knew the people of his neighborhood would not march again toward the Susquehanna: their own homes were in danger. The enemy was within six or seven miles of Tolheo. Weiser had just heard from William Parsons, who wrote in great distress of the murder of Hartman in St. Anthony's Wilderness. "I have not lived long in the World," said Parsons, "and yet I have lived too long." [10]

There was much to be done, and no machinery for doing it: assembling the people and protecting the farms, rousing the government in Philadelphia, distributing the arms Benjamin Franklin had sent up to Reading, protecting friendly Indians, saving the whole edifice of Indian alliances which the hotheads among the people (who wanted to shoot all Indians at sight, and be paid for it, too—they demanded a scalp bounty) were likely to bring down about their ears. Why had not Scaroyady and the Belt been sent on to Weiser's at Heidelberg? This was no time for a council at Harris'. Were the settlers there holding the Indians back? Early on the morning of November 2 he sent Sammy, who had returned from Reading, express to John Harris' with an invitation to the Indians to come to his house.

Weiser himself planned to take a party over into St. Anthony's Wilderness to bring out the settlers who remained there. For this purpose he had sent for his son Peter, who in response came from Reading with about fifteen men. But Weiser now had to wait for word from Harris' before he could stir. His house was the channel through which flowed what little intelligence could be gathered from the frontier, and at all costs there must be no slip in connections with the loyal representatives of the Six Nations remaining in the province.

While he waited for Scaroyady and the Belt, his brain whirled with thoughts of the danger to which his family and the plantation were exposed. "had we but good regulation," he wrote to the Governor at night, November 2,

with gods help we Could Stand at our place of abode, but If the people fail, (which I am a feared they will, because Some goes, Some wont. Some mocKs. Some pleads religion and a great Number of Cowards,) I Shall think of myn and my familys preservation and quit my place, If I Can get none to Stand by me to defend my own house. but I hope you will Excuse this Hury, I have no ClerK now. and had no rest this Several days nor Nights hardly.[11]

He did not go into St. Anthony's Wilderness. Scaroyady turned up suddenly, demanding that he be taken at once to Philadelphia. The old chief, never very patient, was now thoroughly angry with Pennsylvania. It was no time to offend the Six Nations viceregent from the Ohio. Unfortunately at just about this same time there came a letter from the Governor (dated October 31, but delayed a day or two in town) appointing him a colonel and telling him to go ahead and save the country.

Weiser was torn two ways. The commission called him to stay; Scaroyady urged him to go. What was he to do?

Governor Morris to Conrad Weiser [12]

Philadelphia October 31ˢᵗ 1755

Sir,

I had the pleasure of receiving Your favor of the 30ᵗʰ Instant and of being thereby set right as to the Indians passing the Mountains at Tolheo which I am glad to find was a false alarm. I heartily commend your Conduct and Zeal and hope you will continue to act with the same Vigor and Caution that you have already done, and that you may have the greater Authority I have appointed You a Colonel by a Commission herewith.

I have not time to give you any Instructions with the Commission but leave it to your Judgment and discretion which I know are great to do what is most for the safety of the people and service of the Crown. . . .

I have only to wish you all imaginable success and to recommend it to you to Continue your Care and Diligence for his Majesties Service.

I am Sir

Your most Humble Servant

ROBERT H MORRIS

The Governor's instructions were loose; Scaroyady's demands were firm. Weiser delayed his journey with Scaroyady, therefore, only long enough to dash off instructions to some of his neighbors, and then went to town with the Indians.

Conrad Weiser to John Artz and others [13]

Dear Friends and Neighbors!

I inform you that I am virtually compelled to go off to Philadelphia in all haste with these Chiefs of the Indians living on the waters of the Susquehanna, They want no more words, but deeds,—and they tell me it appears, that I am their good and loving friend! But they see that I do not have it in my power to do what I think is right and proper in Indian affairs, they are now resolved to have a yes or no answer from the Governor and Assembly—and since the affair that they have privately imparted to me is so very important I must go with them without delay for the best interests of the country.

Meanwhile you must do your duty like honest men, and set a guard near Dietrich Six's of at least 50 men and more so the settlements can have warning where the enemy will be breaking in upon them, and since the Governor of Pennsylvania in this time of pressing need has selected me (not of my seeking) for Colonel of the militia soon to be established and has installed me with full powers under his Hand and Seal. I accordingly herewith appoint Johannes Artz, William Risser, Johannes Ekert, Johannes Meyer and Friederick Robel to represent me in place and person in making such arrangements and giving such orders, with all gentleness yet in full earnest, as may be for the people's safety, [and] to tell fractious persons to their faces that they will be looked on and

treated as enemies of their country and good-for-nothing parasites upon the common weal;   My journey to Philadelphia will be all for the best,   I am
                                    Your obedient servant and true Friend
                                                      C. W.

To Johannes Artz and the other
above named inhabitants of
Heydelberg
            the 5th Nov. 1755
            at 8 o'Clock in the morning

                                    II

Weiser and Scaroyady made such good time that the Governor's Council, assembled in Philadelphia on Friday, November 7, received a letter from Germantown of the same date "at 6 o'clock in the evening," announcing Weiser's arrival there with Andrew Montour, Scaroyady, "and drunken Zigrea." [14]

The Council was reconvened next morning and the Governor welcomed the Indians and desired their advice. Scaroyady was glad to give it. "Brethren," he said: "Since we saw one another last Affairs have taken a great turn. We have now need to look about us in this dangerous time. I came down on purpose to encourage both Governor, Council, Wisemen and Warriors." He went on to say that the Ohio Delawares, prodded by the French, had proclaimed war on the English, and that they had sent two messengers to the Big Island on the Susquehanna who had made the following declaration:

When Washington was defeated, We the Delawares were blamed as the Cause of it. We will now kill. We will not be blamed without a Cause. We make up three Parties of Delawares. One Party will go against Carlisle;   One down the Sasquehannah;   and I myself with another party will go against Tulpohoccon to Conrad Weiser. And We shall be followed by a Thousand French and Indians, Ottowawas, Twightwees, Shawonese and other Delawares. [15]

Scaroyady was not content to talk only to the Governor and Council. He had a message, he declared, from the Susquehanna Indians to the people of Pennsylvania, and to the people of Pennsylvania (through their elected representatives) he would give it. In other words, he desired to be heard in public and before the Assembly.

Accordingly a joint meeting of the Council and the Assembly was held in the State House at three o'clock that afternoon; [16] and there, before the Governor, Council, Assembly, the Mayor and Aldermen of Philadelphia, and many citizens, Scaroyady made his final appeal for deeds, not words, from Pennsylvania. Speaking "with great Force and Energy, and with apparent Grief and Concern," [17] as we are told, he urged the English "to act like Men, and be no longer like Women, pursuing weak Measures, that rendered their Names despicable," but to take up the hatchet and join the Six Nations and the Indians on the Susquehanna against the French. "I want you to open your hearts," he said, "I want to look into their Insides. I must now know if you will stand by us, to be plain, if you will fight or not. . . . Be persuaded that we are determined to know the certainty of your Measures before we take any of our selves." [18]

Taking two belts of wampum tied together in token of the union of the Six Nations and their tributaries on the Susquehanna, he threw them on the table and demanded a response without delay.

Governor Morris, whom Benjamin Franklin described as "the rashest and most indiscreet Governor that I have known," [19] thanked Scaroyady for his visit, but regretted that it was impossible to give an answer at this time. That, he indicated as he turned to the Speaker of the Assembly, was a matter that lay in the hands of the Assembly. He desired that body to return to its House and (in all but so many words) to repent.

Richard Peters once described Governor Morris as "a kind amicable sensible Man, but with a wrong turn of mind." This was one of his wrong turns. The Assembly, more than a little piqued, met his first desire by returning to their House; but, as for the second, they adjourned and left the Governor—and the Province—flat. When His Excellency was apprised of this turn of affairs (Richard Peters performed the pleasant duty of telling him) he threw up his hands and announced that he was leaving town at once—going to the back counties. The Council was startled, knowing this to be a very wrong turn indeed. In the emergency, "The first thing that occurred," we read in their minutes, "was to send for Mr Weiser and the Indians . . ." [20]

Scaroyady and the rest, informed of the Governor's intention, conferred among themselves and then spoke to His Excellency through Conrad Weiser:

. . . if you go we shall take all for lost, and therefore We request you in the most pressing terms not to go, but to stay with your Council and Assembly and come to a Determination on the important Point we have spoken to you upon. We declare if we fail in this present Application we will not come here again nor trouble ourselves further with the Province but leave it to its own Destruction and provide for our own safety in some other place and in the best manner we can.[21]

The Governor stayed.

On Wednesday, November 12, the impatient Scaroyady having waited four days for his answer, the Assembly tossed back to the Governor the shuttlecock of the disputed money bill (which the Governor, it will be recalled, because of the terms of his commission from the Penns was unable to sign), and the matter was left exactly where it had been before Scaroyady spoke. The chief was sent for and informed of the impasse. He assured the Governor that this meant the absolute defection of the Delawares, and left with Colonel Weiser for the frontier.

Ten days had been lost. The Susquehanna Delawares had been pushed into Onontio's lap. "*Hinc illae Lacrymae!*" wrote William Peters (brother of the secretary) after three years of Indian war: "thus the grand crisis was neglected & that critical & most favorable Opportunity of fixing & securing those Indians in our Interest . . ." [22]

Conrad Weiser managed to save something out of the ruins of the conference. By his own steadiness and good sense he restored some portion of the confidence in the English colonies which Scaroyady and his companions undoubtedly desired to feel. Andrew Montour went so far as to leave his wife and children with the English. Scaroyady, with all his irritability and explosiveness, was a man of principle; and he now proved himself a better friend to the English than they deserved to find in him after presenting him with the spectacle of hosts quarreling in the presence of their guest. Scaroyady was a second Shickellamy in his devotion to the Iroquois-English alliance, and he had no intention of throwing it away merely because the intrigues of the French on the Ohio and the slow-wittedness of the authorities in Philadelphia had now imperiled it.

When the old chief finally left Philadelphia, he left it entrusted with a dangerous mission to Onondaga, where he was (1) to lay before the Great Council (if he survived the journey through what was, in part at least, enemy country) the defection of the Delawares; (2) to discover whether the Six Nations themselves were, as George Croghan said they were, for reasons of policy inciting the Delawares against the English; and, (3) to propose to the Onondaga Council to correct their rebellious nephews and take the hatchet out of their hands. On his way north he was to visit all the Indian towns along the Susquehanna up to its headwaters, keeping his eyes open, gathering intelligence, and calling on all Indians to assist Brother Onas.

Scaroyady believed, as Weiser did, that the Susquehanna Indians (Delawares, Shawnees, etc.) were not yet lost. But it was known that they were in a precarious position: threatened by the Indians from the Ohio, and threatened also by Pennsylvania settlers who could not distinguish friend from foe but only knew that Indians killed and therefore must be killed. On November 9 the Indians at Wyoming had told Charles Broadhead that they were gravely disturbed. They had heard nothing from Colonel Johnson, nothing from Brother Onas, nothing from the Six Nations; ". . . and now we hear the Hatchets are a flying about our Ears, which puts us in Fears, & makes us believe we are in great Danger . . ." [23] It was part of Scaroyady's mission to bring reassurance to the Susquehanna Indians before the Delawares and Shawnees from the Ohio stampeded them into some bloody incident that would force them, through fear of English reprisals, to ally themselves with the French.

When Scaroyady left, it was already known well enough that the Ohio Delawares and Shawnees were on the warpath, led by Shingas, the Beaver, and Pisquetomen—three brothers, and nephews of the late Chief Olumapies (Sassoonan) of Shamokin. [24] It was not known that a new leader had arisen among the Susquehanna Delawares, namely Teedyuscung (the Moravian convert Daniel, *alias* Honest John, of the Shecomeco mission) who was already lifting his voice and his hatchet against Brother Onas, and sending his ambassador, by name Cut-Fingered Peter, with scalps and belts of wampum to the Six Nations.[25] There was soon to be apprehension enough among Daniel's late Brethren, the Moravians. "The Savages have made it clear," wrote Spangenberg at Bethlehem, December 9, 1755, "that they will lay in Ashes first *Bethlehem*, then *Easton*, then *Nazareth*, and then the remaining *Settlements* in the *Fork*, & massacre everyone." [26]

III

While Weiser was in Philadelphia, the Governor received bad news from the west. "The great Cove and kennalaways is all Burned to Ashes," wrote Adam Hoops, November 6.[27] Wild rumors were circulating about the activities of "Shingas the Terrible" and his Delaware warriors. ". . . it is really very Shocking," wrote Hoops, "to See an Husband looking on while these Indians are Chopping the head off the Wife of his Bosom, and the Childrens blood drank like Water by these Bloody & Cruel Savages as We are Informed has been the Fate of many . . ." [28]

For some days, however, after Hoops wrote there was a lull, and the Governor, on November 15, expressed his hope "that the Indians have Stopd their Progress." By an ironical coincidence, that was the day on which the Indians for the first time came over the Blue Mountains into what is now known as Lebanon Valley and attacked the settlements there.

Peter Spycker to Conrad Weiser [29]

Tulpehoccon y[e] 16th
November 1755

Conrad Weiser Esq[r]

John Anspack and Frederick Reed came to me and told me the miserable Circumstance of the People murdered this side the Mountain. Yesterday the Indians attacked the Watch killed and wounded him at Derrick Sixth, and in that Neighbourhood great many in that night. This morning our people went out to see, came about 10 o'clock in the morning to Thomas Bower's house finding a Man Dead killed wth a Gun Shott. Soon we heard a noise of firing Gunns, Running to that place, and found four Indians sitting on Children scalping, 3 of the Children are dead, and 2 are alive the Scalps are taken off; hereafter we went to the watch House of Derrick Sixth where the Indians first atacked, finding 6 Dead Bodies, 4 of them scalpt, about a mile this side the Watch house as we went back the Indians set fire to a Stable & Barn, where burnt the Corn, Cows and other Creatures, where we found 7 Indians, 5 in the House eating their dinner and drinking Rum which was in the House and 2 outside the House, we fire to them but in vain, the Indians have burnt 4 Plantations more the above account told me Peter Anspack, Jacob Caderman, Christopher Noacre, Leonard Walborn told me in the same manner, George Dollinger & Adam Dieffenbach Sent me word in the same manner.

Now we are in great Danger for to Lose our Lives or Estates, Pray therefore for help, or else whole Tulpehoccon will be ruined by the Indians in a

short time, and all Buildings will be burnt down & the people scalped, therefore you will do all haste to get people together to assist us. The Assembly
can see by this work how good and fine friends the Indians are to us, we
hope their Eyes will go open & their Hearts tender to us, and the Governors
the same, if they are true Subjects to our King *George* the second, of Great
Britain, or are willing to deliver us in the hands of these miserable Creatures.—
I am,
Your Friend
PETER SPYCKER

NB   the People is fled to us from
the Hills. Peter Kryger and
Jn° Weiser are the last—

At Reading Weiser found everything in an uproar: drums beating, bells
ringing, all the people under arms and expecting an attack that night.[30]
Messengers from Tulpehocken poured in with ever growing tales of disaster. The frontier seemed to be caving in on Reading while the two
branches of the government in Philadelphia settled down comfortably
to their game of political chess.

Though we may agree with the Assembly that it was right to tax the
Proprietory estates, and though we may be convinced that the whole
proprietorial system of government was wrong, yet we must still feel with
Weiser and the people of Reading that this was not the time for debating
abstract principles of government. It was a time to save the lives of threatened frontiersmen with their women and children. The Governor was
under oath not to accept the defense bill in the form in which the Assembly
sent it to him. The Quaker Assembly knew this very well. Some of its
members supported the bill in its present form as a means of breaking the
proprietorial government; others, it was suspected, as a means of preventing
defense measures altogether.

The rasher spirits in Reading were for burning the houses of the few
Quakers in that town, and were with difficulty restrained.

The report ran about town that a battle was in progress between the
Indians and the whites. But it was murder rather than battle that Weiser's
volunteers had to cope with, and there was no chance of winning a clear
victory over an enemy who struck secretly and then vanished into the
woods. Nevertheless, the guard Weiser had set at Dietrich Six's gave a
good account of itself. The Delawares had found a lion in the path. "The
Enemy not beat but scared off," was Weiser's summary of the affair, which
in its way was one of the decisive engagements of this war.

Conrad Weiser to Governor Morris [31]

Honoured Sir!

On my Return from Philadelphia I met in the Township of Amity in Berks
County, the first News of our cruel Enemy having invaded the Country this
Side of the Blue-Mountain, to witt, Bethel and Tulpenhacon. I left the Papers
as the were in the Messengers Hands, and hasted to Reading, where the Alarm

and Confusion was very great. I was obliged to stay that Night, and part of the next Day, towitt, the 17ᵗʰ of this Instant, and sot out for Heidleberg, where I arrived that Evening. Soon after, my Sons Philip and Fredrick arrived from the Persuit of the Indians; and gave me the following Relation, towitt, that on Saturday last about 4 of the Clock, in the Afternoon, as some Men from Tulpenhacon were going to Dietrick Sixˢ Place under the Hill on Shamokin Road to be on the Watch appointed there, they were fired upon by the Indians but none hurt nor killed, (Our People were but Six in Number, the Rest being behind), upon which our People ran towards the Watchhouse which was about one half of a Mile off, and the Indians persued them, and killed and Scalped several of them. A bold Stout Indian came up with one Christopher Ury who turned about and shot the Indian right through his Breast; The Indian dropt down Dead, but was dragged out of the Way by his own Companions (he was found next Day and scalped by our People) The Indians devided themselves in two Parties; Some came this Way to meet the Rest that was going to the Watch, and killed some of them, so that six of our Men were killed that Day and a few Wounded. The Night following the Enemy attacked the House of Thoˢ Bower on Swartaro Creek. They came to the House in the Dark Night, and one of them put his Fire-Arm through the Window and shot a Shoemaker (that was at Work) dead upon the Spot. The People being extreamly Surprized at this sudden Attack, defended themselves by firing out of the Windows at the Indians. The Fire alarmed a Neighbour who came with two or three more Men; they fired by the Way and made great Noise; scared the Indians away from Bowers House, after they had set fire to it, but by Thomas Bowers Deligence and Conduct was timely put out again, So Thoˢ Bower with his Family went off that Night to his Neighbour Daniel Schneider who came to his Assistance. By 8 of yᵉ Clock Parties came up from Tulpenhacon & Heidleberg. The first Party saw four Indians running off. They had some Prisoners whom they scalped imediately. three Children lay scalped yet alive, one died since, the other two are like to do well. Another Party found a Woman just expired with a Male Child on her side, both killed and Skalped. The Woman lay upon her Face, my Son Fredrick turned her about to see who she might have been, and to his and his Companions Surprize they found a Babe of about 14 Days old under her, raped up in a little Cushion, his Nose quite flat which was set right by Fredrick, and life was yet in it and recovered again. Our People came up with two Parties of Indians that Day, but they hardly got sight of them. The Indians Ran off Imediately; Either our People did not care to fight them if the could avoid it or (which is more likely) the Indians were alarmed first by the loud Noise of our Peoples coming, because no Order was observed. Upon the whole, there is about 15 killed of our People, Including Men, Women and Children, and the Enemy not beat but scared off. Several Houses and Barns are Burned. I have no true accound how many. We are in a Dismal Situation, some of this Murder has been comitted in Tulpenhacon Township. The People left their Plantation to within 6, or 7, Miles from my House. I am now Bussy to put Things in Order to defend my House against another Attack.

Guns and Ammunition is very much wanted here, my Sons have been obliged to part with most of that, that was sent up for the Use of the Indians. I pray your Honour will be pleased, if it lies in your Power to send us up a Quantity upon any Condition. I must stand my Ground or my Neighbours will all go away, and leave their Habitations to be destroyed by the Enemy or our own People. This is enough of such Meloncolly Account for this Time. I beg to Conclude, who am

Sir

Your very obedient
CONRAD WEISER

Heidleberg in Berks
County, November 19th
1755

P: S: I am creditable informed just now, that one Wolf a Single-Man, killed an Indian, the same Time when Ury killed the Other, but the Body is not found yet; The Poor Young Man since died of his Wound through his Belly.

This letter alarmed Governor Morris. He saw that behind these apparently senseless cruelties lay a concerted policy, all the more dangerous since it was not the outcome of mere blood hysteria, which must soon subside. It was a planned attack, not only on the general morale of the province, but also on its economic foundations.

Governor Morris to the neighboring governors [32]

Sir/

By the enclosed Intelligence you will see that the Indians have pass'd the sasquahana and laid waste the settlements at a place Calld Tulpehockin which was one of the best peopled and most fruitful parts of this Province and lyes within about seventy miles of this city. The People, who are under no kind of discipline and mostly without arms, are flying before them and leaving the Country to their Mercy. By the manner of ye attacks these Savages have made upon the different parts of this Province there is reason to believe their main body is more numerous than Scalping partys generally are and as they destroy cattle & Horses and Burn & destroy every thing before them it seems to be their intention to disable us from furnishing Provisions & ye expected Assistance in another Campaign against Fort Duquesne, for which this province was certainly most conveniently situated and best circumstanced but will it self stand in need of the aid of the other Colonys if these cruel Ravagers are suffered to go on . . .

How successful the enemy was in spreading fear and the spirit of rebellion among the people of Pennsylvania, is seen in a second letter written by Weiser to the Governor on November 19.

Conrad Weiser to Governor Morris [33]

May it please the Governor!

That Night after my Arrival from Philadelphia, Emanuel Carpenter and Simon Adam Kuhn, Esq^{rs} came to my House, and lodged with me. They acquainted me that a Meeting was appointed (of the People of Tulpenhacon & Heidleberg and adjedent Places) in Tulpenhacon Township at Benjamin Spycker's early next Morning. I made all the Hast with the Indians I could, and gave them a Letter to Thos McKee, to furnish them with Necessaries for their Journey. Scarujade had no Creature to ride on. I gave him one. Before I could get done with the Indians 3 or 4 Men came from Benjaⁿ Spycker's to warn the Indians not to go that Way; for the People ware so enraged against all the Indians,   & would kill them without Destinction. I went with them;   so did the Gentlemen beforenamed. When we came near Benjamin Spickers I saw about 4 or 500 Men, and there was a loud Noise;   I rode before, and in riding along the Road (and armed Men on both Sides of the Road) I heard some say, Why must we be killed by the Indians and we not kill them? why are our Hands so tied? I got the Indians to the House with much adoe, where I treated them with a small Dram, and so parted in Love and Friendship. Capt Diefenbach undertook to conduct them (with five other men) to Susquehannah. After this a Sort of a Counsel of Warr was held by the Officers present, the Gentlemen beforenamed and other Freeholders. It was agreed that 150 Men should be raised imediately to serve as Outscouts, and as Guards at Certain Places under the Kittitany Hills for 40 Days; That those so raised   to have 2 Shillings Per Day, & 2 Pound of Bread. 2 Pounds of Beaff and a Jill of Rum, and Powder & Led. (Arms they must find themselves) This Scheme was signed by a good many Freeholders and read to the People. They cried out that so much for an Indian Scalp they would have (be they Friends or Enemies) from the Governor. I told them I had no such Power from the Governor nor Assembly. They begun, some to Curse the Governor; some the Assembly;   called me a Traitor of the Country who held with the Indians and must have known this Murder before hand. I sat in the House by a Lowe Window, some of my Friends came to pull me away from it, telling me some of the People threatned to Shoot me. I offered to go out to the People and either Pasefy them or make the Kings Proclamation;   But those in the House with me would not let me go out. The cry was. *The Land is betrayed and sold*. The Comon People From Lancaster County were the worst. The wages they said was a Trifle and said some Body pocketed the Rest, and they would resent it. Some Body had put it into their Head that I had it in my Power to give as much as I pleased. I was in Danger of being Shot to Death. In the mean Time a great Smoke arose under Tulpenhacon Mountain, with the news following that the Indians had comitted Murder on Mill Creek (a false alarm) and set fire to a Barn. most of the People Ran and those that had Horses Rode off without any Order or Regulation. I then took my Horse and went Home, where I intend to stay, and defend my own House as long as I can,   There is no Doings with the People without a Law or Regulation by the Governor and Assembly. The people of Tulpenhacon all fled;   till about 6 or 7 miles from me some few remains. Another such Attack will lay all the Country Waste on the west side of Schuylkill.

I am

Sir
your Most obedient,
CONRAD WEISER

Heidleberg in the
County of Berks
November 19th 1755

The great need was powder, lead, muskets, blankets, and a decent measure of military discipline. Quaker opposition to a militia law made the last, for the time being, impossible; and money for supplies lay locked up in the disputed money bill. Between pacifism and absentee government, the Province seemed likely to succumb.

I laid before the House one Letter from Mr Weiser [wrote Peters] wherein he says positively that if the Express does not bring up Powder, Lead &

Blankets, y^t County will be deserted as far as Reading. . . . The Pannick is inconceivable in every Part of the Country. . . . In the midst of all this Misery, the Citizens are doing their Business as usual, with out much seeming Concern; they neither muster, nor arm, nor fortify, nor make one Effort for the Relief of the Back Inhabitants, but meet in the coffee House, wait and see the Issue of Matters between the Govr & Assembly, & receive the Women from Carlisle, Lancaster & Reading, who are leaving their Families with as much Ease as if they were come upon an ordinary Visit.[34]

Threats of direct action poured in from the frontiers upon the city. "There are within this few weeks upwards of 40 of his Majesty's subjects massacred on the Frontiers of this and Cumberland C^y," wrote the Reverend John Elder of Paxton, "besides a great number carried into Captivity; and yet nothing but unseasonable Debates between the two parts of our Legislature . . ."[35]

"The People are so incensed," wrote Weiser to Morris, "not only against our cruel Enemy the Indians, but also (We beg leave to inform your Honour) against the Governor and Assembly, that we are afeard they will go down in a Body to Philadelphia and commit the vilest Outrages. They say, they will rather be hanged than to be butchered by the Indians . . ."[36]

The threat was carried out. A mob descended on the city. The Assembly passed a modified money bill and a militia law. The sequence of events leading to this change of heart in the government is as follows:

Saturday, November 22: Governor Morris received a letter from Thomas Penn offering a free gift of £5,000 to assist in the defense of the province.[37]

Monday, November 24: This gift was formally announced to the Assembly.[38]

Tuesday, November 25: A body of several hundred people, mostly Germans from the frontier, came "to implore the protection of the Assembly and to pray it to interrupt their fruitless disputes"; [39] and the Mayor, Aldermen, and Common Council of Philadelphia presented a Remonstrance to the House. "Let it be no longer said," ran the Remonstrance, "that while we are daily hearing so much concerning Privilege and Right, we are in the mean time deprived of that most essential Right and great first Privilege, (which GOD and Nature gave us) of defending our Lives, and protecting our Families." [40]

That same day the Assembly passed a militia law [41] (it had been introduced earlier by Benjamin Franklin) and sent it up to the Governor. They also voted to draw up a new bill to make money available for defense without taxing the proprietorial estates.

Though the militia law had a pacifist joker concealed in its terms, it still made possible the raising of an army with a measure of cohesion if not with much semblance of discipline. Ex-Governor Hamilton sat down with Benjamin Franklin and other commissioners to lay plans for defense.

The money bill became law on November 27, 1755. On that day Peters wrote to Weiser:

Write to Mr James Hamilton and M^r B: Franklin for what you want and direct your Letters to the Committee of assembly for the disposal of the £60,000 granted for the Countrys Use by Act of Assembly. God bless you . . . The man will tell you y^t I have take true Pains for to get you the Powder Lead & Blanketts, which is sent by the express order and Approbation of the Governor [42]

Within a few days Conrad Weiser was sent for to Philadelphia again, and the organization of a real army for Pennsylvania had begun.

CHAPTER 47

... *Watches an Army Grow*

I

THE winter of 1755–56 saw the gestation of Pennsylvania's army. We have already seen how the Governor, on October 31, made Weiser a colonel—of nothing. The commission did not change the situation. Already Weiser, with Read and other magistrates and freeholders, was doing all possible to raise men locally and put up resistance.

But the defense of the colony was in private hands. There was no constitutional army—only a multitude of armed bands without proper officers and with next to no discipline. ". . . every man is a Captain," wrote James Read, "and the proper Officer has little notice paid his orders." [1] There was little cohesion, no central organization, no plan of campaign. In a word, there was no military machine, but only a collection of scrap.

The building of an army out of this junk heap affords an interesting study. It might seem to us now that it would have been well, once the militia law was passed and money appropriated, to scrap the defense forces that had sprung up along the frontier, melt them down and construct a totally new army out of them. But that was impracticable. Such a course would have left the frontier open at a crucial time, and would have wholly undone an already bewildered border population. Instead, the Governor and commissioners made an army out of the material they had on hand, adding to it, stiffening it, improvising daily, meeting each emergency as it came, slowly evolving a plan of campaign in which every frontier unit should have its place, and thus muddling their way through into the middle of the year, when they were able to show a well-shaped Pennsylvania Regiment with a First, Second, and Third Battalion—east of the Susquehanna, west of the Susquehanna, and at Shamokin where the Susquehanna forks. So it came about that Conrad Weiser, who in October had organized a three-day army of his own, who in November had been appointed a colonel without a regiment, and who by January had come to be known as Colonel of the Berks County Regiment, became in May 1756, Lieutenant Colonel of the First Battalion of the Pennsylvania Regiment, with a major, captains, lieutenants, ensigns, and five hundred enlisted men under him.

It was the pressure of the back settlements that had at last forced action on the Broad Brims of Philadelphia, and it was the continued pressure from such populations that kept a nervous Governor and a balky Assembly busy evolving a coördinated plan of defense. Shippensburg, Carlisle, Paxton, Reading, Bethlehem, Easton—the same story came from all of them: scalpings, mutilations, the burning of houses and barns and cattle.

Weiser's town of Reading presented a typical scene. It was filled with refugees, frightened, destitute, planless. "The People of this Town and County are in very great Consternation," wrote Weiser to the Governor.

Most of this Town are but day labourers, owing Money, are about to leave it, they have nothing at all to support their Familys. All Trade is stoped, and they can get no employment, and without the Govern[t] takes about 30 or 40 of them into pay to guard this Town, they must go off and the rest will think themselves unsafe to Stay, & the back Inhabitants will have no place of Security left for their Wives and Children when they are out either against their enemy, or taking care of their Plantations & Cattle . . .[2]

Weiser ordered munitions from Lancaster and other necessaries from Philadelphia. He kept guards posted in town and sent out scouts into the valley. At the same time he gathered what information he could of the plans of the enemy (who had a rendezvous in the Red Valley behind the Second Mountain), and sent couriers to warn outlying settlements of impending attacks. "About a Quarter of an hour before we left home," wrote the people of the Forks of the Delaware in a petition to the Governor just after the Gnadenhutten disaster, "we receiv'd a Message that Nine Families were cut off the other side of the Mountain which alarm came a short time after we received a Letter from Conrad Weiser informing us of our Danger by Way of the West Gap of the Mountain." [3]

After passage of the militia law and money bill, Weiser, as has been noted, was sent for express to Philadelphia. A "Plan of Operations" was being concerted between the Governor and a Committee of the House. Blockhouses, it was decided, were to be built and companies of rangers under regular pay were to be established all along the Blue Mountains. The situation at Tulpehocken and Heidelberg was at first the most pressing and received first attention. But while the Governor and commissioners were considering where to post men for the defense of Berks County, word came of the attack on Gnadenhutten. Benjamin Franklin, in whom all parties had confidence, was accordingly put in charge of the defense of Northampton County.

The Governor issued a flood of military commissions. When he inopportunely (in the middle of December) departed to attend a conference with General Shirley in New York, he left blank commissions with James Hamilton, who continued Morris' indiscriminate hand-outs. Hamilton admitted afterwards that most of the officers he commissioned were men of no character.[4] Conrad Weiser also received blank commissions—to be filled in by him, but submitted to the Governor for approval.[5] One of Weiser's first recommendations for a commission was on behalf of "M[r] Christian Bussey the Doctor of this Town." [6] We shall hear more of this "hearty and very worthy person" [7] in the months that followed.

Officers were appointed for a company in Lebanon Township (north of Schuylkill Gap), and for one in Bethel Township [8] (near Dietrich Six's). Weiser distributed 130 men over his part of the frontier.

II

Meanwhile he kept his eye on the prime source of trouble, which lay behind the Blue Mountains. Unlike most settlers, he could still see the situation from the Indian point of view, and he was intent upon separating friend from foe. The Ohio Delawares, whom he had found to be a poor lot of riff-raff when he was among them in 1748, were now wholly in the French interest, as he knew. But he refused to give over the Susquehanna Indians, among whom he had many friends. He advised calling them to a conference at Harris' Ferry, and set out for that place to make arrangements. He sent notices to the Indians on the West Branch of the Susquehanna, while the Governor sent a message, by Aaron Dupui and Charles Broadhead, inviting the Indians on the North Branch of the Susquehanna to attend at "the beginning of the next Moon," [9] that is to say, on January 1.

The Governor's message was never delivered. While Weiser was hurrying from Philadelphia to Harris', Broadhead's plantation and others in the Minisink region were attacked. Weiser heard the news as he approached Reading. The frontier was again in an uproar, and Weiser had to break his journey at Reading to put some order into a panic-swept mob.

"This Country is in a dismal Condition," he wrote to the Governor: "believe me kind Sir that it cant hold out long. Consternation, Poverty, Confusion, Parties is every where   If no haste is made for our Relief, I cannot stay but must move with my Family to any place of better security than this. I can add nothing agreeable . . ." [10]

Reading was a detail in the military campaign, and there were officers appointed to attend to it. But the diplomatic campaign among the Indians of Pennsylvania rested wholly on Weiser's shoulders, and this had to be attended to at Harris'. He hurried on.

At the Ferry he received bad news from the Belt and the Broken Thigh: the French Indians had persuaded the Delawares at Nescopeckon on the Susquehanna, halfway between Shamokin and Wyoming, to allow their town to be used as a place of rendezvous by the enemy; the Shickellamies and others of the Six Nations had fled to the Iroquois country.[11]

Preparations, nevertheless, went ahead for the conference. The Governor and commissioners were to meet Weiser at Reading. Benjamin Franklin, meanwhile, who had for the moment turned into military channels the same ingenuity that he had hitherto applied to printing, electrical experiments, and politics, addressed to "Messrs Wiser, Seely, and Read" at Reading some instructions for their conduct of Indian warfare.

B. Franklin to Messrs. Wiser, &c.[12]

Easton, Dec. 30th, 1755.

Gentlemen—We are just on the point of setting out for Bethlehem, in our way to Reading, where we propose to be (God willing) on Thursday evening. The commissioners are all well, and thank you for the concern you express for their welfare. We hope to have the pleasure of finding you well. No news this way, except that Aaron Dupuis's barn was burnt last week, the Indians still keeping near those parts.

In haste, gentlemen, your humble servant,

B. FRANKLIN

INSTRUCTIONS

Monday morning, 10 o'clock

The fifty arms now sent are all furnished with staples for sling straps, that if the governor should order a troop or company of rangers on horseback, the pieces may be slung at the horseman's back.

If dogs are carried out with any party, they should be large, strong, and fierce; and every dog led in a slip string, to prevent their tiring themselves by running out and in, and discovering the party by barking at squirrels, &c. Only when the party come near thick woods and suspicious places, they should turn out a dog or two to search them. In case of meeting a party of the enemy, the dogs are all then to be turned loose and set on. They will be fresher and finer for having been previously confined, and will confound the enemy a good deal, and be very serviceable. This was the Spanish method of guarding their marches.

A party on the scout should observe several rules to avoid being tracked and surprised in their encampments at night. This may be done sometimes when they come to a creek or run, by entering the run and traveling up the stream or down the stream, in the water, a mile or two, and then encamp, the stream effacing the track, and the enemy at a loss to know whether the party went up or down. Suppose a party marching from A intends to halt at B, they do not go straight to B and stop there, but pass by at some little distance, and make a turn which brings them thither. Between B and C two or three sentinels are placed to watch the track, and give immediate notice at B, if they perceive any party pass by in pursuit, with an account of the number, &c., which enables the party of B to prepare and attack them if they judge proper, or gives them time to escape. But I add no more of this kind, recollecting that Mr. Wiser must be much better acquainted with all these things than I am.

Yours, &c.

Would it not be better for the people in each district, township, or neighborhood, to collect their families, stock, grain, and fodder, in some proper place in the neighborhood, and make a stockaded enclosure, and remain there during the winter. I say would not this be better than leaving every thing to be destroyed by the Indians, and coming down into the thicker settlements to beg for subsistence?

You are to dispose of the arms for the best defence of the people, where they were most wanted, and with the governor's approbation. Half-past 12 P.M.

The Governor and Richard Peters arrived in Reading at noon on a cold New Year's Day, and an hour later Franklin, Hamilton, and Fox came in from Bethlehem with an escort of militia.[13] Richard Peters, who had taken cold the night before at John Pott's house in Pott's Grove, observed with no sympathetic eye the "intolerably great" panic of this "wretched village." "The Country People expect the Indians in ten Days to fall on some part of the Country, that being their time of the Moon, but I hope they are not true prophets. What may be I cant say but for any thing I see at present five hundred Indians may lay as far Waste before them as they please." [14]

"I have disobliged Col. Weiser in not bringing him a sword," he wrote (for the eye of his brother William,—and then changed his mind and crossed it out); "I promised him one at New York but it was forgot, and if I have not one to present to him before I return all will be to pieces" [15]

Weiser informed the Governor of what he had learned at Harris', and advised changing the place of treaty to Carlisle.[16] On January 3 an Indian runner came from Bethlehem with news of a second disaster at Gnadenhutten. The soldiers recently sent there had been attacked by a large force of Indians and driven back through Lehigh Gap. "We have repeated Accounts," wrote Peters wildly, "that the whole Body of Indians is against us, and Mr Weiser is of that Opinion and thinks that no Expence should be saved nor time Lost in engaging the Southern Indians, for without their Assistance our Country will be overrun, as the Peoples Fears rather increase than otherwise, and no Body can be got to fight." [17]

In the near panic that descended on the commissioners, orders were sent to Captain Wayne in Northampton County to increase his company and offer a scalp bounty to his men: "forty Pieces of Eight for every Indian they shall kill & scalp." [18] Franklin was sent off to Gnadenhutten, accompanied by a lieutenant and twenty men of Captain McLaughlin's company (who left without paying their bills), while Captain McLaughlin himself with thirty men prepared to set off with the Governor, Peters, Weiser, etc., for Harris'—fresh dispositions having first been made for the guard at Reading and for patrols along the Blue Mountains west to the Susquehanna.

Like a cloud over all the Governor's plans hung the absence of any report from Scaroyady and Montour. Many weeks had gone by since they had left Tulpehocken under Captain Dieffenbach's escort. There was a rumor that they had been killed—worse, that they had deserted to the enemy. Weiser, no less than the Governor, wanted to know what the Six Nations were doing. Had they forgotten the chain of friendship? Would they send warriors to help Pennsylvania? Or were they themselves joining the Delawares in the woods?

If Franklin's electrical experiments had then borne the fruits that are familiar to us today, the Governor would have heard over the radio, before he left (freshly barbered) [19] for Weiser's at Heidelberg, the message that Scaroyady dictated at Oquage near the headwaters of the Susquehanna to the Reverend Gideon Hawley for despatch to Brother Onas. It was a disturbing message. "I have but just escaped with life," said Scaroyady. The Delawares at Wyoming and at Tioga (where Conrad Weiser had smoked a pipe in 1737) were in the French interest. All Indians seen traveling on the frontier, warned Scaroyady, were to be regarded as enemies, since the friendly ones had either left for the Six Nations country or kept themselves strictly at home. The Susquehanna Delawares "declare, in plain Terms," he said,

That they are determined to fight the English, as long as there is a Man left; that when they have conquered the English, they will turn their Arms against those Indians who will not join with them now.

I am arrived here and now feel safe and easy, but it is with much difficulty that I have come thro' the Settlement of the Delawares. . . . When I return shall go by the way of Albany, for there is no going back by the way I came.

You may expect to hear from us again by the next opportunity. . . . I advise you to lay stil, and not come against your Enemies this way 'til you have further Intelligence. But you'll guard your Frontiers well and keep Scouts out constantly.[20]

After a night at Weiser's, where Peters paid a pound "to Davies yᵉ School Master for Journey to York & Cakes," [21] the Provincial Secretary and the Governor continued their journey, stopping to bait their horses "at Boogers near yᵉ Moravian house on Quittapohilla." [22] They had dinner at Galbraith's (site of the modern Hershey), and came to John Harris' house on Wednesday evening, January 7. Next day they had a conference with the Belt and the Broken Thigh, Weiser interpreting; and in the afternoon, after fording the Susquehanna (at a cost to Peters of a shilling and sixpence for a guide), came to Carlisle in the rain. At 7 o'clock that evening, Mr. Peters "greasd" his sore throat. Next morning Peters was blooded, and found a congenial companion in William Logan, just arrived, who complained of the ride, the damp, and his rheumatism, and talked much about his sense of duty.

Some days were wasted waiting for George Croghan, who was expected to bring a lot of Indians down from Aughwick. Weiser seems to have spent the interval on a visit to his own plantation, for we find record of his selling "two Reading lottery tickets" on January 10 "at Womelsdorff" to Jacob Shirman (who promised to pay "the day after the lottery is drawn"), two to Fredrick Teisinger "on his wadges for the Watech," one to George Mayer—"N. B. John Zerbe Brother in Law"—, and some to "Christian Ruth and Peter Fleck in Company two Reading." [23] Perhaps on this flying visit to his command he attended the muster of Captain Jonas Seely's new company of twenty-seven men on this same day at Reading. Certainly the wretched captains needed all the moral support the presence of their colonel could give them in order to keep some sort of discipline among their troops, for the Assembly's militia law was so tender of the consciences of enlisted men that it left discipline to the free consent of the soldiers. On January 12 Captain John Van Etten's men signed an agreement that "whoever shall get drunk, desert, or prove cowardly in Time of Action, or disobedient to our Officers, shall forfeit his Pay." [24] Since the pay was at the rate of six dollars a month and since they signed on for only one month at a time, the prospect of punishment can have held few terrors for thirsty guardsmen.

Conrad Weiser returned to Carlisle, where Croghan turned up at length, but with only half a dozen Indians. He hoped that more would yet come, including the White Mingo; but he feared that "if anything hindered the White Mingo from coming, it would be hearing that the Belt was already at Carlisle," for "that great Differences had arose between the White Mingo and the Belt about a Successor to Tanacharisson." [25] Richard Peters, who had had to be blooded again the day before but was not feeling too wretched to enjoy a bit of gossip, wrote in his diary: "Great Dissensions betwⁿ the White Mingo & other Branches of the halfe Kings family of one party & the Belt & his family of the other party about yᵉ Succession."

Croghan, always quick to find differences between the English and their allies, brought alarming news. Delaware Jo, whom he had sent to the Indian town of Kittanning and to Fort Duquesne for intelligence, reported that at Kittanning there were "above one hundred English Prisoners big and little," and that the commander of Fort Duquesne had some time past succeeded in inducing a party of Six Nations warriors to offer the French hatchet to the Delawares and Shawnees.[26] It was Croghan's opinion that the Six Nations, in fear of being totally extirpated between the French and the English, had offered to incorporate the Delawares, Shawnees, Munsies, and Nanticokes into the Six Nations if they would join them and their allies in driving the English back as far as the South Mountains; after which the Six Nations expected, on concluding an alliance with the southern Indians (Cherokees and Creeks), they could easily drive the French from the Ohio "by Cutting off the Communications between their Forts and Starving them out." [27] All the Six Nations except the Mohawks and the Oneidas were reported to be involved in this vast scheme, which anticipated the conspiracy of Pontiac, and the later visions of the Shawnee Tecumseh.

Conrad Weiser had no great faith in the dependability of Croghan's reports. He preferred to go to the sources himself. Accordingly he talked with Silver Heels, who had recently visited Nescopeckon. Silver Heels had there seen 140 warriors do a war dance in preparation for a foray against Pennsylvania; but he told Weiser he was sure the Six Nations were not consenting or privy to all this.

The Belt in council next day corroborated Silver Heels' opinion, and laid the whole blame for the war on a secret treaty between the French and the two tribes, Delaware and Shawnee.

The Carlisle conference accomplished little. It had been intended to rally the Susquehanna Indians and give them confidence in Pennsylvania. But there were hardly any Indians there to rally. Those that were there— the Belt, Silver Heels, Newcastle, Jagrea, Seneca George, David, and Isaac —did not receive comfort: they gave it.

We are sorry our Number is not greater [said the Belt], but few as we are, we are all Warriors, and at your Service whenever you call upon us. We esteem the Blood that has been shed in this Country as running from our own Veins, and as the French are the Cause of it, we esteem them our Enemies, and shall, whenever you think proper severely revenge it upon them.

. . . as you have sent Messages to the Six Nations in their great Council, we think it more prudent to wait their Return, that we may know their Resolutions; and this we are the rather inclined to, as we ourselves, by your Messengers Scarrooyady and Montour, sent a Message of our own to enforce yours, and giving thereby our Sentiments to the United Council—And we would not have you uneasy at not receiving an Answer, for the Season of the Year is bad, and the Members of the great Council live remote from each other, and require Time to get together.[28]

He advised the building of a fort at Shamokin—now and not later. It is impossible to overemphasize the importance that the Indians attached to the building of that fort. Indeed, they looked upon its construction as a test of Brother Onas' competence and sincerity—as the province was to learn with embarrassment a few months later. ". . . and we desire also," continued the Belt, "that you would place some proper Person to live always there to manage Indians Affairs (mentioning Conrad Weiser or in case of his Refusal some other proper Person) that we may have him to advise with in all difficult Matters, and that this may be a Place of Refuge in times of Distress for us with our Wives and Children to fly to for our Safety, and be also a Security for you . . ." [29]

Shortly before the Governor's departure, an Indian named John King came in with news that Delaware Jo (Croghan's spy) had gone over to the French, and that the White Mingo had left this country and gone north to Oneoquage. It was a disagreeable note on which to end the conference.

Richard Peters, having previously paid his two doctors, now tipped the servants (Betty in particular, she getting 7/6), tossed a few coins to the beggars, and paid the washerwoman 24/6 for his and the Governor's wash.[30] The Carlisle Conference was ended.

III

The next two or three weeks were a whirl and scramble for Weiser. There was a new line of forts to attend to. The building of a fort at Shamokin would have to be delayed, it was decided by the Governor and commissioners, until the ice broke up on the Susquehanna; but meantime a chain of forts was rushed up, ten or twelve miles apart along the Blue Mountains from the Susquehanna to the Delaware, and more men were enlisted to garrison them.

Each enlisted man was to be strongly recommended (so ran the instructions issued to all officers) "to provide himself with a Gun, an Hatchet, one Pound of Powder, four Pounds of Bullets or Swan Shot and Six Flints," and to keep his gun in good condition.[31]

Franklin was building a fort at the Lehigh Gap (Fort Allen) and Captain Morgan another on the Schuylkill (Fort Lebanon); but "the Principal and only Regular one," as the Governor wrote, "is at a pass called Tolihaio which I have named fort Henry." [32] This was at Dietrich Six's, on the Shamokin Trail under Round Head.

To this place Captain Christian Busse was ordered, on January 25, with a company of fifty men to erect a stockade with all speed.[33] Weiser's subsequent relations with this most competent officer afford some of the pleasantest passages in the Colonel's military career.

February 1, Busse wrote to say that he and his men had reached Bosehair's the night before; that they had immediately made a barricade round the house five feet high. He was joined by Dietrich Six and George Grove, the nearest neighbors, who had been driven by the Indians from their homes.[34] Busse and his men were alarmed every night by the Indians, whose tracks they found going deep into the settled country. The barricade was surrounded by woods, which enabled the enemy to creep up unnoticed and fire on the "Centinels." The fire of the Indians was particularly dangerous, since they commonly used rifles, which had a longer range than the traditional army musket.

Wolves came over the mountains, and tore open the new graves. "One man was quite eaten—only his jacket left." [35] Another, partly eaten, Captain Busse buried again as decently as he could.

Meanwhile his men, with the help of hands from the neighborhood, were erecting the fort near-by. It was finished by the end of March, and the company moved in with all their supplies.

The best picture of Weiser's life during the weeks following the Carlisle Conference—his military activities and his family sorrows—is found in a letter he wrote to Major Parsons, once his neighbor at Stonykill under the Blue Mountains and now the chief citizen and military commander of Easton.

Colonel Weiser to William Parsons [36]

philad^ia February the 13th 1756

Dear Sir

Your letters of the 21 of dec^r and that of the 20th of January I received. the first I Could not answer being oblidged to go with the Govr to Carlile and every Hour of the day gave me Some new trouble, the Second I postponed till now being oblidged after my return from Carlile, to wait on the Govr & Comissioners in Reading Imediatly, and from there make another Journey to John Harris ferry, and from there directly by the way of my own house tho. to this town. where I arrived on the 6th of this Instant. I acknowledge I might have found a leisure Hour to write a few lines to you but that would have not ben Satisfactory neither to you nor me. I am at present, reading a letter from Scaruiody and Andrew Montour wrote by one Gidean Hawly a Missionary at Canohoghquaocky on SusqueHana about 40. or 5 Miles this Side Oneido in which they Inform the govern^or that with difficulty they passed by Nest-KopecKon. Woyomock and Tia-ogon, the delawares being turned oppen Enemys to pensilvania and those of the 6 nations Scattered among them under great Concern, and would by no means join the delawares, and that the Said two Messengers of ours are well assured that the Six nations had then (to wit January th 5) Sent a message to the delawares to order them to desist from Killing the people of pensilvania, but that the delawares paid no regard to it and that the Counsil of the Six nation were then Sumonsed to meet at onontago and our two Messengers would their attend and Solicidite our Cause. and that they had Strong hopes of Success, we expect them here every day with Mr Daniel Clause. by whome we will have the result of General Johnson Treaty which he was to hold at his Seat with the Chiefes of the Six nations on the 23 or 24 of last month. I Sent also two yong Indians from John Harris^s to NesKopeckon. to learn what Numb^r of Indians are there and whether any french men are among them. &c. I Expect them every day back If they are not Cut of by the Enemy they left John Harris on the 2^d Instant, one of them is the noted Aroson by us Called Silverhill. as to other affair. Capt Christ^n Bussey is Building a Stockade ford near dietrich Six he has 50 men in his Company and the people helps, there is 30 men at Samuel Hunter Mill under Capt McKee. Item 50 men at Manidy and big Suartaro under Capt Smith. 50

men under Captn Jacob Morgan at ford libanon and Bern township there is
at present no body at your house but your tenant I have recomended it very
Much to Captn Bussey to do what he Can for Honest Martin, he promised
he would we have in Reading (I Cant tell whether 25. 30. or more of the
Indepent Companys from new york, they behaved hitherto very well to the
people I hope they will Continue So, you have by this time heard of the
Mischief done by the Indians (as it is in the news) over SusqueHana in Shear-
mans Valey and I Expect Some Mischief will be done Soon about our way,
the people begine to be Secure again, and are tired of Keeping Watch

but my good friend I must acquaint you now with another piece of news
which gives me and my old womin a great deal of trouble. to witt my dear
Son in law Mr Heintselman the younger lutherian Minister in this town departed this life last Munday and is very much lamented by his Congregation.
Neighbours and by all most every body that Knew him. yesterday he was
Burried. the day before yesterday his witow was delivered of a healthy and
well Shaped Son, you Can think how moving It was to me and my wife (She
has ben here this 4 weeks) to See the poor orphan. & his dead father and the
Mother the witow Sheding tears over both. However all this and a great many
more affliction Comes from the hand of a Mercyfull god, and I will bear with
it. I worship him and pray that he would be pleased for his great names Saik
to grant our Bleeding Country peace again, and in the mean time Comfort the
fatherless the wounded the dieing, and teach our hands to fight Such a Cruel
an Enemy, & would the people of pensilvania obey him he would rout our
Enemy Soon

Willm parsons Esquire

I again promise to be more deligent in writing to you in particular If any
thing of moment Should happen when I Came here my deceas^d Son in law
was Exceedingly glad to See me, he Spoke to the last minute he had to live,
So that he Could be understood, when I think on him I Cant help to Shed
tears. in Short I thought he would be a Comfort to me & my old womin in
our old days bear with me. and beliefe that I am
Your true old friend and humble Servant

CONRAD WEISER

P S. Be pleased to give my hearty respects to Captn oglevie I am Informed
he is in Eastton

I Came down here to wait on the Governor & the Gentlemen Comissioners
in order to get pay for the men we the Setlers about tulpehocKin hired to
Serve as a gard along Kititany hills we have met but with very little Success
yet but retain hopes to do, Christian lauer is with Adam Read Esqr Come
yesterday

here is a Strong talk of peace licke to be made between the two Contenting
Crowns, Item of a new governor. M^r peters has ben very bad with a Sore
trode, is Some what bether

Mr Benjamen franklin was Choosen Colonell last night by Milition Officiers
of this town. Mr Masters lev^T Colonell one. McCall Major

Despite the help of stockades and patrols, the condition of the settlements
along the Blue Mountains was still pitiful. Refugees were streaming east.
Henry Melchior Muhlenberg, who visited Bethlehem at the end of March,

notes that the Moravians had given shelter to about eight hundred fugitives
at one time. He crossed the Lehigh and met a woman eighty-eight years
old, who had had to fly from home with nothing to call her own but a
small bundle of clothes. "She wept bitterly at being compelled to journey
into a strange land at her great age, but took comfort in God's word and
desired the dear Lord would take her out of the harsh world to everlasting
peace." [37]

In one house farther down the valley Muhlenberg found six families,
with thirty children, who had fled from Heidelberg Township. Their
wretchedness, he said, was indescribable. "The old folks wring their hands,
weeping and bewailing their extremity: the children are all crying for
something to eat and drink . . . In short they are walking, standing, lying
all about, and the few household things they have brought with them are
so scattered and mixed no one knows what he has any more." [38] At Gottfried Knauss's he found six more families from Heidelberg, with twenty
small children, some of them sick, in addition to the landlord's ten.

CHAPTER 48

. . . *Appeals to Thomas Penn*

COLONEL WEISER was sensitive to the distress suffered by the settlers along the frontier entrusted to his care. But he was sensitive also, as no other man was, to the suffering of the colony's loyal Indians. He could not rid his mind of the plight of such people as the Shickellamies and Jonathan, with their wives and children. The war had made the borders as unsafe for the better sort of Indian as it was for the white man. Already there had appeared among Pennsylvania's frontiersmen the symptoms of a disease that was to ravage the borders for many years afterwards: an insane lust for Indian blood that was satisfied only by indiscriminate slaughter.

Journal of Conrad Weiser's Proceedings at
John Harris' Ferry [1]

[Heidelberg, February 4, 1756]

. . . On the 31st of last Month one James Young came over from Tobias Hendricks, and told me privately in the Presence of John Harris, that above 15 Men with Arms came that Day to Tobias Hendricks in order to come to this Side of the River to kill the Indians at John Harris's, judging them of being guilty or privy to the Murder committed a few days ago in Sherman's Valley; and that he had much ado to stop them, and desired me to take all the Care possibly I could. I thereupon sent a Letter with said Young Express to the Magistrates and the Principal Inhabitants in Carlisle, to desire them to caution the People of Cumberland against such imprudent Behaviour, of which nothing but a general War with all the Indians could be the Issue, a copy of their Answer is hereunto annexed. I took for granted what they said, and sent immediately another Express by James English and Jagrea (now called Satacaroyies) to bring the Indians that remained in Carlisle since the last Treaty away to John Harris's Ferry, there to remain with the rest till the Governor's Order should be known. I wrote to those Gentlemen to hire a Waggon for the Indians, if needful.

I thought it not prudent to inform the Indians of this Affair, but several People that came from over the River knew of it, and the Indians came to hear of it. I had a good deal of Trouble to quiet their Minds (if I did at all). Satacaroyies and Newcastle went to Michael Taeffs that night, and Newcastle got in the night light headed, he looked upon every Person as an Enemy, and would persuade Satacaroyies to run away with him; he himself made off privately next morning, and had not been heard of, when I left John Harris's, which was on the 2d Instant in the Afternoon. Michael Taeff and Satacaroyies declared before me that he had no Liquor, and I am persuaded Satacaroyies would not have come back so sober in the morning as he did, if they had had any Liquor. I sent Word all about to the People to take care of the said Newcastle, if he should be seen any where; he had no Arms with him.

I think it highly necessary that the said Indians should be taken care of deeper within the Inhabitants; for should they suffer by our foolish People, we should lose all Confidence and Honour with the rest of the Indians. Submitted to his Honour the Governor his Council, and the Assembly

By their faithful Indian Interpreter

CONRAD WEISER

With these happenings in mind, Conrad Weiser, when he despatched Silver Heels and David from Harris' to Nescopeckon for intelligence of the enemy, sent with them a personal message for his Indians friends:

I sent also a String of Wampum all white to Jonathan John Shikcalamy, and his Brothers, to invite them to come to my House, if they could be found, gave a written Pass to Aroas [Silver Heels] and David, and ordered them to carry a Silk Handkerchief upon a Stick on their Return, and that only two should come before and keep the Path. The old Belt gave them a long Lesson, they all looked very serious. Aroas said he would be back in ten days or in 15 at farthest; if not then we might think he was dead . . .[2]

Weiser did not know at this time that Jonathan had joined Scaroyady and Montour in their dangerous journey through the Delaware country to the Six Nations.

The Governor sent special instructions to Captain McKee of Hunter's Fort above Harris' on the Susquehanna about looking out for these Indians and providing an escort to "Conduct them safe" to Colonel Weiser's house.[3]

On February 21, Silver Heels, David, and the Shickellamies turned up in Philadelphia.[4] The messengers had found Nescopeckon deserted, and they learned that Wyoming would be death for them to enter. They had accordingly sent a message to the Shawnee chief, Paxinosa, who lived nearby. Paxinosa deliberated with his people, and returned this answer by James Logan:

. . . we think it is in vain to speak one word more to our Grandfathers, the Delawares—I spoke so often to them to the same Purpose, till at last they threatened to knock me on the head; and what can I do since Scarroyady a Man of Authority among the Six Nations, and of great Experience and Eloquence could not prevail on them—They would not so much as touch his Belts he laid before them. They throwed them on one side with their Pipes, and gave him ill Language.[5]

On Sunday Conrad invited Tachneckdorus (John Shickellamy) and his wife to breakfast, and asked many questions, which were freely answered. The Delawares on the North Branch of the Susquehanna, reported John, were enemies to the English, but the Shawnees were neutral. When asked if any of the Six Nations ever went on Delaware war parties against the English, John replied:

Uncle, I will tell you the Truth, let the most high (Supreme Being) hearken to what I say and chastise me if I hide any thing from you, or tell you a Lie. We have been in great Extremity for want of Provisions, the Delawares told us, that a large Country was deserted by the English on the River Delaware, and the Houses full of good Provisions, Flour, Bacon, Pork, Fat Hogs &c[a] my two Brothers went with the Delawares to fetch Provisions from Delaware, the lame one [James Logan] whom you know very well could not perform the Journey, but staid by the way, the younger went on, and after they (his Company) had gathered some fat Hogs to drive them away, the English unexpectedly came upon them, killed one of the Delawares, and put the rest to Flight, and regained every thing, and my Brother came away without any thing; he told me his Heart did bleed to see Indians and English fight, and he assured me he did not fight against the English, but gave Way.[6]

On Tuesday, February 24, the Indians were received in formal council at the State House, and again on Thursday. The Belt held the limelight. He reported the success of his son-in-law's expedition to Wyoming. At great length and with much ceremony he outlined the course of Indian relations with the English, using the familiar metaphor of the ship tied to the bushes. Prompted, no doubt, by the sight of what George Washington at about the same time called the "fatal lethargy" of the colonies, he ended with a piece of advice that Governor and Council might have taken as the strongest admonition:

Brethren, We advised you, when at Carlisle, immediately to build a Fort at Shamokin; we repeat our Advice, and earnestly entreat you will not delay the doing it—Such Indians as continue true to you want a Place to come to, and to live in Security against your and their Enemies—And to Shamokin when made strong they will come and bring their Wives and Children with them; and it will strengthen your Interest very much to have a strong House there. Indeed you lose Ground every day till this be done—Pray hasten the Work, the Warriors say they will go along with you, and assist you in building a Fort there [7]

To this request the Governor did not reply for a week, and when he did it was to say that the fort would be built after Scaroyady and Montour had returned with "agreeable news" from the Six Nations.

Weiser's patience broke. The knowledge that the great Indian alliance of which the province had been so proud was crumbling because of the stupidity, slyness, greed, cowardice, and brutality of Governor, politicians, rum traders, pacifists, and frontiersmen; and the knowledge that his own friends, white and brown, were being sacrificed to slaughter by a fatuous government that would neither fight nor retreat and seemed incapable of taking any positive action, caused him to sit down and write an appeal to the Proprietor, Thomas Penn, entreating him to come to America (where he should have been all this time) and try to get the government into some sort of working order.

Conrad Weiser to Thomas Penn [8]

Honoured Sir
    Permit me to declare, that It was not forgetfullness of duty nor gratitude, that I never wrote to you ever Since you left this your province, being well assured that the Governor the Secretary and others of your friend would omit nothing worth notice to Inform you off and I Could not write bare Ceremonies or Compliments It is what I never learned nor Can I persuade meself by what Knowledge I had of Your Honour, that you Expected Such from your Known

friends. but now dear Sir I Can not forbear of writing a few lines to let you Know that the Suffering people of this your province *Cries loud for your presence* I have not words Sufficiantly to Express meself nor Can this piece of paper bear what would be Sufficiant but mine and a great many other peoples prayers to the most high are. that he would direct your ways So that the good people of (at present unhappy) Pensilvania might once more be So happy as to have your Honour among them, I am Sorry to Say that not every body is of the Same mind with me, but your Honours presence and love of Justice & good Nature would in my humble opinion gain them all. If I was So happy as to have two or three Hours Conversation with you, or with your Honoured Brother Mr Rich^d penn I flatter meself Several things in this province would Soon alder for the better, Especially Indian affairs I fear that the rudness law less ness. and Ignorance of the back Inhabitants not only of this, but also of the Neighbouring provinces Will bring a General Indian Warr over us. they Curse & damn the Indian and Call them Murdering dogs into their faces without distinction When on the other hand these poor Indians that are still our friends doe not Know where to go for Safety, in the woods they are in danger of being Killed, or their yong men joining our Enemy, among us they are in danger of being Killed by the Mob, and what is pity full, we have litle or no Government within our doors, things are So much aldered Since your Honour left this province that it would require a learned pen to give a full & Just account of it. I must Conclude with declaring that I am a faithful Subject of his Majesty King George—and a hearty well wisher of your Honours person and noble family, and Shall during the few days I have to live yet. remain

Philadelphia
february the 28
1756
to the Honourable
Thomas penn Esquire

Sir
your very obedient and
humble Servant
CONRAD WEISER

This letter was enclosed in one from Richard Hockley, at whose house on Society Hill Conrad Weiser was a frequent visitor.

Richard Hockley to Thomas Penn [9]

Philad^a March 2nd 1756

Honoured Sir
. . . Conrad Weiser desired me to forward a Letter to You without taking the least notice to anyone here, I know nothing of the Contents of it, neither does anyone here as he tells me. I see he is very uneasy and told me he had a great mind to leave the Province, but I hope he will not as he is a usefull sensible Man and of great Integrity. . . . I see so much Deceit and Hypocrisy that I am truely tired of this world, and yet can't forbear secretly hopeing at times that I shall live to see You get the better of them all in every respect . . .

Meantime John Shickellamy had received a present of twenty-eight pieces of eight, and had left for Nescopeckon to bring his brothers and their families down to safety.[10] John made good time, and in a little over a month was back in the settlements with his two brothers, their wives, and children.

Thomas McKee to Edward Shippen [11]

Foart at Hunters Mill, Ap[11] 5th 1756

S[r]

I Desire to let you No that John Secalemy Indian is Com here y[e] Day before yesterday about 4 oclock in y[e] afternoon, & Gives me an account that there is a Great Confusion amongst y[e] Indians up y[e] North branch of Susquehannah, the Dalewars are aMoving all from thence to ohio and wants to Persuad y[e] Shanoues along with them but they Decline Goeing with them that Course as they Still Encline to Joine with us, the Shanoues are Goeing up to a Town Called Teaoga where there is abody of y[e] Six Nations and there they Intend to Remain, he has brought Two More men Som Women & Som Children along with him and Sayeth that he Intends to live & Die with us and Insists upon my Conducting him down to where his Sister and Childer is at Canistogo and I,m Loath to leave my Post as his Honour was offended at y[e] last time I did but Can,t help it, he Desires to acqueint you that his Sisters Son was kill,d at Penns Creek in y[e] Scrimege wth Cap[t] Patterson, this with Due Respects from

Sir your Hum[l] Ser[t]

THOM[s] M[c]KEE

On Sunday, March 21, 1756, Scaroyady and Andrew Montour came at last to Philadelphia under escort of Daniel Claus.[12] With them were Weiser's adoptive brothers, Moses the Song and Jonathan Cayenquiloquoa, the latter with his wife. Jonathan and his wife had been missing for some time and were thought to have been killed by the Delawares. We may imagine Weiser's pleasure at finding them safe, and the joy of the two boys from the Academy.

But a shadow fell over the welcome. "Fatigue and fresh Fish of which the Indians are fond," writes Richard Peters, "threw them into pleuritick Disorders, and they had like to have all dyed, but with the favour of Providence, one only dyed, a Warrior of Note and Brother to Conrad Weiser who was buried with the Honours of War." [13]

It was Moses the Song, whom we have met carrying Captain Stobo's letter from Fort Duquesne after Washington's defeat at Fort Necessity.

"Last Monday," wrote Daniel Claus to William Johnson, "the 29. of March dies Moses Moye Mishes Son who came down with me, he fell sick on Sunday Night at 12, o Clock and expired the next Night about 2 in the Morning he was buried honourably in the English Churchyard, and your honour will find a paragraph about it in the News papers. Skaronyade begs your honour to acquaint the Relations with it." [14]

It is recorded in the minutes of the provincial council that the usual condolences were made. The Indians received ten strouds, ten shirts, and "a Piece of Handkerchiefs to cover his Grave." [15] The Governor's Council, the Commissioners, the officers of the militia, and the principal inhabitants of Philadelphia attended the funeral.

CHAPTER 49

... Sends Scaroyady
the Scalp He Forgot

I

THE death of Moses seemed an omen. The Indians found no health in Pennsylvania. Daniel Claus wrote to William Johnson on April 5:

This Province at present is in a most deplorable Situation The Gov^rs Party and the Quakers (whose head is Mr Franklin) are continually in Dispute with one another, and nothing but Confusion reigns here; the Enemy as reported is descending upon them with a Body of 1600 Strong; Mr Peters is Sometimes most distracted and dreads its Ruin if things go on as they do The 60,000 pound raised lately are expended to one quarter and no body knows what good was done thereby.[1]

Everything was in a mess. Capt. Busse was writing to Weiser for pay for his troops. Peters was writing to Weiser for minutes (for which Weiser was not responsible) of the late conference. Governor Morris was appealing to him for advice on all manner of things from dealing with the Indians to dealing with New York. The line of forts along the Blue Mountains was proving less effective than had been hoped.

... for want of a regular supply of Provisions [wrote Peters to Penn, April 28] "and of Arms and Amunition the Garrisons can neither Scout nor Range, nor in case of Attack defend their Forts. The Commissioners say they have found all Persons concerned in a Confederacy to cheat the Province & to do no duty and are extreamly incensed against the Officers and Men on this Account, and what will be done with the Forts whether burnt or stronger Garrisons placed in them I cannot tell. The Commissioners are forever complaining that the Money melts fast and does no good through the Dissolutions, Extortions Cowardice and backwardness of the People and this Language dispirits every one, for tho' it may be true yet such a Lamentation about it does but hurt the Publick cause.[2]

The steadiest party in the province and its chief anchor up to this time had been the group of Six Nations Indians headed by Scaroyady, the Belt, Jonathan, and the Shickellamies. Now these very men, disillusioned at last, were resolved to leave the province and seek refuge among the Six Nations in the north. "We are amazed," said Scaroyady, April 10, "to find you still sitting with your Hands between your Knees." [3] "I plainly foresee," wrote Claus, "Indian affairs must drop in this Province as there will be no Indians." [4]

The Governor made spasmodic efforts to hold them. He offered Claus a captain's commission, proposing that he head a band of fifty or sixty Indians from New Jersey. Claus declined to commit himself before he had consulted Scaroyady.[5]

Then the Governor called in Scaroyady and his associates before the Council, made a formal declaration of war against the Delawares, and offered the Six Nations, in the person of Scaroyady, a hatchet.[6] At the same time he offered a scalp bounty, ostensibly to encourage the Indians, really "at the pressing Instance of all the Inhabitants" except the Quakers.[7] A price list was published for Indian commodities: prisoners and scalps, male and female, children and adults, ranging from $150 for a living adult male "above Twelve Years old" to $50 for a female scalp.[8] He renewed his old promise to build a fort at Shamokin.

Weiser was opposed to the scalp bounty (it was a menace to friendly Indians, whose scalps were the most easily procurable), but he favored the declaration of war as a means of bringing the Delawares to their senses and of convincing Scaroyady and the Six Nations that the English meant business and were not afraid to fight.

Two days after the hatchet was offered, Scaroyady made his formal reply. Weiser was the interpreter. "You have indeed tried all amicable Means with those and with the Six Nations," said the Chief, "but as all have proved ineffectual, you do right to strike them. . . . We heartily approve of your Resolutions; awake, shake off your Lethargy; stand up with your Hatchet in your Hand, and use it manfully." [9] He agreed to take up the hatchet, but warned the English against making a feeble peace —one that would leave them and their Indian allies insecure. The Indians with him danced the war dance, "the Indian call the Belt singing with a Belt in his hand."

Meanwhile opposition to the declaration of war had developed. The Quakers brought pressure. On Monday, April 12, the Governor and Council met to discuss the whole matter afresh. The Quakers presented an address "bearing their Testimony against War." [10] Difficulties about the wording of the declaration were considered, and Conrad Weiser was "desired" to consult Scaroyady. Scaroyady could not at the moment be conferred with, being in liquor.[11] He might better have remained in that condition, for when he came to himself again and was told of this new piece of Brother Onas' confusion, he was ready to throw Pennsylvania to the dogs.

On the afternoon of April 14 he came with others to the Governor "and desired Mr Weiser might be sent for; he came with Reluctance, and then Scarroyady acquainted the Governor, that he proposd to depart for the Six Nation Country, in three Days, and take all the Women with him, and all the Men, except three, Aroas, Seneca George, and Cassiowea, or Newcastle." [12]

"I was much surprized at this Resolution," said the Governor later in a report to the House, adding with round-eyed innocence, "I am fearful some Discontent has given Rise to this sudden Resolution, tho I know of no Reason they can have for it." [13] Meanwhile Weiser kept the Governor in hand at the conference, advising him to say no more to the Indians than that he would send for them and take leave of them when everything was ready. The Governor directed Weiser to do what he could to persuade them to stay with the province, and there the matter rested for the moment.

The blame for the loss of her Indian allies need not be placed wholly at the feet of Pennsylvania herself. English affairs up and down the coast were in confusion. Intercolonial jealousies and rivalries added a bewildering background to affairs already sufficiently tangled within each province. "Sr Wm Johnson is very angry with this Government," wrote Peters to Weiser, April 5, "& I believe at the Instigation of Sr Charles Hardie or our old Sly Friend Mr Delancy." [14]

A story had got about that Weiser was to supplant Johnson as Superintendent of Indian Affairs. Weiser himself was entirely innocent,[15] but Shirley's party in New York was toying with the idea, and Richard Peters, with his "dark manner" of expressing himself where trouble was brewing, did nothing to stop it.

I think I was asked at New York by Mr William Alexander [wrote Peters to Thomas Penn] wether Conrad woud Accept of an Employ in the six Nation Country in case Mr Shirley and Mr Johnson shoud not make up their differences and I laugh'd at the fancy and said no more than that Mr Shirley must not risque matters with Col. Johnson or with the Six Nations.[16]

The Indians themselves, who usually showed more steadiness in council than the whites, were all at sea, and the government at Philadelphia found it impossible to learn from them exactly what had happened in the recent conference at Onondaga.[17] Scaroyady had reported that the Six Nations had determined to cut the Delawares off if they did not listen to reason and stop killing the English. The written report that came to hand from Sir Charles Hardy made no mention of any such threat.[18] Andrew Montour said that such action had been agreed upon by the Six Nations in private council. Daniel Claus said that nobody had heard it.[19]

The truth is that the Iroquois themselves were more than a little evasive at this time. They were undecided and hesitating. They leaned to the English, their hereditary friends, but were appalled at the fatuity of the present colonial governments, and would not commit themselves to what seemed at the moment to be a dying cause. The French, on the other hand, knew what they were about, and were becoming increasingly dangerous to the Confederation. "The Iroquois are beginning to fear us," wrote Bigot to the Minister in France. "All the Indians are on our side, and this paralyzes the English." [20]

II

Not three days but two weeks elapsed before the Indians left for New York; and in the meantime Weiser had innumerable conferences with them, with the Governor, and with some newcomers in the field of Indian affairs, a group of Quaker politicians headed by Israel Pemberton. Weiser had other matters as well to attend to in Philadelphia. There were the affairs of his daughter Margaret (Heintzleman's widow), and Jonathan Cayenquiloquoa's sons at the Academy. The minutes of the Assembly for April 16 record the following motion passed:

That as Cayenquiloquoas is a principal Person among the Six Nations, and is desirous to have his Sons educated among the English, and as this House are of Opinion, that the same may be attended with very good Consequences not only to the Proprietaries of this Province in Particular, but to the British Interest in America in general, we will defray all such reasonable Expences as shall arise thereupon, for such time as it shall be judged necessary.[21]

The Governor was in a state of perpetual tantrums. It was not his custom to spare a meal or a bottle, but the confused affairs of the Province now threatened to interfere with both. On April 16 the House passed a resolution declining to make preparation for the proposed military campaign. A few days later the Governor received a letter, written April 16, from Sir Charles Hardy of New York, expressing the hope that, since the Six Nations were arranging for a peace between the Delawares and the English, the province of Pennsylvania would not (as it had already done) declare war on the Delawares.[22]

Mr. Claus's refusal of the captain's commission put the Governor into such a rage that he "would not," as the Council minutes record, "after this admit him to his Sight." [23] The "tedious Ceremonies" of the Indians were a further exasperation to him. Indian expenses were no less an annoyance to the Assembly. The Governor and the House bickered over the reward to be given Scaroyady and his companions for their signal service to the province in the northern reconnaissance. Scaroyady and Montour expressed "some uneasiness" over the delay. The House, appealed to, threw the matter back to the Commissioners. In the end it landed in Conrad Weiser's lap.

Weiser had repeated interviews with the Indians, the Commissioners, and the Governor. On April 17, toward the end of the day, after waiting about for some time in his lodging, entertaining the Indians and attending to his correspondence, expecting momentarily a call from the Governor which never came, he at last presented himself uninvited at the Governor's residence. Finding His Excellency engaged, Weiser sat down and put his thoughts on paper.

Conrad Weiser to Governor Morris [24]

May it please the Governor
I was required by some of the Gentlemen of the Commissioners to wat on your Honour about this time in order assist in Setling the presents for Scaruiady and other Indians now in town. and as you are engaged in Company I thought it as Convenient to put my thoughts about that affair in writing. which are as folows

To Scaruiady a Sute of Cloath and 40 or 50 dallers in money to And^w Montour as the Governor & the Gentlemen the Comissioners pleases, he is to have more than Scaruiady and he Can talk with your Honour & the Comissioners himself

Jonathan was not hired by the Government but went up with the two former at their request and Suffered or underwent the Same danger he should have a Sute of Cloathes.

the rest Should all be Cloathed and a few Dollers in their Pocket. If any Stays with us they Should fare as well as those that goes away

Silver Hill Should be bribed to Stay.

The womens Should have Each a Strowd Matchcoat a Shirt a pair of Indian Stocking a few dressed dear Skins for shoes   perhaps undressed will do for those that Stay   the above is my Simple opinion which Submit to your Honour   who am your very obedient

CONRAD WEISER

Aprill the 17
at about 5 in the afternoon

III

It was about this time that a move for peace was started by the Quakers. With the approval of the Governor and the assistance of Conrad Weiser, who acted as chief interpreter, they held conferences with the Indians at Israel Pemberton's on April 19, 21, and 23, at which the good offices of the Friends were offered to bring about a peace between the Delawares and the English.[25] Scaroyady, no doubt as much bewildered by this sudden turn of events as by all the other developments of the last few weeks, welcomed the proposal, but gave warning that it would be unsafe to send white men into the Indian country. He suggested instead that Newcastle, Jagrea, and William Lacquis should take the message; ". . . if they have their throats cut," he said, "you cannot then hear from them, but it may please the most high that they may return Messengers of Peace." [26]

It was so decided, and all arrangements were made for the despatch of the three Indian messengers. They were reported to have left for Bethlehem with Bishop Spangenberg on the 23rd, but on the morning of the 26th the same three Indians, who were not so much afraid of having their throats cut as they were of having their liberties curtailed, came to the Governor to inform him that Scaroyady (who had left for New York the day before) had had no right to send them and that they declined to go on his errands; that they were not, however, unwilling to go, but merely determined to go of their free will; and that, if the Governor had any message to send to the Delawares by them, they would take it.[27] The Governor thereupon sent for Weiser and, after consultation, delivered a message to the three Indians to this effect: that the Six Nations commanded the Delawares to lay down the hatchet; that, if the Delawares hearkened to this advice, the English, though they were prepared to avenge the blood that had been spilled, might be induced, by the influence of the Six Nations, not to prosecute the war but to overlook the past and build a lasting peace. Paxinosa, the Shawnee chief who had remained loyal to the English, was invited to come down from the neighborhood of Wyoming to the English settlements under escort.

The three messengers set off. There was every reason for haste. The situation was already bad enough on the frontier, where the Indians were scalping and burning almost at will. Now that the leaves were breaking out it was feared that the new cover thus offered to scalping parties would enable them to carry everything before them.[28]

Weiser at the time had no better prevision than anyone else of the long

series of conferences with the Delaware chief, Teedyuscung, which was
to ensue from this embassy. Weiser was living from day to day, oppressed
by the darkness and muddle about him. Government policies changed from
hour to hour to meet new pressures as they arose: now from the Germans
or the Scotch-Irish on the frontier, now from the Quakers in Philadelphia;
now from Scaroyady who approved of the Declaration of War, now from
Sir William Johnson who did not. Issues were not yet clarified, the ranks
of the belligerents were not yet fixed. Even the United Six Nations, once
Pennsylvania's Rock of Gibraltar, were divided into three camps: pro-
French, pro-English, and neutral.

One thing stood out clearly: the existence of Pennsylvania and the rest
of the English colonies was threatened by a possible alliance between the
French and all the Indians. Force had to be met with force, and those of
the Six Nations who were still inclined to the English had to be convinced
that the English colonies were a good risk; but at the same time it was
wisdom to break up the new order in the woods, based on French hegem-
ony, by making a separate peace if possible with the Delawares. The French
on Pennsylvania's borders were not in themselves dangerous. They were
strong only through the Indian allies Dumas had won for them.

For this reason Weiser, who had advised the declaration of war, now
backed Newcastle's peace message to the Delawares.

Meanwhile Scaroyady, Jonathan, Montour, and other Indians had left
for New York on April 25. Scaroyady, for all his beautiful speeches at the
Quaker conferences, was in a mood as fretful as the Governor's, and his
irritation was not softened when he discovered that he had "forgot the
Scalp without the Belts, it was left at Mr Weiser's Lodging," and had to
get Daniel Claus to write a letter to the Provincial Secretary asking him
to have the scalp "sent after him." [29]

CHAPTER 50

... Meets King Teedyuscung

I

THE declaration of war against the Delawares had not had the effect desired. The opposition to the measure expressed by the Quakers in Philadelphia and by the government of New York had shown Scaroyady and the Six Nations that English councils were still divided. Pennsylvania, fearing the defection of her Indian allies, felt the necessity of making a peace at almost any price with such of the Delawares as could be brought to it. The Ohio Delawares were known to be directly under the influence of the French, so much so that Delaware scalping parties were even officered by Frenchmen. But it was hoped that the Susquehanna Delawares might be brought to lay down the hatchet.

The three Indian emissaries proceeded to Bethlehem, where they were joined by Captain Augustus, alias George Rex, a Delaware "of a great Family" and Elder of the Indian congregation. Here they were provided with food, kettles, tomahawks, guns, tobacco, and ten pieces of eight each.[1] They set off again, May 1, with David Zeisberger and other Moravians as escort.

In these perilous times when Indians were liable to be shot at sight in the woods for the sake of the scalp bounty, it was necessary for them to have a token to distinguish them as friends. The token by which Scaroyady and his party were to be recognized when they approached any English fort was, as they explained in a farewell message to the Governor, "a Club'd Musket and Green Boughs in our Hats." [2] They requested that, after twenty days, the commanders of the forts should keep a lookout for them.

While the province awaited the return of the four Indians from the North Branch of the Susquehanna, there were important developments nearer home. Weiser and the Governor made a flying trip to Harris' Ferry to speed the departure of the troops for Shamokin.[3] The army of Pennsylvania was stiffened, at least in its bookkeeping, and a "List of Officers in the three Battalions of the Pennsylvania Regiment" [4] was issued, with "Conrode Weiser" Lieutenant Colonel of the First Battalion (commissioned as of May 5, 1756) supported by Major William Parsons, Captains Christian Busse, Jacob Morgan, John Wetterholt, Frederick Smith, Jacob Orndt, John Van Etten, George Reynolds, and "Captain Lieutenants" Samuel Weiser, Philip Marsloff, Jacob Wetterholt, Samuel Humphrey, Andrew Engel, James Hyndshaw, Philip Weiser, Anthony Miller, and Sam Allen.

In England Thomas Penn, having received Weiser's letter and others telling of the confusion in the province, had appointed a new governor, "Mr Denny a Gentleman of the Army," [5] recommended by His Royal Highness the Duke of Cumberland, who was soon at sea in more senses than one. "It gives us great concern," wrote the Proprietor to Weiser, "that the situation of our Country shou'd oblige you to write in the manner you have done to me . . . Col. Denny has orders and brings with him very good inclinations to restore peace among yourselves . . ." [6] The new governor was soon busy paving Pennsylvania with good intentions.

To Richard Hockley, Penn wrote in some anxiety about Conrad Weiser:

We hope Conrad Weiser does not resolve to leave our Province; has he any Temptations from Shirley to assist him? I think Johnson does not wish him at New York—I cannot perfectly understand the hints you give, tho' I guess at them, you will do every thing in your power to prevent Conrad Weyser's leaving us.[7]

The news of Colonel Denny's appointment was, according to Richard Peters, received as a Quaker victory by Israel Pemberton, who at the coffee house announced the appointment "with a Triumphant Sneer." [8] Peters himself had forebodings. "I am in pain about my own Conduct," he wrote to Thomas Penn, June 3, 1756, "as I know him [Denny] to be haughty and overbearing, and at this time of Life I cannot put up with affronts or sleights." [9] A few days later he offered Penn a tentative resignation [10] as secretary ("I woud be left to my Option whether to resign or not")—to strengthen his hand with the new Governor in the dark days that lay ahead.

II

The four Indian messengers appeared with their green boughs in twenty days, and a courier was sent from Bethlehem to inform the Governor of their arrival there.[11] Augustus reported to Bishop Spangenberg that the Six Nations had sent the Delawares a belt with these words: "Leave off Kill^g ye white People, It is none of Your Business, You are but Women you know." [12] Augustus reported, further, that the Delawares were ready to make peace.

Governor Morris to Conrad Weiser [13]

Paxtang May 25th 1756.

Sir

NewCastle and the other Indians Employd by me upon a Message to the Northwest Branch of Sasquahana are returned, and Mr Peters informes me that they decline Saying any thing of the business they have been employd about, til they See me, and have your assistance, you will therefore give your attendance at Philad^a as Provincial Intrepeter as soon as you Possibly can.

I am Sir   Your Most Humble Servt

Rob^T H: Morris

To Conrad Weiser Esqr

Weiser hurried to Philadelphia and there took down in writing the report of Newcastle, Jagrea, and William Lacquis [14] (Augustus having remained with his flock at Bethlehem). Finding Wyoming deserted, they had gone on to Tioga, where they found great numbers of Indians. They summoned a conference and delivered the Governor's message, first giving wampum to clear the dust from their hearers' eyes, cleanse their stuffed throats, and bore open their ears. To the Governor's offer to cover with sand the blood that had been shed and to bury the hatchet under the roots of a great tree, Paxinosa, the Shawnee, replied that he would rejoice to take hold once again of the old treaties of William Penn.

Teedyuscung spoke for the Delawares. This picturesque figure, who was to leave a streak of blood, flame, and rhetoric across the next seven years of Pennsylvania's history (until the Six Nations executed him in 1763 by burning him while he lay drunk in his cabin), had once been known among the English as Honest John. A Jersey Indian by birth, a basket- and broom-maker by trade,[15] he had been with the Moravians at Shecomeco, where he cultivated a "poor sinner feeling" [16] and impressed the missionaries as hearty if not faithful.[17] The Moravians finally baptized him (giving him the name of Gideon), but with some hesitation, "because of his wavering disposition." He confessed at his baptism that he had been a bad man all his life, and "had no power to resist evil." He wept and trembled during the ceremony, and said that "he had never before been so desirous to be delivered from sin" [18]—a feeling which subsequent events gave him many opportunities for recapturing. His chief temptations were wine, women, and scalps.

Teedyuscung (i.e., *One Who Makes the Earth Tremble*),[19] said that the dark cloud was almost dispelled, and desired Brother Onas and the people of Pennsylvania to spit the bitterness out of their mouths. "We have laid aside the Hatchet," said Honest John; uttering, nevertheless, the caution— perhaps to protect himself in the future record in view of the scalpings that he knew very well were soon to come—that he did not speak for the Ohio Indians, who were under the influence of the French.[20]

Conrad Weiser's report being presented to the Council, June 3, the Governor proclaimed a thirty-day suspension of hostilities,[21] this to be observed, of course, only with respect to the Delawares living east of the Susquehanna River. The next step was to send the Indian messengers back to Teedyuscung with a formal invitation to a peace conference. But this the Governor was too busy to attend to at once. He was away at New Castle, and Weiser had his hands full keeping peace with the three Indian messengers who were becoming uneasy lest their long absence from Tioga should make the Delawares there think either that they had been killed or that the English were not in earnest about the peace.

Newcastle was particularly on edge, worrying about a niece whom he had left at Michael Taafe's on the Susquehanna with the understanding that the Governor should have her brought to Philadelphia. She had not come. When the Governor at length returned, Weiser was able to smooth out the misunderstanding; and Newcastle, assured that the girl this time would certainly be sent for, prepared to return to Teedyuscung.[22]

When he left, he took with him a quantity of belts and an invitation to a treaty to be held at Conrad Weiser's. "Brethren," ran the Governor's message, "that both you and I may have an Opportunity of making those mutual Declarations at a publick Convention, I now kindle a Council fire at the House of Conrad Weiser, who is one of the Council of the five Nations and the publick Interpretter of this Province." [23]

Weiser explained to the Governor that "it was Necessary to name a particular Place But the Indians were Notwithstanding Allways at Liberty to name another, and he beleaved from Something that Captain Newcastle had droped, the Indians would Chuse the forks of Delaware." [24] A belt of fourteen rows accompanied this part of the message.

When Newcastle and his Indians left, the commanders of the forts along the Blue Mountains were instructed to keep watch again for their return. "Their Signal will be a red flag with the Union in the Corner," ran the instructions given Colonel Clapham, who was charged with the building of the fort at Shamokin, "or if that should be lost they will carry green Boughs or Clubd Muskets, will appear open and Erect and not approach you in the night." [25]

For the moment, the country was at peace. The new leafage springing in the forest had not brought the expected flow of blood. For six weeks the Delawares had lain quiet.

Good news meanwhile had come from Scaroyady. He and Montour had despatched a messenger, by name Ogaghradarisha, to Pennsylvania bringing permission from the Six Nations to build the fort at Shamokin, and with a request that a second fort be built at Adjouquay, fourteen miles above Wyoming—a place from which, it was explained, "an old woman may Carry a heavy Pack of skins . . . to the Minisink and return . . . in two Nights." [26]

Weiser, after spending a few days at Heidelberg and Reading attending to the affairs of his home, farm, and battalion, was again summoned to Philadelphia, this time for a conference with "the old man Ogaghradarisha." [27]

There were some difficulties about Ogaghradarisha's messages. For one thing, it seemed strange that the Six Nations should have asked Pennsylvania to build a fort at Adjouquay, since the lands there never had been bought of the Indians. It was plain that the request had come, not from the Onondaga Council, but from some Indians at Tioga. Weiser, consulted, advised referring the matter to the Six Nations proper, and awaiting their decision.

Newcastle meanwhile had gone to Tioga and delivered the Governor's message. The invitation was accepted. Teedyuscung, who now called himself "King," came back with Newcastle as far as Bethlehem, having first sold "an English Female Prisoner for a Horse to perform his Journey." [28]

From Bethlehem, where he left the King, Newcastle hurried on to Philadelphia. He besought the Governor not to delay, since "The times are Dangerous the Swords drawn and Glittering all Around you." [29] King Teedyuscung had sent a special message: ". . . at the forks of Deleware we will sit down and wait there and shall be ready." [30]

There was need enough for haste. After a quiet spring, the enemy had begun scalping again. Four people were killed in the Hole near Swatara Creek (now Monroe Valley), one of them Conrad Weiser's eighteen-year-old nephew, a son of his brother Frederick.[31] "The people," wrote Weiser, "are again in a great Consternation."[32] Colonel Clapham had, by July 4, got his Shamokin detachment no farther north than Robert Armstrong's, some twenty miles above Harris' Ferry. The commissioners, said Weiser, were "as nigh as nine pence is to ten to disband him."[33]

"Just at this Moment," wrote Weiser to the Governor, July 11, "my Son Sammy arrived from Fort Henry, and tells me that there had been an Engagement at Caghnekacheeky, wherein twelve on our side were killed, and Six Indians; That our People kept the Field and scalped the Indians, and that the Indians ran off without any Scalp. As bad News as it is I wish it may be true."[34]

People were afraid to gather in the harvest without military guards, and the forts were too thinly garrisoned to give protection to everyone. So great was the demand for help that on July 15 Captain Busse had only four men left in Fort Henry, and had to refuse a request from Bixler to send a guard for his harvesters who, having heard a loud noise in the woods, refused to work without protection.[35] It grieved the Captain to see the grain left standing, but he could do nothing.

The problem of the Indian refugees was becoming acute again. John Shickellamy, insulted by the inhabitants round McKee's, was determined to leave the white settlements altogether; and the matter of Newcastle's niece was proving less simple to adjust than had been expected.

Richard Peters to Conrad Weiser [36]

Philadelphia 11th July 1756

Sir

Capt McKee brought down the Indian Girl and left her agreeable to the Governor's Order at Springetsbury, but Jagrea and Ogaghradaricha went against Capt McKees Will and brought her to Town to Mrs Boyle's along with John Shickalemy's Wife, who was at Connestogoe and came to Mr McKee's and insisted on coming with him to Town. I understand She intends to return with the old Man to Sasquehannah, I suppose to her Husband, but this may not perhaps be proper, and it will be better to keep her here—If you think so, the Governor desires You will take measures to detain her.

The Governor was at Newcastle when Capt McKee returnd with the Girl from Taaffe's, and being told that She was at Boyle's in Town, he was very angry, upbraided Thomas McKee with Want of Obedience to his Orders, and gave him very sharp Reproof. He said in Excuse for himself, that he could not hinder it. The Girl was ordered back to Springetsbury, and in an hour's Time she ran away and was absent in the Woods all night. I sent McKee in the morning to search for her, and he found her, and brought her to Town, and then the Governor determined with his Council to send her under the Care of James Ennis to your House till Newcastle's Return. The Governor is downright angry with Thomas McKee, and he as much displeased with the Governor, so that I have had a sad time of it.

You are desired to examine John Skick Calamy's Wife, closely, and to dispose of her or keep her at your House as You shall judge best. . . .

> I am
> > Sir
> > Your affectinate
> > humble servant
> > > RICHARD PETERS

Ogaghradarisha was given a pass to enable him to proceed through the settlements to Conrad Weiser's. All persons were ordered to suffer him to pass "without Molestation Tho' on Sunday." [37]

III

At Fort Johnson, Sir William, having recently been confirmed in his appointment as sole superintendent for Indian affairs in the northern colonies, sought to achieve a spectacular success by a policy of appeasement toward the Delawares. The social and political gifts that had won him such huge successes among the English on both sides of the ocean were now to bring in a new era in Indian relationships. Of the conference held at Onondaga in July 1756, he wrote:

I concluded this Treaty by taking off the Petticoat, or that invidious name of Women from the Delaware Nation which hath been imposed on them by the 6 Nations from the time they conquered them, In the name of the Great King of England their father and on behalf of all their Brethren the English on this continent, and promised them I would use my influence and best endeavors to prevail with the six Nations to follow my example, the Deputies of the Six Nations who were present approved of this measure, but said they were not a sufficient number nor properly authorized to do it on behalf of their constituents, however they would make their report and press it on them.[38]

Under these pleasant words the watchful Iroquois deputies concealed their real sentiments, though their evasive answer might have been taken by Johnson, if he had been able to see beyond his nose, as a clear indication of their disgust. The Six Nations did not forget. In the stormy conference held at Easton two years later their anger flashed out against the English for making so much of the Delawares and in particular for making Teed-yuscung "a great man." They taunted the Delawares with having let a stranger take off their petticoats without making men of them, so that they merely ran around naked.

It was to take all Weiser's skill and influence with the Confederacy to undo the harm Johnson's playboy gesture had done. If Delaware petticoats were to be removed, it must be done by the Six Nations and by no one else.

Teedyuscung, who arrogated to himself the rôle of a plenipotentiary representing no less than ten nations (Delawares, Shawnees, Mohicans, Munsies, and the Six Nations), assumed the air of a benevolent patriarch and held it as long as he was comfortably in liquor. From Bethlehem he had moved, escorted by a detachment under William Parsons, to Easton.

"The King took a short Nap by the Way," wrote Parsons. ". . . He was very good Humoured the whole Journey but thought it long before he could get any Rum. I furnish'd them with one Bottle, a little more than a pint, at their first Coming and have this Minute (10 o'Clock) furnish'd a second." [39]

Orders were sent from the Governor to Parsons, to collect food and engage all available houses in town for the accommodation of the Governor and his party; and to Colonel Weiser "to call together such Detachments of the several Companies on the frontiers, as could safely be spared," [40] and march them to the place of treaty. To do this was to inflict a hardship on the farmers, who needed protection in harvest time; but there was no choice in the matter, for the large number of Indians assembling at Easton made the presence of a strong guard there a necessity.

At the last moment, July 22, the Governor decided to change the place of meeting from Easton to Bethlehem, and issued orders to that effect, word of which coming to Teedyuscung at Easton, the King of Ten Nations sent a stern reply that served to put the Governor straight in no time:

Brother, [he said] I am very glad to hear from you. At the Distance of 400 Miles from hence I received your Invitation to come and make peace. I understood that you had laid a Junck of Fire here at Easton that I might come and smoke my Pipe by it. Brother since you sent that Message I am come, and will stay here, And I cant understand what you mean by sending me about from place to place, like a Child. [41]

Governor Morris came to Easton.

Weiser marched into town with twenty-two men of his Reading company and a few detachments collected along the way. [42] At Bethlehem he had been joined by Lieutenant Engel with thirteen hungry men, without provisions or a farthing of money, who had walked thirty-seven miles the day before through the rain, being lost in the woods. Captain Busse ordered breakfast for them, and the guard, thus strengthened, went on to Easton, where they arrived on Tuesday, July 27, before noon.

IV

Throughout the conference Teedyuscung held the spotlight, being designed both by nature and by art to catch and hold attention. He was a well set-up man, tall, raw-boned, impressive; and his suit, "a fine dark brown Cloth Coat laced with Gold which he now wears"—the French had given it to him recently at Niagara—matched his complexion. [43]

From an unofficial report, in which the personal diary of William Parsons, who had attended the King for some days before the Governor arrived, is blended with official matters written by Richard Peters, the whole being endorsed by Conrad Weiser as "a true account of what passed between the Governor and the Indians in my presence at Easton," we get the following highlights.

The King and his wild Company were perpetually drunk, very much on the Gascoon, and at times abusive to the Inhabitants, for they all spoke English more or less, The King was full of himself, saying frequently, That which Side soever he took must stand, and the other fall; repeating it with Insolence That he came from the French who had pressed him much to joyn them against the English, That now he was in the middle between the French and English quite disengaged from both Sides, and whether he joyned with the English or French, he wou'd publish it aloud to the World, That all Nations might know it; At other times he declared he did not come to the English for the Sake of what they wou'd give him, but to Establish an Everlasting Peace and Friendship with them, which if they wou'd accept of, They shou'd find him a true and usefull Friend. That he was born among the English some-where near Trenton and is near fifty Years old. He is a lusty raw-boned Man, haughty & very desirous of Respect and Command. He can drink three Quarts or a Gallon of Rum a Day without being drunk—He was the Man that per-suaded the Delawares to go over to the French, and then to attack our Frontiers, and he and these with him have been Concerned in the Mischief done to the Inhabitants of Northampton County . . .

The Town's People Observed That the Shirts which the Indian Women had on were made of Dutch TableCloths, which it is supposed they took from the People they murdered on our Frontiers. . . . The Governor invited Teedyus-cung and the Indians to dine with him, But before Dinner the King with some of them came to the Governor and made the Governor four Speeches giving four Strings of Wampum after the Indian Manner; One to brush the Thorns from the Governor's Legs, Another to rub the Dust out of his Eyes, to help him to see clearly, Another to open his Ears to enable him to hear them patiently, And the fourth to clear his Throat That he might speak plainly— Then Teedyuscung entered upon a rambling Conversation saying that he was made King by ten Nations, Being asked what ten Nations, He answered The united Six Nations, Mohocks, Onondagoes, Oniedas, Senecas, Cyugas, and Tuscaroras and four Others, Delawares, Shawanes, Mohickons and Munsies; who wou'd ratify what he shou'd do—He carried the Belt of Peace with him, and whoever wou'd might take hold of it. But as to them that refused; The rest wou'd all joyn together and fall upon them . . .

Teedyuscung urged the Governor to begin Business, saying the time was precious and those who sent him wou'd be uneasy, expecting to see him by a certain Day which was not farr off. To which the Governor declared that he was ready, and as uneasy to begin Business as he, but he waited for Mr Weiser who being of the Council of the six Nations and the Provincial Interpreter, it was necessary he shoud be present. At which the King Expressed his Satisfaction, said the Governor was in the Right and his Uncles wou'd be better satisfied to have Mr Weiser present.

The Governor and Indians then went to Dinner, escorted by a Detachment of the first Battalion of the Pennsylvania Regiment; After Dinner the King expressed great Satisfaction with the Governor's Behaviour to him and in a polite Manner acknowledged his Mistaken Oppinnion of the Designs of the Government, which some People about him had represented, before he set out to be unfavourable to the Delawares; But he found it the reverse. He frequently said he wou'd open all his Soul to the Governor, and tomorrow produce his Authorities, by which it wou'd appear, he did not come of his own head, but by Express Direction of his Uncles the Six Nations; he did not indeed come to treat, but to look about him and try what Reception he shoud meet with and what wou'd be said to him by this Government, of whose Sincerity there had been some Doubts, after which he was ordered by his Uncles to report all he shou'd see and hear, to them. And as by the Kindness already shewn him his Doubts were removed and he saw clearly the End, wou'd be good—His Uncles and the Delawares wou'd come together and conclude a firm Treaty—

At a Council held at Easton Tuesday the twenty seventh Day of July 1756, . . .

Mr Weiser coming to Town the Governor proposed to open the Conferences, but on his saying he was a Stranger to Teedyuscung, and it wou'd take up some time, at least a Day, to be rightly informed of his Temper and Expectations, it was deferred 'till to Morrow. Capt Newcastle came to the Governor, much in Liquor, Tho' otherwise a very sober Man; and requested a Council might be called, saying he had something of a particular Nature to communicate, with which being obliged, he acquainted the Governor That the Delawares had bewitched him and he shou'd dye soon; The Govenor wou'd have rallied it off, but he grew more serious and desired this Information might be committed to Writeing and incerted in the Minutes of Council, and sent to the six Nations; That if any harm came to him, They might know to whom to impute it, and not charge others with it. Teedyuscung he declared had warned him in a friendly manner; That he wou'd not live long having overheard two Delawares say They wou'd put an End to his Life by Witchcraft; And whilst he was speaking Teedyuscung mistrusting what Newcastle was upon bolted into the Room; fell into a violent Passion with Newcastle, who he supposed had been telling the Governor foolish Words, and desired he might not be regarded in anything he shou'd say on such a foolish Subject, Exclaiming, He bewitched! The Governor was too wise to hearken to such silly Stories, And then left the Room in as abrupt a Manner as he entered it— After he was gone The Governor Endeavoured to shew NewCastle that he was in no Danger, but he made no Impression, NewCastle still urging That his Information might be taken down and in Case of his Death, be communicated in a special Message to the six Nations which was promised, and he then withdrew, to appearance more composed—

At a Council held at Easton Wednesday the 28th day of July 1756 . . .

Mr Weiser informed the Council That the King and the principal Indians being all yesterday under the Force of Liquor, he had not been favoured with so good an Oppertunity as he coud have wished, of making himself acquainted with their History, but in the main, he believed Teedyuscung was well inclined; He talked in high Terms of his own Merit; But Expressed himself a Friend to this Province. . . .

To the Surprize of Every Body Capt Newcastle was seized this Morning with a violent Pleurisy and thought to be in great Danger, but on loosing some Blood and taking proper Physick the Violence of the Distemper abated and he recovered.[44]

Later, on this same day, the conference blazed into its fullest brilliance. There were present: the Governor; William Logan, Richard Peters, Benjamin Chew, and John Mifflin of the Governor's Council; three members of the Provincial Commissioners; King Teedyuscung and fourteen other chiefs; Conrad Weiser, Interpreter for the Six Nations; Benjamin "that speaks English," Interpreter for the Delawares; John Pumpshire and Joseph Peepy, Delawares; officers of the Royal American Regiment and of Weiser's battalion of provincials; magistrates and freeholders of Easton and neighboring communities; "and about thirty Citizens of the City of Philadelphia." [45]

Teedyuscung made a great speech:

Brother, Hearken to what I am going to say, I declare in the most solemn Manner, That what I now Relate is the Truth. Abundance of Confusion, Disorder and Distraction has arisen among the Indians. from People taking upon them to be Kings and Persons of Authority. In every Tribe of Indians there have been such Pretenders, who have held Treaties, sometimes publick, and sometimes in the Bushes; Sometimes what these People did, came to be known, but frequently it remained in Darkness, or at least no more was imparted to the Publick, than they were Pleased to Publish. To some they held up their Belts, but others never saw them; This bred among the Indians great Heart Burnings and Quarrels, and I can assure you, That the present Clouds do in a great Measure owe their Rise to this wild and irregular way of doing Business—the Indians sensible of this Mistake of our Ancestors; are now determined to put an End to this Multitude of Kings, and to their dark way of Proceedings; They have agreed to put the Management of their Affairs into the Hands of a very few, and These shall no longer have it in their power to huddle up and give partial Representations of what is done. I assure you that there are only two Kings appointed to transact Public Business of which I am one, having the Management of Publick Affairs Committed to me by ten Nations, to whom I am accountable. For the future Matters will goe better on both Sides, You as well as we will know Who we are to deal with—[46]

From this point, we follow the Colonial Records:

"We must beseech the most High to Scatter the Clouds which have Arisen between us, that we settle Peace as heretofore."
A String.
"Brethren, the English, and Particularly the Governor of Pennsylvania:
"You know you have invited me here. I come, therefore; my Uncles, the Six Nations, will Confirm what I say. In your Messages to the Indians at Diahoga, you Signified to us that you heard we were in want and Distress, which to be sure we were, and pitied us & our poor Wives & Children; we took it kindly and as a word that came from your heart; now is the time for you to look About and Act the part of a Charitable and wise man; be, therefore, strong; Be Assured, that tho' I am poor I will do my Share. Whatever Kindness you do to me or my People, shall be published to ten Indian Nations; we won't hide any Presents you shall give us, every body shall know that we have heard your good words; we will not do as others & some of our Uncles, the Six Nations, have done, sneak away and hide your words and Presents in the Bushes; but shall publishe far and near that all may Join with us. Exert yourselves now in the best manner you can, and you will Obtain your End. . . ."
Being asked if he had done Speaking, he said he had for the present; "the main thing," he added, "is yet in my Breast (laying his hand to his heart), but

this will depend on what words the Governor will speak to us;" then he repeated the Delaware word "Whish Shiksy," the same in Mohock Language as Jago, with great Earnestness and in a very Pathetick Tone. Mr. Weiser, who knew the word to have a very extensive and forcible sense, desired the Interpreter to ask him what he meant by "Whish Shiksy" on this particular Occasion, and Explained himself in the following manner: "suppose you want to Remove A large Logg of Wood that Requires many Hands, You must take pains to gett as many together as will do the Business; if you fall short of one, tho' ever so weak, all the Rest are to no purpose; tho' this being in itself nothing, yet if you Cannot move the Logg without it, you must spare no pains to gett it; Whish Shiksy, be Strong; look round you; Enable us to get every Indian nation we can; put the means into our heads; be sure perform every Promise you have made to us in Particular, do not Pinch matters neither with us nor other Indians; we will help you. But we are poor & you are Rich; make us strong and we will use our strength for you; and besides this, what you do, Do Quickly; the times are Dangerous, they will not Admit of Delay; Whish Shiksy, do it Effectually, and do it with all **Possible Dispatch.**" [47]

The Governor took *Whish Shicksy* to heart, and next day, after consultation with Conrad Wieser, delivered his reply. Presenting Teedyuscung with a string of wampum to open his ears, he ran over the history of the war and the negotiations that had led to the present meeting.[48] He assured the King that the people of Pennsylvania were disposed to renew their ancient friendship with the Indians, invited him to return with all his people to receive presents to relieve their distresses, and proposed that they bring with them all the prisoners they had taken during this war and deliver them up as a token of their sincerity. For, he said, adopting the Indian metaphor,

. . . tho' Peace may be made from the Teeth outwards, yet while you retain our Flesh & Blood in Slavery, It cannot be Expected we can be friends with you, or that a Peace can come from our hearts I repeat this Article of the Prisoners as a necessary Condition of Peace and desire you will Consider it as such.[49]

Teedyuscung replied with a dramatic gesture. "Brother," he said, taking a large belt of wampum in his hands: "At the very time Newcastle came with your last messages I was in treaty with the Six Nations, and Received this Authority from them," lifting up the Belt; "this Belt denotes that the six nations by their Chiefs have lately renewed their Covenant Chains with us, formerly we were Accounted women, and Employed only in womens business, but now they have made men of us, and as such are now come to this Treaty having this Authority as a man to make Peace." [50]

There was some mystery about that belt. Weiser asked Newcastle what messages had actually been received by the Delawares at Tioga from the Six Nations, and got a picturesque (but only partially printable) reply, which he put down in a literal translation that found its way into the conference records:—

Taken from Captⁿ Newcastles Mouth by Mr Weiser
31st July 1756 [51]

The large Belt given by Teedyuscung was sent to the Delawares by the Council of the Six United Nations with a Message to the following Purport

Cousins the Delaware Indians

You will remember that you are our women, our Forefathers made you so, and put a Petty Coat on you, and charged you to be true to us and lye with no other man. But of late you have suffer'd the String y^t ty'd your Pettycoat to be cut loose by the French and you lay with them and so became a common Bawd, in which you did very wrong and deserved Chastisement, but notwithstanding this we have still Esteem for you . . . We advise you not to act as a Man yet but be first instructed by us and do as we bid you and you will become a noted man.

Cousins

The English & French fight for our Land, Let us be strong and lay our hand to it, and defend it. In the meantime turn your Eyes & Ears to us and the English our Brethren & you will live as well as we do.

To Weiser there was no mystery. Teedyuscung was deliberately misinterpreting the belt and declaring the independence of the Delawares. This action, following Johnson's, would raise suspicion among the Six Nations that the English were playing a double game: from one side of their mouths recognizing the suzerainty of the Six Nations; from the other acknowledging the independence of the Delawares. Weiser was uneasy. Teedyuscung was a new man to him, perhaps more dangerous than his drunken wind-baggery led most of those who heard him to suspect. The Moravians had accepted him as a convert. The Quakers at the conference were impressed with his idealism and desired to make him and his people a special present from "the children of William Penn." Where would this end?

Whatever his doubts and fears, Weiser had to let the situation unfold itself, and meanwhile there were plenty of things to distract his mind. On Friday the 30th he held a court-martial for the trial of two soldiers of Captain Insley's company.[52] On the same day the Governor received a letter from the Secretary of State in London, enclosing His Majesty's declaration of war against France, news that was solemnly announced to the people while Weiser's troops, drawn up in three divisions, stood under arms and fired three volleys at the close.

It was decided by the Governor and Council, on the advice of Newcastle and Weiser, to accept the Independence Belt and to give in return a belt large enough to dilate the King's expansive soul. To this end all available wampum, white and black, strung and loose, was assembled, and five thousand new pieces were fetched from Bethlehem. A number of Indian women were gathered in a room to make a belt according to the Council's specifications. It was to be "a fathom long & sixteen Beads wide, in the Center of which was to be the figure of a man, meaning the Governor of Pennsylvania, and Each other side five other figures, meaning the ten Nations mentioned by Teedyuscung."

The King, getting wind of this activity, and putting his own interpretation on it, made a scene. According to the Council minutes,

The King who was very Irregular in his visits, as well as his Discourses, bolted all of a Sudden in to the room and with a high tone of voice spoke as follows, vizt

"Brother,—I desire All that I have said and you have said to one another may be taken down Aright, some speak in the Dark, do not let us do so let all be Clear and known, what is the Reason the Governor holds Councils so Close in his hands, & by Candle light, the five nations used to lett him set out of doors like women, if the five nations still make him a woman they must But what is the Reason the Governor makes him a woman (meaning why he Confers with Indians, without sending for him, to be present and hear what passes), The Governor answered, that he held Councils on a hill, has no Secrets, never sits in swamps, but speaks his mind Openly to the world; what hapens here he has Aright to hear, the women were sent for to make a belt, not to Council; the six nations may be wrong, they are not under his Direction, and therefore he is not answerable for their Conduct, if they have not treated the Delewares as men; the Chief thanked the Governor, seemed well pleased & said tomorrow he would speak more, what he had to say was from the six nations; He that wont make peace must die, A String [53]

On Saturday, July 31, a good-sized present (to which the Quakers contributed largely) was given to the Indians, and the King and the Governor made appropriate speeches of leave taking. The Governor urged Teedyuscung to work in collaboration with Newcastle for "A speedy & Honourable Peace." Teedyuscung replied that "his heart & ours should be one . . . for if different liquors are put in a Cask & shaked they will mix & Come one." He added as an afterthought that he had a large family and needed a horse to carry provisions to them. Horse and provisions being supplied, the conference broke up. Teedyuscung set off for Tioga with his sons, son-in-law, grandson, counselor, and attendants; the Governor for New York to meet General Shirley; the Council for Philadelphia; and the detachments from the First Battalion of the Pennsylvania Regiment which had served under Weiser as guard, to their various posts along the Blue Mountains.

At "Bethlehem's Inn" on August 1, Lieutenant Colonel Weiser ordered dinner for forty-eight men at a cost of one pound, seventeen shillings, and sixpence. "Here," he notes in his *Account of Expences*, "Lieutenant Engels Men Seperated, And went towards their Fort. They had no Money at all I gave them Ten Shillings to buy some Provision by the Way for themselves." [54]

The Colonel reached Reading with his company on the evening of August 2.

CHAPTER 51

. . . Puts Down Mutiny

THE meeting with Teedyuscung at Easton in July had done no more than open the way for peace negotiations. Rhetoric had been exchanged, but no commitments. The Governor had invited Teedyuscung to bring all his people to a second conference, there to receive a quantity of presents—on condition that English prisoners be brought in and set free. Whether Teedyuscung really intended to make peace was not known. Even during the conference, reports came in of renewed scalping on the border, and after the conference such atrocities became common. Was Teedyuscung's dissociation of himself from the Ohio Delawares perhaps no more than a device to keep the record straight while his warriors massacred the harvesters along the frontier?

Weiser thought Teedyuscung double-faced, but what lay behind his evasive rhetoric he did not know. Was the King false from stupidity or cunning? The whole scheme of Indian relations had of late become so tangled and unstable that the interpreter could not even be sure the Six Nations were altogether frank with him. Were they using Teedyuscung, as the latter claimed they were, as their agent in an attempt to defend Indian lands from the English as well as from the French? "The English & French fight for our Land," Newcastle had reported the Six Nations as saying to the Delawares at Tioga, "Let us be strong and lay our hands to it, and defend it."

After the conference Newcastle was secretly despatched to the north to learn whether the Six Nations were back of Teedyuscung and whether Pennsylvania was to take this pompous windbag at his own valuation.[1] Was he a mere king of vaudeville? Was he a temperamental fellow who "took miff" [2] at the government's failure to take sufficient notice of him— a man whose resentment would pass quickly after the shedding of a little blood? Was he an honest patriot engaged in a war of liberation for the Delawares? Or was he in truth the leader of ten tribes engaged in a vast scheme of Indian intrigue which threatened the existence of the English colonies?

Whatever his motives and credentials, this was certain: the French could use him. If Weiser had known what was going on in the mind of Dumas, who was studying the Indian situation closely from his post at Fort Duquesne, he would have had ample reason to fear Teedyuscung. Dumas' policy, which had striking success for a time, was first to control the Six Nations Indians on the Ohio (who were gathered about Captain Chauvignerie at Fort Machault), and then, through the Six Nations, to control their tributaries.

Montcalm's success at Oswego on August 15 gave Dumas' policy an impetus that soon affected Teedyuscung, for, as Parkman says, the capture of

Oswego "wrenched away from the British alliance the Western Nations of the Iroquois and left only the Mohawks unquestionably true."

For the moment, however, Teedyuscung seemed to be more a nuisance than a peril. By the middle of August he and his entourage had got no farther on their way to Tioga than Fort Allen (which William Parsons heard they had turned into a dram shop) [3] and whence he sent his "Love to all his frends in Bethlehem and Eston," and assured them that when he had boasted in conference that he had killed some of the English, he had merely been "in Drinck."

True to his peaceable principle that "if different liquors are put in a Cask & shaked, they will mix and Come one," the King stayed on at Fort Allen mixing his drinks and his squaws. We should not, however, blame the resulting confusion to the garrison so much on Honest (but too Amiable) John as on Lieutenant Miller, "that little impertinant Body which your Honour saw at the Tavern on Quittopolela Spring," [4] as Major Parsons described him to Governor Morris, who kept the King drunk in order to cheat him of the sixteen deerskins he had with him in a bundle intended as a present for the Governor. The Lieutenant got the skins—but at the expense of all discipline in the fort.

On the night of August 5, liquor running freely, Corporal Christian Weirick quarreled with the Indians and ran amok. He knocked Lieutenant Miller down; attempted, as Captain John Nicholas Wetterholt tells us, to tear John White to pieces, and "drove about the Fort like a Beast. . . . Then he went and broke the stones from the Chymney back and threw them into the Window and cursed furiously and said that he would kill one of the 4 Reading Town Soldiers or would Stab or Shoot Serjeant White." [5] He seized four guns, tried to shoot the place up, and said no men should live that day. The guard refused orders to arrest him.

Weiser, who had been having a few days of comparative quiet at Reading, presiding at the Court of Common Pleas, received a frantic letter from Captain Reynolds, the officer in command at Fort Allen, about the "bad affair" that had occurred during his absence.[6]

Before Weiser intervened, Major Parsons had sent orders to Captain Jacob Orndt of nearby Fort Norris to place Lieutenant Miller under arrest. Whereupon the Lieutenant threatened, as Orndt reported, that "the feirst men that Would Touch him he would Cut an arm from his boty" [7]— and the Battalion had mutiny on its hands.

It was unfortunate that the new governor's first contacts with Colonel Weiser's Battalion should have been in connection with this fracas at Fort Allen. But so it was. Colonel Denny arrived in Philadelphia on August 20, and was the same day proclaimed governor. Next day this "very genteel" [8] member of the Society of Dilettanti (who had in 1744 presented the society "with a portrait of himself in Roman dress by George Knapton," [9] but whose romantic days being now past covered himself with a "brown fustian coat" that toned with his brown fustian mind) sent instructions to Colonel Weiser.

Governor Denny to Colonel Weiser [10]

Colonel Weiser   Philadelphia 21 Aug[t] 1756
Sir.

Having received Information that the Indians have threatned an Attack upon Bethleham and that numbers of them are hovering about Fort Allen in a very suspicious manner. I think it necessary for the security of that post of the Province to send you this Information and to order you to proceed to Bethleham or Fort Allen with all convenient dispatch and to Assemble there or in such other place as you may Judge best such detachments from the several Companies of your Battallion as the Intelligence shall receive may make necessary and you will make such disposition of those Troops and give them such orders as you may Judge most for his Majesty's Service and the safety of the Inhabitants taking care to be explicit in those Orders as the nature of the Service will admit of—

And being informed that great disorders have been committed by the Officers at Fort Allen and some other Officers of your Battalion you will without delay make a strick enquiry into their behaviour as well with regard to the Indians as in their Military Capacity of which you will make a full report to me and till you can receive my Directions thereupon you will put the Officers or any of them that you shall Judge Culpable under Arrest or suspend them from Acting as Officers till my pleasure is known as you shall Judge best, and that the service may not in the mean time suffer you will Appoint proper Persons to Act in the Places of those you shall so Arrest or Suspend returning to me their Names and your Opinion of their fitness for those Stations. . . .
I am   Sir,
                                          Your humble Servant
                                          WILLIAM DENNY

No sooner had Weiser set out for Bethlehem and Fort Allen to investigate the rumor of an impending Indian attack and the mutiny Captain Reynolds had on his hands, than letters were dispatched to inform him of another mutiny at Fort Norris. The guard at this latter place, according to Captain Orndt,[11] had refused to arrest a disobedient sentry, and the company, siding with the guard, made the Captain feel, as he put it, like a prisoner in their midst. The company, meanwhile, sent to "their Colonell Weisser" a "Complen" of their own, asserting, among other things, that their captain withheld their rum, that one of their sergeants drank too much, and that they could not eat the meat "for stink and worms." [12]

It was a pretty kettle of fish, but, with the aid of Major Parsons, Weiser quickly straightened everything out. In the end Lieutenant Miller surrendered himself, young Captain Reynolds and his detachment were transferred to Fort Norris, and Captain Orndt (really an efficient officer who later won distinction for himself as Major Orndt before the French and Indian War was over) was moved to the important station at Fort Allen. The "mutinies" had had no serious military consequences, but on the new Governor's peevish and supercilious mind they had left an unfortunate impression of the colonial forces under Weiser's command.

Colonel Weiser's complaints addressed to the Governor against the conditions out of which the disturbances had grown were too warm and unstudied to win His Excellency's admiration for the backwoods commander who had written them.

Colonel Weiser to Governor Denny [13]

Honoured Sir

I take the freedom to trouble your Ho[nour with] these few lines Now I am pretty Sure that my Le[tter] dated at Bethlehem August the 27 last past Sent [by] favour of Major parson must have Come to hand before now and as it Contained only a part of an answer to your Honours orders to me dated August the 21 last [past] I think it necessary to add that . . . the province of Pensilvania [has not] much Credit of late, because a great many of the men Employed in the Service have not received pay for some months, and I hear both officiers & Comon men are very Much discontent for Some of them are allmost Nacked and the fall of the year is Coming on, I have Expended above . . . 100 hundred pound pensilvania Currancy for prov[isions] to some of the Companies according to agreement with [the] Gentlemen the Comissioners of the province and I never received one farthing of Solary as yet and I do not Know how long I Can Stay at my place people are Moving every day away from under the mountain and leave their plantation because for fear of the Cruel Savage Eneemy and it Can not be Expected that these few Men now posted under Kittitany hills Can gard the Countrey against the Invasion of the Barbarians the frontier is too large and the woods to thick though the range every . . . day according to orders given them yet we hear of frequent Murder Comited by these Cruel Enemys and of some being tied with Cords and lead into Captivity and all this makes no more Impression upon the most part of the people of pensilvania no more than If a lim of a tree had Struk one of their Creatures. god help us . . .

There could never be sympathy between a self-important martinet just out from Lord Chesterfield's England and a full-blooded, outspoken, tumultuous enthusiast whose genius sprang directly out of the American forest.

CHAPTER 52

. . . *Sees Teedyuscung Sober*

SEPTEMBER 1756 was a bad month for Pennsylvania. "The Country," wrote Peters to Penn, "is in a more deplorable Condition yⁿ ever." [1] The French had recently unleashed a fierce drive from the west. After the Indians had taken Fort Granville on the Juniata, almost all the inhabitants of Cumberland County left their plantations. People were even beginning to leave York County on a rumor that the Indians had attacked and killed some persons below the South Mountains. The fall of Oswego had all but wrecked the English alliance with the Six Nations. Killings were resumed in Berks County and farther east. Even Colonel John Armstrong's successful attack on the Indian town of Kittanning, which he had destroyed, and the death of the great Delaware warrior, Captain Jacobs, was no offset to the list of disasters. There was panic again. Conrad Weiser feared lest the back inhabitants might come to an accommodation with the French and Indians "on condition of being rendered secure in their Possessions." [2]

John Shickellamy, who some months before had fled from McKee's in fear of his life, turned up at Bethlehem, half starved. He was escorted by two Moravians to Philadelphia, where he told how he had been wandering for days in the woods without a gun, in danger from the settlers. ". . . he thought it very hard," he told Weiser, who had been sent for express to meet him, "that there was no Body that Spoke in his favour among them people on SusqueHana, tho they all Knew that he was a Constant friend to the people of Pensilvania. that he desired them to give him a Safe gard to Convey him to his uncle, C- Weiser but they would not do it, and said that CW. was as great a Rogue as him Self" [3]

Weiser, it appears, remained in Philadelphia for several weeks. He had much conversation with John Shickellamy, who had, only two months past, been to Onondaga to learn the disposition of the Six Nations toward the present war and to find out whether Teedyuscung spoke with authority. He had seen the Belt (Tohashwughtonionty, the Seneca) and Silver Heels (Aroas). [4] The Mohawks, Oneidas, and Onondagas, he reported, were hearty for a war against the French, and the Cayugas were neutral. But this information was old, antedating the capture of Oswego, and could not now be relied on. As for Teedyuscung, he was the chief man at Tioga, said John, and had been advised by the Six Nations to make peace. He had no other authority. Personally, said John, he hated the sight of Teedyuscung and "would not speak to him so only saw him at a distance." [5]

Conrad gave John a present of lead, powder, flints, "a Kitle Pretty Big," shirts, stockings, matchcoats, vermilion, needles, awl blades, knives, a little rum, an "ivory Cum," "a Speckticle"; and he added thereto "Horses & Sadle & Bridle to put goods to Shomocken part to give to the poor Some to Sell." [6]

Weiser had been dabbling again in Assembly politics.

Richard Hockley to the Penns [7]

Philadᵃ Sepʳ 19ᵗʰ 1756

Hon'd Sirs

. . . I delivered your message to Conrad Weiser who receiv'd it kindly and since that your letter which pleases him very much   he is in town at present and told me he would write by this ship and give his letter to me to forward if he does I shall send it,   my house is open to him which he frequents without yᵉ least ceremony, he is a valuable Man and your fast Friend,   I expect he will be returned as a Member for Berks the ensuing Election—

Richard Hockley was too sanguine. The elections went against the proprietorial party, and another pacifist Assembly was returned. Weiser was never to have a seat in the House.

If September was a bad month for Pennsylvania, October promised to be a worse one. The one thing best calculated to take the backbone out of a government trying to end an Indian war was provided by a letter from Lord Loudoun, received late on Friday night, October 1: "a Letter," wrote Peters, "of the most extraordinary nature that was ever wrote to a Governor." [8]

"I do hereby for the future for bid you or your Government," said the new Commander-in-Chief of the British forces in America, "from Confering or Treating with these Indians in any shape or on any Account whatsoever . . ." [9] All Indian negotiations were to be left to Sir William Johnson.

"I . . . shall only observe to you," wrote Peters to Penn, October 2, "that if Indian Affairs are taken out of the Hands of the Government so as neither to suffer the Governor to confer nor Treat with Indians, all our friendly Indians will turn against us, and we shall have the most lamentable Winter." [10]

Word came from Ogaghradarisha that the French and their Indians, a thousand in number, were coming to besiege the fort at Shamokin. The Governor and Benjamin Franklin set out early in the month for Harris' Ferry and Carlisle to take measures for a counter offensive, like that launched so successfully against the Delawares at Kittanning. Weiser was to have gone with them, but, being ill of "an intermitting Feaver," he was unable to leave his house.[11] Toward the middle of the month, Peters relayed to him information received from Major Parsons to this effect: "Teedyuscung has collected the English Prisoners and is with them at Wyomink waiting to know if we will receive him . . . An Express is gone to him to come & stay at Easton till the Govʳ send further to him. I advise you of this yᵗ you may be in readiness to do your part." [12] At the same time an express was sent for the Governor. Nothing must interfere with the Delaware negotiations.

From other quarters equally important news was coming in. Captain Newcastle who, it will be remembered, some time before had run away in a fit of light-headedness, came to Philadelphia in October having found his head but lost his heart. He brought with him a beautiful young wife and important news from the Six Nations. The news was that Teedyuscung had no authority from his Uncles to treat with Brother Onas.

The Governor, when he arrived in the capital, declined to hold the proposed conference with Teedyuscung—not because of anything the Six Nations had said, but because an Indian treaty would be contrary to Lord Loudoun's instructions. The Council argued with him, insisting that, Loudoun or no Loudoun, the Proprietors had, by the terms of their charter, the right to negotiate with the Indians; and that "the Prop⁵ & Government of Pennsylvania," as Peters wrote afterwards to Thomas Penn, "have had more Interest with and influence upon the Six Nations than ever Sʳ Wᵐ Johnson can have." [13]

Denny at length agreed to a compromise. He despatched Colonel Weiser (whom Captain Newcastle had himself fetched from Berks County) to Easton with an invitation to Teedyuscung to come down to Philadelphia. If Denny's military conscience must be bruised by contravening Lord Loudoun's orders, at least his body should not be committed to the inconvenience of a journey to the frontier.

Newcastle did not accompany Weiser to Easton. He had traveled for the last time on behalf of Pennsylvania. He lay critically ill with the smallpox in Philadelphia.

Weiser delivered the Governor's invitation to King Teedyuscung, presenting a string to wipe the royal traveler's sweat from his body. Teedyuscung took ten or fifteen minutes to deliberate upon his answer. "Mr. Pemberton used to say," we read, "that, after he [Teedyuscung] had dranken a half a gallon of rum, he was a match . . . for the . . . Governor of Pennsylvania, Mʳ Denny." [14] What use the King made of his ten or fifteen minutes Weiser does not tell us, but when the time was up he was more than a match for Mr. Denny.

Brother, the Governor of Pennsylvania, [he said] you remember very well that in time of darkness and Danger I came in here at your invitation and at this place (meaning Easton) we kindled a small Council Fire to which I am now returned and several other Indians of different Nations, and some more are by the way to come, so that if you shoud put out this little Fire it will be said of it that it was only a Jack Lanthorn (what the Germans call Irrwish) kindled on purpose to deceive those that approach it, therefore Brother I think it by no means adviseable to put out this little Fire but rather to put more sticks upon it, and I desire that you will come to it as soon as possible, bringing your Old and Wise Men along with you, and shall be very glad to see you here.[15]

When Weiser's very ample report of this rebuff reached Philadelphia, the Governor was incensed both with Teedyuscung and with the Colonel, but he went to Easton. It was not the last time that Weiser disturbed Denny's haughty inaccessibility to common sense and publicly put the Governor in the wrong, nor the last time that the Governor smarted at being set right by a man who could not read Caesar's *Commentaries* in the original. The Reverend Richard Peters, who also found Weiser much too trying an illustration of the text which informs us that the children of this world are sometimes wiser than the children of light, perceived that he had in even so poor an instrument as Governor Denny (whom he despised) a weapon which might be useful in the hour of vengeance.

How long, O Lord, how long?

II

The Governor traveled as far as Bethlehem without a guard. At this point his journey was interrupted by a rumor, brought him by David Zeisberger, that the Indians around Easton were gathering for mischief. Weiser, hearing of this, promptly investigated. Finding that not only was this story of a "mighty Pannick" among the whites unfounded but also that the only source of danger lay in the Indians' impatience at the Governor's delay, he sent word to that effect to His Excellency, who accordingly came on to Easton on the morning of Monday, November 8. It unfortunately happened that the Governor, by taking an unanticipated route, managed to miss Teedyuscung and Weiser who had come out with an escort to meet him. But the absence of *éclat* on his arrival was made up for during the days that followed.

Denny liked to do things in style, and he disliked Indians (who entertained indelicate notions about that part of the anatomy which modest persons concealed under a wig). For these two reasons he saw to it that he was attended by a large guard as long as he remained in Easton. The guard was composed of units of the Royal Americans and of the Pennsylvania Regiment. Weiser, before he left for Easton, had bought flags: "Two pound ten Shill^g . . . for Colours for the Province Service." [16]

At three o'clock on Monday afternoon, November 8, His Excellency the Governor "Marchd from his Lodging to the place of Conference Gaurded by a party of the Royal Americans in the front & on the Flanks and a Detachment of Colonel Wieser,s Prevential in sub Divisions in the Rear with Colours flying Drums Beating & Mussick Playing *and all the honours Due to a Person of his Rank*." [17] (In the manuscript note from which this is taken the italicized portion has been crossed out by a cautious pen, and this part of the record did not go into the Council Minutes.) A special Order of March was drawn up, and for the next ten days this ceremonial accompanied the Governor when he went to the place of conference.

It was the most colorful air the drab little "Town in the Forks"—a huddle of log houses gathered about a stone jail—had ever put on. The men and women from the town and surrounding settlements were reinforced by citizens of Philadelphia. Benjamin Franklin was there with some of the commissioners and dozens of Quakers, including Israel Pemberton. There were plenty of frontiersmen in buckskins and beavers. Some thirty or forty Indians were on hand, mostly Delawares, half a dozen Iroquois, two Shawnees. It was known that many more Indians were in the outskirts (these had given rise to the rumors of trouble), but they were afraid to come in under the eye of the troops. Not many of the Indians present were in blankets, for most of them were Jersey Delawares whose contacts with the whites had made them drab in costume as well as in morals; but their long black hair, brown faces, clear mild eyes, and good carriage would have made them look distinguished in anything. There were regulars in red coats with white buttons, marching smartly behind a band, and detachments of Weiser's volunteers with nothing much to distinguish them from the crowd but their muskets, tomahawks, scalping knives, and "colors."

There were, in addition, for those who had eyes to see, romantic delights of another order. I like to think that, in the sight of the Reverend Richard Peters, who enjoyed *Pamela, or Virtue Rewarded*, the following description of the treaty setting, written by the Reverend Thomas Hopkinson, secretary at an Easton treaty held five years later, might have found favor:

> *Mid the Deep murmur of the lofty groves*
> *which nod o'er Lehigh's Sylvan painted Stream,*
> *all fancy-fired the muse enraptur'd loves*
> *wand'ring, to meditate poetic Theme.*
> *Serpentine waters mid the lofty hills*
> *in Broad meander lead th' astonish'd Eye,*
> *from massy rocks here the cool Stream distills*
> *there distant mountains melt into the Sky*
> *the gay musicians of the groves around*
> *In cadence Sweet attune their warbling Song*
> *their warbling Song the darksome caves resound*
> *and light wing'd breezes bear the strains along.*[18]

The conference lasted ten days. Teedyuscung ("an *Apostat,* who has raised himself to a King,"[19] growled Bishop Spangenberg in neighboring Bethlehem) was in great form. This was due, not to increased sobriety on his part, but to the excellent coaching of the Quakers, who found in him a rod to scourge the Governor.

Teedyuscung opened the conference with the old ceremony of opening the Governor's eyes and ears that he might give the necessary attention to what was to be said. The Governor responded by opening Teedyuscung's eyes and ears, and also clearing a passage from his heart to his mouth—a significant detail. Teedyuscung assured the Governor that the evil rumors lately circulated were no more to be regarded than the whistling of birds. The Governor replied that no heed ought to be paid to their chirping. That concluded the first day's activities.

On later days they got down to business. The Governor repeated his request that all English captives (only five of whom had been brought in) should be released. Teedyuscung replied politely by requesting the Governor to "throw down the Fence"[20] that confined some of his "Brethren and relations in the Jerseys" (they were in jail for one misdemeanor or another).

With a belt of ten rows Teedyuscung reminded the Governor of "the Ancient League and Covenants" made by their forefathers, and with a

belt of seven he suggested that it now lay in the Governor's power to act
the benevolent part toward the Indians of William Penn.

On November 12, Governor Denny thanked Teedyuscung for his affectionate reference to William Penn and then, rejecting Weiser's advice
for that of more dubious counselors, prodded Teedyuscung with a question that deflected the conference from the road of peace to the road of
confusion and war.

As we are now met together at a Council Fire kindled by us both, and have
promised on both sides to be free and open to one another, I must ask you how
that League of Friendship came to be broken? Have we, the Governor or
People of Pennsylvania done you any kind of Injury? . . . speak your mind
plainly on this head, and tell us if you have any just cause of Complaint, what
it is, That I may obtain a full Answer to this Point, I give this Belt.[21]

Weiser recognized this for what it was: a maneuver by Israel Pemberton's Quakers to escape the political consequences of Pennsylvania's military unpreparedness (for which they were responsible) by blaming the
war itself on the Proprietors. For this purpose Pemberton proposed to
raise the ghost of the Walking Purchase, by having the Governor ask the
Indians if they had any complaints.[22]

The Indians [wrote Weiser afterwards] would have been glad if they were
never put to answer that Question; and it was a very absurd one in the
Indian Light, for they wanted nothing but forgiveness, and old Friendship
restored. they had in their Way asked Pardon for what had then passed.
Witness what they said to Capt Newcastle & Jagerea. of purging us from the
bitterness of our Heart and cleaning our inward Part from the overflowing of
our Gall. See Treaty 1756 in Easton. Page
I was not pleased with the Question, but protested against it. Some of the
Six Nations were out of Humour with it, saying to me in Private, why does
the Governor ask such a Question, now the Thing is made up? Will he begin
to raise another Quarrel? Why you forgave our Nephews the Delawares, and
what need you ask such Questions; Indeed Teedjouskong would have openly
scolded had he not been prumped with an Answer from that Party which so
manifestly endeavoured to ruin the Proprietaries Intrest and Character. for
I remember by my Journal then kept, that, that Evening, when we came out
of the Conference, between Light and Dark I walked between John Pompshire
& Moses Dideamy. Israel came and pulled Moses by his Arm or Garment and
they walked behind the House, and had some talk together, and I, and Pompshire walked slow, Pomshire asked me. Do you see them two walk behind
the House? Yes said I, and what Harm (I kept to myself as if I was ignorant
of the Design of Israel) O, Mischief is going on, said Pompshire, Israel is
wicked. Moses did not stay long. when he overtook us! Pompshire asked him,
what did Israel say? Moses made Answear nothing. No says Pompshire I know
what he said, for he spoke to me the same Thing I believe; well said Moses!
Israel told me that now was our Time to speak bold, and to be strong and
fear nothing, and to remember well what was said to us by him before.
Indeed Teedjouskon was more honest than Israel. Teedjouskon gave several
Reasons and Israel meant only one in the Discourse with Moses. In Short the
Question was unreasonable; unmannerly, and withal offencive. But how could

the Governour help it, so many Counsellors, Comissioners, noted Quakers, pressing him to put that Question. if he had refused they would have no Doubt declared him an Heretic in Church, and State. Many Expressions Teedjouskon made use of, were no Indian Phrases, and he could not afterwards answer to them, before he spoke with Israel, or some others; This very Thing cost Pennsylvania much Blood and Treasure.

Teedjouskon now seeing, that he had such an applauseable Cause for striking the English, he committed Murder on his Return, in Order to sell Peace the Dearer, and to make him the greater Man.[23]

On the unlucky thirteenth of November Denny repeated his question, and Teedyuscung, after some hesitation, replied by raising the issue that was to bedevil all future relations between the Delawares and Pennsylvania. The Indians, said Teedyuscung, had been deprived of their lands by fraud; and, what made it worse, they felt that they were despised by the white men for allowing themselves to be swindled.

When the Governor asked Teedyuscung to be specific, the King replied with a reference to the Walking Purchase. I quote from Weiser's manuscript version:

This very ground I Stand on was our land & Inheritance—Bargains or [are] bargains, and we Stand by them, tho we Should have had only pipes which will be brock tomorrow for Some of our land. but we think we Should not be [ill] used on this account by those very people who now enjoy the fruit of our land nor be Called fools for it.[24]

The Walking Purchase had been referred to, but there was more in Teedyuscung's mind than he dared to say in public. What lay behind his extremely guarded references to the land, Conrad Weiser set himself to find out. The results of his investigation he wrote down in a document that cuts through the tangles of legal argument on the one hand and sentimentality on the other which together have cluttered up the ensuing years of debate over the matter of the Delaware lands; and he shows clearly the point at which the Indians felt themselves to be not merely "taken in" (that they could pass over, for, as Teedyuscung said, "bargains are bargains") but actually robbed of what was theirs by every principle of law and justice. The document has come down to us in several versions. I quote the one written in Sammy's hand, since it undoubtedly comes closest to his father's original.

Memorandum, taken at Fort Allen, November the 26th 1756 [25]

As I came along this Morning from Nicklaus Opplingers, Joseph Deedemy kept me Company, for the most Part, and sometimes Jn Pomshire: we began to discourse about this present Indian Warr; I asked them several questions and so did they me: among other Things I told them, that for my Part, I did not understand Deejoskon clearly, in his Speech about the Cause of the Warr; now and then he blamed the English in General; then the Proprietaries of Pennsylvania, and then the Indians for being too Credulous and foolish to believe the French. Sometimes said the French's Success, Wealth & Power prevailed upon you all and so on Joseph Deedemy told me that every thing was agreed upon in the Indian Counsel what should have been said; that their King Deedjoskon had every Thing in his Heart what to say before he came to Easton, and there his Memory, but being too often overcome with strong Liquor he spoke confuse; tho' nothing that was wrong or false in itself; only not in such Order as he ought to have done, and one Passage he never mentioned at all which drawed the Delaware Indian's Heart from the English and their Indian Ally.

Querry. what is that? Answer, Deedjoskon should have given an Account of the Differences that have arose some Time ago Between the Delaware-Menessing Indians and the Minquos, and should have told the Governour of Pennsylvania how the Later have cheated the Former out of a great Deal of Land on the River of Delaware & sold it to the Proprietaries of Pennsylvania: That the Minqous had abused the Delawares some Years before—greatly in Philadelphia, as if the Delaware & Menessink Indian were their Dogs, and that Canassatego, then Speaker among the Minquos, ordered them away from their own Land, and said he would give them Lands on Susquehannah River, and instantly ordered them to Settle there, which the Delaware and some of the Menessink Indians did in Order to prevent Mischief: That then Canasatego sold that Land to the Proprietaries of Pennsylvania: They, the Delaware and Minessink Indians made no Reply against it, thinking themselves safe enough on Susquehannah; but about three Years ago a Company of New-England-Men came down Susquehannah and took openly Draughts of all the good Spots of Lands and perhaps of all. When the Indians asked why they did so? they boldly answered, that so many hundred Families from New-England would come and settle there. *This is our land* says *the Indians Setled on it.* No, answers the Others the Land is none of yours; it belongs to the Minquos, you are only their *Tenants, Slaves, Dogs* (as it sounds in an Indian Ear) That thereupon the Delawares sent a large Body of their people as their Deputation to the Mohawks Country to protest against the New-England People or any other white, to settle there, and to complain of the Mohawks proceeding, and to tell them plain; if they the Mohawks would not prevent the New-England People from setling on Susquehannah they the Delawares would go over to Ohio to the French in hopes to receive better usage from them. That the Mohawks then denied every Thing, and said the New-England People stole there, and had no leave of them for any Lands on Susquehannah, and never would sell them any; and that the New-England-People nor any white should never settle there: That the Deputation went home again, and they the Delaware and Menessink Indians, being so farr satissfied, but that they soon were informed by some of the Minquos themselves, that, that Land had actually been sold to the New England People; and that the Mohawks had received large Consideration for them, and that the Mohawks had deceived the Deputies of the Proprietaries of Pennsylvania, who were about buying it, and the Minquos all had promised the Proprietaries of Pennsylvania that they should have the Preference if ever it should be sold; Querry, what did your People say then? answer, they were terrible angry, and Suspected that they would be cut off, and by that Alarm rosen perhaps by ill designed People, our Indians gathered at Tiaogon to see what would be the Consequence; either they would join the French or maintain their Lands; but that a great many went over to the French from Time to Time, and came back with Messages till the Warr broke out.

I said I wished that this Story had been told at the Treaty. answer, Deedjoskon was afraid of the Minquo Indians that were there, least they might misrepresent the Story when they come home. The Minquo Indians (said Deedemy again) have from the Beginning cheated our Nation, and got our Forefathers to call them Uncles, by Deceit and Art, and at last said they conquered our Forefathers. Querry, why, is it not so? Answer: No the Minquos stood in Need of our Forefathers Assistance, and got some of their cunning Men, to come down to our Forefathers, with the News, that a Certain Nation from the West, was preparing to come and cut our Forefathers off, and some other came of the same Sort as Deputies with howling and Lamentations, songs over our Death (who were to be killed) and so our Forefathers entered into a League with them, and rather fought their Battles, than the Mohawks should have fought ours.

Both these Indians were desirous or rather insisted upon, that I should use my Endeavour with the Governour and people of Pennsylvania, to lay out a large Tract of Land on Susquehannah and secure it so to their Posterity, that none of them could sell, and no Body buy it;   That the Delawares would for the most Part, if not all come and live on it and be reconciled to the People and Government of Pennsylvania forever. I promised to do it. Deedjoskon told me much the same Story as before mentioned before we parted, with very little Differences, and desired of me as to obtaining Lands for them.

November 16 Teedyuscung presented the Governor with fifteen deerskins "to make Gloves of," and the Governor presented the Indians with four hundred pounds worth of assorted goods.

The conference ended next day with speeches of condolence for the death of Captain Newcastle. Not all the care of Dr. Graeme, nor the kindness of the Quakers, who looked after him during his illness, had availed to save him. Before he died, he requested that he be buried in the Quaker burying ground; [26] and there, accordingly, he was laid to rest, a "vast Train" of townspeople attending.

It might be added that Newcastle's young widow, "Maryred," [27] while waiting to be sent from Philadelphia to the Mohawk country, begged about town for some weeks after the funeral. Weiser, when he returned to Philadelphia, did what he could for her with little gifts, but his patience broke when she came one day to beg a pair of worsted stockings. He sent her over to the Reverend Mr. Peters for accommodation. [28]

To return to Easton: Weiser marched out of town with the Indians, November 18, and brought them to Bethlehem, where they were lodged, not among the Moravian Indians, but on the other side of the Lehigh, in a house which was described as "quite full of them." [29] At Bethlehem there ensued some difficulty between Teedyuscung and his wife. He could not get her away in the morning. "she wanted to stay in Bethlehem, because for his debauched Way of Living," wrote Weiser; "he took all the Children but one from her. at the Brethern's Request I interceded, and prevailed to go with her Husband. We left Bethlehem by Ten of the Clock." [30]

On the 22nd, after some bickering about a horse the King wanted ("*What is a Horse* to the Governor of pensilvania?" he said) [31] Weiser took his leave of the genial old murdering beggar:

Deedjoskon, quite sober, parted with me, with Tears in his Eyes, recommended Pompshire to the Government of Pennsylvania, and desired me to stand a Friend to the Indians, and give good Advice till every Thing that was desired was brought about; Though he is a Drunkard and a very Irregular man, yet he is a Man that can think well, and I believe him to be sincere in what he said.[32]

CHAPTER 53

... *Becomes a Fallen Tree*

I

AFTER the second Easton conference, Teedyuscung loitered again in the neighborhood. When smoke from burning houses was seen hanging in the air, suspicion arose that ceremonial wampum had been insufficient to clear the passage from the heart to the mouth of the Delaware peacemaker.

Auckon, "a young Indian Man," informed Horsfield at Bethlehem on December 1 that he had met four Delawares near Wyoming, all painted and dressed for war, and that three Cayugas who had attended the Easton conference were now "gone towards Allemangle to Kill the White People." [1] The news came too late to prevent the disaster that fell on Berks County.

A letter to Weiser from Lieutenant Engel, who commanded Fort Everett in the wild Allemangel region (so named because it was "lacking in everything") tells the story.

Lieutenant Engel to Colonel Weiser [2]

November 29th 1756

My greetings to you Lieutenant-Colonel Conrad Weiser I report to you by these few lines that another disaster has fallen on Lynn Township nine miles from the road we rode over, five miles from Mr. Eberits house, there was a man by the name of Jacob Stein Bruch who had moved from his place to the Oley Hills, Now it happened that he came up to look at his place afterwards going to his neighbor's house, whose name was Balsar Jäger to stay there overnight, when he Jacob Steinbruch came into the house, he said, how comes it that his dogs did not bark, As he said this the dogs barked then the Father and Son went to the door, and asked Who is there Nobody answered them, just then a shot came through the window and hit Jacob Steinbruch in the breast, That happened on November 28 at twilight when one begins to light the lights, The Father and Son went into the attic and broke through the roof Thereupon an Indian jumped over the fence into the woods Then the Father came down and told his Wife and Daughter to run away, and the Father went out of the house. Then two more Indians sprang out of the stable, and ran after the Daughter and beat her and took her away with them She was 10 or 11 years old The Father ran after the Indians and shot at them to rescue his Daughter but they took her away with them, then he came about 12 o'clock at night to my sergeants at Mr. Ebenrits house Then at 2 o'clock at night he came to me and told me then I immediately took 10 men with me and also Mr. Ebenrit to investigate, but when we came there, we found a Blanket in the field and one at the corner of the house and a spear which you will receive, We looked everywhere for tracks but could not find any, Then I had the man buried, The people are terribly frightened

466

and are leaving their Places and my soldiers say they have had the spear of
this Indian in their hands at Fort Elling.

From me ANDERES ENGEL
Commander in Allen-Mangel

This to Conrad Weiser
Lieutenant Colonel living in Tholpenhocken in Bergs County.
by John Everett.

Things grew quiet again along the Blue Mountains, and soon people
were coming back to their plantations. They began even to lay out new
towns and to speculate in real estate.[3] Hope springs eternal. One cause of
this lull in the Delaware attacks was that Dumas, the genius of the Ohio,
had left Fort Duquesne and gone to Montreal, where we find him on December 13 taking part in a great Indian conference.[4] But this good fortune
(for the English) was not known to the authorities of Pennsylvania, and
they remained constantly on the alert for an ill wind from the west.

If with the withdrawal of Dumas from the Ohio the situation was improved in the West, it was deteriorating nearer home. Sir William Johnson
appointed George Croghan as his deputy agent to transact Indian affairs
in Pennsylvania. Governor Denny, a stickler for the rules, thenceforth
tried to push Weiser out of the Indian scene altogether, and told him to
devote himself to his military duties.

"Is it true that you are become a fallen Tree?" asked Jonathan Cayenquiloquoa, April 28, in Reading: "That you must no more engage in Indian Affairs neither as a Counsellor nor Interpreter?"

"I told him it was true," writes Weiser; "That the King of Great Britain
had appointed Warruychyockon [Johnson] to be manager of all Indian
affairs . . . And that accordingly the Great General that came over the
Great Waters, had, in the Name of the King, ordered the Government of
Pennsylvania to desist from holding Treaties with the Indians. And the
Government of Pennsylvania will obey the King's Command; And conse-
quently I, as the Government's Servant, have Nothing more to do with
Indian Affairs."

"O sad!" said Jonathan. "But *Olia* (Comrade, the Stile we give one another) I heard you have engaged on another Bottom. You are made a
Captain of Warriors and laid aside the Counsel Affair, and turned a Soldier."

"*Olia*," replied Weiser, "what You say is true. But . . . *Olia*, don't
charge me with such a thing, as that I take greater Delight in War than in
Civil Affairs. I am a man for Peace, and If I had my wish there sho^d be
no War at all, at least not on this Side the Great Waters."[5]

Conrad Weiser at this time may have been glad enough to step aside as
well as he could from "council affairs," for the confusion that had oppressed him when he had been unable to see through the schemes webbed
about him had turned to disgust now that he saw only too well. The
machinery of government had all but broken down. It appeared not only
that the Quakers were carrying on separate negotiations with the Indians,
setting them against the government and so prolonging the war, but also

that Sir William Johnson, entrusted with the administration of Indian affairs for the northern colonies, was secretly using his power to wreck Pennsylvania's arrangements. When the Easton treaty was in the air, Johnson

. . . was so disturbed at this [I quote from Peters' letter to the Proprietaries, February 14, 1757] that several Mohocks were dispatched one after another to prevent Teedyuscungs coming to Easton with Messages and Belts from him acquainting them that he had rec^d Information that he would be killed and all his Men with him by the Governor of Pennsylvania if he trusted himself at Easton. This was told by Geo: Croghan (in his Cups I suppose to some of his Intimates) and transpired and was told me by Mr Logan in such a manner as it may be depended upon. Gracious Heaven! what can the English Expect will become of them. will their Arms have Success amidst so much Hypocrisy & Dissumulation! [6]

II

Everyone in Pennsylvania—Indians no less than whites—was astonished at the appointment of George Croghan, a man "of a broken Fortune . . . a meer Tool and Cypher," as Isaac Norris described him: "I am persuaded he can never do any Honor to Sr Wm Johnson or to the Commiss^n he holds under him as it is of too much Importance for his Abilities, or at least for his involved dependant Condition." [7] The minutes of Council for December 14, 1757, note that the members were not a little surprised at the appointment, "knowing Mr. Croghan's Circumstances," [8] which were these: He had recently thrown up his captain's commission and the command at Fort Shirley (Aughwick) because his accounts were "overhauled." He was much in debt and in fear of prosecution—"under the protection of a Law not yet confirmed at Home." [9] This last circumstance was not altogether regretted in government circles. It gave a handle to a man whose loyalty to the province and to the British cause in general was in some question.

Croghan's fumbling activities during the spring of 1757 concerned Weiser little, except in so far as they helped to precipitate the crisis of 1758, to resolve which was to be Weiser's last major service to the province. Croghan sapped confidence all round. He offended Mr. Atkins, the Superintendent of Indian affairs for the southern district; he offended the Cherokees, the Ohio Indians, the Six Nations; he disgusted Peters, the Council, the Governor, and the Quakers—giving the latter some cause for their interference in Indian affairs.

Weiser, on instructions from Philadelphia, came to Croghan's assistance at Lancaster in May 1757, helping him to prepare his speeches and to set the crooked straight. Things were crooked enough. The Indians were scattered and drunk. Even Scaroyady had been in trouble. Cursed, it was said, with "a Very bad Wife," [10] he had got into a brawl on the road, and was "much beat & bruised." Two white men went to jail over the affair. The faithful Scaroyady—sound of mind and body—soon recovered and set off with twelve warriors to scour the woods about Shamokin for enemy Indians, who were reported to be in the neighborhood.[11]

If Scaroyady's bad wife was in a position to set things in a broil, much more so was Governor Denny, "a Triffler, Weak of Body, peevish and adverse to Business": [12] "The Govern[r] (poor little Body) seems quite irresolute, ready to receive any impression for a Moment, & as ready the next to have it effac'd— In short He is a wavering, Weak, unstable Creature [this last word was crossed out in the original] Gentleman, & under his Administration, Lord have Mercy on us—" [13]

Scaroyady's wife had another partner in disharmony: Israel Pemberton. In the absence of Teedyuscung (who "hated the Light and would not appear," [14] said Weiser), Israel Pemberton and his Quaker contingent tried to keep the land grievance to the fore, and to that end stroked and coddled such Indians as they could reach. But Weiser was a match for them at Lancaster and spoiled their maneuvers. "So much Labour," says Weiser sarcastically of Pemberton's unsuccessful Indian lobby; "so much Silver Ware; so many Visits made to their Camp, by great Men *All Lost*, all this presents, Trouble, and Art, to prevail nothing." [15]

"Damn the rascals," he imagines the disappointed Israel saying of the Indians; but no, blame for failure of the Quaker lobby must not be laid at the feet of the Indians; it must be laid at the feet of Conrad Weiser:

An unlucky Fellow, [Conrad refers ironically to himself] a Poor Rascal who had nothing to give them, no not one Shilling. but to our Surprise a Man of Credit among them came one Morning to them, and admonished them as his Countrymen, among whom he was naturalized, told them, or advised them, to Act the Part of Gentlemen, to stick by the Truth, and fear nothing, made such an Impression on them, that notwithstanding all the Arts and Expences, the three words wanted could not be brought from them (Onas cheated us).[16]

The greatest task with which Weiser was confronted at Lancaster was to divert the Governor's petulance into channels least dangerous to the country of which he was the head. When "honest Little Abraham" [17] (a Mohawk, son of Hendrick's brother Abraham), mindful of the fact that the Delawares had said they no longer acknowledged the Six Nations as a whole but only the Senecas to be their Uncles, advised caution and patience, and proposed that Brother Onas send an invitation to Teedyuscung *by way of the Senecas*, whose country, he explained, being the West Door of the Six Nations was the proper passageway in wartime for messages to the Confederacy and its tributaries [18]—Governor Denny declared in a pet that he would send no such invitation nor allow one to be sent: "an End shou'd be entirely put to any further Treaties in this government."[19] It was drawn to the Governor's attention that to reject little Abraham's advice would offend the Six Nations. Denny was more afraid of offending Lord Loudoun. But Weiser and Croghan worked to good effect on His Excellency, in the end preparing a speech for him, which he delivered, assuring Little Abraham that he found his advice "good and wholesome" and would accordingly invite Teedyuscung and the Senecas to a treaty.

III

The coming treaty was much on Conrad Weiser's mind. He knew, as no other man knew, what had to be done and how difficult it was to do it. It was not just a matter of getting Teedyuscung to bury the hatchet and smoke a peace pipe. A little rum might accomplish that. What was wanted was a peace that should endure: a peace based on the satisfaction of legitimate grievances and at the same time one that gave the Delawares a stake in preserving it.

To this Weiser, who in the spring had been preparing for the government a special report on the Delawares,[20] their history, their relation to the Six Nations, and their relation to the province, bent his mind. The conclusion to which he came was that the Proprietaries should set aside a considerable territory for this footloose nation, a permanent reservation of land which, once assigned to them, should be inalienable.[21] The Delawares should be given a home *forever*.

This policy of "fixing the Indians on Lands where they may remain undisturbed" was accepted by Thomas Penn.[22] So far so good. But the manner of doing this had to be watched lest the remedy prove worse than the disease. No action should be taken except through the medium of the Six Nations. To deal with the Delawares directly might bring down the Great Confederacy on Brother Onas's track, and the Six United Nations were still powerful enough to threaten the existence of the English colonies.

There was the problem: to continue peace negotiations with Teedyuscung and the Delawares without recognizing their independence of the Six Nations. It was a nice problem under any circumstances. What made the successful handling of it doubly precarious at this time was that the only man in the province who fully understood the pitfalls to be avoided was *persona non grata* with all the cooks who had their ladles in the broth.

Among these latter were the newcomers on the Indian scene, Israel Pemberton's Quakers, who, intent on restoring the political prestige they had lost because of the state of military unpreparedness in which the province found itself when war came in 1755,[23] now whited themselves for war— war against sin and the Proprietors of Pennsylvania—and who marched under a banner bearing the device: *The Friendly Association for regaining and preserving Peace with the Indians by pacific Measures*.

All the advantages which the retirement of Dumas from Fort Duquesne had given Pennsylvania, were offset by Pemberton's fanaticism; for, as soon as Teedyuscung's support from the French on the Ohio began to fail, support from Pemberton's Friendly Association sprang up in its place.

"Israel Indeed," snorted Weiser to his pen, "who prumped Teedjouskon, all along is a Politician, but Teedjouskon is not for he told so many Lies about his Right to the Land in the Forks, and on the other Side of the Mountains, that he is ashamed of himself now, and so must be his Promptor, if any Shame can find Place in him as yet." [24]

Eager, self-righteous, furtive, and complacent, Israel Pemberton "threw

his dirt about him" (said Peters) with such vigor that the next peace conference with Teedyuscung was turned into a farce-tragedy; and James
Pemberton laughed when his brother had stirred up the Indians to such an
extent that they blacked themselves and prepared for mischief.

Uneasy lies the head that wears a crown—

except, of course, the crown of Israel Pemberton, for his scalp had been
made secure by private dealings with Teedyuscung.

CHAPTER 54

. . . Watches Israel Pemberton

I

WHERE was Teedyuscung? He had been expected by George Croghan and the Governor at Harris', at Lancaster, at Philadelphia. Jonathan had expected to find him at Bethlehem or Easton. The King was as elusive as a black fly in June.

The question of his whereabouts was answered on the afternoon of July 4, when the commander at Fort Allen received a letter addressed

To M^r
Jacob Ornt at
furt allin these [1]

Wanomong June 26th 1757

Sir/

I have Com Down as far as Wanomong   I am in grat Want of brovision for I am to stea heare tell all the Chief of the InDian Com Down   I Desire of your favour to senD me Send Some brovision and SiX Quarts of Run   I Desire moses Tattamy to Com Up to meet me at Wanomong   it is from your FrenD

TATEUSCOUNG

On the same day (July 4) word was despatched to the Governor that "a large Body of Indians" had attacked and burnt Broadhead's house in the Minisink, near the Delaware Water Gap above Easton—attacked boldly, within sight of Fort Hamilton itself. Captain Van Etten had driven the enemy off, but not before John Tidd had been killed, scalped, and inhumanly mangled.[2]

Rum and scalps. The signs were unmistakable. Teedyuscung was indeed on his way.

There was fear at Easton. "Your Honour will be pleased to consider the Defencelessness of this little Town," wrote William Parsons to the Governor, "which stands upon the very Land which the Indians claim, and is upon that Account alone much more in danger of an Attack from the Savages than any other place." [3]

This appeal from Parsons put the Governor in an awkward position. It was apparent that Easton needed a guard; but to supply one from Colonel Weiser's battalion at the moment was next to impossible, since, on the Governor's own instructions, Weiser had sent large detachments to Fort Augusta (to attack which place rumor said the French were now building a road through the forest from Fort Duquesne) and into Cumberland County. The battalion now was almost incapable of holding the line of forts along the Blue Mountains. Even the guard at Reading had been withdrawn. The Indians were burning and scalping in the Tulpehocken Valley.

Busse reported that they were in the Hole. Peter Gersinger had been "shot and scalped behind his Plow" somewhere between Fort Henry and Fort Northkill.[4]

Weiser, meanwhile, not knowing that Teedyuscung was so close at hand, was making a formal inspection of the forts covering Easton (Allen, Norris, Hamilton). We learn from Captain Van Etten's journal that on July 1 the sentry at Fort Hamilton reported "hearing music," which the Captain rightly interpreted as indicating the approach of Colonel Weiser.[5] The Colonel promptly appeared, spent the night at the fort, inspected the garrison and equipment, and marched off again with his bugler and attendants.

While Weiser was hurrying back to the Schuylkill, Teedyuscung turned up at Fort Allen. There Captain Orndt, what with Indians and the discipline of his own forces, had worries enough on his mind.

Captain Orndt to Colonel Weiser [6]

[Fort Allen, July 5, 1757]

To the honourable Colonel C Weiser
Sir

These are to inform you that Detiuscung is arrived here Yesterday ev'ning and there be at present about 200 Indians with him with young and old— Detiuscung is intended to stay here about five or six days and in this Time he expects one hundred of the Seneka Indians here and then he is intended to go to Easton in hopes to meet with his Honour the Governor

I am inform'd that Lieut Miller is run away with another Man's Wife and I hope you will inform his Honour the Governor how necessary it is that I might have another Lieutenant. . . .

I am, Sir, &c.—
JACOB ORNDT

Provisions running short at Fort Allen, Captain Orndt had to march with the Indians, three days later, to Easton. On the way an accident occurred which, it was feared, in the tension then prevailing might have serious consequences. One of the Indians (William Tattamy, the interpreter's son) went off by himself toward Bethlehem, and "a foolish wite boy aboud 15 years of eage," as the good Captain wrote to Governor Denny, "followed him, and Shot him in the Right Thigh of the out sid bone, but not morterly."[7] What made matters worse, was that Major Parsons was absent from Easton when Orndt arrived, so that the captain of Fort Allen had to remain at Easton with his guard to see that there were no fallings out "between Wite Peoble and the Indians."[8]

In Philadelphia pressure being brought to bear on Governor Denny, he was made to see that he must go to Easton, where Teedyuscung awaited him. Now Denny was no less a stickler for safety than for etiquette; and, being confronted with the prospect of going himself to Easton, he made up his mind quickly about the advisability of denuding the frontier of men. He ordered Weiser to make up a strong guard for Easton.

Colonel Weiser to Governor Denny[9]

Honoured Sir

I received both your Comands that of the 7 and that of 9 Instant upon receipt of the first I wrot to Capt Bussey & others to keep so many men in Readeness and Capt Busse arrived at my house when your Express arrived. we have ordered things so that about 110 men of the first Battalion will be in Easton towards the latter end of this week I ordered Som from every Company even from Capt Smiths on Suartaro to Capt von Ettens at fort Hamilton only Some of Capt Smiths mens time being out on the 6 of this Instant I Supose about one half of his Company I wish your Honour had Sent his discharge, he wont inlist the men a new, and by all what I Can learn abuses the officers under him, and hase never Sent me a Journal nor Muster Roll. the lieut⁺ & Insign Complains bitterly against.

What the Consequence will be of takeing So many men away from the frontiers is as yet unknown, most every day Murder is Comited at and about tulpehockin, but last friday 4 have ben Killed & Scalpd and four more Carried off all women & children about 8 miles from my house the Bushes are thick the Indians [lay loe] and watch their oppertunity. the people of tulpehockin are moving away their best Effect and wifes & children the road to Reading is Some times Couved with waggons loaded with houselegood Reading is full of Women & children and not one men of this Battalion to gard them only the few Inhabitants two Indians have been Seen about half a Mile of the town upon Rising ground. it is thought they came as Spies . . .[10]

I Intent to Set out presently for Easton by me Selve and Insign Biddle one Coman Soldier, to do what Service I Can before your Honours arrival which I wish to be as Soon as possible. I can not well be spared in my neighbourhood. . . .

Reading July the
12 in the Morning
  1757

Things were so bad in Tulpehocken that Pastor Kurtz told Pastor Handschuh that no person left his house now without a gun, even to visit a neighbor; that people scarcely dared let their children go out of doors to play; that he himself had three refugee families living with him, which brought the number of the children in the house up to fifteen; and that he had a soldier standing guard at his door. "Last Wednesday a Woman and 2 Children were carried off by the Indians, 5 Miles from here." [11]

Richard Peters to Colonel Weiser [12]

Philadelphia 13 July 1757

Sir

The Governor received your very affecting Letter this day at 12 o Clock. He knows too that Teedyuscung is at Easton waiting wᵗʰ Impatience. and yet he has ordered me to tell you by Express that he will not stirr from this City till he knows for certain that there is a Sufficient Guard at Easton.

Issacher Davies was sent up wᵗʰ the Indians and a Set of Instructions to provide Lodging for four members of Council, & he reports that there is not a Bed or Lodging Room to be taken for yᵉ Council, except what is at Mʳ Parsons House wᶜʰ will hold no more than the Govʳ & some other person. Mʳ

Hamilton Mr Chew & Mr Mifflin therefore did Say positively that they will not go till they have a place provided for them to Sleep in let it be where it will.

I must Desire you will write to the Governor by the Return of the Express on these two Points first that an Escort or Guard is actually at Easton & secondly that Lodgings fit & decent be provided for Mr Hamilton Mr Chew & Mr Mifflin besides ye House of Wm Parsons where the Govr will be & insists that I shall be there too for convenience of Business.

These two Points settled, the Govr will set off the Moment he receives your Letter. I am in ye utmost concern for our most unhappy Situation.

Dr Sir

your m^t hble

Servt

RICHARD PETERS

dont detain ye Express

When Weiser arrived at Easton, July 14, he found the air tingling. The wave of Indian attacks all along the frontier kept the town in a state of near panic. Teedyuscung, whom Weiser greeted on arriving, hoped no ear would be given "to the singing of Birds in the woods." [13] Pumpshire was desired by His Majesty to say that the ominous black wampum in the belt now delivered was to be explained as merely intended to set off "the Ten white Spots, Signifying ten Nations that came with Teedyuscung." [14]

On July 17, "about Sunset," wrote Weiser to Denny,

We were alarmed by a Woman who came running into Town as if distracted and reported that her Husband and some of her Children were killed by the Indians, and soon after some of her Children came with the same Report. I ordered ten Men on Horseback to go to the Place with all possible Speed (The Place being but two Miles from this Town) who returned and said that the Alarm was false. They found the Man alive and undisturbed, no Indians having been there.[15]

The guard was assembling, piece by piece. Busse was bringing up detachments from Forts Swatara, Henry, Lebanon (on the Schuylkill), Allemangel. Other detachments were coming in from Forts Norris and Hamilton. There would soon be more than one hundred men on hand. And they were needed—not to protect the white people but to protect the Indians. On July 16 Weiser took down a sworn statement by one Matthew Lowry that "a great number of the people of new Jersey had agreed and Signed to Come to Easton to Cut off the Indians that are now there." [16]

When the guard was assembled ("in the whole of 105 Men including Officers"),[17] Weiser wrote to assure the Governor that all was well, and to hasten His Excellency's arrival. Nothing could go wrong. In Teedyuscung's entourage Weiser had been pleased to find "one Cappach Piton, an old Acquaintance of mine . . . who never was down yet as long as I can remember. He is a sincere, honest, old Man." [18] The King himself was on his best behavior and easily pacified. An "armband and two Rist bands" for himself, and "2 Rist bands 4 Dozen hachiefs" and six silver crosses for his wife helped to clear the spring of his good humor. Indeed, Weiser had the "good Luck" to pacify both the white people and the Indians.

I have been obliged [he informed the Governor] to put one of the Jersey People under an Arrest, and another into Prison, but at the Instance of Teddyuscung I discharged them again, with a Caution to behave better for the future. . . . The Indians are altogether good humoured, and Teedyuscung, considering how much he loves strong Liquor, behaves very well, and I have not seen him quite drunk since I came to this Town. I find that they are desirous to come to a lasting Peace with us.[19]

On receiving these assurances, William Denny hid his scalp under a wig and came to Easton.

II

Major Parsons, having gone to the seaside for his health (his days were now numbered), had left his house for the Governor's accommodation. Nathaniel Vernon engaged to provide "fress Provisions On Every Day . . . such as fowls, Beeff, Motton, Veal, Bred & Butter." [20] Mr. Issacher Davies was deputed by the Provincial Secretary to look after "Beds, Bedding, Sheets, Table Linnen, & other Linnen necessary for the use of a Family . . . Kitchen Furniture, wood, and water." [21] Nicholas Scull undertook "to Provide Servants what Shall be Necessary for ye Governour." [22] Peters ordered clean beds "in good & respectable Houses" for the members of Council.

There was only one hitch for the Governor. "No Coock," runs a note in the *Archives*, "Can be Gott at East Town." [23] There were several hitches for the Council. "I have ben out to looke and Send others out," wrote Weiser, July 15, "and find that good beds and Clean rooms are either Scares or taken up." [24] In Parsons' old house (the Governor had Parsons' new house) were two clean rooms: "the beds I Call good," said Weiser, "but perhaps them Gentlemen will differ with me in opinion. let them peradvent[r] Send beds in a Waggon . . ." The Colonel and his officers had rooms in Adam Yohe's Tavern. He would gladly, he said, give up his own room to the use of the Gentlemen of the Council if they liked, but he feared that for them a public house would "perhaps not Suit So Well."

King Teedyuscung lodged at Vernon's tavern, where he was near the fountainhead itself: the source of "fowls, Beeff, Motton, Veal," and rum. The cleanly Israel Pemberton brought his own bed with him. He found himself "well accommodated" [25] in a little house behind Paul Miller's place (adjoining Yohe's tavern) which he shared with his brother "Johny," the Quaker Daniel Stanton, and the Presbyterian Charles Thomson, who was the teacher in the Quaker school in Philadelphia. James Pemberton, who came late, found himself "agreeably situate" in another house which he shared with some Friends who had "Everything in neat order." James wrote to his wife: ". . . the woman thou wen't with me to Germantown to seek for as a maid . . . is our housekeeper." [26]

The letters from Easton of these Pemberton brothers are full of meals and beds. Such creature comforts were not to be despised: they kept one ready, like oil in the virgins' lamps, for the call when it came. There was work in the vineyard. Tares must be rooted out, the "cruelty" and "injustice" of a "Weak & Wicked ministry" [27] (represented by Denny, Weiser, and Croghan) must be frustrated. The fruits of "patience" and "prudence" were at last at hand; the days of "calumny" and "contumely" past. "The time we have long been waiting for, seems now to be come, in wch we may do ourselves & the Truth we profess the Justice due." [28] The Friends were "instruments." In the hands of a Power, they were irresistible. Within a few days of the opening of the conference Israel was able to boast that the plans of the wicked had been "remarkably frustrated" and their councils "confounded." [29] What that meant to Weiser, the government, and Pennsylvania's conduct of the war, will soon be seen.

Denny and Peters arrived on Wednesday, July 20. The Governor was bored at the prospect of dealing with an Indian potentate who under a shed by day slept off his nightly potations; but Denny had enough regard for his scalp to attend to the niceties of forest etiquette. There was need of tact. As the crowds assembled in town, there came a change over Teedyuscung. Some saw a connection between this change and the arrival of the Quakers, who proceeded at once on their arrival, with the purest of intentions, to put Teedyuscung on his guard against government sculduggery. The pleasant mood in which Weiser had first found the King soon changed to one of petulance and spleen.

When the King greeted the Governor, he complained that Conrad Weiser had deceived him: had "broke his Word with him" by not letting him know, as he had promised to do, of the Governor's approach in sufficient time to enable him to go out to meet His Excellency in the outskirts of the town "according to an antient Custom with the Indians." [30]

Trouble flared up again over Teedyuscung's mother-in-law. It was darkly suspected that she was being detained wrongfully at Bethlehem. Instructions were despatched to have her sent at once to her daughter at Easton.

Peter Boehler to Governor Denny [31]

Bethlehem Jul. ye 22^d 1757

May it please Your Honour

When Capt Arnd delivered Your Honours Letter requiring that the Mother of Teedeysung's Wifes Mother might be forwarded to Easton, she was gone over the River on the Top of the Mountain to pick Huckleberries, & it being now five oclock is not expected home till in the Evening. When she comes home, we shall let her Know the Gouvernours Pleasure & on our Part, do all we can, to prevail with her to go to morrow morning to see her Daughter Neither I, nor any of our Brethren, that are concerned with the Indians here in Bethlehem have heard a Word of Teedeyscungs' or his Wifes Desire that her Mother should come to Easton & on that Account am sorry that Your Honour had such groundless Information, as if we had prevented her going thither,

Hoping that Your Honour will do us that Justice as to clear us from such an Aspersion at least in Your own Mind
I am

Your Honours
most obedient & most
obliged humble Serv[t]
PETER BOEHLER

The Quakers might think Teedyuscung a noble savage perverted by a vicious "ministry"; the Moravians, who knew Gideon better, had fewer illusions.

The treaty opened on July 21 in a confusion of tongues and haberdashery. There was the Governor, accompanied by Richard Peters, Benjamin Chew, and other Gentlemen of the Council. There were commissioners and members of the Assembly. There were Weiser's militiamen, equipped with new uniforms (green coats, red shirts, and leather leggings), as also with muskets, cartouche boxes, bayonets or tomahawks, and scalping knives. There were numbers of Quakers, well fed, sober, and sharp eyed. There were the citizens of the frontier town itself, and people from outlying parts, some of them from New Jersey across the river, who had come in to see the show. And there were Indians of all sorts and sizes: "159 of Teedyuscung's Company, that is to say, 58 Men, 37 Women, and 64 Children; . . . 119 Senecas, and others of the Six Nations, viz[t], 45 Men, 35 Women, and 39 Children," [32] and others, bringing the number to close on three hundred.

There was a great flashing of wrist bands, "Silver gagetts," brooches and crosses, and a great fluttering of linen—if French Margaret, who was present with her family, and the wives of Teedyuscung and his counselors knew how to put to best advantage the "Silver truck" and handkerchiefs by the dozen which they received from Weiser and others on behalf of the Proprietors at the conference.[33] "To M[r] Wiser," runs one item in the Penn Accounts, "for y[e] Sineckes 8000 Wampum 3 arm bands 1 Rist band 8 Dozen hachefs."

There was color in the mixed costumes and complexions gathered under the "booth" specially erected for the conference; and the headgear that was doffed (where doffing was possible) was as various as the river and valley and mountain landscape outside: Broadbrims, coonskins, tricornes, turkey feathers, scalplocks, and rabbit tails.[34]

Weiser attended as "Interpreter for the Province." He interpreted the Governor's speeches to the Six Nations. He also wrote the speeches for the Governor to deliver—which His Excellency did in refined and emasculated versions. But Weiser was not responsible for the treaty. George Croghan was in charge (on their "father" Johnson's commission, as Weiser explained to the Indians). Thomas McKee was "Interpreter for the Crown." John Pumpshire and Moses Tattamy were interpreters for Teedyuscung.

Proceedings opened with the usual figurative ceremonial. Teedyuscung wiped the Governor's eyes with a handkerchief, cleared his ears with a feather, and declared himself ready with a remedy to cure the sore at the Governor's heart. All this was conventional and expected. What followed was not. Since his memory was weak, said the King, "he desired he might have a Clerk to take Minutes along with the Governor's Clerk." [35]

Next day the Governor thanked Teedyuscung for his kind speeches, and introduced George Croghan as the agent of Sir William Johnson and the Crown. He passed over Teedyuscung's request for a secretary as contrary to the precedent already established at Lancaster by William Johnson's agent.

By that speech the Philistines were delivered into Israel's hand. His party had known of Teedyuscung's desire for a clerk before the Governor had heard of it. The Quakers insisted (without convincing George Croghan) that they had not planted the idea in Teedyuscung's head: he had thought it out by himself, at Wyoming, after the last conference (i.e., "a long hour by Shrewsbury clock"). However that may be, the idea, once planted, was cultivated assiduously by Israel Pemberton, and not allowed to die as Teedyuscung himself seemed disposed to let it. In conference on July 22, Teedyuscung expressed himself as quite satisfied with the Governor's ruling. But that night Pemberton hunted the King out to make him change his mind.

Israel Pemberton did not possess "a fugitive and cloistered virtue." On the contrary, he ran for his immortal garland with a deal of dust and sweat. Teedyuscung, whom Pemberton intended to use as a rod on others' backs, was of too easy and amiable a disposition for the Higher Venegance. He needed stiffening. Accordingly Israel, who had come out in a rash of spiritual poison ivy (he diagnosed it himself as "Christian Tenderness"), followed Teedyuscung at night into Yohe's tavern intending to administer to him a headier dose than the tavern keeper knew how to concoct. He meant to teach the King his grievances.

Extract from Colonel Weiser's Journal [36]

[Easton, July 22, 1757]

In the Evening as I came from Council & sat with Benjn Lightfoot in my Room Israel Pemberton came up Stairs, opened the Door & looked in, and said, Oh! I thought there was no Body there. I desired him to come in but he repeated the same and went away to the next Room where Capt[ns] Bussé and Orndt were with Teedyuscung, Pompshire and Moses Tatamy & others. After a while, when Ben: Lightfoot was gone, I went to see Teedyuscung in the said Officers Room; but he was then gone & soon returned & seemed to be pretty warm and spoke to me to this Purport, That He was led by the Nose by the Governor ["at the same time laying his Hand to his Nose and shaking it," adds Christian Busse in a later deposition], but that he would have his own Clerk and that he had as much Right to a Clerk as the Governor had. I told him he might speak to the Govern[r] Himself & that I would not carry that Message.

That was on Friday. To George Croghan on Saturday Teedyuscung presented an ultimatum: no clerk, no treaty. Croghan thought it best, for the sake of peace, to yield. Accordingly, when the conference was resumed on Monday, Teedyuscung called for Charles Thomson ("Master of the Publick Quaker School in the City of Philadelphia" and house companion at Easton of Israel Pemberton), who thereupon took his seat at the table beside the regular clerk and proceeded to take minutes.

We are "not without hopes," wrote Israel Pemberton to Dr. John Fothergill, "the same good providence which has remarkably interposed and Conducted hitherto will leade to a final happy Conclusion to the Exaltation of the Testimony of Truth & the Confusion of its adversaries . . ." [37]

Perhaps it was the heady scent of the forests about Easton that had stirred in the breast of this gentle Quaker the very spirit of the old Scotch Covenanters.

The conference moved on, with the slow and dignified progression of Indian parliamentary practice, from the clearing of blood from the seats of council to the redressing of grievances and the making of plans for a durable peace.

The land grievance, said Teedyuscung, was "not the principal Cause, that made us Strike our Brethren the English yet it has caused the Stroke to come harder, than it otherwise would have come." [38] What hurt most was not that the land had been taken from them, but that no part of it had been reserved for the Indians' permanent settlement. It seemed that he was dropping the complaints about fraud he had made at the last Easton treaty, but the point needed elucidation. Governor Denny requested Croghan to hold a private conference with Teedyuscung to clear up what was "dark and confused" in his speech.

At 9:30 A.M. on Saturday, July 30, Teedyuscung came with his counselors to Croghan's house. Of this conference at Croghan's a report reached the Governor, written entirely in Charles Thomson's hand (though unsigned), to the following purport. Teedyuscung had said, "The Complaints I made last fall, I yet continue," [39] and he had gone on to elaborate four points:

1. He wished to see "the Writings and Deeds" on which Brother Onas grounded his claim to the land.

2. He demanded satisfaction if it was found that any lands had been bought of Indians who had no right to sell, or that the Proprietors had taken more land than the deeds properly entitled them to.

3. He wanted a tract set aside, containing some two million acres (a plan was appended, in what appeared to be Thomson's hand, showing a great arc pivoting on Shamokin, taking in the Great Island on the West Branch of the Susquehanna, reaching to a point not far below Tioga on the North Branch, and including the Wyoming Valley), to be held inviolate for the Delawares forever.

4. He desired to receive for himself and his people instruction in house building, religion, reading, and writing.

Was this simple common sense and justice, or an ingenious political maneuver? The fourth point was unexceptionable, and so were the others —if it were not for the fact that they opened up an old quarrel on which the Six Nations had passed judgment in 1742. The face was the face of Teedyuscung, but the voice was that of Israel Pemberton.

The Governor and Council, after considering this report, called in Weiser and Croghan to confer with them about it. Weiser expressed surprise that Teedyuscung should have spoken thus, "Teedyuscung having not only at Fort Allen on his going last from Easton, but again his coming to the Treaty, told him that they did not want to continue the Dispute about the Lands." [40] Croghan, referring to Teedyuscung's second point, said the Delawares admitted that the Proprietaries had made fair purchases of the lands from the Six Nations, but contended that the Six Nations were not the rightful owners of the land. "Mr Croghan, and Mr Weiser and all present were of Opinion, that if the Delawares shou'd persist in this manner of proceeding, it would occasion a Breach between the six Nations & them, of which the Consequences at this time might be very fatal . . ." [41]

Several days were consumed in fruitless discussion of land grievances. Teedyuscung declined to accept William Johnson as arbitrator of the land dispute, as the Proprietors had proposed. But at a council held in Weiser's lodging the King appeared more placable. He desired only to see the deeds of the "Back Lands, which are the main Points . . . As soon as that is done," he said, "I will not say one Word more, about the Differences or Lands, but confirm the Peace as soon as that is done." [42]

For the moment peace seemed to be just around the corner; but the oddest of crises arose to make the parties involved forget land matters in concern for their scalps. Israel Pemberton and his friends were by this time sure that something was going wrong. Charles Thomson, three days after his appointment as Teedyuscung's secretary, thought he had ferreted out a government plot to keep Teedyuscung in liquor "to unfit him to say anything worthy of being inscribed by his Secretary. On Saturday," as he wrote to his friend Rhodes,

under pretence of rejoicing for the victory gained by the King of Prussia & the arrival of the Fleet, a Bonfire was ordered to be made & liquor given to the Indians to induce them to dance. For fear they should get sober on Sunday & be fit next day to enter on business, under pretence that the Mohawks had requested it another bonfire was ordered to be made & more liquor given them. On Monday night, the King was made drunk by C. Weiser, on Tuesday by G. Croghan; last night he was very drunk at Vernon's and vernon lays the blame on the Comin & G. Croghan. He did not go to sleep last night. This morning he lay down under a shed about break of day & slept a few hours. He is to speak this afternoon. He is to be sure in a fine capacity to do business. But thus we go on. I leave you to make reflections. I for my part wish myself at home.[43]

A few days later Thomson nervously set off an explosion that might have laid the town of Easton in ruins.

On Tuesday, August 2, the Governor sent word to Teedyuscung that he would meet him in public conference at five o'clock in the afternoon. Weiser ordered up his red-shirted guard to conduct His Excellency to the booth. A message came from the interpreter Pumpshire and a certain James Davies ("one of Teedyuscung's Counsellors") that the King was in liquor and the conference would have to be postponed. The Governor ordered Weiser to discharge the guard, and went out. Israel Pemberton was sure that it was Croghan who had made Teedyuscung drunk, and whose servant had spread the report that the King was incapable of business. But, says Pemberton, Teedyuscung (under care of persons whom he does not name) so far recovered himself as to be "more fitt for business than expected." [44] He came to the place of treaty, waited there for an hour, and then sent Mr. Thomson to express his displeasure at being kept waiting and to demand an explanation from the Governor. Peters, in the Governor's absence, explained that the meeting had been put off at the particular request of Pumpshire and a member of Teedyuscung's own council.

Thomson was angry. "Teedyuscung is sober," he declared, and went off in a huff.

Pumpshire and Davies appeared a few minutes later to offset whatever Thomson might have said.

"The King," they insisted, "and many of the Indians are very drunk, and it would not be proper to meet this afternoon."

When Thomson returned Peters' answer to the Indians, they "were so enraged," writes Israel Pemberton with enjoyment, "that they blacked themselves for Warr loaded their Arms & sev[eral] of them prepared to go off, it was only with some difficulty they were prevented, & their resentment Allay'd." [45]

James Pemberton was even more exultant:

they loaded their Guns & began to Collect with a design to frighten or realy to do mischief [he wrote to his wife] & some here think it would have been the case if some of the Commissioners & ffrds had not interposed. the Govern^r & some of Councill shew'd the greatest Signs of terror & Amasem^t B Chew it is said went ab^t Ringing his hands and crying for mercy & help like a Child, & James Hamilton was in danger some of the rest it is likely took care to secure themselves out of ye way of danger. that I find they are Alive but Ben. Still looks very pale. [46]

James Hamilton's danger was real enough. He and Chew "happening to be at or near ye place where ye s^d Tumult arose," so runs a statement signed by William Peters and Jacob Duché, Jun.,

a Young Indian, who was blackt, was seen to follow them & to present his Gun at Mr Hamilton, as he was returning back into ye Town, but before he had fired some person interposed, seiz'd him & wrested his Gun from him, w^{ch}, on examination, was found loaded wth Powder & a chaw'd Bullet—Tho' this Young Indian was ye K'g Teedyuscung's Son, yet it was not judg'd proper to take any other Notice of ye Affair than to double ye Sentrys. [47]

Next day James Pemberton wrote again to his wife, asking her not to make known what he had mentioned about Ben Chew, "as it may perhaps have been aggravated tho' there is no doubt he was much frightned." [48]

Under the conference shed on the day after the fracas, the Governor sat ill at ease. Only a few days before, Richard Peters had received a letter from ex-Governor Morris expressing the hope that he might return to Philadelphia with his scalp [49]—a remark that now seemed in ill taste. Denny delivered himself before Teedyuscung of a labored speech about lands and titles and the means by which His Majesty's government could adjust such matters to Teedyuscung's satisfaction. He talked about ministers, proprietaries, governors-in-chief, Sir William Johnson and his Deputy Agent George Croghan; and he delivered a belt by way of emphasis.

Teedyuscung replied fretfully that what the Governor had said was "as a Rumbling over the Earth, or Confusion about Lands," [50] and that two things were wrong with his speech.

When the Governor asked if he would let him know what those two things were, he replied rudely, "No, let the Governor find them out."

At this point, Weiser tell us, a murmuring arose among the chiefs of the Delawares. In the turmoil that ensued the conference minutes fall into confusion. Weiser, in a deposition made two or three days later, gives us the best clue we have to what went on:

This Deponent Conrad Weiser says that observing this uneasiness among the Delaware Chiefs he not understanding their Language askd one of the Six Nations who sat near him & understood Delaware to tell him what was said by the Indians who he observed were in Council together. and in answer the said Six Nation Indian said they were angry wth Teedyuscung for dwelling so long upon the Land Affair, That the Delaware Indian Lapachpiton whom this deponent knows to be of great Reputation among the Indians interrupted Teedyuscung whilst he was speaking to y[e] Governor, and in an angry way askd him, Why did you bring us down? We thought we came to make Peace with our Brethren the English, but you continue to quarrel about y[e] Land affair which is Dirt. A Dispute we did not hear of till now. I desire you to enter upon the Business we came down for which is Peace. And further said that thereupon all or most of the Indians gave Sounds of Approbation. This Deponent further says, that he instantly wrote down these words as they were spoke to him by y[e] s[d] Six nation Indian and gave the Writing to y[e] Governor just as Teedyuscung took y[e] two Belts & was beginning to speak to y[e] Gov[r] [51]

In the last sentence, Weiser refers to the most dramatic incident of the treaty. The King rose, dark and commanding, took up two belts tied together, and, in one of those spectacular reversals to which he was temperamentally inclined, held out his hand to the Governor in token of peace.

Governor Denny, taken aback (as were also the Quakers), rose a trifle uncertainly to meet him.

Now, as I have two Belts [said the King] and Witnesses are present who will speak the same, by these Belts, Brothers, in the presence of the Ten Nations, who are witnesses, I lay hold of your Hand (taking the Governor by the Hand) and brighten the chain of Friendship that shall be lasting; and whatever Conditions shall be proper for us to agree too, may be mentioned afterwards: This is the Time to declare our mutual Friendship. Now, Brother, the Governor, to confirm what I have said, I have given you my Hand, which you were pleased to rise and take hold of; I leave it with you. When you please, I am ready, Brother, if you have any thing to say as a token of confirming the Peace, I shall be ready to hear; and as you arose, I will rise up, and lay hold of your Hand. To confirm what I have said, I give you these Belts.[52]

He presented the two belts tied together, picked up another belt, and went on speaking.

If the Governor please, I have a word or two more to say to you, In remembering the old ancient Rules of making Friend[p] I remember I was formerly represented as a woman by my Uncles, the Six or Five Nations; but they gave me a pipe, and good Tobacco; those present know it to be true; and what I say is in behalf of all those present, and those far off. That Pipe and good Tobacco of Friendship I now deliver to you. Brother, when you shall smoke that good Tobacco, it will give you such a Relish, that you shall feel it as long as the Sun Shines. That very good Tobacco and Pipe, that I shall deliver into your Hand, represents among us a perpetual Friendship. Now I deliver you an equal part of it, and I desire it may be a lasting Comfort in this World, and the World to come.[53]

This was not amusing to the Pembertons. "a peace was Concluded," wrote James Pemberton, who was disappointed as well as bewildered at the turn things had taken, but resolved to put the best face on it, "tho' seemingly contrary to the Inclination of the Councellors on our side. & had it not been for the Steady Resolut[n] of the Indians, it would not have been done & was very little expected when the Conference began yesterday morning that it appears to be a Providential Interposition which baffled the wickedness of our deluded Rulers." [54]

Next day there was a great banquet at Vernon's, attended by "the Governor, his Council, the Speaker, and Members of Assembly, the Commissioners and Gentlemen in Town, the Delaware King, his Counsellors, Warriors, and all the Indians, Men, Women, and Children, in number about Three Hundred." [55]

After dinner peace was formally proclaimed. Colonel Weiser's troops were drawn up in front of the company and fired three volleys.

"The Governor," it is recorded, "afterwards continued his Entertainment at which there was a great Chearfulness. At night was a large Bonfire, and variety of Indian Dances."

IV

William Smith, first Provost of the University of Pennsylvania, wrote some satirical verses (supplying his own annotations) that convey a sense of the petulant futility with which the conference impressed intelligent bystanders.

A Dialogue between his H——r, the G———r and F——d I——l P————n on the Arrival of Teedyuscung the Delaware Chief, at Easton, July, 1757.[56]

The G———r

An Indian Treaty is a solemn Thing—
You know Sir W———m's * Agent for the K—g.

* Sir W———m J———n

If G——rs should act, it is not right;
But the poor Br——n are excluded quite.

I——l P————n

Thee wilt again present our Gifts—Govr—What then?
No more Peace-offerings from the Sons of P—n—
Arm, arm, ye gallant Few, and treat no further,
Nor meanly heap Rewards on those † who murder.
F——d l——l mourn, for lo, I send thee greeting.
Thy next Attempt will prove a silent Meeting.

† The Delawares & Shawanese, many of whom are now said to be out on scalping
Parties

O Tempora! O Mores! which may be interpreted, Pray Heav'n amen[d
the] Manners & the Times!

What had the conference accomplished? Very little. Certainly it had
not brought peace. Blood streamed on the frontiers again that fall. At
Easton there had been (after squalls) a handshake, a dinner, a bonfire,
presents, words about peace; but there had been no settlement of issues.

The debate over the Delaware land grievance had led nowhere. It could
lead nowhere except to a war with the Six Nations. The dispute had been
settled by Canasatego and the Onondaga Council in 1742. To disturb that
settlement was the road to a war more terrible than that under which the
province was already bending.

In the opinion of Conrad Weiser, the Walking Purchase was not the
real issue dividing the Delawares from the province. Said Weiser:

I never heard of a regular Complaint made by an Indian Councel against the
Proprietors of Pennsylvania, of being wronged out of Land. It is true some of
the Stragglers among 'em when they wanted more Rum, would frequently
complain and say they had been cheated; which will be the Case allways as
long as there are any Indians, and as long as they can get Rum.[57]

The real issues were concealed in the meshes of French power politics,
especially after Lydius' purchase of the Wyoming Valley in 1754 and Braddock's defeat in 1755.

After the conference, some Indians told Weiser "that Israel Pemberton had given them a Rod to scourge the white People."[58] These words
were to run like a refrain through the proceedings of the next few years.
Israel Pemberton was what has been called "a good man in the worst sense
of the word." He was virtuous undoubtedly, and he followed the gleam;
but he was self-righteous, censorious, and impatient of any light but his
own. Assured of the purity of his own motives, he never stopped to examine
the purity of his logic; and now, to right an old injustice, he was prepared
to commit a hundred new ones.

Most of the lands in the province had been honestly purchased. Even
the Walking Purchase, shady though its execution was, had been undertaken with what was a just purpose in the main: to put an end along the
Delaware River to a system of blackmail and extortion. It is true that the

Indians, ignorant of the white man's conception of land as real estate or property, and of a purchase as giving the right not merely to use the land but also to expel the original dwellers upon it, had unwittingly sold their birthright. But, as Weiser keenly noted, if the principles on which Israel Pemberton attacked the proprietaries' land policy in Pennsylvania were followed to their logical conclusion, it would be necessary to return the whole continent to the Indians—an end which Pemberton and his Friends, comfortably ensconced in businesses dependent on the proper settlement of the province, by no means had in mind.

To roll back the tide of settlement, even to undo the Walking Purchase, would in 1757 have involved a greater injustice than the one thus sought to be redressed. Thousands of white men had innocently settled with their families on these lands and were already farming them. The removal of these settlers now would have been unjust to them, even if it had been possible. Whatever one may say of the ethics of colonization ("they count this the most just cause of war, when any people holdeth a piece of ground void and vacant, to no good nor profitable use, keeping other from the use and possession of it," wrote Sir Thomas More of his Utopians), the whites were in America to stay—a fact to which the Pembertons, with their soft beds in Philadelphia, themselves bore sufficient witness.

Israel Pemberton may have been right in exposing individual frauds practised on the Indians, and he may have been right in raising the ethical problems involved in the relations between white men and Indians and between the Six Nations and their tributaries. But he was not content to raise problems; he attempted to settle them himself without possessing an adequate knowledge of the background. He did not understand the Indians; he did not know their history. He had no comprehension of Pennsylvania's relations with the Six Nations. He saw in the tears of King Teedyuscung, shed on parting from people who had loaded him with gifts, only a mark of Divine intervention; and he looked on Croghan, Peters, Denny, and Conrad Weiser as men of sin who must be watched at every turn and thwarted in all their designs.

He did not understand what effect his revelation of disunion in English councils must have on these French-incited Delawares. He did not understand the effect on the Six Nations of his encouragement of the Delawares to "speak out boldly" and assert their independence. He did not know that in angering the Six Nations he was kicking away one of the main props of Anglo-Saxon security in America. He did not know that his conduct was prolonging the war, weakening the Delawares, and pushing King Teedyuscung to his death.

Conrad Weiser could have told him (he had learned it at Ephrata) that, while it is well to keep before one the vision of the ideal, it is necessary also, whether in church affairs or international affairs, to know the ground on which one treads.

Besides the matters aired openly at Easton, there were other and deeper issues in the background, chief among these being the proprietorial system of government—a system that left "half the convex world" between the governing authority and the people governed. But this, at the moment, did not concern Conrad Weiser. Though he was well aware that the system under which the colony labored was rotten and could not long endure, he was at the moment intent on winning a war. If that war were lost, the question of responsible government would cease to exist.

CHAPTER 55

... *Examines La Chauvignerie*

THE Easton conference of 1757 had done little good. It had left the situation on the Ohio (whence came the chief threat to Pennsylvania) unchanged; and it had left the situation to the north changed for the worse. The Six Nations Indians who attended the conference were all eyes and ears. They said nothing, but they watched with close suspicion the movements of Teedyuscung and Israel Pemberton; and in the Quaker support of the King's demands they recognized a challenge to their own sovereignty. They went away angry and contemptuous. They saw that Brother Onas was not master in his own house, and they feared that he no longer had the power to support them as in the days when Logan, Weiser, and Shickellamy had forged an alliance underpinning the Six Nations empire.

"At this Treaty," said Weiser, "the Indians learned our Weakness, by being Informed of our Divisions." [1]

"Shure those people Must be Mad," wrote Croghan of the Quakers, "for in My opinion they are Seting up yᵉ Indians to Claime yᵉ Whole province." [2]

"This conduct of theirs," said Croghan again, "has in a great measure destroyed His Majesty's Indian Interest to the Westward." [3]

But as the conference broke up, Weiser's eyes were not fixed on these distant horizons. He attended wearily (his health was breaking) to the thousand personal details pressed on him by the departing Indians. He gave orders for their entertainment at Bethlehem on their way to Fort Allen and the Indian country. The Stewards of Bethlehem, in their statement of account against the Province, noted that, on instructions from Colonel Weiser, they gave breakfast, August 9, to seventy-five Indians with half a gill of rum each and a pint of cider, gave dinner the same day to 170 Indians, and supper to 215. The 215 had breakfast, dinner, and supper, with rum and cider, for five days more. [4]

French Margaret was supplied with "3 new hunting saddles," "2 snaffle bridles," and twenty gallons of rum with "4 caggs" to put it in. [5] She and her Mohawk husband, Peter Quebec, were given special passes to take them through the white settlements. [6] Weiser had no great confidence in French Margaret. She was known to have killed a female prisoner recently because the poor woman could not walk fast enough on the trail. But French Margaret was a daughter of Madame Montour and had to be cultivated. Down whose throat her four kegs of rum were to flow, we do not know. She was a prohibitionist at home. She had told Brother Mack, when he visited "French Margaret's Town" at the mouth of Lycoming Creek in 1753, that she did not allow the use of rum in her town and that her husband had not drunk rum for six years. [7] Perhaps she wished merely to keep her followers quiet on the trail. Perhaps her husband wished to make up for lost time.

Paxinosa, the Shawnee chief, who had come in with Abraham (the

Mohican) and a company of fifty-seven Indians on the second last day of the conference, was provided, on Weiser's order, with a pair of spectacles, a pair of buckles costing a shilling and eightpence, and some pipes and tobacco. Abraham got sixpence worth of fishhooks. Teedyuscung, King of ten nations, got "a comb, snuff, gingerbread, and sope" to the tune of one shilling and tenpence.[8]

At Bethlehem the gentle Moravians steeled tomahawks for the Indians, repaired saddles, shod horses, and mended pans. A shroud had to be made for "Bill Tattamy," who had died of his wound. For one Indian or another Weiser bought shoes, ribbons, a ten-shilling shirt, a "Handcher Chev" worth 7/6, a pair of stockings. To Lapachpiton he gave two pounds in cash. This last item appears twice on the account submitted to the government, on the debit and on the credit side, its second appearance as *Contra Credit* being explained in a meticulous note as forty shillings "Cappack pitton left in my hand when he was drunk and I Could not Stay till he was Sober & charged on the debt^r Side." [9]

When Weiser got back to Reading, he was worn out and things worried him. There was much bad news. The Indians were murdering around Manada Gap, Indian Town Gap, and the Swatara region. In Bethel Township, "as John Winklepleigh's two Sons, and Joseph Fishbaugh (a soldier in the Pay of the Province) when they went out, about Sun-rise, to bring in the Cows, they were fired upon by about fifteen Indians; one of them was scalped, the other got into the House before he died; and the soldier was wounded in the Hand." [10] In Hanover Township, four miles from the Blue Mountain, Leonard Long's son was shot at his plow and scalped. John Graham's cattle were killed at Indian Town Gap. "In one of the Houses they left a scalping Knife, and had killed and scalped a Mare." [11] Isaac Williams' wife was killed and scalped in sight of her house, "she having run a little Way, after three Balls had been shot through her Body . . ." [12] In the week of September 18 it was reported that twenty-two persons had been killed in Hanover Township alone. On September 30 the five children of Peter Walmer were carried away, four girls and a boy.[13] As if these terrors were not enough for the inhabitants, "there is now such a severe Sickness in these parts (the like of which has not been known)," says an anonymous writer, "that many Families can neither fight nor run away . . ." [14]

The letters of Conrad Weiser during the next few months make unhappy reading. He was ill. Never one to give in, he kept up his correspondence, but it was querulous and hysterical. He was worried by the new wave of Indian attacks, worried by the Quaker attempt to drag him through the muck of the Delaware land grievance, worried by the illness of Major Parsons, worried by the virtual break-up of his battalion through the Governor's meddling, worried by the malicious gossip that was circulating about him.

Weiser had never been popular. The rougher sort of frontiersman hated him for his Indian sympathies. That he had grown used to. But when he heard that gossip was running about in Philadelphia to the effect that he was afraid of Indians, he lost his temper. Unstrung with fatigue and a sickness like palsy that had seized him, he allowed the imputation of cowardice to torture him, and he sent Benjamin Franklin an ill-advised letter to publish in the *Pennsylvania Gazette*. It appeared in the issue of August 14, 1757.

Advertisement in the Pennsylvania Gazette [15]

Reading, August 10, 1757.

Whereas I have been informed that a Report has been spread in Philadelphia, that in my last Tour from Fort Allen to Fort Hamilton I should have been told by a friendly Indian of ten or twelve Enemy Indians being encamped at a small Distance from me, and that I might easily have killed or taken them all; and that I (though I had above twenty Men with me) should have gone another Way on Purpose to avoid coming to an Engagement with them: In Vindication of my Character, I do inform the Publick, that the foresaid Report is notoriously false, which I can prove, by substantial and credible Witnesses, who accompanied me in that Tour; and that the Authority of such Report must be a base Slanderer.

CONRAD WEISER

Despite his failing health, Weiser came to Philadelphia in September to confer with the Governor and Council about the Wyoming affair. Teedyuscung had requested the building of a fort and houses for the Indians at Wyoming, the Assembly had pressed compliance upon the Governor, and the Council recommended that Conrad Weiser be given the management of the whole affair.

Conrad Weiser declined, for two sound reasons. "I am in a very low State of Health," he informed the Council, "and cannot, without great Hazard, undertake any Journey; besides, if the Six Nations should not be pleased with the building of a Fort at Wyomink, they would blame me more than any body else, because they would have it to say, that I knew their Rights, &cᵃ, . . ." [16] In his place, four men were commissioned to this business: John Hughes, Edward Shippen, James Galbreath, and Charles Beaty.

Other requests from Teedyuscung were referred to Weiser, and his sentiments were expressed in writing with something of his old vigor. He doubted the wisdom of the Governor's sending (at Teedyuscung's desire) a black belt inviting the King's ten nations to go to war against the French. He feared the Delawares might say that Pennsylvania "made Peace with them, in order to make them fight our Battle . . ." He opposed offering the Indians a price for scalps (as Teedyuscung again requested) "for fear we must then pay for our own Scalps . . ." [17]

The rumor got about that Colonel Weiser was about to resign his commission. Captain Daniel Clark so reported to Major Burd [18] of Fort Augusta, who had aspirations for the Colonel's shoes. It is not known whether Weiser at this time really intended to resign, or whether the rumors were being put about to lead him to take the step. Certainly Edward Shippen desired advancement for his son-in-law, James Burd; and as certainly "old

Mr. Shippen" knew how to put pressure on Governor Denny. The political toils were closing round Conrad Weiser.

The Philadelphia trip did Weiser's health no good. It left him lame: "I Belief I got Cold in my Knees the last time I was in philad^{ia}," [19] he explained to William Parsons. But he stuck to his job, trying to pull together the forces in his battalion which Governor Denny had dispersed, and so to withstand the renewed fury of Indian attack.

"I cannot describe the Consternation the people are in, in these parts," he wrote to the Governor, October 1. "I humble intreat your Honour to pity our Cause and give orders that the men belonging to the first Battalion of pensilv^{ia} regiment now at fort augusta may all return to their proper or former Station . . ." [20]

Colonel Weiser to Major Burd [21]

Heidleberg in the County of
Bercks October the 3. 1757

Dear Sir

I can not Blame you, If you reckon me among the worst of Corespondents, you ever had, a good many of my friends give me that very Character, tho I Could Say Some thing in my defence. I have Spent the latter end in June and begining of July, in visiting the forts on the East Side of SusqueHana, I was but two days at home when I was ordered to fort Allen to meet TeediousKon, and attend the treaty at Easton, after 4 weecks Spent disagreeable I got home, and soon got the Intermeting feaver, and Bloody flux—before I got over it, I was ordered to Come to philadelphia, about Some Indian affairs, which Journey took me three Weeks, and all the time our unhappy back Inhabitants were Murdered & Carried into Captivity, I got home the first day of this Month, and found the people in these parts in the Greatest Consternation, and a great many Killed within this three Weeks last past. His Honour the Governor among other articles in the Instruction he gave me last ordered me to recall Captn Wetherholts with fifty men of my Battalion from fort Augusta, in these words. "*as Captn Wetherholts has* a Comand of one hundred men of your Battalion at fort augusta and one half may now be Spared you will order the Captain and fifty men, that is to Say Eighteen men drafted out of your own Company ten out of the late Captain Smiths twelve out of Captn Busseys and ten out of his own Company, to return to the Battalion, and on their arrival You will order them, to their respective Companys." &c

Captain Wetherholts I hear is gone home in a very poor State of health (I have not Seen him as I was in philadelphia) I hope you will permit lieut^{t} Humphrey to bring the men down, with the draft from Capt Morgans Company in Stead of Wetterholts, and if you would be pleased to Send the whole hundred If there be as many (besides Captn pattersons Company) you will do a piece of great Service to me and the back Inhabitants of the East Side of SusqueHana the Governor promised to Send for the rest Soon (Excepting Captain Pattersons) I Can not help thinking but that I have reason to Complain, besides the men at fort augusta, belonging to my Company I am obliged to Garrison Hunters fort, which allways was Garrisoned by Augusta Regiment. I have a frontier to gard, above a hundred mile in lenght the men not paid a farthing for this four Months past, and Several other bad Circumstances which this paper Cant bear macks every thing very disagreeable, I Expect

the paymaster here Soon to pay of the Battalion their arrears. and If you
would Sent the remainder of the hundred men to Come and receive their pay
and provide for the winter, I will even Send them or others in their Stead to
fort augusta again. If required, and these men would all the while in their
March Serve as wood rangers, I hope Care will be taken of the Sick, that If
the Can not travle by land they may be Sent by water or Keept in the
Hospital, as you will Judge best

in philadelphia every thing looks disagreeable between the Governor and
the Comissioners or rather the assembly. the fort and houses promised to be
Build for the Indians at Wayomock wont be finished this year perhaps not
began, the treating Bill the Governor rejected. and the Assembly wont Suffer
him to name the Comissioners for to Carry on that trade, nor will he Suffer
them to name them, because the put in Members of their house So we must
loose what little Interest we have as yet with the Indians because for our
domestick quarrles

I saw old Mr Shippen in philadelphia the Capt his Son. and Capt loiyd they
are all well, a great many Sick are up and down in the Country Some Sick
persons haveing ben Killed by the Indians because they Could not leave their
Beds

Of forein news we have nothing Material. the King of prussia^s affairs looks
Some thing dull Since the Battle with Marshal traun or taun the austrian
General. the french made themselves Master of Some provinces in Germany to
wit East friesland, Hessen, and a great part of Hanover. I must Conclude and
not tire your patience. I wish you health and happiness with all me heart.
who am   Dear Sir
                                            your very humble Servant
                                                 CONRAD WEISER

pray give my Kind respect to the officiers
at fort augusta and particularly to M^r
Bard your Comissary

To the Governor (through Peters) Weiser wrote urgently for the return of more men from Fort Augusta than his original instructions had
called for.

Colonel Weiser to Richard Peters [22]

                                        Heidelberg, in Berks, Octr 4, 1757.

Sir:

I did not think on the Post till he entered my doors, else I would have wrote
particularly to the Governor, tho I have ben very Buisy with writing to the
Comanding officers of the several forts under my Care. It is now Come so farr
that murder is Comited allmost every day; there never was such a Consternation among the people, they must now leave their houses again, with their
Barns full of Grain; five Children have ben Carried of last Friday, some days
before a sick man killed upon his bed, begged of the Enemy to shoot him
through his heart, which the Indian answered, I will, and did so. A girl, that
had hid herself under a Bedsted, in the next room, heard all this, two more
families were about that time destroyed. Inclosed is the Journal of last month
of my Ensign at North Kill, Capt. Bussey lies dangerously sick at John Harris.
I hear he is tired of every thing; I have neither men nor a sufficient n'br of
officers to defend the Country. If his Honour would be pleased to send orders

for to recall all the men belonging to my Battalion, from fort Augusta, he would justly bring upon him the blessing of the most high. I can not say no more. I think meselfe unhappy, to fly with my family in this time of danger I cant do. I must stay, if they all go. I am now preparing to go to fort Henry, where I shall meet some officers to consult with, what may be best to be done. I have ordered ten men, with the Governors last orders, to fort Augusta; I shall overtake them this Evening at fort Henry, and give them proper instruction. For Gods sake, dear Sire, beg of the Governor, press it upon him in my behalf, and in behalf of this distrest inhabitants, to order my men back from fort Augusta I will give my reason afterwards, that I am in the right.
I Conclude with my humble respects to his Honour,

And remain, Kind Sir

Your most humble Servant,
CONRAD WEISER

Excuse my hurry.

Governor Denny sent immediate instructions to Burd to send Weiser the additional troops asked for.

Weiser paid a visit to Busse at Harris', and there received news of the capture of a French cadet at Fort Henry on October 12. He hurried back to Heidelberg, to which place Sammy (on instructions from his father) with a ranging party from the fort at Swatara Gap which he then commanded, had brought the prisoner for examination.

Michael La Chauvignerie, a lad some seventeen years of age, was a son of the commandant at Fort Machault (Franklin, Pa.) on the Allegheny. Although he looked wild as well as worn at the time of his capture and was found to have taken part in no less than three raids into the Swatara region, he turned out, when washed and fed and removed from the scene of war, to be a very pleasant, home-loving young man.

The story of his adventures, as told to Weiser and others, gives as clear a picture as we can find of the kind of warfare against which the First Battalion was attempting to defend the Province. It was the strategy of the French by directing these lightning Indian raids along the border, to lay waste the frontier settlements, cripple the colony's wealth in crops and cattle, drive mobs of refugees in on the centers of population and trade, and disrupt the normal economy of the country.

Chauvignerie had left Fort Machault on September 11.[23] He had with him a French companion, La Jardin, and thirty-three Indians. Among these were two chiefs, La Grande Terre and Maconse, the latter, who had a brother in Pennsylvania, acting as guide. They had traveled for two weeks over very mountainous country when they met another party of Indians returning from an expedition and bringing back with them some trophies: one scalp and three prisoners—a man and two women. The returning party gave their male prisoner to Chauvignerie's Indians; whereupon most of these latter decided to rest on their borrowed laurels and go home. Chauvignerie went on, and twelve Indians with him. They crossed the Susquehanna, picked up the Shamokin Trail, followed it for a while, and then left it to come out at Swatara Gap and enter what is now called Lebanon Valley. On their way they passed many deserted farms; but four miles from the Gap, on Read's Creek, they came upon the still inhabited house of Peter Walmer.

Saur's newspaper of October 15 regaled its readers with some details of what ensued.

News comes from Quittobohille that in Lancaster County on Oct. 1 Indians came to Peter Wamfflers House, while he and his wife were in the fields, bringing in a Wagon with hay. The Indians took 5 Children off with them, 4 girls and one boy; the smallest Child is scarce a Year old and cannot walk yet; they took from the House all they could carry: the rest they destroyed, scattered the flour, spilled the honey, broke the pots and windows and tore up the beds.[24]

In half an hour Chauvignerie and his Indians were off again, headed for the Ohio. They had done what they had come to do: with small risk they had got a little booty and some good prisoners (the Indians were fond of children, and white children made very good Indians when they grew up). Before they left, according to Chauvignerie, they "took some cloathes for the children, . . . afterwards took some horses at another place about three leagues off and put the children on them"; hurried off through St. Anthony's Wilderness past abandoned farms where they saw nothing alive but geese and other fowl. They were careful to make no fires at night except in deserted houses.

On October 3 they recrossed the Susquehanna toward the west. While they were making what speed they could with their child prisoners and other booty (which unfortunately included little food), Chauvignerie discovered that he had dropped from his blouse the piece of bread which was his only ration. He turned back along the trail to look for it. The Indians went on. By the time he had made up his mind that further search was useless, night had fallen and caught him alone in the woods. He could neither catch up with his party nor make them hear him. He fired his gun, but there was no response. He wandered about, searching for his men for two or three days; and then, being afraid of starving, he determined to return to the English settlements. He passed the Susquehanna again, found the Shamokin Trail, and crossed the mountains. He could not remember how long he had been alone in the woods. He thought it was seven days; "But I may have forgot a Day," he told Colonel Weiser, "as I was in great Distress." [25]

On October 12 a sentry at Fort Henry observed what appeared to be "a French Deserter or Spy" [26] coming down the hill and making for Dietrick Six's house. The commanding officer being informed despatched an officer and two men to arrest him. He was held in the fort until Sammy appeared with orders to take him to the plantation at Heidelberg. There, on October 5, Weiser examined him "by such an Interpreter as I could get," [27] and then hurried on with him to Reading to examine him again next day "upon Interrogatories" with the more competent assistance of James Read and Captain Oswald, the latter an officer of the Royal American Regiment.

The Colonel was not chiefly interested in the prisoner's personal adventures. He wanted to know about the movements of the Indians, their leaders, their prisoners, the condition of Fort Machault, its garrison, and the Indians around it. Chauvignerie gave crisp and intelligent answers. La Grande Terre was "the Indian Commander" of his party, and Maconse was the guide. Fort Machault covered two acres. It had bastions and six swivel guns. There were fifty French regulars there and forty Canadians. There were no Indians at the fort. His father, the commander, had three prisoners as servants. The Indians had a great number, but they could scarcely be persuaded to part with them.

A few days later, under guard of some of Captain Oswald's regulars, the young cadet was sent to Philadelphia, where he was once more examined, this time by Chief Justice Allen. Chauvignerie was not unhappy. He wrote to his father, January 3, 1758:

I am in the hands of a good Governor, who, out of Consideration for You, has taken great Care of me, They overwhelm me with Kindnesses, they look after all my Wants, I am very well fed, he has given me my Freedom in a little Town called Germantown which is two Leagues from Philadelphia where I spent two Months in Prison. . . . I hope to See you again soon because there is going to be an Exchange of Prisoners with the English . . .

I am, my very dear Father and dear Mother with most profound respect, your very humble and very obedient Son *La chauvignerie fils.*[28]

Later in the spring, as we learn from a letter written by General Abercromby to William Pitt,[29] steps were taken for young Chauvignerie's exchange; and we are entitled to believe that the hopes expressed in his letter of embracing his father and mother with "tender love" the marks of which he promised to show them as long as he lived, were soon in process of being fulfilled.

CHAPTER 56

. . . Hears from Richard Peters

AFTER the disappearance of Chauvignerie's party, the frontier was comparatively quiet for a time. "I hear of no news on the frontiers," wrote Weiser to James Young, the Paymaster, on October 27, "and wish I may not hear of any more." [1] But if there were no murders there were plenty of other distractions for the Colonel's mind. With winter approaching, he needed blankets for his men, and all the forts were short of flints.[2] Sickness was all about. "Several Women & children are Swipt off by this raging distemper." [3] Major Parsons' health was not improving.

"I was glad to hear you was returned from the Jerseys to Easton," wrote Weiser to Parsons, October 23, "but Could have wished in a better State of health then when you went, I am now lame and can hardly walk over the floor . . . My wife joins with me in our respects to you, and very heartly wish that you may recover your Strenght and Health again Dear old friend yours Conrad Weiser" [4]

There was more trouble about the disposition of the troops. The Governor at Weiser's entreaty had ordered his men down from Fort Augusta. He now ordered a company up again. Denny's commands to that effect reached Weiser on the evening of October 31, through Edward Shippen (father-in-law of the commander at Fort Augusta), who was on his way to Wyoming via Fort Augusta with the Indian commissioners. Weiser's company was to be their escort.

Colonel Weiser to Edward Shippen [5]

Sir

I hereby acknowledge the receipt of yours with the inclosed from the Governor, I Could have wished I had received it at fort Heinry where I have ben this 3 or 4 day, I Just now returned home. I am Some what Surrprized that I must Send again, it is but a week ago, Since about a hundred men of my Battalion returned from fort augusta where there is Still a Company of my Battalion left those that returned are mostly in a bad State of health, however I must obey orders, and will dispatch an Express to Captain Wetterholts at Maxidany Imediatly for Some men and So on their way as farr as Susque-Hana as Soon as possible, I am

Sir
your most humble Servt
CONRAD WEISER

Heidleberg in
Bercks—Oct the 31.
by Sun Set
please to Mention my Compliment to the Gentlemen Comissioners I heartily wish you all a good Journey and Safe return

So the battalion had to be bled again. Since there was no company in reserve that could be sent with the Indian commissioners, it was necessary to make up a company in such a way as to avoid seriously depleting any single garrison. This took time, since the forts were strung out over a hundred miles. Meanwhile the commissioners, who had gone on to Fort Hunter, complained about the delay. On November 3 they notified the Governor (but not Colonel Weiser) that they would not wait, but were going on with another escort.[6]

Before the company Weiser was gathering could reach the Susquehanna, things had happened. We had better let Weiser tell the story.

Colonel Weiser to Governor Denny [7]
"by way of Journal"

[November 10, 1757]

Honoured Sir

I received your Comand per Express from new Castel I received on the 31 of oct^r last Past in the Evening When I Just Came from fort Heinrey & dispatch an Express Imediatly to Capt Wetherholts in Linn township North Hampton County ordering him to send Lieut Wetterholts with 14 privat men with all possible Speed. I wrote by Express to fort Williams & Hunter & Heinry to Send their quota in proportion according to the demand Wetherholts March^d the 3te by the Way of reading where they arrivd on the 4ten in the Evening an unhappy affray happen^d between Some of them and Some of the regulars encamped at Reading in the quarter of Wetherholts' men. in which Affray Several of Wetherholts men where wounded and most all of them Imprisoned. (The particulars of this affray I leave to the Gentlemen that have ben on the Spot to Inform) I heard of it by Lieut^t Wetherholts next day, and was Extremely Concern^d because for the Service those men were on.

The night's doings at Peter Feder's tavern provided a juicy morsel for the readers of Saur's newspaper:

Another Report from Reading informs us, that some of the Provincials and the Troops from England, gathered in Peter Feder's house, and had a brotherly quarrel; they fought so well with their brethren, shot and slashed, that, between 60 and 70 Men were wounded. . . . they smashed windows and everything they could break in the house, as if they were out after the French and Indians.[8]

Meanwhile Captain Sammy (whom the Colonel had appointed to the command of the Wyoming party's escort since he could speak Mohawk and might therefore be of special assistance to the commissioners) had set out for the Susquehanna. The story grows more confused, and Weiser's letter with it.

Conrad Weiser to Governor Denny (continued)

. . . On the 6 I Sent orders to the Comanding officier in fort Heinry to Sent 15 other men in Stead of Wetherholts men to folow Capt Lieut^n Weiser who was then on his March to Hunters fort—I have ordered him to Comand the Company I Sent of my Battalion. thinking, that the public Service might require it and the Gentlemen Comissioners Stand in need of an Interpreter to the 6 nation Indians (Insign Kern March^d Imediatly with these 15 men). I Set

out for Reading that day, and found things as I was inform^d   the men being
let out of goal, I ordered L^t We [therholt] to proceed on his March with as
many of his men as where able to march Some haveing ben Wounded that I
thought best to Send them to their old Station   Wetherholt march with nine
of his men on the 7 Instant with orderers to folow Samuel Weiser to fort
Hunters and further . . . [in] hopes of overtaking him Otherwise If no hope
to overtake him then to return to the fort on Suartaro and make report to me
and receive further orders

by Sam^1 Weisers last letter on his March, he acquainte me that he Intended
to leave Hunters on the 8th Instant. he Could not tell whether or no the Comissioners were there yet or not.

I am Sorry I had no longer time So that the Soldier I sent might have ben
better provided for the winter season, It gave Some trouble that I was
obliged to Send again to fort Augusta & Wayomock, many of my men Coming
from fort augusta but a few days ago . . . in very poor State of Health

I take this apportunity to begg leave of your Honour to lay before my
Grievances by the first apportunity about the payment of the Battaleon under
my Comand and Especially that of my Company, I am more than Sixty pounds
out of pocket and that in Such a way that your Honour I belief will not
Justify   I will not trouble your Honour any further at present . . .

This letter was scarcely out of Weiser's hands when he received one
from Richard Peters. It was the letter the Provincial Secretary had been
itching to write for seven long years—ever since the dispute over the
Mahanoy lands.

Lord, in the day of vengeance, try him.

It is not proposed here that the letter was written solely on Peters'
initiative. There were others who had more to gain than he from Weiser's
surrender of his military commission. Edward Shippen, for instance, had
a son-in-law. The Governor may quite honestly have felt that the battalion
needed new leadership under a younger and more professionally minded
man. But the task of eliciting Weiser's resignation was one congenial to
Peters' pinchbeck soul, and he threw himself into it with zeal.

Quivering with malice, he addressed to "Collonel Weiser at Reading" a
letter so full of gossip, slander, petty meanness, and hypocrisy, that it affords the best portrait we have of the Reverend Richard Peters' Mr. Hyde.

Richard Peters to Conrad Weiser [9]

[Philadelphia, November 9, 1757]

Dear Sir

At Newcastle I received from my Brother your Lre to him of the 27th 8^ber
with the Paper inclosed. On this Subject I will write some other time. When
I returnd with the Governor from the Newcastle Assembly I found the Conversation was mostly upon the State of your Battalion. It was said that the men
were left to themselves—that two or three were together in farm Houses. that
more men were enlisted by some Captains than their Companys for three years
or during the War and yet many who were only enlisted for a year were not
discharged tho the Governor gave frequent Orders that these shoud be dis-

charged—that tho several wanted Arms there were fifty good Ones in the Collonels House that the Powder & Lead were suffered to be at Easton & Reading tho' the men wanted it in their Companies—that several old unfit men were enlisted & that your own Company was the very worst of all—In short that the officers are under no Command—have not nor do now scout or range and that this Battalion is almost useless. Your friends on this Occasion are much grieved and know not what to say—they hear further that a man is kept in your house to make shoes which you sell to the Men and that you are grown a great Lover of money. The Captains of your own Battalion say they have never received explicit and clear Orders about Enlisting, nor have seen the Beating orders. You may remember the Govr desird you to furnish every Captain with a Copy of the Beating Orders given you. In short, Dear Sir, I cannot help mentioning what is said.

On the other hand the Governor expressly declares that His Orders are never obeyed and is very much displeased.

The Serjeant has staid a long time & people press upon me. I can not add at present more than that I am

Dr Sir

Your affectionate
humble Servant
RICHARD PETERS

Conrad Weiser to Richard Peters [10]

Heidleberg November 17th 1757.

Sir

I was favoured with yours of the 11th Instant, & am very sorry to hear so many Complaints against me & my Batalion. I must say they are either thro' Malice or Ignorance; and I will now trouble You with an Answer to some of the Charges.

First it is said "That the Men were left to themselves, and that two or three were together in Farm Houses." A Charge, of which I am quite ignorant. I have, from time to time, given Orders to the Contrary, which I can make appear. It is true, with Respect to Captain Wetherholts, that at Justice Everitts, where his Company are posted, there being no House capable of Containing so many Men, He quartered them in the Neighbourhood, continuing to range the Country, of which I have before Informed the Governor.

As to the Charge about enlisting, every Captain in my Batalion had Orders to recruit for three Years—and to complete their Companies, to 53 Men, Including 2 Serjeants, 2 Corporals & a Drum. If the Captains have enlisted more, they have suffered for it, as I have also, having lost above forty Pounds by it. I had in my Company, five Men over and above my Complement, and the Commissary refused paying 'em, tho' the most of 'em had five Months pay due and I was obliged to pay them out of my own Pockett, & discharge them. Is it for this Reason, that they call me a Lover of Money? If it be I readily Acquiesce. With Regard to there being more Men in my Batalion than the Complement, this would not have happened, had it not ben for some verbal Encouragement I received from Some of the Gent. Commissioners, who upon being informed of my Batalion's being too full, assured me that they would pay fourteen Hundred Men, and they knew that neither the Augusta Regiment nor the second Batalion (but particularly the Augusta Regiment) had not their full Complement. And had the Commissary paid us Monthly, According to the Governor's Promise, We should only have lost the Pay of the Supernumeraries for One Month. But in my Opinion We are wronged out of the Pay for the Supernumeraries for five Months, and no One has suffered more by this Article than myself.

I cannot remember that the Governor ever gave me Orders to discharge all those who were enlisted only for One Year; but for to discharge 'em gradually, as We got others for three Years, and allways to keep the Companies full.

And As to, the Charge about Arms & Ammunition, I have made the several Captains and Commanders of Companies acquainted that they might send for what Supply they thought proper and whenever they sent, they received what they requested. As to the Ammunition in Reading it was brought and unloaded there, without a Line or any Direction whatsoever. As there is no Magazine provided by the Province in these Parts it cannot be in a safer or in a better Place being in the keeping of an honest Man, who distributes, or delivers it out according to my Order.

With Respect to the other Charge, for enlisting old, disabled Men &. I acknowledge that at first *elderly*, but not *unfit*, Men were enlisted, but are since discharged, as We could procure other and better Men in their Places.

That my own Company is the worst of all, and that the Officers are under no Command, is what I absolutely deny, and am sorry that the Commissary did not Intimate this, when He was here.

In Answer to what is said of my Batalion's being allmost useless I shall observe that if it is now thought so, It is not long, since it has been looked upon in that light. I have been obliged to send two Companies over Sasghehannah into Cumberland County upon an Alarm occasioned by discovering several Places where Indians had lodged. Sometime after upon an Alarm of Fort Augusta being in Danger of an Attack, Three Companies of my Batalion were sent to their Reinforcement, at Sundry times. These three Companies remained there all Summer, One still remains there, and two of 'em lately returned, of whose Condition, the Commissary of the Musters was an Eye Witness. Another Company is marched with the Commissioners, to Wyoming. The remaining Part of my Batalion are scattered from Hunters Fort on Sasghehannah, to Depuys on Delaware. A Frontier too large to be protected by the Small Number of Forces left in this Batalion.

I cannot help observing that tho' I have frequently been obliged to send large Detachments from my Batalion, to the Assistance of the other Forces, when thought in Danger, Yet I never have rece^d the least Assistance tho' We have such an Extent of Country to defend, which has been repeatedly and allmost constantly attack'd by the Enemy. Another thing I cannot omit. When Intelligence was received that a large Body of Indians had crossed Sasghehannah abov Fort Augusta, supposed to be about One Hundred, and intended to fall in near Schuylkill, I only rece^d bare Accounts of it, without any Orders for Assistance, tho' the Information proved true, and that Party of the Enemy, actually Invaded the Settlements on Schuylkill, and did Considerable Damage, tho' not so much as might be expected from so great a Number. My Batalion has been considerably weakened, by the Resignation of Reynolds & Smith & the Dismission of Vanetta, and other Vacancies, not filled up. There are now five Vacancies in my Batalion, five Officers absent on Command at Fort Augusta, & Wyoming, and Captn Bussé lyes sick incapable of Duty. From such Deficiencies it may easily be judged what Difficulties I am under.

If any Captain in my Batalion will say that He has received no explicit

Orders about recruiting, or has not a Copy, or has not Seen the Beating Orders I must say He is a Lyar.

The Charge about the Shoemaker is scandalous & malicious, & undeserving of Notice—but if You require it I will answer it in my next. Above all I am sorry his Honour the Governor should charge me with disobeying his Orders. That I have obey'd his Orders punctually, in all Instances (save once whereof his Honor was acquainted and satisfy'd) I think I can maintain and have Reason to remember some Orders whereby I have suffered, particularly that for keeping two Saddle Horses at each Fort, the one to alarm the neighbour-hood in Case of an Attack, the other for the more speedy forwarding Intelli-gence &ca, from fort to fort or to the Commanding Officer. These Horses with Saddles were Accordingly provided and used in the Service, and an Account amounting to upwards of One Hundred Pounds was laid by me bef: the Commiss^{rs} who absolutly refused Payment alledging that the Governor had not consulted with them about the Matter. And perhaps my desiring Pay-ment of the just Account, considerable Part whereof I had paid out of my own Pockett and am answerable for more, is another Reason of being called a Lover of Money.

I have constantly endeavoured to give the Back Inhabitants all the Protection in my Power, and allways understood that it was for that End that the Batalion was raised; and if that does not please I have only one Offer more to make, which is my Resignation, which shall be Immediately on their doing me and my Batalion Justice.

I hereby send the Journalls of the several Captains and Commanders of Forts in my Batalion, as also the Return of the Batalion which I desire may be laid before his Honour the Governor in Order to Justify my Officers.

I have nothing further to add at present, but am

Sir
Your humble Servant
Conrad Weiser

P.S.
  I have a Lameness in my hand
and can scare hold a Pen
in my Hand.
        C W.

CHAPTER 57

. . . *Dislikes Governor Denny*

I

ONE day in January 1758, a party of ten men went over the Blue Mountains, as we read in Saur's *Pensylvanische Berichte*, February 18, 1758, to hunt deer and visit their deserted plantations. They saw some Indians and lifted their flintlocks to shoot. The Indians, instead of taking cover, stood still and shouted: "Stop! We are friends!"

The whites replied, "If you are friends, leave your weapons behind you and come here."

The Indians laid down their tomahawks and guns, walked over to the white men, and said, "We are friends and your Brothers. *It is no mor Warr.*"[1]

It was not the peace pipe smoked the summer before at Easton that had caused the change in the woods, but something that had taken place on the Ohio. It was over a year now since Dumas had left Fort Duquesne, and his successor, as General Montcalm noted in a letter of April 10, 1758,[2] had not been so successful in holding the Indians.

Conrad Weiser learned from the Indian Will Sock that sometime during the winter of 1757–58 the commander at Fort Duquesne had gathered the chiefs of the Wyandots, the Onigh-Calliackon, and the Missisaugas to feast on a Big Fat Bear (by which he meant the Six Nations); and that the chiefs of these three nations had refused to eat his roast and declared their intentions to die with the Six United Nations.

"Eat your roast yourselves," they said to the Frenchmen, and kicked the commandant's war wampum under his feet.

"Children," said the French officer with rueful humor, "I have built a large fire and burned the roasted [bear] meat."[3]

Already in March 1758, it was reported in Philadelphia that Shingas the Terrible was coming in to make peace. With that announcement the Delaware War seemed really to be over.

But there was a canker in the rose. By his manner of appeasing the Delawares, Brother Onas had angered the Six Nations and had good reason to fear them. Not only Pennsylvania but the whole of British North America, now acting as a unit under the command of Lord Loudoun, had of late so mishandled its relations with the Iroquois Confederacy that the old chain of friendship forged by Weiser, Logan, and Shickellamy was ready to snap. The colonies were in real danger of a Six Nations war.

"I have been told that he [Lord Loudoun]," wrote Goldsbrow Banyar to Sir William Johnson,

has expressed so warm a Resentment against those Nations, that if I did not think it would abate before his Lordship proceeded to Action, I should be greatly alarmed with the Apprehensions of an approaching War with those

People, more to be dreaded in my opinion than the War we sustain already against five times their Number. Let the Situation of those People be considered, and though they are not so powerful in themselves or their alliances as formerly yet we should soon severely feel the Weight of their Resentment.[4]

The handling of this situation, when it came to a head at Easton in the fall of 1758, was to be Conrad Weiser's most signal service to his country.

No hope of reward, not even the reward of public recognition, moved the old interpreter at this time. A new breed of creature filled the places of authority whence in happier times recognition and honors would surely have come to him. Denny, Peters, Israel Pemberton— Is there a story in Aesop about a chicken, a fox, and a lamb that set out to bring a lion down? There should be.

Conrad Weiser was moved by something deep within him—natural honor, love of country, religion—which enabled him to remain upright, even though he had to stand aside, while others (in the language of the Good Book) moved forward on their bellies.

II

Late in November Richard Peters wrote a personal letter to Weiser summoning him to Philadelphia. The Colonel intimated in his reply that he took commands from his superior officer, and would leave his post when, but not until, the Governor sent for him. ". . . it will be somewhat a troublesome Journey to me at Present," he wrote, November 30, "as I have not the Use of my right Hand. It is about two Weeks ago that in my sleep I got a lameness in my Hand, though without Pain, which still continues. Some say it is a Palsy; but however I will make a Shift to come down if otherways my Health will Permit, as Soon as the Governor gives me Leave." [5]

Colonel Weiser had as good as offered his resignation. The next step was up to the Governor, but the Governor had no mind for business. The matter dragged on for weeks. Meanwhile Weiser carried on. He enlisted men. He examined the muster rolls and journals of the officers. He issued reprimand where the work of the garrisons appeared slack, and demanded strict compliance with the orders about ranging and pursuit of the Indians. He called for lists of all persons killed and captured since the beginning of the war. He wrote to Philadelphia for a clarification of the instructions about recruiting, requested that such new regulations made by the Governor as related to his battalion should be communicated to him without delay. He asked that he be informed (the Governor was careless about these things) what commissions had lately been issued and what reports had been received from the commissioners whom Captain Sammy had escorted into the Wyoming Valley.

Colonel Weiser's commission was renewed December 1.[6] Lieutenant Hyndshaw wrote from the Wind Gap December 2 to express regret that, though his company was complete, its effectiveness was ruined by being so dangerously divided (he had had to supply men for the escort of the Wyoming commissioners).

. . . my thus Dividing my Company [said Hyndshaw] in Such smal Numbers is difficult to me, besides it exposes the Men to danger which if more in Number it might perhaps be prevented, my thus Dividing of the Men I must say is not your Orders to me, but I hope, and has alwise found you, tender and Compassionate to a poor desteressed Country, which gives me Comfort that you will not take it amiss for my thus doing, nor Suffer me to Receive any hurt or blame thereby, could I have more Men Allowed me I could be of more Service to my Country I think and not without Reason. that there is not one Company in Your Battalion Patrolles so much as mine. . . . I desire your favour, if you Please to Acquaint me, the Reason why His Honour our Governor is so long a filling up the Vacantees of Commissions in Your Battalion and if Benjamin Shoemaker is anywise likely of having the Lieu^ts Commission in my Company which through you He makes great dependence on. . . . I am with wishing you and your Spouse and the Rest of your family, Very good Health, and am
Dear Sir—Your reall Friend and Most Humble Servant   James Hyndshaw.[7]

Conrad Weiser to Richard Peters [8]

Heidleberg in the County of Bercks
december the 14 1757

Sir

I have been lame in my wrist for four weeks past and Could no make use of my right hand as usual, I had it plistered and Cold Came into it, by which It grew very bad but is now growing better, and I Intent (God Willing) to be in philadelphia next week, bring ing with me all the papers you requested

Captn Bussey is not wholy recovered nor is it likely that he will, he is for the most part of the time lighthead^d . . .

Zigerea Signified to Samy Weiser, when last at fort augusta, that he wanted to talk with me very Much about very particular things I wish the poor felow was with me for a day or two

I received no letter nor list of the officers by last post as you was pleased to promise in your last, but It does not matter now. the time wont be long before I Shall have the Satisfaction to be once more in town Excuse my Scriblings for the above Said reason. If you please mention my best respects to his Honour the Governor I have nothing to add but am

Sir
your most h^ble Servant
Conrad Weiser

ps: every thing is quiet up here Since
the murder of Robeson & Ball in Hanover which
Murder I have reason to Suspect to have ben Comited by Some Indian from fort a. g a.

Three days after Weiser wrote that letter preparatory to handing in his papers, Major William Parsons died in Easton. The old company of volunteers that had saved the province in 1755 was breaking up.

Weiser went in to town a few days after and awaited the Governor's pleasure. He waited for a month. We find him "putting up some Books" at the shop of Armbruster, the German printer, on Thursday, December 29.[9] The Governor kept dilly-dallying with him and with Major Burd of Fort Augusta, who also had been given leave of absence at this time and called to town. The retiring Colonel and the entering one were alike disgusted.

Early in the new year Weiser's patience snapped and he took the Governor by the beard.

Conrad Weiser to Governor Denny [10]

[Undated]

Honoured Sir.

It is this day two weeks Since I arrived in philadelphia at your Honours request I had a Strong hope to get an answer to my letters of the 26 and 27 of the month last past, in which I Set forth the wreched Condition of the back Inhabitants of this province on the East side of the river of Susquehanna and some of the soldiers in the first Battalions of pensilvania regiment, but now I begin to despair of meeting with any Sucess, or favourable answer, tho attended so long—and the back Inhabitants are Continually Murdered and carried   into Captivity, and three Companys Consisting of 150 odd men of the Batalion I have the Honour to Comand lie inactive (as to the ranging part) at fort augusta. Your Hon[r] Knows they weer Sent up there first by your order accasioned by an alarm that the french were on their march, to attack fort augusta. and tho that alarm prooffed false, and augusta regiment must now be full, I Can not obtain the liberty or orders from you Honour to recall the men from fort augusta, to their old Station Where the Inhabitants Since their absence have ben Continually Murdered and Carried into Captivity, in a most Cruel manner. *It is true,* one hundred and fifty nine men, were rased by your Honours order for three months, to replace those, that were gone to fort augusta, but these mens time has ben out for Some weeks and they are gone off having meet with no further encouragment, It is probably that If your Honour had permited to recall my men from fort augusta according to my request the last murder on Suartaro &ca would not have ben comited for how is it possible for to garrison fort Henry *with 30.* The fort on Suartaro *with 30* and Hunters fort with 100 men and also to Send out strong ranging parties between Said forts? I Must think that your Honour tooke Some dislick to me—If so, or If your Honour thinks it better for his majestys or the province Service or your more Ease, that I should resiyne please to Say So. I Can prooff by Substantial Evidence that I had inclination So to do, Some time ago, Your Secretary is not Ingnorant, of this, my inclination, and Will now do it If your Honour require it, and I will make room for a better man: for the better his majesty and my Country is Served, the greater Satisfaction it will be to me, tho I am not tired of Serveing my king and my Country, and will do it when I am not in Comission or pay in the best manner I Can, but at this Junctur, I think with Submission neither meselfes, nor the Battalion I have had the honour hithertoo to Comand. nor that part of the Country that was Comited to my Care, had Justice done . . .

It seems that this letter had enough bite in it (the old lion's teeth were still sound) to stir His Excellency to action, for on January 8 we find Edward Shippen writing to his father to announce that "Conrad Weiser has resigned, and a commission is making out for Mr. Burd as Lieutenant Colonel. . . . Mr. Burd is not certain," continues Shippen, "when he shall leave town. The Governor is so dilatory, that no business can be done with him." [11]

Weiser remained in Philadelphia for a few days longer, trying without success to get a settlement of his accounts. He wrote a letter to Timothy Horsfield at Bethlehem informing him of his resignation.

Conrad Weiser to Timothy Horsfield [12]

philadelfia January the 16
1758

dear Sir

yours of the 27 of last month I received in phil[ia]   I am Sorry I was not a home when the letter was delivered to my wife, who sent it to me p[r] post, . . .

I am detained here this 3 Weeks about Setling Accounts, but must go home without do it   I have resigned my Comiss[n] as leut[t] Coll. in Pensilvania regiment & Major Will Burd the Comanding officer at fort augusta now here in this town got it, tho with my Consent I did resign voluntarely

I have lost the use of my right hand, most altogether, by a fit of a palsy, but it Seam's to grow better,   you will therefore Excuse this Scrall the inclose[d] I desire you will forward to fort Allen with my Compliment to Capt ornd, and If time admits acquaint him of my resignation,   I pray that a Corespondence may be Kept up between me and you as neighbours upon the frontiers. I am your hearty wellwisher and   dear Sir

Your humble Servant
Be pleased to remember me to   CONRAD WEISER
my friends in Bethlehem

There was a great show of housecleaning after Weiser left the battalion. Burd proposed to reorganize the defense of the province, disbanding some of the garrisons, and gathering a striking force to be used in enemy territory. He sent Lieutenant Kern on a tour of inspection from Depuy's Fort on the Delaware to Fort Hunter on the Susquehanna. With few exceptions Kern found the men "in Good order," though the equipment was spotty. Colonel Burd himself inspected the garrison at Fort Henry, now under Captain Sammy's command.

"Had a review this morning at 9 A. M.," he writes, February 22; "found ninety soldiers under good command, and *fine fellows*." [13]

He marched the same day to Conrad Weiser's (presumably to "see & examine" the letters and orders relating to the battalion) [14] and spent the night there. There was no hard feeling.

Later in the year Thomas Penn sent a letter to Conrad by the *Earl of Leicester* Packet in which he expressed concern that Weiser's bad health had caused him to resign his command; added that, after all, a man so useful in Indian affairs should not be exposed to other dangers; expatiated on the desirability of Weiser's continuing his assistance in the important matter of clearing the Proprietaries' good name from the imputation of unjust dealing with the Indians; and subscribed himself "Your very affectionate Friend." [15]

Part V

THE CHAIN HOLDS

CHAPTER 58

... *Comes to the Aid of* *General Forbes*

I

THOUGH relieved of his military command, Weiser was under no temptation to slip back into the twilight and take his ease. There was still the church, the law, Indian affairs, and the thousand and one odds and ends of public life that beset a man who has once been a leader in his community.

From the 14th to the 17th of February, we find him in Reading presiding at the Court of Common Pleas. On March 6 he presided at the Orphans Court. March 15 he sent, with his endorsement, a petition to the Governor from citizens of Bern Township and adjacent parts for soldiers (the garrison at Northkill having been disbanded) to protect their homes.[1] There was reason, they thought, to expect an Indian attack, and they were right. On April 5, four men in neighboring Bethel Township were killed and scalped [2]—four days after Saur's newspaper had reported that Teedyuscung had given a great leap for joy on hearing that Shingas the Terrible was coming in from the Ohio to make peace.

Saturday, March 11, Teedyuscung passed through Germantown to Philadelphia with four chiefs from distant nations, ambassadors for peace —all nice, quiet men, said Saur's newspaper, who would not touch strong drink since they believed it disturbed their intellects.[3] They had traveled on snowshoes, and it had taken them no less than forty-seven days to reach Bethlehem. They had brought strings of wampum with them and a peace pipe, beautifully designed, which they hoped to smoke with the Governor. They had hoped also to seize and hold fast the peace belt by which Teedyuscung and his allies had been bound at Easton. This sounded well. Was Teedyuscung proving really to be an apostle of peace?

On Monday the Governor sent a string of wampum to wipe "the snow out of their Eyes and Ears." Teedyuscung wiped the Governor's eyes and ears with another string, and sent word that he would call on Brother Onas and bring his clerk with him. The Governor sent back word that Teedyuscung was welcome but not the clerk. Teedyuscung replied that he was tired of waiting, was at dinner, and would bring his clerk with him or not come at all.[4]

On Tuesday Teedyuscung met the Governor in council. "Brother," he said, "I come here. this is our house. . . . I have very weighty matters to speak. . . . About the Clerk when I speak to you I shall bring my Clerk wth me." [5]

With deputies at hand from the Ohio and beyond, it was evident that weighty matters indeed were in the air. It was no less evident that more

skilful hands than Denny's and Peters' were needed to handle them successfully. Conrad Weiser was sent for.

"Teedyuscung is in Town," wrote Peters the same day, "with some
Deputies of his Nation from Diahogo who bring good news, (as it is said
for they had not yet delivered their Speeches) that our Peace Belts are
accepted by several Indian Nations and particularly by some of the Ohio
Indians. . . . Pray hasten." [6]

Before Weiser reached Philadelphia, Teedyuscung (who would "do
nothing but in the most popular and publick Manner") [7] had explained in
public conference that since the last Easton Conference he had given "the
Halloo" to "all the Indians Nations in this Part of the World," and that
the said nations had sent a pipe, two or three whiffs from which would
dispel any dark clouds that might have arisen; that all the Indian nations
from sunrise to sunset had sent a belt, the two ends of which they themselves held, in hopes that the English would take hold in the middle. There
were in all eighteen nations, including Teedyuscung's original ten. Among
the new ones were the Twightwees of the Far West and the Nalashawana
who lived north of New England. Teedyuscung presented a belt of ten
rows, with the figures of two men in the center taking each other by the
hand: this to represent Teedyuscung and the Governor of Pennsylvania.

With a second belt, of twelve rows, he blinded the eyes of the French,
that they might not see the Indians who lived behind them passing by to
make friends with the English. With a belt of eight rows he begged God
to bless their endeavors. With a belt of seven rows he desired the Governor
to push on in the good road of peace. [8]

The Governor smoked a peace pipe with Teedyuscung (*He Who Makes
the Earth Tremble*) on the very day an earthquake was felt in Philadelphia. [9] On the same day Governor Denny made his reply to Teedyuscung's
belts—before Conrad Weiser arrived and without benefit of his advice.
The Governor agreed with Teedyuscung and tried to imitate his rhetoric.
He embraced Teedyuscung's eighteen Indians nations (the King was fast
becoming the Father of All) and accepted them as allies of the English.
With a belt, he also blinded the eyes of the French and stopped up their
ears. With another belt he praised Teedyuscung's ability. With still another he signified that, though contrary winds should throw hail, snow, and
rain in his face, it would not stop him in his labors for peace.

This was all very beautiful. But one thing had been overlooked. Neither
party had blinded the eyes of the Six Nations, who were a jealous people
and did not recognize the right of their nephews, the Delawares, to deal
in matters of peace and war with any nations whatsoever between the sun-
rise and the sunset.

Weiser was on hand to take part in the conference held on Saturday,
March 25. He was in time to hear Teedyuscung recommend rewards for
his interpreter (Isaac Still) and ten messengers. He heard the King propose
that the Governor pay the debts that he (the King) had been obliged
to run up at two or three taverns in town through the necessity he had
been under of treating his followers.

The speech the Governor made in reply that day was in a different tone from anything that had preceded it. It bears the mark of Conrad Weiser's mind. Without the bombast and grotesquerie of Teedyuscung, it yet followed the vein of Indian metaphor; but its metaphors were such as Conrad Weiser had learned from the Six Nations at Onondaga, and it avoided the political pitfalls the Governor had been tumbling about in.

"We Remember very well," said the Governor to Teedyuscung, adopting the tried Indian rhetoric that expresses tones of thought without making commitments,

how kindly you received our Forefathers when they first arrived in this Country, You secured their Ship to the Bushes and kindled up a fire for them, You entertained them with the Best you had and you must remember the Mutual Friendship that subsisted between us since that time and hope those black Clouds that came from the North will be now intirely Dispelled, as the greatest part of them already are . . .

You may remember, that at first when the Clouds were beginning to be dispelled, a little foot Path was opened by Fort Allen to Wioming for our Messengers to pass thro' with Messages; but as now the Clouds are intirely dispelled between us, and the Indians on Susqueannah, I think it necessary to Open a great Road, that is, from Diahogo and the Heads of the Susqueannah down to Fort Augusta, called by the Indians Shamokin, where you will always find a Kind reception, Entertainment, and Protection in your Road to Philadelphia.[10]

The Governor ended with a statement that the transactions of this conference would be laid at once before His Majesty's Commander-in-Chief in America and also before Sir William Johnson, who no doubt would find them agreeable. This was intended to forestall criticism from Abercromby (who had succeeded Loudoun) and Johnson. It may also have been intended to prevent the Six Nations, who would certainly be informed of these proceedings by Johnson, from thinking that Brother Onas was playing tricks behind their backs, i.e., dealing secretly with an independent Delaware nation.

To Colonel Washington Governor Denny wrote a letter the same day informing him of the peace Pennsylvania had just concluded with the Indians on the Ohio, and requesting him to restrain the Cherokees who, it was known, were "come down to go to War" in that region.[11] The Cherokees, who were of Iroquoian stock, were believed to find their chief satisfaction in a war against the French in the fact that it gave them an opportunity of striking at their ancient enemies the Shawnees and the Delawares. Weiser's influence seems apparent in that letter, though the request to write it had come from Teedyuscung.

"I have reason to believe," it ran, "that the Cherokees hate the Delawares and Shawanese and do not desire they should become our Friends but would have them all destroyed, having Long born them great Enmity, so that it is a nice point how to Communicate this News to them without giving them disgust . . ."[12]

It was a nice point indeed. Two months later a party of Cherokee warriors presented themselves in Philadelphia, assuring their brethren that, having received "a Message from the King of Great Britain, to come to War against the French," they were on their road against the enemy to knock his brains out, and had already been so successful as to kill two Shawnees.[13]

It should be mentioned that one prime result of this conference in March was the sending of Frederick Post, a Moravian, with peace belts to the Ohio—an expedition carried through with the utmost skill and in face of the greatest dangers. We shall hear of it later.

II

Weiser had not long been home from the conference when he received another urgent summons to Philadelphia, this time to confer with General Forbes, who was preparing a second expedition against Fort Duquesne.

Richard Peters to Conrad Weiser [14]

Friday past 1.0 Clock
28 Apr. 1758

Dear Sir

The Governor and Brigadier General Forbes will want your Advice and Services in Indian Affairs, and send this Express jointly to desire you will come immediately to confer with them. You will be so good as to pardon me for giving you so short notice, But several Dispatches just come to hand must stop till your Arrival here, and matters of the greatest Moment are under Consideration hasten therefore as as fast as you can to assist in the Consultations and bring with you a mind disposed to concur in, and personally execute, Such measures as shall be agreed upon. I am writing by order of the Governor & General who greet you with their best wishes. I am

Dr Sir
Your most
humble Servt
RICHARD PETERS

When Weiser came to the city, he found General Forbes worried about the Cherokees, and Teedyuscung more than worried. There were seventy or eighty Cherokees reported to be in the vicinity of Carlisle, much dissatisfied. Sir William Johnson was bungling. What could Conrad Weiser do about it?

Brigadier General Forbes to General Abercromby [15]

[Philadelphia, May 4, 1758]

Sir

. . . There having already a Capt (Called the Raven) and 30 men gone away home disgusted, for want of the necessary Supplies promised them, and I wish I may be able to prevent this discontent from Spreading, for which purpose I think of sending old Conrad Weiser with all that I can pick up of Indian things, up amongst them, to make a parsimonious distribution among them from time to time.

. . . I am this moment informed that there are 6 or 8 Cherokees arrived here and that they are to be followed by 60 or 70 this afternoon. Poor Tediuscung is in a terrible pannick nor do I well know what to do with him, or how to dispose of them. . . .

Y^r most ob^t & most hum^le Servt
Jo Fforbes

Forbes was depending on Weiser's advice, and was rather irritably insistent on getting it. The General was sickening to his death. Peters wrote some weeks later (May 22), Weiser in the meantime having gone home, to say that "The General takes it amiss that you do not come to Town. He has as I hear told several people that he depends on Your advice. . . . I think it woud be for your Interest and the publick good if you coud come and confer a little with the General." [16]

May 5 Weiser attended the Governor's Council. It was decided, with General Forbes's approval, that Teedyuscung's request for the building of houses for the Indians at Wyoming should be granted.[17] The chief was called in and so informed. Teedyuscung thanked the Governor, assured him he would press on with the work of peace, would not listen to bad news—and would the Governor grant him a favor since he had never asked him for one before? James Perry, "a hearty, stout Man," whom Teedyuscung said he did not know personally but with whose military bearing he had been impressed, he desired should be made a captain in the army.

The Governor expressed his regret that the request had not come sooner, since all the captains' commissions were now filled; but said he would give the man a lieutenant's commission if Teedyuscung would raise some good troops for him to command.

Teedyuscung returned thanks.

A rumor was circulated at this time that the Indian Will Sock and a Cayuga friend had been tampering with the Conestoga Indians near Lancaster. Weiser was asked to stay in town and investigate. He interviewed the two Indians, William Sock (a son of Betty Sock) and Jorachquison, in the presence of his old friends Jagrea and Seneca George. There was apparently nothing in the Conestoga story. The Indians known to be leaving there were merely going up the river on a hunting trip.[18]

But Weiser learned from Will Sock, who had recently come down from the Seneca country, some other news of such importance that he put it down in writing. It was presented to the Governor in Council by Jagrea, Will Sock, and the Cayuga, on Monday, May 8; the absence of Conrad Weiser himself being explained by them as due to his "haste to return home." He had to preside at the Orphans Court in Reading on Wednesday.

It appeared from Weiser's statement that the sachems of the Six United Nations had recently held a great council in the Seneca country, at which they had decided to send messengers to all the Indians on the Ohio, the St. Lawrence, and the Susquehanna, desiring them to desist from using the hatchet against either the French or the English. All the Indians were to be neutral for a time. Meanwhile the Six Nations were to send a large delegation to Pennsylvania to discuss matters of great consequence with Brother Onas.[19]

From other sources it became known that the Six Nations were debating their final course in the conflict between France and England in America. Three courses were open to them: to preserve their neutrality; to join the French against the English; to join the English against the French. While these great matters were under consideration by the Six Nations, Indian affairs were "in suspense," as William Johnson put it.

The suspense was not to be lifted until the conclusion of the conference at Easton in October 1758. Meanwhile, Weiser's interview with Bill Sock had given clear warning that a showdown was coming between the Six Nations and the English over Teedyuscung and the Delaware pretensions.

III

The news of General Forbes's expedition against Fort Duquesne put new spirit into Pennsylvania's army.

" 'Tis odd," wrote Captain Lloyd to Major Joseph Shippen, "but certainly true, that the company at Fort Henry, who before used to sing psalms fervently every day, have, ever since the news of the expedition, sang nothing but songs of mirth, and seem to have certainly forgot their psalms." [20] Acres of rich lands on the Ohio were being promised to the soldiers. One fellow at Fort Henry, so said the Captain, swore he would desert, if left behind in garrison, and follow the regiment to the west.

This kind of campaigning was alien to Conrad Weiser's spirit. But the staff work required for it was still in his vein. Forbes used his advice about the Indians; Colonel Bouquet depended on him for procurement of wagons. Weiser organized the wagon service from Berks County: contracted for the wagons, horses, and drivers; named appraisers; appointed wagon masters.

Colonel Bouquet to Conrad Weiser [21]

Carlisle 5th June 1758

To Conrad Weiser Esqr
Sir

Besides the 60 Waggons that I have required from your County for the Transport of Provisions to [the] Frontier, and which I expect will be sent immediately to the appointed Places, more will be wanted for the Expedition. Therefore I must beg the favour of you to use your Influence to fill up as many of the Printed Contracts as you Can: & to appoint a Day and Place to receive them.

I do empower you hereby to name and appoint Appraisers to Value the Waggons & Horses in Behalf of the Crown, jointly with those appointed by the Magistrates in behalf of the Owners.

If some money in Advance is wanted to enable any Poor farmer to fit out his Waggons, you will draw upon Mr Adam Hoops for the necessary Sum And he shall inform you of the time the said Contracted Waggons shall be wanted.

I inclose you an advertisement, which you may alter as you think necessary

There must be a Waggon Master appointed to every 30 Waggons of your County—

Mr Hoops informed me of a very fit Man whose name I have forgot, who was recommended by you. I beg you will appoint him one of the Waggon Masters, and if the five Shillings per Day don't appear to him sufficient, I will add something to it (for him alone)

I am Sorry, my Dear Colonel to give you all this trouble, but I know that you will do Chearfully anything to forward his Majesty's Service
I am   &ca

Conrad Weiser to Colonel Bouquet [22]

Most Noble Colonel

Your favours of the 30 of May and 5th of June with the advertisement to the Inhabitants in the County of Bercks are Come to hand, I am Sorry that I was not at home. the Governor haveing Called me to Philadelphia, on Indian Affairs, where also Mr Read was, I was dispatched Imediatly and Comeing to Reading employed a Clerk to make me out Several Copies of the advertism^t and as the time was but Short, I ordered that the Inhab^ts should met me in Reading to Contract for Waggons according to Your direction. Where I have ben Buisy with, this 3 or 4 days (I arrived but last Sunday) and about 23 have Contracted with me—We have a Set of people here that will not only do Nothing, in this affair, but by their Exemple and Ill will, puts Mischief into others. Whereof the Waggon Master John lesher will Inform you Particularly, I have appointed him a Waggon Master according to your Order, and your Honour will find he will Answer the end—he is a noted freeholder here, and he can be but a looser upon the whole by his leaveing his plantation, Mills Iron Work &ca. but his Majesties Servies he has at heart, and therefore will go.

. . . this day is the last day that I wait for people to Come in to Contract. haveing applied for a press warrant to his Honour the Governor before I left philadelphia, which is Come up now, I shall send the Constable to press Waggons & Horses, Sufficient (and according to your Order).

I am much concerned for the backwardness of some our Religious people (as they pretent to be) and hope their Ill behaviour will not be Imputed to the whole County, and indeed not to all of that set, for some of them have done their Share towards this present Service, Some people in the poor town of Reading rose ten pound by Subscription to give to a Waggoner of their town to go for their share. I have nothing further to trouble your Honour with at present but promise to do my Endeavour to get the rest of the Waggons with all possible Speed. I wish you health and happiness and pray sincerly that the most high may prosper your undertaking and Bless his majestys armes.—

I am

Most noble Colonel
Your very obedient and
humble Servant
CONRAD WEISER

Reading June the 14 1758
Excuse my Scralls I have no
Clerk at present to make out fair Copies

PS. dear Sir. I Can not help recomending my dear Son Samy to your paternal Care: I dont mean to Spare him let him do his duty and behave as a Couragies Soldier on all occasions, but he may want Conduct and good advise from a Gentleman of your Experience: Mr Read is not returned as yet from philadelphia,

Weiser kept his head through all the suspicions, delays, complaints, and quarrels that beset the organizing of such a service. Farmers were indifferent and kept their best horses at home. The wagoners were jealous of the wagon masters.

The General was uneasy, finding everything ready for his expedition in June except the wagons for transport and supply.

"Coll¹ Weiser," wrote Adam Hoops, "is the only magistrate who has Shewn a publick Spirit & Zeal for his Majestys Service . . ." [23]

At length the wagon train was in motion. Wagons were assembled from all over the province in the meadows at Carlisle. From Carlisle they went to Fort Loudoun and back; others went from Fort Loudoun to Fort Lyttleton and back; and still others went to Raystown, and so on. ". . . the Pennsylvania phalanx," as the exuberant Captain Lloyd put it, was about to "thunder with irresistable fury at the gates of Fort Duquesne." [24]

General Forbes and the last of Colonel Montgomery's Highlanders left Philadelphia on June 30. The country was anxious and expectant. For the benefit of the Council (to whom Conrad Weiser had complained of the disloyalty of Christopher Saur's editorial utterances) Peter Miller of Ephrata translated an article from Saur's newspaper praising the General and expressing the hope that soon "we shall be able to mention some thing about him Hero like."

No pain of body could break Forbes's spirit, but he suffered as much mental agony at Carlisle as a man could suffer who had the example of Braddock to dispirit him. At Carlisle Forbes found everything in confusion. He put the camp in some order, but the wilderness about him refused to be mastered. Forbes knew what Teedyuscung reported from the Ohio, but did Teedyuscung know what he was talking about? There were conflicting reports about the Indians. There was no sure knowledge of the size of the French forces. The defeat of Abercromby by Montcalm at Ticonderoga had, it was supposed, released fresh French troops for the defense of Fort Duquesne. It was of the last importance to learn what the French were doing in the Ohio Valley. Forbes had sent out no fewer than five hundred provincials and Indians in scouting parties; but still he could get no reliable intelligence of the French at Fort Machault and Fort Duquesne.

As usual in times of crisis, Pennsylvania turned to Conrad Weiser. Late in July General Forbes sent to Richard Peters a letter of credit for four hundred pounds to be used as a fund for procuring the best intelligence possible "of the Affairs upon the Ohio with regard to me. So lose no time," he said, "in making use of some of it either by your own or Co¹ Weisers means to get me the perfectest knowledge of what is doing in those parts that is possible." [25]

Richard Peters to Conrad Weiser [26]

Philadelphia 28 July 1758

Dear Sir

On this unfortunate Retreat of General Abercromby and the Slaughter of his best Officers there is ye greatest reason in the world to believe the French will draw off some of their Indians & Canadians for the Relief of the Ohio: in which case the Burthen of the War will fall on General Forbes Now how to come at the Knowledge of the French Force at Fort Duquesne & Wenango is the difficulty . . .

Now Sir as the Preservation of this Country does in my Opinion absolutley depend on the Conquest of the Ohio this year the Indians changing fast for us in those Quarters as you will perceive by the enclosed from Major Orndt, and as the State of Affairs shoud & must be known to give our little Army its full weight, I can see no other way than for you to proceed to Fort Augusta and myselfe to go instantly to Bethlehem If you cant go yourselfe send Captn Busse from Fort Allen cross the Country with an Escort. Heaven & Earth shoud be raised on this Occasion. From Fort Augusta Captn Busse in case you cannot go shoud proceed to Wyomink and try to get a Trusty Indian there. Tho the Indians I shall employ at Bethlehem will go by the way of Wyomink and therefore this place may be left to me.

I have sent Lawrence Burke to Niagara as thro that Pass the French & Indians must pass and their Numbers will be best known.

Frederick Post has repeated directions to send off from the Ohio as soon as he comes there two or three Delawares to the General their Signal is this, they are to fasten their Match Coat to a long Pole & holding it up waive it to & fro. Of this be sure take notice. Over & above this they may be furnish'd with a yellow Stripe of Shalloon to lop about their head & Arm & an English Flag may like wise be used. but the Match Coat is the best as they only make use of it in their approaches to the English Fronteer or Army & the Enemy cannot find any thing about them shoud the Messengers be searched. I send you two flaggs & Six Stripes of yellow Shalloon. The greatest care will be required on the part of the Indians when they approach the Army—Scouting Parties are thick up & down in the Woods & they may run Risques. I wish you coud think of some way of these Spies coming to the General with Safety; for my own part I find difficultys & danger will attend this access to the Generals Camp. Where it can be done without much loss of Time these Indian Messengers shoud come to Fort Augusta or Fort Allen or Fort Henry & be escorted to the General but where this cannot be conveniently done, then how to get safe into ye Camp without being fired on by the scouting Parties y^t will be all around the Camp is the difficulty. Pray think of it and give the proper Instructions.

I send you Thirty Pounds of which you be as careful as if it was for ye Subsistence of your Wife & Family. When that is gone send your Accounts & you shall have more. Perhaps it is too little, if so I will send more.

Prepare as soon as your Court is over or before if you can to go to the Mohock Castles. Not a moment is to be lost. This will be insisted upon. . . .

I need not press Secrecy. Let no man know any thing of this. Tell the Indians to say nothing but wherever they come in to apply to ye Commanding Officer for an Escort to ye General.

I understand that Humbus an Indian at Shamokin has not been rewarded for a Scalp he brought in. He may perhaps be the best you can get to go, and if so this uneasiness about the Scalp shoud be removed. and the matter settled to his Satisfaction. . . .

Conrad Weiser to Richard Peters [27]

Reading, July the 29th, 1758
at 5 in the Afternoon.

Sir,

I can but acknowledge the receipt of yours by Mr. Benjn Davis' Express. I shall do all what lies in my power in the mentioned Service. I Intend to set out for Carlisle pleas God, to-morrow in the after noon, or towards the Evening, to wait on General Forbes. I can say no more at present, but on my return, which I hope will be about the time of Reading Court, I will give you all the Intelligence I can.

I am, Sir
your very obedient,
CONRAD WEISER

Weiser made a flying trip to General Forbes at Carlisle, returning in time to preside at the Court of Common Pleas in Reading, August 8. On the journey he had his son Benjamin with him. They went by way of Harris' Ferry, whence Weiser sent an "express" to Fort Augusta.

Just what arrangements he made with the Indians cannot be said with certainty; but it would appear that he got in touch with the Indian Humbus (or Hambies), a warrior then at Fort Augusta. "Captain Hambies" was quick with the tomahawk, a trifle irascible, but useful in an emergency. He had recently killed another Indian, one James Cotas, "in the Dead time of the night," over a quarrel originating in "some difference as hunters." [28]

Weiser had better success in his message to Humbus at Fort Augusta than Peters had with his messengers, Zacheus and Jonathan (a Mohican), sent from Bethlehem to Teedyuscung. Humbus with three Delawares went out to the army in the west, and scouted as far as the French fort at Venango (Fort Machault).[29] Zacheus and Jonathan, returning to Philadelphia on August 9, delivered to the Governor Teedyuscung's reply to his request to send them on with another Indian to the Allegheny. ". . . this is my Answer," said He Who Makes the Earth Tremble: "I do not suffer them to proceed—as it is a dangerous Undertaking." [30]

Even Humbus did not have General Forbes's entire confidence. From Shippensburg on August 28 Forbes wrote to Richard Peters, "Hambies & Teedyuscung's son goes down to Easttown to persuade their friends to come and join me, I wish they may be sincere so pray let them be watched narrowly." [31]

Poor General Forbes. The journey to Shippensburg, to which place he was carried in a litter slung between two horses, had prostrated him. He lay in agony for weeks, while his forces crawled on over muddy roads, not by Braddock's roundabout route but straight over the mountain ridges of Pennsylvania. At last, on November 18, the General was carried at the head of the Highlanders, Royal Americans, and provincials (led by Montgomery, Bouquet, and Washington) into an empty Fort Duquesne.

The enemy, deserted by their Indian allies, had blown up the fortifications, burned the storehouses and barracks. Their commander, with part of his forces, had retired to Fort Machault; another part had gone down the Ohio; some had gone overland toward Presq'isle.

The Ohio Valley was English. The way to the West was open.

CHAPTER 59

... *Sizes up Tagashata*

I

THE Easton Conference in 1758 was the climax of Weiser's activities as an Indian ambassador. The peace there achieved was a monument to his career. It was also a vindication of the Indian policy associated with his name.

But this last triumph was shaped out of such a strange and bewildering tangle of forest statecraft and swamp politics that the quality of the achievement cannot be conveyed in a mere summary. To understand it, we must finger the many strands that went into the making of the pattern.

On July 6, 1758, Governor Denny heard that Teedyuscung, with fifty Indians, had reached Germantown on his way to the city. Some of the Indians were from the Ohio. One of these was Pisquetomen, a brother of Shingas the Terrible. It was of the utmost importance to extend them all courtesies. Accordingly Conrad Weiser, accompanied by two members of the Governor's Council—Richard Peters and William Logan—was sent to meet them, offer the Governor's greeting, and bring them in to town.

Early in the evening they reached Philadelphia, where Weiser expected the Governor himself to be waiting to receive them, as Indian etiquette, and the etiquette of all civilized countries, demanded. But Denny was a man of moods and indisposed to walk in the cool of the evening with savages.

When Weiser learned of the Governor's reluctance, he took his pen and flung a lifetime of independence into a letter of remonstrance in which already one can hear the peal of the Liberty Bell.

Conrad Weiser to Richard Peters [1]

Mr Peters

Sir If the Governor wont meet the Indians this Even ing only to Shake hands with them, and Signify his Satisfaction to See them in town, and leave Buis ness to other day, when they are recovered from their fatigue, I will Say that he does not act the part of a Well wisher to his Majestys people, & Interest, at this Critical times,—you may let him Know So. here is my hand to my Say ing So—I am Sir a loyal Subject and a Will Wisher to my Countrey

CONRAD WEISER

Philadelphia July
the 6. at half
an hour after five

The conference that began the next day was not one to catch the public ear. Its importance lay in the overtones. Teedyuscung had given the halloo across the Allegheny Mountains to the Indians of the sunset. They had, however, heard him but little. "The Reason is," he reported them as saying, "you have not spoak loud enough." [2] Now he proposed to put both hands to his mouth and give a whoop that all nations must hear.

It had long been suspected that Teedyuscung was "a man of Straw, set up by the Quakers." It was certain that he was not the person of consequence, with eighteen nations at his beck, he gave himself out to be. But he was not altogether clown. There were elements of danger in his braggadocio that spoiled the comedy. He had bluffed his way into the hearts of the Friendly Association, and they honestly believed him to be a great and good man whose struggle to obtain freedom from the Six Nations and justice from the Proprietors deserved the support of all right-thinking men.

Disturbing evidence had been accumulating that the Six Nations were resentful of his pretensions and of Pennsylvania's submission to them. "He speaks of himself in a Stile of Consequence," wrote Johnson, "which I am fully convinced belongs to no single Indian upon the Continent . . . it will not in my humble Opinion, be advisable to give Tediuscung this exclusive Distinction in publick Treaties & Negotiations, as it will tend to give umbrage to the other Indians. . . ." [3]

The resentment of the Six Nations was hastening to a climax. Eyendeegen, a Seneca, appeared in Philadelphia early in August to announce that the Six Nations were coming to speak to Brother Onas. Seven or eight from his town had been at the last Easton conference, "but they had little to say then, because our Cousin Teedyuscung was busy, and we had not time to say any thing. We only came to hear him, Now when we come we will speak for ourselves fully." [4]

Teedyuscung himself had told the Governor the Six Nations were coming. "I am not going to tell you any great matter," he said casually to the Governor at the end of the July conference, "but I would let you know, that there are four Messengers sent to invite the Senecas and other Indians to a Conference; when they come, I will let you know, and then I will meet you at Easton, where our Council Fire still burns; I reckon they will come very soon." [5]

Denny, feeling a certain tingling in the region of the scalp, said that Philadelphia would be a better place to meet them.

"You are right," said Teedyuscung, letting him down gently; "but it will shew a bad example to our Children, to have one fire here, and another there. I must keep to my Council Fire." [6]

And he did.

II

To no single person and to no single nation can be given the honor of calling the Easton peace conference of 1758. Teedyuscung, backed by the Pennsylvania Assembly, Governor Denny, and General Forbes, had proposed a conference early in the year to bring the western Indians into alliance with the English. At the same time the Six Nations, incensed at Teedyuscung's pretensions, and "Afeared," as Croghan put it in a letter to Johnson of April 14, "that ye Delaways and Shannas wants to Settle a firm pace with ye English Independent of them . . . ,"[7] proposed to come to Pennsylvania and attend to the peace negotiations themselves. Johnson least of all deserves credit. He was for and against the treaty as the political winds blew, at one time inviting the Six Nations to send delegates and at another time forbidding them to go. In the end he gave his approval, on instructions from General Abercromby (to whom General Forbes and Governor Denny had both appealed). Johnson declined to attend himself, though Forbes and Denny thought his place at this crucial time was by the Easton council fire. Instead, he sent George Croghan as his deputy, with Andrew Montour as an interpreter.

September 13, Weiser was directed (from Philadelphia) to prepare for the conference. He was to go to Easton and there, as the Indians assembled, he was to make himself acquainted "wth every Indian of consequence" and learn the conditions on which they were willing to terminate differences, not only with Pennsylvania, but with the other colonies as well.[8] To help him extend civilities, five thousand white and five thousand black pieces of wampum were sent him.

During the conference, by instructions from Philadelphia, all money paid to the Indians was to pass through his hands. According to his accounts, disbursements began on September 18,[9] which we may therefore take to be the day on which he took over his duties.

All but a fragment of Weiser's journal at this conference has been lost; but we have, in addition to the full minutes preserved in the Council records, a set of Weiser's accounts, letters of Quakers attending the meetings, and the racy diaries of Attorney-General Benjamin Chew and Secretary Peters.

The student of these manuscript pages may think he finds himself in a world of strange values, betokened by belts of wampum, hatchets, scalps, and peace pipes. But if his patience permits him to look beneath the symbols of Indian speech and to study the men who took part at Easton and the issues over which they struggled, he will find the same tangle of forces as those that continue to drive our modern world: ambition, idealism, fear; the defense of systems of government and ways of life; the making and breaking of empires.

The actual management of the treaty was not, except during one crucial incident, in Weiser's hands. It was in the hands of Tagashata, George Croghan, Richard Peters, Israel Pemberton, Teedyuscung, and Governor Denny. Weiser's part was to save it from its managers.

The private records of the conference tell a confused story of conflicting interests: colonial, imperial, international. So many causes had to be taken care of: the common cause of all the English colonies in America; the personal interest of the Proprietors of Pennsylvania; the people's cause, which Israel Pemberton seemed (to Richard Peters and others) to think was invested in his own person; the rights of the Six Nations, represented by two mutually distrustful factions, that of the Senecas led by Tagashata and that of the Mohawks led by Nickas; Teedyuscung's cause, which meant

independence for the Delawares and importance for himself; and the cause
of Governor Denny's comfort and dignity.

In a way it was Richard Peters' treaty, and he never did a better piece
of work. He was the clearing house. Reports from all sides found their way
to him, and he issued the necessary orders. But Peters could have done little
by himself. Behind the scenes there was always Conrad Weiser, gathering
intelligence, giving presents, and at crucial moments offering advice which
neither Indian chief nor colonial governor found it safe to reject.

The conference was long and the proceedings involved. As the inter-
minable Indian preliminaries dragged on, settling questions of precedence
and jurisdiction among the tribes and between the Indians and Brother
Onas; and as the schemes of Quakers, Proprietors, Conoys, Nanticokes,
Six Nations, and Delawares grew toward a head, the patience of Governor
Denny snapped. So did Teedyuscung's, Israel Pemberton's, Richard Peters',
Nickas', and Tagashata's. Explosion after explosion rent the air and set
the town by the ears. Israel Pemberton called William Logan a liar. Benjamin Chew had a mind to hit Israel "a Slap in the Chops." [10] Teedyuscung
told the Cayugas to wear his petticoat.

Through it all Conrad Weiser controlled himself and played his game
with a cool head. There were enormous stakes involved: nothing less than
the control of a continent. Weiser's object was to cement English friendship both with the Six Nations and with the Delawares. He had to bring
about a peace that should embrace not only the Susquehanna Indians but
those on the Ohio as well, and to draw these latter away from the French.
(It must be remembered that Forbes was not yet in Fort Duquesne.) Besides, the peace with the Delawares had to be concluded in such a manner
as to leave undisturbed Six Nations' claims to sovereignty over their
nephews.

Teedyuscung was the crux of the problem. The Six Nations, accustomed
in their own Confederation to exercise the lightest kind of sovereignty,
were disposed to keep only the shadow of jurisdiction over the Delawares,
to allow them independence *de facto* if not *de jure*. But Teedyuscung made
such a compromise impossible. Day after day, whether drunk or sober, he
insulted his Uncles, called them fools, told them that they could do nothing
without him, that he was King and what he did not do should not stand.
With such a man there had to be a showdown. On the outcome of that
showdown hung the issue of peace or war on the Susquehanna, on the
Ohio, on the Mohawk, even in a measure on the Saint Lawrence.

The handling of that crisis when it came was, at the wish of the Six
Nations and with the consent of Governor Denny, left to the management
of Conrad Weiser.

III

Weiser was at Easton from September 18 to October 28 (this is the time
covered in his "Memorand of the Mony by me paid away to the Indians
in Easton").[11] For three weeks the Indians straggled in, in small groups and

large. Delawares and Shawnees came from the Ohio; Conoys, Nanticokes,
Tuteloes, and more Delawares from the Susquehanna; Mohicans, Pump-
tons (or River Indians), and still more Delawares from the Delaware River
and parts adjacent in New Jersey. From the Niagara region there came
great numbers of Senecas, Keepers of the West Door of the Long House;
from the Albany region came Mohawks, Keepers of the East Door; and
from the Six Nations territory in between (the middle fires of the Long
House) came Cayugas, Onondagas, Oneidas, and Tuscaroras: in all, 501,
according the Quaker count. Conrad Weiser counted 390, not including
Delawares.

Among the Indian celebrities present [12] when the conference was finally
assembled, we find:

Nickas Karaghiaghlalie, a Mohawk chief;

Tagashata, a Seneca chief;

Thomas King, alias Sagughsuniunt, an Oneida chief;

Last Night, a Conoy chief;

Abraham, a Mohican chief;

French Margaret with her husband, Peter Quebec.

Nickas brought with him only a small Mohawk delegation: "one women
& two Boys" (his wife and two sons). Tagashata's Seneca delegation of
eighty-three persons was made up as follows: eight council chiefs, including Kayenquaraghton, a war captain with thirty-six warriors; twenty-eight
women; and ten children. The size of this delegation showed the supreme
interest the Senecas took in the Ohio country, the fate of which was to
be decided at this conference, and the determining weight of their nation
among those of the Confederacy in deciding the current issue of peace or
war.

The next largest delegation was that of the tiny Nanticoke nation, which
mustered in to the number of fifty-seven. Their supreme interest was in
presents.

Some came for business and some for a jamboree. The rum business
boomed. Teedyuscung led off with a carnival of almost continuous drunk-
enness. During the early days of the conference his intervals of sobriety
were just long enough to let him repeat in cold blood the insults he had
hurled at the Six Nations under the venial warmth of drink. Israel Pemberton's followers, who had come determined to make a great man of
Teedyuscung, preened him to such heights of vainglory that he grew
completely reckless and crowed insults from his rum barrel sufficient to
make Tagashata's scalp lock stand on end. He had formerly boasted himself king of eighteen nations. He now added one more to the number and
called himself King of the Quakers.

When Weiser, some time afterwards, read in Thomson's *Enquiry* that
Frederick Post had delivered to King Beaver (brother of Pisquetomen and
of Shingas the Terrible) a message "from your Children the *Friends*,"
indignant comment spurted from his pen:

from your Children the Friends   O fye, O, fye! The Quakers submit to the
Barbarians, to the Murderers and Heathens; Submit to their Chastisement,

why so? If Teedjouskon or the Delawares are our Rulers, Israel will be the sole Monarch, for then we will be governed by the Indians, the Indians by Israel Pemperton. & Israel Pemperton by the D——l

This is no wild Humour. In one of the Treaties at Easton, it will be found that Teedjouskon (Israels King) by a Belt of Wampum offered to reign over us, and demanded Submission, offered us a Petticoat and a Pipe with good Tobacco, the same as his Ancestors received from the, then, five Nations. A Certain Officer [Lt. Col. Weiser?] took the Belt in Anger from the Table, & would not suffer and Answer to be made, to such an Imputant and Extravagant Demand; Judging it was to the Dishonour of his Sovereign, & a Disgrace to Pennsylvania and he told him, that if he insisted upon an Answer to that Belt: The Point of the Sword should decide it, upon the first mention thereof.[13]

At Easton the drinking grew ever wilder. Vernon, the innkeeper, complained that the Indians had broken into his cellar and stolen rum and wine. Not only Teedyuscung, but other chiefs as well, were perpetually drunk and incapable of business. When the Governor tried to put a stop to the orgy, normal restraints having proved unavailing, by having sentries set over the rum barrels, Israel Pemberton's party uttered a howl against infringement upon the liberties of the people.

To see events in their order and watch the growing tension, we must return to the early days of the conference before the Governor's arrival.

Under date of September 24, the single fragment preserved from Weiser's Easton journal gives us a glimpse, as though through a door crack, of the scene in Vernon's tavern: "I arrived at Vernon's with some of the Head Men of the Several tribes then in Easton. Thomas King had three Waiting Men Sitting behind him upon the floor they Looked as if they were Slaves" [14]

George Croghan to Richard Peters [15]

Easton, Sept. 26th, 1758

Sir,

I have Wrote ye Governor a Long Letter which you will See, as the Indians has been allways Drunk Mr Wiser Nor My Self Could Nott Do any business with ye Indians I Suspect that Teedyuscung is kept Drunk hear on purpus to Serve Some End, Butt I hope on ye Governors perusing My Letter he will Tak Such Steps as will prevent Such Abuses on his Government, there Must in my opinion be Something Very Extroynery in Vew or Else the Comm^{rs} wold Neaver have ordred their Comeseray heer to give out So much Liquer itt Looks bad in them I think to putt Such Confidence in So Infamous a Vilian att this Time. . . .

I am S^r y^r Most Obeident Servant
GEO: CROGHAN

P.S: Youl Excuse boath Writing & peper
and geuss at My Maining fer I have
this Minnitt 20 Drunken Indians About
Me I shall be Ruin^d if ye Taps are Nott
Stopt itt Dose Nott Cost Me less than £3 a Day
on ye Indians Extraguenty.

Richard Peters came up in haste, arrived in Easton on Thursday the 28th at 12 o'clock, and proceeded at once to put things to rights.[16] Some of his efforts were schoolmasterish and ineffective. "This morn," he wrote in his diary for September 30, "I sent Sheriff to Teedyuscung to insist on his keeping Sober. He sent me word I was no Govr & he did not regard what I said . . . desired And. Montour to keep sober and come to me every morning."

But Peters' activities were not confined to admonition. He attempted, successfully, to coördinate the efforts of the many men who were engaged in the task of feeding, sheltering, amusing, placating, and advising five hundred Indians—as well as the smaller but quite as difficult group of white people who had come up from Philadelphia.

On Weiser chiefly devolved the task of attending to the Indians' comfort. He had struggled with it before Peters' arrival, greeting the delegates on their arrival, looking after their wants, and extending to them the small courtesies that always touched the hearts of these warm-hearted people. He was mindful alike of the memory of the departed and of the needs of the living. Nothing could have been better calculated to please his Indian friends than the gifts he gave, not only to the chiefs, but also to the children and the grandchildren of old friends who were now with Hiawatha. In his account "against the Honourable the proprietors of Pensilvania," we find record of presents "To Canasategos Grand Daughter" (⅞) and "To shickelimys grand Children" (15 shillings).[17]

He never forgot the young folk. They had pennies and sweets from him. In his statement of account appears an item of five pounds and four shillings "To small money to the Children & to pay Caks peaches apels during the Time before the Secretary Came.[18]

On the afternoon of September 28, Weiser, Croghan, and the Mohawks at Easton received messengers from Tioga saying that Tagashata was approaching with a company of Senecas, Cayugas, Onondagas, Munsies, Mohicans, and Shawnees, with some additional Indians from the Ohio— about ninety in all. Tagashata desired that flour should be sent to them, and that wagons be got ready at Fort Allen to bring them from that place to Easton. Peters had the flour sent, added twelve gallons of rum, engaged two Indians as an escort for the provisions, arranged for the wagons, and notified the officer commanding at Fort Allen. Next day Weiser reported that the Indians had got as far, perhaps, as Wyoming. Montour had word that "Tagashata had received several Belts from Six Nations Munsies and Mohickons desiring to remonstrate ag[t] Teedyuscung after trying all fair reproofs in private." [19]

Croghan was worried. He had expressed his fears a few days before in a letter to Sir William Johnson:

I have a bad opinion of this Treaty y[e] Indians are Much Divided and Jelious of Each other. y[e] Muncys & Mohickenders Dispise Teadyuscung as Well as y[e] Six Nations and y[e] Quaker party hear I faer will Indevour to Supert him if So y[e] Six Nations will be much Displesd with us and Indeed they are unready [already?] Jelous of itt [20]

On the afternoon of September 29 Weiser attended a meeting held by some hundred Susquehanna Indians under the conference shed. Teedyuscung turned up fresh from a dinner of "Roast Porck & Trout" with Richard Peters,[21] and went among the Indians calling them fools to treat with the white men.

"I know better," he said; "I will never make peace with them."

He went on to abuse the Six Nations.

Peters was sent for and came rather nervously, waiting till Teedyuscung had departed before he ventured to present himself under the shed. The Indians gave him a petition, enforced with appropriate Belts, asking for "Guns Paint Cloaths for ye Men and Women."

The Secretary was at a loss. He had no authority to grant such a request. He was about to decline the belts when Weiser interposed, saying that such an action would be taken as an affront. Peters accordingly accepted the wampum with as good a grace as he could.[22]

Next day a Tuscarora Indian gave Teedyuscung a beating "for affecting the Great man, and suffering ye Jersey Militia to bring him to the Ferry and give him a battery by way of Salute." Weiser was present when Teedyuscung came to Peters' lodging, accompanied by Abraham, to ask the Secretary's pardon for his ill behavior of yesterday. The King was advised to ask pardon also of his Uncles, the Six Nation; "wch he said he woud." [23]

Word reached Easton on Sunday that Tagashata and his host were at Fort Allen, and that Tagashata desired to see "Mr Weiser or Croghan or Montour." [24] Croghan objected to Weiser's going. In the end Montour, Nickas, and Captain Nelson were sent with a sufficiency of ceremonial belts "to take the Senecas by the hand." [25]

At noon on Monday, October 2, Weiser came to Peters to tell him that the Ohio Indians were coming. Frederick Post, the brave Moravian who had carried peace belts to the western Indians, after an exciting journey to the very walls of Fort Duquesne, had returned with the best of news for General Forbes. He brought with him Shingas' brother, Pisquetomen, who with others was coming to the treaty at Easton by way of Heidelberg—intending to pick up Conrad Weiser at his house and bring him along, having heard that "he had quitted the Business of Interpreter."

Daniel, Post's companion on the journey, had already arrived at Easton. He had left the Ohio only seventeen days before, and it was only twenty-four days since he had been inside Fort Duquesne. The Indians there, he reported, had had no word of peace from Pennsylvania until the arrival of Post. Teedyuscung's halloo had not reached their ears, his belts had not been forwarded. They must, thought Daniel, have been put in somebody's bosom and forgotten.[26]

Daniel reported, further, what General Forbes wanted to hear: that the French on the Ohio had not been strengthened by reinforcements from Canada. On the contrary, they were thinking of moving away from Fort Duquesne: "they had a Canoe ready," they said, "and woud go away when they pleased."

Daniel was a true apostle of Teedyuscung: he was loyal to the party that offered the best price. Having seen the weakness of the French on the Ohio, he put himself behind the English and urged them to be strong.

"The French," he said, "they were but as an handful of Corn, quite in y^r power."

He did not inform Weiser that while on the Ohio he had sold Frederick Post to the French for value received, and had failed to deliver only because of the staunchness of Pisquetomen, who carried Frederick Post in his bosom, and because the Ohio Delawares, having given Post the protection of their Fire, refused to break the laws of hospitality.

The day after Daniel's arrival, Timothy Horsfield came over from Bethlehem with a letter from Post himself cautioning everyone against Daniel, whom he thought to be "a Spy sent by the French." [27] Weiser got a faithful Indian to watch both Daniel and Teedyuscung. These two gentlemen were observed to be in council with a few other Indians all Wednesday morning. "Daniel had spread a great many Belts on a Matchcoat laid upon ye Ground wch Mr Weiser took to be private Belts sent by ye French to Teedyuscung." [28]

Weiser was busy keeping an eye on the past as well as on the future. Since the purpose of the conference was to arrange peace, and since it was necessary before the quarrel could be settled to find out what it had been about, Weiser carried his investigations into the original causes of the war. Teedyuscung had said (on occasion) that land frauds had caused the war with the Delawares, but nobody except the Quakers took Teedyuscung very seriously. Weiser had long since convinced himself that "land fraud" was little more than a convenient slogan which the French and the Quakers used to incite the Delawares against Pennsylvania's Governor and Council.

On October 5 Weiser showed Peters a paper, which Teedyuscung and others had signed the day before, "purporting that the Carolina People had crucified a Shawonese Chief," [29] and that this was the real cause of the war, the Shawnees having called on the Delawares to join them in revenging themselves on the English.

At seven o'clock in the evening an officer arrived with Pisquetomen, and delivered to Peters the Journal of Frederick Post. When Weiser read it next morning, he found corroboration of Teedyuscung's story. The Shawnees were said to have started the war in revenge for the killing of one of their chiefs by the Carolina people.

It was about this time that Weiser received a message from a Shawnee, Ackowanothio, who lived on the Ohio. Whether the speech was delivered by Ackowanothio himself, or whether he had sent it by Pisquetomen, Daniel, or some other Indian from the Ohio, is not known. Two copies have been preserved, both written in a clerk's hand, one of them, however, ending with four words written in by Conrad Weiser himself: "Gave a large String. *to Conrad Weiser Interpreter.*" [30]

Is it possible that Ackowanothio was Weiser's old friend, Kakowatchiky, (Kakowatchy, Cacowachico) the Shawnee chief whom Weiser had visited

with Zinzendorf in the Wyoming Valley and who had since moved out to
the Ohio on the invitation of the Shawnees settled there? Weiser had
visited him at Logstown in 1748 and given him a present from Brother
Onas. He was then already failing; but next year, though blind, he attended
a meeting with some Frenchmen and drove them away. In 1752 James
Patton found him "lying bed-rid." [31] But the old chief clung to life. In 1755
he sent a message to Brother Onas through some Wyandots on their way
to Philadelphia.[32] Was he now in 1758 sending his last words of advice to
Brother Onas? The evidence is too slight for a final conclusion. We know
only that Ackowanothio was a person of importance and someone in whom
Weiser had sufficient confidence to take his advice seriously—so seriously
that on the strength of it he warned against General Forbes' advancing too
hastily into the Ohio Valley.

The Speech of Ackowanothio [33]

an old Indian on the Ohio in behalf of the
Delaware Indians and others living on the
Waters thereof.   September 1758—

Brethren the English, you wonder at our joining with the French in this
present War. Why can't you get get Sober and think impartially? Does not
the Law of Nations permit, or rather Command us all, to stand upon our
Guard in Order to preserve our lives, the lives of our Wives and Children,
our Property and Liberty? Let me tell you this was our Case: have a little
patience. I will tell you, Brethren, your Nation allways shewed an Eagerness
to settle our Lands, cunning as they were, they always encouraged a number
of poor People to Settle upon our Lands: We protested against it several
Times, but without any redress, or help.—We pitied the poor People:—we did
not Care to make use of Force, and indeed some of those People were very
good People and as Hospitable as we Indians, and gave us Share of what little
they had: and gain'd our Affection for the most Part; but after all we lost
our hunting Ground: for where one of those People settled, like pigeons, a
thousand more would Settle, so that We at last Offered to sell it, and received
some Consideration for it:—and so it went on till we at last jumped over
Allegeny Hills and settled on the Waters of Ohio. Here we tho't ourselves
happy!—We had plenty of Game, a rich and large Country, and a Country
that the most High had Created for the poor Indians, and not for the white
People.—O how happy did we live here!—but alas! not long. O! your
Coveteousness for Land at the risque of so many poor Souls, disturb's our
Peace again. Who should have thought, that that Great King Over the Water,
whom you always recommended as a tender Father to his People, I say, who
should have thought that that Great King should have given away that Land
to a parcel of Covetous Gentlemen of Virginia called the Ohio Company! who
came immediately and offered to Build Forts among us, no doubt, to make
themselves Master of our Lands and make Slaves of us. To which We could
not agree, notwithstanding their fair Words. *Onontio* our Father heard this
with his own ears, went home and prepared, in his turn, to take our Lands
from us as we or some of us, Suspected. He made a Proclamation to us in the
following Manner. "Children, the King of England has given your Lands on

the Ohio to a Company of wicked Men in Virginia, who, I hear are preparing
to come and take Possession with a strong hand;   be on your Guard, don't let
them make the least Settlement on Ohio, they will within a few Years settle
the whole: they are as numerous as Muskeeto's and Nitts in the Woods: if
they get once a fast hold it will not be in your Power to drive them away
again;   if you think you can't keep them off tell me so and I will keep them
off." *Brethren,* We never lik'd the French;   but some of the Six Nation, in
particular some of the Seneca's came with the French and took Possession on
the Heads of Ohio;   we did not like it, and therefore sent several Messages
to them to turn about and go the way they came to prevent Mischief, but to
no Purpose. The French being numerous and supported by the aforesaid
Seneca's and other Indians, we were obliged to be Still, and by their Craftiness
and Presents we were brought over to their Side of the Question;—But a great
number of us stood Neuter.

Now Brethren, when that great General Braddock landed at Virginia with
Orders from the King of England to drive away the French from Ohio and
take Possession himself of that fine Country for the English, the French did
let us know immediately and told us, Children, now the Time is come of
which I often told   such an Army is coming against you, to take your Lands
from you and make Slaves of you—You know the Virginians;—they all come
with him.—If you will stand your Ground I will fight with you for your
Land, and I don't doubt we will Conquer them. The French General's words
by the Assistance of the Priests had great influence with the Indians on the
Ohio, brought the Shawanese over in a body to them, they being wrong'd in
Carolina and Imprisoned and had their Chief hanged or put to death in a cruel
Manner. These Shawanese brought over the Delawares to their Measures;
they, the Delawares were drove from their Lands: it being sold by the Mohocks &c. to the New England People, and just then some of the Delawares
came to Wyomock, much incensed against the English, and were easily
brought over to the French and Shawanese.

Now Brethren, all this, with many other Abuses, we suffer'd from our
Brethren the English, yet our Heart is much afflicted, there remains Sparks of
love in it towards our Brethren the English; were we but sure you will not
take our Lands on the Ohio, or the West side of Allegeny Hills from us:—
we can drive away the French when we please, they have even promis'd to
go off when we pleased: provided we would not suffer the English to take
possession of the Lands (for as the French says) we can never drive you off
you are such a numerous People: and that makes us afraid of your Army,
which should not have come so nigh us,   we don't know what to think of it.—
We sent you Messages of Peace, you receiv'd them kindly, and you sent us
Messages of Peace, we receiv'd them kindly, and sent back again more stronger
Words: Why did not your Army stay at Ray's Town, 'till Matters had been
settled between us. We still suspect you Covet our Lands on the Ohio, for
you came against us;   but we never heard as yet what you intend to do (after
you have drove away the French) with the Forts and Lands on Ohio.

Brethren, one thing more sticks in our stomach, which is, That we cannot
thoroughly believe you that you are in Earnest to make Peace with us; for
when we lived among you, as sometimes it would happen, that our young men
Stole a Horse, kill'd a Hog, or did some other mischief, you resented it very
highly, we were imprisoned &c. Now we have kill'd and taken so many of
your People, will you heartily forgive us and take no revenge on us.

Now Brethren, consider all Things well and be assured that We, the Indians,
are heartily inclin'd to make a lasting Peace with you.
    Gave a large *String* to *Conrad Weiser*
Interpreter

[Endorsed] Indian Speech
          Inclosed in Mr Weisers Letter
          of 15 Novr 1758

October 5 was a great day. In the evening at six o'clock Tagashata came
to town, accompanied by the Cayuga Chief Tokahayon and a crowd of
followers.[34]

The Senecas were a formidable sight. Dressed in shirts, blankets, leggings,
and "sepacks" (heavy moccasins) like most of the Six Nations Indians, and
adorned with paint—white, black, red; in bars, parallel stripes, or zigzags
from brow to chin—the Senecas were further distinguished by nose ornaments that gave them a strange and forbidding appearance as befitted
members of the nation that ranked as the Keeper of the Western Door
and War Leader of the Six Nations.

The gristle between the nostrils they have bored through, and in this hole
they have a small piece of brass wire in form of a ring from which they suspend a flat three-cornered seband-stone, downwards of a breadth of two
fingers. This stone is unceasingly dangling right before their mouth and the
lips, that they cannot eat or drink without the greatest inconvenience unless
they are to hold up the stone with one hand.[35]

The newcomers received a salute from Major Orndt's provincials, and
Weiser escorted the chiefs to Vernon's tavern.

It had been intended to offer the last arrivals the usual compliments of
welcome that same evening, but the Indians being found dispersed,
"Teedyuscung half drunk Isaac Stille no better," it was advised by Nickas
and others "to let it alone till morning." [36]

Next day Tagashata and Tokahayon politely turned the tables on their
host. At Adam Yohe's they made speeches to Richard Peters, expressing
their joy at seeing him and reminding him of their old acquaintanceship at
Albany in 1754. Later they called on Peters at his lodging "with all their
men women & Children." The Reverend Richard unbent to the tune of
seven shillings (distributed among the women, with an encore of three
shillings and sixpence), two bottles of wine, and a bowl of punch.[37]

Tagashata gave out information at Easton that conflicted with Daniel's
report from the Ohio. Large reinforcements, he said, had gone to Fort
Duquesne, and the Indians there gathered from all adjacent parts were
prepared to assist the French.

Weiser kept a wary eye on Tagashata. The Seneca nation (of which
he was a leading chief) being near neighbors to the French at Niagara and
being more or less dependent on them for trade, had earned a reputation
for French leanings. Tagashata himself was thought to have been out on
the warpath against Pennsylvania. Indeed, Teedyuscung had informed
Weiser in Philadelphia "that Tagashata was his adviser & Bror . . . and

went out wth the Scalping Parties." [38] For information about Tagashata, Weiser relied chiefly on two men, Nickas the Mohawk and Tokahayon the Cayuga. Nickas was, of course, an old friend and wholly reliable. Tokahayon he knew by reputation to be trustworthy and a man whom it would be profitable to make a friend of. To this end Weiser gave him a "fine New fashioned Pip" and further gifts amounting in value to nine pounds.[39]

There were other gifts charged by Weiser to the Proprietors at this treaty, among them presents "To Nickes," "To Nickes Sons," "To Nickes's Family"; to Thomas King and other Six Nations chiefs; "To Capⁿ Thomas and Sam Squirrel"; "To Assary quo alias Abraham"; "To four Indians Each a Doller." [40] These kept open the channels of intelligence—a service that was becoming increasingly important as Indian relations deteriorated and headed down hill toward the conspiracy of Pontiac, which lay only a few years distant in the future.

Tagashata, Weiser learned, was to be trusted. Nickas reported that, while it was true Tagashata had been "privy to the Senecas joining Teedyuscung" (he would own as much in public), nevertheless Tagashata was now for peace, and had, indeed, broken with Teedyuscung. When he had advised the latter to lay down the hatchet, Teedyuscung rejected his advice and insulted him by throwing his petticoat (always metaphorically) at the Senecas and telling them to wear it.[41]

"I am a man," said Teedyuscung.

CHAPTER 60

... *Finds the Indians*
Unacquainted with Hours

I

ON Saturday, October 7, Weiser went out with Major Orndt, Richard Peters, and Charles Swaine to meet Governor Denny. They encountered him a couple of miles from town, and brought him in by two o'clock. An hour later Benjamin Chew, also just in from Philadelphia, presented himself at the Governor's house to pay his compliments, and found His Excellency already worked up into a sputtering passion.

It was over the wagons. Sir John Sinclair, it seems, had been complaining that the colonials were not supplying wagons enough for General Forbes. Governor Denny was resolved to have those who held back, concealing their wagons, sent pinioned to Philadelphia to be "swinged" by Sir John. Ben Chew, the Attorney-General, remarked that such conduct would be illegal, dangerous, and dishonorable. The Governor turned on him "in a very insolent taunting way," and issued some bullying orders to Captain Nelson.[1]

"What a Strange Peevish petulant Creature it is," wrote Chew in his diary.[2] And a changeable, he might have added; for a few days later word came from Philadelphia that Sir John Sinclair "was gone out of Town abruptly having as it was thought reced a Check from yᵉ Govʳ abᵗ Waggons."[3]

Teedyuscung called on the Governor to welcome him to town and to tell him that he (the King) had hallooed the peace so loud that all the nations as far as the Twightwees had heard it and were now come to this place of treaty. He proceeded to wipe the dust and sweat from Denny's face and to pull the briars out of his legs; and he desired that His Excellency should extend the same courtesies to the Indians on the morrow. The Governor limbered up sufficiently in conversation, carried on through the Delaware interpreter Isaac Still, to tell Teedyuscung of recent English military successes. Unfortunately His Honor was so carried away by his subject that he went on to say that the English now "had the Indians in a Pound," they had better watch out. Peters intervening to explain that the Governor was not speaking for himself but only reporting the sentiments of others by way of information, the King was satisfied and the matter passed off without any trouble.

Weiser was desired to arrange with Peters the ceremonies for the next day, and to determine what the Governor was to say. It was decided that His Honor was to speak "only in yᵉ Ceremonial way," business to be left till another time. The reason for this will appear later.

The Governor, who "did not incline to have company"[4] that evening, quarreled with Peters for allowing his nephew, Jemmy Peters, and young Andrew Allen (son of the Chief Justice) to be in the house with him.

"What!" fumed His Honor, "is it come to this that I am to have boys' company! It is indecent. Tell the boys to go away."

Peters did so, as he confided to his Pepysian diary; after which he "just staid Supper & retired to bed."

The conference opened on Sunday, October 8. Under the conference shed, at about two o'clock, the Governor welcomed Tagashata and the Indians, duly wiped the sweat from their eyes, and cleared the council seats of blood that their clothes might not be stained nor their minds disturbed.

Conrad Weiser, pleading that "his Memory did not serve him to remember the Several Ceremonies" appropriate to the occasion, desired Nickas to interpret the speech into the language of the Six Nations. Andrew Montour interpreted for the Delawares.

Tagashata responded in form, extending his thanks, and returning with apologies the belt of invitation which, he said, had "reached our Towns about the time that the leaves put out last Spring," but which the Senecas had been unable to accept at that time because of their fear of the French, who were near them. He returned also a second belt of invitation sent more recently through Sir William Johnson, in response to which they were now come.

Meanwhile "Teedyuscung sat by," as Ben Chew records: "seem'd low-spirited, & eclipsᵈ but said Nothing." [5]

Members of the Friendly Association arrived that day, some before and some after the conference. They let it be known at once that they were on to everything. They had as good an intelligence service as Weiser's—but it was Denny, Peters, Croghan they were watching. They had a copy of the Council's report and of the Proprietary instructions—"In short," wrote Peters, "they know every thing." Israel Pemberton did not conceal the fact that there was going to be no nonsense at this treaty. Right would triumph. Teedyuscung would be set on high.

It might have been expected that, after all the delays, the conference would have moved briskly forward from this point to attack the serious issues still remaining to be settled between Brother Onas, the Delawares and Shawnees, and the Six Nations. But that was not in accordance with the tradition of Indian councils, nor, indeed, was such a course possible. This was no ordinary council between two peoples. It was an assemblage of odd parts collected from many nations and from widely separated sections of the country. Neither the Six Nations nor the English were ready to speak with one voice. Tagashata had his instructions, but they did not cover all the points that he soon saw were to be handled at Easton. The Delawares were not united under Teedyuscung. And the English spoke with two voices: Governor Denny's and Israel Pemberton's.

Above all else, the Six Nations demanded a clear pattern, direction, and leadership in their councils. Merely getting together and threshing things out in public convention was to them unthinkable. An Indian conference was no "forum" in the modern sense. The Six Nations had a horror of impromptus on the public platform. Their love of democratic procedure entailed the instructing of each speaker. His voice must be the voice of a united people, and he must say only what had been agreed upon in private council with other delegates beforehand. There was a further reason for the elaborate care they took in instructing their speakers. The Confederacy was an imperial power, and it must show no fumbling in its councils while the world was looking on. The Six Nations owed much of their prestige to the solid front they had in the past been able to present to their nephews and brethren, and to their unhesitating course in public council.

But here at Easton, where there were several Indian nations represented, and many tribes and factions within each nation, it was especially necessary to hold preliminary councils in order to work out courses of common policy. Croghan "sent for a Belt all white to recommend Unanimity to all yᵉ Indians." [6] For days each nation held its own private councils, in which the views of dissident branches were considered, common policies were worked out, reports were received from other nations of their probable actions; and thus each nation determined in advance what compromises and adjustments might be made, so that the time waste and recriminations of unchartered debate might be avoided.

Weiser understood this, and he made the Governor understand it. But Israel Pemberton scented in the delays of the next few days only another plot of that "rascal" Croghan and of the pack of liars who composed the Governor's Council, a plot to lower Teedyuscung's prestige and conceal proprietorial fraud in the matter of Indian lands. Israel Pemberton was an honorable man, but full of himself. Well meaning and honest but a fanatical partisan, he could see no good in any but the "House of Israel" (as Ben Chew called the Friendly Association, his followers); [7] and he exhibited at this Easton Conference of 1758, the full significance of which eluded him, a suspiciousness, irritability, and contradictoriness bordering on hysteria.

October 9, Governor Bernard of New Jersey arrived with some fanfare by the Philipsburg ferry at half past eleven o'clock, and was taken up to Governor Denny's lodging. Bernard had some matters to adjust with the Minisink and Pumpton (or River) Indians.

The minutes of the Pennsylvania Provincial Council for October 9 and 10 record (through report of "Mr. Weiser," who was the principal go-between) that the Indians were in council, "deliberating on Matters necessary to be adjusted before the meeting," and that they "desired the Governors would not be impatient."

Let us glance for a moment at these inner councils.

On Monday, October 9, Tagashata, who had the business in hand for the Six Nations, began to sift matters by calling the Delawares into council and asking them to tell their Uncles the truth about the war. Why had they struck the English? Was it the French who first persuaded them to it? Were they perhaps striking the English in revenge for the Six Nations' selling of their lands? Or had the English themselves injured them about land matters?

"If your Uncles have wronged you out of any Land," said Tagashata, "pray don't mince the matter. Say so boldly." [8] The Six Nations would put things right.

The Delawares then retired to prepare an answer. What precisely the Delaware answer was has not been recorded. But its general tenor was satisfactory. We learn from George Croghan (at whose house Tagashata's conference had been held) that "Teedyuscung had acknowledged he was addicted to Drink & had been negligent but would leave it to his Unckles to transact business for ye future." [9] That point at least had been settled, and to the satisfaction of the Six Nations—for the moment, that is, for nothing could be settled permanently with King Quicksilver.

The Six Nations went on to dispose of other problems. Weiser received a summons to attend a special council of chiefs. When he came, he found Tagashata and Nickas sitting apart, a committee of two.

Tagashata addressed himself to Weiser, Croghan, and Montour, these latter also being present:

Brothers we have been in Council all day yesterday and to prevent Jealousy we will now tell you what we are about.

The Minisink Indians have given us a String to undertake to manage this Cause wth ye Govr of Jersey as they are women and not in a Condition to travel and dont understand State affairs. They gave 2 Belts to be made use of in doing y^r Business wth ye Gov^rs.

Now Brothers we dont like this Commission in the Least it is given to us and we will tell our Brethren the Minisink Indians so. We are resolved that they shall first discover who gave them ye Hatchet and acknowledge the wrong they have done and promise to be good friends wth their Brethren the English before we can take their Cause in hand. This we desire you will make known to the Govr and his Council y^t they may have patience. tell them y^t we are doing their Business & they shall hear from us every time when Occasion requires. [10]

The conditions imposed on the Jersey Indians must also be complied with by the Pennsylvania Delawares. This was the ruling of the Six Nations. It was therefore necessary, before any serious business could be transacted with the Delawares at Easton, that the offending parties should "take out the Hatchet from their Brethren and the English Heads" and "cure the wound." [11]

The question of priorities having been settled, there still remained the question of precedence. Should the Delawares speak in the ceremony of removing the hatchet, or should the Six Nations speak for them? Would it be the proper thing for the Governor, as host, to make the opening gesture? For two days Weiser, though he was constantly in attendance on the Indians, was unable to make any satisfactory report to the Governor and Council. That the Indians should have their way in determining the order of ceremony was allowed, but what procedure they would finally determine upon no one could guess. To the last, Weiser was not sure that the Governor might not be called upon to speak first, and he advised Denny to have a speech ready. A speech was accordingly prepared, shown to members of the Council and the Assembly, and submitted to Weiser for his approval, he being called in specially for this purpose.

On Wednesday, October 11, the tension came near to the breaking point. The Indian councils were coming to an end. Decisions were being made. The hour for the public conference was set, and changed, and changed again. Weiser was kept flying back and forth between the Indians and the Governor with announcements and contradictions.

At nine o'clock in the morning he "came to tell ye Govr y^t the Indians woud speak this fore noon." [12]

At half past ten he came to tell the Council that "the Indians and Quakers were all to gether in the Lutheran Church."

Mr. Chew went over to investigate, and, after passing what appeared to be a sentry, put his head in a window.

I observed a large Assembly of Quakers and Ind^s [he writes in his diary] sitting some round a long Table and others on benches behind with great Solemnity & as much form as is usual in Publick Treaties. Isr^l Pemberton was on one Side about Midway the Table sitting with a Pipe in his Mouth collected in himself in great State. . . . I did not count them but the Whites appear'd to be between 20 and 30. The Number of Indians I think was much greater. I know very few of 'em but distinguish'd Tagashata the Seneca Chief & Tom^s King. As soon as I look^d in Isr^l Pemberton accosted me and asked me to Walk in and Smoak a Pipe with them and I shou'd hear the Roman Oratory reviv^d in Tom^s Kings Speaking, that they were about no harm I excus'd myself from going in saying we were only taking the Air and did not come to interrupt them, he replied they were upon the best Subjects in the World Love and ffriendship I told him they were Noble Subjects and wish all those Success who were sincerely dispos^d to promote & Cultivate them! he then ask^d me if it w^d be unlawful for them to send for a Glass of Wine and drink with their Brethren I said he must judge for himself, But say's he I want the Attney Gen^{ls} Opinion—I jocosely told him if he applied to me as a Lawyer for my Advice I cou'd not give it without a ffee, for it was generally said Advice for Nothing is worth Nothing.[13]

The Indians told Weiser afterwards that they had been invited to the church to meet their Brother Onas, as they thought, "but were deceived, & Now found there were more Onasses than one." [14]

At noon Weiser reported that the Indians were at last assembling, nearly a hundred being already in the shed. Governor Bernard was "uneasy": he wanted his dinner and had invited Governor Denny to dine with him in Philipsburg. Denny was hungry too. After waiting till half past one, he sent Weiser to the Indians to demand a "Peremptory Answer" to the question, "At what hour do we meet?"

Weiser found the Indians dispersed, but he rounded up a few chiefs and drew from them the answer, "4 o Clock."

The governors went to dinner. Whereupon Teedyuscung and the Quakers flew into a passion, saying the Indians were ready and the governors were making them wait.

"High words betw^n Mr. Logan and Israel Pemberton." Logan said the Indians "had appointed 4 o Clock Israel said it was a Lye." [15]

Logan clenched his fist and said he had long borne with his abusive tongue, but would do so no longer; "& said that the Affinity that was between them was the only reason why he did not knock him down." [16]

At half past three Weiser sent Peters a note saying that the Indians had been waiting for over an hour. About the same time, "Mr Growden sent a Note letting us know what a sad ferment was in Town and desird ye Gov^rs to come." [17]

Their Honors arrived, well fed, from Philipsburg "at 4 o Clock P M" and took their places under the conference shed. [18]

II

Who was to speak first?

The Six Nations had decided that Tagashata should, and accordingly the belts and strings of wampum which were to punctuate his address were laid out in order on the table before him. [19]

But, as soon as the company sat down, Teedyuscung sprang up and, holding out strings of wampum, desired he might be heard first.

The Indians showed astonishment. They had had no inkling of this. George Croghan, no doubt suspecting the influence of Israel Pemberton and such-like "busy Mischievous ffelows" [20] (as Chew described them), asked the King if what he was about to say was by commission from the Delaware Council or on the advice of other counselors. Teedyuscung did not reply.

It was an embarrassing moment. Teedyuscung had taken the floor from his Uncle. The walls of decorum were down. Anything might happen. Into the breach stepped Governor Bernard of New Jersey, tactfully desiring to bid the Indians welcome. Since he was an outsider, his speaking first could not so readily be taken exception to as if he had been one of the regular contenders for that honor. Governor Bernard gave his welcome, and added a plea for brotherly love.

When Bernard sat down Teedyuscung stood up again and desired all present to give ear. He had, in fact, nothing of importance to say; it was merely a Sir Roger de Coverley gesture. He wished to feel his importance, to show his position, and to act the part of a father to his children.

"As you, my Brethren," he said to the two governors with a comprehensive sweep of the imagination, "desired me to call all the Nations who live back, I have done so; I have given the Halloo, and such as have heard me are present. Now if you have anything to say to them, or they to you, you must sit and talk together." [21]

Tagashata then rose, icy, composed. With admirable brevity he dismissed the meeting. "It has pleased the Most High," he said, "that we meet together here with Chearful Countenances, and a good deal of Satisfaction; and as publick Business requires great Consideration, and the Day is almost spent, I chuse to speak early tomorrow morning." [22]

Before the meeting broke up, Governor Denny had to get his oar in. He asked for despatch, "and desired the Chiefs would fix the Time of meeting."

This they declined to do, "saying, they were unacquainted with Hours, but would give Notice when they were ready." [23]

The day's strain and this final rebuff were too much for Governor Denny. Before the evening was over he had worked himself up into a passion against the innkeeper Vernon in Easton and against the Proprietor, Thomas Penn, in England. Poor Richard Peters was dragged in on this latter affair, receiving instructions to write to Penn informing him of the Governor's displeasure at not having received an immediate reply to a recent letter of his.

Peters "settled" the minutes he had taken during the conference, "and went to Bed."

At eleven o'clock next morning the Governors and the Council went to conference under the shed. No Indians were there. After waiting for some time, Denny asked where the Quaker Council House was or the Lutheran Church: "may be ye Indians might be there." [24]

At length the chiefs arrived. After they had seated themselves, "Teedyuscung came in wth Pisquetomen Drunk. Teddy," wrote Peters, "had a Bottle of Rum wth a Straw Cork wch he put under ye Table & wch C Read overset y^t ye Rum might run out." [25]

It might have been better if Charles Read (of New Jersey; a "tool of I. P.") had let nature take its course and allowed Teedyuscung to drink himself under the table. As it was he remained vociferously awake throughout the conference, "& swore in English prodigiously." [26] He declared "that he was King of all the Nations & of all ye world & ye Six Nat^s were ffools & . . . did not know how to behave to ye English & that the way to be well used by them was to make war on them & cutt their Throats." [27]

The Indians, even Teedyuscung's own counselors, were angry with him, but they controlled themselves and appeared to pay him little attention. The conference proceeded under Tagashata's leadership with great solemnity, Weiser translating the speeches for the Six Nations. No one translated for the Delawares that day, Teedyuscung being too drunk to understand anything.

Tagashata, representing the Six Nations, spoke on behalf of the Indians "living at Wioming and on the Waters of the River Susquehannah."

"Brethren," he said: "We now remove the Hatchet out of your Heads that was struck into them by our Couzins, the Delawares; it was a french Hatchet that they unfortunately made use of, . . . we take it out of your Heads, and bury it under ground, where it shall always rest, and never be taken up again." He laid a belt upon the table.

As for the Ohio Indians, he continued, taking up eight strings of black wampum, "We have told all these that they must lay down the French Hatchet, and be reconciled to their Brethren the English . . . We, the Mohocks, Senecas, and Onondagas, deliver this String of Wampum to remove the Hatchet out of your Heads, that has been struck into them by the Ohio Indians, in order to lay a Foundation for Peace." [28] He laid the eight black strings upon the table.

As Tagashata sat down, the Cayuga Chief Tokahayon rose, and, holding three strings of wampum in his hand, addressed the governors on behalf of the "younger Nations" of the Confederacy, the Cayugas, Oneidas, Tuscaroras, and those still more recently accepted into the Confederacy—the Tuteloes, Nanticokes, and Conoys. With three strings he widened the road from their country to Easton and washed away the blood that had stained it. Then, taking up a large belt, he apologized in particular for the young men of his own Cayuga nation who had gone out four times to strike the English. The French, he said, had stolen them away "like a thief in the Night . . . and corrupted them to do Mischief." [29] He asked forgiveness for these young men, and, with a belt ten rows in width, he took the hatchet out of the heads of "all the English."

This ceremonial concluded, the way was open for peace.

The Governor's Council sat up all night preparing an answer to Tagashata and Tokahayon. "Mr Weiser read his private Journal to them in wch is inserted at large Nickas Enquiry of the Cause of the War." [30]

Weiser's journal has been lost, but Ben Chew has left a good summary of it in his diary:

In ye Evening Mr Weiser inform'd us that he had some time ago employ^d Nichas a Mohock Chief to find out if possible from Teedyuscung ye true Reason in private Conversation why he struck us, on wch Nichas made him this report.

That on his first application to Teedyuscung he c^d get Nothing from him, but he desir'd him to enquire first of ye Minisinks, & have they had assign'd their Reasons, he w^d give his. He then went to ye Minisinks who said they were women & wore Pettycoats & c^d not speak but the Senecas were their Mouth & their ffathers. Nichas then applied to Tagashata who gave this Account. That after they had heard the Delawares had struck us, they Sentt to them to know ye Cause & Teedyuscung brought 'em a bundle of Scalps, which they threw away & were surpriz^d & told him he had murder'd their Brethren ye English & reprimanded him Severely for it, on wch he threw down his Petty coat, saying he was Now a Man & they might wear it 'emselves that he had taken up ye hatchet & was able to fight all his Enemies & w^d not obey 'em or hearken to their Advice. Then Nichas went to Tohaajo ye Cayuga Chief who denied they knew or were made acquainted wth Teedyuscung's striking us before he did it, but Afterwards he came to their Town and told them the Shawanese by the Seneca's Advice had induced 'em to take up ye Hatchet agst us, but Now they deny it, & ye English w^d come & cut him off, & requested ye Cayugas to join him wch they rejected. He then s^d he w^d go over to the ffrench. They advis^d him ag^t it & told him ye french w^d not keep him under their wing longer than he acted as they pleased & then they w^d throw him into the Lake. The Senecas may say what they will we know how it is but he went away much Dissatisfied. Nichas then return'd again to Teedyuscung & demanded on ye behalf of his Uncles ye Mohocks that he w^d Now tell him ye true Cause of ye War. Teedyuscung s^d ye Reason was the English had cheated him of a great Many Lands, & Now claim'd his Land at Wyomink & were going to drive him off. Niccas answer'd that he knew better, as as to

Wyomink, they had no Right to Lands there,   he lied & insisted on knowing the Truth, on wch Teedyuscung S^d well Uncle Now I will tell you ye real Truth, You know ye Virginians some Years ago killed some of ye Shawonese & among the rest one of their great Men. The Shawanese to revenge this join'd ye ffrench, when ye Troubles began between 'em & ye English & invited us by a Belt to take up the Hatchet wth them putting us in Mind that one of us was unjustly hanged Some years ago at Amboy in ye Jerseys & they seduced us but Ive return'd them ye Belts & thrown it in their ffaces & am sorry for it.

CHAPTER 61

... Saves the Easton Peace
Conference from Disaster

I

DESTINY had marked Friday the thirteenth of October as the day of calamity for the conference. The proceedings began pleasantly enough. The Governor made a long and friendly speech, punctuated with a plenitude of belts, working up to a request for the return of prisoners as an earnest of the Indians' sincere desire for peace.

Pisquetomen delivered a message from the Ohio Indians, in the name of King Beaver, Shingas, and others, proposing peace and asking that, when peace was concluded at Easton, the terms of it should be sent to the Ohio, where all nations would join and hold it fast. Three strings of wampum accompanied the message: one for the Governor, one for Teedyuscung, and one for Israel Pemberton.

As the Governor, who distributed the strings, handed Israel Pemberton his, he was overheard to say "jocosely" to those sitting by him, "I hope he will soon be favour'd wth another String wch he richly merrits." [1]

The Governor, well pleased with himself, was about to close the conference when Nickas got up and opened the flood gates of disaster. He spoke for some time, "wth an Apparent Warmth & Resentm^t in his fface & manner turning frequently & pointing to Teedyuscung who sat by, Israel Pemberton Said loud enough to be heard by many round ye Table that it ought not to be interpreted because it wou'd make a difference among the Indians." [2]

Weiser was ordered to interpret it, "but he said he did not chuse to do it Mr Montour might do it." [3]

Andrew Montour did not choose to do it either. He referred it to Weiser again.

After a pause Weiser said it might be better if the speech were interpreted to the Governor and Council *in private conference*.

He was told to ask the Indians how they wanted it done, in public or in private.

In public they said at first; but a few minutes later, after Weiser had talked with them quietly, they changed their minds and said that, at Weiser's request, "they consented that it should be interpreted in the Morning at a private Conference." [4]

That evening, Peters writes, between six and seven o'clock, the Governor and Croghan came to drink tea with him. They were full of the conference, and both blamed Weiser for his conduct. They did not understand that the old Interpreter had just done one of the wisest things in his career. He had postponed an open quarrel between the Six Nations and Teedyuscung, giving time for anger to cool and for statesmanship to get control of slipped tempers. Neither he nor Hercules could have dammed the wrath of the Six Nations at Teedyuscung's assumption of powers that did not belong to him, but he had diverted that wrath into safer channels. What they said in public, once it was translated and put into the records, must be acted upon, or else, as the Indians expressed it, they would be known as liars: but what was said in private might serve to clear the air for the moment and then as much of it as seemed expedient might be forgotten. Besides, it was better that, after the first shock of Teedyuscung's humiliation, he should be given time to find some hole or corner for escape (as the old rogue knew so well how to do) when he came to explain his retreat to his public. Otherwise the conference was threatened with what Pemberton called "the gloomy prospect of an open variance." [5]

Next day, Saturday, most of the Indians were drunk and the private conference had to be postponed. Weiser this day had his hands full with the Quakers. They were in a turmoil. They called a number of the Indians together and told them to forget what Nickas had said. So far so good. But they went on to say that Croghan was responsible for the attack on Teedyuscung: It was a plot to "give the 6 Nations an ascendancy over ye Delawares that did not belong to them, but that Teedyuscung was a Man of Resolution & great Influence among Numerous Tribes of Indians & wou'd not Submit to it, & that a bloody War w^d be ye Consequence." [6]

The Quakers said openly that Teedyuscung would be supported against the Six Nations. "In vain," wrote Peters, "did Mr Weiser relate to them y^t the first principal and real cause of this difference was entirely owing to the insolent Speeches of Teedyuscung." Weiser complained afterwards that "tho he had mentioned ye matters of Fact in y^r order yet they [the Quakers] seemed not to mind them." [7]

The cat was now out of the bag. For better or for worse "the House of Israel" was dedicated to the task of making a great man of Teedyuscung.

In the records of the Friendly Association we find the following remarkable avowal made by "a member" (surely Israel Pemberton) concerning Teedyuscung: ". . . he is really more of a politician than any of his opponents, whether in or out of our Proprietory Council, and if he could be kept sober, might probably soon become Emperor of all the neighboring nations." [8]

Israel did not know the Six Nations.

II

On Sunday morning, October 15, the two governors with their Councils and Commissioners met the chiefs of the Six Nations in a private room at Scull's.

Nichas, the Mohock Chief, [we read in the minutes] stood up, and directing his discourse to both Governors said:

"Brothers, We thought proper to meet you here, to have some private discourse about our Nephew Teedyuscung.

"You all know that he gives out, he is a great Man, and Chief of Ten Nations this is his Constant Discourse. Now I, on behalf of the Mohocks, say, we do not know he is such a great Man. If he is such a great Man, we desire to know who made him so. Perhaps you have, and if this be the case, tell us so. It may be the French have made him so. We want to enquire and know whence his greatness arose."

Tagashata on Behalf of the Senecas, spoke next.

"Brethren: I, for my Nation, say the same that Nichas has done; I need not repeat it. I say we do not know who has made Teedyuscung this great Man over Ten Nations; and I want to know who made him so." [9]

Assarandonquas spoke to the same effect for the Onondagas; and after him Thomas King, the Oneida, holding in his hand a belt of six rows, spoke for all the remaining members of the Confederacy down to the recently admitted Nanticokes and Tuteloes:

On their Behalf I now tell you, we none of us know who has made Teedyuscung such a great Man; perhaps the French have, or perhaps you have, or some among you, as you have different Governments and are different People. We for our parts intirely disown that he has any Authority over us, and desire to know from whence he derives his Authority.[10]

The Six Nations had taken charge of the treaty. From that point on, Teedyuscung, Israel Pemberton, and Governor Denny were kept on the side lines.

On Monday afternoon the Indians assembled in full force, Six Nations, Delawares, and all, to hear Governor Denny's reply to the question, "Who made Teedyuscung a great man?" Denny's speech had been carefully drawn up in advance, and, being submitted to the Indian Commissioners appointed by the Assembly, had received their approval.

This was to be a day of decision. The Indians were "sober to a man." [11] During the morning the chiefs were in council. Weiser was sent to them to desire them to let him know when they were ready. He reported that they were "busy in Settling matters betw[n] higher and inferior nations." [12] The governors and the gentlemen of their councils waited.

It was not until one o'clock that the public conference began. The Six Nations took charge. They called for the reading of the minutes of Sunday's private conference.[13] The minutes were accordingly read and interpreted into the Delaware tongue for the benefit of Teedyuscung. The Six Nations had been insulted in public. Their dignity was to be as publicly restored.

Governor Denny spoke, holding in his hand the belt wherewith the Six Nations had denied Teedyuscung to be a great man. He explained that, when Pennsylvania first invited the Delawares to the Fire at Easton, Teedyuscung came and said he represented ten nations. Pennsylvania then believed him and treated with him as an agent for peace.

I can only speak for myself, [said the Governor] and do assure you, that I never made Teedyuscung this great Man, nor ever pretended to give him any

Authority over you; and I must do him Justice to declare to you, that, at our former publick Treaties, Teedyuscung never assumed any such Power, but on many Occasions, when he spoke of you, called you his Uncles and Superiors. . . .

If any others have made Teedyuscung so great a Man, as to set himself above you, I am sorry for it. It is more than I know, and they who have done it must answer for themselves.[14]

At the conclusion of his speech, the Indians laughed and said, "See, he pities Teedyuscung." [15]

Governor Bernard spoke, assuring the Six Nations that he still considered Teedyuscung their nephew.

Then Tagashata rose to speak to the Delawares. He reminded his Nephews of their earlier promise to return all their prisoners, and he instructed them to perform their promise.

Robert White, a Nanticoke, next rose, conscious of his new authority as a chief of the Confederated Nations. His was no longer an insignificant nation, such as had provided comic relief at the great Onondaga Conference of 1743, but one which was entitled to call the Delawares nephews. He spoke to them truly like an uncle. What had they done, he demanded, with the peace belts, one a fathom long and twenty-five rows wide, which his people had sent to the Delawares from Otseninky? We want to know, he said, "what is Become of these Belts; may be they may be under Ground, or they have swallowed them down their Throats"—i.e., sold them for rum. He desired an answer in public conference, and he laid down a string of wampum to enforce his demand.[16]

The Quakers were excited and angry. They said: "the Six Nations might say w^t they would ag^t Teedyuscung he should be a great man." [17]

Next day, rum being kept from the Indians and their heads being in consequence clear for business (again at the sacrifice of what the House of Israel called Liberty and Privilege) they were in their tribal councils all day. They sent repeated messages to desire Governor Denny not to be impatient or hurry them: "they had not the use of Pen & Ink as we had, and it took a great deal of time to do Business, & to so order matters as they depended solely on y^r Memories." [18] They were "settling matters of Consequence betw^n them and their Cousins." [19]

At first each nation counseled separately; afterwards all nations gathered under the shed.

"Old Ted," wrote James Pemberton to his wife that day, "looks very Serious & [I] believe is very thoughtfull how he shall acquitt himself of Some matters." [20]

The day was lowering. Tempest was in the air as well as in the councils. Tagashata, Tokahayon, Nickas, and Teedyuscung consulted with Weiser and Peters about a message to the Ohio Indians. They complained that Pennsylvania was niggardly in the matter of wampum: "ye belts shoud be as large again & more of them." [21]

"It raind hard." Governor Bernard came from Philipsburg, fussing about a horse thief he had apprehended. The two governors went together to the conference shed, only to be informed by Weiser that the Indians were busy and could not meet them.

After dinner Ben Chew and Israel Pemberton met on the street and quarreled over the conduct of the treaty, in particular about George Croghan, whom Israel called "a Rascal and Vilain." Chew flared up. Pemberton said he meant no affront—why was he so warm?

"Indeed," wrote the Attorney-General in his diary, "I only wanted a fair Opportunity to hit him a Slap in the Chops . . ." [22]

Nature herself subscribed. Peters records of the afternoon, "a most violent Gust of Thunder and Lightning."

By next day the Quakers had recovered their composure and confidence. ". . . the schemes laid to depose Old Ted are not Like to succeed," wrote James Pemberton to Hannah his wife.[23] Conrad Weiser suspected that messages were passing between Israel Pemberton and the Indians. Teedyuscung "was wth Israel Pem almost all day," wrote Peters. "M[r] Logan and I saw Teedy at Israels door & Is went round & came thro Sculls yard." Chew heard that the Indians were about to make Teedyuscung a king. Somebody was certainly making mischief. Israel Pemberton was giving presents to the Indians. By means of these, it was feared, he might gain all his points, "unless," as Peters observes, "some Goods were put into y[e] hands of C Weiser." [24]

The conference under the shed began about half past eleven and lasted till nearly four o'clock. Nickas explained to the governors that, the Counselors having expressed themselves, it was now for the Warriors to speak, and that Thomas King had been appointed to deliver their words. Tom King accordingly rose and, addressing himself "as well to all concerned in Publick Affairs, Governors and their Councils, and Indian Chiefs and their Councils as to Warriors of all Nations, White People and Indians," he desired they should attend carefully, since what he was going to say "would serve to regulate the Conduct of English and Indians to each other." Holding eight strings of black wampum in his hand, he entered upon an explanation of the origin of the war, which he traced to the same causes as those we have already seen outlined in Ackowanothio's message to Conrad Weiser.

With three strings of white wampum he requested the Governor of Pennsylvania to return to the Six Nations that part of the Albany Purchase which lay, still unsettled and unpaid for, beyond the Alleghenies. These Ohio lands were their hunting grounds. Their warriors and hunters disapproved of that part of the sale and declined to confirm it.

When he sat down, the Six Nations chiefs were asked if they had anything more to say. They said "that they had done; and having eased their Minds of all that lay heavy upon them, they would return home." [25]

But not so Teedyuscung. Nerves braced with a shot of Israel Pemberton's militant pacifism, the King "arose, and spoke." [26] It was noticed that as soon as he opened his mouth the three senior chiefs of the Six Nations got up and went out, one after another, "seemingly much displeased." But Teedyuscung went on and, as well as he could, stuck to his old rôle. After some remarks about nine Delawares killed at Goshen, he traced the migrations of last year's fathom-long, twenty-five-rowed peace belt, which he said he supposed had gone through all his Uncles. He repeated his charge of land frauds against the Proprietors, and enlarged it to include the lands "from Tohiccon as far as the Delawares owened"—which, he added casually, meant as far as the heads of the Delaware River [27] (it will be remembered that the Delaware River heads near the Schoharie in the Mohawk country). Then he took up a large belt to address "his Uncles the United Nations"; but, finding their principal chiefs had departed, "he let it alone." Indeed, he could do no other. Tom King refused to hear him in their absence.[28]

III

Old Ted could sleep well that night. He had for the moment turned the tables on his Uncles. "Matters seemd now to be brought to a Crisis," wrote Chew.

Teedyuscung had renewed the Charges of Fraud against the Prop[rs], & set up a Claim not only to the Lands between Tohickon & the Kittachtinny Hills which were the Subject of our former Disputes but to the Lands above the Hills to the Head of the Delaware. & that in y[e] presence and hearing of the Six Nations.[29]

The Province had deeds from the Delawares (confirmed by the Six Nations) to the Land at Easton, and a deed from the Six Nations for lands north of the Hills. The Province was, however, anxious for peace and prepared to pay almost any price for it, as Israel Pemberton knew. But to appease Teedyuscung by paying him for lands already bought from the Six Nations would be to deny the sovereign rights of the latter. It was a nice point, requiring, as the Attorney-General said, "a great deal of Skill & Caution." Conrad Weiser was therefore employed to sound the Six Nations and, "if he found them well affected, to put it boldly to them & know explicitly how far they woud go on this occasion." [30]

It was 1742 all over again. Weiser found the Six Nations indisposed to enter into the dispute about the lands below the Hills (the Walking Purchase) to which they said "they had no right . . . nor ever claimd any," though they recognized that the release they gave for these lands in 1736 and their removal of the Delawares from them in 1742 was "an acknowledgment that they were convinced we had fairly bought them of the Indians." [31] But they positively affirmed their right to the lands beyond the Hills, acknowledged they had sold a large part of them to Pennsylvania and been paid for it, and said they would stand by that sale in public. This assurance from Weiser that the Six Nations would stand by the purchase of 1749, and the drawing up by Benjamin Chew of a release from the Proprietors to the Six Nations of the Ohio lands (which Weiser and Peters were empowered to sign), were the principal cards Governor Denny held in his hands when he came to the next session of the conference.

Israel Pemberton had good cards, too. On Thursday evening he had the Indians dine with him and the Quakers at Scull's,[32] "and distributed a good many Presents among the Indians . . ." On the morning of the conference, the Governor having had a sentry placed over Vernon's liquors so that Indians heads might again be kept clear for business, the Quakers interfered, and there ensued what we might call the Battle of the Rum Barrels. Fox and Galloway, says Chew, "made the Streets resound with the Epithets Liberty & Privilege" and "seemd determin'd to kick up a Riot . . ." The Governor was stiff, Vernon angry. It took all the Attorney-General's industry and tact (a commodity with which he was not too well supplied) to suppress the "confounded Fracas." [33]

All day Thursday Conrad Weiser was busy interviewing, carrying messages, explaining deeds to the Indians. Pisquetomen was pressing to be sent off with his message to the Ohio. Peters made out passports for him. The Indians were hurrying from their houses. Excitement was unbounded. Governor Bernard came over to read a long draught of his next speech, which was to be delivered to the Minisinks. Croghan reported that the Indian Sam Evans claimed the land on which Philipsburg stood. The Minisinks had claims against Jersey amounting to £2,500. "Quakers will make Claims enough," wrote Peters. The Secretary became ill and could eat no dinner.

Meanwhile both parties had gone into a huddle with their Indians: the Six Nations at Weiser's, the Delawares at Israel Pemberton's. Israel ("Impudent Scoundrel," Peters calls him in telling of the incident) tried to steal a march on his antagonist. He opened the door of Weiser's room and called out Robert White, the Nanticoke. Now, Robert White did not like Weiser. Possibly the Interpreter had told him (truthfully) that he was a pompous ass. Be that as it may, when Robert White went out, it was suspected that he told Pemberton about the dicker he and Last Night (the Conoy chief) had been trying to make with the Proprietors about an island at the mouth of the Juniata; for afterwards Israel came to say that no fresh purchases ought to be made, since the Ohio Indians had claims in some places. Pisquetomen (to follow this flurry to its end) said they had none. Israel temptingly countered by saying that Pisquetomen himself had a right to lands in Jersey; "but," writes the Reverend Richard, "yᵉ Indian honester yⁿ Israel said he had not."

The Six Nations worked hard on Thursday, and to good effect. Teedyuscung reduced his claims. He admitted to Weiser, as he did afterwards in private to the Governor, that the Delawares did not claim lands high up on the Delaware River—these belonged to their Uncles, the Six Nations.[34]

Friday, October 20, was a bad day for Richard Peters. The wind was in the east and cold. Conrad Weiser called him up before seven o'clock to report that the Six Nations would not meddle with any dispute about the lands of the Walking Purchase. Peters fussed about for hours in the raw air before he could get the Six Nations chiefs together to settle finally the message Pisquetomen was to take to the Ohio. The Secretary's indisposition grew worse. He was blooded (for fifteen shillings), and was advised to keep away from the conference shed—which he did, and thereby missed hearing one of the gems of Indian oratory.

But it was a good day for Pennsylvania. Teedyuscung, in an early conference at Weiser's with the Six Nations chiefs, acknowledged that he and his people had no right to lands above the Kittatinny Hills. It only remained for him to say so in public, lest, as Chew put it, "when the Six Nations backs were turned Teedyuscungs friendly Incendiaries woud prevail with him to deny it."

Teedyuscung made a clean job of it. Under the conference shed, in the presence of all, Indians as well as whites, he withdrew his claims to land on the Delaware—to any land at all—and threw himself on the generosity of his Uncles.

He did it with dignity and skill. He made an abject surrender, and yet, like a conjurer, he pulled the honors out of his matchcoat sleeve. The speech he made contains the best single passage spoken in all the Easton conferences, perhaps in all the Indian conferences held in Weiser's lifetime. As we read his words about the *Bird on a Bough*, we forget the straggling Jersey Delaware who spoke them, forget the consequential, rum-swilling King of shreds and patches. We hear rather the voice of his people, the lament of a vanishing race.

Teedyuscung addressed himself to the Six Nations, and, speaking as a wanderer who knew not where to lay his head, asked that he and his people be given a deed for land in the Wyoming Valley that they might have a home to leave to their children.

"Uncles," he said, holding in his hand a belt of twelve rows,

I sit here as a Bird on a Bow; I look about, and do not know where to go; let me therefore come down upon the Ground, and make that my own by a good Deed, and I shall then have a Home for Ever; for if you, my Uncles, or I die, our Brethren the English will say they have bought it from you, & so wrong my Posterity out of it.[35]

There are three manuscript versions of the speech. One, Andrew Montour's translation, is short and freakish. It represents Teedyuscung as asking his Uncles to look upon him "as a Person Sitt^g on a Twig." [36] A second, long and colorless, is Isaac Still's. It is followed in the manuscript with this note: "N.B. The Above is agreeable to Isaac Stills Interpretation but according to Conrad Weisers Interpretation it was—See C. Weiser's Interpretation." [37] The third is the one I have quoted. It appears anonymously in the official minutes of the treaty, but it is almost certainly Conrad Weiser's. It is the only one of the three not expressly attributed to either of the other two interpreters. It is written in the manner of Conrad Weiser. Presumably Weiser conferred with Peters before the minutes were "written fair," and offered his own transfusion of the other two translations, for elements of both are found in it.

Was Peters referring to Weiser's rendering of Teedyuscung's speech when he wrote to him a few weeks later saying, "The Indians Speech seems very natural"? [38] Weiser knew something of the Delaware tongue, much of the Indian mind and poetry. The speech as it stands in the minutes has the color, cadence, and understanding of Indian metaphor that stamped Weiser's literary property as clearly as the brand CW marked his cattle. Richard Peters, who prepared the minutes, was neither an Indian scholar nor a creative artist. He could never have invented these speeches nor given them their flavor. But he was a man of some literary judgment. He admired Richardson's *Pamela* [39] and Weiser's woodnotes. In entering Indian speeches in the minutes, he tried to preserve as nearly as possible their native form and color. We are therefore to thank him as well as Weiser (and we should add the printers Franklin and Hall, who first published them) for preserving the greenwood quality of this distinctive literary product, Pennsylvania's Indian treaties.

IV

Friday's conference cleared the air. Even the Quakers for the most part approved—Israel Pemberton dissenting.

James Pemberton asked Chew to go and have a talk with Israel.

I told him [writes Chew] "that his Brother was a violent unmannerly Brute & I was unwilling to trust myself in his Company because if he tooke the same Liberties wth me he had done wth others I shoud not keep my hands off him. If he woud conquer his Passions & become a rational Creature I shoud have no Objections to confer with him on this or any other Occasion. He censured his Brother & said that he was of a very unhappy temper and often did things he was afterwards sorry for &c [40]

The peace conference now moved rapidly ahead. The day that saw Teedyuscung's surrender was important for several additional reasons. For one thing, in a private conference attended by the Six Nations chiefs, Teedyuscung, and two members of Governor Denny's Council, it saw the preparation of the message to the Ohio Indians. Peters, confined by his indisposition dinnerless to his room, drew up final passports for Pisqueto-men and his party bound for the West.

The Six Nations had the conference well in hand. Over their nephews they had resumed their benevolent protectorate. They promised to recommend Teedyuscung's request for lands "to the great Council Fire at Onondaga" for settlement. When Governor Bernard proposed to settle the Minisink and Wapping claims to lands in New Jersey for what he described as the "extraordinary Price" of eight hundred Spanish dollars, the Minisinks appealed to their Uncles. The Six Nations, by Thomas King, said

. . . that it was a fair and honourable Offer, and that if it were their own Case, they would chearfully accept of it; but as there were a great many Persons to share in the Purchase Money, they recommended it to his Excellency to add Two Hundred Dollars more; and if that was complied with, the Report of it would be carried to all the Nations, and would be a proof of the Affection and Generosity of their Brethren the English on this Occasion, and would be very agreeable to them.[41]

Tuesday, October 24, Weiser and Peters signed the release of the Ohio lands, and presented it to the chiefs of the United Nations in a private conference at Adam Yohe's.[42] Two days before this, Benjamin Chew and Israel Pemberton had buried the hatchet. They had some talk, wrote Peters, in which Pemberton asked pardon and acknowledged that he was in the wrong. The watchful Secretary notes that the reconciliation was witnessed by Hugh Roberts.

There was reconciliation all round, for whites and Indians, both within and without their various councils. Israel Pemberton lent wampum for the making of a Peace Belt. Only Governor Denny failed to catch the peace spirit. He was "excessively peevish." On Sunday he "packd up all his Things in a huff & said he woud go to morrow morning." [43]

"Swaine said ye Govr was mad—there was no meaning in anything he did, all was Passion & Pet." [44]

On Monday a friend of Tagashata's died. The burial and condolences took time and delayed the public conference. The peace belt grew hot in the Governor's hand. He would have flung it in the Indians' faces if he could have found them. He "was so angry y^t no one coud speak to him. . . . at 3 o Clock went to ye Shed and because Indians were not in it but lying round nor Govr Bernard there he swore and stampt and said he was ill usd. I told him"—it is Peters' voice we hear—"he woud spoil ye whole Treaty, his behaviour was shocking."

When the Indians did at last assemble, Governor Denny went through the formalities of healing wounds, removing grief, and burying the hatchet. Then, with a large peace belt which James Davies and the Jersey women had made the day before, he "brightened the chain of Friendship" and confirmed the "Antient Union."

There followed three days of rejoicing, with speeches, presents, and feasting. But Governor Denny was tired of savages. He took an abrupt leave before the ceremonies were concluded, "and mounted his horse for Bethlehem," as Peters informs us. "Swaine told me," adds the Secretary, "ye Govr was 70 years old worn out tho but 48. y^t he was unfit for business, and shoud go home directly. Mr Boyle said he was ye most troublesome peevish man he ever saw." The Six Nations chiefs asked Weiser to go with them "to search him if he was a man or woman."

The Easton Conference of 1758 brought an end to the war in the west. Frederick Post set out from Easton, October 25, bound again for the Ohio. He went by way of Reading, where he met Pisquetomen. They conferred at Weiser's house, and went on together with news of the peace concluded at Easton, news which was to strip the French at Fort Duquesne of all their Indian allies and clear the way for General Forbes.

This treaty struck the blow, wrote Col. Bouquet, "which has knocked the French in the head . . ." [45]

At the same time it strengthened the Six Nations. Post reported from the Ohio a few weeks later that their prestige had never been so high.

Tarachiawagon once more, as at Lancaster, had held up the sky for his Indian brethren. But he could no longer hold up the sky for himself. Sir William Johnson had not only deprived him of authority; he was now trying also to deprive him of esteem. The Indians at Easton told Weiser that Sir William "woud not let him be called longer by his Indian Name Tarachia Wagon [the Holder of the Heavens] it was too high a name. They might call him by his first name Segoruras [the Killer]." [46]

CHAPTER 62

... *Presides at the Quarter Sessions*

I

THE Lutherans in Reading being without a preacher, it was natural that they should turn to Conrad Weiser to find one for them. From the beginning he had watched over the little flock of Trinity. He had selected the ground—two lots at the northwest corner of Prince and Thomas Streets (now Sixth and Washington)—and had seen to the erection of the little log church. Since then he had brooded over the wretched cavalcade of itinerants, among them that "Wicked drunken felow" [1] Wortman, who had preached from its pulpit. There had been occasional days of light, as when Muhlenberg visited them and took the service, or Pastor Kurtz of Tulpehocken. But Muhlenberg and Kurtz had many other charges. Trinity needed a resident pastor. Some members of the congregation suggested inviting Pastors Kurtz and Schaum to take the Reading pulpit in turn. But Weiser advised sending a call across the sea for a preacher of their own and for some financial help toward paying his salary.

It must have been soon after Weiser's return from Easton that the letter was written to Ziegenhagen and Albinus, "Preachers in the High German Court Chapel" in London. The copy preserved in the Krauth Memorial Library at Mount Airy Lutheran Seminary, Philadelphia, is undated; but it is endorsed by Ziegenhagen as received January 14, 1759.[2] It is in German, of Weiser's composition. The style is unmistakable: like a storm in the mountains, valleys lit by streaks of lightning and the air filled with rumbling thunder.

Their "Worshipfulnesses" (*Wohl Ehrwürdige*) are informed of the plight of the congregation, consisting of some ninety families out of a total of about two hundred German families in this war-ruined, sect-ridden county seat of Berks. They have done their best to support a Lutheran preacher, and indeed have had various "Guest Preachers"—about whom in general the less said the better "lest we thoughtlessly dishonor the True Servants of God who have now and then as occasion served preached God's Word earnestly among us. In short, we have no preacher." Could their Reverences send them an Evangelical Lutheran of irreproachable life, modest yet enthusiastic, who could stand up against the criticism he would have to meet from the other sects? If not, would they offer their advice? —and "God himself might show the ways and means." They could give their preacher no other riches than a parsonage and forty pounds a year— *Pensilvanisch*. They knew a preacher could not live properly on less than sixty pounds; but if God pleased to send peace again they might give more.

The letter was signed (in his old bold hand, his lameness now troubling him only in cold weather): "Conrad Weiser a Magistrate of the County of Bercks aforesaid." Below his, all the elders (seven, of whom Peter

Weiser was one) put their signatures, and fifteen other members of the congregation.

The conclusion of this incident is found in a letter from Muhlenberg to Ziegenhagen.[3] The Reading Lutherans, after sending their letter to London, decided after all to go ahead on their own and invite a certain Herr Hausihl of Frederickstown, Maryland. Conrad Weiser said he had no objection provided it was understood the preacher from Maryland came only for two years or until the man they had written to London for arrived. Mr. Hausihl came. They liked him so well they invited him to stay for three years. "He promised Mr. Weiser," says Muhlenberg, "that he would readily make way, when the preacher they asked for came from Europe." He stayed on at sixty pounds a year, and, being a man of character and intelligence who could give the congregation unity and leadership, he laid the foundations of a strong Trinity Church.

However bitter the sects might be, they found a common home in the house of Conrad Weiser, who could still worship with the Lutherans, the Reformed, the Moravians, and the German Baptists. When the Reformed congregation of Reading, which had been meeting in private houses and sometimes in the Lutheran Church, wanted to build a church of their own, they turned to Conrad Weiser to get the land for them. About five years before this, that is, on May 20, 1754, he and Isaac Levan had taken out a patent for two lots on the northeast corner of Prince and Thomas Streets for a meetinghouse. Now, on March 5, 1759, Levan and Weiser deeded the land to Francis Wenrick, Yeoman; Wolfgang Hagka, Locksmith; George Diehl, Cordwainer; Jacob Tick, Carpenter,—"Trustees and Elders for the Religious Society of Dutch reformed Calvinists in Reading."

Now this Indenture Witnesseth [runs the deed] that the said Conrad Weiser and Isaac Levan do hereby Acknowledge and Declare that altho' the said two Lots of Ground was taken up by and purchased in their names aforesaid Yet in Fact the same was purchased for the Site of a Meeting House intended to be erected thereon and Burying Ground for the said Society of Dutch reformed Calvinists and was so granted to them in Trust and of Intent and Purpose that they shou'd Reconvey the same to the said Trustees and Elders of the said Meeting . . .[4]

Weiser was looking to the end. He wished to set all in order now, so that there should be no confusion following his death. He had had enough trouble in his lifetime with warrants, patents, returns, and all the clerkly processes connected with the sale of Reading lots—for which he had been appointed one of three commissioners. "I wish I have never undertook that troublesome business," he wrote to Peters, April 24, 1753, after Jacob Heller and Michael Greter had both applied for lot No. 310. "I gave Jacob the return and ordered him to go and get a patent or be h—g^d which he would, I was then quite out of Humour."[5]

Besides this matter of the Reformed Church grounds, he wanted to clear up the trouble over the Reading schoolhouse. The town had a school board, of which Conrad Weiser was a member. Several years before, they had joined with the Lutherans in a lottery (authorized by Governor Morris at the request of Weiser and Peters) to raise money for the school and the church. But the lottery was a failure, a third of the tickets being left on the trustees' hands and the rest being drawn "very unlucky." Weiser, therefore, on March 18, 1760, wrote to Richard Peters asking that the original agreement be suspended and that the school be taken over by the "trustees general of the freeshools." He also desired to deed over the house and lot (the title to which was in his name), and asked Peters to arrange this matter for him. "I want to part with the title to prevent trouble to my family and the people Concurned. life is uncertain." [6]

Conrad and Ann Eve had never entirely severed relations with their friends in the Ephrata Kloster. During the winter of 1758–59, Sister Flavia paid them a visit, as we learn from her subsequent letter dated January 16, 1759,[7] addressed to her "Dear Friend Conrad Weiser in Reding." In this letter she sends hearty greetings to all, and announces her safe return home. At the Kloster both brothers and sisters have great pleasure in hearing of her visit—and especially "Brother Friedsam" [Conrad Beissel].

"May God send his blessing, that we may end our few remaining days in his presence. For the harvest approaches and the days draw to an end . . ."

II

Relieved of his army commission, Weiser turned vigorously to the business of the Berks County courts. He presided at the Quarter Sessions, heard cases, conducted examinations, received petitions, appointed road viewers, issued summonses, mittimuses, recognizances, and search warrants. Many small disputes he adjusted out of court, such as that between Richard Peters and Peter Brown over twenty acres of land.

On February 26, 1759, Weiser and Jonas Seely issued an order to the Overseers of the Poor to take into their care "a Female Child named Elizabeth, aged about five Months," born in the common jail—her mother, "Elizabeth Grouel Widow," having been convicted of murder and sentenced to be hanged. The overseers were instructed "not to fail under Penalty of Twenty Pounds" to "Provide for the same, as a Parishioner; Until the said Child is fit to be bound out to Service— As the Law in that Case doth direct and appoint . . ." [8]

"At a Court of General Quarter Sessions of the Peace and Goal Delivery, held at Reading in and for the County of Berks the fourteenth Day of November & in the Year of our Lord one thousand seven hundred and Fifty nine Before Conrad Weiser Esquiere and his Associates Justices &c—" William Stiegel (the "Baron Stiegel" of blue glass fame) presented a petition for the laying out of that part of the road from Elizabeth Furnace which intersected the Berks County line. Viewers were appointed and the "Road laid out by Order." [9]

During the August term Weiser's old friend Captain Busse died. The story is written into page 19 of Weiser's Account Book: [10]

1759	august term	£	s.	d
Received by a Collection from Several Gentlemen dinning at Mr Edward drury's in Reading for the then sick Captain Bussey to Support him in his distress the Sum of £ 6. 2. 6		6.	2.	6

he died the evening folowing
the money was laid out for his Burrial in the folowing
manner, to wit.

to 18 yards of Crap for mourning veils to those
that Carried the death body to the Grave & to the
Minister & Chanter at 2/6 per yard 2. 5.00
to the Minister in Cash (funeral Sermon) 00.10.00
to the Chanter for bespeaking necessary thing
and giving notice to the people of the town 00. 6.00
for digging of the Grave 00. 6.00
for the Coffin to philip weis paid by me to
philip Jacob Meyer 00.14.00
to Andrew Engel for a Supper to Some that
Sat up with the deceased and other Serviceable
friends 1. 8. 6

Though Conrad Weiser no longer had the confidence of those who pulled the strings of government in Philadelphia and London, he was still the chief magistrate in his own community and the intermediary between the civil and military authorities there. It was in this latter capacity that he helped Sheriff Thomas Lincoln (whose brother John was the great-grandfather of President Lincoln) in what we might call *The Case of the Countryman's Fiddle.*

This involved one of the two civilian complaints that he presented in a letter of January 1, 1759, to Lieutenants Allen and Meyer. The letter shows Justice Weiser in good form: courteous, friendly, informal, but very much to the point.

He begins by wishing his good friends a happy New Year, with all the usual appurtenances, and then moves straight to business. Complaints have been brought to his notice, which he hopes they will excuse him for now obtruding upon their attention. The first, submitted by Mr. James Whitehead, a lawyer, is against Lieutenant Allen, who is said to have tried to make a man pay forty shillings he did not owe, and, on failing in that attempt, to have snatched from the man's hand an order on the paymaster. The paymaster has already been informed of this, has stopped payment on that order, and will see justice done to the original holder.

"The second complaint," writes Weiser, "comes through Mr Lincoln Sherriff of this County . . ." It is to the effect that Lieutenant Meyer

. . . hired a poor old man at the White Horse [Tavern], with a promise of food and drink, to come to Reading with his fiddle and help the recruiting officers by playing. But they tried by all manner of devices to make him enlist, did not give him his victuals, he paid his own reckoning, they took his fiddle away from him and did not give it back . . . I would offer Herr Meyer the friendly advice to give orders that the old fellow's fiddle be given back to him. . . . I assure you two gentlemen my friends, that I wish you well and will be glad to do anything that may tend to your credit and advantage, and I beg you not to take this amiss, if it were not my duty, I would not concern myself with such matters—I am Esteemed Sirs Your obedient Friend & Servant Conrad Weiser.[11]

III

In the spring of 1759 Weiser was engaged by Colonel Bouquet to get together a brigade of wagons from Berks County for the provisioning of the army at Fort Pitt. He had to contract for, appraise, and pay for wagons; to hire horses and drivers; to buy oats, rye, and spelts, and find bags to put them in. More than that, he had to overcome the apathy of "stupid, obstinate, narrow sighted People" (as Colonel Bouquet described them) whose horizon was bounded by their own rail fences, people who either cared nothing at all of what happened as far away as the Ohio, or, like John Hughes, saw a government "plot" in every army order.[12]

It was humdrum, tedious work, but Colonel Weiser (as he was still some-times called) was a man to make drama even out of a wagon train. He warned Bouquet at the outset that sufficient wagons could not be got without press warrants. When he received orders "for the Impressing of Waggons for the King's Service" and presented them to the assembled justices of the county on June 18, there was a storm. Conrad Weiser pro-vided the lightning and James Read the thunder. James Read, Prothonotary, lover of strong drink and good Latin, read the governor's press warrant aloud.

". . . all seemed very willing to obey and do what lay in their Power," wrote Weiser in a letter which he sent to Bouquet at Lancaster, "except Mr Read, who rose many Questions, and asked me whether I was an Officer of the Army? Where is your Contract with the General? What Authority have you to demand Waggons?" [13] The incident so much impressed itself on Weiser's mind that a week later he described it again to Colonel Bouquet —the first letter having failed to reach him, since the "fool" of a soldier who had engaged to carry it, finding the Colonel gone from Lancaster, had not had the wit to forward it to him.[14] From the two letters together the following account is woven.

Weiser laid the governor's order and the act of Assembly before the Justices. "There is the governor's Warrant," he said; "there is the Law." [15] He then presented his written demand for thirty-nine wagons.

Mr. Read read it to the justices and flung it on the table, refusing to sign any press warrant.

I took my Paper up [said Weiser] and desired in the Civilest Manner Possible a written answer from the Justices which Mr Read opposed. I then indorsed Mr Reads answer on my Paper which he had thrown down, and

show'd what I had wrote to Mr Seely, to know whether I had put it down
right. Mr Read snatched it out of his Hands . . .[16]

Weiser walked away and left the justices to think things over. After
they had conferred a while, they sent two of their number to inform Mr.
Weiser of their acquiescence. The warrants were ready next morning, and
Weiser hired three constables to carry them to every township.

Sebastian Zimmerman, "a noted freeholder of good reputation," who
had served as a wagon master under General Braddock, was, on Weiser's
"nomination," appointed wagon master of "this first Brigade," [17] and early
in July received his instructions. He was to load 180 bushels of rye at
Frederick Weiser's in Heidelberg, 278 bushels of oats at Peter Kucher's
in Lebanon, 240 bushels of oats at Pastor Stoever's on the Quittapahilla—
these and other loads to be delivered in Carlisle or taken on to Fort Bedford as should be determined later. He was to see that the hired boys and
drivers looked well after the horses, and that they camped at night where
water and pasture were convenient for the animals. There was to be no
quarreling in the brigade, and lazy drivers were to be punished. Whatever
happened, the wagon master was to think always of one thing: to do what
was best for the public service.

"In conclusion," wrote Weiser, "I commend you to God's care and wish
you a good journey." [18]

Even with press warrants, the magistrates found trouble enough in getting wagons. Refusal to obey a warrant brought a fine of forty shillings,
this to be expended on the poor of the township. The law, wrote Weiser
to Bouquet, was "somewhat lame." In some communities men were encouraged to pay the fine; ". . . so a township may Compound with it self
and send no Waggons the fines continues among themselves . . ." [19]

Bouquet was discouraged at "the backwardness of the People of Penn-
sylv^a and near total Stagnation of Waggons." "We crawl here," he wrote,
"upon an ungrateful Soil that produces nothing but thorns." [20] But his
complaints were not directed at Berks County. Conrad Weiser kept his
brigade full.

IV

As we follow the story of Weiser's life, we find ourselves so much dependent on government reports, ecclesiastical records, and such-like public
papers, that we have missed seeing Justice Weiser in his moments of relaxa-
tion. We should like to see him for a moment toasting his toes by the fire,
or playing with the children. It is fortunate for us that among his papers
he has preserved something that gives us such a glimpse.

On a sheet of paper containing the single fragment of his 1758 Easton
Journal, is another item that Conrad thought worth preserving, no doubt
for its family interest. It is written in his good bold hand and meticulously
endorsed "Ein Rätssel [A Puzzle] N° 40." [21] Had the Justice taken the
trouble to write it down, and to work it out as he does, for the benefit of

his own son Benjamin, now fifteen or sixteen years of age, or had he gone to all this trouble for the sake of little John Peter (twelve or thirteen years of age) who since the peace at Easton had very likely resumed his visits to the farm?

However that may be, here is Justice Weiser with his slippers on and the children around him:

A father sends 3 daughters to market with apples   To the first he gives 10 to another 30   to the third 50. with instructions that none shall charge more than the others. The one who makes the best sale shall marry first   she must get no more money than the others. Question how can the father's wishes be fulfilled. *facet*

The first had 10 apples sold 7 for a penny	1
She still has three which she sold for 3 pence apiece	9
makes in all	10 pence
The 2nd had 30 apples she sold 28—	4
and two more at 3 pence —	6
makes—	10
The third had 50 apples she too sold	
7 for a penny and had one left	
The 49 came to 7 pence	7
She sold the one left over for —	3
	10

For another intimate glimpse we have "mister Conrad Weissors Bill" [22] from the shoemaker, John Wittman for 1758–59, giving what we might call an angling shot of the Weiser family. There are shoes for Mr. and Mrs. Weiser, shoes for Ben, shoes for the Maid, and Wolf and Tromer, shoes for "the little boy." Mrs. Weiser's new shoes cost four shillings, Conrad's cost seven shillings and sixpence, Ben's seven shillings, the Maid's five shilling and sixpence, the little boy's three shillings. Ben was hard on shoe leather. He had five pairs of shoes in one year, with half a dozen mendings.

v

Despite the many activities he had to occupy his mind, the year 1759 was an unhappy one for Conrad Weiser. His world was breaking up. The little group of officers with whom, during the war years, he had been most intimate, was disappearing. William Parsons had died in 1757. Dr. Christian Busse died in 1759.

His own family was disintegrating. Peter had set up for himself as a saddler in Reading, Frederick as a "yeoman" at Heidelberg. Philip had his own family. He was the oldest son, but he was ailing and his father could rely on him little. Maria, Muhlenberg's wife, lived at a distance. Margaret, widow of the young preacher Heintzelman, had made a second marriage, distasteful to her father. Benjamin was still at home, but his father felt that the boy should be sent to Philadelphia for more schooling. Sammy was a captain now in the Second Battalion, serving with the forces covering Fort Pitt and its supply lines. Sammy had always been intimate with his father, and had followed most closely in his steps, both in Indian affairs and in the army. During the winter of 1758–59 he was stationed at Fort Ligonier, and was reported to be doing well. "I have had much talk with Col Bouquet about Sammy," wrote Peters, March 2, 1759, "of whom he speaks very favourably." [23]

A few weeks after this bit of good news about Sammy, there came bad news from Sammy himself.

"English Copy of Capt Weisers Letter to his father" [24]

[Fort Ligonier, April 1, 1759]

dear father. Herewith I let you Know that I am as yet in good Health, thanks be unto God, I hope the Same with you and my dear Mother. Sisters & Brothers, Since the Mitel of february last I received no letter from you, whether they have ben Stopt or no, I Cant tell There is from Carlile an opportunity at least every fort night to Send letters. Things goes here So, that I am tired of the Service, tho I did my part allways Chairfully, there are not 25 men in this Garrison that have not the Scurvy, they die vast, Some have Swelled limbs Can neither move bakwards nor forwards. In Short, there are here So many miserable objects among the Soldier. that one Cant look on them, without Compassion, and what wonder. we had in four months last past not a bit of meat but rotten, and hard Salted Borck, and the flour is all in Balls and the breath made thereof eats quite bitter, we have had long Since promised fresh Beaf, but to no purpose, like all other promises, If this people must Stay four weeks longer here, they will all die without Exception God knows that no body Cares for us, we are abused in all respect

I hope you have by this time acquainted Coll. Bouquet & Mr Peters, that I want to quit the Service, and get leave to resign, we have not heard a word yet whether there are troops Comeing up for our relief or not whether we will get pay or when. So much I am asure that there are not Six pensilvania Soldiers here that are Capable of going on another Expedition without first being recruited and Curred in the Inhabitant part, I have eat nothing this 6 days past but bread and Some Green which now begines to Come out, two officiers had poisoned themselves with greens, but they are well again. Captⁿ Wetherholts lies Sick by the way he had leave to go home from pitsburrg Lieutᵗ Conrads life is doubted at the Same fort Several are deathly Sick of my Company. I do what I can (and that is but little) but I have nothing. Lieutᵗ Humphry will Inform you of what passes for news here. which is not much . . .

Conrad Weiser to Richard Peters [25]

Reading Aprill the 19 1759

Sir

Yester day I received a letter of son Samy, I translated in English and Send hereby for your perusal and whom Soever you will Show it, Samy wrot so to his beloveth father, who dont doubt the truth thereof, and his father Sends a Copy to an old friend of hisen, make what use you please thereof for the good of the Service and poor forsaken people.—

I will Send this day my Sons Peter & Benjamen to meet him with a spare horse to Carlile or—fort Loudon, tho I have reason to doubt whether ever I Shall See him again in Pensilvania, what grieves me most is that I Consented to his Excepting of a Comission at first, and that I inlisted So many men, and Consequently made them miserable. The partiality, the disorder, the malice. the in Justice to the meaner Sort will ruin us at last. If ever the present time dont. I think we may well apply to us what the prophet Says Esai 59 v. 9 . . . 15. but what Shall I Say or do I Conclude and wish for better times, If not to be Seen by me. the posterity may. I wish you health and happiness. and remain

dear Sir
your very humble servant
CONRAD WEISER

Richard Peters was honestly glad to serve his old associate in this matter, as indeed in any matter tending to diminish the importance of the Weiser connection. "Out of respect to you & Sammy," wrote the Secretary, "& in obedience to the dictates of my own Understanding I applied for yᵉ Acceptance of Sammys Resignation. & I hope I have given you a Comforter in your advanced Age." [26]

The name of "Capᵗ Samˡ Weiser" was struck from the list of officers, May 15, 1759.[27]

With Sammy at home, Weiser found opportunity to continue Benjamin's schooling.

I Intent to Send my Son Benjamen to philadⁱᵃ Some time next weke to Shool [he wrote to Peters, June 12, 1759]. he can read and write a litle English and the German. I think the time he went to the accademy Shool was for the most Part lost. he provided not Much. how things are there now, I dont Know, would be rather inclined to Send him there again, Ben: wants to go to Mr. dove, who is a Stranger to me, but as he erected his Shool in opposition &ca. I would rather Choose Some other place. I beg a word of your advise—

I find here in Reading (as well as you in philadelphia) that things grow worse & worse. Some Gentlemen here are ploting agt. me. I Shall act oppenly without ploting and show them what they are about. . . . I get Ill linguage. . . . I wish you health, Christian patience. and happiness—[28]

His own stock of patience, never a large one, was draining away fast. The Assembly put off paying his accounts. He wrote angrily to Peters. "Your letter," responded Peters, "gives me pain of heart." But Peters was unable to get his accounts settled.

Richard Peters was unchanged. Bold for righteousness and Richard Peters, he still laid traps for his honest friend, Conrad Weiser. When in March 1759 Weiser was needed in town on some Indian business, Peters tried to put Weiser's back up and make him refuse to come. "You know there are some Indians in Town," wrote Peters, March 2, 1759, "& I moved that you shoud be Sent for provided an order for Pay wou'd be given by some or other but none chusing this I with just Indignation declared that I woud not be concerned on sending for you & that till your Accounts were paid off you had more Spirit than to come." [29]

To Thomas Penn the Secretary expressed a deal of "just Indignation" against Conrad Weiser for his unreasonableness in pursuit of his money. "I am sorry to see Conrad Weiser so unreasonable," [30] responded the Proprietary, instructing Peters to pay him no money for accounts chargeable to the Assembly. Peters had helped to maneuver Weiser into the position of a football between the Proprietors and the Assembly—kicked by both sides.

Times were indeed changing, and Peters' world as well as Weiser's was breaking up. Peters' shafts did not always find a mark; and sometimes, when they found it, they were returned to him with a vengeance. He used his sharp tongue at the expense of Colonel Bouquet. Now Colonel Bouquet was not only one of the truest gentlemen in Pennsylvania at that time, but also one of the toughest. Peters' words came back to him in a reprimand from Thomas Penn, and the Secretary wrote a personal apology to the officer whom history remembers as the hero of Bushy Run.

"I meant not to disoblige," said Peters. "If I speak what appears to me right in a disagreeable manner, it is a misfortune and as my friends tell me I do often err in this point I will endeavour to alter, but I am afraid of the force of habit." [31]

The world had changed also for Governor Denny. This good dilettante was now out of office and, though no longer in fear of his scalp, was in tantrums about his honor. If Edward Shippen of Philadelphia is to be believed, the ex-Governor carried pocket pistols when he went out for fear of insults: "I dont wonder at his Apprehensions," wrote young Shippen to his father, "Since if his Conscience be awake, he must Tremble at the Sight of every honest Man." [32]

CHAPTER 63

. . . Hears of Mischief
Hatching in the Woods

ON November 23, 1759, Christopher Saur's *Pensylvanische Berichte* announced the capitulation of Quebec. That meant the virtual end of French rule in America. It is an odd coincidence that next day Conrad Weiser made his will. His work was done.

January 2, 1760, he wrote to Colonel Bouquet, congratulating him on his safe return from Pittsburgh.

I would have Come to lancester to wait on you [he said] but being troubled with a Cold at present which prevents me. but If your Honour Stays Some days in lancester I will take a ride over. I should be glad If yourself would Setle with Mr Keemer about his Waggon Mastership . . . recommend him to you to have his accounts closed. . . . Kind Sir Excuse my Scrolls my right hand is in Cold Weather very lame. I Conclude with wishing a happy new year . . .[1]

It was a time of elation for the English colonies. Duquesne, Niagara, Quebec! Only the capitulation at Montreal remained for the control of the better part of the continent to pass into English hands. But it was not a time of elation for Conrad Weiser. He knew that success is often more dangerous than failure. He had urged caution on General Forbes, advised him not to advance precipitately into the Ohio Valley, lest the Indians should think the English had come not to free their lands but to steal them. Forbes nevertheless had gone ahead, had taken Fort Duquesne, rebuilt it as Fort Pitt, and established a permanent garrison there with covering forces at Bedford and Ligonier.

What Weiser feared happened. The Indians took fright. They were, in fact, losing their importance. They no longer held the balance of power between the French and the English. They were now only a small cog on a big English wheel. Not only the Delawares and Shawnees, but also the Senecas (most numerous among the Six Nations), the Twightwees, Wyandots, Pottawattamies, and Ottawas of the West saw their danger and united to remove it. The English colonies found that the new allies which the peace at Easton in 1758 had brought them were not permanently to be relied on. Certain great men among the western tribes needed to be watched. Among these was Pontiac, the Ottawa, who had helped to defeat Braddock at the Monongahela in 1755.

Late in November 1759, two Indians from the Ohio were brought by Teedyuscung to Philadelphia. They conferred with the new Governor, James Hamilton, and also with the Quakers. They invited Teedyuscung and "all the Tribes of Indians settled on the Waters of the Susquehanna" to come to a great concourse of Indians to be held beyond the Ohio in the spring, there "to consult what measures to take in the present conjuncture of their affairs." [2]

Following the visit of these Ohio Indians there were whisperings, which persisted throughout the winter and on into the spring, of some great stroke being prepared against the English. Conrad Weiser's Indian friends were uneasy. John Shickellamy sent for Conrad.

Captain Trump to Conrad Weiser [3]

[Fort Augusta, January 28, 1760]

Sir!

Yesterday a mingo Indian arrived here with the inclosed String of Wampum from John Shickelemy, requesting you might meet him here, in ten Days from that Time: he begs you'l send me Word by the Bearer whether you intend meeting him here, as he intends staying here but a short Time, but Oblidged to return, immediately to his Town

> I am Sir, Your
> Humble Servant
> LEVI TRUMP

Conrad Weiser to Captain Trump [4]

[Reading, February 3, 1760]

Sir

Yours of the 28th last past came to Hand last night, for which I thank you, but as I am at present lame and oblidged to keep my Room, It is impossible for me to make the Journey, be pleased to Acquaint John Shickalemy of this, I am very glad in the Mean Time to hear from him, and should be more so; if he would, (if he is in Health) come and Visit me, with a Couple of his Friends or Brothers I should make them heartily wellcome, for which Purpose I send him the inclosed String of Wampum He may safely come by the Way of Fort Henry. Your care will provide necessaries for him. with my hearty good Wishes to you and other Gentlemen officers at Fort Augusta I remain Sir

> Your very humble Servant
> CONRAD WEISER

Colonel Burd's Diary at Fort Augusta [5]

[February] 17th Sunday. Had a Councill with John Schicalemy & the other Indians delivered John Shicalemy a string of Wampom from Conrod Wieser Esqr John Schicalemy desired me to Acquaint Mr Wieser that he and some others of his freinds would go to Visit Mr Wiser the Middle of nixt Month.

Conrad Weiser to Governor Hamilton [6]

Reading february the 18. 1760

Honoured Sir

It is about two weeks ago, when I received the Express from fort augusta, forwarded by Captain Trump at the Instance of John Shickelimy, now a noted man among the Indians on the waters of that river, with a Streng of Wampum. a Copy of Captn Trumps letter is here inclosed, I Imediatly after the receipt thereof Sent a Copy of the letter and my answer to it to the

Secretary, whether the letter miscarried or the Secretary being from home I dont Know,   I was desireous to have Some thing of an answer to it. tho' as I then thought Johns invidation might not Signify much. yet I am Since Informed by some Soldiers Coming from fort augusta, that the Indians about there are much displeased, and the invidation might be of Some Consequence. If your Honour orders it Sammy Weiser Shall go up to fort augusta for Intelligence. my answer to John ShicKelimy was. that I Could not travle by this Severe weather and that I was lame. but gave him a Kind invidation by a Streng of Wampum to Come with his Brother or Some other friend to See me and Conferr with me of things he had on his mind—and I would make them wellcome. I have nothing to add, but am,

Honoured Sir,
Your very obedient and most
humble Servant,
CONRAD WEISER

To Governor Hamilton

Please to turn over

I give my best Compliments to your Honour, and if it is your Commands, that I Shall go to Fort Augusta, according to   the within Letter of my Father, I will with Pleasure obey Your Honours Command, who am

Your Honours most
obedient & very humble
Servt
SAM^L WEISER

Richard Peters to Conrad Weiser [7]

Philadelphia 21 February 1760

My dear Sir

Mr Hockley & I have been put to the trouble of a Journy to Carlisle from whence we return'd late on Sunday Night

I found your letters y^t had been deliverd in my Absence & shewd them to the Govr, who was of Opinion that you might have sent your Son tho you could not go yourself. This morning his Honour shewd me yours of the 18th Instant & ordered me to acquaint you that he is of Opinion your Son shoud go up & see & confer wth Jno SheckCalamy as it is a very critical time & if John be sincere he may communicate many things which at this time may prove of great Service. It is said the Indians are every where plotting to betray the Garrisons & to do some great Stroke & Samuel is desird to let the Commanding Officer at Fort Augusta know this. Col. Mercer is there & will have the Command during Col Burds absence wch may be five or Six Weeks. Mercer is prudent and will sift SheckCalamy well along wth Sammy. If you have not heard any thing since the date of your Letter. The Governors orders Sammy to set out directly for Fort Augusta to take the best measures for conferring wth SheckCalamy

Two Indians I am informd are found dead near Carlisle supposed to be murdered by some of the Inhabitants. This gives me the utmost Pain as it may throw great difficulties in ye way of a Peace. . . .

RICHARD PETERS

The Govr acknowledges Sammys
Letter wrote on the back of
yours & thanks him

Sammy got off to Fort Augusta a few days later, conferred with John Shickellamy, presented some strings of wampum, and gave John Petty (the youngest of the Shickellamies) a gift of fifteen shillings.[8] But Sammy's visit was not enough. There was something on John Shickellamy's mind that he wanted to tell Conrad himself. "my son Samuel," wrote Weiser to Bouquet, March 15, "is returned from fort Augusta he brought no Particular news only the Indians are some what uneasy about the fort some of them will soon Come to pay me a visit . . ." [9]

The Indians had reason enough to be uneasy. During the winter a Delaware Indian known as Doctor John, who lived in a cabin on Conodoguinet Creek, was heard to boast at Peter Tittel's house in Carlisle that he had "killed Sixty white People & captivated Six," and would do as much again if war were renewed. He asked a certain Thomas Evans in the house if he would like to taste death.[10] He spoke contemptuously of the soldiers, saying that they were good for nothing, that he and two or three other Indians would drive the whole lot of them, adding that the white people had killed his Captain Jacobs (at Kittanning) but that *there was another greater than Captain Jacobs still alive.*[11]

One night soon after this loose talk at Tittel's, some white men broke into the cabin where Doctor John, his wife, and two children were sleeping, killed them with axes, and scalped them.[12] The news crackled through the woods like a fire. Everywhere the Indians were alarmed and sullen. Colonel Burd at Fort Augusta, anxious to allay their fears, sent a message inviting all the Indians in the neighborhood to a conference. "They were so affected by this Affair," he wrote, "that they declin'd meeting me in the Fort, saying that perhaps I might cut them all off; there is seldom less than 100 Indians here and often 200 and upwards." [13] He met them outside the walls, assured them that the murderer if found would be brought to justice, and that a reward was offered for his capture. He read the Governor's Proclamation to this effect. "The Indians answered it was well and that they would give an answer to the Proclamation when the Strawberries were ripe." [14] The Colonel's assurances seemed to have set the Shamokin Indians at ease, but, as Burd observed, no one knew what was actually going on in their minds.

Teedyuscung came to Philadelphia and met the Governor and Council on March 29. "There lye some dead bodies between us, uncover'd on the ground," said Teedyuscung, "which fill our hearts with Grief and our Eyes with Tears, so that we can neither see nor speak to one another untill they be put out of our sight." [15]

The Governor, who was well aware that only a spark was needed to set off an explosion among the Indians, promised to make every endeavor to find the murderers and punish them. As for the dead bodies, he said, he buried them deep in the ground, and to confirm it he presented a string of wampum. With another string he wiped Teedyuscung's tears from his eyes.

To this Teedyuscung responded: "Brother you have really covered the dead, I will make it known wherever I go." [16]

To make Teedyuscung's halloo the more effective, he was fitted out with "a good suit of Cloaths, Hat &ca that he may make an Appearance answerable to the Occasion," [17] and was entrusted with presents ("some silver Ornaments") for King Beaver, Shingas, Delaware George, and other dignitaries. He was accompanied, when he set out for the concourse in the west, by a retinue of two white men (Frederick Post and John Hayes), two Indian interpreters (Moses Tattamy and Isaac Still), and Teedyuscung's son, Captain Bull.[18]

Meanwhile John Shickellamy continued to hang about Fort Augusta, buying Jewsharps, getting his frying pan and axe mended, having his tomahawk brazed,[19] and asking to see Conrad Weiser. Something was on his mind. "Jnᵒ Shekalemy," wrote Colonel Mercer from the fort, "does not go to Col Weisers but is desireous of Seeing him here, so I send to let him know . . ." [20]

It is easy enough now to understand poor John Shickellamy's dilemma. He knew what was plotting in the woods, and no doubt wanted to let Conrad know—without betraying himself to the watchful vengeance of the disaffected Indians (now numbering most of the inhabitants of the forest) who threatened to kill all those of their own race who would not turn against the whites.[21] (Our old acquaintance Jagrea was killed, it is said, because he would not attack the English.) John was afraid to go down into the settlements. He was afraid, moreover, even if Weiser came to him, to tell Conrad all he knew. But he wanted to say enough to set him on the trail of discovering for himself the mischief that was hatching in the woods; and he wanted, perhaps as much as anything else, Tarachiawagon's advice on how to guide himself in a world of changing loyalties.

Tarachiawagon ("You Must Hold up the Sky for Us"—so Chief Loft translated the word for me on the Six Nations Reserve near Brantford), Father of the Peoples, was never more needed than now.

Colonel Mercer sent for Conrad Weiser express, but the message came too late. Weiser had left with Sammy for Philadelphia, to settle his "Accounts for Wagons &cᵃ with the Genˡ," as Peters explained to Mercer.[22]

John Shickellamy had been for some time getting ready to set off for Onondaga, promising to submit to the Great Council the proposal of Brother Onas to build a proper road over what was then known as the Shamokin Trail.[23] But still John hung around, until he learned on the 4th of May that Weiser was in Philadelphia and could not possibly come "to see his old friend SheekCalimy." [24]

When, on May 5, John at last set off for Onondaga, expecting to be back in two months, Conrad Weiser had just two months and one week to live.

May was a happy month for the Weisers. On the 28th Sammy was married.[25] The bride was Judith Levan, daughter of Isaac Levan, a Reading merchant. The day before, Israel Jacobs had charged to Conrad Weiser's account a matter of twelve pounds and six shillings worth of wine and punch,[26] intended, no doubt, to give the Weiser circle (justices, sheriffs, clerks, the shoemaker, the maid, workers on the farm and at the tannery, as well as relatives and a host of others who still looked on the Weisers as friends and protectors) a share in the family celebration.

Sammy's marriage was the last family event of which we have record during Conrad's lifetime, and it is a fitting place at which to leave the story of the hearth that had been Conrad's prime concern for forty years. Yet it was not Sammy but Teedyuscung and John Shickellamy by whom Conrad Weiser's personal story was to be carried to its strange climax.

Teedyuscung, with his new hat and imposing retinue, had proceeded up the Susquehanna to Tioga and beyond, summoning councils preparatory to his going, with a grand halloo, across the Alleghenies and the Ohio to the great concourse in the West. But there was something mysterious about the journey. On July 1 the two white men who had been in his party turned up at Bethlehem with word that they had been denied passage through the Seneca country.[27] Hayes's diary is full of strange portents.

On Tuesday, May 27, at Asinsan, he writes, "about one Clock, Daniel Benet Came Down from the Mingo[s] town, and told us that they Bid us Welcome to this town, but if we Came any farther they would Rost us in the fire . . ."[28] A strange welcome, it seemed, from Pennsylvania's allies, the Six Nations.

There were stranger things yet to be learned from these Indians on the Seneca border.

Wed'y, 28. The Indians told us that S[r] William Johnstone has Corespond-ence with the French; some told us to Go home and Bury the Indians that were Kiled Near Carlisle, or they would Come and Bury them them selves Soon.[29]

They heard a wild tale about horses in the moon.

Mon'y, [June] 2d. We were Diverted with a strange Storey that they told us of the Indians at Diahogo, Seeing a Vision in the Moon on May the 29th, Viz., that they Saw 2 horses in the Moon, one Came from the East, the other from the West, and they fought a battle, and the Eastrly horse prevailed and threw the other Down and fell a top of him, and then Men appeared about one foot Long from the East and Drove all before them; the Indians were very Much Grieved at this Strange sight, and wanted to Know our opinions of it, but we thought best to say nothing about it [30]

That evening messengers whom they had sent to the Seneca town re-turned with peremptory orders to the white men to go back: "fer they Durst not trust us because of them that was Killed over Sisquhana." Teed-yuscung and his Indians might go on, but no white man was to pass through this country.

Frederick Post was a brave man, as he had demonstrated in his earlier journeys to the Ohio (where one morning he had recovered his strayed horse from under the very walls of Fort Duquesne), and he and Hayes, at Teedyuscung's request, decided to defy the Seneca prohibition. The party advanced upstream to Paseckachkunk, where they found the Indians gathered from all the little towns around to see the outcome of the white men's daring. Some Mohawk chiefs arrived and repeated the ban: "for there was an old agreement that no white man Should pas throw their Country for fear of Spyes to see their Land."

Mon'y, 16th. We got our final Answer to Go home, and they were Sorry that we were in Teeduscungs Bosom, for they Said they feard it would be bad for them, and the Delawares on Sisquhana, for perhaps there would Rise a storm, and the Limbs would fall and Knock our Brains out, and they and the Delawares would be Sorry for it, Lest they Should be Blamed for it, and that they Had begun a good Work of peace themselves, and was Going to Alegeny soon to Confirm it; But was positive in their Answer that we must Go home . . .[31]

Looking back on this episode with our knowledge of what came after, we see the stage being set for the greatest of all Indian dramas—the Conspiracy of Pontiac. The woods were no longer free, as Weiser had known them, to white men. This was the Indians' country, and the Indians were becoming conscious of themselves, not as so many nations, but as a single race. Great events were shaping. The conspiracy was, of course, only in its incubation period. Pontiac was still sizing up the English. He had yet to have his famous meeting with Captain Rogers and his Rangers.

Conrad Weiser had for years been in charge of Pennsylvania's Indian intelligence service. He was the one man living who might have detected the plot before it was mature. Johnson was too busy with military affairs. Croghan and Montour—who could trust them? Montour was at this time whining about not having received his deserts from Pennsylvania; Croghan was reporting from the Ohio that all was well.

When Post and Hayes got back to Bethlehem with their tales about woods closed to white men, storms rising, limbs falling, brains being knocked out, horses fighting in the moon, and the white people being all driven into the sea,[32] Conrad Weiser had just twelve days more to live.

CHAPTER 64

. . . Goes to His Father

I

THE last twelve days of Conrad Weiser's life were not wasted.
He had a talk with "two Indians." Was this the long-deferred talk with John Shickellamy (and some other Indian, perhaps Conrad's brother Jonathan) who had just come back from Onondaga? Conrad learned from them that something on a vast scale was indeed hatching in the woods. They could not tell him too much. They were torn between two loyalties, to their father's friend and to their own flesh and blood; and they were in fear of their lives. But they told him enough to let him understand the tremendous import of what was impending and the need of getting to the bottom of it himself.

July 3   The two Indians told me that the French Indian (so they called him) that was last Winter in Philad pretending to be a Messenger from the Ohio Indians reported on his return that the Quakers in Philadⁱᵃ gave him a rod to chastise the people Setling on the Indian Lands on the other side the Apalakin Mountains and to take Courage the Majority of the People of Pensilᵛᵃ was on the Indian side of the Question . . .[1]

At this point a mist covers Conrad Weiser's path, and we see no more of him for some days. What use he made of his information, how he employed the first nine of the ten days that remained to him, we do not know. Whether he took this, his last journal (of which this small fragment alone has come down to us), himself to Philadelphia or sent one of the boys with it, whether he made preparations for a journey of investigation to the Ohio, are questions to which there are neither letters of his own nor government records to give us an answer. When the mist clears he is already at journey's end.

On the morning of Saturday, July 12, he left Reading in company with Sir John Sinclair, the Quartermaster General, who was on his way to Fort Pitt. Whether Weiser intended to go with him, on behalf of the intelligence service, to the fort that had been erected so close to the old Logstown he knew, it is impossible to say. Henry Melchior Muhlenberg speaks of his father-in-law as merely paying a visit to the farm, but perhaps Muhlenberg did not know what was going on. If Weiser were setting out for the west to investigate such a plot as the two Indians had hinted at, he would not have talked freely about it (if for no other reason than to save the lives of his Indian friends) and Muhlenberg would have had no means of knowing. Be that as it may, Weiser got no farther than Heidelberg. He was taken ill soon after leaving Reading and suffered great pain. Sir John (considerate of nothing but his own puffy dignity) "left him on the road," as Edward Shippen afterwards told Colonel Burd, "on Accoᵗ of his being a little disordered." [2] Conrad was scarcely conscious when the horse brought him back to the spring beside the old Heidelberg home. After Sir John had left him on the road, "he continued ill," wrote Shippen, "& in a Stupid Condition till night & then expired."

Muhlenberg tells us that he died at noon on Sunday of the *Colica pituitosa*.[3]

His body lay in the house for two days and nights—*in der Stille*, as Muhlenberg wrote to the Fathers at Halle, so that the Interpreter, who in his last years had been too much occupied (as his son-in-law thought) with military matters and business of state, was given "time to balance his account before the Throne of Grace." [4]

The good pastor need not have been so much concerned about his father. Conrad Weiser had already balanced his account. He had served his fellow men unstintingly as farmer, churchman, ambassador, soldier, and judge. If further evidence is needed, Muhlenberg himself provides it:

Two weeks before his death his son-in-law and daughter paid him a last visit on his estate at Heidleberg where he had most of his children around him. He spoke of his past life, recalled the countless blessings the forgiving Father in Christ the good shepherd of the sheep had shown him, spoke with tears of the immeasurable Love, Goodness, Grace, Pity, Patience, Forbearance and Tolerance which the Lord through Christ's intercession and forgiveness had promised and bestowed upon him! and sang some hymns with his family from the depth of his heart, so that one could see how the foundation [laid] in youth . . . of which Christ Jesus is the corner stone, had remained intact, though the superstructure of wood, hay, and stubble had been burnt away . . .

On Monday preparations were made for the funeral. At Peter Spycker's in Tulpehocken Frederick bought twenty-four yards of mourning crêpe, five yards of muslin, two pounds of nails, two pounds of tobacco, one dozen pipes, four yards of black ribbon ("del[d] to Philip"), a ten-pound loaf of sugar, and six pounds of rice. Israel Jacobs supplied 1¾ gallons of wine and 5½ gallons of rum.[5]

On Tuesday the body was laid to rest in the family burial plot beside the house,[6] on the little eminence whence Round Head may be seen. Pastor Kurtz, Sr., preached the funeral sermon. Conrad Weiser, who knew his Bible through and through, would have been pleased with the texts: *Genesis* XV, 15, and *Psalms* LXXXIV, 12.[7]

And thou shalt go to thy fathers in peace thou shalt be buried in a good old age.
O Lord of hosts, blessed is the man that trusteth in thee.

The Ephrata Diary recorded the death of "Brother Conrad Weiser." The Bethlehem Diary noted that he had died suddenly and had been buried on the farm beside his father's grave.

A sandstone slab was placed at his head, with this crude (and inaccurate) inscription:

> *Dieses ist*
> *die Ruhe Staette*
> *des weyl Ehren*
> *geachten M. Con*
> *radt Weisers. der*
> *Selbige gebohren*
> *1696 d 2 November*
> *in Astaet im Amt*
> *Herrenberg im wit*
> *tenberger Lande*
> *Und gestorben*
> *1760 d 13 Julius*
> *ist alt worden*
> *64 Jahr 3 M 3 wch* [8]

Beside this stone now stands another for Ann Eve. At the feet of Conrad and Ann Eve, in a semicircle, are a few small stones, untrimmed, uninscribed. Tradition tells us that some of these mark the graves of Indians who desired to be buried with Tarachiawagon. Their names have not come down to us.

In government circles his death made scarcely a ripple. Peters arranged with the family to have his papers, such as were wanted, removed to Philadelphia. Peters knew well enough that Conrad Weiser had been the cornerstone of the colony's successful Indian policy, but the Secretary found it pleasanter to pity Conrad than to praise him. In writing to Sir William Johnson, Peters spoke of "poor Mr Weiser." Johnson, more self-contained and less self-deceived than Peters, referred to his one-time rival merely as "Conradt Weiser deceased."

What Peters wrote to Thomas Penn on July 26 is not known; but that the Reverend Richard pursued Weiser after death is made evident enough by Penn's reply: "Your account of Conrads unprepared State of Mind I did not expect to hear as he was always esteemed a very religious Man." [9]

It was a poor triumph for Peters. He himself was no longer *persona grata* with the Proprietor, who had reprimanded him only a few weeks before Conrad's death, and, a few months later, accepted his resignation with disconcerting calmness. "Your reasons for withdrawing from Business," wrote Penn, December 12, 1760, "carry great force with them, and no doubt you act right in following the dictates of your own Conscience." [10] Peters gave up state affairs and retired to the incumbency of St. Luke's, Philadelphia, where his neighbors' faults might be castigated with less danger of reprisal.

Thomas Penn's opinion of Weiser was somewhat higher than Richard Peters might have desired. "I am much concerned to hear of Conrad Weyser's Death," he wrote to Richard Hockley, "as he was a very honest useful Man, and I think it will be long before we find another equal to him—" [11] ". . . the confidence both the Indians as well as the Government had in him," he wrote to Governor Hamilton, "was a vast addition to his importance." [12]

July 31 the heirs gathered for the proving of the will.

In the name of God. Amen. I Conrad Weiser of the Town of Reading in the County of Berks in the Province of Pennsylvania Gentleman being of perfect health of Body and of sound and disposing Mind & Memory (blessed be God for the same) yet considering the uncertainty of human life and desiring to quit myself as far as I may of the Cares of this World do make this my Last Will and Testament hereby revoking and making void all other and former Wills by me heretofore made. . . . I give devise and bequeath unto my beloved Wife Ann Eve the Messuage and Lot wheron I now live in the Town of Reading . . . Item I give devise and bequeath unto my said Wife [Ann] Eve and to her Heirs forever my Lot [of] Ground situate on Callowhill Street in the said Town of Reading mark'd in the Plan of said Town N° 72. . . . Item I give and bequeath unto my said Wife two of my best featherbeds of her own choice, All my Kitchen Utensils and the Sum of fifty pounds current money of Pennsylvania . . . Item I give devise and bequeath unto my four Sons Philip Frederick Samuel and Banjamin, that is to say to each of my said Sons . . . the part or share to him allotted in a Draught or Plan sign'd with my own proper hand and to this Annexed of all that my Plantation in Heidelberg in the said County of Berks and my several Tracts of Land lying contiguous containing in the whole about Eight hundred And Ninety Acres . . .

Item I give devise and bequeath unto my Children Philip, Frederick, Peter, Samuel, Benjamin, Maria Mühlenberg and Margaret Fricker All those my Lands lying beyond the Kittochtinny Mountains and all My Grants or Rights to Lands lying beyond the same Mountains . . .[13]

There was a special provision for little Israel Heintzelman. Ann Eve, Peter, and Samuel were appointed executors. Even Richard Peters noted that Weiser's family had been well provided for.

In the presence of Maria, Philip, Frederick, and Margaret, the executors made an inventory of the "Goods and Chattels." [14] These were appraised by Christopher Witman and others. On August 30 a "Vandue" was held, for which the sons "Philip Fridrich Peter Saml." provided two pounds, six shillings, and ninepence worth of punch.[15]

We do not know what became of his library of 145 books and pamphlets —a library that contained four Bibles, a dictionary, some law books, books on heraldry and genealogy (the *Neüremberg Wapen Kalendar*, and *The Wirtemberg Genealogy*), "Eight Books of the Doctrine & Worship of the Brethren at Ephrata," "Six Books concerning the Doctrine &c of the Unitas Fratrum," two hymn books, Voltaire's *Life of Charles XII of Sweden*.

We do not know what became of his "Chamber Organ & Musick Books belonging thereto," the "Book of Medicine," "An old Leather Trunk and two small D° with Drugs in them," "Writing Paper, Blank Bonds, Sealing Wax, Wafers," "A Black Walnut Desk," "A large Map of Pennsylvania framed," "A large prospect of Philadelphia," "Two Indian Blankets," "His Riding Horse and Saddle," "A pair of Saddle Bags," "His Cane Sword and Pistols," "A fowling Piece," and "A Blunderbuss." [16]

II

It is said that George Washington once spoke these words by Weiser's grave: "Posterity will not forget his services." But Conrad's best epitaph was spoken by his old friend, Seneca George. At the opening of the Treaty at Easton, August 3, 1761, the chief rose, and, holding in his hand a white belt of wampum marked with four black streaks, said:

Brother Onas: We, the seven Nations, and our Cousins are at a great loss, and sit in darkness, as well as you, by the death of Conrad Weiser, as since his Death we cannot so well understand one another; By this Belt we cover his Body with Bark.[17]

On June 24, 1763, Pastor Muhlenberg visited the old plantation at Heidelberg. He found Frederick just returned from the border with news of an Indian attack.[18] Pontiac's War was on. Frederick had gathered in the cattle from the fields and was preparing to defend his house. It was said that fifteen hundred people had already been killed. Troops were once more on the frontier. John Jacob Wetterholt, who had served under Colonel Weiser in the old First Battalion, was in command of a company.

On October 8, 1763, Lieutenant Dodge scrawled a note to Horsfield at Bethlehem:

M[r] horsfield Sir Pray send me help for all my men are killed But one and Cap[t] Wetherholt is almost Dead . . . He is shot thru the Body for god sake send me help these from me to serve my Contry and king so long as i live
Send me help or I am a Dead man
thes from me Ly[t] Dodge
Sarg[t] meguier is shot threw the Bodey—
Pray send up the Docter for god sake—[19]

The wounds of Pontiac's War were not to be healed for a hundred years. Henceforth along the frontier "the only good Indian was a dead Indian." Under the sod at Heidelberg lay Tarachiawagon, who had held up the sky while he lived, but took with him into his grave the last hope of understanding between the white man and the red.

> *Hearken ye!*
> *We are diminished.*
> *Woe! Woe!*
> *The clear places are deserted!*
> *Woe!*
> *They are in their graves—*
> *They who established it—*
> *Woe!*
> *The great League . . .*
> *Their work has grown old.*
> *Woe!*
> *Thus are we become miserable.*[20]

But that is not the note on which to end the life of Conrad Weiser. He was a man of faith: faith in God, faith in his fellow men, faith in America. In that faith he had built churches and towns, he had set up a flag on the Ohio. Following him, America marched into the West. He had made it possible for an Abraham Lincoln to grow up in Indiana.

Out of war he had wrung safety for his people, and the opportunity to build a great civilization on the labors of free men.

> *And they that shall be of thee shall build*
> *the old waste places: thou shalt raise up the*
> *foundations of many generations; and thou*
> *shalt be called, The repairer of the breach,*
> *The restorer of paths to dwell in.*
> —Isaiah, LVIII: 12

ABBREVIATIONS USED IN THE
NOTES

A.P.S.—American Philosophical Society, Philadelphia.

Arch. der Br.—Archiv der Brüderunität, Herrnhut, Saxony (photostats of these Moravian records are in the Library of Congress, Washington, D.C.).

Corr. of C. W.—Correspondence of Conrad Weiser.

C.R.—Pennsylvania *Colonial Records.*

Hall. Nach.—Hallesche Nachrichten. Unless otherwise specified, the edition of 1886 and 1895 is referred to (Vol. I, Allentown, 1886; Vol. II, Philadelphia, 1895).

H.S.P.—Historical Society of Philadelphia.

L.C. of P.—Library Company of Philadelphia.

P.A.—Pennsylvania Archives.

Pa. Mag.—Pennsylvania Magazine of History and Biography.

P.P.—Provincial Papers, Department of Archives, Harrisburg.

P.R.O.—Public Records Office, London.

Prov. Rec.—Provincial Records (minutes of the Governor's Council), Department of Archives, Harrisburg.

S.P.G.—Society for the Propagation of the Gospel.

NOTES

CHAPTER I

1. "Petition of Thomas Benson": *Documentary History of the State of New York,* III, 557 ff.
2. *Journal* of the Rev. John Sharpe, June 13, 1710: Am 1365, H.S.P.
3. W. A. Knittle, *Early Eighteenth Century Palatine Emigration* (Phila., 1937), p. 144.
4. "Petition of Thomas Benson": *Doc. Hist. of the State of N.Y.,* III, 558.
5. Conrad Weiser's *Autobiography,* p. 3 (the German original in the possession of Mrs. Howell Souder, 1709 67th Avenue, Philadelphia). A microfilm of this manuscript is at the H.S.P., Philadelphia. For other versions of this famous "Diary" see: "Friederich Weisers Buch," Ohio State Museum, Columbus, Ohio; Library of Congress, Washington, D.C.; Collections of the Historical Society of Pennsylvania (1853), I, "Copy of a Family Register in the handwriting of Conrad Weiser . . . Translated from the German by Hiester B. Muhlenberg, M.D., of Reading, Pa."; *Olde Ulster, An Historical and Genealogical Magazine,* II, 199, 229; *Pan-Germania,* Sept.–Oct., 1912; "Private Journal of Conrad Weiser, taken from a copy in possession of Daniel Rupp of Lancaster, Pa., which had been copied from the original in possession of Dr. Hiester Muhlenberg, of Reading, Pa.," Mayer MS., II, 130–7, Hist. Soc. of the Reformed Church; "Conrad Weiser's Tagebuch," *Der Deutsche Pionier* (Cincinnati), II, 182–6 and 216–21; C. Z. Weiser, *The Life of (John) Conrad Weiser* (Reading, 1876), 440–9; etc.
6. Eugen Schopf, pastor of Grossaspach 1893–1919, "Hans Conrad Weiser, Vater und Sohn," in *Blätter des Altertumsverein für den Murrgau (Beilage zum Murretal-Boten Backnanger Tageblatt,* No. 49, July 24, 1925).
7. Von Alberti, *Württembergisches . . . Wappenbuch,* II, 1032.
8. Schopf, *op. cit.*
9. *Ibid.*
10. *Ibid.*
11. C. Z. Weiser, *Conrad Weiser* (Reading, 1876) p. 10.
12. Schopf, *op. cit.*
13. Life of Weiser by H. M. Muhlenberg, in the Muhlenberg Diaries, Krauth Memorial Library, Lutheran Theological Seminary, Mt. Airy, Pa.; *Hall. Nach.,* II, 445, 453.
14. This information was given to me by Hans Th. von Wasielewski, who visited Grossaspach in 1937 in search of Weiser material.
15. Eugen Schopf, *J. K. Weiser, Vater und Sohn* (Stuttgart, 1938), p. 11.
16. Schopf, *Blätter des Altertumsverein,* July 24, 1925.
17. W. A. Knittle, *Early Eighteenth Century Palatine Emigration* (Phila., 1937), p. 4.
18. Schopf, *op. cit.*
19. Conrad Weiser's *Autobiography.*
20. Knittle, *op. cit.,* 14.
21. *Ibid.*
22. *Autobiography.*
23. Schopf, *op. cit.*
24. *Ibid.*
25. Knittle, *op. cit.,* 28.
26. *Ibid.,* 54 ff.
27. *Ibid.,* 56.
28. *Ibid.,* 60.

29. *Ibid.*, 274.
30. *The Tatler*, No. 41, July 14, 1709; No. 51, August 6, 1709.
31. Knittle, *op. cit.*, 67.
32. F. R. Diffenderfer, "The German Exodus to England in 1709," *Publications of the Pennsylvania German Society*, VII, 301.
33. *Documents Relative to the Colonial History of the State of New York*, V, 87.
34. *Ibid.*, V, 88.
35. *Ibid.*, V, 113.
36. *Ibid.*, V, 118.
37. *Ibid.*, V, 121–2.

CHAPTER 2

1. *Documents Relative to the Colonial History of the State of New York*, V, 121.
2. *Ibid.*, V, 181.
3. *Calendar of State Papers*, 1711–1712, pp. 97–8.
4. *Calendar of State Papers, America and West Indies*, 1710–1711, # 317.
5. W. A. Knittle, *Early Eighteenth Century Palatine Emigration* (Phila., 1937), 169.
6. *Ibid.*, 168.
7. *Documentary History of New York*, III, 656.
8. *Ibid.*, III, 676.
9. Knittle, *op. cit.*, 152–3.
10. *Autobiography.*
11. *Ibid.*
12. *Documents Relative to the Colonial History of the State of New York*, V, 214.
13. Papers relating to the French Refugees, etc., p. 56, Dreer Collection, H.S.P.
14. See letter from Gov. Hunter to the Lords of Trade, Sept. 12, 1711: *Docs. Rel. to the Col. Hist. of the State of N.Y.*, V, 262–5.
15. Journal of the Rev. John Sharpe, Nov. 6, 1711: Am 1365, H.S.P.
16. C.O. 324–34, p. 170, P.R.O., London; *Doc. Hist. of N.Y.*, III, 707–14; *Ecclesiastical Records of the State of N.Y.*, III, 2168.
17. Gov. Hunter to Secretary Popple, July 25, 1715: *Docs. Rel. to the Col. Hist. of the State of N.Y.*, V, 418.
18. C.O. 324–34, p. 170, P.R.O.; *Doc. Hist. of N.Y.*, III, 707–14; *Ecc. Rec. of the State of N.Y.*, III, 2168.
19. *Autobiography*
20. *Ibid.*

CHAPTER 3

1. *Doc. Hist. of N.Y.*, III, 901; *Ecc. Rec. of the State of N.Y.*, III, 1969; J. W. Lydekker, *The Faithful Mohawks* (N.Y., 1938), p. 35.
2. Letter from William Andrews to the S.P.G., March 9, 1712/3: Lydekker, *Ibid.*, 35.
3. *Autobiography.*
4. W. Andrews to the S.P.G., Oct. 17, 1714, "At ye Queens Forte by the Mohawkes Castle": Lydekker, *op. cit.*, 45.
5. *Ibid.*, 38.
6. *Ibid.*, 37.
7. *Ibid.*
8. *Ibid.*
9. *Ibid.*, 40.
10. "Daniel Claus' Narrative" (*Society of Colonial Wars in the State of New York*), Vol. A, No. 9, New York, 1907) makes it clear that Conrad Weiser first lived with the Mohawks in the upper Schoharie Valley. In his account of his journey in 1750 to the Six Nations country, he says, "Mr. Claus . . . sat out with Col Weiser . . . to Albany from thence to Schohairee where Mr. Weiser first lived & learned the 6 Natn.

Language . . ." There remains the question whether Weiser first lived at "Eskahare" (Schoharie) or whether he lived at Karighondonte's town some eight miles to the south, both towns being on the upper Schoharie Creek. Evidence that he lived at Karighondonte's town (usually called the Wilder Hook) is this: Weiser never refers to Indians at Schoharie, but he does refer to his Indian friends in the other neighborhood. Writing of his journey with Daniel Claus in 1750, he tells of making a special visit to his "old Friends and Acquaintance" at "a small Mohock's Indian Town about eight miles Southwards" (see p. 307). Further, Weiser showed familiarity with the trails that fanned out in all directions from the Wilder Hook, but in 1750 he got lost trying to follow the trail leading from the village of Schoharie to the Lower Mohawk Castle—a trail with which he would surely have been familiar if the Indian town of Schoharie had once been his home.

11. Lydekker, *op. cit.*, 37.

12. Jonathan Cayenquiloquoa is repeatedly spoken of as Weiser's brother by adoption. The evidence that Moses was also a brother is this: Richard Peters, in a letter of April 25, 1756 (Penn MSS., Official Correspondence, VIII, 71, H.S.P.) speaks of the recent death and burial in Philadelphia of an Indian "Warriour of Note and Brother to Conrad Weiser." We know from other evidence that it was Moses who had died.

13. Horatio Hale, *The Iroquois Book of Rites* (Phila., 1883), p. 79.

14. *Ibid.*, 172 ff.

15. William C. Reichel, *Memorials of the Moravian Church* (Phila., 1870), I, 92, n.

16. *Conrad Weisers Beschreibung der Indianer in Mitheilungen an Christoph Saur* (published partly in Saur's newspaper and partly in his almanac during the years 1746–1748. The transcript from which this extract has been translated is in the Juniata College Library, Huntingdon, Pa. The first paragraph of the quotation is from Part III of the letter to Saur, the second from Part I. Parts I and II of this letter have been printed in the *Pa. Mag.*, Vol. I, 163 and 319, Vol. II, 407. An English translation of Part I was printed by Franklin and Hall, 1757 (Api. 282, H.S.P.); a manuscript translation is in the Ridgway Library, L.C. of P. A translation of Part III is in the H.S.P. (Am. 541).

17. Lydekker, *op. cit.*, p. 38.

18. Horatio Hale, *op. cit.*, pp. 37–8.

19. James Logan to John Penn, Dec. 18, 1730: Penn MSS., Off. Corr., II, 145, H.S.P.

20. *C.R.*, III, 474.

CHAPTER 4

1. *Autobiography.*

2. William Andrews to the S.P.G., Oct., 17, 1714: Lydekker, *The Faithful Mohawks* (N.Y., 1938), 44.

3. *Docs. Rel. to the Col. Hist. of the State of N.Y.*, V, 373.

4. The inclusion of the Tuscaroras is commonly assumed to have taken place shortly after the Treaty of Utrecht in 1713; but Mr. Lydekker adduces evidence that the fusion was not later than 1710, when the Iroquois chiefs in England, in an address to Queen Anne, referred to their people as "the Six Nations." See *The Faithful Mohawks*, 28, n. 1.

5. Survey of church and fort, *Doc. Hist. of N.Y.*, III, 602.

6. C.O., 324–34, p. 170, P.R.O.; *Doc. Hist. of N.Y.*, III, 707–14.

7. Jeptha R. Simms, *Frontiersmen of New York* (Albany, 1882), 125.

8. C.O., 324–34, p. 170, P.R.O.; *Doc. Hist. of N.Y.*, III, 707–14.

9. *Autobiography.*

10. Chief Joseph Montour of the Six Nations Reserve, Ont., gave me this interpretation of the word Mohawk in 1936. He told me that he had seen a drunken Mohawk, to whom he had partially explained the meaning of the term, beat his breast and cry, "Look at me: I am a *Mohawk*, a man-eater!" The Mohawks, according to Chief Montour, at one time called the Delawares "Witches,"

11. *Autobiography.*

12. See Chapter 10, p. 87.

13. Conrad Weiser's letter to Saur, Part I. See Chapter 3, n. 16.

14. *Autobiography.*

15. *Ecclesiastical Records of the State of N.Y.,* III, 2001.

16. "the first and nearest to Schenectady was named Kneskerns dorf. (2) gerlachs. dorf. (3)   fuchsendorf   (4) Hans george schmids dorf   the (5) Weisers or Brunnendorf. (6) Hartmans dorf the 7th Oberweissers dorf, . . ."—*Autobiography.* See Frank E. Lichtenthaeler, "The Seven Dorfs of Schoharie" (*Historical Review of Berks County,* January 1944), for evidence that the elder John Conrad Weiser's first home in this valley was at what is now known as the town of Schoharie rather than at Middleburgh.

17. *Autobiography.*

18. This saying was given me by the late C. C. Gingrich of Lawn, Pa.

19. Judge John M. Brown, *A Brief Sketch of the First Settlement of the County of Schoharie by the Germans* (1816; reprinted by the Schoharie County Historical Society, 1940), p. 5.

20. Jeptha R. Simms, *History of Schoharie County* (Albany, 1845), p. 51.

21. Brown, *op. cit.,* 8.

22. See the excellent story, under this name, of the early Schoharie settlement by Walter D. Edmonds, *The Saturday Evening Post,* March 2, 1935.

23. C.O., 324–34, p. 170, P.R.O.; *Doc. Hist. of N.Y.,* III, 707–14.

24. *Docs. Rel. to the Col. Hist. of the State of N.Y.,* V, 656.

25. Simms, *Hist. of Schoharie County* (Albany, 1845), p. 61.

26. Brown, *op. cit.,* p. 9.

27. Simms, *Hist. of Schoharie County,* p. 56.

28. *Doc. Hist. of N.Y.,* III, 687.

29. July 22, 1715: *Doc. Hist. of N.Y.,* III, 688.

30. July 25, 1715: *Docs. Rel. to the Col. Hist. of the State of N.Y.,* V, 418.

31. Simms, *Hist. of Schoharie County,* 60.

32. Knittle, *Early Eighteenth Century Palatine Emigration* (Phila., 1937), p. 297.

33. See the Cope List, H.S.P.

34. C.O., 324–34, p. 170, P.R.O.; *Doc. Hist. of the State of N.Y.,* III, 707–14.

35. Julius Friederich Sachse, "The Fatherland": *Publications of the Pennsylvania German Society,* VII, 171.

36. Brown, *op. cit.,* pp. 9–10.

37. C.O., 324–34, p. 170, P.R.O.; *Doc. Hist. of N.Y.,* III, 707–14.

38. *Ibid.*

39. Brown, *op. cit.,* 10.

40. *Ibid.*

41. See Letter of Attorney to Conrad Weiser *et al.,* August 16, 1719: Library of Congress, Washington (transcript from P.R.O.)

42. *Autobiography.*

43. C.O., 324–34, p. 170, P.R.O.

44. Secretary Clark to Walpole, Nov. 27, 1722: *Doc. Hist. of N.Y.,* III, 717.

45. See Weiser's Memorial, Oct. 20, 1720: Library of Congress (from P.R.O.); *Calendar of State Papers, America and West Indies,* 1720–1721, pp. 182–3.

46. *Autobiography.*

47. Simms, *Hist. of Schoharie County,* p. 64.

48. *Ibid.*

49. See Richard Peters' Diary at Easton, 1758, H.S.P.

CHAPTER 5

1. *Autobiography.*

2. Philadelphia Wills, 1747–1763, p. 986, Genealogical Society of Pennsylvania, Phila.

3. Life of Weiser, by H. M. Muhlenberg, in the Muhlenberg Diaries, Krauth Memorial Library, Mt. Airy Lutheran Theological Seminary; *Hall. Nach.,* II, 445–53.

4. *Doc. Hist. of N.Y.,* III, 571.

5. See Simmendinger List, Knittle, *Early Eighteenth Century Palatine Emigration* (Phila., 1937), 194.

6. *Hall. Nach.*, I, 176–8.

7. *Autobiography.*

8. See Weiser's Journal of his journey to Onondaga (Chapter 10, p. 86). April 3, 1737, he reached Otseninky and wrote, "I was at this place in 1726."

9. See Letters Patent issued to Conradt Weiser, Johannis Lawyer, and Peter Wagoner, July 8, 1725: Department of State, Albany, N.Y.

10. *Ibid.*

11. See Articles of Agreement between "Capt Conradt Wyzer of Minesink . . . and John Crook Junior of Kingston," April 5, 1726: Penn MSS., Pennsylvania Land Grants, IX, 23, H.S.P.

12. Logan Papers, Blue Letter Books, III, 105–6, H.S.P.

13. *Autobiography.*

14. The evidence for this route is presented by Frank E. Lichtenthaeler, in "They Drove Their Cattle Overland," the *Historical Review of Berks County*, July 1940, p. 111. See also Paul B. Mattice's reply in "The Palatine Emigration from Schoharie to the Tulpehocken," the *Historical Review of Berks County*, October 1944.

CHAPTER 6

1. Lightfoot Papers, Road MSS., H.S.P.

2. Road petition presented at the Quarter Sessions, Philadelphia County, March 1733.

3. List of officers, 1731–1741, private Sessions Docquet for Appointing Officers, Prothonotary's Office, Courthouse, Lancaster, Pa.

4. *Autobiography.*

5. *C.R.*, III, 350.

6. *C.R.*, III, 327.

7. A. H. Smyth, *The Writings of Benjamin Franklin* (1905), I, 366–7.

8. P.P., IV, 77; *P.A.*, I, 330.

9. James Logan to John Page, Jan. 3, 1731/2: Dickinson-Logan Letter Book, 34b, H.S.P.

10. Simon Gratz Autograph Collection, Am. Colonial Clergy, H.S.P.

11. P.P., III, 41, 43; *P.A.*, I, 220.

12. P.P., III, 38; *P.A.*, I, 216.

13. *Ibid.*

14. P.P., III, 33; *P.A.*, I, 218.

15. Penn MSS., Off. Corr., II, 181, H.S.P.

16. Dickinson-Logan Letter Book, 36–7, H.S.P.

17. Penn MSS., Off., Corr., II, 181, H.S.P.

18. Thomas Penn to Richard Peters, Jan. 10, 1756: Penn Letter Books, IV, 205–7, H.S.P.

19. Prov. Rec., 1726–1734, p. 184; *C.R.*, III, 429.

20. James Logan to John Penn, Aug. 2, 1731: Logan Papers, II, 7, H.S.P.

21. Logan Letter Books, III, 342–3; Penn MSS., Off. Corr., II, 191, H.S.P.

22. *P.A.*, First Series, I, 288.

23. C. B. Montgomery of Philadelphia tells me that Thomas Webb is thought to have been a Berks County man.

24. Prov. Rec., 1726–1734, p. 215; *C.R.*, III, 425.

25. Logan Papers, II, 14; Dickinson Letter Book, 33; Logan Letter Book, p. 42, H.S.P.

26. Prov. Rec., 1726–1734, p. 238; *C.R.*, III, 444.

27. *Ibid.*

28. *C.R.*, III, 472.

29. Prov. Rec., 1726–1734, p. 236; *C.R.*, III, 443.

30. *C.R.*, III, 469.

31. Prov. Rec., 1726–1734, p. 240; *C.R.*, III, 446–7.

32. "Confirmation of Schuylkill Valley Deed," Sept. 7, 1732: Room 220, Case 44-B,

Drawer 2, Department of Archives, Harrisburg. See also *P.A.*, First Series, I, 344–5. July 12, 1742, Conrad Weiser, Benjamin Franklin, *et al.*, witnessed the confirmation of the deed by Lingahonoa, "one of the Schuylkill Indians."

CHAPTER 7

1. James Steel to John Taylor, Phila., June 21, 1733: Taylor Papers, XV, #3089, H.S.P.

2. See "Draught of Cunrad Wiser's Land Situate on a branch of Tulpehoccon Creek in the County of Lancaster. Surveyed By Vertue of 2 Warrt^s each for 100^a the one dated the 17th of 8ber 1734 the other dated the 24th of 7ber 1735 Survey'd May ye 12th 1736 Per William Parsons": Copied Surveys, C—224, p. 72, Land Office, Harrisburg.

3. "Patent to Cunrad Wiser 200as": Patent Book, A—8, p. 83, Land Office, Harrisburg.

4. Conrad Weiser's Account Book is owned by Mrs. K. T. Anderson, Augustana College and Theological Seminary, Rock Island, Ill. The H.S.P. has a photostatic copy, and the Historical Society of Berks County a microfilm copy, of this valuable book.

5. *Chronicon Ephratense; a History of the Community of Seventh Day Baptists at Ephrata, Lancaster County, Penn'a,* by Lamech and Agrippa," translated from the original German by J. Max Hark, D.D. (Lancaster, 1889), p. 4.

6. *Chronicon Ephratense*, p. 54.

7. *Ibid.,* 58.

8. *Ibid.,* 135.

9. *Ibid.,* 31.

10. *Ibid.,* 32.

11. *Ibid.,* 43

12. *Ibid.,* 32.

13. *Ibid.,* 132.

14. Christopher Marshal's Diary, ed. D. M^{c}N. Stauffer, II, 158, H.S.P.

15. See Rev. P. C. Croll, *Annals and Historic Landmarks in the Lebanon Valley* (Phila., 1895), 43–5.

16. See Henry Melchior Muhlenberg's biographical sketch of his father-in-law, Muhlenberg Diaries, Krauth Memorial Library, Mt. Airy Lutheran Theological Seminary; *Hall. Nach.,* II, 445 ff.

17. *Ibid.*

18. Schmauk, *The Lutheran Church in Pennsylvania* (Phila., 1903), p. 479.

19. Weiser to Brunnholtz, Feb. 16, 1747: Juniata College Library, Huntingdon, Pa.; Krauth Memorial Library, Mt. Airy, Pa.; Fresenius, *Bewährte Nachrichten von Herrnhutischen Sachen,* III, 844–74; *Hall. Nach.,* I, 190–2.

20. *Ibid.*

21. See "The Confusion at Tulpehocken," by J. Taylor Hamilton, *Transactions of the Moravian Historical Society,* IV, 235 ff.

22. *Ibid.*

23. Weiser to Brunnholtz, Feb. 16, 1747: Juniata College Library, Huntingdon, Pa.

24. *Tr. Mor. Hist. Soc.,* IV, 235 ff.

25. Weiser to Brunnholtz, Feb. 16, 1747.

26. *Chronicon Ephratense*, p. 64.

27. *Ibid.,* 71.

28. *Ibid.,* 66.

29. *Neun und Neunzig Mystische Sprache* (Phila., 1728).

30. *Chronicon*, p. 33.

31. *Ibid.,* 88.

32. *Ibid.,* 69.

33. The title page of the *Chronicon Ephratense* attributes the authorship to "Lamech and Agrippa." Agrippa is the Latin form of the name Jabez. Jabez was the name Peter

Miller assumed among the Brethren in Zion. For further evidence that Miller was the author, see Christopher Marshal's Diary (Albany, 1877), pp. 122 and 151: Aug. 15 and Dec. 27, 1777. Peter Miller left the manuscript with Marshal to correct.

34. See *Rev.* III, 8.
35. *Chronicon,* pp. 71-2.
36. *Ibid.,* 72.
37. *Ibid.*

CHAPTER 8

1. See John Philip Boehm, "Faithful Letter of Warning," August 23, 1742: William John Hinke, *Life and Letters of Rev. John Philip Boehm* (Phila., 1916), 353-4. See also P. C. Croll, *Annals of Womelsdorf* (no imprint), Chapter 6; and Julius F. Sachse, *The German Sectarians of Pennsylvania,* I, 242-4.
2. *Brief Conrad Weisers nach London,* Nov. 27, 1752: Halle Documents, Vol. I, Krauth Memorial Library, Lutheran Theological Seminary, Mt. Airy, Pa.
3. *Chronicon Ephratense,* p. 74.
4. *Ibid.*
5. *Vide Exod.* II, 21; IV, 25.
6. *Chronicon Ephratense,* pp. 74-5.
7. *Ibid.,* 77.

CHAPTER 9

1. Logan Papers, X, 59, H.S.P.
2. *Ibid.*
3. *Ibid.*
4. *Ibid.,* X, 60.
5. Logan Papers, II, 57, and X, 63, H.S.P.
6. Logan Papers, X, 59.
7. *Ibid.*
8. *Ibid.*
9. Conrad Weiser to James Logan, Sept. 25, 1736: Charles Roberts Autograph Collection, Haverford College.
10. *Ibid.*
11. "Indian Treaty at Lancaster," June 22, 1744: Pennsylvania Archives, H.S.P.
12. "Memorial of the Six Nations, 1744," Division of Manuscripts, Library of Congress, Washington, D.C.
13. Prov. Rec., 1734-1737, p. 92; *C.R.,* IV, 82.
14. Andrew Hesselius' Notes on his Journey to America and back to Sweden 1711 to 1724, July 20, 1712: Am. 211, H.S.P. The original manuscript is in the Royal Library at Stockholm, where C. Stille ordered it translated in 1888.
15. Prov. Rec., 1734-1737, p. 92; *C.R.,* IV, 82.
16. P.P., VI, 63; *P.A.,* First Series, I, 694-7.
17. Prov. Rec., 1734-1737, p. 98; *C.R.,* IV, 88.
18. Penn MSS., Accounts, Large Folio, I, 53, H.S.P.
19. Conrad Weiser to James Logan, Oct. 27, 1736: Logan Papers, X, 65, H.S.P.
20. Logan Papers, XI, 25, H.S.P.
21. Facsimile of Thomson's *Inquiry into the Causes of the Alienation of the Delawares and Shawanese Indians* (Phila., 1867), 70.
22. "Observations, made on the Pamphlet, intitled, 'an Inquiry into the Causes of the Alienation of the Delaware and Shawano-Indians from the British Interest.' by Conrad Weiser. Chiefly on Land Affairs": Moravian Archives, Bethlehem, Pa.
23. Logan to Weiser, Oct. 18, 1736: Logan Papers, X, 64, H.S.P.

24. *Ibid.*
25. *Ibid.*
26. *Ibid.*
27. Weiser to Zinzendorf, July 7, 1742: Rep. 14. A., Nr. 25, Arch. der Br.
28. "A Copy of Mr Chew's Private Diary during the Treaty at Easton In October 1758," Thursday, Oct. 19: Am. 043, H.S.P.
29. *Ibid.*
30. Book of Indian Deeds, p. 43, Department of Archives, Harrisburg; *P.A.* First Series, I, 498-9.
31. *Ibid.*
32. Logan Papers, X, 65, H.S.P.
33. Penn MSS, Indian Affairs, I, 39, H.S.P.
34. *Ibid.*
35. Penn Letter Books, I, 189, H.S.P.

CHAPTER 10

1. *C.R.*, IV, 203.
2. James Logan to Gov. Clark of New York, Feb. 1, 1737/8: Logan Papers, X, 69, H.S.P.
3. Logan Papers, X, 66, H.S.P.
4. Logan Papers, X, 58, H.S.P.
5. Penn MSS., Private Correspondence, II, 163, H.S.P.
6. *Ibid.*
7. Conrad Weiser to Richard Peters, March 15, 1754: Corr. of C. W., I, 44, H.S.P.; Boyd, *The Susquehanna Company Papers* (Wilkes-Barre, 1930), I, 63.
8. *Ibid.*
9. The German version (incomplete) was until recently in the possession of C. W. Unger of Pottsville, Pa. A microfilm copy of this manuscript is in the H.S.P. The translation by Hiester H. Muhlenberg is printed in Schoolcraft's *History, Condition and Prospects of the Indian Tribes of North America* (Phila., 1854), IV, 324-41. It is printed also in the Rev. W. M. Beauchamp's *Life of Conrad Weiser* (Syracuse, 1925), pp. 12-27. For the shorter English version, see: Society Collection, Conrad Weiser's Journal to Onondaga, H.S.P.; Penn MSS., Indian Affairs, I, 42, H.S.P.; Moravian Archives, Bethlehem, Pa. In the version here printed, Hiester Muhlenberg's translation has been followed in the main, with occasional correction of place names. I have thought it a safer guide to the identification of places if these names were spelled as Weiser himself spelled them in the original manuscript.
10. Weiser's route may be followed now by motor car. The road runs north of Montoursville, at first along the west bank of the Loyalsock, then through a narrow valley up into the mountains, past Wallis Run and down to Lycoming Creek at Fields Station or Bodines.
11. About three-quarters of a mile south of Grover this stream is seen, near the railroad track, to make a sharp turn to the north. The surface water flows into Towanda Creek, but in time of flood water on adjoining lands to the south is found flowing into Lycoming Creek.

CHAPTER 11

1. Logan Papers, X, 70, H.S.P.
2. Logan to Weiser, Aug. 6, 1737: Peters MSS., I, 30, H.S.P.; Logan to Gov. Gooch, Sept. 21, 1737: Logan Papers, X, 58, H.S.P.; Logan to Gov. Clark, Feb. 1, 1737/8: Logan Papers, X, 69, H.S.P.
3. Logan Papers, X, 58, H.S.P.
4. Logan Papers, XI (Indian Affairs), 28, H.S.P.; *C.R.*, IV, 245.
5. *C.R.*, IV, 245.

6. Penn MSS., Ind. Aff., I, 46, H.S.P.
7. Stump had put his mark, May 12, 1737, to a receipt for £10 from James Steel.
8. Logan Papers, X, 70, H.S.P.
9. *C.R.*, IV, 668.
10. Steel to Smith, April 29, 1735: Letter Book of James Steel, 1730–1741, p. 96, H.S.P.
11. *Ibid.*
12. April 18, 1735: Pennsylvania Journal, I, 147, H.S.P.
13. *P.A.*, First Series, I, 539.
14. *P.A.*, First Series, I, 540.
15. Penn MSS., Ind. Aff., VIII, 259, H.S.P.
16. *P.A.*, First Series, I, 541.
17. Letter Book of James Steel, p. 156, H.S.P.
18. *Ibid.*
19. Etting Coll., Miscellaneous MSS., I, 95, H.S.P.
20. John Watson to Israel Pemberton, Aug. 9, 1757: Etting Coll., Misc. MSS., I, 90, H.S.P.
21. Richard Smith's Journal of 1769 (N.Y., 1906), p. 79. On June 9 he lodged at night with Edward Marshall, "who lives on an island 35 Miles above Trenton . . . This Marshal is the Man who performed the famous Walk for the Proprietaries of Pennsylvᵃ in 1733 [sic], for which as he tells us, he has never yet recᵈ any Reward."
22. Penn MSS., Off. Corr., III, 55, H.S.P.
23. Penn Letter Books, I, 224, H.S.P.
24. Penn MSS., Ind. Aff., I, 46, H.S.P.
25. Peters MSS., I, 30, H.S.P.
26. Letter Book of James Steel, p. 182, H.S.P.
27. Penn MSS., Ind. Aff., I, 46, H.S.P.
28. Richard Peters' draught of treaty, Aug. 1, 1739: Pennsylvania Archives, H.S.P.

CHAPTER 12

1. *Chronicon Ephratense* (Lancaster, 1889), p. 83.
2. This legend is still current at Ephrata.
3. Julius F. Sachse, *The German Sectarians of Pennsylvania* (Phila., 1899), pp. 359 ff.
4. *Ibid.*, I, 362.
5. *Ibid.*, I, 319.
6. *Account Books Kept by Benjamin Franklin*, ed. George Simpson Eddy (N.Y., 1928), p. 52. For facsimile of this account, see Sachse, *Sectarians*, I, 327.
7. *Chronicon*, p. 108; Sachse, *op. cit.*, I, 353.
8. Sachse, *op. cit.*, I, 358.
9. Sachse, *op. cit.*, I, 357–62.
10. Sachse, *op. cit.*, I, 368 ff.
11. *Chronicon*, Chapter XIX.
12. *Chronicon*, pp. 125–7.
13. Franklin's Ledger D, p. 39, A.P.S.
14. Sachse, *op. cit.*, I, 377 ff.
15. Pennsylvania Journals, H.S.P.
16. Sachse, *op. cit.*, I, 377 ff.
17. *Ibid.*
18. *Ibid.*, I, 386.
19. *Chronicon*, p. 127.
20. *Ibid.*
21. Logan to Weiser, July 25, 1740: Peters MSS., I, 45, H.S.P.
22. *C.R.*, IV, 433.
23. *Autobiography.*
24. *Sectarians*, I, 386; *Chronicon*, p. 120.
25. *Chronicon*, p. 132.

CHAPTER 13

1. *Chronicon*, p. 109.
2. *Ibid.*, p. 120.
3. Rep. 14.A., Nr. 18, p. 55, Arch. der Br.
4. *Chronicon*, p. 137.
5. *Ibid.*, p. 133.
6. *Ibid.*
7. *Ibid.*, p. 137.
8. *Ibid.*, pp. 131-2.
9. *Ibid.*, p. 132.
10. *Ibid.*, p. 103.
11. *Ibid.*, p. 84.
12. Penn MSS., Ind. Aff., IV, 30, H.S.P.
13. *Chronicon*, pp. 82-6.
14. Rep. 14.A., Nr. 16, p. 112, Arch. der Br.
15. Conrad Weiser to Count Zinzendorf, Dec. 1, 1745: Rep. 14.A., Nr. 25, p. 23, Arch. der Br.

CHAPTER 14

1. Corr. of C. W., I, 6-7, H.S.P.
2. Richard Peters to Thomas Penn, Oct. 8, 1741: Letter Books of Richard Peters, IV–VIII (1737-1750), H.S.P.
3. Maria Dickinson Logan Collection, H.S.P.; Corr. of C. W., I, 8, H.S.P.; Penn MSS., Off. Corr., III, 195, H.S.P.; Society Collection, H.S.P.; "Ein Wohlegemeindter und Ernstlicher Rath an unsere Lands-Leute die Teutschen, Folio 2pp. an Election circular, Phila. 1741, Benj. Franklin."—See Seidensticker, *First Century of German Printing in America* (1893), p. 14.
4. Pennsylvania Archives, H.S.P. The manuscript shows corrections in the hand of James Logan. It is printed here as Weiser wrote it. The endorsement, "Translation of Dutch printed Paper oct 1741," is in the handwriting of Richard Peters.
5. Letter Books of Richard Peters, No. IV, p. 18 (reverse), H.S.P.

CHAPTER 15

1. *The Journal of John Wesley*, Feb. 18, 1738.
2. Peters MSS, I, 84, H.S.P.
3. Rev. Levin Theodore Reichel, *The Early History of the Church of the United Brethren (Unitas Fratrum) Commonly Called Moravians in North America* (Nazareth, Pa., 1888), p. 69.
4. *Ibid.*, p. 70.
5. *Ibid.*, p. 69.
6. *Ibid.*, pp. 57-8; Loskiel, *History of the Missions of the United Brethren Among the Indians in North America* (London, 1794), p. 4.
7. Reichel, *op. cit.*, p. 90.
8. Rep. 14.A., Nr. 16, p. 222, Arch. der Br.
9. Richard Peters Letter Books, IV–VIII, H.S.P.
10. Sachse, *Sectarians*, I, 427.
11. *Chronicon Ephratense* (Lancaster, 1889), p. 146.
12. Reichel, *op. cit.*, p. 97.
13. Rep. 14.A., Nr. 16, p. 231, Arch. der Br.
14. Weiser to Brunnholtz, Feb. 16, 1747: Juniata College Library, Huntingdon, Pa.; Fresenius, *Bewährte Nachrichten von Herrnhutischen Sachen* (Franckfurt am Mayn, 1746-1751), III, 844-74.

15. *Ibid.*
16. *Ibid.*
17. Reichel, *op. cit.,* pp. 104-5.
18. Conrad Weiser to Count Zinzendorf, March (?), 1742: Rep. 14.A., Nr. 25, p. 29, Arch. der Br.
19. Reichel, *op. cit.,* p. 105.
20. *Ibid.*
21. Weiser to Brunnholtz, Feb. 16, 1747: Juniata College Library, Huntingdon, Pa.
22. *Ibid.*
23. Count Zinzendorf to Conrad Weiser, April (?), 1742: Rep. 14.A., Nr. 14, p. 65, Arch. der Br.
24. Sachse, *Sectarians,* I, 416-7.
25. Weiser to Zinzendorf, Jan. 12, 1741/2: Rep. 14.A., Nr. 25, p. 3, Arch. der Br.
26. Weiser to Zinzendorf, Nov. 26, 1742: Rep. 14.A., Nr. 25, p. 15.
27. Weiser to Zinzendorf, Jan. 12, 1741/2: Rep. 14.A., Nr. 25, p. 5.
28. Conrad Weiser to Gottlob Büttner, June, 1743: Rep. 14.A., Nr. 25, pp. 19-20.
29. Weiser to Zinzendorf, March (?), 1742: Rep. 14.A., Nr. 25, p. 29.
30. *Ibid.*
31. Rep. 14.A., Nr. 15, p. 21.
32. Rep. 14.A., Nr. 25, p. 23.

CHAPTER 16

1. William C. Reichel, *Memorials of the Moravian Church* (Phila., 1870), I, 72.
2. Penn MSS., Ind. Aff., IV, 30, H.S.P.
3. *C.R.,* IV, 413.
4. Richard Hockley to Thomas Penn, June 27, 1742: Penn MSS., Off. Corr., III, 221, H.S.P.; *Pa. Mag.,* XXVII, 433.
5. James Logan to Conrad Weiser, June 28, 1742: Peters MSS., I, 88, H.S.P.
6. Richard Peters to Thomas Penn, July 9, 1742: Peters Letter Books, IV-VIII, H.S.P.
7. Prov. Rec., K (1737-1747), 245; *C.R.,* IV, 563.
8. "Indian Charges July 5th 1742": Penn MSS., Accounts, Large Folio, I, 55, H.S.P.
9. Prov. Rec., K, 245; *C.R.,* IV, 564.
10. *Ibid.*
11. Prov. Rec., K, 249; *C.R.,* IV, 570.
12. Prov. Rec., K, 249; *C.R.,* IV, 572.
13. Prov. Rec., *ibid.; C.R.,* IV, 571.
14. Prov. Rec., K., 252; *C.R.,* IV, 574.
15. *C.R.,* VII, 327
16. Prov. Rec., K, 255; *C.R.,* IV, 578-9.
17. *Ibid.*
18. D. J. Brinton, *The Lenâpí and Their Legends* (Phila., 1885), p. 121.
19. Rumors sprang like weeds out of Canasatego's grave. Daniel Claus thought he had been poisoned by the French. For other explanations of his death and the circumstances connected with it, see Chapter 38.
20. Prov. Rec., K, 255-6; *C.R.,* IV, 580.
21. Brinton, *op. cit.,* p. 115.
22. Prov. Rec., K, 256; *C.R.,* IV, 581.
23. Prov. Rec., K, 257; *C.R.,* IV, 583.
24. *C.R.,* VII, 651.
25. Peters MSS., I, 89, H.S.P.

CHAPTER 17

1. Gov. Thomas to Conrad Weiser, Feb. 26, 1741/2: Peters MSS., I, 73, H.S.P.
2. Rep. 14.A., Nr. 25, p. 29, Arch. der Br.

3. William C. Reichel, *Memorials of the Moravian Church* (Phila., 1870), I, 30.
4. *Ibid.*, I, 65.
5. De Schweinitz, *The Life of David Zeisberger* (Phila., 1870), p. 108.
6. *Ibid.*
7. Rep. 14.A., Nr. 15, p. 17, Arch. der Br.
8. Rep. 14.A., Nr. 25, p. 9, Arch. der Br.; Moravian Archives, Bethlehem.
9. Gov. Thomas to Conrad Weiser, Sept. 9, 1742: Peters MSS., I, 94, H.S.P.
10. Weiser to Brunnholtz (Answer to Question 8), Feb. 16, 1747: Juniata College Library, Huntingdon, Pa.; Krauth Memorial Library, Mt. Airy, Pa.; Johann Philip Fresenius, *Bewährte Nachrichten von Herrnhutischen Sachen* (Franckfurt am Mayn, 1746-1751), III, 844-74.
11. James Logan to Gov. Clarke, March 30, 1742: Reichel, *Memorials*, I, 15, n.
12. "Zinzendorf's Narrative of a Journey from Bethlehem to Shamokin, in September of 1742": Reichel, *Memorials*, I, 78.
13. "Zinzendorf's Observations Concerning the Savages . . .": Reichel, *Memorials*, I, 18.
14. "Zinzendorf's Narrative," Reichel, *Memorials*, I, 91.
15. Reichel, *op. cit.*, I, 64.
16. *Ibid.*, 66.
17. Rep. 14.A., Nr. 16, p. 187, Arch. der Br.
18. Rep. 14.A., Nr. 16, p. 43.
19. Reichel, *Memorials*, I, 84-5.
20. *Ibid.*, 86.
21. Weiser to Brunnholtz, Feb. 16, 1747: Juniata College Library, Huntingdon, Pa.
22. Reichel, *op. cit.*, pp. 95-6.
23. *Ibid.*, 98.
24. Peter Böhler writing from Bethlehem, Oct. 14 (New Style), 1742: Rep. 14.A., Nr. 27, p. 33.
25. Reichel, *op. cit.*, 102.
26. *Ibid.*
27. *Ibid.*, 103.
28. Weiser to Brunnholtz, Feb. 16, 1747: Juniata College Library.
29. *Ibid.*
30. Reichel, *op. cit.*, 111 and 113.

CHAPTER 18

1. Weiser to Brunnholtz, Feb. 16, 1747: Juniata College Library, Huntingdon, Pa.
2. Prov. Rec., K, 270-2; *C.R.*, IV, 630-3.
3. Prov. Rec., K, 272; *C.R.*, IV, 634.
4. Prov. Rec., K, 274; *C.R.*, IV, 637.
5. Prov. Rec., K, 273; *C.R.*, IV, 636.
6. Prov. Rec., K, 277; *C.R.*, IV, 640-1.
7. Prov. Rec., K, 277; *C.R.*, IV, 642.
8. Prov. Rec., K, 278: *C.R.*, IV, 642-3.
9. *Ibid.*
10. *Ibid.*
11. *Ibid.*
12. Prov. Rec., K, 278; *C.R.*, IV, 644.
13. Prov. Rec., K, 283: *C.R.*, IV, 653.
14. Corr. of C. W., I, 33, H.S.P.
15. MS.: "Janontowano."
16. Prov. Rec., K, 278-9: *C.R.*, IV, 644-6.
17. Corr. of C. W., I, 33, H.S.P.
18. This custom originated in an early religious festival among the Iroquois, the Festival of Dreams, which lasted several days and nights, during which time everyone expected to receive from his friends whatever he had dreamed of. See *Jesuit Relations*

(ed. Thwaites, Cleveland, 1896) XLII, 165: "It would be cruelty, nay, murder, not to give a man the subject of his dream; for such a refusal might cause his death. Hence, some see themselves stripped of their all, without hope of retribution; for, whatever they thus give away will never be restored to them, unless they themselves dream, or pretend to dream, of the same thing. But they are, in general, too scrupulous to employ simulation, which would, in their opinion, cause all sorts of misfortunes. Yet there are some who overcome their scruples, and enrich themselves by a shrewd piece of deception."

19. J. M. Hubbard, *Red Jacket and his People* (Albany, 1886), pp. 41–2.

CHAPTER 19

1. Peters MSS., I, 108, H.S.P.
2. Prov. Rec., K, 281; *C.R.*, IV, 649.
3. Prov. Rec., K, 280; *C.R.*, IV, 647.
4. Prov. Rec., K, 280; *C.R.*, IV, 648.
5. Prov. Rec., K, 281–2; *C.R.*, IV, 650.
6. Prov. Rec., K, 284; *C.R.*, IV, 654.
7. "Extracts from Mr. Lewis Evans' Journal. 1743," T. Pownall, M.P., *A Topographical Description of such parts of North America as are contained in The (annexed) Map of the Middle British Colonies, &c. in North America* (London, 1776). See also Lawrence Henry Gipson, *Lewis Evans* (Phila., 1939).
8. *Observations Made by Mr. John Bartram, In his Journey from Pensilvania to Onondaga, &c.* (London, 1751), p. 11.
9. *Ibid.*
10. *Observations*, p. 12.
11. Evans' Journal.
12. *Observations*, p. 13.
13. Evans' Journal.
14. *Observations*, p. 16.
15. *Observations*, p. 21.
16. "Spangenberg's Notes of Travel to Onondaga in 1745," ed. John W. Jordan, *Pa. Mag.*, II, 432.
17. *Observations*, pp. 21–2.
18. *Ibid.*, p. 24.
19. *Ibid.*, p. 31.
20. *Ibid.*, p. 37.
21. *Ibid.*, pp. 38–9.
22. Evans' Journal.
23. This legend was told me, June 10, 1937, by Mrs. Kellogg, an Indian scholar of the Oneida nation, then living on the site of the old Council House at Onondaga.
24. *Observations*, p. 40.
25. Prov. Rec., K, 287; *C.R.*, IV, 660.
26. *Observations*, p. 40.

CHAPTER 20

1. Bartram's *Observations* (London, 1751), pp. 40–1.
2. *Observations*, p. 43.
3. *C.R.*, IV, 660–1.
4. *Ibid.*, 667.
5. *Observations*, p. 45.
6. Prov. Rec., K, 288; *C.R.*, IV, 661.
7. *Ibid.*
8. Prov. Rec., K, 288; *C.R.*, IV, 662.
9. *Ibid.*

10. Prov. Rec., K, 288; *C.R.*, IV, 662–3.
11. The ritual of these beautiful ceremonies has been recorded by Horatio Hale in *The Iroquois Book of Rites* (Phila., 1883), pp. 117–39.
12. Prov. Rec., K, 288–91; *C.R.*, 663–8.
13. *Observations*, pp. 62–3.
14. Prov. Rec., K, 291–2; *C.R.*, IV, 668.
15. *Observations*, p. 63.
16. *Ibid.*, 65.
17. *Ibid.*, 68.
18. *Ibid.*, 71.
19. *Ibid.*, 73.

CHAPTER 21

1. Benjamin Franklin's Ledger D, p. 93, A.P.S.
2. Weiser to the Vorsteher at Ephrata, Sept. 3, 1743: Miscellaneous Collection, Department of Archives, Harrisburg; Lebanon County Historical Society, Lebanon, Pa.; Rev. C. Z. Weiser, *The Life of John Conrad Weiser*, second edition (Reading, 1899), pp. 128–30.
3. Conrad Weiser to Count Zinzendorf, Oct. 17, 1743: Rep. 14.A., Nr. 25, p. 18, Arch. der Br.
4. Sachse, *Sectarians*, I, 260; II, 139–40.
5. *Chronicon Ephratense*, p. 163.
6. Rep. 14.A., Nr. 16, p. 113, Arch. der Br.

CHAPTER 22

1. Prov. Rec., K, 291; *C.R.*, IV, 667.
2. P.P., VIII, 59; *P.A.*, First Series, I, 643–4.
3. P.P., VIII, 66; *P.A.*, I, 649.
4. P.P., VIII, 61; *P.A.*, I, 646.
5. P.P., VIII, 62; *P.A.*, I, 647.
6. P.P., VIII, 63; *P.A.*, I, 648.
7. *Ibid.*
8. Prov. Rec., K, 298–9; *C.R.*, IV, 680–5.
9. Pennsylvania Archives, H.S.P.

CHAPTER 23

1. Richard Peters to Penn, March 7, 1743/4: Richard Peters Letter Books, IV–VIII, H.S.P.
2. Richard Peters to Penn, May 31, 1744: *Ibid.*
3. Peters MSS., II, 2, H.S.P.
4. Peters MSS., II, 12, H.S.P.
5. Peters to Penn, Aug. 2, 1744: Peters Letter Books, IV–VIII, H.S.P.
6. Peters MSS., II, 16, H.S.P.
7. "Zinzendorf's Narrative," W. C. Reichel, *Memorials of the Moravian Church* (Phila., 1870), p. 72.
8. Witham Marshe, *Journal of the Treaty at Lancaster in 1744* (Lancaster, 1884).
9. Peters MSS., II, 16, H.S.P.
10. Marshe, *op. cit.*, pp. 11–2.
11. *Ibid.*, p. 12.
12. "Memorandum of Indian Expences": Peters MSS., II, 16, H.S.P.
13. Peters to Penn, Aug. 2, 1744: Peters Letter Books, IV–VIII, H.S.P.
14. *Ibid.*

15. *Ibid.*
16. *Ibid.*
17. Marshe, *op. cit.*, p. 12.
18. Peters to Penn, Aug. 2, 1744: Peters Letter Books, IV–VIII, H.S.P.
19. *Ibid.*
20. "The Indian Treaty as Literature," by Lawrence C. Wroth, *Yale Review*, July 1928, p. 749.
21. Peters to Penn, Feb. 8, 1744/5: Peters Letter Books, IV–VIII, H.S.P.
22. Prov. Rec., K, 315–6; *C.R.*, IV, 706–7. See also Franklin's report of this treaty, reproduced in *Indian Treaties Printed by Benjamin Franklin* (Phila., 1938), ed. Julian P. Boyd.
23. Prov. Rec., K, 316; *C.R.*, IV, 708.
24. Prov. Rec., K, 322; *C.R.*, IV, 717.
25. Prov. Rec., K, 324; *C.R.*, IV, 720.
26. Marshe, *op. cit.*, p. 24.
27. Prov. Rec., K, 324; *C.R.*, IV, 721.
28. Marshe, *op. cit.*, June 30.
29. Prov. Rec., K, 332; *C.R.*, IV, 733.
30. Prov. Rec., K, 334; *C.R.*, IV, 737.
31. *P.A.*, First Series, I, 658.
32. Prov. Rec., K, 334; *C.R.*, IV, 736.
33. Horatio Hale, *The Iroquois Book of Rites* (Phila., 1883), p. 74.
34. C. W. Canfield, *Legends of the Iroquois* (N.Y., 1902), pp. 137, 216 (n.).
35. See Rep. 14.A., Nr. 15, p. 17, and Nr. 16, p. 187, Arch. der Br.
36. Rep. 14.A., Nr. 16, p. 260, *ibid.*
37. See Chapter 61, p. 552.
38. *C.R.*, IV, 667.
39. Peters MSS., II, 16, H.S.P.

CHAPTER 24

1. *The Lees of Virginia* (N.Y., 1935), p. 54.
2. *Ibid.*, p. 58.
3. Hamilton to Penn, July 10, 1750: Penn MSS., Off. Corr., V, 27, H.S.P.
4. Peters MSS, II, 19, H.S.P.
5. See version compiled by Abraham H. Cassell and translated by Miss Helen Bell, *Pa. Mag.*, I, 319, and II, 407.
6. Peters MSS., II, 22, H.S.P.
7. *Translation of a German Letter wrote by Conrad Weiser, Esq; Interpreter, on Indian Affairs, for the Province of Pennsylvania* (Philadelphia: Printed and Sold by B. Franklin, & D. Hall): Api., 282, H.S.P. See also copy in the Ridgway Library, L. C. of P.
8. *Ibid.*
9. The third section of "Conrad Weisers Beschreibung der Indianer in Mitheilungen an Christoph Saur" is translated here from the copy at Juniata College, Huntingdon, Pa. A translation of the part beginning, "Chastity is a virtue with them," is filed, Am. 541, at the H.S.P.

CHAPTER 25

1. *C.R.*, IV, 746.
2. Conrad Weiser to James Logan, Sept. 29, 1744: P.P., VIII, 76; *P.A.*, First Series, I, 661.
3. *C.R.*, IV, 744.
4. See notice in the *Pennsylvania Gazette*, Dec. 6, 1744.
5. *Hall. Nach.*, I, 337.

6. Moravian Archives, Bethlehem. The letter is endorsed, in Spangenberg's hand: "Conr. Weiser an br. Pyrlaeus. Von dem Mordbrennern."

7. P.P., IX, 3; *P.A.*, First Series, I, 672.

8. The Courthouse, Lancaster, Pa.

9. *P.A.*, First Series, I, 665.

10. Weiser to Peters, Jan. 2, 1744/5: P.P., IX, 1; *P.A.*, First Series, I, 665.

11. P.P., IX, 3; *P.A.*, First Series, I, 671.

12. Continuance Docquet, Feb., 1744/5, Prothonotary's Office, Courthouse, Lancaster, Pa.

13. Henry Eyster Jacobs, "The German Emigration to America," *Publications of the Pennsylvania German Society*, VIII, 93.

14. Muhlenberg's Diary, *ibid.*, p. 92.

15. *Hall. Nach.* I, p. 117; Dr. John Ludwig Schulze, *Reports of the United German Evangelical Lutheran Congregations* (extracts from the *Hall. Nach.* translated into English), I, 176–8. See also *The Journals of Henry Melchior Muhlenberg*, tr. by Theodore G. Tappert and John W. Doberstein (Phila., 1942), pp. 102–3.

16. Rep. 14.A., Nr. 25, p. 23, Arch. der. Br.

17. Henry Muhlenberg to Conrad Weiser, Dec. 27, 1750: Ministerium of the Evangelical-Lutheran Church, deposited in the Krauth Memorial Library, Mt. Airy Lutheran Theological Seminary.

18. Life of Weiser by H. M. Muhlenberg, Krauth Mem. Lib.; *Hall. Nach.* II, 445–53.

CHAPTER 26

1. Peters MSS., II, 23, H.S.P.

2. P.P. IX, 3; *P.A.*, First Series, I, 671–2.

3. Peters MSS., II, 25, H.S.P.; *P.A.*, First Series, I, 664.

4. Peters MSS., II, 23, H.S.P.

5. P.P., IX, 3; *P.A.*, First Series, I, 671.

6. Peters MSS., II, 32, H.S.P.

7. *Ibid.*, 30.

8. "Extract of the Subscribers [Conrad Weiser's] Journal, taken New York, July y[e] 15th 1745": Horsmanden Papers, No. 20, p. 87, note (g.), New York Historical Society.

9. J. W. Lydekker, *The Faithful Mohawks* (N.Y., 1938), pp. 56–7.

10. Corr. of C. W., I, 12, H.S.P.

11. *Diary of David McClure* (N.Y., 1899), p. 56.

12. *Translation of a German Letter wrote by Conrad Weiser* (Phila., by B. Franklin).

13. Spangenberg's Journal, June 9 (N.S.): ed. John W. Jordan, *Pa. Mag.*, II, 424 ff.

14. Bishop Cammerhof's Letters to Zinzendorf, 1747–1749, Sunday, Jan. 14: tr. by John W. Jordan, H.S.P.

15. Conrad Weiser to Count Zinzendorf, Dec. 1, 1745: Rep. 14.A., Nr. 25, p. 23, Arch. der Br.

16. Prov. Rec., K, 363; *C.R.*, IV, 780.

17. Prov. Rec., K, 363; *C.R.*, IV, 781.

18. *Ibid.*

19. Prov. Rec., K, 364; *C.R.*, IV, 781.

20. Spangenberg's Journal, June 21 (N.S.).

21. *P.A.*, First Series, I, 662.

22. Horsmanden Papers, No. 20, pp. 82–9, New York Historical Society.

23. Conrad Weiser's account with the Government of Virginia: Corr. of C. W., I, 12, H.S.P.

24. *C.R.*, IV, 772.

25. *The Autobiography of Benjamin Franklin*, ed. Carl Van Doren (N.Y., 1940), pp. 360–2. Franklin's account is not very trustworthy, and it is difficult to date the conversation here described. How are we to explain Canasatego's mention of "the many Years since they had seen each other"? During Canasatego's lifetime, Conrad Weiser visited Onondaga in 1737, 1743, and 1745. There is no reason to suppose that Weiser had

seen Canasatego before 1737. When he met him at Onondaga in 1743, it was after seeing him only a few months before in Philadelphia. When he met him at Onondaga in 1745, it was after seeing him only a few months before at Lancaster. It would appear that Benjamin Franklin, who wrote this in his old age, was inventing detail for verisimilitude.

26. Note (e) in the Horsmanden manuscript: "These Indians are descended from a Branch of the Mohawk Nation, who many y^{rs} Since being accepted as Hostages by the ffrench, were at length seduced by the Artifices of the Priests, to desert this Countrey, & take up their Residence altogether in Canada, & having been converted to their Superstition, & reconciled to their foolish Customs, to Say their Prayers by Tale of Beeds. The English Mohawks, by way of Derision call y^m y^e *Praying Indians,* The French, Kocknewage's."

CHAPTER 27

1. Penn MSS., Ind. Aff., I, 49, H.S.P.
2. "Memorandums taken by Conrad Weiser in Albany at the Treaty with the Indians held in October 1745": Penn MSS., Ind. Aff., I, 46, H.S.P.; *Indian Treaties,* ed. Julian P. Boyd (Phila., 1938), pp. 309–11.
3. *Ibid.*
4. Gov. Thomas to Thomas Penn, Dec. 11, 1745: Penn MSS., Off. Cor., IV, 55, H.S.P.
5. Penn MSS., Ind. Aff., I, 49, H.S.P.
6. James Logan to Richard Peters, Dec. 8, 1745, "C. Weiser has so filled me with indignation against that Monster of a Man as he himself calls him Govr Clinton, that I can by no means be easie without expressing my thoughts to thee . . .": Logan Papers, X, 73, H.S.P.
7. Penn MSS., Ind. Aff., 49, H.S.P.
8. Penn MSS., Off. Corr., IV, 55, H.S.P.

CHAPTER 28

1. Penn MSS., Off. Corr., IV, 51, H.S.P.
2. Peters MSS., II, 46, H.S.P.
3. Rep. 14.A., Nr. 25, p. 23, Arch. der Br.
4. Peters MSS., II, 49, H.S.P.
5. *Ibid.*, 48.
6. *Ibid.*, 50.
7. Du Simitière Papers, Yi 966, Ridgway Library, L.C. of P.
8. *Ibid.*
9. Letters about the Lancaster Confusion, Jan. 5–Feb. 9, 1746: Muhlenberg Diary, PM 95, A-1742-8, Krauth Memorial Library, Mt. Airy; *Journals of H. M. Muhlenberg,* tr. by Tappert and Doberstein (Phila., 1942), pp. 112–4.
10. Spangenberg, July 23, 1746: Rep. 14.A., Nr. 18, p. 136, Arch. der Br.
11. Feb. 15, 1746: Reichel, *Memorials of the Moravian Church* (Phila., 1870), p. 64.
12. Spangenberg, July 23, 1746: Rep. 14.A., Nr. 18, pp. 136, 142.
13. Rep. 14.A., Nr. 16, pp. 205–8.
14. Rep. 14.A., Nr. 18, p. 132.
15. Box 2-a, Depositions, etc., Society Collection, H.S.P.
16. Rep. 14.A., Nr. 18, p. 121.
17. Rep. 14.A., Nr. 18, p. 108.
18. Rep. 14.A., Nr. 18, p. 132.
19. Peters MSS., II, 51, H.S.P.
20. Corr. of C. W., I, 14, H.S.P.
21. Peters MSS., II, 55, H.S.P.
22. Rep. 14.A., Nr. 18, p. 136.
23. Peters MSS., II, 58, H.S.P.

24. *C.R.*, V, 40.
25. *Ibid.*, II, 48, 49.
26. *Ibid.*, II, 50.
27. Bishop Cammerhof's letters to Zinzendorf, tr. J. W. Jordan, March 20–9, H.S.P.
28. March 30, 1748: Peters MSS., II, 100, H.S.P.
29. Corr. of C. W., I, 15, H.S.P.
30. *Ibid.*
31. Corr. of C. W., I, 15½, H.S.P.
32. *Ibid.*
33. *Ibid.*
34. Corr. of C. W., I, 13, H.S.P.
35. Prov. Rec., L, 321; *C.R.*, V, 285.
36. Weiser to Zinzendorf, May 16, 1742: Rep. 14.A., Nr. 25, p. 7.
37. *Ibid.*
38. Weiser to Brunnholtz, Feb. 16, 1747. This date, May 1743, is given by the version in the Krauth Memorial Library, Mt. Airy.
39. Rep. 14.A., Nr. 18, p. 124.
40. David Bruce's Journal at Shecomeko, May 12, 1746: Am. 708, H.S.P.
41. *Hall. Nach.*, I, 244.

CHAPTER 29

1. Diary of Nicholas Kurtz, Jan. 11, 1747: Krauth Memorial Library, Mt. Airy, Pa.; *Hall. Nach.*, I, 199; Baumgarten, *Theolog. Bedenken*, VI, 673 ff. Here as elsewhere material is found in the original diaries not printed in the *Hallesche Nachrichten*.
2. Answer to Ninth Question, Weiser to Brunnholtz, Feb. 16, 1747: Juniata College Library, Huntingdon, Pa.; Krauth Memorial Library, Mt. Airy, Pa.; Fresenius, *Bewährte Nachrichten von Herrnhutischen Sachen* (Frankfurt und Leipzig, 1748), III, 844–74.
3. Weiser to Zinzendorf, Aug. 24, 1742: Rep. 14.A., Nr. 25, p. 13, Arch. der Br.
4. Muhlenberg to Weiser, Feb. 28, 1747: Krauth Mem. Lib., Mt. Airy, Pa.; *The Historical Review of Berks County*, Vol. IV, No. 4, p. 115.
5. James Logan to Conrad Weiser, Feb. 25, 1747: Peters MSS., II, 73, H.S.P.
6. Peters to Weiser, Feb. 25, 1747: Peters MSS., II, 72, H.S.P.
7. Muhlenberg to Weiser, Feb. 28, 1747: see note 4 above.
8. For Pennsylvania German aids to teething, see the *Publications of the Pennsylvania German Society*, XLV, 119–20, "Folk Medicine of the Pennsylvania Germans," by T. R. Brendle and C. W. Unger: "For dentition . . . suspend a rabbit's tooth about the child's neck." The late Dr. George Wheeler has suggested to me that a wolf's tooth may have been used to like purpose. There were many such remedies used in the old days. Brendle and Unger continue: "To ease dentition for a child hang a mouse by a string until it is dead, then tie the string about the child's neck and leave it there until it drops off; . . . tie around a child's neck a string by which three mice had been hanged."
9. Vol. 12, p. 490, Recorder of Deeds, Berks County Courthouse, Reading, Pa.
10. Docket No. 2—No. 34, August Sessions, 1747, Bern Township, Quarter Sessions, Lancaster County Courthouse, Lancaster, Pa.
11. No. 33, Docket Drawer 1740 to 1762, May Sessions 1747, Quarter Sessions, Lancaster County Courthouse.
12. March 8–23, 1747: Bishop Cammerhof's Letters to Zinzendorf 1747–9, tr. by John W. Jordan, H. S. P.
13. *Ibid.*, May 22–24, 1747.
14. See Conrad Weiser's letter, Sept., 1747: Fresenius, *Bewährte Nachrichten*, III, 822–30.
15. June 29, 1747: Bishop Cammerhof's Letters to Zinzendorf, H.S.P.
16. Weiser's letter of Sept., 1747, *loc. cit.*
17. *Hall. Nach.*, I, 201–2.

18. Cammerhof to Zinzendorf, Nov. 17, 1747: *loc. cit.*
19. Dated "Dolpehacken den 10 October."
20. Cammerhof to Zinzendorf, Nov. 17, 1747: *loc. cit.*
21. *Hall. Nach.,* I, 201–2.
22. De Schweinitz, *Life and Times of David Zeisberger* (Phila., 1870), p. 60.

CHAPTER 30

1. P.P., X, 10; *P.A.,* First Series, I, 761.
2. P.P., X, 2; *P.A.,* First Series, I, 757.
3. P.P., X, 10; *P.A.,* First Series, I, 761.
4. William H. Hill, *Old Fort Edward* (Fort Edward, N.Y., 1929), pp. 27 ff.
5. *Ibid.*
6. *The Papers of Sir William Johnson,* ed. James Sullivan (Albany, 1921), I, 65–6.
7. P.P., IX, 69; *P.A.,* First Series, I, 749–50.
8. P.P., IX, 71; *P.A.,* First Series, I, 751.
9. P.P., X, 10; P.A., First Series, I, 761.
10. *P.A.,* First Series, I, 766.
11. P.P., IX, 71; *P.A.,* First Series, I, 751.
12. P.P., X, 10; *P.A.,* First Series, I, 762.
13. Ledger D, 342, A.P.S.
14. Peters MSS., II, 78, H.S.P.
15. Prov. Rec., L, 76; *C.R.,* V, 120.
16. P.P., X, 18; *P.A.,* First Series, I, 771–2.
17. Diary of Johann Nicholas Kurtz, Sept. 30, 1747: Krauth Mem. Lib., Mt. Airy, Pa.
18. Cammerhof to Zinzendorf, tr. John W. Jordan, Nov. 17, 1747, H.S.P.
19. P.P., X, 10; *P.A.,* First Series, I, 762.
20. *Ibid.*
21. Logan Papers, X, 76, H.S.P.
22. Peters MSS., II, 81, H.S.P.
23. Cammerhof to Zinzendorf, tr. John W. Jordan, Nov. 17, 1747, H.S.P.
24. *Ibid.*
25. Logan Papers, XI, 33, H.S.P.; *C.R.,* V, 136.
26. Peters MSS., II, 83, H.S.P.
27. Corr. of C. W., I, 18, H.S.P.

CHAPTER 31

1. Peters MSS., II, 112, H.S.P.
2. Friday, Nov. 18/19, 1748: Moravian Archives, Bethlehem, Pa.
3. PW 42, D 1, Ministerium of the Evangelical Lutheran Church of Pennsylvania and Adjacent States, Krauth Memorial Library, Mt. Airy, Pa.
4. The letter is endorsed, "Copy to Spangenberg, Febr. 13 1747/8"
5. *Pensylvanische Berichte,* April 16, 1748.
6. For an account of what follows, see Muhlenberg's Diary, *Hall. Nach.,* I, 380–2; Handschuh's Diary, *Hall. Nach.,* I, 165 ff.; Kurtz's Diary, *Hall. Nach.,* I, 202 ff.

CHAPTER 32

1. Prov. Rec., L, 103; *C.R.,* V, 138.
2. Prov. Rec., L, 74; *C.R.,* V, 119.
3. Burton J. Hendrick, *The Lees of Virginia* (N.Y., 1935), p. 61.
4. Peters MSS., II, 83, H.S.P.
5. Conrad Weiser to James Logan, Nov. 13, 1747: Logan Papers, X, 78, H.S.P.

6. Peters to the Proprietaries, Nov. 19, 1747: Peters Letter Books, IV–VIII, #7, pp. 1, 2, H.S.P.

7. Weiser to Logan, Nov. 13, 1747.

8. Prov. Rec., L, 115; C.R., V, 146.

9. Peters to Proprietaries, Nov. 19, 1747.

10. Prov. Rec., L, 117–8; C.R., V, 148.

11. Ibid.

12. Prov. Rec., L, 360; C.R., V, 309.

13. "Lancaster July 1748 the Counsil on Indian Affairs to Michall Gross," item under date of July 25: Pennsylvania Archives, H.S.P.

14. Prov. Rec., L, 362; C.R., V, 311.

15. Prov. Rec., L, 367–8; C.R., V, 314.

16. Peters MSS., II, 89, H.S.P.

17. Peters to the Proprietaries, May 11, 1748: Penn MSS., Off. Corr., IV, 93, H.S.P.; Peters Letter Books, IV–VIII, H.S.P.

18. Weiser to Peters, March 28, 1748: Peters MSS., II, 99, H.S.P.

19. John Ludwig Schulze, Reports of the United German Evangelical Lutheran Congregations in North America (Phila., 1880), I, p. 195; Hall. Nach., I, 165.

20. For an account of these comings and goings, see Conrad Weiser's letters to Richard Peters, July 10, 14, 17, 1748: P.A., First Series, II, 8–10.

21. July 27, 1748: Peters Letter Books, VII, H.S.P.; Indian Treaties, ed. Julian P. Boyd (Phila., 1938), p. xlix.

22. Weiser to Peters, July 14, 1748: P.P., X, 33; P.A., First Series, II, 9.

23. P.P., X, 38; P.A., First Series, II, 11–2.

24. Peters MSS., II, 106.

25. Prov. Rec., L, 421 ff.; C.R., V, 348 ff.

26. Prov. Rec., L, 425–6; C.R., V, 348.

27. Peters to the Proprietaries, Oct. 26, 1749: Peters Letter Books, IV–VIII, #7, H.S.P.; Penn MSS., Off. Corr., IV, 245–9, H.S.P.

28. Oct. 2, 1748: Box N to W, Maria Dickinson Logan Papers, H.S.P.

29. Prov. Rec., L, 435; C.R., V, 357.

30. Prov. Rec., L, 433; C.R., V, 356.

31. Prov. Rec., L, 436; C.R., V, 358.

32. Conrad Weiser Papers, H.S.P. Another copy is preserved in the Moravian Archives, Bethlehem, Pa. See also I. D. Rupp, Early History of Western Pennsylvania (Harrisburg, 1846), Appendix, pp. 13 ff.

33. Penn MSS., Off. Corr., IV, 163, H.S.P.

34. Corr. of C. W., I, 18, H.S.P.

35. Ibid., II, 27.

CHAPTER 33

1. Bishop Cammerhof's Letters to Zinzendorf, tr. by John W. Jordan, Feb. 10–6, 1748, H.S.P.

2. Ibid.

3. Ibid.

4. De Schweinitz, Life and Times of David Zeisberger (Phila., 1870), p. 149.

5. Ibid., p. 150.

6. Journal of the Shamokin Mission, Dec. 6, 1748: Moravian Archives, Bethlehem, Pa.

7. Ibid.

8. New York State Museum, Bulletin 113, Archeology 13, Civil, Religious and Mourning Councils and Ceremonies of Adoption of the New York Indians, by William M. Beauchamp (Albany, 1907), p. 383.

9. Journal of the Shamokin Mission, Dec. 8, 1748.

10. Ibid., Dec. 9, 1748. See also John H. Carter, "Shickellamy," Northumberland County Historical Society, III, 42. Carter tells of the exhuming in 1860 of a grave thought to be Shickellamy's, containing 400 beads, some bells and dangles for breech

pants, copper rings, bracelets, an iron tobacco box with a small quantity of tobacco in it, a fishing line, a needle, a penny, a halfpenny, a copper medal (identified as one struck in England in 1714), a scalping knife, a musket barrel, a ceremonial iron tomahawk, flint arrow heads, a stone paint cup filled with vermilion, an iron pipe of peace with the tomahawk broken off, an old English white clay pipe, and a green glass bottle with a long neck. A boulder monument to Shickellamy, "Diplomat and Statesman," was erected in 1915 near the site of this grave by the Augusta Chapter of the D.A.R., in coöperation with the Pennsylvania Historical Commission.

11. Journal of the Shamokin Mission, Dec. 12, 1748.
12. P.P., X, 70; *P.A.*, First Series, II, 23.
13. John Shickellamy. According to Carter, *op. cit.*, his name, Tachnechtoris, means "a wide-spreading oak."
14. Horatio Hale, *The Iroquois Book of Rites* (Phila., 1883), p. 153.
15. C. Hale Sipe, *The Indian Chiefs of Pennsylvania* (Butler, Pa., 1927), p. 164.
16. Colonel Cresap was not responsible for these murders.
17. From "Notes on the State of Virginia," *The Writings of Thomas Jefferson* (N.Y., 1894), III, 156–7.
18. Horatio Hale, *op. cit.*, p. 129.

CHAPTER 34

1. Anthony Palmer to Gov. Ogle, Jan. 25, 1748: *Archives of Maryland*, XXVIII, 415.
2. P.P., X, 42; *P.A.*, First Series, II, 15.
3. To Richard Peters: P.P., X, 70; *P.A.*, First Series, II, 24.
4. Peters to the Proprietaries, April 29, 1749: Peters Letter Books, IV–VIII, #7, H.S.P.
5. Weiser to Peters, May 8, 1749: Corr. of C. W., I, 19, H.S.P.
6. Richard Peters to Thomas Penn, July 5, 1749: Penn MSS., Off. Corr., IV, 219, H.S.P.; Richard Peters' Letter Books, IV–VIII, #7, H.S.P.
7. Conrad Weiser's Account, "Indian Expences in the Year 1749," June 22–4: Gratz Collection, H.S.P.
8. Richard Peters to Thomas Penn, July 5, 1749. See note 6 above.
9. *Ibid.*
10. *Ibid.*
11. *Ibid.*
12. Penn MSS., Off. Corr., IV, 237, H.S.P.
13. Du Simitière Collection, Yi 966, Ridgway Library, L.C. of P.
14. *Ibid.*
15. *Ibid.*
16. Peters MSS., II, 122, H.S.P.
17. Du Simitière Coll., Ridgway Library, L.C. of P.
18. Sept. 11, 1749: Penn MSS., Off. Corr., IV, 237–9, H.S.P.
19. Weiser's "Indian Account on their Return 1749," Corr. of C. W., I, 21, H.S.P.
20. Penn MSS., Off. Corr., V, 59, H.S.P.
21. Penn Letter Books, II, 297, H.S.P.

CHAPTER 35

1. Peters MSS., II, 115, H.S.P.
2. Muhlenberg Diaries, Vol. XXXV, pp. 141–2, Krauth Memorial Library, Mt. Airy, Pa. Excerpts from this letter may be found in *The Historical Review of Berks County*, Vol. IV, No. 4, p. 116,
3. Peters to the Proprietaries, May 11, 1748: Peters Letter Books, IV–VIII, #7, H.S.P.; Penn MSS., Off. Corr., IV, 93, H.S.P.
4. Peters' Letter Books, H.S.P.; Penn MSS., Off. Corr., IV, 219, H.S.P.
5. William J. Mann, *The Life and Times of Henry Melchior Muhlenberg* (Phila., 1888), p. 240.

6. *Hall. Nach.*, II, 98.
7. Feb. 27, 1749/50: Penn MSS., Off. Corr., IV, 193, H.S.P.
8. *Ibid.*
9. *Ibid.*
10. P.P., XI, 4; *P.A.*, First Series, II, 45.
11. Penn MSS., Off. Corr., IV, 239, H.S.P.
12. Cop. Survey, B-21, p. 103, Land Office, Harrisburg.
13. Penn MSS., Off. Corr., IV, 189–91, H.S.P.
14. Penn Letter Books, II, 103, H.S.P.
15. Penn MSS., Off. Corr., V, 3–11, H.S.P.
16. Penn Letter Books, II, 306 ff., H.S.P.
17. Penn MSS., Off. Corr., V, 57–61, H.S.P.
18. Charles Fisher Snyder, "Conrad Weiser in the Susquehanna Valley," *Proceedings of The Northumberland County Historical Society*, VI, 57.
19. Penn MSS., 1720–1766, Supp., p. 55 (top), H.S.P.
20. Peters to Penns, Sept. 28, 1750: Penn MSS., Off. Corr., V, 57 ff., H.S.P.
21. *P.A.*, II, 41.
22. Penn MSS., Off. Corr., V, 3–11, H.S.P.
23. Corr. of C. W., I, 27, H.S.P.
24. Penn Letter Books, II, 305, H.S.P.

CHAPTER 36

1. Prov. Rec., K, 281; *C.R.*, IV, 648.
2. Peters to the Proprietaries, July 10, 1750: Penn MSS., Off. Corr., V, 29, H.S.P.
3. *Ibid.*
4. Prov. Rec., M, 62; *C.R.*, V, 435–6.
5. Peters, July 10, 1750, *ibid.*
6. *Ibid.*
7. Phila., 1900, pp. 213–4.
8. Prov. Rec., M, 64–5; *C.R.*, V, 440.
9. Prov. Rec., M, 67; *C.R.*, V, 443.
10. Peters, July 10, 1750: *ibid.*, 31.
11. Peters MSS., III, 20, H.S.P.

CHAPTER 37

1. Peters MSS., III, 5, H.S.P.
2. Parkman Papers, Massachusetts Historical Society, Boston. A digest of this letter, in Conrad Weiser's hand, is in the Peters MSS., III, 6, H.S.P.
3. Peters MSS., III, 9, H.S.P.
4. Peters MSS., III, 10, H.S.P.
5. Penn MSS., Indian Affairs, IV, 5, H.S.P.
6. Corr. of C. W., I, 27, H.S.P.
7. Penn MSS., Off. Corr., V, 27, H.S.P.
8. Penn Letter Books, III, 22, H.S.P.

CHAPTER 38

1. W. M. Darlington, *Christopher Gist's Journal* (Pittsburgh, 1893), pp. 221–2.
2. Penn MSS., Off. Corr., V, 35, H.S.P.
3. "Daniel Claus' Narrative," *Society of Colonial Wars in the State of New York*, Vol. A., No. 9 (N.Y., 1907).
4. *C.R.*, V, 470.
5. Muhlenberg's Journal, *Hall. Nach.*, I, 509 ff.

6. Bethlehem Diary, Friday, Aug. 17/28, 1750: Bethlehem, Pa. The note runs: "At noon we had an unexpected Visit from Conrad Weiser, who, on his way to Onondago, where he has a Commission from the Governor *relating to the Ohio-Company* (*as he intimates*) [the words in italics are crossed out in the Diary] came here with his Travelling Companions and receiving a friendly Invitation stayed with us for a little While.

"He had planned to meet his Son-in-law here, the celebrated Mühlberg . . . who was making a visit to Esopus and was to accompany his Father-in-law a good part of his Journey. And they did meet here as arranged and spent a couple of Hours with us."

7. Muhlenberg's Journal, Aug. 17, *loc. cit.*
8. Reichel, *Memorials of the Moravian Church,* I, 46.
9. Muhlenberg's Journal, Aug. 20, *loc. cit.*
10. Prov. Rec., M, 84; *C.R.,* V, 470.
11. Muhlenberg's Journal, Aug. 22, *loc. cit.*
12. Prov. Rec., M, 84; *C.R.,* V, 470.
13. "Daniel Claus' Narrative," *loc. cit.*
14. Prov. Rec., M, 85; *C.R.,* V, 471–2.
15. "Daniel Claus' Narrative," *loc. cit.*
16. Prov. Rec., M, 86; *C.R.,* V, 472–3.
17. Prov. Rec., M, 86; *C.R.,* V, 474.
18. Prov. Rec., M, 87–8; *C.R.,* V, 474–6.
19. Rep. 14.A., Nr. 16, p. 185: Arch. der Br.
20. Penn MSS., Ind. Aff., I, 69, H.S.P.
21. Prov. Rec., M, 88; *C.R.,* V, 476.
22. Journal of Conrad Weiser to Onondaga, 1750: Am, 183 (back of p. 13), H.S.P.
23. Rep. 14.A., Nr. 18, pp. 274–8, Arch. der Br.
24. *Ibid.,* p. 319.
25. Prov. Rec., M, 88–9; *C.R.,* V, 476–8.
26. William Johnson to Gov. Clinton, Jan. 22, 1748/9: *The Papers of Sir William Johnson,* Vol. IX (Albany, 1939), p. 36.
27. Prov. Rec., M, 89; *C.R.,* V, 478.
28. "Daniel Claus' Narrative," *loc. cit.*
29. Prov. Rec., M, 90; *C.R.,* V, 479.
30. Muhlenberg's Journal, Sept. 22, 1750: *Hall. Nach.,* I, 513.
31. Halle Documents, Vol. I: Krauth Memorial Library, Mt. Airy, Pa.
32. Sept. 30, 1750: Penn MSS., Off. Corr., V, 63, H.S.P.
33. Corr. of C. W., I, 28, H.S.P.
34. C.O. 5–1344, P.R.O.

CHAPTER 39

1. Peters to the Proprietaries, July 12, 1750: Penn MSS., Off. Corr., V, 35, H.S.P.
2. Thomas Penn to Richard Peters, Oct. 12, 1750: Peters MSS., II, 111, H.S.P.; Penn Letter Books, II, 246–7, H.S.P.
3. Peters MSS., III, 35, H.S.P.
4. Corr. of C. W., I, 35, H.S.P.
5. "Croghan's Account of Indian Affairs": Penn MSS., Ind. Aff., I, 51, H.S.P. "In April 1751, the Governor sent me to the Ohio with a Present of Goods, the Speeches were all wrote by the Provincial Interpreter, Mr Weiser."
6. *C.R.,* V, 526.
7. Peters to the Proprietaries, May 11, 1748: Penn MSS., Off. Corr., IV, 93, H.S.P.; Peters Letter Books #7, H.S.P.
8. Penn MSS., Off. Corr., IV, 219, H.S.P.
9. Penn MSS., Off. Corr., IV, 185, H.S.P.
10. May 11, 1748, *loc. cit.*
11. Peters to the Proprietaries, Sept. 28, 1750: Penn MSS., Off. Corr., V, 57–61, H.S.P.
12. *C.R.,* V, 479.

13. Sept. 28, 1750: *loc. cit.*

14. James Hamilton to Conrad Weiser, April 27, 1751: Peters MSS., III, 38, H.S.P.

15. *C.R.,* V, 541–3.

16. Corr. of C. W., I, 22, H.S.P.

17. Du Simitière Coll., Yi 966, Ridgway Library, L.C. of P.

18. Cayenquarachton himself reappears at Easton in October 1758, where he receives three pounds and fifteen shillings from Conrad Weiser. See Weiser's Accounts: Peters MSS., V, 57, H.S.P.

19. Rudolph Bonner "conducted a tavern for a long time" on the Manatawny Road at Methacton, Worcester Township, Montgomery County. See "Genealogical Data relating to the German Settlers in Pennsylvania," compiled by Edward W. Hocker, 1935, p. 105: Vg 1675, H.S.P.

20. *Documentary History of New York,* VI, 703.

21. *Documents Relating to the Colonial History of the State of New York,* VII, 717.

22. *The Papers of Sir William Johnson* (Albany, 1921), I, 342.

23. *Ibid.,* p. 344.

24. "Daniel Claus' Narrative," *loc. cit.*

CHAPTER 40

1. Peters MSS., III, 27, H.S.P.

2. *Ibid.,* 54.

3. James Hamilton to Conrad Weiser, March 11, 1752: Gratz Coll., Governors of Penna., Case 2, Box 32, H.S.P.

4. Penn MSS., Additional Miscellaneous Letters, I, 76, H.S.P.; Penn MSS., Off. Corr. V, 225, H.S.P.

5. Peters MSS., III, 55, H.S.P.

6. Prov. Rec., M, 153; *C.R.,* V, 569.

7. Prov. Rec., M, 154; *C.R.,* V, 571.

8. Peters to the Proprietaries, 1752: Penn MSS., Off. Corr., V, 199, H.S.P.

9. Peters to the Proprietaries, Dec. 14, 1752: *ibid.,* 311.

10. Peters to the Proprietaries, June 19, 1752: *ibid.,* 245.

11. See Albert T. Volwiler, *George Croghan and the Westward Movement* (Cleveland, 1926).

12. Conrad Weiser to Richard Peters, July 20, 1747: *P.A.,* First Series, I, 762; Peters to the Proprietaries, Feb. 15, 1749/50: Penn MSS., Off. Corr., IV, 185, H.S.P.

13. Peters to the Proprietaries, June 26, 1756: Gratz Coll., p. 66, H.S.P.

14. Bouquet to Gen. Gage, Dec. 22, 1746: quoted by Charles A. Hanna, *The Wilderness Trail* (N.Y., 1911), II, 32.

15. Henry Fox, Secretary of State: quoted by Volwiler, *op. cit.,* p. 109.

16. Gov. Hamilton to Gov. Sharpe, Jan. 7, 1754: *P.A.,* First Series, II, 114.

17. John Langdale to Col. Bouquet, Pittsburgh, March 5, 1761: 21646, Letters of Bouquet, pp. 75–6, British Museum, London.

18. Israel Pemberton to John Fothergill, Easton, August 3, 1757: Pemberton Papers, Etting Coll., II, 27, H.S.P.

19. March 16, 1752: Penn MSS., Off. Corr., V, 217, H.S.P.

20. *Ibid.*

21. July 7, 1752: Peters MSS., III, 58, H.S.P.

22. Peters MSS., III, 60, H.S.P.

23. Halle Documents, Vol. II, pp. 1040–1: Krauth Memorial Library, Mt. Airy, Pa.

24. Peters MSS., III, 57, H.S.P.

25. Richard Peters to Conrad Weiser, Jan. 3, 1752: Peters MSS., III, 53, H.S.P.

26. Peters MSS., III, 61, H.S.P.

27. *Ibid.*

28. Penn Physic MSS., Accounts, XI, 39, H.S.P.

29. Peters MSS., III, 69, H.S.P.

30. Daniel Claus to Gov. Hamilton, Jan. 10, 1754: *P.A.,* First Series, II, 116.

31. Penn MSS., Off. Corr., VI, 115, H.S.P.
32. Penn MSS., Add. Misc. Letters, I, 80, H.S.P.
33. *Ibid.*
34. Peters to the Proprietaries, May 3, 1753: Penn MSS., Off. Corr., VI, 47–9, H.S.P.
35. Corr. of C. W., I, 17, H.S.P.
36. Corr. of C. W., I, 38, H.S.P.
37. *Ibid.*, 17.
38. Conrad Weiser to Richard Peters, Feb., 1753 (?): Corr. of C. W., I, 17, H.S.P.
39. *Ibid.*
40. "A Paragraph of a Letter wrote by Wᵐ West to the Governor of Pennsylvania, Susquehana May 7ᵗʰ 1753": Add. MSS., 1403, p. 178, British Museum.
41. *Ibid.*
42. Penn MSS., Off. Corr., VI, 39, H.S.P.
43. Conrad Weiser to Gov. Hamilton, June 25, 1753: Berks and Montgomery Counties, Misc. MSS., p. 51, H.S.P.
44. Corr. of C. W., I, 42, H.S.P.
45. See Peters to the Proprietaries, Sept., 1753: Penn MSS., Off. Corr., VI, 105–7, H.S.P.
46. *C.R.*, V, 642.
47. Prov. Rec., M, 205; *C.R.*, V, 642; Peters MSS., III, 74, H.S.P.
48. *C.R.*, V, 646.
49. Prov. Rec., M, 208: *C.R.*, V, 646.
50. Prov. Rec., M, 207; *C.R.*, V, 644–5.
51. Prov. Rec., M, 207; *C.R.*, V, 645–6.
52. Prov. Rec., M, 207–8; *C.R.*, V, 645–6.
53. Prov. Rec., M, 208–9; *C.R.*, V, 646–7.
54. William M. Beauchamp, in *The Life of Conrad Weiser* (Syracuse, 1925), p. 95, notes that "Alexander Colden was youngest son of Cadwallader Colden, famous as the author of the History of the Five Nations . . ."
55. Penn Letter Books, III, 276, H.S.P.
56. Peters to the Proprietaries, Nov. 6, 1753: Penn MSS., Off. Corr., VI, 115, H.S.P.
57. Gov. Hamilton to Conrad Weiser, Sept. 21, 1753: Peters MSS., III, 76, H.S.P.
58. Edward Shippen to James Burd, Lancaster, Sept. 23: "Mʳ Weiser wrote me yesterday that he expected Mʳ Peters to be at his house to night by a Letᵗ which the Governor had sent him; . . . Mʳ Weiser hopes to have my Company at the Treaty . . ."—Shippen Papers, Vol. I, Correspondence, p. 149, H.S.P.
59. *C.R.*, V, 664.
60. Peters to the Proprietaries, Nov. 6, 1753: Penn MSS., Off. Cor., VI, 115, H.S.P.
61. *Ibid.*
62. Prov. Rec., M, 222; *C.R.*, V, 666.
63. Prov. Rec., M, 224; *C.R.*, V, 668.
64. Prov. Rec., M, 224; *C.R.*, V, 669.
65. Prov. Rec., M, 229; *C.R.*, V, 676.
66. Prov. Rec., M, 230; *C.R.*, V, 677–8.
67. *Ibid.*
68. Prov. Rec., M, 231; *C.R.*, V, 679.
69. *Ibid.*
70. Penn MSS., Off. Corr., VI, 115, H.S.P.
71. Prov. Rec., M, 234; *C.R.*, V, 684.
72. *C.R.*, V, 686.
73. Conrad Weiser to Richard Peters, Nov. 16, 1753: Peters MSS., III, 78, H.S.P.
74. *Ibid.*
75. The letter as here presented is made up of two fragments preserved in separate places: Corr. of C. W., I, 62, and II, 25, H.S.P. The two pieces are written in the same bold hand that Conrad used at this time, and they both deal with matters of concern in the fall of 1753. Weiser's letter to Peters of Nov. 16 in that year gives evidence that the Ohio letter was sent to Col. Taylor: "I had a letter by Mʳ Price from Coll. Taylor of virginia a principle Member of the ohio Company who is desirous to Know the

truth of Matters about ohio, but I can not at present answer it, Should therefore be glad to See a printed Copy of the Comissioners report at the treaty at Carlile."

CHAPTER 41

1. Corr. of C. W., I, 43, H.S.P.

2. Conrad Weiser to Richard Peters, Feb. 7, 1754: Berks and Montgomery County Misc. MSS., p. 55, H.S.P.

3. See Conrad Weiser's letter to Bethlehem (undated), Rep. 14.A., Nr. 25, p. 28, Arch. der Br. See also: Leonhardt Schnell's letter from Lancaster to Br. Peter at Bethlehem, Feb. 6, 1754, Rep. 14.A., Nr. 25, p. 27; Weiser's letter to Bethlehem of Feb. 20, 1754, ibid.; and a letter from Bethlehem, March 19, 1754, Rep. 14.A., Nr. 27, pp. 119 ff.

4. Rep. 14.A., Nr. 25, p. 28, Arch. der Br.

5. Conrad Weiser to Richard Peters, Feb. 7, 1754: Berks and Montgomery Counties, Misc. MSS., p. 55, H.S.P.

6. Prov. Rec., M, 293; C.R., V, 769.

7. Corr. of C. W., I, 44, H.S.P.

8. March 25, 1754: Peters MSS, III, 91, H.S.P.

9. Prov. Rec., M, 315; C.R., VI, 24.

10. Berks and Montgomery Counties, Misc. MSS., p. 57, H.S.P.

11. Penn Physick MSS., Accounts, XI, 52, H.S.P.

12. Prov. Rec., M, 324; C.R., VI, 36–7.

13. Penn MSS., Ind. Aff., II, 9, H.S.P.; Du Simitière Coll., Ridgway Library, L.C. of P.

14. Corr. of C. W., I, 31, H.S.P

15 Berks County Deeds, B-1, p. 377, Courthouse, Reading, Pa.

16. Deeds 1736–1759, Am 995, No. 170, H.S.P.

17. Thomas Penn to Richard Peters, Feb. 1, 1754, Penn Letter Books, III, 303, H.S.P.; March 9, 1754, ibid., p. 307, H.S.P. See also Hall. Nach., II, 228; H. W. Smith, Life and Times of William Smith (Phila., 1880), I, 40 ff.; William Smith to Samuel Chandler, May 30, 1754, Minutes of the German Free Schools, p. 33, Brinton Coll., H.S.P.

18. Peters MSS., III, 99, H.S.P.

19. Penn Letter Books, III, 330, H.S.P.

20. Prov. Rec., M, 333; C.R., VI, 49.

21. P.A., First Series, II, 145.

22. Prov. Rec., M, 375; C.R., VI, 112.

23. Prov. Rec., M, 376; C.R., VI, 112.

24. "Expences with the Indians of the Six united Nations in Albany during the time of the Treaty," July, 1754: Penn MSS., Accounts, Large Folio, II, 12, H.S.P.

25. "Observations, made on the Pamphlet, 'an Inquiry into the Causes of the Alienation of the Delaware and Shawano-Indians from the British Interest.' by Conrad Weiser," note on p. 78: Moravian Archives, Bethlehem, Pa.

26. C.R., VI, 80.

27. C.R., VI, 111.

28. Ibid.

29. Prov. Rec., M, 379; C.R., VI, 118.

30. Prov. Rec., M, 380; C.R., VI, 119.

31. Prov. Rec., M, 381–2; C.R., VI, 119–21.

32. Inquiry into the Causes of the Alienation of the Delaware and Shawnee Indians (1759).

33. Conrad Weiser's "Observations," on p. 77 of Thomson's book.

34. Weiser's "Observations" on p. 78.

35. Ibid.

36. Weiser's "Observations" on p. 82.

37. Weiser's "Observations" on pp. 78–9.

38. P.A., First Series, II, 559. Cf. Daniel Claus to Richard Peters, July 10, 1755: The Papers of Sir William Johnson, Vol. IX (Albany, 1939), pp. 199–200.

39. P.A., First Series, II, 175.

40. Papers Relating to French Refugees: Colonial and Indian Affairs, Dreer Coll. p. 36, H.S.P.

41. *Ibid.*, p. 62.

42. Richard Peters to Conrad Weiser, Nov. 8, 1754: Corr. of C. W., I, 48, H.S.P.

43. *Johnson of the Mohawks* (N.Y., 1930), p. 165.

CHAPTER 42

1. Prov. Rec., M, 369; *C.R.*, VI, 103.

2. Prov. Rec., M, 367; *C.R.*, VI, 100.

3. Lawrence Henry Gipson, *Zones of International Friction* (N.Y., 1939), p. 298.

4. Aug. 14, 1754: Berks and Montgomery County Papers, 1693–1869, p. 181, H.S.P.

5. *The Papers of Sir William Johnson* (Albany, 1921), I, 409–10.

6. William Trent to James Burd, July 7, 1754: Papers of the Shippen Family, XV, 119, H.S.P.

7. See *Memoirs of Major Robert Stobo* (Pittsburgh, 1854), pp. 86–92; *C.R.*, VI, 141, 162.

8. Prov. Rec., M, 412; *C.R.*, VI, 162.

9. Prov. Rec., M, 395; *C.R.*, VI, 141.

10. Minutes of the German Free Schools, p. 43, Smith Papers, Brinton Coll., H.S.P.

11. Penn MSS., Off. Corr., VI, 219, H.S.P.

12. Prov. Rec., M, 399; *C.R.*, VI, 146.

13. Conrad Weiser's original manuscript is in the Berks County Historical Society Museum, Reading, Pa. See also Prov. Rec., M, 403 ff.; *C.R.*, VI, 150 ff.

14. Prov. Rec., M, 402; *C.R.*, VI, 149.

15. Berks County Hist. Soc.; Prov. Rec., M, 407 ff.; *C.R.*, VI, 155 ff.

16. Pennsylvania Archives, H.S.P.

17. George Croghan to Gov. Hamilton, Sept. 27, 1754: Penn MSS., Off. Corr., VI, 221, H.S.P.

18. Papers Relating to French Refugees, Colonial and Indian Affairs, Dreer Coll., p. 62, H.S.P.

19. Daniel Claus to Richard Peters, Oct. 29, 1754: Pennsylvania Archives, H.S.P.

20. Arthur Pound, *Johnson of the Mohawks* (N.Y., 1930), p. 172.

CHAPTER 43

1. Conrad Weiser to Richard Peters, Oct. 12, 1754: Corr. of C. W., I, 47, H.S.P.; Julian P. Boyd, *Susquehanna Company Papers*, I, 136. See also "Account of my Expences to Shamokin in building House for James Logan in the Year 1754 in September & October": Reformed Church Historical Society, Lancaster, Pa.

2. Corr. of C. W., I, 47, H.S.P.

3. *Ibid.*

4. *P.A.*, First Series, II, 178.

5. Richard Peters to Conrad Weiser, Oct. 25, 1755: Corr. of C. W., I, 59, H.S.P.

6. Conrad Weiser to Richard Peters, Oct. 12, 1754: Corr. of C. W., I, 47, H.S.P.

7. Peters to Parsons, Nov. 7, 1754: Misc. MSS., Northampton County, 1727–1758, p. 139, H.S.P.; Weiser to Peters, Oct. 16: Papers Relating to the French Refugees, Colonial and Indian Affairs, Dreer Coll. H.S.P.

8. Parsons to Peters, Nov. 9, 1754: Misc. MSS., Northampton County, 1727–1758, p. 139, H.S.P.

9. *P.P.*, XIII, 80; *P.A.*, First Series, II, 193.

10. *C.R.*, VI, 269; *C.R.*, VI, 252.

11. *C.R.*, VI, 187.

12. *Papers of Sir William Johnson*, II, 611; IX, 589.

13. "Daniel Claus' Narrative," *loc. cit.*

14. Prov. Rec., M, 476; *C.R.*, VI, 243.
15. Account of the Proprietaries with Richard Peters, Albany Indian Purchase, Feb. 15, 1755: Penn MSS., Ind. Aff., III, 59, H.S.P.
16. Prov. Rec., M, 503; *C.R.*, VI, 279.
17. Gov. Morris to Isaac Norris, Jan. 17, 1755: Geo. W. Norris Coll., H.S.P.
18. *Papers of Sir William Johnson*, IX, 148.
19. Account of the Proprietaries with Richard Peters, Albany Indian Purchase, *loc. cit.*
20. Prov. Rec., M, 513; *C.R.*, VI, 291-2.
21. Gov. Morris to Conrad Weiser, Jan. 22, 1755: Peters MSS., IV, 2, H.S.P.
22. Smith Papers, "German Free Schools," p. 64, Brinton Coll., H.S.P.
23. Thomas Penn to Richard Peters, Oct. 17, 1754: Penn Letter Books, IV, 4, H.S.P.
24. Notes of Trial, Weiser vs. Achmooty, Oct. 18: Yates Papers, Box 1791-1794, H.S.P.
25. Weiser to Peters, March 8, 1755: Corr. of C. W., I, 50, H.S.P.
26. Letter from Conrad Weiser, April 12, 1755: Corr. of C. W., I, 53, H.S.P.
27. *Ibid.*
28. Samuel Weiser to Nicholas Scull, June 9, 1755: Copied Surveys, B-19, p. 28, Land Office, Harrisburg.
29. Charles Fisher Snyder, "Conrad Weiser in the Susquehanna Valley," *Northumberland County Hist. Soc.*, VI, 58.
30. Peters to Weiser, March 15, 1755: Peters MSS., IV, 8, H.S.P.
31. *Ibid.*
32. Thomas Penn to Richard Peters, Aug. 14, 1755: Penn Letter Books, IV, 143-7, H.S.P.; Penn MSS., Supp., XVII, 93, H.S.P.; Boyd, *Susq. Co. Papers*, I, 301.
33. P.P., XIV, 21; *P.A.*, First Series, II, 259.
34. P.P., XIV, 84; *P.A.*, First Series, II, 318-9.
35. May 23, 1755: Peters MSS., IV, 15, H.S.P.
36. March 19, 1755: Balch Papers, Shippen, Vol. I, p. 39, H.S.P.
37. *Papers of Sir William Johnson*, I, 465-6.
38. May 24, 1755: Penn MSS., Off. Corr., VII, 41, H.S.P.
39. Parkman, *Montcalm and Wolfe* (Boston, 1898), I, 209.
40. Report from Philadelphia, July 10: *Pennsylvanische Berichte*, July 16, 1754.
41. Croghan to Johnson, March 14, 1757: *Docs. Rel. to the Col. Hist. of the State of N.Y.*, VII, 270.
42. June 30, 1755: *C.R.*, VI, 457-8.
43. Shippen Papers, Vol. I, Correspondence, p. 215, H.S.P.
44. Prov. Rec., N, 95; *C.R.*, VI, 467-8.

CHAPTER 44

1. See Francis-J. Audet, *Jean-Daniel Dumas Le Héros de la Monongahéla* (Montreal, 1920).
2. Franklin to Jared Eliot, Aug. 31, 1755: Works of *Benjamin Franklin* (N.Y., 1887), II, 412.
3. Audet, *Dumas*, p. 69.
4. *Ibid.*, pp. 22-34. See also Public Archives of Canada, Ottawa, and the Library of Congress, Washington.
5. See Gov. Morris to Col. Innes, July 14, 1755: P.P., XV, 33.
6. See Gov. Morris to Sir Thomas Robinson, July 16, 1755: P.P., XV, 36.
7. Prov. Rec., N, 105; *C.R.*, VI, 480.
8. *C.R.*, VI, 494.
9. For Morris's effort to keep the news secret, see his of July 17, 1755: Peters MSS., IV, 23, H.S.P.
10. Prov. Rec., N, 118; *C.R.*, VI, 494-5.
11. Corr. of C. W., I, 53, H.S.P.
12. Bartram Papers, I, 34, H.S.P. The letter (a fragment) is not signed, but the

late C. B. Montgomery of the H.S.P. has suggested that the style and spelling (cf. Bartram's letter to Collinson of Feb. 4, 1756) point to John Bartram as the author.

13. Prov. Rec., N, 116; *C.R.*, VI, 493.
14. Penn MSS., Off. Corr., VII, 97, H.S.P.
15. See Swaine to Morris, July 23, 1755: Penn MSS., Off. Corr., VII, 97, H.S.P.
16. Peters MSS., IV, 37, H.S.P.
17. Corr. of C. W., I, 55, H.S.P.
18. *C.R.*, VI, 522. See also Du Simitière Coll. Ridgway Library, L.C. of P.
19. Prov. Rec., N, 161; *C.R.*, VI, 553.
20. *Ibid.*
21. Prov. Rec., N, 173; *C.R.*, VI, 568.
22. *Prov. Rec.*, N, 192; *C.R.*, VI, 589-90.
23. Conrad Weiser's "Memorandum," Aug. 23, 1755: Penn MSS., Accounts, Large Folio, II, H.S.P. See also Account of the Prop. with Richard Peters, Aug. 23, 1755: Penn Physick MSS., Accounts, XI, 105, H.S.P.
24. Peters Accounts, Aug. 23, 1755: Penn MSS., Ind. Aff., III, 59, H.S.P.
25. Penn Physick MSS., Accounts, XI, 105, H.S.P.
26. Prov. Rec., N, 192; *C.R.*, VI, 589.
27. Penn MSS., Accounts, Large Folio, II, H.S.P.
28. June 26, 1755: Photostats of Franklin data, J. P. Morgan Library, A.P.S.

CHAPTER 45

1. Audet, *Jean-Daniel Dumas* (Montreal, 1920), pp. 22-34.
2. *C.R.*, VI, 640.
3. Prov. Rec., N, 214; *C.R.*, VI, 614.
4. Prov. Rec., N, 237; *C.R.*, VI, 649-50.
5. Peters to Weiser, Oct. 18, 1755: Corr. of C. W., I, 59, H.S.P.
6. *C.R.*, VI, 645.
7. Prov. Rec., N, 243; *C.R.*, VI, 648.
8. Prov. Rec., N, 241; *C.R.*, VI, 646.
9. Prov. Rec., N, 242; *C.R.*, VI, 647.
10. William Trent to James Burd, Oct. 4, 1755: Parkman, *Montcalm and Wolfe* (Boston, 1898), I, 354-5.
11. *C.R.*, VI, 654, 657.
12. John Harris to Isaac Norris, Oct. 27, 1755: Du Simitière Coll., Ridgway Library, L.C. of P.
13. Weiser to Parsons, Oct. 28, 1755: Horsfield Papers, I, 69, A.P.S.
14. John Harris to Gov. Morris, Oct. 28, 1755: Du Simitière Coll., Ridgway Library, L.C. of P.
15. Conrad Weiser to Gov. Morris, Oct. 31, 1755: Du Simitière Coll., Ridgway Library, L.C. of P.
16. Horsfield Papers, I, 39-41, A.P.S.
17. *C.R.*, VI, 649-50.
18. Prov. Rec., N, 244; *C.R.*, VI, 649.
19. Wm. Bird to James Read, Oct. 27, 1755: Muhlenberg Papers, in possession of C. W. Unger, Pottsville, Pa. See also Edward Shippen of Lancaster to John Harris, Oct. 29, 1755: *C.R.*, VI, 655.
20. Conrad Weiser to James Read, Oct. 26, 1755: *C.R.*, VI, 650-1.
21. *C.R.*, VI, 657.
22. Prov. Rec., N, 245; *C.R.*, VI, 651.
23. *Ibid.*
24. Oct. 27, 1755: Penn MSS., Off. Corr., VII, 141, H.S.P.
25. Letters of Peters to the Proprietaries, Gratz Coll., p. 1, H.S.P.
26. Prov., Rec., N, 249-51; *C.R.*, VI, 656-9.
27. The commonly accepted versions of this episode are much confused. The late Dr. George Wheeler of Philadelphia has given an excellent account of the incident

in a paper read before the Berks County Historical Society, June 14, 1932, and in his "Annals of the Swatara," Chapter 10 (*Schuylkill Press and Pine Grove Herald*, Feb. 10, 1939).

28. Weiser to William Allen, Oct. 30, 1755: *C.R.*, VI, 659.

CHAPTER 46

1. John Harris to Benjamin Franklin, Oct. 31, 1755: Du Simitière Coll., Ridgway Library, L.C. of P.

2. "List of People that took of the Guns or Musquets which came by N. Kintzer's Waggon": Corr. of C. W., II, 17, H.S.P. See also "Account of Sundry Guns &c & Ammunition delivered by Evan Morgan. 1755": Pennsylvania Archives, H.S.P.

3. John Bartram to Peter Collinson, Feb. 4, 1756: Bartram Papers, I, 44, H.S.P.

4. Prov. Rec., N, 257; *C.R.*, VI, 667.

5. Weiser to Gov. Morris, Oct. 31, 1755: Du Simitière Coll., Ridgway Library, L.C. of P.

6. *Ibid.*

7. Prov. Rec., N, 259; *C.R.*, VI, 669.

8. Conrad Weiser to James Read, Nov. 1, 1755: Du Simitière Coll., Ridgway Library, L.C. of P.

9. *Ibid.*

10. Oct. 31, 1755: Lancaster County Misc. Papers, 1724–1772, p. 105, H.S.P.

11. P.P., XVI, 9; *P.A.*, II, 453.

12. Prov. Rec., N, 252; *C.R.*, VI, 660.

13. Moravian Archives, Bethlehem, Pa.

14. Prov. Rec., N, 268; *C.R.*, VI, 681.

15. Prov. Rec., N, 270; *C.R.*, VI, 683.

16. *C.R.*, VI, 685.

17. Penn MSS., Ind. Aff., III, 66, H.S.P.

18. Prov. Rec., N, 272; *C.R.*, VI, 685.

19. June 26, 1755: Photostats of Franklin data, J. P. Morgan Library, A.P.S.

20. Prov. Rec., N, 274; *C.R.*, VI, 688.

21. *Ibid.*

22. P.P., XV, 57.

23. Prov. Rec., N, 327; *C.R.*, VI, 752.

24. Letters of Peters to the Proprietaries, Nov. 15, 1755, Gratz Coll., p. 15, H.S.P.

25. *C.R.*, VII, 49, 141.

26. Rep. 14.A., Nr. 18, p. 428, Arch. der Br.

27. P.P., XVI, 32; *P.A.*, First Series, II, 474.

28. P.P., XVI, 16; *P.A.*, First Series, II, 463.

29. Prov. Rec., N, 287; *C.R.*, VI, 703–4.

30. *C.R.*, VI, 705.

31. P.P., XVI, 55; *P.A.*, First Series, II, 503–4.

32. P.P., XVI, 85.

33. P.P., XVI, 57; *P.A.*, First Series, II, 504.

34. Letters from Peters to the Proprietaries, 1755–1757, Photostats, pp. 20–1, H.S.P.

35. Prov. Rec., N, 287; *C.R.*, VI, 704.

36. P.P., XVI, 63; *P.A.*, First Series, II, 511.

37. *P.A.*, Eighth Series, V, 4150.

38. *Ibid.*

39. Arthur D. Graeff, "The Relations Between the Pennsylvania Germans and the British Authorities (1750–1776)," Vol. XLVII of the *Publications of the Pennsylvania German Society*.

40. *P.A.*, Eighth Series, V, 4152.

41. *P.A.*, First Series, II, 517.

42. Peters MSS., IV, 45, H.S.P.

CHAPTER 47

1. To Richard Peters, Nov. 18, 1755: Penn MSS., Ind. Aff., II, 47, H.S.P.
2. *C.R.*, VI, 760.
3. "The Humble Petition of the Inhabitants of the Forks of Delaware," undated: Du Simitière Coll., Ridgway Library, L.C. of P.
4. Peters to the Proprietaries, Feb. 23, 1756: Gratz Coll., p. 25, H.S.P.
5. *C.R.*, VI, 760.
6. Prov. Rec., N, 334; *C.R.*, VI, 760.
7. *Ibid.*
8. *C.R.*, VI, 755.
9. Prov. Rec., N, 328; *C.R.*, VI, 753.
10. Prov. Rec., N, 334; *C.R.*, VI, 760.
11. See Conrad Weiser to Gov. Morris, Dec. 22, 1755: *C.R.*, VI, 763.
12. *Memoirs of Benjamin Franklin* (Phila., 1840), I, pp. xviii–xix.
13. See Morris to Strettle, Jan. 1, 1756: Penn MSS., Off. Corr., VIII, 1, H.S.P.; Carl Van Doren, *Benjamin Franklin* (N.Y., 1938), p. 248.
14. Jan. 1, 1756: Penn MSS., Off. Corr., VIII, 1, H.S.P.
15. *Ibid.*
16. Minutes of Commissioners, Jan. 2: Pennsylvania Archives, H.S.P.
17. *Papers of Sir William Johnson*, II, 401–2.
18. P.P., XVII, 1; *P.A.*, First Series, II, 543.
19. Richard Peters' Diary, Jan. 6, 1756, H.S.P.
20. Penn MSS., Off. Corr., VIII, 5, H.S.P.
21. Peters' Diary, Jan. 7, 1755, H.S.P.
22. *Ibid.* The party had, no doubt, stopped at *Peter Kucher's*. See Miss Olive S. Kreider's "Development of East Lebanon," *Lebanon County Historical Society*, XI, 169 ff.
23. Corr. of C. W., I, 64, H.S.P.
24. *P.A.*, First Series, II, 547.
25. Prov. Rec., N, 355; *C.R.*, VI, 784.
26. Prov. Rec., N, 353; *C.R.*, VI, 781.
27. Penn MSS., Off. Corr., VIII, 9, H.S.P.
28. Prov. Rec., N, 358; *C.R.*, VII, 4.
29. Prov. Rec., N, 359; *C.R.*, VII, 6.
30. Peters' Diary, H.S.P.
31. Corr. of C. W., I, 61, H.S.P.
32. Prov. Rec., O, 37–8; *P.A.*, First Series, II, 370.
33. *P.A.*, First Series, II, 547.
34. A digest of this letter is in the Muhlenberg Papers in the possession of C. W. Unger, Pottsville, Pa. See also H. H. Muhlenberg, "A Forgotten Retrospect," *Berks County Historical Society*, 1926.
35. Letter from Capt. Busse, undated: Muhlenberg Papers, *loc. cit.*
36. Horsfield Papers, I, 103, A.P.S.
37. H. M. Muhlenberg's Diary, March 30–April 3: Vol. XIX, p. 1, Krauth Memorial Library, Mt. Airy, Pa.; *Journals of H. M. Muhlenberg*, tr. by Tappert and Doberstein (Phila., 1942), p. 388.
38. *Ibid.*

CHAPTER 48

1. Prov. Rec., O, 23–4; *C.R.*, VII, 34–5.
2. Prov. Rec., O, 23; *C.R.*, VII, 34.
3. P.P., XVII, 27; *P.A.*, First Series, II, 564.
4. *C.R.*, VII, 47.

5. Prov. Rec., O, 39; *C.R.*, VII, 49.
6. Prov. Rec., O, 42–3; *C.R.*, VII, 52.
7. Prov. Rec., O, 44–5; *C.R.*, VII, 54.
8. Penn MSS., Off. Corr., VIII, 61, H.S.P.
9. *Ibid.*, p. 57.
10. *C.R.*, VII, 54.
11. P.P., XVIII, 8; *P.A.*, First Series, II, 615–6.
12. Peters to the Proprietaries, April 25, 1756: Penn MSS., Off. Corr., VIII, 71, H.S.P.; Gratz Coll., p. 40, H.S.P.
13. *Ibid.*
14. *Papers of Sir William Johnson*, II, 438.
15. Prov. Rec., O, 62; *C.R.*, VII, 70.

CHAPTER 49

1. *Papers of Sir William Johnson*, II, 438.
2. Peters to the Proprietaries, Gratz Coll., p. 39; Penn MSS., Off. Cor., VIII, 73–4, H.S.P.
3. *C.R.*, VII, 79.
4. *Papers of Sir William Johnson*, II, 439.
5. *Ibid.*, p. 440.
6. *C.R.*, VII, 75.
7. Peters to the Proprietaries, April 25, 1755: Penn MSS., Off. Corr., VIII, 71, H.S.P.
8. Prov. Rec., O, 68; *C.R.*, VII, 76.
9. Prov. Rec., O, 71; *C.R.*, VII, 79.
10. Prov. Rec., O, 75; *C.R.*, VII, 83.
11. *C.R.*, VII, 87.
12. Prov. Rec., O, 81; *C.R.*, VII, 90.
13. Prov. Rec., O, 82; *C.R.*, VII, 92.
14. Peters MSS., IV, 52, H.S.P.
15. Peters to the Proprietaries, June 1, 1756, Gratz Coll., p. 52, H.S.P.
16. *Ibid.*
17. *C.R.*, VII, 70–1.
18. *C.R.*, VII, 100.
19. *Papers of Sir William Johnson*, II, 440.
20. April 12, 1756: *Report on Canadian Archives*, 1899, Supp., p. 166.
21. *P.A.*, Eighth Series, V, 4228 ff.
22. *C.R.*, VII, 102.
23. Prov. Rec., O, 85; *C.R.*, VI, 95.
24. P.P., XVIII, 27; *P.A.*, First series, II, 628.
25. Etting Papers, Misc. MSS., I, 84 ff., H.S.P.
26. *Ibid.*, p. 86.
27. *C.R.*, VII, 105.
28. Peters to Proprietaries, April 25, 1756: Penn MSS., Off. Corr., VIII, 71, H.S.P.
29. P.P., XVIII, 42; *P.A.*, First Series, II, 646.

CHAPTER 50

1. Spangenberg to William Logan, May 2, 1756: Misc. MSS., Bethlehem and Vicinity, Northampton County, 1741–1849, p. 39, H.S.P.
2. Prov. Rec., O, 109; *C.R.*, VII, 119.
3. *C.R.*, VII, 121–2. See also Capt. Busse to Lt. Col. Weiser, May 12, 1756: Corr. of C. W., II, 59, H.S.P.
4. Pennsylvania Archives, H.S.P.
5. Penn-Hamilton Corr., p. 36, H.S.P.
6. Penn Letter Books, IV, 302–5, H.S.P.
7. *Ibid.*, IV, 304–5.

8. Peters to Proprietaries, Gratz Coll., p. 53, H.S.P.
9. *Ibid.*
10. *Ibid.*
11. May 21, 1756: Misc. MSS, Bethlehem and Vicinity, 1741–1849, p. 29, H.S.P.
12. *Ibid.*, p. 35.
13. Etting Coll., II, Governors, p. 14, H.S.P.
14. Penn MSS., Ind. Aff., II, 83, H.S.P. See also *C.R.*, VII, 137 ff.
15. Conrad Weiser's "Observations," Moravian Archives, Bethlehem, Pa.
16. David Bruce's Journal at Shecomeko, Jan. 26, 1746: Am. 708, H.S.P.
17. *Ibid.*, April 5, 1746.
18. George Henry Loskiel, *History of the Mission of the United Brethren among the Indians in North America*, tr. La Trobe (London, 1794), II, 124–5.
19. "Mr. John Pemberton informed me that the meaning of Tidiuscung (the name of a celebrated chief of the Indians) is *one who makes the earth tremble*."—Benj. Smith Barton Box of MSS., Commonplace Book, 1789, H.S.P.
20. Prov. Rec., O, 132; *C.R.*, VII, 141.
21. Penn MSS., Ind. Aff., II, 89, H.S.P.
22. *P.A.*, First Series, II, 685.
23. Prov. Rec., O, 137–8; *C.R.*, VII, 146.
24. *Ibid.*
25. P.P., XVIII, 79; *P.A.*, First Series, II, 668.
26. Prov. Rec., O, 149; *C.R.*, VII, 158.
27. Prov. Rec., O, 147; *C.R.*, VII, 156.
28. Penn MSS., Ind. Aff., II, 101, H.S.P.
29. Prov. Rec., O, 190; *C.R.*, VII, 199.
30. Prov. Rec., O, 189; *C.R.*, *ibid.*
31. Horsfield Papers, I, 173, A.P.S.
32. *Ibid.*
33. *Ibid.*
34. P.P., XIX, 23; *P.A.*, First Series, II, 697.
35. Corr. of C. W., I, 76, H.S.P.
36. Peters MSS., IV, 66, H.S.P.
37. P.P., XIX, 24.
38. *P.A.*, Second Series, VI, 453–4.
39. Horsfield Papers, I, 229, A.P.S.
40. *Ibid.*, p. 233.
41. P.P., XIX, 45; *P.A.*, First Series, 721–2.
42. "Account of the Expences of Conrad Weiser in his March with his Company and several Detachments of other Companies to Easton": Corr. of C. W., I, 77, H.S.P.
43. "Minutes of Indian Conferences held at Easton," July 25, 1756: Indian Treaty Box, H.S.P.
44. *Ibid.*
45. Prov. Rec., O, 198; *C.R.*, VII, 207.
46. "Minutes of Indian Conferences," *loc. cit.*
47. *C.R.*, VII, 208–9.
48. *C.R.*, VII, 210 ff.
49. Prov. Rec., O, 202; *C.R.*, VII, 210.
50. Prov. Rec., O, 203; *C.R.*, VII, 213.
51. Pennsylvania Archives, H.S.P.
52. Horsfield Papers, I, 249, A.P.S.
53. Prov. Rec., O, 208; *C.R.*, VII, 219.
54. Corr. of C. W., I, 77, H.S.P.

CHAPTER 51

1. *C.R.*, VII, 222.
2. Peters to Proprietaries, Gratz Coll., p. 67, H.S.P.

3. Horsfield Papers, II, 285, A.P.S.
4. *Ibid.*
5. *Ibid.*, p. 253.
6. Northampton County Misc. MSS., 1758–1767, p. 53, H.S.P.
7. Misc. MSS., Bethlehem and Vicinity, 1741–1840, p. 49, H.S.P.
8. *Pa. Gazette*, Aug. 26, 1756; *Pa. Mag.*, XLIV, 102.
9. *Pa. Mag.*, XLIV, 100.
10. Horsfield Papers, II, 292, A.P.S.
11. Misc. MSS., Beth. and Vic., p. 49, H.S.P.
12. Northampton County Papers, p. 223, H.S.P.
13. Corr. of C. W., II, 123, H.S.P.

CHAPTER 52

1. Sept. 4, 1756: Peters to the Proprietaries, Gratz Coll., pp. 81 ff., H.S.P.
2. Prov. Rec., P, 24; *C.R.*, VII, 245.
3. P.P., XIX, 99; *P.A.*, First Series, II, 778.
4. *Ibid.*
5. *Ibid.*
6. Peters MSS., IV, 75, H.S.P.
7. Corr. of Penn Family, 1732–67, p. 96, H.S.P.
8. Peters to the Proprietaries, Gratz Coll., p. 93, H.S.P.
9. Prov. Rec., P, 44; *C.R.*, VII, 270.
10. Peters to the Proprietaries, Gratz Coll., p. 93, H.S.P.
11. Prov. Rec., P, 69; *C.R.*, VII, 302.
12. Corr. of C. W., I, 85, H.S.P.
13. Peters to the Proprietaries, Gratz Coll., p. 96, H.S.P.
14. Commonplace Book, 1789, Benj. Smith Barton Box of MSS., H.S.P.
15. Prov. Rec., P, 74–5; *C.R.*, VII, 310.
16. Oct. 28, 1756: Misc. MSS., 1744–1859, Northern Interior and Western Counties, p. 11, H.S.P.
17. P.P., XXI, 27; *C.R.*, VII, 314.
18. Du Simitière Coll., Yi-2, Ridgway Library, L.C. of P.
19. Dec. 10, 1756: Rep. 14.A., Nr. 18, p. 465, Arch. der Br.
20. Prov. Rec., P, 93; *C.R.*, VII, 334.
21. Prov. Rec., P, 83; *C.R.*, VII, 320.
22. See Theodore Thayer: *Israel Pemberton King of the Quakers* (Phila., 1943), pp. 183–4.
23. Conrad Weiser's "Observations," Moravian Archives, Bethlehem, Pa.
24. P.P., XXI, 55; *P.A.*, First Series, III, 39.
25. *C.R.*, VII, 431–2; Pennsylvania Archives, H.S.P.
26. *Some Chapters in the History of the Friendly Association* (Phila., 1877), p. 61.
27. Weiser to Peters, Dec. 31, 1756: *P.A.*, First Series, III, 87.
28. *P.A.*, First Series, III, 86–7.
29. Rep. 14.A., Nr. 18, p. 468, Arch. der Br.
30. P.P., XXI, 37; *P.A.*, First Series, III, 66.
31. P.P., XXI, 76; *P.A.*, First Series, III, 86.
32. P.P., XXI, 38; *P.A.*, First Series, III, 68.

CHAPTER 53

1. Horsfield Papers, II, 328, A.P.S.
2. Berks and Montgomery County Papers, p. 61, H.S.P.
3. Busse to Weiser, Jan. 10, 1757: Corr. of C. W., II, 23, H.S.P.
4. Audet, *Dumas* (Montreal, 1920), p. 83.
5. Prov. Rec., P., 217–8; *C.R.*, VII, 491.

6. Peters to the Proprietaries, Gratz Coll., p. 135, H.S.P.
7. Isaac Norris Copy Book of Letters, p. 79, H.S.P.
8. *C.R.*, VII, 355.
9. Isaac Norris Copy Book of Letters, p. 80, H.S.P.
10. William Logan to Gov. Denny, May 6, 1757: Logan Papers, XI, 48, H.S.P.
11. *Ibid.*
12. Peters to the Proprietaries, Gratz Coll., p. 94, H.S.P.
13. John Baynton, May 18, 1757: Gratz Coll., H.S.P.
14. Weiser's "Observations," Moravian Archives, Bethlehem, Pa.
15. *Ibid.*
16. *Ibid.*
17. *Ibid.*
18. Little Abraham showed a sound knowledge of Iroquois constitutional law. See "The Traditional History of the Confederacy of the Six Nations," ed. Duncan C. Scott, F.R.S.C., *Transactions of the Royal Society of Canada*, 1911, p. 223. When the Confederate Council was first organized, Deganaweda is reported to have said: "These two Chief Warriors [of the Senecas] shall represent the door of the Confederacy, (Ka-noh-hah-ge-ko-wah) meaning the great black door, through which all good and evil messages must come to reach the Confederate House of Lords or Council, and if any person or Nation has any news, message or business matter to lay before the Confederate Council he or they must come through this door."
19. *C.R.*, VII, 524.
20. See Peters to Weiser, Feb. 15, 1757: Corr. of C. W., II, 31-b, H.S.P.
21. Feb. 14, 1757: Peters to the Proprietaries, Gratz Coll., pp. 135 ff., H.S.P.
22. Thomas Penn to R. Peters, June 21, 1757: Penn Letter Books, V, 143, H.S.P.
23. See Theodore Thayer: *Israel Pemberton—King of the Quakers* (Philadelphia, 1943), p. 98.
24. Weiser's "Observations," Mor. Arch., Bethlehem, Pa.

CHAPTER 54

1. P.P., XXII, 67.
2. *C.R.*, VII, 621.
3. Misc. MSS., Bethlehem and Vicinity, 1741–1849, p. 55, H.S.P.
4. *C.R.*, VII, 621.
5. Van Etten's Journal, July 1, 1757, H.S.P.
6. P.P., XXIII, 2; *P.A.*, First Series, III, 207.
7. *P.A.*, First Series, III, 209.
8. *Ibid.*, p. 210.
9. Corr. of C. W., II, 73 and 83, H.S.P. Two fragments are here interwoven. They are both written on the same kind of paper and in the same stage of Weiser's changing handwriting.
10. Here ends the fragment on p. 73.
11. Halle Documents, II, 1108, Krauth Memorial Library, Mt. Airy, Pa.
12. Peters MSS., IV, 99, H.S.P.
13. P.P., XXIII, 11; *P.A.*, First Series, III, 216.
14. *Ibid.*
15. P.P., XXIII, 15; *P.A.*, First Series, III, 221.
16. Corr. of C. W., II, 85, H.S.P.
17. P.P., XXIII, 15; *P.A.*, First Series, III, 221.
18. P.P., XXIII, 13; *P.A.*, First Series, III, 218.
19. P.P., XXIII, 15; *P.A.*, *ibid.*, pp. 221-2.
20. P.P., XXIII, 4; *P.A.*, *ibid.*, p. 209.
21. *P.A.*, *ibid.*, p. 208.
22. P.P., XXIII, 209; *P.A.*, *ibid.*, 209.
23. *Ibid.*
24. P.P., XXIII, 12; *P.A.*, *ibid.*, p. 217.

25. Israel Pemberton to his "beloved Spouse," July 21, 1757: Pemberton Papers, XII, 46, H.S.P.

26. James Pemberton to his wife, Aug. 4, 1757: Pemberton Papers, XII, 56, H.S.P.

27. Pemberton Papers, XII, 55, H.S.P.

28. Etting Coll., Pemberton Papers, II, 26, H.S.P.

29. *Ibid.*, p. 27.

30. Prov. Rec., Q, 1; *C.R.*, VII, 649.

31. P.P., XXIII, 24.

32. Prov. Rec., Q, 1; *C.R.*, VII, 649.

33. "A Count of Wampum & Silver Truck," July 19, 1757: Penn MSS., Accounts, Large Folio, IV, 34, H.S.P.

34. See Andrew Hesselius's *Notes on his Journey to America*, July 20, 1712: Am. 211, H.S.P.

35. Prov. Rec., Q, 3; *C.R.*, VII, 652.

36. Corr. of C. W., II, 77, H.S.P.

37. Etting Coll., Pemberton Papers, II, 27, H.S.P.

38. Prov. Rec., Q, 22; *C.R.*, VII, 676.

39. Prov. Rec., Q, 23; *C.R.*, VII, 677.

40. Prov. Rec., Q, 28; *C.R.*, VII, 683.

41. *Ibid.*

42. Prov. Rec. Q, 36; *C.R.*, VII, 693.

43. *Pa. Mag.*, XX, 422.

44. Etting Coll., Pemberton Papers, II, 27, H.S.P.

45. *Ibid.*

46. Pemberton Papers, XII, 55, H.S.P.

47. *P.A.*, First Series, III, 276.

48. Pemberton Papers, XII, 55, H.S.P.

49. Peters MSS., IV, 104, H.S.P.

50. Prov. Rec., Q, 41; *C.R.*, VII, 699.

51. P.P., XXIII, 65; *P.A.*, First Series, III, 257.

52. Prov. Rec., Q, 50; *C.R.*, VII, 700.

53. *Ibid.*

54. Pemberton Papers, XII, 55, H.S.P.

55. Prov. Rec., Q, 62; *C.R.*, VII, 705.

56. William Smith Coll., Vol. VI, Early Papers, etc., H.S.P.

57. P.P., XXIV, 63; *P.A.*, First Series, III, 313.

58. *P.A.*, Eighth Series, VII, 5552.

CHAPTER 55

1. P.P., XXIV, 63; *P.A.*, First Series, III, 314.

2. P.P., XXIV, 74; *P.A.*, *ibid.*, p. 319.

3. Croghan to Johnson: *Docs. Rel. to the Col. Hist. of N.Y.*, VII, 321–4.

4. Reichel, *Memorials of the Moravian Church*, I, 349.

5. *Ibid.*, p. 331.

6. P.P., XXIII, 64.

7. Reichel, *op. cit.*, p. 331, n.

8. *Ibid.*, p. 333.

9. Penn MSS., Accounts, Large Folio, II, 35, H.S.P.

10. *Pa. Gazette*, Aug. 18, 1757.

11. *Ibid.*

12. *Ibid.*

13. George Wheeler, "Annals of the Swatara," Chapter 15: *Schuylkill Press and Pine Grove Herald*, March 17, 1939. For date of the attack on the Walmer homestead, see Weiser's letter to Peters of Oct. 4: *P.A.*, First Series, III, 283.

14. *Pa. Gazette*, Aug. 18, 1757.

15. Issue of Aug. 18, 1757, p. 3.

16. Prov. Rec., Q, 98; *C.R.*, VII, 735.
17. *Ibid.*
18. Sept. 27, 1757: *Shippen Papers*, ed. Thos. Balch (Phila., 1855), p. 98.
19. Horsfield Papers, II, 407, A.P.S.
20. Commission on Indian Affairs, Autograph of the Members, #51, 1–122, Emmett Coll., N.Y. Free Library.
21. Shippen Papers, III, Corr., p. 63, H.S.P.
22. *P.A.*, First series, III, 283.
23. For a full account of Chauvignerie's adventures, see George Wheeler, *op. cit.*
24. *Pensylvanische Berichte*, Oct. 15, 1757.
25. *P.A.*, First Series, III, 295.
26. *Ibid.*, 293.
27. P.P., XXIV, 42; *P.A.*, First Series, III, 294. A copy of the Examination of Chauvignerie is in the Manuscript Division, Library of Congress.
28. P.P., XXV, 3.
29. C.O. 5–50, p. 39, P.R.O.

CHAPTER 56

1. Corr. of C. W., II, 97, H.S.P.
2. Horsfield Papers, II, 407, A.P.S.
3. *Ibid.*
4. *Ibid.*
5. Shippen Family Papers, XV, 127, H.S.P.
6. *C.R.*, VII, 772.
7. Corr. of C. W., II, 103, H.S.P.
8. *Pensylvanische Berichte*, Nov. 16, 1757.
9. Corr. of C. W., II, 101, H.S.P.
10. *Ibid.*, p. 105.

CHAPTER 57

1. See *Pensylvanische Berichte*, Feb. 18, 1758.
2. Audet, *Dumas* (Montreal, 1920), p. 91.
3. Prov. Rec., Q, 270; *C.R.*, VII, 120.
4. *Papers of Sir William Johnson*, II, 749–50.
5. Peters MSS., IV, 126, H.S.P.
6. P.P., XXV, 2.
7. Corr. of C. W., II, 113, H.S.P.
8. Peters MSS., V, 11, H.S.P.
9. "Trial of Wm. Smith," Papers of the Rev. Wm. Smith, Brinton Estate, H.S.P.
10. Corr. of C. W., II, 125, H.S.P.
11. *Shippen Papers*, ed. Thos. Balch (Phila., 1855), p. 105.
12. Horsfield Papers, II, 413, A.P.S.
13. Journal of Col. J. Burd, Feb. 16–Aug. 31, 1758: Vo N* .25, Vol. III, H.S.P. Cf. *P.A.*, First Series, III, 353.
14. See Peters' letter to Lt. Col. Burd, Jan. 18, 1758: Papers of the Shippen Family, III, Corr., H.S.P.
15. Dec. 6, 1758: Penn Letter Books, VI, 14–5, H.S.P.

CHAPTER 58

1. *P.A.*, First Series, III, 361–2.
2. Corr. of C. W., II, 61, H.S.P.
3. *Pensylvanische Berichte*, March 18, 1758, p. 3.

4. *C.R.*, VIII, 29–30.
5. P.P., XXV, 51.
6. Corr. of C. W., II, 127, H.S.P.
7. *Papers of Sir William Johnson*, II, 814.
8. *C.R.*, VIII, 33 ff.
9. *C.R.*, VIII, 43 ff.
10. Prov. Rec., Q, 202; *C.R.*, VIII, 55.
11. Prov. Rec., Q, 203; *C.R.*, VIII, 57.
12. Prov. Rec., Q, 204; *C.R.*, VIII, 57.
13. Prov. Rec., Q, 275; *C.R.*, VIII, 125.
14. Peters MSS., V, 41, H.S.P.
15. *Writings of Gen. John Forbes*, ed. A. P. James (Menasha, Wis., 1938), p. 85.
16. Peters MSS., V, 46, H.S.P.
17. May 3, 1758: *Letters of Gen. John Forbes to Gov. Denny* (Pittsburgh, 1927).
18. *C.R.*, VIII, 116–21.
19. *Ibid.*, 119.
20. May 15, 1758: *Shippen Papers*, ed. Thos. Balch (Phila., 1855), p. 121.
21. 21652, p. 31, Bouquet Papers, Haldimand Coll., British Museum.
22. Canadian Archives, Ottawa, Canada.
23. Adam Hoops to Henry Bouquet, June 26, 1758: 21643, p. 129, Letters to Bouquet, Haldimand Coll., British Museum.
24. *Shippen Papers*, p. 121.
25. Corr. of C. W., II, 133, H.S.P.
26. *Ibid.*
27. *P.A.*, First Series, III, 500.
28. P.P., XXVII, 33; *P.A.*, First Series, III, 481.
29. See Col. Burd to Gov. Denny, Aug. 18, 1758: Peters MSS., V, 51, H.S.P.
30. P.P., XXVII, 56; *P.A.*, First Series, III, 509.
31. Peters MSS., V, 52, H.S.P.

CHAPTER 59

1. Nead Coll., H.S.P.; *P.A.*, First Series, III, 439.
2. P.P., XXVII, 50; *P.A.*, First Series, III, 460.
3. *Papers of Sir William Johnson*, II, 824.
4. Prov. Rec., Q, 310; *C.R.*, VIII, 151.
5. P.P., XXVII, 50; *P.A.*, First Series, III, 468.
6. *Ibid.*
7. *Papers of Sir William Johnson*, II, 820.
8. Corr. of C. W., II, 135, H.S.P.
9. Peters MSS., V, 57, H.S.P.
10. "A Copy of Mr Chew's Private Diary during the Treaty at Easton In October 1758," Oct. 17: Am .043, H.S.P.
11. Peters MSS., V, 57, H.S.P.
12. P.P., XXVII, 95.
13. Conrad Weiser's "Observations," Moravian Archives, Bethlehem, Pa.
14. Corr. of C. W., II, 139-a, H.S.P.
15. P.P., XXVII, 68; *P.A.*, First Series, III, 544.
16. Journal of Richard Peters at Easton, 1758, H.S.P.
17. Peters *MSS.*, V, 57.
18. *Ibid.*
19. Peters' Journal, Sept. 29.
20. *Papers of Sir William Johnson*, III, 4.
21. Peters' Journal, Sept. 29.
22. *Ibid.*
23. *Ibid.*, Sept. 30.
24. *Ibid.*, Oct. 1.

25. *Ibid.*, Oct. 2.
26. *Ibid.*
27. *Ibid.*, Oct. 3.
28. *Ibid.*, Oct. 4.
29. *Ibid.*, Oct. 5.
30. P.P., XXVII, 69.
31. C. Hale Sipe, *The Indian Chiefs of Pennsylvania* (Butler, Pa., 1927), p. 109.
32. *C.R.*, VI, 568.
33. P.P., XXVII, 69; Penn MSS., Ind. Aff., III, H.S.P.
34. Peters' Journal, Oct. 5.
35. Journal of Andrew Hesselius, Aug. 23, 1721, H.S.P.
36. Peters' Journal, Oct. 5.
37. *Ibid.*
38. *Ibid.*, Oct. 6.
39. Peters MSS., V, 57, H.S.P.
40. *Ibid.*
41. Peters' Journal, Oct. 12.

CHAPTER 60

1. Chew's Diary, Oct. 6, H.S.P.
2. *Ibid.*, Oct. 8.
3. Peters' Journal, Oct. 11, H.S.P.
4. *Ibid.*, Oct. 7.
5. Chew's Diary, Oct. 8.
6. Peters' Journal, Oct. 9.
7. Chew's Diary, Oct. 16.
8. Peters' Journal, Oct. 9.
9. *Ibid.*, Oct. 10.
10. *Ibid.*
11. *Ibid.*
12. *Ibid.*, Oct. 11.
13. Chew's Diary, Oct. 11.
14. *Ibid.*, Oct. 12.
15. Peters, Oct. 11.
16. Chew, Oct. 11.
17. Peters, Oct. 11.
18. *Ibid.*
19. *C.R.*, VIII, 179.
20. Chew, Oct. 16.
21. Prov. Rec., Q, 335; *C.R.*, VIII, 180.
22. Prov. Rec., Q, 336; *C.R., ibid.*
23. *Ibid.*
24. Peters, Oct. 12.
25. *Ibid.*
26. *Ibid.*
27. Chew, Oct. 12.
28. Prov. Rec., Q, 337; *C.R.*, VIII, 182.
29. *Ibid.*
30. Peters, Oct. 12.

CHAPTER 61

1. Chew's Diary, Oct. 13, H.S.P.
2. *Ibid.*
3. Peters' Journal, Oct. 13, H.S.P.
4. Prov. Rec., Q, 344; *C.R.*, VIII, 190.

5. Pemberton Papers, XIII, 1, H.S.P.
6. Chew, Oct. 14.
7. Peters, Oct. 14.
8. *Some Chapters in the History of the Friendly Association,* (Phila., 1877) I, 97 ff.
9. Prov. Rec., Q, 344–5; C.R., VIII, 190.
10. Prov. Rec., Q, 345; C.R., VIII, 191.
11. Peters, Oct. 16.
12. *Ibid.*
13. *C.R.,* VIII, 192.
14. Prov. Rec., Q, 346–7; C.R., VIII, 193.
15. Chew, Oct. 16.
16. Prov. Rec., Q, 348; *C.R.,* VIII, 195.
17. Peters, Oct. 16.
18. Chew, Oct. 17.
19. Peters, Oct. 17.
20. Pemberton Papers, XIII, 1, H.S.P.
21. Peters, Oct. 17.
22. Chew, Oct. 17.
23. Pemberton Papers, XIII, 2, H.S.P.
24. Peters, Oct. 18.
25. Prov. Rec., Q, 352; C.R., VIII, 199.
26. Prov. Rec., *ibid.;* C.R., VIII, 200.
27. Prov. Rec., Q, 353; C.R., VIII, 201.
28. Chew, Oct. 18.
29. Chew, Oct. 19.
30. *Ibid.*
31. *Ibid.*
32. *Ibid.*
33. Chew, Oct. 20.
34. Peters, Oct. 20.
35. Prov. Rec., Q, 355; C.R., VIII, 203.
36. Logan Papers, XI, 54, H.S.P.
37. P.P., XXVII, 89.
38. Peters MSS., V, 61, H.S.P.
39. Peters Letter Books, #5, undated, but following a letter of March 8, 1741/2, H.S.P.
40. Chew, Oct. 20.
41. Prov. Rec., Q, 360; C.R., VIII, 209.
42. Peters, Oct. 24.
43. Peters.
44. *Ibid.*
45. Volwiler, *Croghan* (Cleveland, 1926), p. 139.
46. Peters, Oct. 15.

CHAPTER 62

1. Oct. 13, 1753: Peters MSS., III, 77, H.S.P.
2. John Nicum Coll., Archives of the Lutheran Theological Seminary, Mt. Airy, Pa.
3. *Hall. Nach.,* II, 257–8.
4. Berks County Deeds, A-2, pp. 114 ff., Courthouse, Reading, Pa. See also Bennett Nolan, *The Foundation of the Town of Reading* (Reading, 1929), p. 149.
5. Peters MSS., III, 69, H.S.P.
6. Peters MSS., III, 86, H.S.P.
7. Misc. MSS., Department of Archives, Harrisburg.
8. Historical Society of Berks County, Reading, Pa.
9. Office of the Clerk of the Quarter Sessions, Courthouse, Reading, Pa.
10. Mrs. K. T. Anderson, Augustana College, Rock Island, Ill. Reproductions are filed in the H.S.P. and the H.S. of Berks County.

11. Corr. of C. W., II, 145, H.S.P.
12. John Hughes to Col. Bouquet, Aug. 10, 1759: 21644, Letters to Bouquet, Haldimand Coll., p. 298, British Museum.
13. Corr. of C. W., II, 71, H.S.P.
14. *Ibid.*, p. 159.
15. *Ibid.*
16. *Ibid.*, p. 71.
17. Weiser to Bouquet, May 25, 1759: 21644, Letters to Bouquet, Haldimand Coll., British Museum.
18. Corr. of C. W., II, 161, H.S.P.
19. Weiser to Bouquet, Aug. 7, 1759: 21644, Haldimand Coll., f. 290, British Museum.
20. Fort Bedford, August 13, 1759: 21652, p. 141, Bouquet Corr., Haldimand Coll., British Museum.
21. Corr. of C. W., II, 139-a, H.S.P.
22. *Ibid.*, p. 137.
23. *Ibid.*, p. 149.
24. *Ibid.*, p. 151.
25. *Ibid.*, p. 155.
26. *Ibid.*, p. 157.
27. P.P., XXVIII, 84.
28. Peters MSS., V, 79, H.S.P.
29. Corr. of C. W., II, 149, H.S.P.
30. Penn Letter Books, VI, 178, H.S.P.
31. Feb. 22, 1760: 21645, p. 59, Letters to Bouquet, Haldimand Coll., British Museum.
32. Nov. 26, 1759: Shippen Papers, ed. Thos. Balch, I, 74, H.S.P.

CHAPTER 63

1. 21645, p. 3, Letters to Bouquet, Haldimand Coll., British Museum.
2. *P.A.*, First Series, III, 698.
3. P.P., XXX, 4.
4. *Ibid.*, p. 5.
5. Diaries, Fort Augusta, Feb. to Nov., 1760: 973, 2-D 54, A.P.S.
6. Gratz Coll., Colonial Wars, Case 4, Box 9, H.S.P.; *P.A.*, First Series, III, 701-2.
7. Corr. of C. W., II, 169, H.S.P.
8. P.P., XXX, 21.
9. Box 14-a, Colonial Wars, Society Coll., H.S.P.
10. See Deposition, P.P., XXX, 14.
11. P.P., XXX, 15, 17.
12. P.P., XXX, 48.
13. Burd to Bouquet, Fort Augusta, March 1, 1760: 21645, p. 59, Letters to Bouquet, Haldimand Coll., British Museum.
14. Fort Augusta Diaries, Feb. 27: 973, 2-D 54, A.P.S.
15. Prov. Rec., R, 63; P.P., XXX, 22; *C.R.*, VIII, 464.
16. Prov. Rec., R, 70; *C.R.*, VIII, 467.
17. P.P., XXX, 25, 26.
18. P.P., XXX, 40.
19. Shamokin Day Book, 1759-1760, p. 268, H.S.P.
20. Shippen Papers, V, 31, H.S.P.
21. See letter from Spangenberg, Bethlehem, April 27, 1759: Rep. 14.A., Nr. 18, p. 493-4: Arch. der Br.
22. P.P., XXX, 46; *P.A.*, First Series, III, 727.
23. P.P., XXX, 47.
24. *Ibid.*
25. Rec. of St. Michael's and Zion Church, Phila., Coll. of the Gen. Soc. of Pa., Ph, 4 L, p. 182, H.S.P.
26. Corr. of C. W., II, 175, H.S.P.

27. *P.A.,* First Series, III, 737.

28. *Ibid.*

29. *Ibid.*

30. *Ibid.,* 738.

31. *Ibid.,* 740.

32. Journal of Chr. Fred. Post, June 10, 1760: Gen. Soc. of Pa., Binghurst, Claypoole, etc., Papers, Part II, pp. 477 ff., H.S.P.

CHAPTER 64

1. Diary of Christopher Marshall, I, 8, H.S.P.

2. Shippen Papers, V, 79, H.S.P.

3. Biographical Sketch of Conrad Weiser, Muhlenberg Diaries, Krauth Memorial Library, Mt. Airy; *Hall Nach.,* II, 445-53. Dr. J. DeWitt Kerr, Lebanon, Pa., after examining the records of Weiser's previous illnesses, diagnoses the case as renal or biliary colic induced by kidney stone.

4. *Hall. Nach.,* II, 364-5.

5. Corr. of C. W., II, 173, H.S.P.

6. *Hall. Nach.,* II, 364-5. See the records of Augustus Church, Trappe, Pa.: "July 15, 1760   Conrad Weiser, my father-in-law b. .... Heidelberg by Pastor Kurtz"—*Pub. of the Pa. German Soc.,* VII, 528.

7. Muhlenberg, *loc. cit.*

8. In the Conrad Weiser Memorial Parl, Womelsdorf, Pa.

9. Penn Letter Books, VI, 311-4, H.S.P.

10. *Ibid.,* p. 344.

11. *Ibid.,* p. 323.

12. *Ibid.,* VII, 67.

13. Register of Wills, Courthouse, Reading, Pa.

14. "Inventory and Appraisement of the Estate of Conrad Weiser Esqr deced. Exhibited by Peter Weiser and Samuel Weiser, two of the Executors. Feby 18. 1762": Register of Wills, Courthouse, Reading.

15. "Conrad Weiser Dr. to Isl. Jacobs": Corr. of C. W., II, 175, H.S.P.

16. Inventory, *loc. cit.*

17. *C.R.,* VIII, 631. See also "Indian Treaties and Conferences," Hildeburn Box, H.S.P.

18. *Hall. Nach.,* II, 531.

19. Misc. MSS., Northampton County, 1741-1849, Bethlehem and Vicinity, p. 135, H.S.P.

20. Horatio Hale, *The Iroquois Book of Rites* (Phila., 1883), p. 153.

INDEX

Struensen, Rev. ——, 257
Stump, Christopher (Stoffel), accompanies CW to Onondaga (1737), 77 ff., 95
Sturmfeder, Baron von, 4
Stuttgart, 4 f.
Suartaro. *See* Swatara.
Sunbury. *See* Shamokin.
Surractoga. *See* Saratoga.
Susana. *See* Benezet, Susan.
Susquehanna Company, 351 ff.
—— River, 25 f., 36, 41, 49, 65, 77, 82 ff., 88 f., 155, 158, 274, 353, 396 ff., 404, 409, 422
—— River, West Branch (Otsinachson), 79 ff., 114, 145 ff., 368, 374, 396
—— Valley, highway between Six Nations country and Pennsylvania, 26, 35
Susquehannocks, 192, 358. *See also* Conestogas.
Swahatawro. *See* Swatara.
Swaine, Charles, 387 f., 533, 551
Swatane. *See* Shickellamy.
Swatara Creek, 31, 35, 155, 400, 412, 425, 443, 489, 493 f., 505
——, Fort, 475, 498, 505
—— Gap, 493 f.
Swegatsy. *See* Oswegatchie.
Swift, Jonathan, 7
Swiss *Beby*, 174, 243
Syracuse. *See* Onondaga.

Taafe, Michael, 428, 441 ff.
Tabea, Sister. *See* Thoma, Anna.
Tachanuntie. *See* Tocanuntie.
Tachnechdorus. *See* Shickellamy, John.
Taeff, Michael. *See* Taafe.
Tagashata, Seneca Chief, at Albany (1754), 359; at Easton peace conference (1758), chaps. 59-61 *passim;* removes Delaware hatchet from the head of Brother Onas, 539
Tagerhidonty. *See* Spangenberg.
Taghneghdoarus. *See* Shickellamy, John.
Tahashwangarorus. *See* Shickellamy.
Tahgahjute. *See* Logan, James, Tahgahjute.
Takanuntie. *See* Tocanuntie.
Takareher, Tuscarora Indian, 126
Talheo. *See* Tolheo.
Tan Weson, brother of Andrew Montour, 345
Tanacharison, the Half King, Seneca Chief, 364 ff.; at Logstown, 268 f.; at Carlisle (1753), 345 f.; death, 374
Tarachiawagon (Holder of the Heavens), Iroquois deity, 20, 194 f.
——, CW's Indian name, 134, 159, 193 ff.,

220 ff., 268 f., 281, 314, 329 ff., 552, 567, 572, 574
Tat's Gap, 305
Tatemy. *See* Tattamy.
Tateuscung. *See* Teedyuscung.
Tatler, 7 f.
Tattamy, Moses, Delaware interpreter, 122, 125, 478 f., 567; discusses land issue with CW, 461 ff.
——, William, son of Moses Tattamy, Delaware Indian, 473, 489
Tawagarat, Six Nations warrior, 80 ff.
Taylor, John, of Lancaster County, 50
——, Col. John, of Virginia, 348, (n. 75)
Teaoga. *See* Tioga.
Tecumseh, Shawnee Chief, 232, 258, 423
Tedarighroano. *See* Tuteloes.
Teeduyscung (Honest John or Gideon), Delaware Chief, 125, 131, 409 f., 457, 468, 490, 513, 516, 518, 566; early life and character, 409, 441; accepts Pennsylvania's peace overtures, 441; king of ten nations, 444; summons Gov. Morris to Easton (July 1756), 445 ff.; declares Delawares to be men, 449; his motives, 452; orgy at Fort Allen, 453; his authority questioned, 456 ff.; summons Gov. Denny to Easton (Nov. 1756), 458 ff.; discusses causes of the war, 463; desires a reservation for his people, 464; has difficulty with his wife, 464; approaches Fort Allen, 472; at Easton (1757), 474 ff., 488 f.; has trouble over his mother-in-law, 477 ff.; demands a clerk, 479 f.; raises the land issue, 480, 486; offers Gov. Denny a peace pipe, 484; conference in Philadelphia (March 1758), 509 ff.; at Easton peace conference (1758), chaps. 59-61 *passim;* king of eighteen nations, 521; "King of the Quakers," 524; king of all nations, 539; withdraws all claims, 549; makes "Bird on Bough" speech, 549; invited to Indian concourse beyond the Ohio, 563 ff.; death, 441, 486
Teisinger, Frederick, 422
Terachjoris, Mohawk Chief, 17
Tetamy. *See* Tattamy.
T'girhitonti. *See* Spangenberg.
Thanachrishon. *See* Tanacharison.
Thanieson, Seneca Chief, 268
Thoma, Anna (Sister Tabea), 174
Thomas (Brant's son), Mohawk Chief, 227
——, Capt., an Indian, 532
——, George, Governor of Pennsylvania, 100, 108 ff., 126 ff., 134 f., 147, 153 f.,